**RAND MᶜNALLY**

Twin Cities

streetatlas

Contents

Introduction

Maps

Lists and Indexes

Cover photo: Musician Snoopy hanging out in West St. Paul, Minnesota. Photo ©Steve Skjold/Alamy.

 **RAND MᶜNALLY**

Rand McNally Consumer Affairs
P.O. Box 7600
Chicago, IL 60680-9915
randmcnally.com
For comments or suggestions, please call
(800) 777-MAPS (-6277)
or email us at:
consumeraffairs@randmcnally.com

Using Your Street Atlas

The PageFinder™ Map

> Turn to Page C to locate the PageFinder™ Map. Each of the small squares outlined on this map represents a different map page in the Street Atlas.

> Locate the specific part of the metropolitan area that you're interested in.

> Note the appropriate map page number.

> Turn to that map page.

The Index

> The Street Atlas includes separate indexes for streets, schools, parks, shopping centers, golf courses, and other points of interest.

> In the street listings, information is presented in the following order: city, map page number, and grid reference.

STREET		
City	Map #	Grid
N Monticello Av		
CHCG	2976	C2
CHCG	3032	C3
LNWD	2920	C2
Montrose Av		
CHCG	2917	A7
SRPK	2917	A7
SRPK	2973	C1

> A grid reference is a letter-number combination (B6 for example) that tells you precisely where to find a particular street or point of interest on a map.

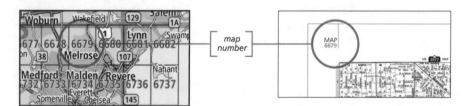

missing pages?

Please note that map pages in this book are numbered according to Rand McNally's page numbering system, not according to traditional page numbering. For this reason, your book may look as though it is missing pages. For example, one page might contain map number 3034 while the following page has map number 3089. The quickest way to resolve any confusion over page numbering is to consult the PageFinder™ Map in the front portion of the Street Atlas.

The Detail Maps

> Each detail map is divided into a grid formed by rows and columns. These rows and columns correspond to letters and numbers running horizontally and vertically along the edges of the map.

> To use a grid reference from the index, search horizontally within the appropriate row and vertically within the appropriate column. The destination can be found within the grid square where the row and column meet.

> Adjacent map pages are indicated by numbers that appear at the top, bottom, and sides of each map.

> The legend explains symbols that appear on the maps.

PageFinder™ Map

PageFinder™ Map
U.S. Patent No. 5,419,586
Canadian Patent No. 2,116,425
Patente Mexicana No. 188186

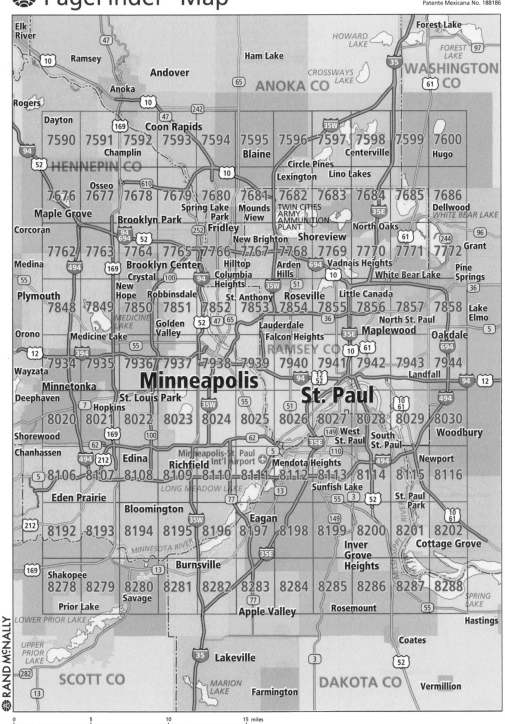

7590	7591	7592	7593	7594	7595	7596	7597	7598	7599	7600
7676	7677	7678	7679	7680	7681	7682	7683	7684	7685	7686
7762	7763	7764	7765	7766	7767	7768	7769	7770	7771	7772
7848	7849	7850	7851	7852	7853	7854	7855	7856	7857	7858
7934	7935	7936	7937	7938	7939	7940	7941	7942	7943	7944
8020	8021	8022	8023	8024	8025	8026	8027	8028	8029	8030
8106	8107	8108	8109	8110	8111	8112	8113	8114	8115	8116
8192	8193	8194	8195	8196	8197	8198	8199	8200	8201	8202
8278	8279	8280	8281	8282	8283	8284	8285	8286	8287	8288

Place names appearing on the map:

Elk River, Ramsey, Andover, Ham Lake, Forest Lake, HOWARD LAKE, FOREST LAKE, WASHINGTON CO, Anoka, Rogers, Dayton, Coon Rapids, CROSSWAYS LAKE, ANOKA CO, Champlin, Blaine, Centerville, Hugo, HENNEPIN CO, Circle Pines, Lexington, Lino Lakes, Osseo, Maple Grove, Spring Lake Park, Mounds View, TWIN CITIES ARMY AMMUNITION PLANT, Dellwood, WHITE BEAR LAKE, Corcoran, Brooklyn Park, Fridley, New Brighton, Shoreview, North Oaks, Grant, Medina, Brooklyn Center, Hilltop, Arden Hills, Vadnais Heights, Pine Springs, Plymouth, New Hope, Crystal, Columbia Heights, St. Anthony, Roseville, Little Canada, White Bear Lake, Robbinsdale, Golden Valley, Lauderdale, Falcon Heights, North St. Paul, Maplewood, Lake Elmo, Orono, Medicine Lake, MEDICINE LAKE, RAMSEY CO, Oakdale, Wayzata, Minneapolis, St. Paul, Landfall, Minnetonka, St. Louis Park, Deephaven, Hopkins, West St. Paul, South St. Paul, Woodbury, Shorewood, Chanhassen, Edina, Richfield, Minneapolis-St. Paul Int'l Airport, Mendota Heights, Newport, Eden Prairie, LONG MEADOW LAKE, Sunfish Lake, St. Paul Park, Bloomington, Eagan, Inver Grove Heights, Cottage Grove, MINNESOTA RIVER, Shakopee, Savage, Burnsville, Apple Valley, Rosemount, SPRING LAKE, Prior Lake, LOWER PRIOR LAKE, UPPER PRIOR LAKE, Hastings, Coates, SCOTT CO, MARION LAKE, Farmington, DAKOTA CO, Vermillion, Lakeville, MISSISSIPPI RIVER

0 5 10 15 miles
1 in. = 6 mi.

Legend

| Interstate highway |
| Interstate (Business) highway |
| U.S. highway |
| State/provincial highway |
| Secondary state/provincial highway/county highway |
| Trans-Canada Highway |
| Canadian autoroute |
| Mexican highway |
| Other highway designation |
| Exit number |
| Free limited-access highway (with tunnel) |
| Toll highway, toll plaza |
| Interchange |
| Ramp |
| Highway |
| Primary road |
| Secondary road |
| Minor road, unpaved road |
| Walkway or trail |

| One-way road |
| Ferry, waterway |
| Levee |
| Trolley |
| Railroad, station, mass transit line |
| Bus station |
| Park and ride |
| Rest area, service area |
| Airport |
| 1200 Block number |
| International boundary, state boundary |
| County boundary |
| Hospital |
| School |
| University or college |
| Information/visitor center/ welcome center |
| Police/sheriff, etc. |
| Fire station |
| Post office |

| City/town/village hall and other government buildings |
| Courthouse |
| Library |
| Museum |
| Border crossing/ Port of entry |
| Theater/ performing arts center |
| Golf course |
| Other point of interest |

Cities and Communities

Community Name	Abbr.	County	Map Page	Community Name	Abbr.	County	Map Page
* Anoka	ANOK	Anoka	7592	* Medicine Lake	MEDL	Hennepin	7849
--Anoka County	AnkC			* Mendota	MNDT	Dakota	8112
* Apple Valley	APVA	Dakota	8283	* Mendota Heights	MNDH	Dakota	8112
* Arden Hills	ARDH	Ramsey	7768	* Minneapolis	MINN	Hennepin	7938
Bald Eagle		Ramsey	7685	* Minnetonka	MNTK	Hennepin	8020
Bellaire		Ramsey	7771	* Mounds View	MNDS	Ramsey	7681
* Birchwood Village	BRHV	Washington	7772	* New Brighton	NBRI	Ramsey	7767
* Blaine	BLNE	Anoka	7595	* New Hope	NWHE	Hennepin	7850
* Blaine	BLNE	Ramsey	7681	* Newport	NWPT	Washington	8115
* Bloomington	BMTN	Hennepin	8195	Nininger Township	NgTp	Dakota	8288
* Brooklyn Center	BRKC	Hennepin	7765	* North Oaks	NOAK	Ramsey	7769
* Brooklyn Park	BRKP	Hennepin	7678	* North St. Paul	NSTP	Ramsey	7857
* Burnsville	BRNV	Dakota	8282	* Oakdale	ODLE	Washington	7944
* Centerville	CTRV	Anoka	7598	* Osseo	OSSE	Hennepin	7677
* Champlin	CHMP	Hennepin	7592	* Pine Springs	PNSP	Washington	7858
* Circle Pines	CIRC	Anoka	7682	* Plymouth	PYMH	Hennepin	7848
* Columbia Heights	COLH	Anoka	7852	* Prior Lake	PRIO	Scott	8279
* Coon Rapids	COON	Anoka	7593	--Ramsey County	RamC		
* Cottage Grove	CTGV	Washington	8202	* Richfield	RHFD	Hennepin	8110
* Crystal	CRYS	Hennepin	7850	* Robbinsdale	ROBB	Hennepin	7851
--Dakota County	DkaC			* Rosemount	RSMT	Dakota	8285
* Dayton	DAYT	Hennepin	7590	* Roseville	RSVL	Ramsey	7854
* Dellwood	DLWD	Washington	7686	* St. Anthony	STAN	Ramsey	7853
* Eagan	EAGN	Dakota	8198	* St. Anthony	STAN	Hennepin	7853
* Eden Prairie	EDNP	Hennepin	8106	* St. Louis Park	STLP	Hennepin	7936
* Edina	EDNA	Hennepin	8022	* St. Paul	STPL	Ramsey	7941
* Falcon Heights	FLCH	Ramsey	7854	* St. Paul Park	SPLP	Washington	8115
* Fridley	FRID	Anoka	7766	* Savage	SAVG	Scott	8280
* Gem Lake	GEML	Ramsey	7770	--Scott County	SctC		
* Golden Valley	GLDV	Hennepin	7936	Sedil		Dakota	8288
* Grant	GRNT	Washington	7772	* Shakopee	SHKP	Scott	8278
Grey Cloud Island Twnshp	GCIT	Washington	8201	* Shoreview	SHVW	Ramsey	7769
--Hennepin County	HnpC			* South St. Paul	SSTP	Dakota	8028
* Hilltop	HLTP	Anoka	7766	* Spring Lake Park	SPLP	Anoka	7681
* Hopkins	HOPK	Hennepin	8021	* Spring Lake Park	SPLP	Ramsey	7681
* Hugo	HUGO	Washington	7599	* Sunfish Lake	SUNL	Dakota	8113
* Inver Grove Heights	IVGH	Dakota	8200	* Vadnais Heights	VADH	Ramsey	7770
* Lake Elmo	ELMO	Washington	7858	--Washington County	WasC		
* Landfall	LNDF	Washington	7944	* Wayzata	WAYZ	Hennepin	7934
* Lauderdale	LAUD	Ramsey	7853	* West St. Paul	WSTP	Dakota	8028
* Lexington	LXTN	Anoka	7682	White Bear Beach		Ramsey	7685
* Lilydale	LILY	Dakota	8026	* White Bear Lake	WTBL	Ramsey	7771
* Lino Lakes	LINO	Anoka	7597	* White Bear Lake	WTBL	Washington	7772
* Little Canada	LCAN	Ramsey	7856	White Bear Township	WtBT	Ramsey	7684
* Mahtomedi	MAHT	Washington	7772	* Willernie	WILL	Washington	7772
* Maple Grove	MAPG	Hennepin	7677	* Woodbury	WDBY	Washington	8030
* Maplewood	MPLW	Ramsey	7857				

*Indicates incorporated city

MAP
7590

1:30,000
1 in. = 2500 ft.

0   0.25   0.5
miles

SEE C MAP

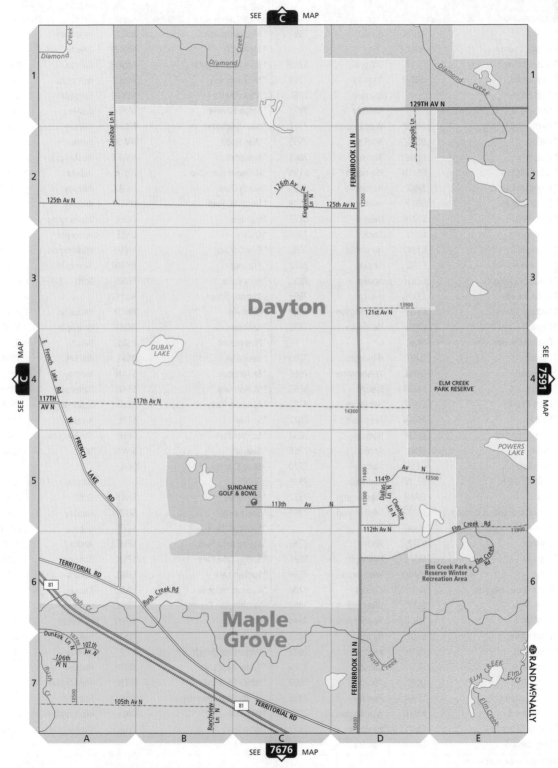

SEE C MAP

SEE 7591 MAP

SEE 7676 MAP

Diamond Creek

Diamond

Diamond Creek

Diamond Creek

Zanzibar Ln N

129TH AV N

Anapolis Ln

FERNBROOK LN N

126th Av N

125th Av N

Kingsview Ln N

125th Av N

12500

Dayton

121st Av N

13900

DUBAY LAKE

ELM CREEK
PARK RESERVE

E French Lake Rd

117TH AV N

117th Av N

14300

POWERS LAKE

W FRENCH LAKE RD

SUNDANCE
GOLF & BOWL

113th   Av   N

114th   Av   N

13500

11400

11300

Dallas Ln N

Cheshire Ln N

112th Av N

Elm Creek Rd

11900

Elm Creek Rd

Elm Creek Park
Reserve Winter
Recreation Area

TERRITORIAL RD

81

Rush Cr

Rush Creek Rd

**Maple
Grove**

FERNBROOK LN N

Rush Creek

ELM CREEK

Elm Cr

RAND McNALLY

Dunkirk Ln N

107th Av N

107th
Av N

106th
Pl N

Rush Cr

10500

105th Av N

Ranchview Ln N

81

TERRITORIAL RD

10400

Elm Creek

A   B   C   D   E

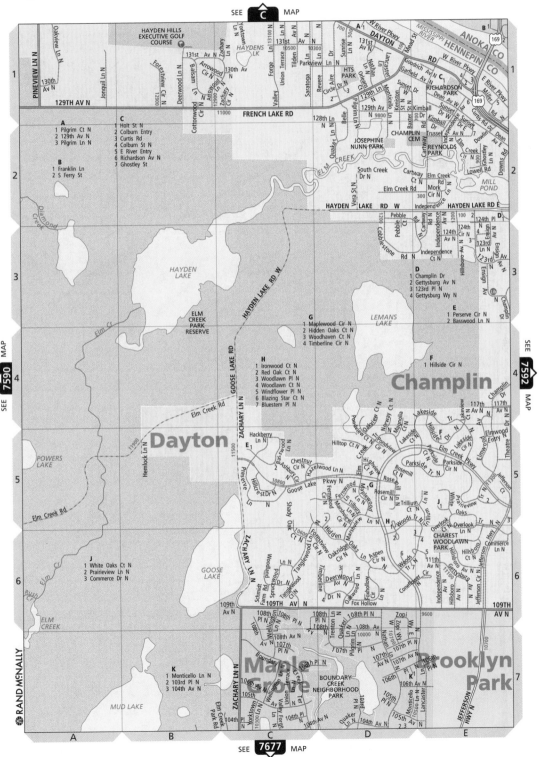

MAP
7591

SEE **C** MAP

1:30,000
1 in. = 2500 ft.

0   0.25   0.5
miles

SEE 7590 MAP

SEE 7592 MAP

SEE 7677 MAP

Dayton

Champlin

Maple Grove

Brooklyn Park

A
1 Pilgrim Ct N
2 129th Av N
3 Pilgrim Ln N

B
1 Franklin Ln
2 S Ferry St

C
1 Holt St N
2 Colburn Entry
3 Curtis Rd
4 Colburn St N
5 E River Entry
6 Richardson Av N
7 Ghostley St

D
1 Champlin Dr
2 Gettysburg Av N
3 123rd Pl N
4 Gettysburg Wy N

E
1 Perserve Cir N
2 Basswood Ln N

F
1 Hillside Cir N

G
1 Maplewood Cir N
2 Hidden Oaks Ct N
3 Woodhaven Ct N
4 Timberline Cir N

H
1 Ironwood Ct N
2 Red Oak Ct N
3 Woodlawn Pl N
4 Woodlawn Ct N
5 Windflower Pl N
6 Blazing Star Ct N
7 Bluestem Pl N

J
1 White Oaks Ct N
2 Prairieview Ln N
3 Commerce Dr N

K
1 Monticello Ln N
2 103rd Pl N
3 104th Av N

HAYDEN HILLS
EXECUTIVE GOLF
COURSE

ELM CREEK
PARK RESERVE

JOSEPHINE NUNN PARK

CHAREST WOODLAWN PARK

BOUNDARY CREEK NEIGHBORHOOD PARK

CHAMPLIN CEM

REYNOLDS PARK

HAYDEN LAKE

POWERS LAKE

GOOSE LAKE

LEMANS LAKE

MUD LAKE

ELM CREEK

MILL POND

ANOKA CO
HENNEPIN CO

RAND McNALLY

MAP
7592

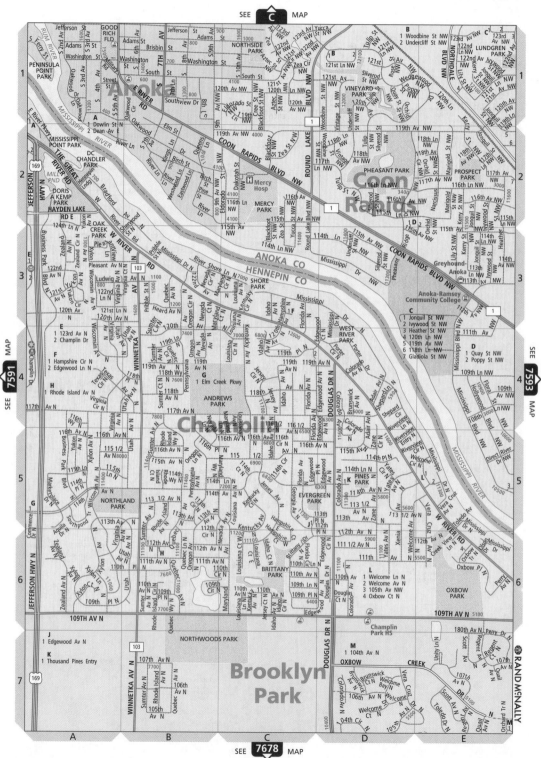

1:30,000
1 in. = 2500 ft.

0   0.25   0.5
miles

MAP
7593

1:30,000
1 in. = 2500 ft.
0   0.25   0.5
miles

SEE C MAP

Coon Rapids

CARDINAL WOODS PARK
WILDERNESS PARK
SAND CREEK SCHOOL PARK
LUNDGREN PARK
THORPE PARK
DEGARDNER PND
LIONS COON CREEK PARK
MALLARY PARK
TOWERVIEW PARK
THOMPSON HTS
Coon Rapids Senior HS
PEPPERMINT STICK PARK
SAND CREEK PARK
ROCKSLIDE PARK
COON RAPIDS SOCCER COMPLEX
Coon Rapids Civic Center
DELTA PARK
HOOVER PARK
CREEK MEADOWS
EPIPHANY PARK
ERLANDSON PARK
DAHLIA PARK
TWIN FLD PARK
RIVERVIEW RES PARK
RIVERVIEW PARK
ROBINSON PARK
AL FLYNN PARK
THOMPSON PARK
LO JACOB SCHOOL PARK
COON RAPIDS DAM REGIONAL PARK
DUNN ISLAND
BROOKLYN PARK
OXBOW CREEK DR

Major roads
NORTHDALE BLVD NW
HANSON BLVD NW
ROBINSON DR
111TH AV NW
COON RAPIDS BLVD NW
CROOKED LAKE BLVD NW
EGRET BLVD NW
MISSISSIPPI BLVD NW
W RIVER RD
NOBLE PKWY
ANOKA CO / HENNEPIN CO

Champlin

SEE 7592 MAP
SEE 7594 MAP
SEE 7679 MAP

MAP
7594

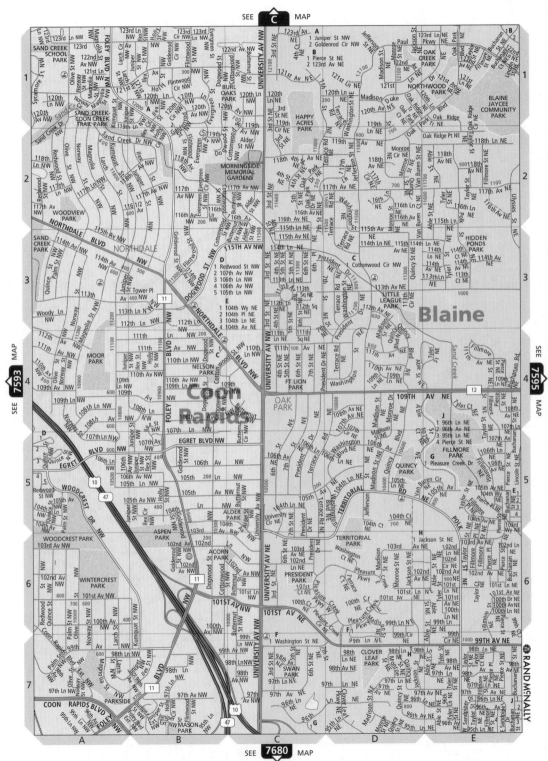

MAP
7595

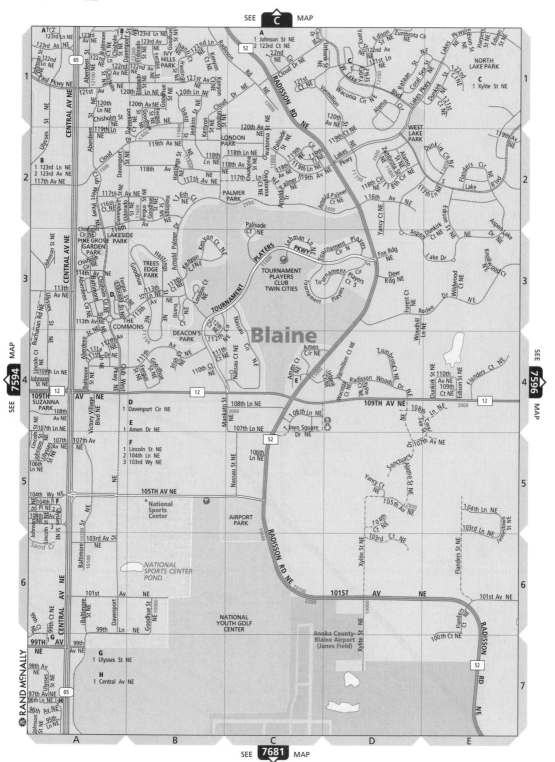

SEE **C** MAP

SEE **7594** MAP

SEE **7596** MAP

SEE **7681** MAP

1:30,000
1 in. = 2500 ft.

Blaine

MAP
7596

1:30,000
1 in. = 2500 ft.
0   0.25   0.5
miles

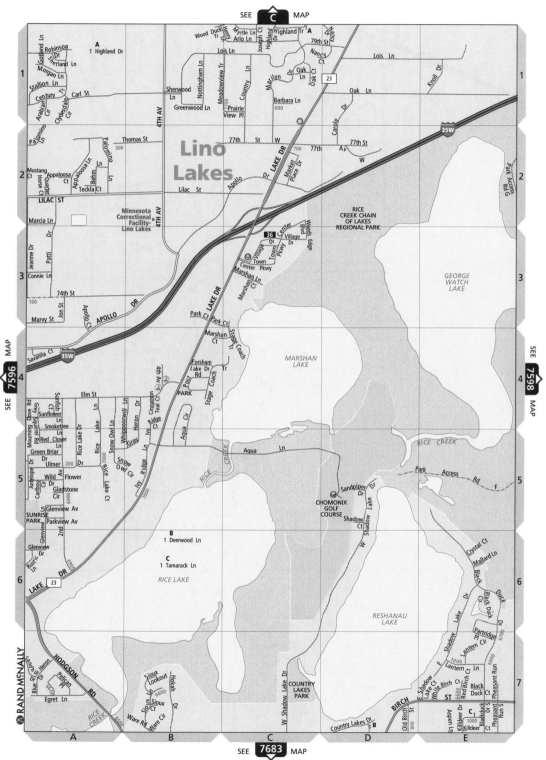

MAP
7597

1:30,000
1 in. = 2500 ft.

0   0.25   0.5
miles

Lino Lakes

RICE CREEK CHAIN OF LAKES REGIONAL PARK

GEORGE WATCH LAKE

MARSHAN LAKE

RICE CREEK

CHOMONIX GOLF COURSE

RICE LAKE

RESHANAU LAKE

Minnesota Correctional Facility- Lino Lakes

SUNRISE PARK

A
1 Highland Dr

B
1 Deerwood Ln

C
1 Tamarack Ln

C₁
1 Killdeer

COUNTRY LAKES PARK

RAND MCNALLY

MAP
7598

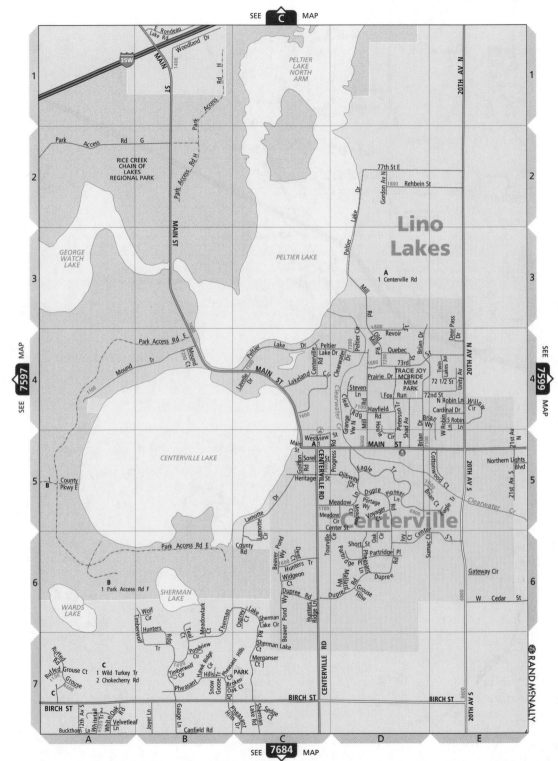

1:30,000
1 in. = 2500 ft.
0   0.25   0.5
miles

PELTIER
LAKE
NORTH
ARM

RICE CREEK
CHAIN OF
LAKES
REGIONAL PARK

GEORGE
WATCH
LAKE

PELTIER LAKE

Lino
Lakes

A
1 Centerville Rd

CENTERVILLE LAKE

Centerville

WARDS
LAKE

SHERMAN
LAKE

C
1 Wild Turkey Tr
2 Chokecherry Rd

B
1 Park Access Rd F

PARK

BIRCH ST

BIRCH ST

BIRCH ST

SEE 7597 MAP

SEE 7599 MAP

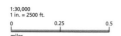

1:30,000
1 in. = 2500 ft.

0   0.25   0.5
miles

MAP
7599

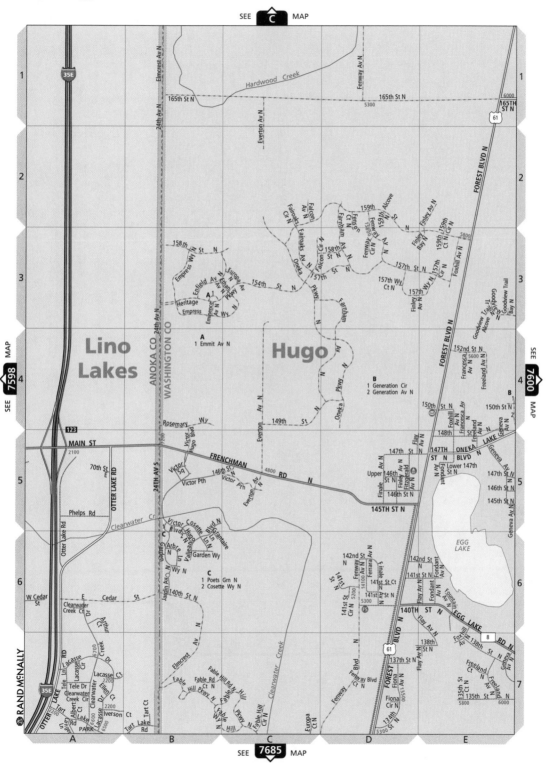

35E

Hardwood Creek

165th St N   165th St N
5300   6000

1

24th Av N

Elmcrest Av N

Everton Av N

Fenway Av N

61   165TH ST N

2

FOREST BLVD N

Falcon Cir N
Falcon Av N
Fairoaks Cir N
Fairoaks Av N
158th St N
Farnham Av N
Fensen Av N   159th
159th Ct N   Alcove St N
Finley Av N   159th
Finley Ct N   Cir N
5800

Fenway Bay N

Oneka Pkwy N

158th St N
Falcon St N
157th St N   Foxhill Av N

5800

154th St N

Empress Wy N
Enfield Av N
Europa Av N
Edwin Av N
Eden Pkwy N

157th Wy
Ct N

157th Wy N   157th Av N
157th Cir N

3

FOREST BLVD N

Goodview Trail
Goodview Trail
Alcove Bay N

A1
Heritage
Empress
Eminence Ct N
Eminence Wy N

A
1 Emmit Av N

**Lino
Lakes**

Hugo

B
1 Generation Cir
2 Generation Av N

152nd St N

Francesca
Av N   5600

Freeland Av N

4

ANOKA CO   24th Av N
WASHINGTON CO

Grandview Av N

Oneka Pkwy N

Oneka Av N

149th St N

150th St N   Foxhill
Av N   150th St N

Freeland Av N   Francesca Av N

B
2

SEE **7598** MAP

Rosemary Wy N

Victor Dr N
Hugo Blvd N
7200

148th St N

147th Av N

Geneva Av N

Geneva Av N   Lake

SEE **7600** MAP

MAIN ST
2100

70th St N

OTTER LAKE RD

24th Av S

FRENCHMAN   RD   N
4800

147th St N
147TH   ONEKA   BLVD
ST N   BLVD

Upper 146th   Finley Av N
146th   Fitzgerald   Av N
St N   Fondant   147th St N
146th St N   147th Av N

Lower 147th
Av N

5

Victor
Sq

Victor Pth
Victor Pth

Everton Av N

Finale Av N
146th St N

145th St N

145TH ST N

EGG
LAKE

Geneva Av N

Phelps Rd

Clearwater Cr

Cosette Wy N

Victor Hugo Blvd N
Vallean
Arbre Ln
Gagne Ln N

Rosemaire
Ln N
Garden Wy

Clearwater Creek

142nd Av N
Fenway Av N
Ferrara Av N
Finale Av N

142nd St N
Fondant Av N
Fondant Av N

6

Otter Lake Rd

Otter Lake Rd
Jardin Av N

C
Wy N
140th St N

C
1 Poets Grn N
2 Cosette Wy N

141st St N

14100 Av N

141st St Ct
141st
St N   141st St Ct
141st
St N   Flay Av N
Fondant Av N

Foxhill Av N

Fountain Av N

W Cedar
St

Cedar   St

Clearwater
Creek Ct N
Arthur
Ct N

141st St
Cir N   5200
5300

8
138th
St N   Foxhill Av N   138th   St N

Freeland
Av N   Geneva Av N

61

140TH   ST   N
Flay Av N

EGG LAKE   RD

RAND MCNALLY

35E

OTTER LAKE

Lacasse
Ln Rd
Tele Dr   Tele Dr
Clearwater
Creek Cir
Albert   Ellen Ct N
Ct N   2200
Iverson

Lacasse
Cir
Lacasse
Ct
2200

Tart Lake Ct

Elmcrest
Av N
Fable Hill
Ct N
Fable Rd
Fable Hill
Pkwy N
Fable
Hill N
Fable Hill
Wy N
Fable Hill
Cir N
Europa
Ct N

137th
St N

FOREST   BLVD   N

Fenway Blvd

Fiona
Av N

Fiona
Cir N

135th St
Ct N
5800

135th St N
6000

7

Clearwater Creek

Fenway Blvd

13th
St N
5300

PARK
Tart   Tart Ct
Lake
Rd

MAP
7600

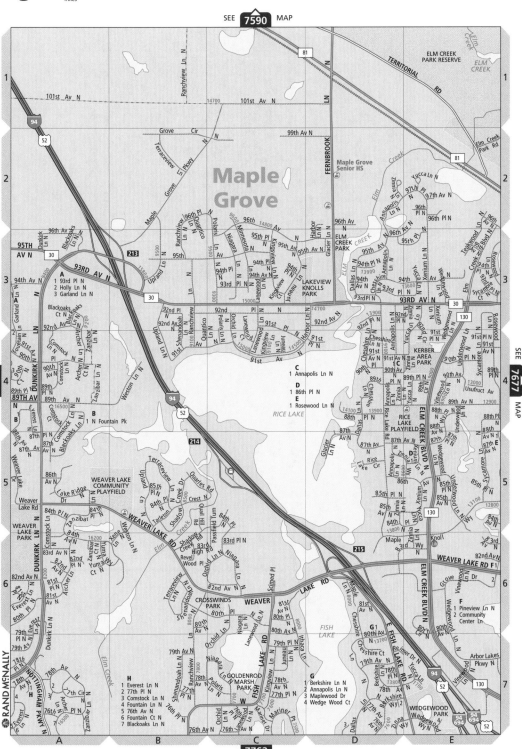

MAP
7676

1:30,000
1 in. = 2500 ft.

0   0.25   0.5
miles

SEE 7590 MAP

SEE 7762 MAP

MAP
7677

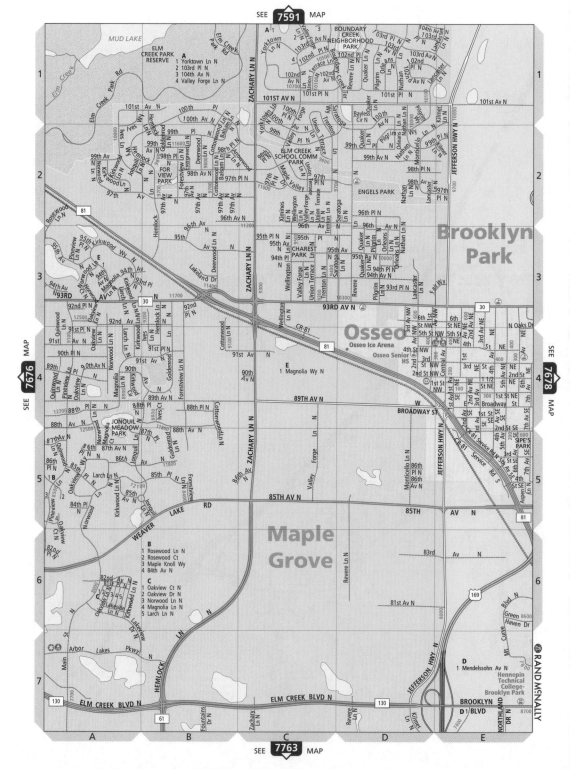

MAP
7678

1:30,000
1 in. = 2500 ft.

0   0.25   0.5
miles

SEE 7592 MAP

SEE 7677 MAP

SEE 7679 MAP

SEE 7764 MAP

Brooklyn Park

Osseo

RAND McNALLY

MAP
7679

SEE 7593 MAP
SEE 7678 MAP
SEE 7680 MAP
SEE 7765 MAP

1:30,000
1 in. = 2500 ft.
0   0.25   0.5
miles

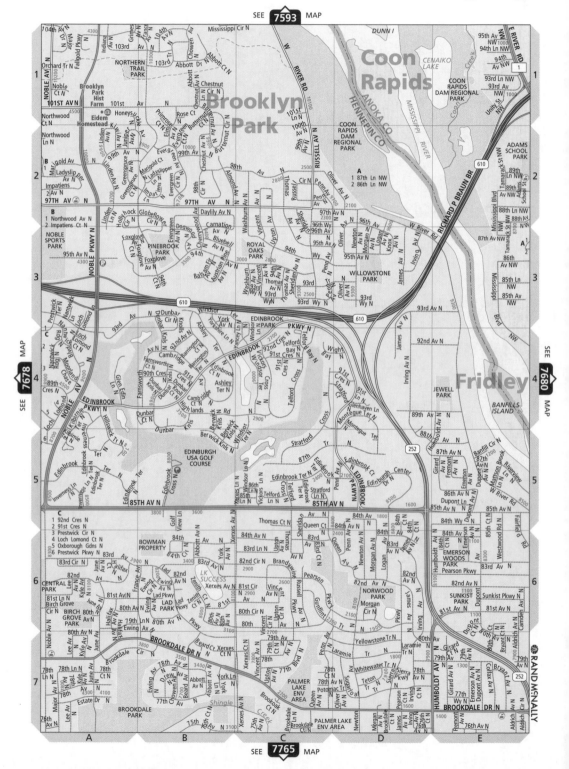

RAND MCNALLY

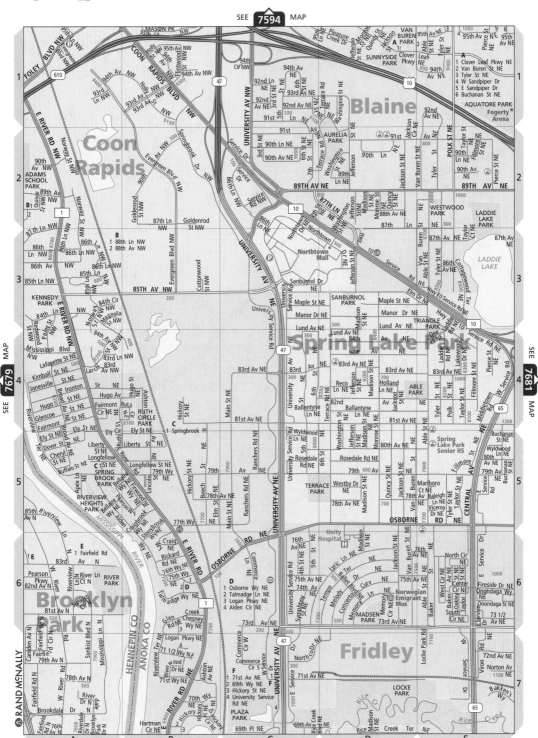

MAP
7680

1:30,000
1 in. = 2500 ft.
0   0.25   0.5
miles

SEE 7594 MAP

SEE 7679 MAP

SEE 7681 MAP

SEE 7766 MAP

RAND MCNALLY

MAP
7681

1:30,000
1 in. = 2500 ft.

0   0.25   0.5
miles

SEE **7595** MAP

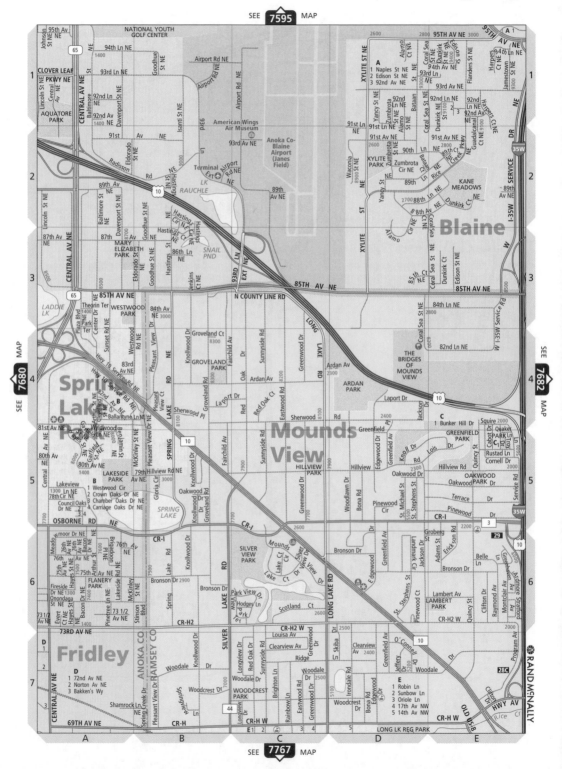

SEE **7680** MAP

SEE **7682** MAP

SEE **7767** MAP

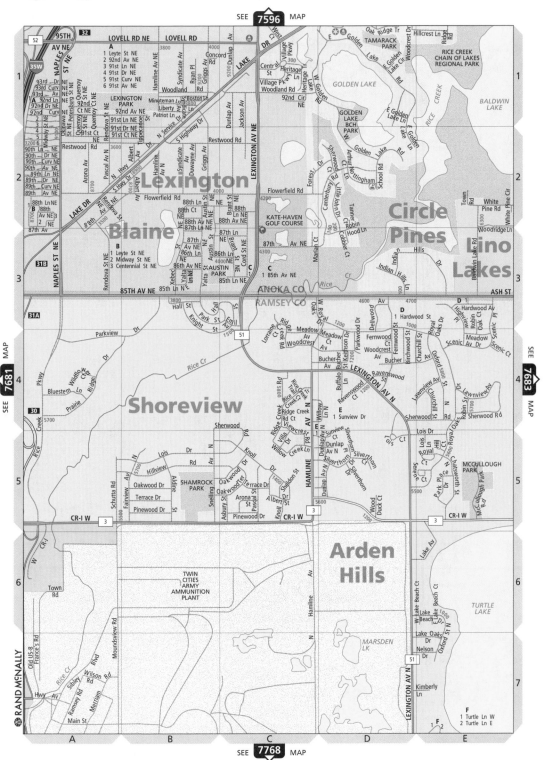

MAP
7683

1:30,000
1 in. = 2500 ft.

0   0.25   0.5
miles

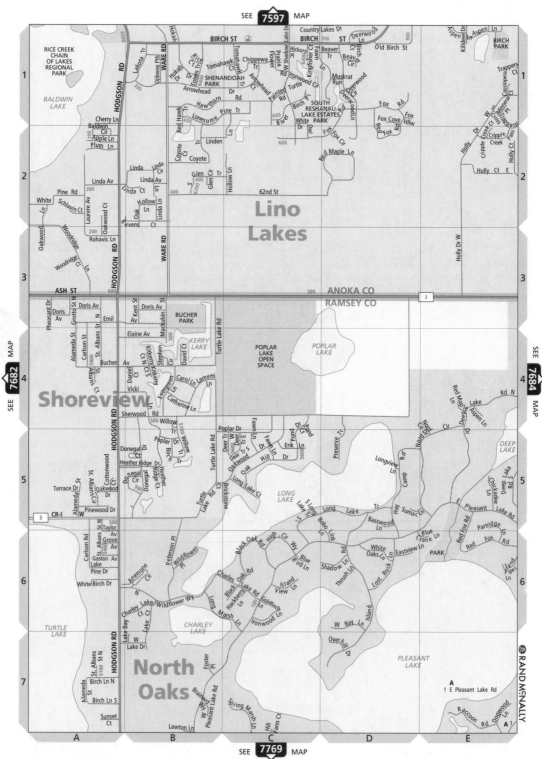

SEE 7597 MAP

Lino
Lakes

Shoreview

North
Oaks

SEE 7682 MAP

SEE 7684 MAP

RICE CREEK
CHAIN
OF LAKES
REGIONAL
PARK

BALDWIN
LAKE

ANOKA CO
RAMSEY CO

POPLAR
LAKE
OPEN
SPACE

POPLAR
LAKE

KERRY
LAKE

BUCHER
PARK

LONG
LAKE

CHARLEY
LAKE

TURTLE
LAKE

PLEASANT
LAKE

DEEP
LAKE

BIRCH
PARK

SEE 7769 MAP

RAND MCNALLY

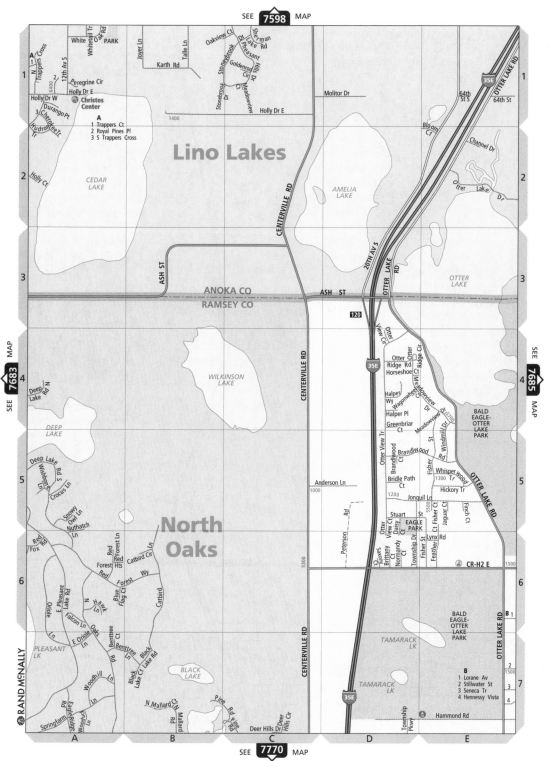

1:30,000
1 in. = 2500 ft.

0   0.25   0.5
miles

SEE 7683 MAP

SEE 7685 MAP

SEE 7770 MAP

Lino Lakes

North Oaks

Christos Center

A
1 Trappers Ct
2 Royal Pines Pl
3 S Trappers Cross

B
1 Lorane Av
2 Stillwater St
3 Seneca Tr
4 Hennessy Vista

CEDAR LAKE

AMELIA LAKE

OTTER LAKE

WILKINSON LAKE

DEEP LAKE

BALD EAGLE-OTTER LAKE PARK

TAMARACK LK

BLACK LAKE

PLEASANT LK

EAGLE PARK

ANOKA CO
RAMSEY CO

RAND McNALLY

MAP
7685

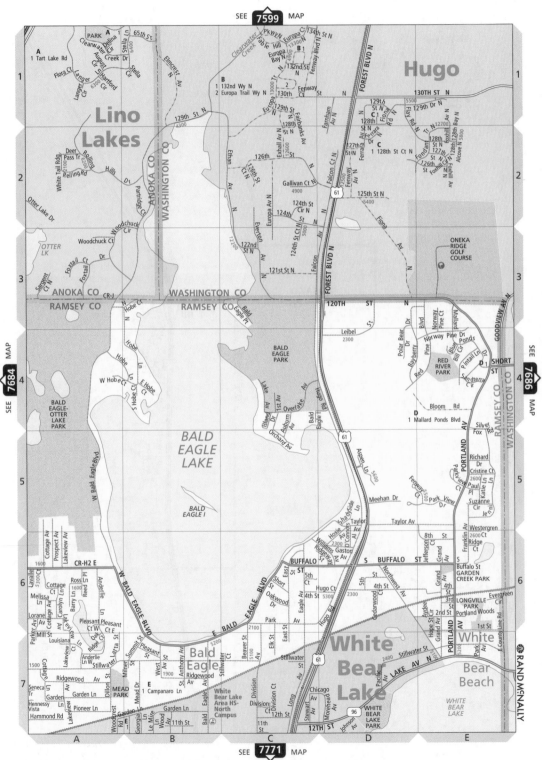

SEE 7599 MAP

SEE 7684 MAP

SEE 7686 MAP

SEE 7771 MAP

Lino
Lakes

Hugo

BALD
EAGLE
LAKE

White
Bear
Lake

RAND MCNALLY

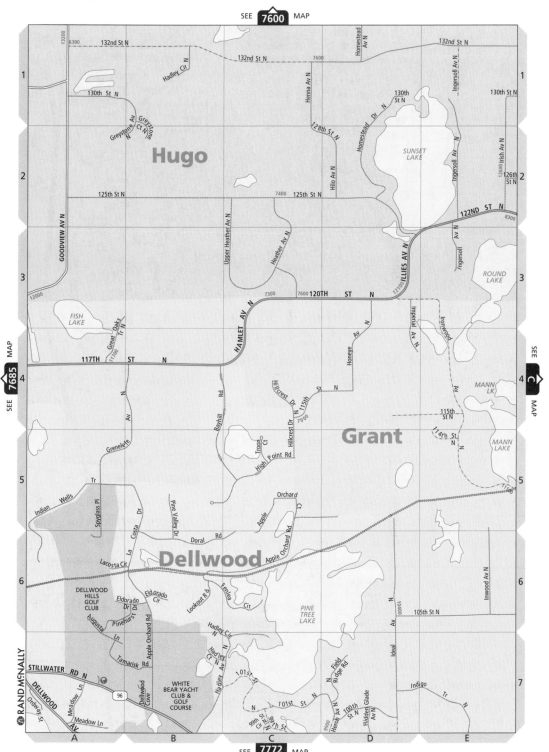

MAP
7686

1:30,000
1 in. = 2500 ft.
0   0.25   0.5
miles

N
RAND MCNALLY

SEE 7685 MAP

SEE C MAP

MAP
7762

1:30,000
1 in. = 2500 ft.

0   0.25   0.5
miles

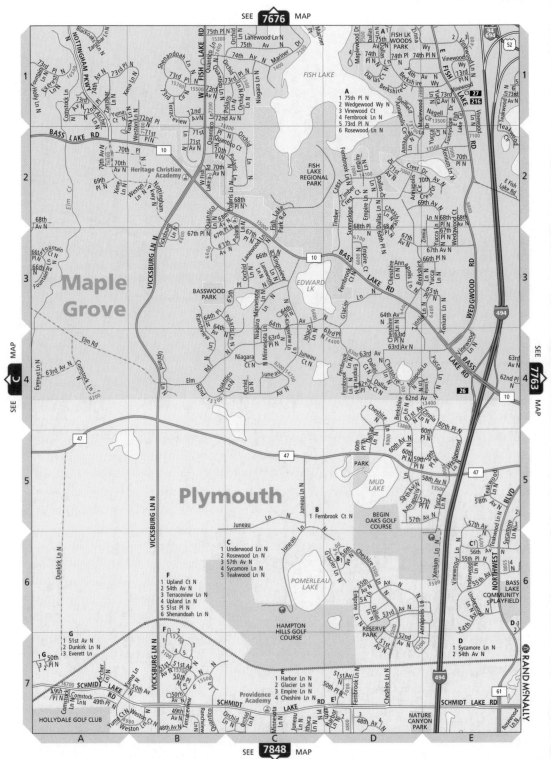

SEE **7676** MAP

SEE **7848** MAP

Maple
Grove

Plymouth

RAND MCNALLY

1:30,000
1 in. = 2500 ft.

0   0.25   0.5
miles

MAP
7763

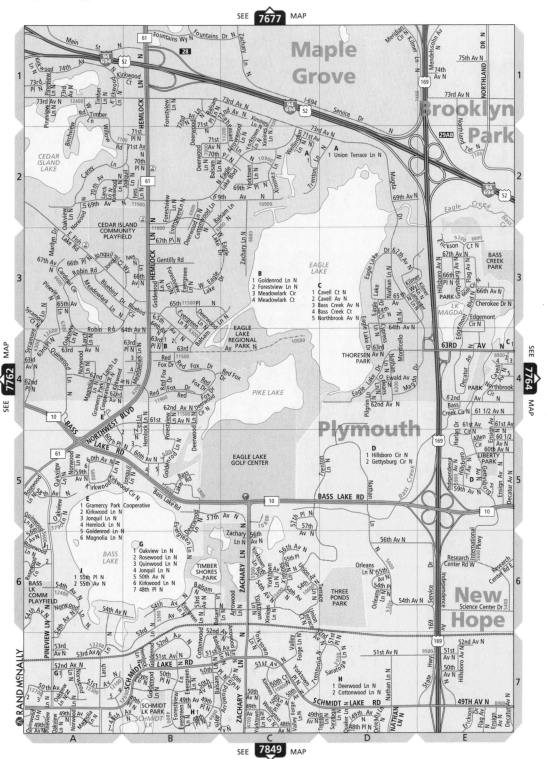

MAP
7764

1:30,000
1 in. = 2500 ft.

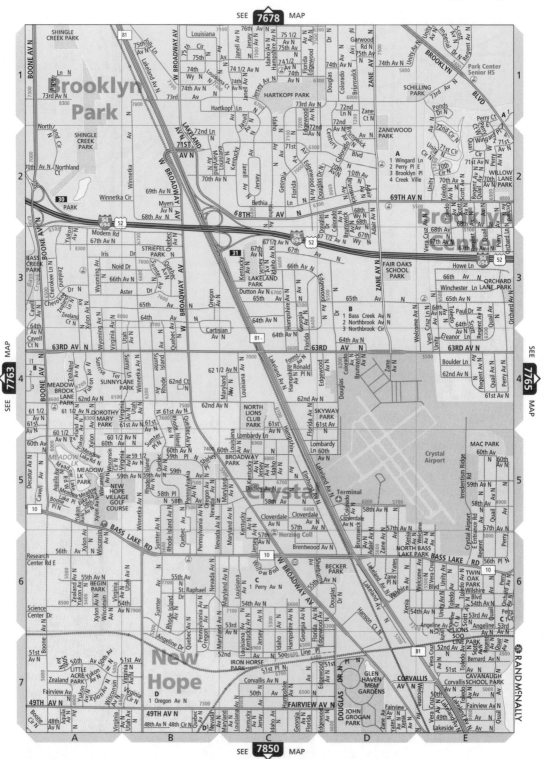

MAP
7765

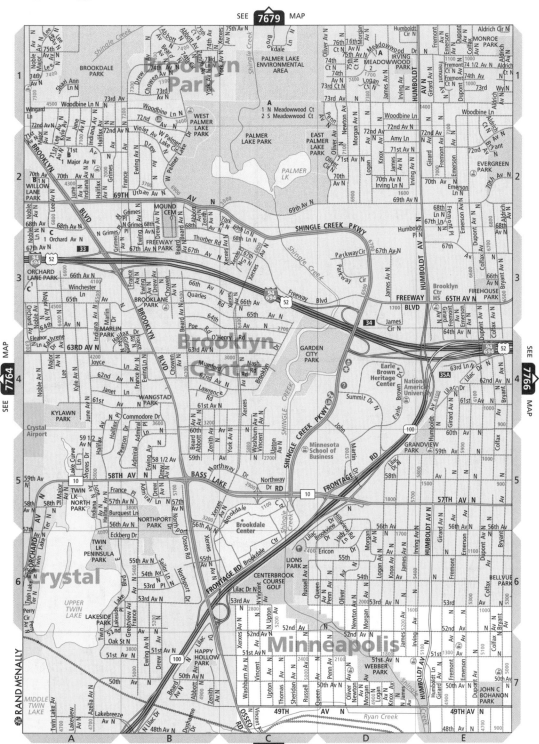

SEE 7764 MAP

SEE 7766 MAP

MAP
7766

1:30,000
1 in. = 2500 ft.

0   0.25   0.5
miles

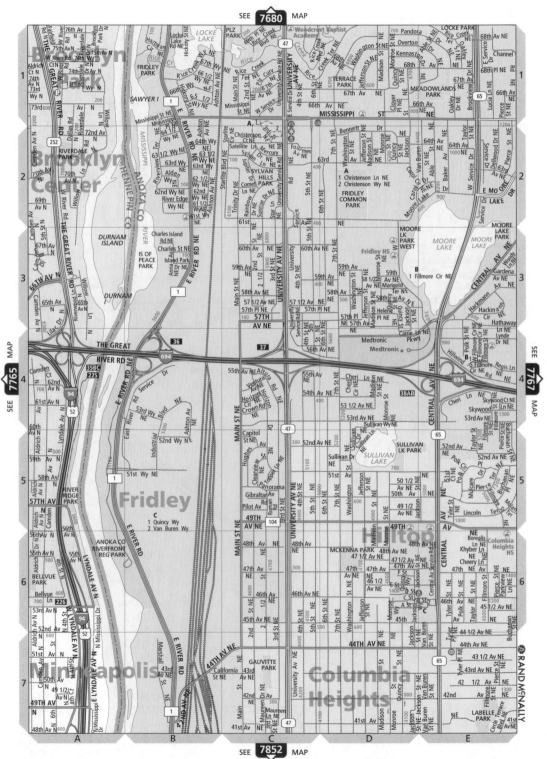

SEE 7680 MAP

SEE 7765 MAP

SEE 7767 MAP

SEE 7852 MAP

RAND McNALLY

MAP
7767

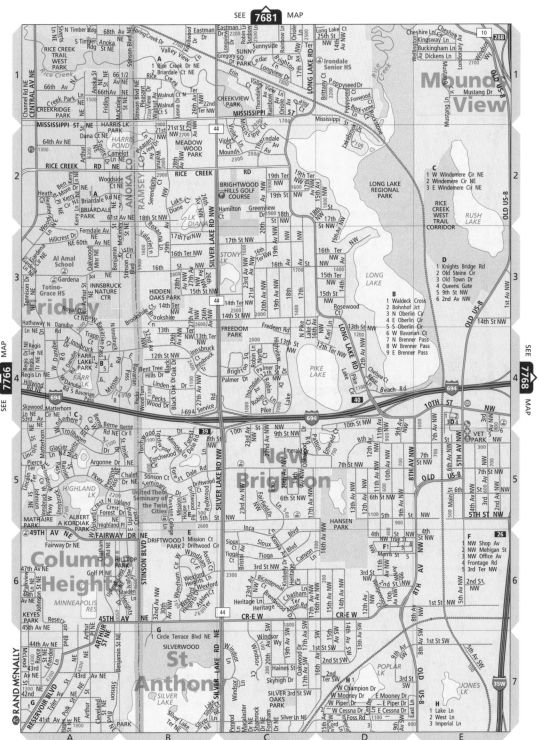

SEE 7681 MAP

SEE 7766 MAP

SEE 7768 MAP

SEE 7853 MAP

MAP
7768

MAP
7769

1:30,000
1 in. = 2500 ft.

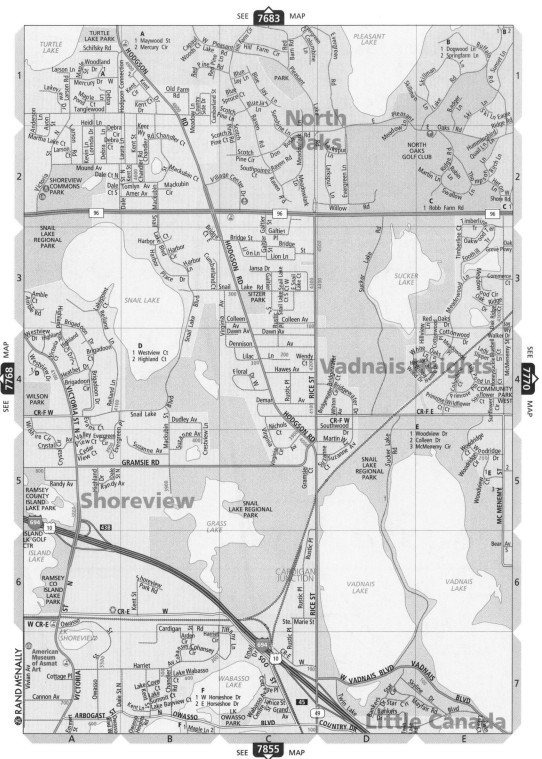

MAP
7770

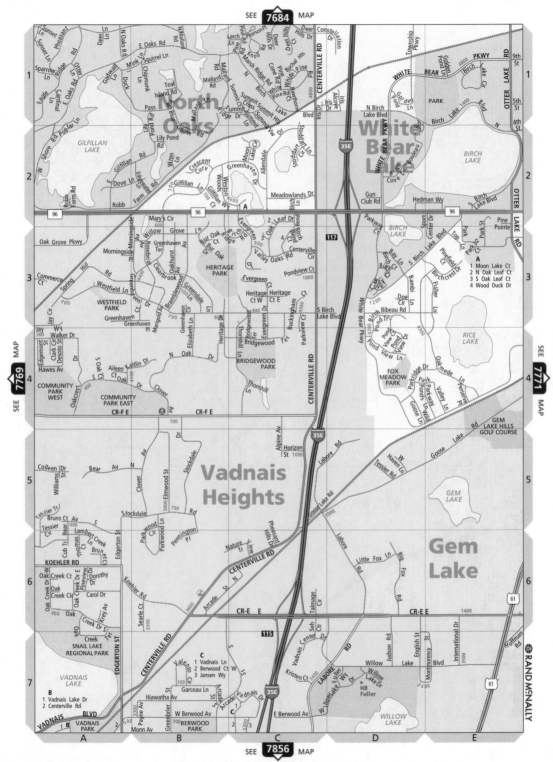

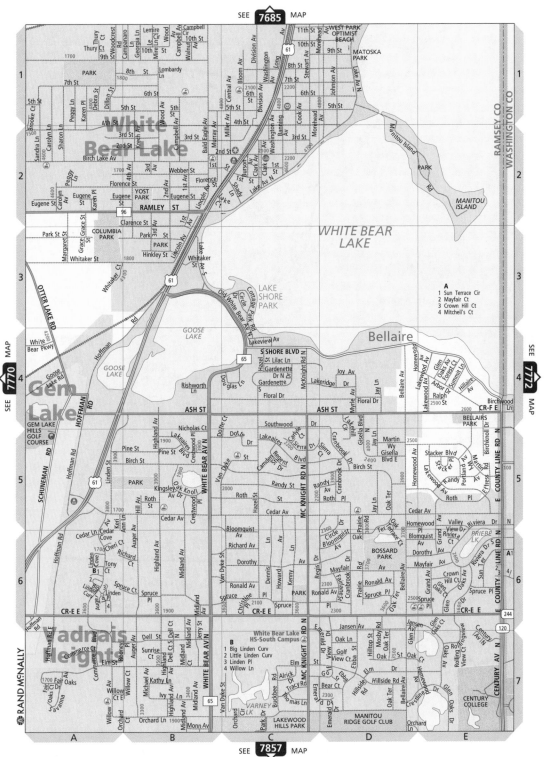

MAP
7771

SEE 7685 MAP

SEE 7770 MAP

SEE 7772 MAP

SEE 7857 MAP

MAP
7772

1:30,000
1 in. = 2500 ft.
0   0.25   0.5
miles

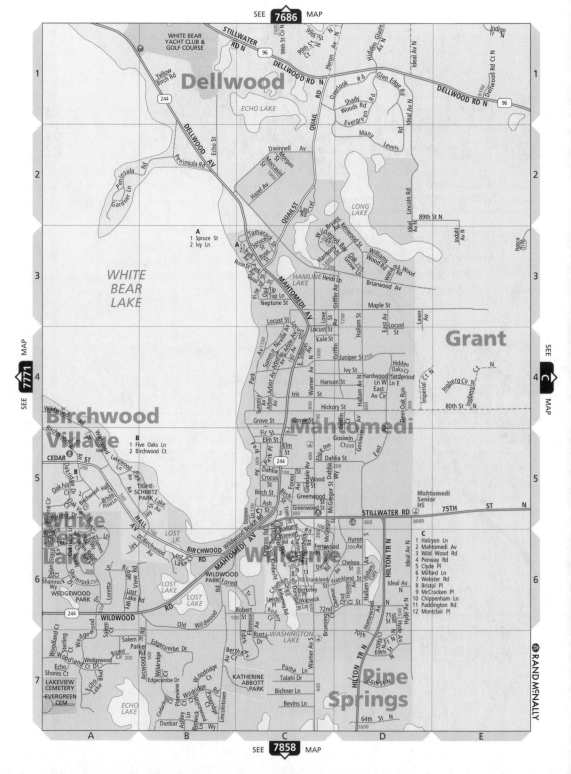

Dellwood

WHITE BEAR YACHT CLUB & GOLF COURSE

STILLWATER RD N

DELLWOOD RD N

DELLWOOD RD N

ECHO LAKE

DELLWOOD AV

WHITE BEAR LAKE

LONG LAKE

HAMLINE LAKE

Grant

Mahtomedi

Birchwood Village

White Bear Lake

Willernie

Wildwood

WASHINGTON LAKE

Pine Springs

LAKEVIEW CEMETERY
EVERGREEN CEM.

ECHO LAKE

A
1 Spruce St
2 Ivy Ln

B
1 Five Oaks Ln
2 Birchwood Ct

C
1 Halcyon Ln
2 Mahtomedi Av
3 Wild Wood Rd
4 Penway Rd
5 Clyde Pl
6 Milford Ln
7 Webster Rd
8 Bristol Pl
9 McCracken Pl
10 Chippenham Ln
11 Paddington Rd
12 Montclair Pl

Mahtomedi Senior HS

STILLWATER RD   75TH   ST N

RAND MᶜNALLY

SEE 7771 MAP

SEE 7858 MAP

MAP
7848

1:30,000
1 in. = 2500 ft.

0   0.25   0.5
miles

SEE 7762 MAP

SEE 7934 MAP

MAP
7849

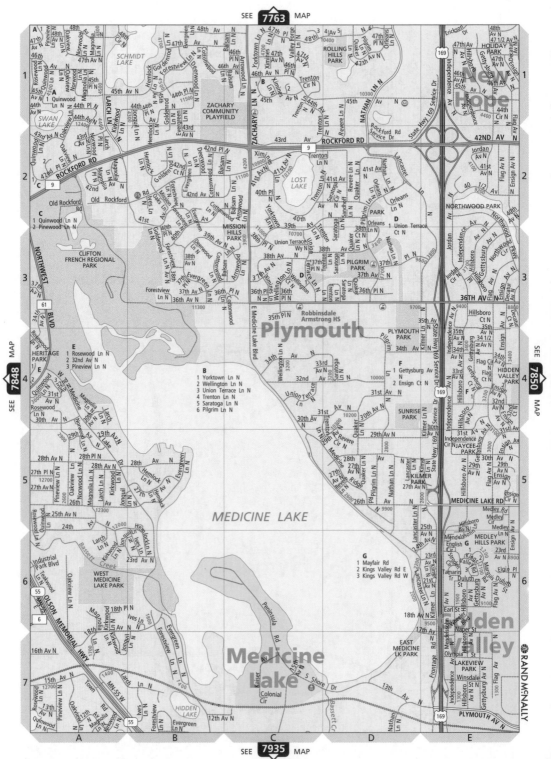

1:30,000
1 in. = 2500 ft.

0   0.25   0.5
miles

RAND McNALLY

MAP
7850

1:30,000
1 in. = 2500 ft.

0   0.25   0.5
miles

SEE 7764 MAP

SEE 7849 MAP

SEE 7851 MAP

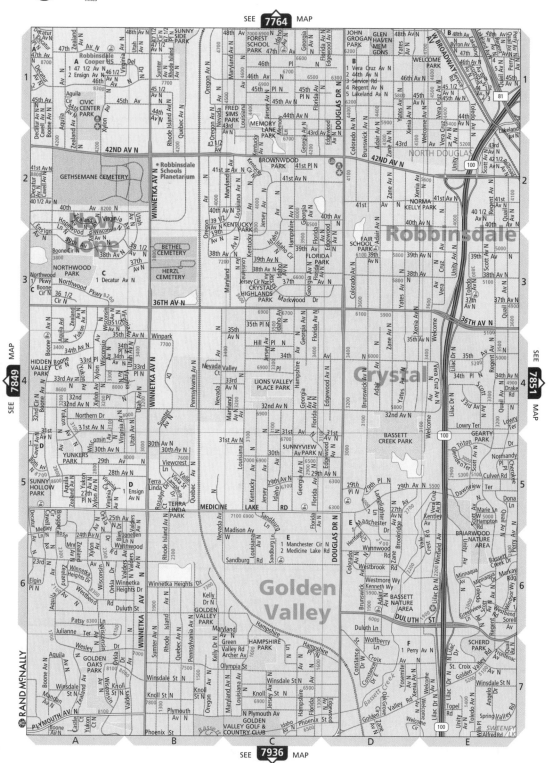

SEE 7936 MAP

MAP
7851

1:30,000
1 in. = 2500 ft.

0   0.25   0.5
miles

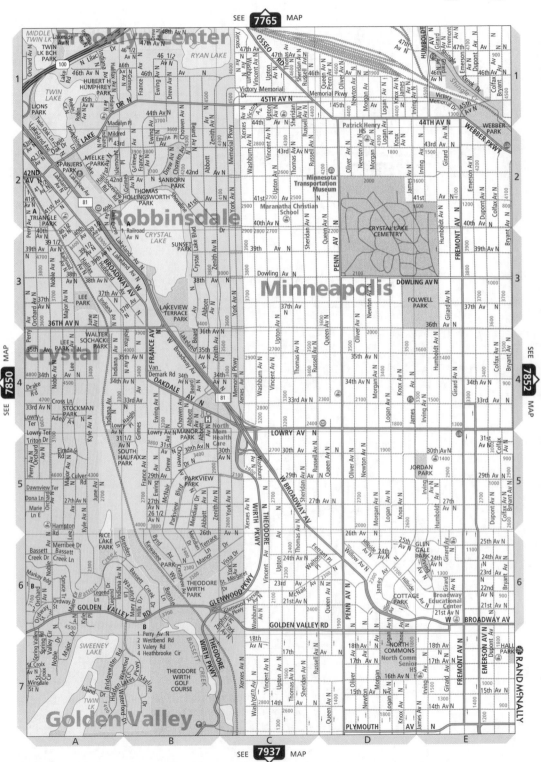

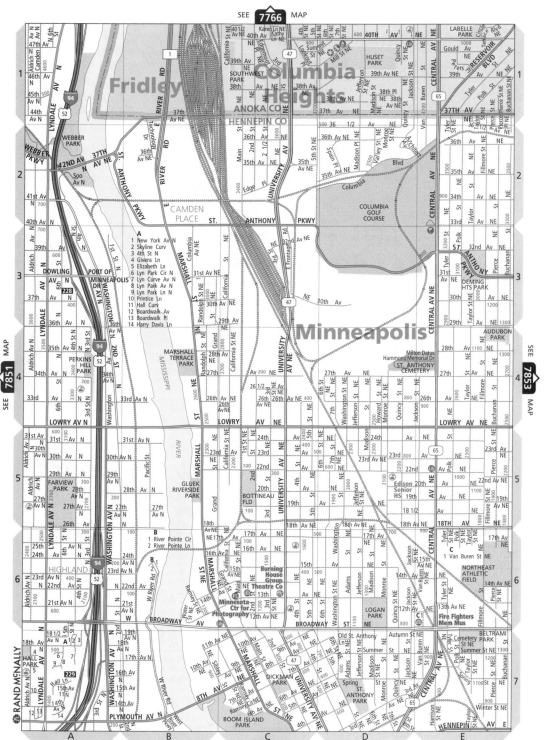

MAP
7852

1:30,000
1 in. = 2500 ft.

0   0.25   0.5
miles

SEE **7766** MAP

Fridley

Columbia Heights

ANOKA CO
HENNEPIN CO

Minneapolis

A
1 New York Av N
2 Skyline Curv
3 4th St N
4 Givens Ln
5 Elizabeth Ln
6 Lyn Park Cir N
7 Lyn Curve Av N
8 Lyn Park Av N
9 Lyn Park Ln N
10 Printice Ln
11 Hall Curv
12 Boardwalk Av
13 Boardwalk Pl
14 Harry Davis Ln

B
1 River Pointe Cir
2 River Pointe Ln

C
1 Van Buren St NE

SEE **7851** MAP

SEE **7853** MAP

SEE **7938** MAP

RAND MCNALLY

A   B   C   D   E

MAP
7853

SEE 7767 MAP

1:30,000
1 in. = 2500 ft.
0   0.25   0.5
miles

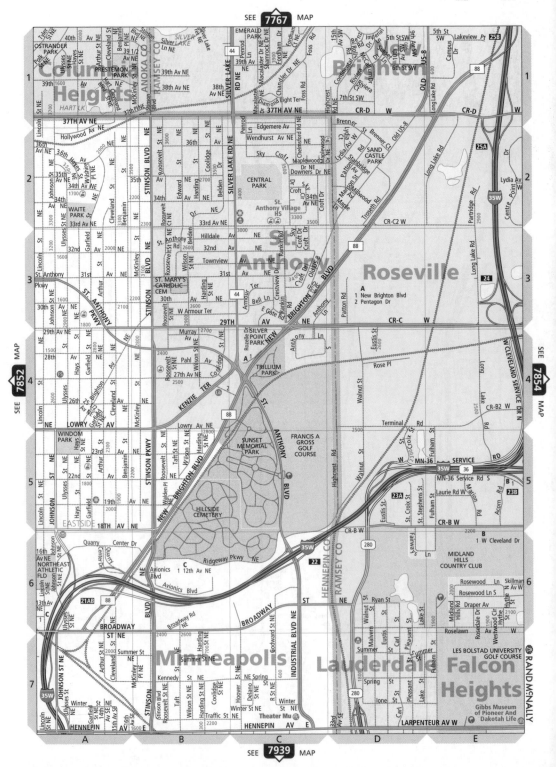

MAP
7854

1:30,000
1 in. = 2500 ft.

0   0.25   0.5
miles

SEE 7768 MAP

SEE 7853 MAP

SEE 7855 MAP

SEE 7940 MAP

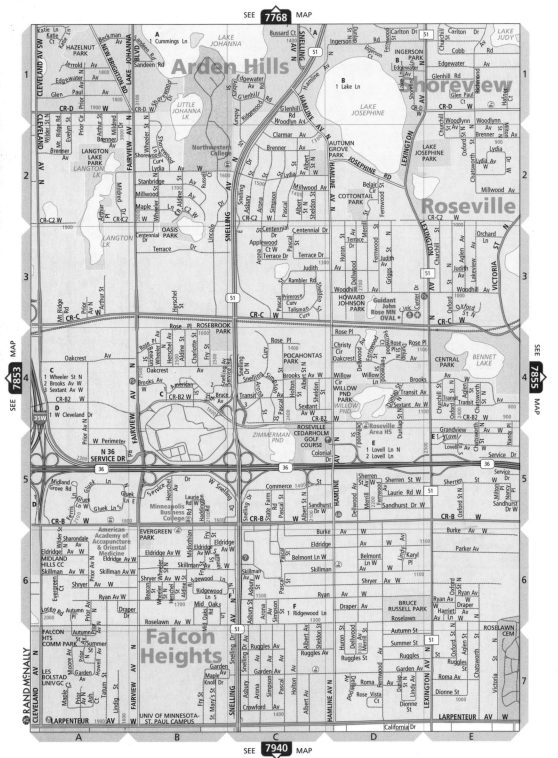

MAP
7855

1:30,000
1 in. = 2500 ft.

0   0.25   0.5
miles

SEE **7769** MAP

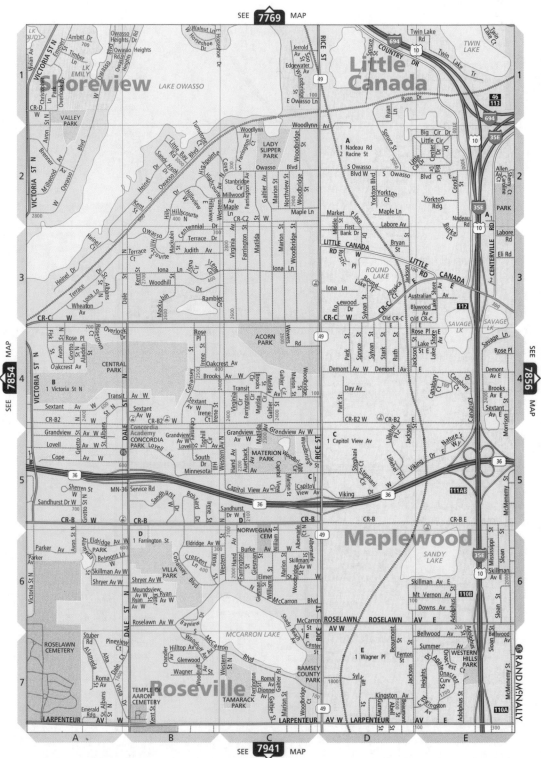

Shoreview

Little Canada

Maplewood

Roseville

SEE **7854** MAP

SEE **7856** MAP

RAND McNALLY

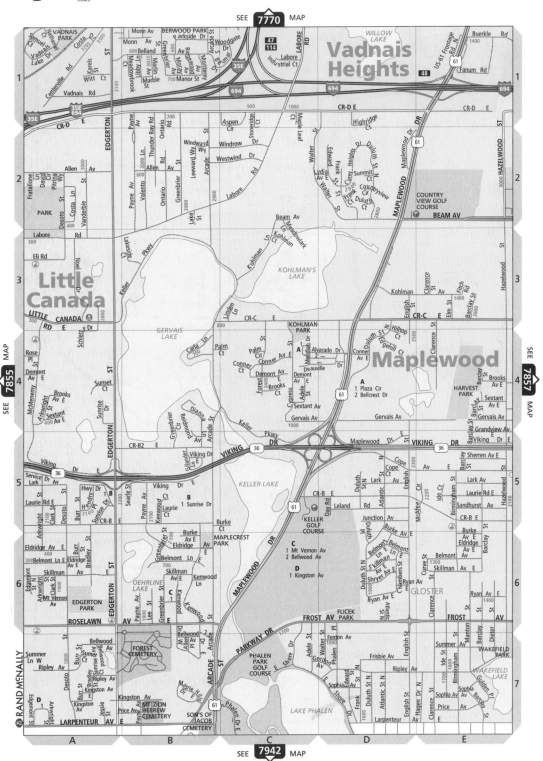

MAP
7856

SEE 7770 MAP

SEE 7855 MAP

SEE 7857 MAP

SEE 7942 MAP

RAND McNALLY

MAP
7857

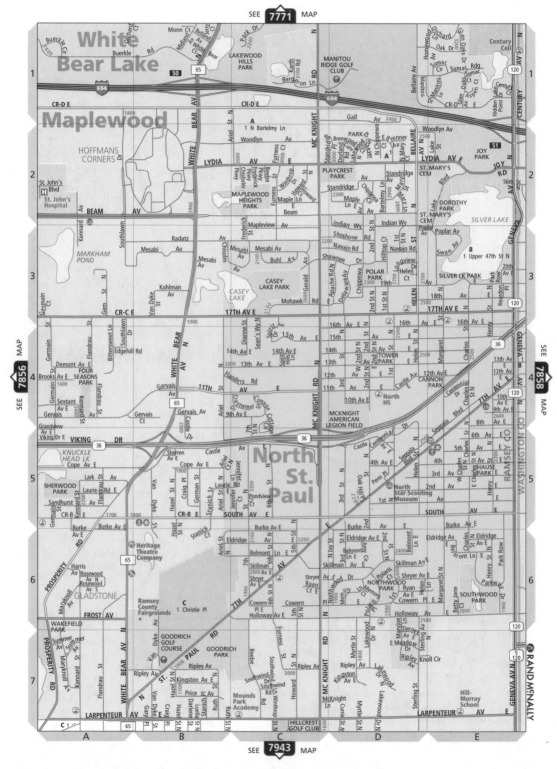

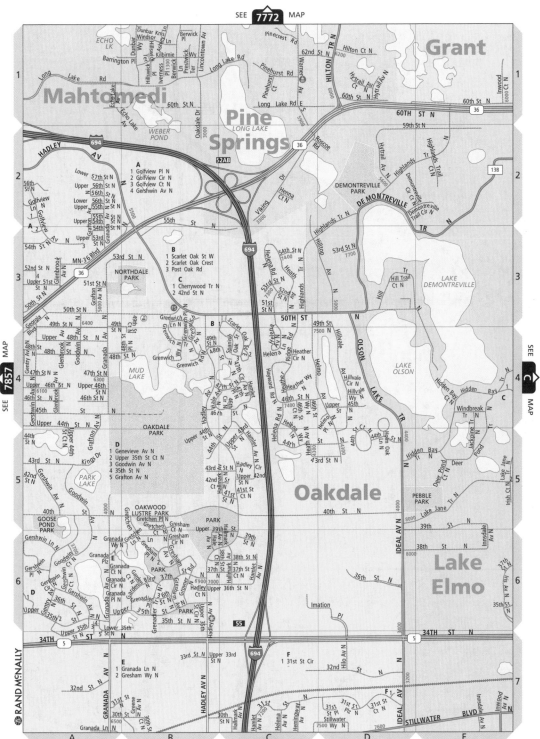

MAP
7858

1:30,000
1 in. = 2500 ft.

0   0.25   0.5
miles

SEE 7772 MAP

Grant

Mahtomedi

Pine
Springs

DEMONTREVILLE
PARK

DE MONTREVILLE

LAKE
DEMONTREVILLE

A
1 Golfview Pl N
2 Golfview Cir N
3 Golfview Ct N
4 Gershwin Av N

B
1 Scarlet Oak St W
2 Scarlet Oak Crest
3 Post Oak Rd

C
1 Cherrywood Tr N
2 42nd St N

NORTHDALE
PARK

MUD
LAKE

LAKE
OLSON

D
1 Genevieve Av N
2 Upper 35th St Ct N
3 Goodwin Av N
4 35th St N
5 Grafton Av N

OAKDALE
PARK

PARK
LAKE

Oakdale

PEBBLE
PARK

OAKWOOD
LUSTRE PARK

GOOSE
POND
PARK

Lake
Elmo

PARK

E
1 Granada Ln N
2 Gresham Wy N

F
1 31st St Cir

SEE 7857 MAP

SEE C MAP

SEE 7944 MAP

MAP
7934

1:30,000
1 in. = 2500 ft.

0   0.25   0.5
miles

SEE 7848 MAP

SEE 7935 MAP

SEE 8020 MAP

SEE C MAP

RAND McNALLY

MAP
7935

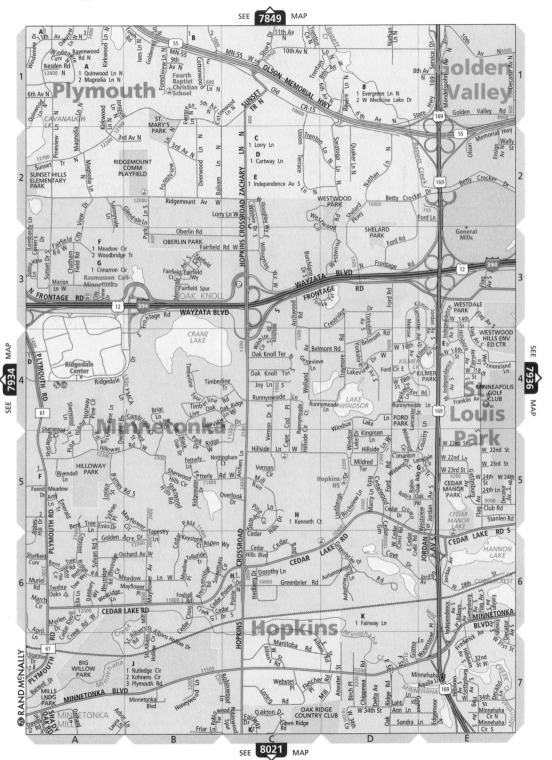

MAP
7936

1:30,000
1 in. = 2500 ft.

0   0.25   0.5
miles

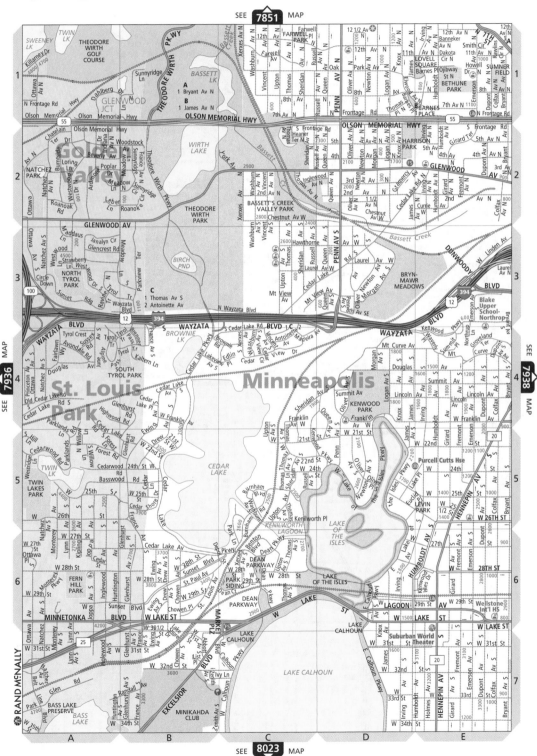

MAP
7938

1:30,000
1 in. = 2500 ft.

0   0.25   0.5
miles

SEE **7852** MAP

SEE **7937** MAP

SEE **7939** MAP

RAND MCNALLY

Minneapolis

SEE **8024** MAP

MAP
7939

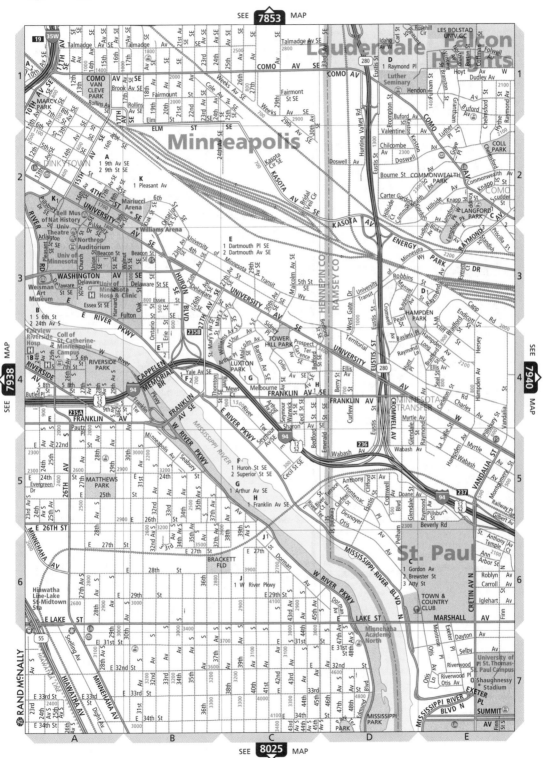

MAP
7940

1:30,000
1 in. = 2500 ft.

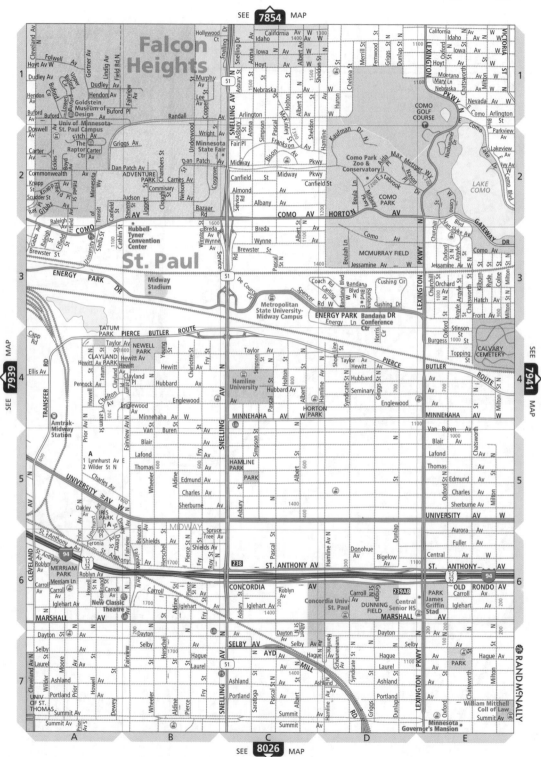

SEE **7854** MAP

SEE **7939** MAP

SEE **7941** MAP

SEE **8026** MAP

Falcon Heights

St. Paul

RAND McNALLY

N
1:30,000
1 in. = 2500 ft.
0   0.25   0.5
miles

MAP
7941

St. Paul

SEE 7940 MAP
SEE 7942 MAP
SEE 8027 MAP

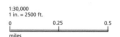

RAND McNALLY

MAP
7942

1:30,000
1 in. = 2500 ft.

0   0.25   0.5
miles

SEE 7856 MAP

SEE 7941 MAP

SEE 7943 MAP

SEE 8028 MAP

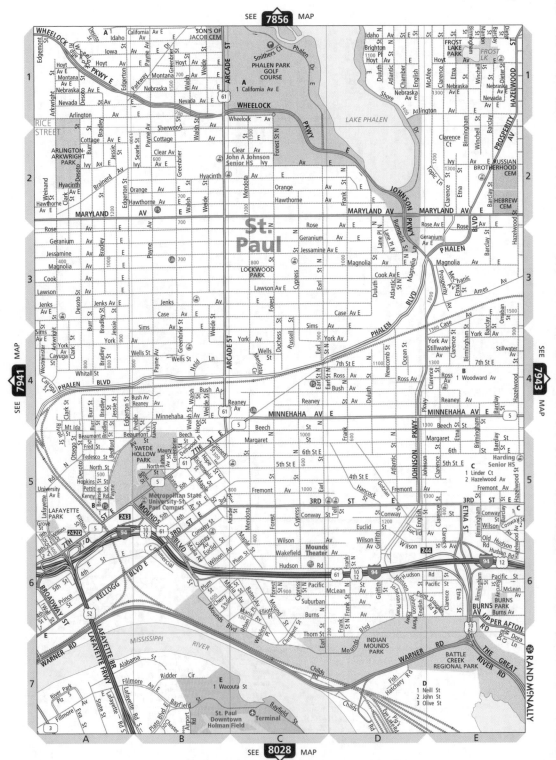

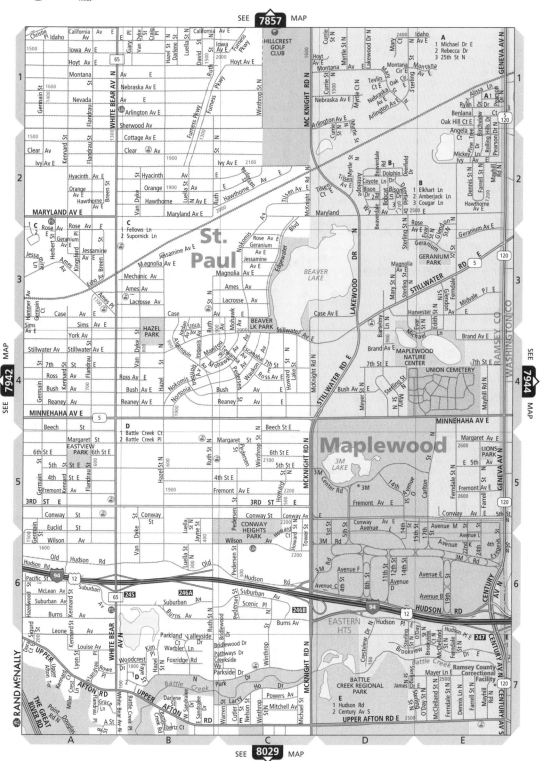

MAP
7943

St. Paul

Maplewood

MAP
7944

1:30,000
1 in. = 2500 ft.
0   0.25   0.5
miles

SEE 7858 MAP

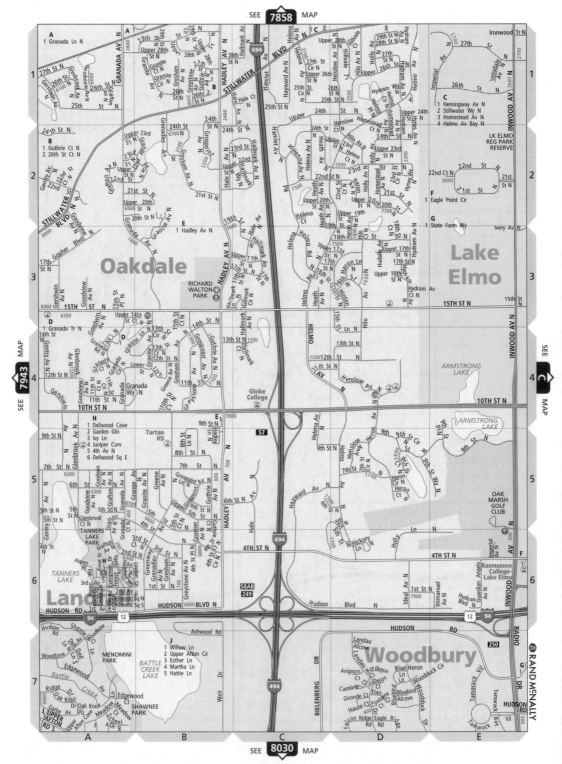

Oakdale

Lake Elmo

Woodbury

Land...

TANNERS LAKE

SEE 7943 MAP

SEE C MAP

SEE 8030 MAP

RAND McNALLY

MAP
8020

1:30,000
1 in. = 2500 ft.

SEE 7934 MAP

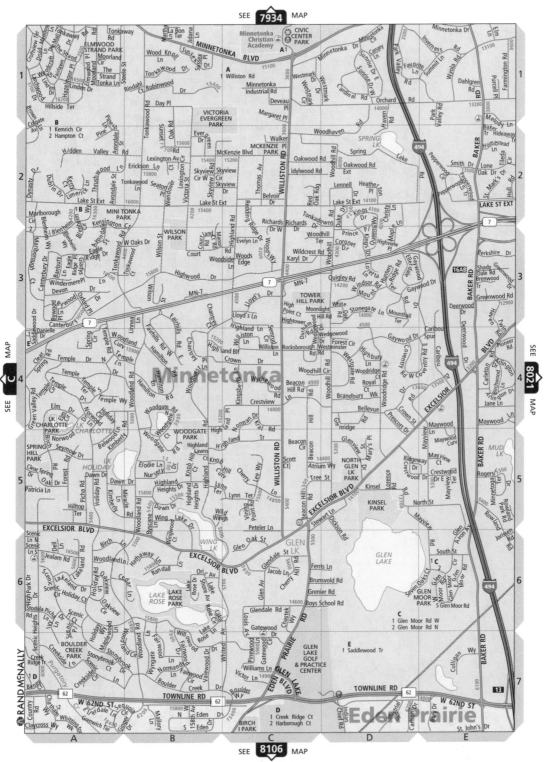

SEE MAP C

SEE 8021 MAP

SEE 8106 MAP

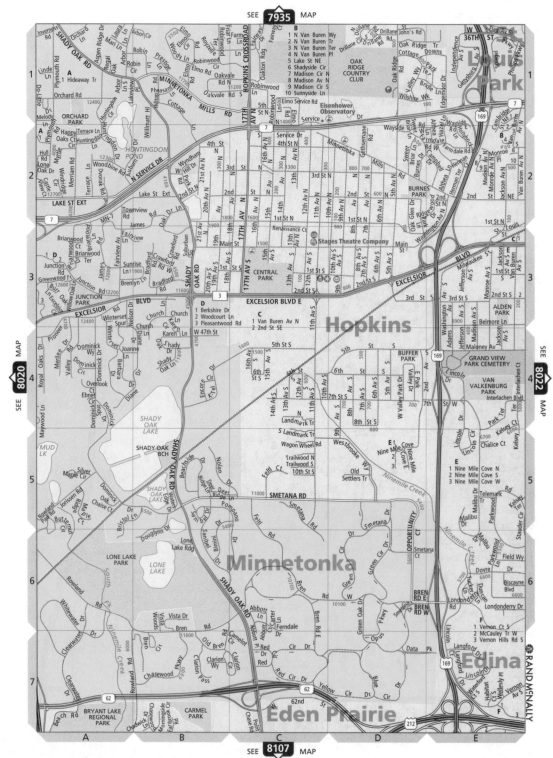

MAP
8021

1:30,000
1 in. = 2500 ft.
0   0.25   0.5
miles

SEE 8020 MAP

SEE 8022 MAP

SEE 8107 MAP

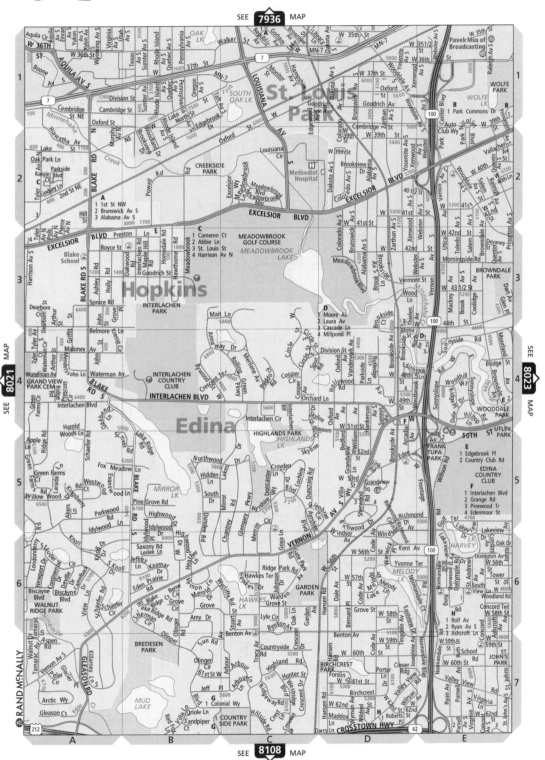

MAP
8022

SEE 7936 MAP

SEE 8021 MAP

SEE 8023 MAP

SEE 8108 MAP

MAP
8023

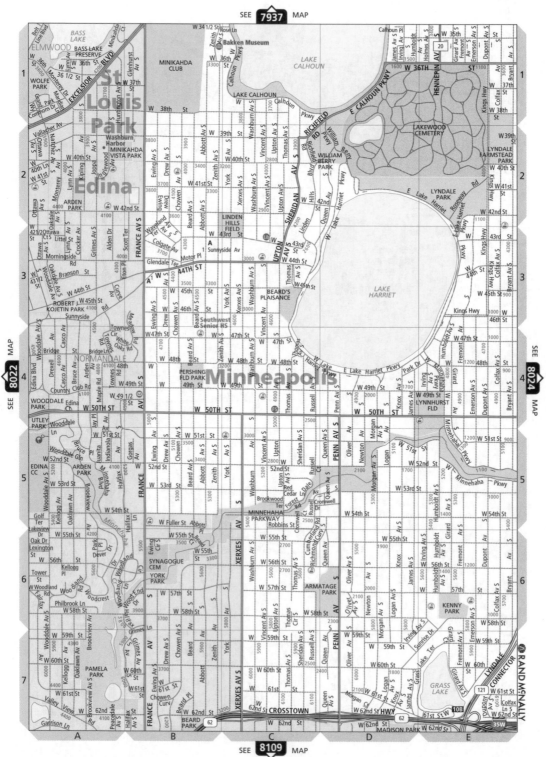

SEE 7937 MAP

1:30,000
1 in. = 2500 ft.
0   0.25   0.5
miles

SEE 8022 MAP

SEE 8024 MAP

SEE 8109 MAP

RAND McNALLY

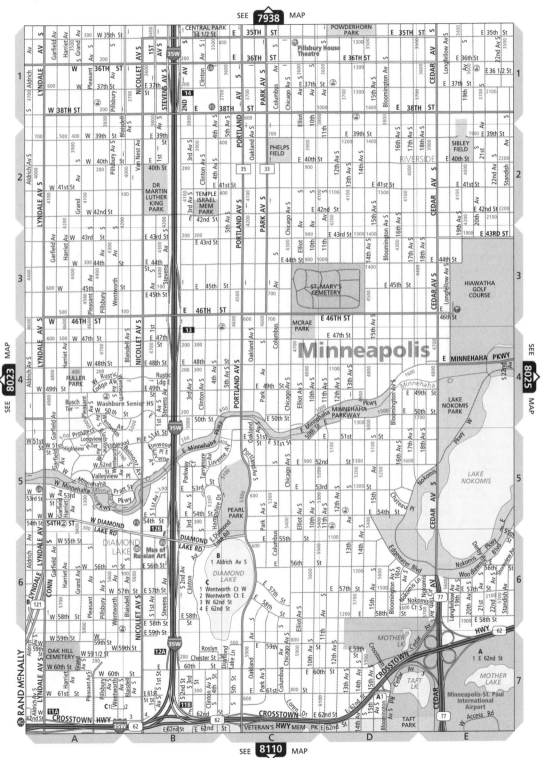

MAP
8024

1:30,000
1 in. = 2500 ft.
0   0.25   0.5
miles

SEE 7938 MAP

SEE 8023 MAP

SEE 8025 MAP

SEE 8110 MAP

Minneapolis

RAND McNALLY

MAP
8025

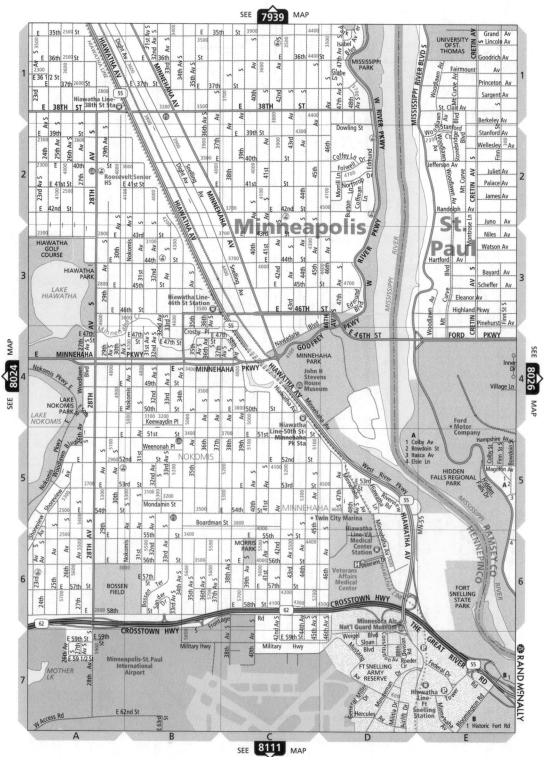

1:30,000
1 in. = 2500 ft.
0   0.25   0.5
miles

MAP
8026

1:30,000
1 in. = 2500 ft.

SEE 7940 MAP

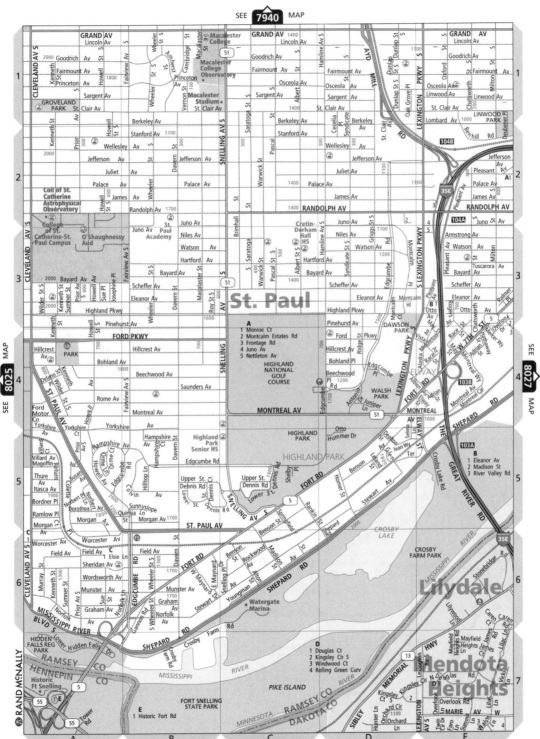

St. Paul

A
1 Monroe Ct
2 Montcalm Estates Rd
3 Frontage Rd
4 Juno Av
5 Nettleton Av

HIGHLAND NATIONAL GOLF COURSE

HIGHLAND PARK

B
1 Eleanor Av
2 Madison St
3 River Valley Rd

Lilydale

Mendota Heights

D
1 Douglas Ct
2 Kingsley Cir S
3 Windwood Ct
4 Rolling Green Curv

E
1 Historic Fort Rd

SEE 8025 MAP

SEE 8027 MAP

SEE 8112 MAP

RAND McNALLY

MAP
8027

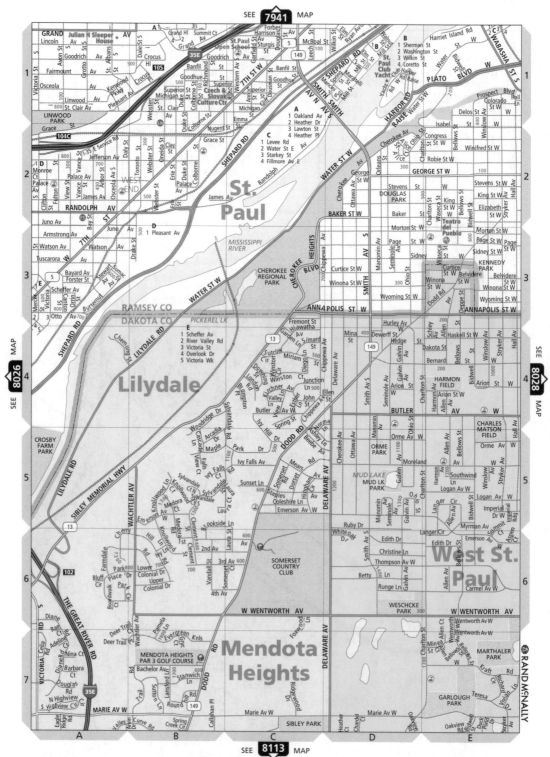

MAP
8028

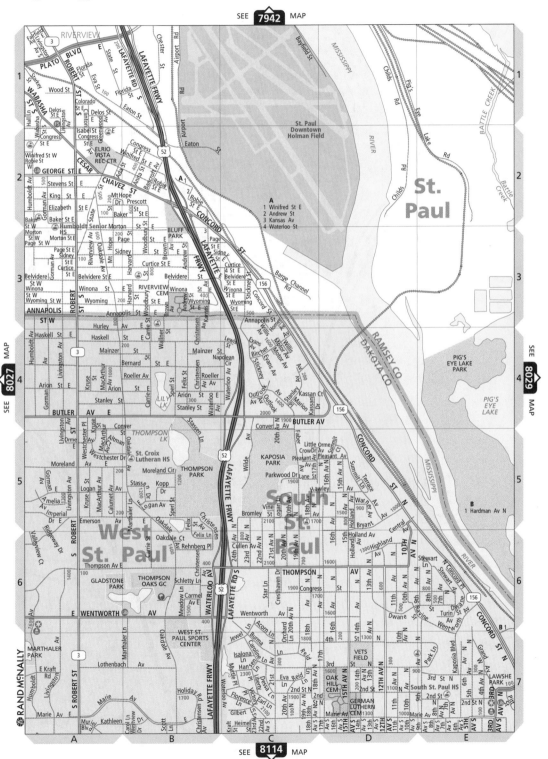

1:30,000
1 in. = 2500 ft.

0   0.25   0.5
miles

SEE 8027 MAP

SEE 8029 MAP

RAND M℠NALLY

MAP
8029

1:30,000
1 in. = 2500 ft.

MAP
8030

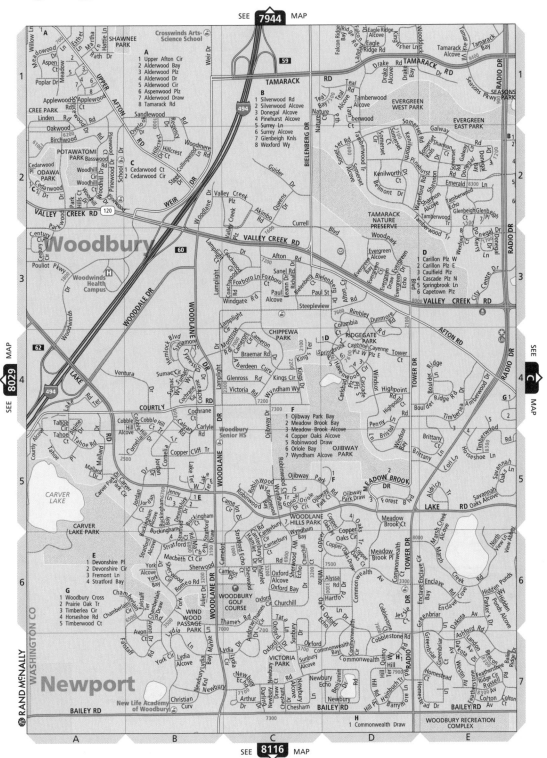

MAP
8106

SEE 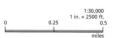 MAP

1:30,000
1 in. = 2500 ft.
0   0.25   0.5
miles

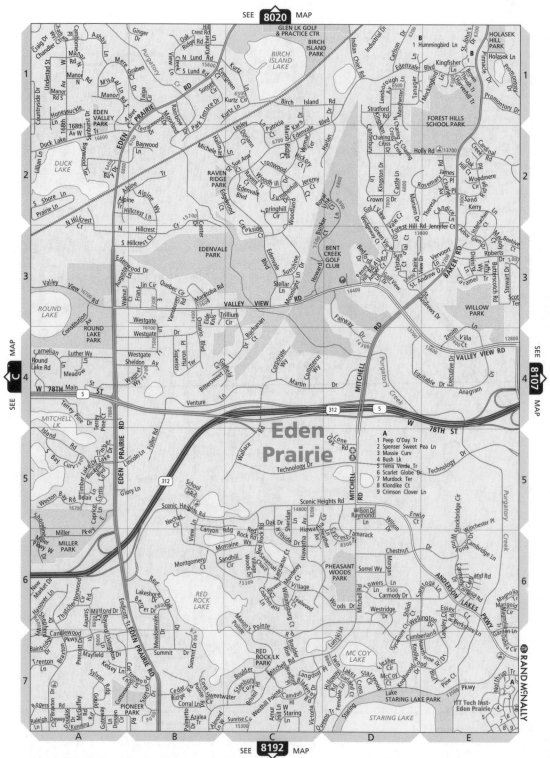

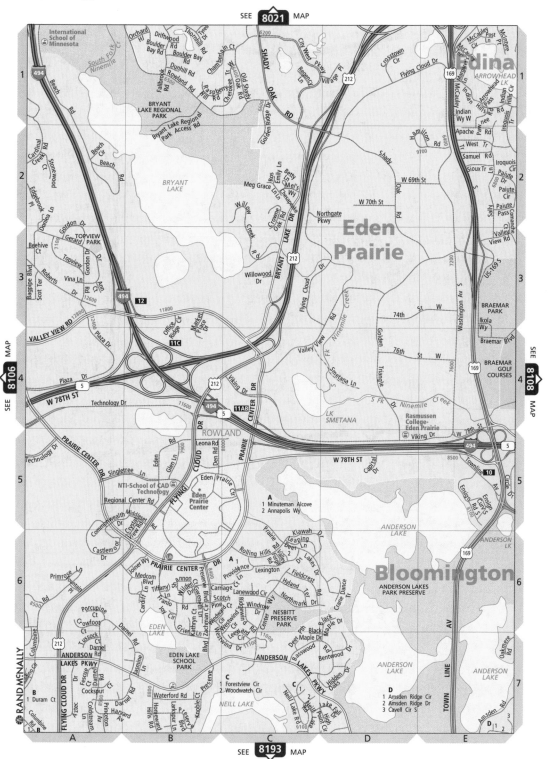

MAP
8107

1:30,000
1 in. = 2500 ft.

miles

SEE 8021 MAP

SEE 8106 MAP

SEE 8108 MAP

SEE 8193 MAP

MAP
8108

1:30,000
1 in. = 2500 ft.

0   0.25   0.5
miles

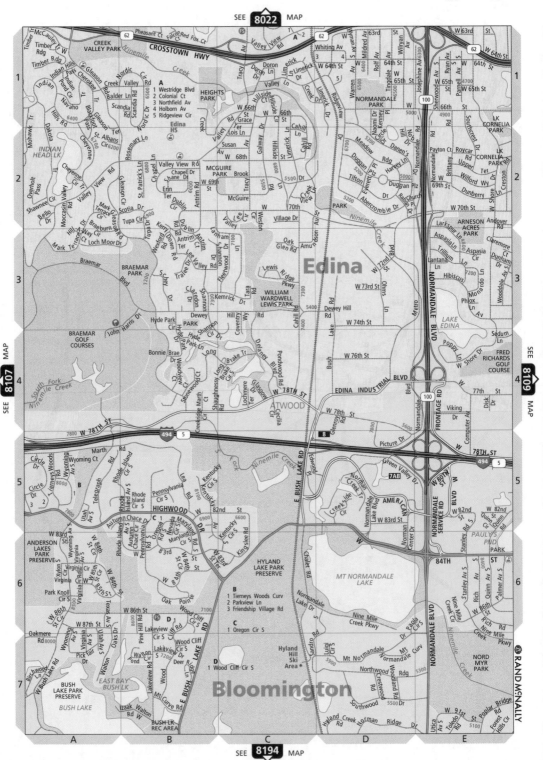

SEE 8022 MAP

SEE 8107 MAP

SEE 8109 MAP

Edina

Bloomington

RAND MCNALLY

SEE 8194 MAP

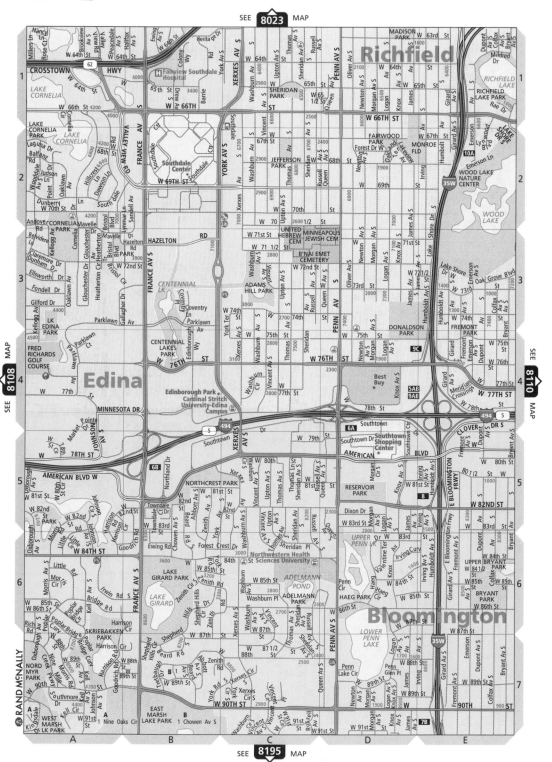

MAP
8109

1:30,000
1 in. = 2500 ft.
0   0.25   0.5
miles

SEE 8023 MAP

SEE 8108 MAP

SEE 8110 MAP

SEE 8195 MAP

Richfield

Edina

Bloomington

MAP
8110

1:30,000
1 in. = 2500 ft.
0   0.25   0.5
miles

SEE **8024** MAP

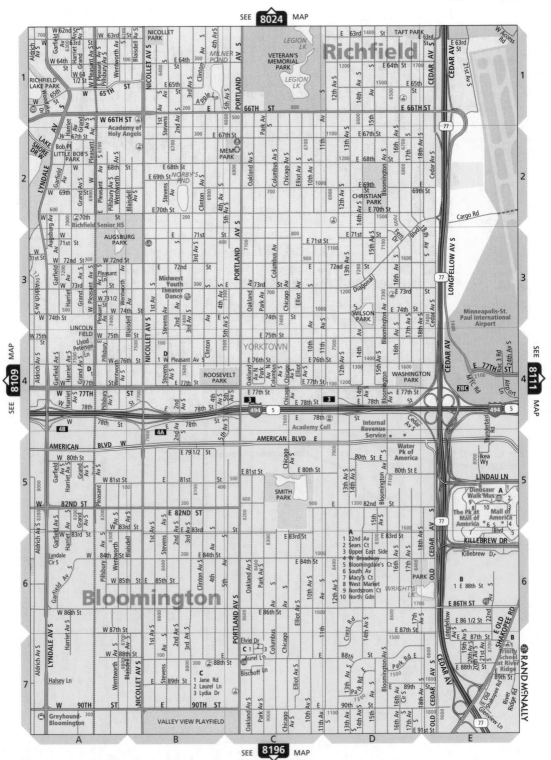

SEE **8109** MAP

SEE **8111** MAP

N

1:30,000
1 in. = 2500 ft.

0   0.25   0.5
miles

MAP
8111

SEE 8025 MAP

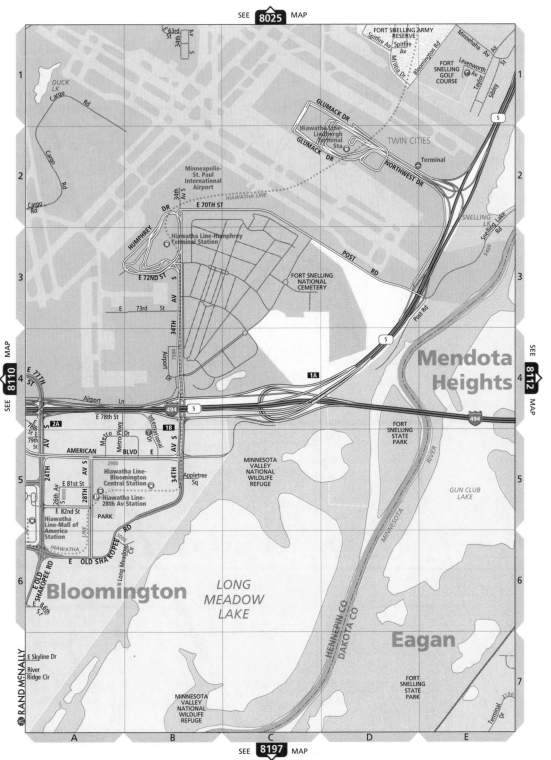

E 63rd St
34th Av S

DUCK LK
Cargo Rd
Cargo Rd
Cargo Rd
Cargo Rd

FORT SNELLING ARMY RESERVE
Spitfire Av   Spitfire Av
Militia Dr
Bloomington Rd
Minnehaha Av
FORT SNELLING GOLF COURSE
Levenworth Av
Taylor
Sibley St

GLUMACK DR
Hiawatha Line-Lindbergh Terminal Sta
GLUMACK DR
TWIN CITIES
Terminal
NORTHWEST DR

5

Minneapolis-St. Paul International Airport

34th Av S
DR
E 70TH ST
HIAWATHA LINE

SNELLING LK
Snelling Lake Rd

HUMPHREY
Hiawatha Line-Humphrey Terminal Station
E 72ND ST

POST RD
FORT SNELLING NATIONAL CEMETERY

34TH AV S

E 73rd St

Airport

5

Post Rd

Mendota Heights

1A

SEE 8110 MAP

SEE 8112 MAP

E 77TH ST
Airport Ln
494
5
FORT SNELLING STATE PARK
494

2A
E 78th St
Metro Pkwy
International Dr
1B
E 78th St E
79th St
AMERICAN
Metro Dr
E
BLVD

24th Av S
26th Av
28TH AV S
34TH AV S

2900
Hiawatha Line-Bloomington Central Station
Appletree Sq

E 81st St

Hiawatha Line-28th Av Station
PARK

MINNESOTA VALLEY NATIONAL WILDLIFE REFUGE

GUN CLUB LAKE

MINNESOTA RIVER

E 82nd St
Hiawatha Line-Mall of America Station
HIAWATHA LINE
E OLD SHAKOPEE RD
Long Meadow Cir

Bloomington

LONG MEADOW LAKE

HENNEPIN CO
DAKOTA CO

Eagan

E OLD SHAKOPEE RD
86th St

E Skyline Dr
River Ridge Cir

RAND McNALLY

MINNESOTA VALLEY NATIONAL WILDLIFE REFUGE

FORT SNELLING STATE PARK

Terminal Dr

SEE 8197 MAP

A   B   C   D   E

1   2   3   4   5   6   7

MAP
8112

1:30,000
1 in. = 2500 ft.
0   0.25   0.5
miles

SEE 8026 MAP

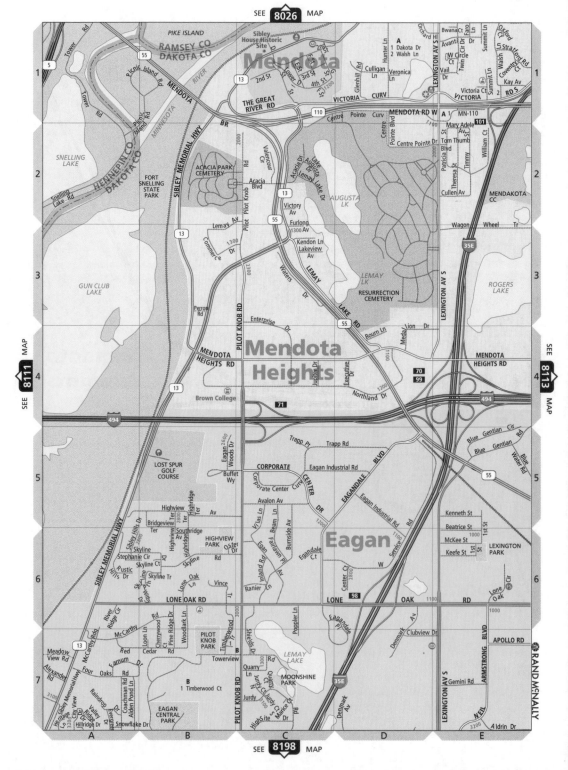

SEE 8111 MAP
SEE 8113 MAP
SEE 8198 MAP

RAND McNALLY

MAP
8113

1:30,000
1 in. = 2500 ft.

0   0.25   0.5
miles

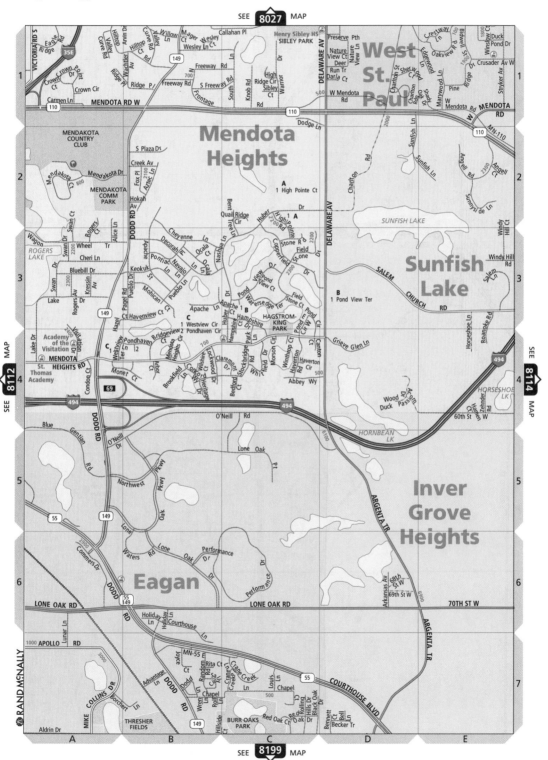

SEE 8027 MAP

West St. Paul

Mendota Heights

Sunfish Lake

Inver Grove Heights

Eagan

SEE 8112 MAP

SEE 8814 MAP

SEE 8199 MAP

A   B   C   D   E

MAP
8114

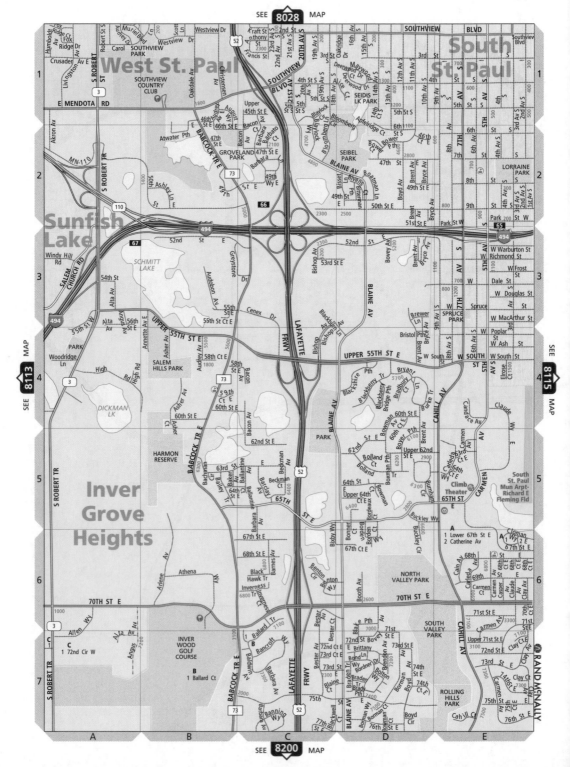

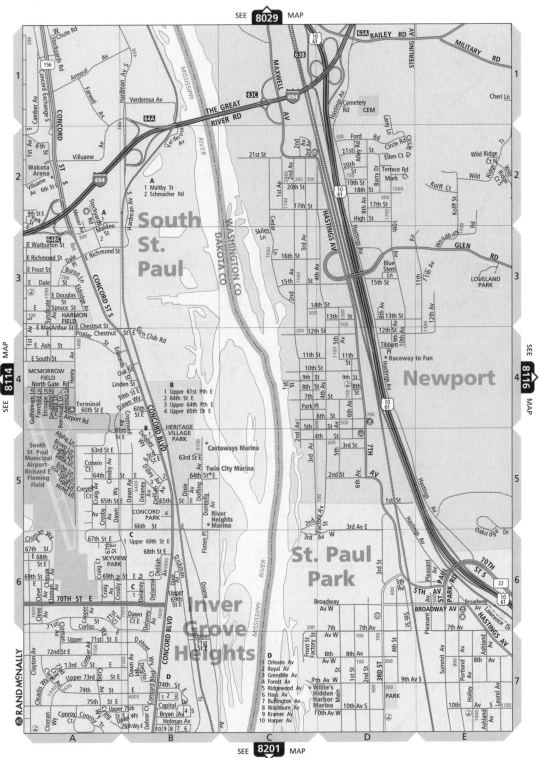

MAP
8115

1:30,000
1 in. = 2500 ft.

0   0.25   0.5
miles

SEE [8029] MAP

SEE [8114] MAP

SEE [8116] MAP

SEE [8201] MAP

South St. Paul

Newport

St. Paul Park

Inver Grove Heights

A
1 Maltby St
2 Schmacher Rd

B
1 Upper 61st Pth E
2 64th St E
3 Upper 64th Pth E
4 Upper 65th Dr E

C
1 Upper 69th St E

D
1 Orleans Av
2 Royal Av
3 Grenoble Av
4 Forest Av
5 Ridgewood Av
6 Hays Av
7 Buffington Av
8 Washburn Av
9 Kramer Av
10 Harper Av

RAND MCNALLY

MAP
8116

1:30,000
1 in. = 2500 ft.

0   0.25   0.5
miles

SEE 8030 MAP

WOODBURY
RECREATION
COMPLEX

RIA
LAKE

LA
LAKE

Newport

6000

Century Av

Catherine Dr

MILITARY RD

Wild Canyon Tr

Wild

Valhalla Dr

WOODLANE DR

Ranch Rd

RADIO DR

Woodbury

Wild Canyon Cir

Canyon Dr

Wild Canyon Ct

Stimson Tr

Crown Ln

5000

Dale Rd

Howkins St

Crackleberry Tr

Crackleberry Bay

Crackleberry Alcove

Crackleberry

Crackleberry Ct

Crackleberry

WOODLANE DR

7000

GLEN RD

GLEN RD

MILITARY RD

RADIO DR

Lynn

Wy

6600

5500

Garden Ct Dr

Deer Tr

Tower Dr

Sunny Hill Dr

SEE 8115 MAP

6000

Av

Kalen Cir

Century

Kalen Kalen Ct

Lynn Wy

Dr

Orchard Ridge Tr

Woodlane Ct

Woodlane Ct

Woodlane Bay

Deer Trail Cir

Fawn Trail

Deer Trail

5700 Cir

SEE C MAP

Summit

6000 Ct S

Summit

Curv

61st St S

Homestead Av

62nd

Homestead

**Cottage
Grove**

Pointe Pl S

6800

Summit Hills Curv

Blvd

Homestead Cir S

Hadley Av S

63rd St S 63rd St

Cir S

Heathstone Hedgecroft

Hinton Av S

63rd St S

Av S

THOMPSON PARK

Thompson Park Curv

Highland Hills Ln S

Highland

Homestead Ln S

65th St S

65th St S

65th St S

65th St S

65th St S

Geneva Av S

B
1 Hidden Valley Pond S
2 Hidden Valley Ter S
3 Homestead Av S

Wildflower Dr

Bluestem Ln S

Hadley

66th St S

66th

67th

Innsdale Av S

66th St S

67th Skip

Inskip

Bedivere

6500

Goldenrod

Cir S

Hadley Cir S

Ct S

A
1 Bluestem Cove S
2 Timber Ridge Ct S
3 Pine Arbor Ln S
4 Pine Arbor Dr S
5 67th St S

Homestead Av Ct S

67th St Ct S

68th

69th

St S

Lincoln Av

Indigo Ct S

Wildrye Cir S

Meadow

Timber Ridge

Timber Ridge

7700

68th St S

Innsdale

St S

Inwood

Cattail Primrose

Av S Ct S

Timber Trail

Timber Ridge Ln S

Timber

Pine Crest Tr S

6100

Pine Arbor Blvd

69th St

Inskip

Ideal

Inskip

C
1 Valerie Ct
2 Elsie Ct
3 Sandy Ct

Granada Ct S

Cattail

Ln S

Timber Ridge Hllw S

Pine Arbor

69th St S

7700

HIGHLANDS PARK

Foxtail

Skylark

Pine Arbor Alcove S

6600

Goodview

70TH

ST S

70TH ST S

22

71st St S

B

Sunflower Cir S

71st St S

Redpine

73rd St

Hidden Valley

72nd

72nd St

Homestead Av S

Imperial Av

72nd St S

Inskip

Inwood

Lawrence

Goodview Av S

11st St S

Prairie

74th St

Bay S

73rd

Cove S

Hidden Valley Ln S

Imperial Av Cir S

Innsdale

PINETREE VALLEY PARK

22

Goodview Bay S

Granada Av S

Granada Bay S

Timber Ridge St S

Timber Ridge Cove S

Hidden Valley Rda S

Hidden Valley

8300

Indian Blvd

Indian Blvd S

Inwood

10 61

C
1 Dr

2 3

Granada Alcove S

74th St S

Burr Oak Av S

Meadow Grass S

Hidden Valley Tr S

73rd St S

73rd St

74th St S

Iden Av S

Illies Av

Imperial

Indian Blvd

Inman Av S

73rd St S

RAND McNALLY

**St.
Paul
Park**

ABDELLA MEMORIAL PARK

Lincoln Av

Selby Av

ST THOMAS AQUINAS CEMETERY

HASTINGS AV

Granada Alcove S

Aspen Cove S

Burr Oak Cove S

Meadow Grass Cove S

HARDWOOD

Harkness Av S

Hidden Valley Ct S

Hinton Park Av S

OAKWOOD PARK

74th St S

Hyde Av S

Ideal

75th St S

Iden Av

Hyde Av S

Immanuel Av

STAD PARK

76th St

Immanuel Av

Imperial Av

Inman Ct S

Inman Tr S

Inman Av S

76th St S

Inskip

Hinton Av S

Homestead Av S

A   B   C   D   E

SEE 8202 MAP

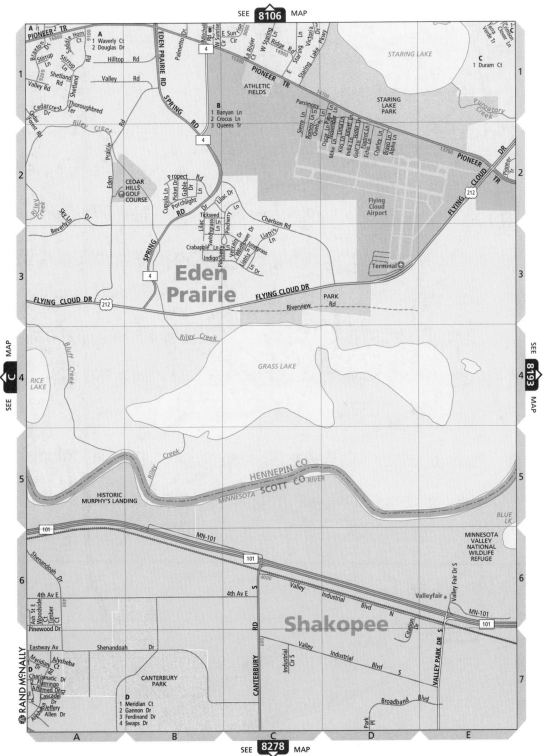

MAP
8192

1:30,000
1 in. = 2500 ft.

miles

SEE 8106 MAP

SEE MAP C

SEE 8193 MAP

SEE 8278 MAP

Eden Prairie

Shakopee

STARING LAKE

STARING LAKE PARK

ATHLETIC FIELDS

CEDAR HILLS GOLF COURSE

Flying Cloud Airport

Terminal

GRASS LAKE

RICE LAKE

HISTORIC MURPHY'S LANDING

HENNEPIN CO
SCOTT CO
MINNESOTA RIVER

BLUE LK

MINNESOTA VALLEY NATIONAL WILDLIFE REFUGE

Valleyfair

CANTERBURY PARK

A
1 Waverly Ct
2 Douglas Dr

B
1 Banyan Ln
2 Crocus Ln
3 Queens Tr

C
1 Duram Ct

D
1 Meridian Ct
2 Gannon Dr
3 Ferdinand Dr
4 Swaps Dr

RAND MCNALLY

MAP
8193

1:30,000
1 in. = 2500 ft.
0   0.25   0.5
miles

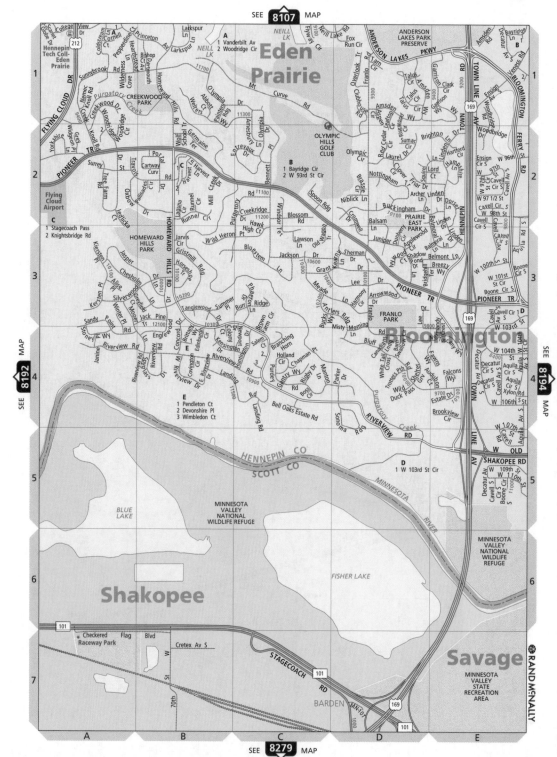

MAP
8194

1:30,000
1 in. = 2500 ft.

0   0.25   0.5
miles

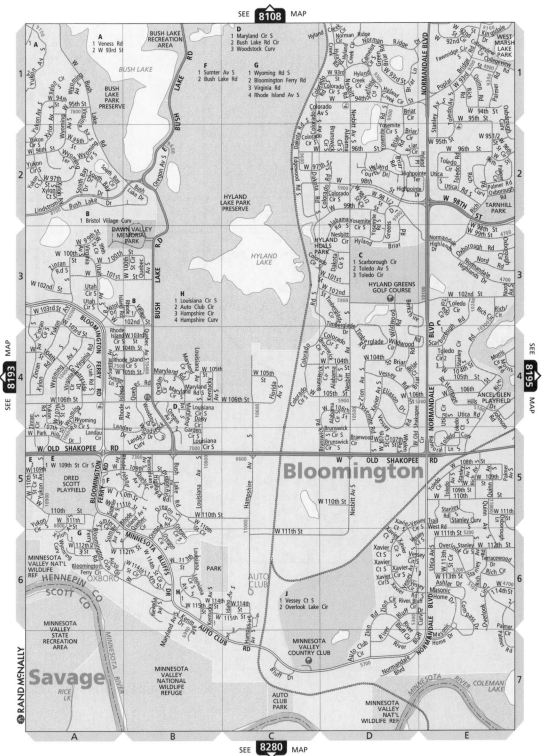

SEE **8108** MAP

SEE **8193** MAP

SEE **8195** MAP

SEE **8280** MAP

Bloomington

Savage

MAP
8195

1:30,000
1 in. = 2500 ft.

0   0.25   0.5
miles

SEE 8109 MAP

SEE 8194 MAP

SEE 8196 MAP

SEE 8281 MAP

A
1 College Heights Cir
2 98th St S Service Rd
3 Pebblebrook Cir
4 Oxborough Rd
5 Nord Cir
6 Normandale Highlands Cir
7 Drew Cir S

Bloomington

Burnsville

RAND McNALLY

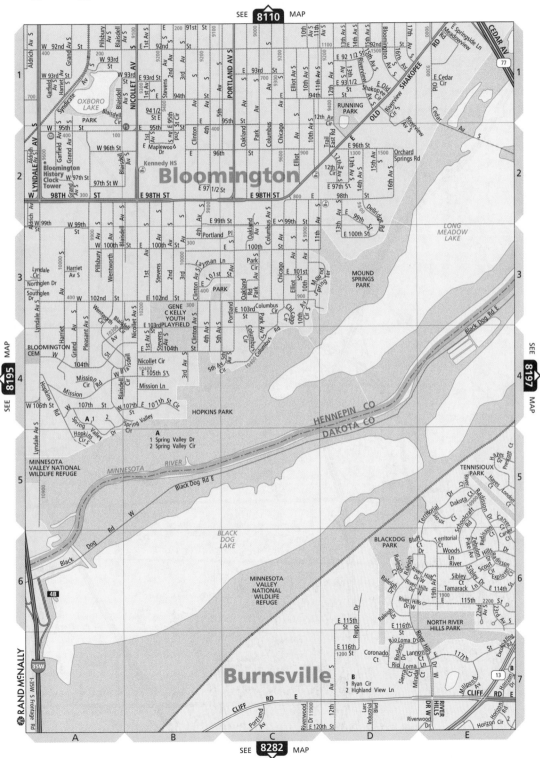

MAP
8196

1:30,000
1 in. = 2500 ft.

0   0.25   0.5
miles

SEE 8110 MAP

SEE 8195 MAP

SEE 8197 MAP

SEE 8282 MAP

Bloomington

Burnsville

RAND McNALLY

MAP
8197

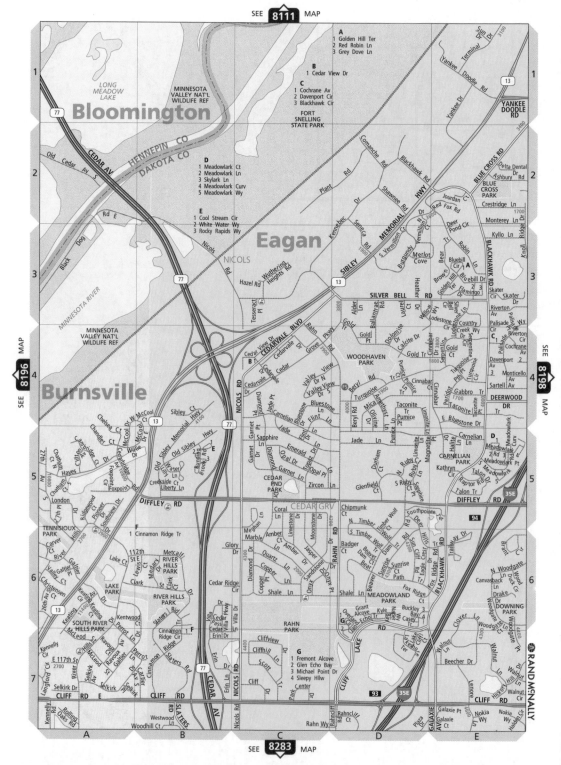

1:30,000
1 in. = 2500 ft.
0   0.25   0.5
miles

A
1 Golden Hill Ter
2 Red Robin Ln
3 Grey Dove Ln

B
1 Cedar View Dr

C
1 Cochrane Av
2 Davenport Cir
3 Blackhawk Cir

D
1 Meadowlark Ct
2 Meadowlark Ln
3 Skylark Ln
4 Meadowlark Curv
5 Meadowlark Wy

E
1 Cool Stream Cir
2 White Water Wy
3 Rocky Rapids Wy

F
1 Cinnamon Ridge Tr

G
1 Fremont Alcove
2 Glen Echo Bay
3 Michael Point Dr
4 Sleepy Hllw
Center

LONG
MEADOW
LAKE

MINNESOTA
VALLEY NAT'L
WILDLIFE REF

FORT
SNELLING
STATE PARK

Bloomington

Eagan

Burnsville

MINNESOTA
VALLEY NAT'L
WILDLIFE REF

MINNESOTA RIVER

NICOLS

HENNEPIN CO
DAKOTA CO

RAND MCNALLY

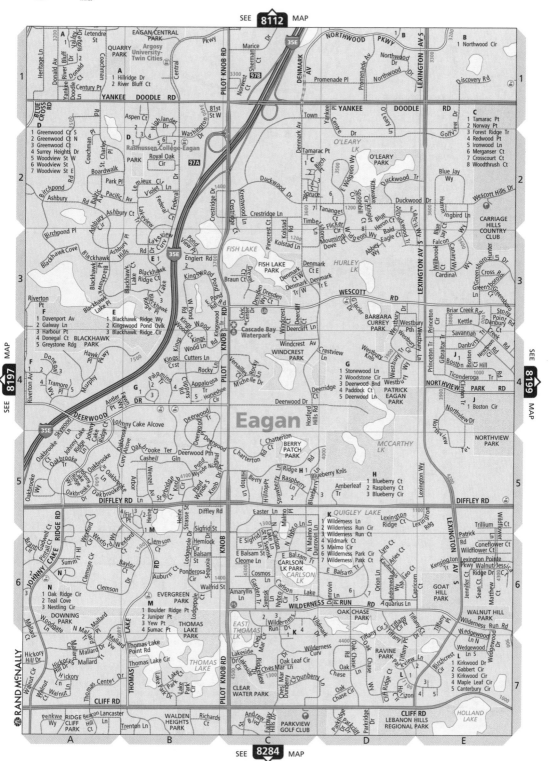

1:30,000
1 in. = 2500 ft.

0   0.25   0.5
miles

Eagan

RAND MCNALLY

MAP
8199

1:30,000
1 in. = 2500 ft.

0   0.25   0.5
miles

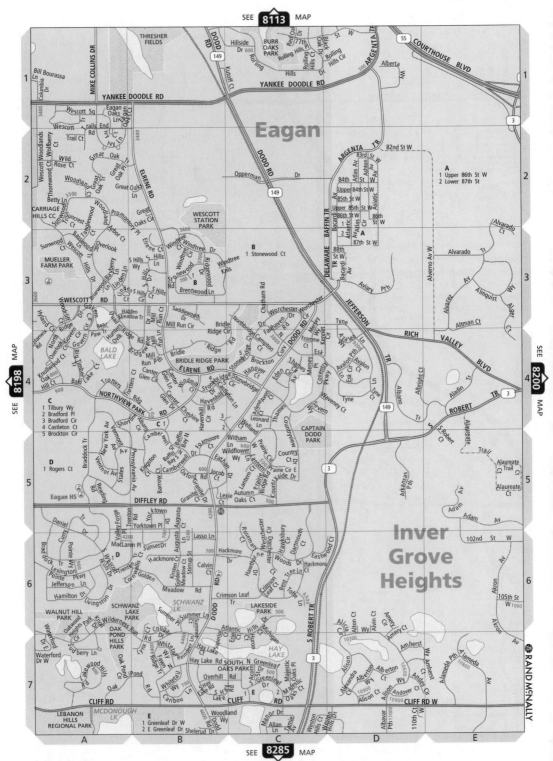

SEE 8113 MAP

Eagan

Inver Grove Heights

SEE 8198 MAP

SEE 8200 MAP

SEE 8285 MAP

RAND MCNALLY

A
1 Upper 86th St W
2 Lower 87th St

B
1 Stonewood Ct

C
1 Tilbury Wy
2 Bradford Pl
3 Bradford Cir
4 Castleton Ct
5 Brockton Cir

D
1 Rogers Ct

E
1 Greenleaf Dr W
2 E Greenleaf Dr

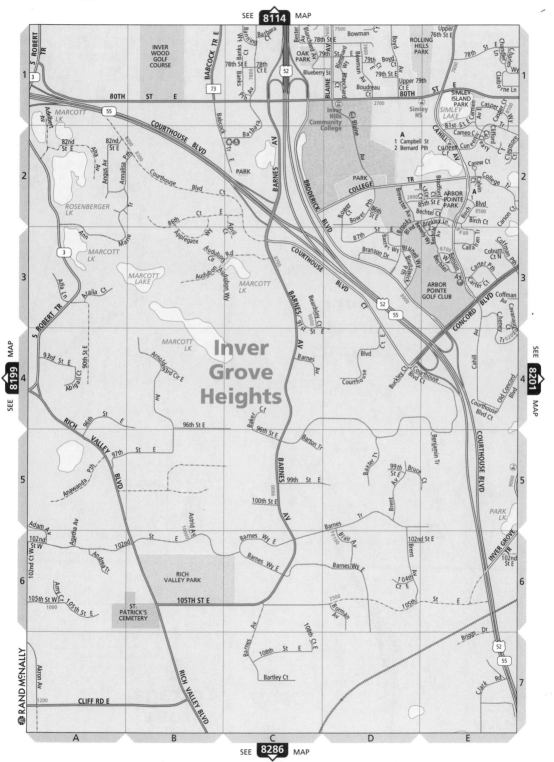

MAP
8200

Inver Grove Heights

MAP
8201

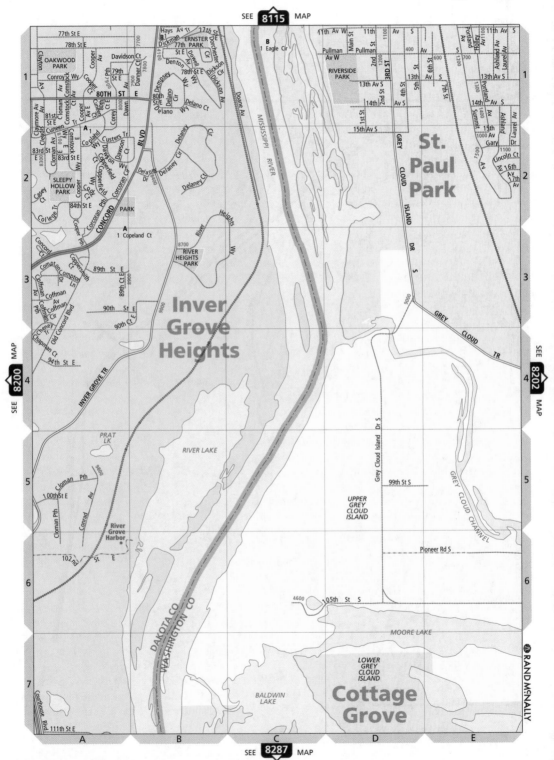

1:30,000
1 in. = 2500 ft.

0   0.25   0.5
miles

SEE 8115 MAP

SEE 8200 MAP

SEE 8202 MAP

SEE 8287 MAP

St. Paul Park

Inver Grove Heights

Cottage Grove

RAND MCNALLY

MAP
8202

MAP
8278

1:30,000
1 in. = 2500 ft.
0   0.25   0.5
miles

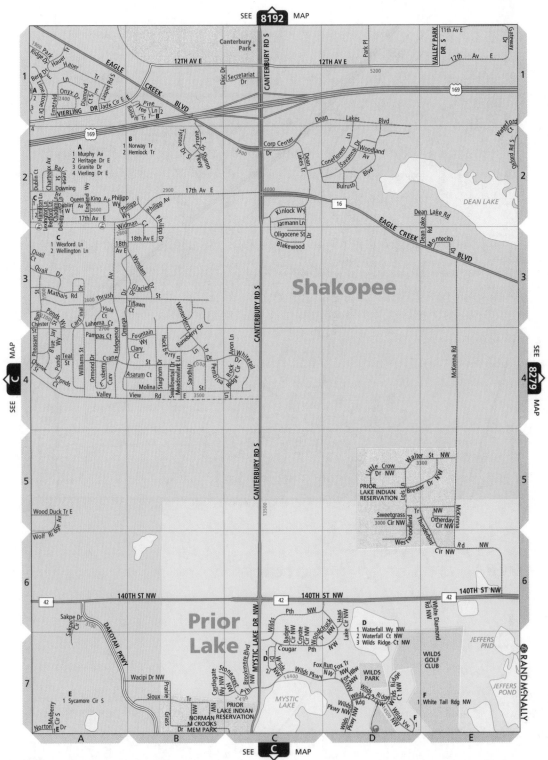

MAP
8279

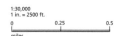

1:30,000
1 in. = 2500 ft.

0   0.25   0.5
miles

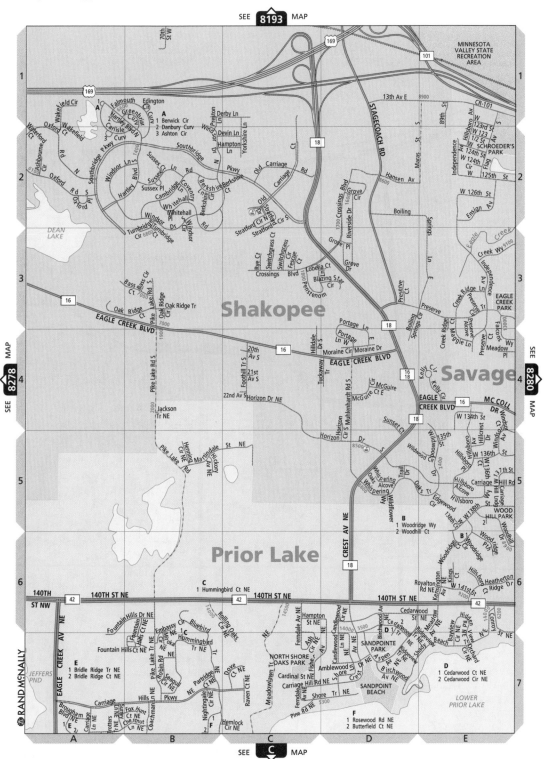

SEE 8193 MAP

SEE 8278 MAP

SEE 8280 MAP

SEE C MAP

RAND McNALLY

MAP
8280

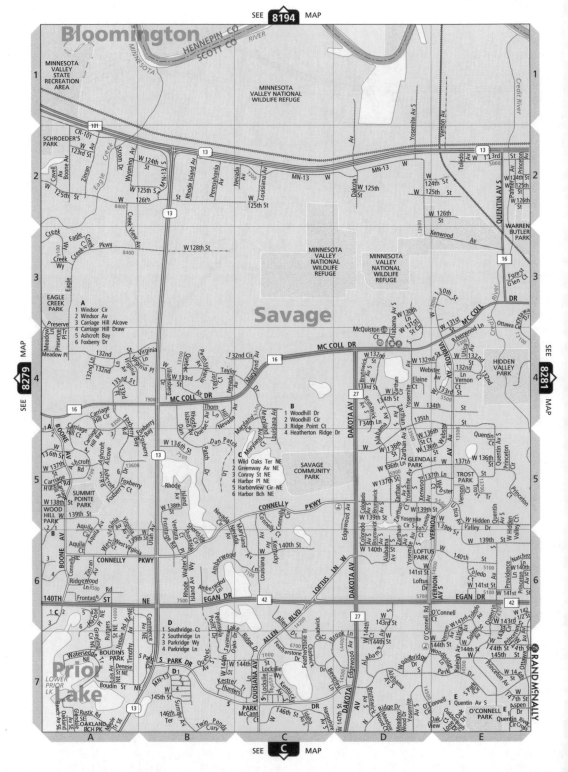

SEE 8194 MAP

Bloomington

SEE 8279 MAP

SEE 8281 MAP

Savage

Prior Lake

RAND MCNALLY

SEE C MAP

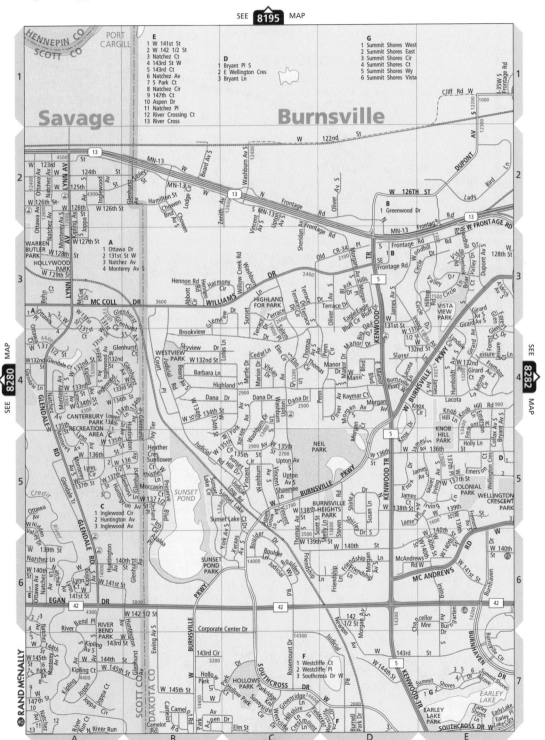

MAP
8281

1:30,000
1 in. = 2500 ft.

0   0.25   0.5
miles

SEE 8195 MAP

SEE 8280 MAP

SEE 8282 MAP

SEE C MAP

PORT CARGILL

HENNEPIN CO
SCOTT CO

Savage

Burnsville

E
1 W 141st St
2 W 142 1/2 St
3 Natchez Ct
4 143rd St W
5 143rd Ct
6 Natchez Av
7 S Park St
8 Natchez Cir
9 147th Ct
10 Aspen Dr
11 Natchez Pl
12 River Crossing Ct
13 River Cross

D
1 Bryant Pl S
2 E Wellington Cres
3 Bryant Ln

G
1 Summit Shores West
2 Summit Shores East
3 Summit Shores Cir
4 Summit Shores Ct
5 Summit Shores Wy
6 Summit Shores Vista

A
1 Ottawa Dr
2 131st St W
3 Natchez Av
4 Monterey Av S

B
1 Greenwood Dr

C
1 Inglewood Cir
2 Huntington Av
3 Inglewood Av

F
1 Westcliffe Ct
2 Westcliffe Pl
3 Southcross Dr W

RAND McNALLY

MAP
8282

SEE 8196 MAP

1:30,000
1 in. = 2500 ft.
0   0.25   0.5
miles

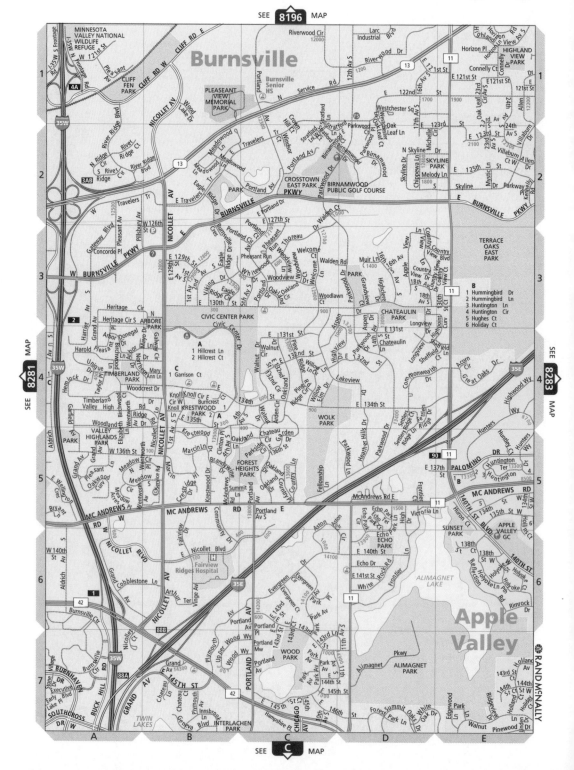

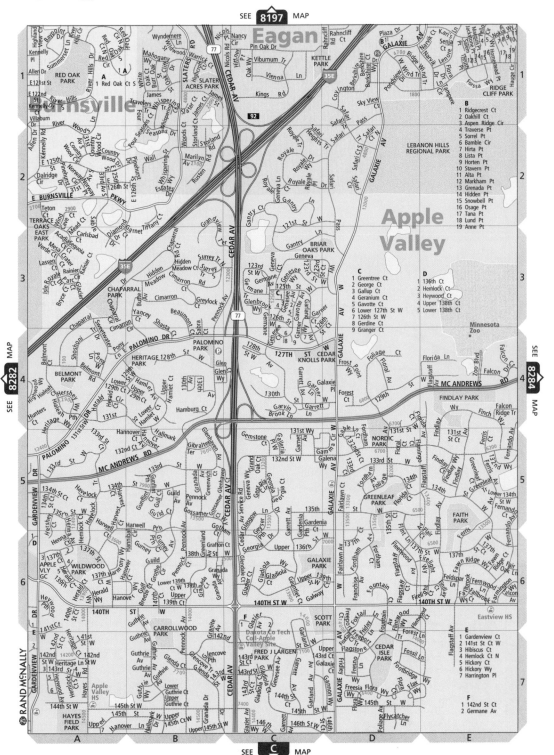

MAP
8283

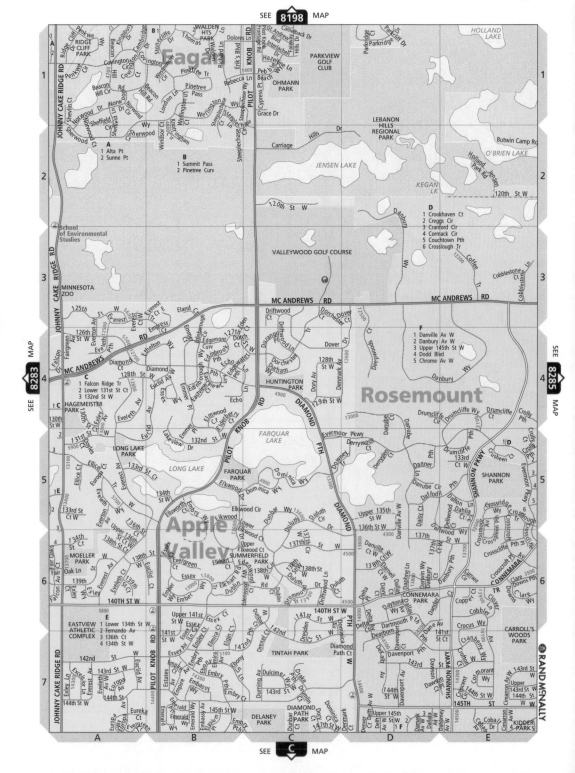

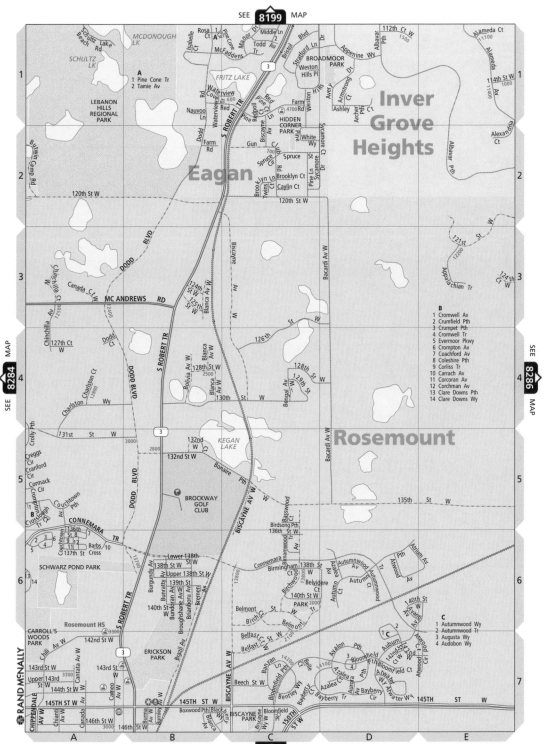

MAP
8285

1:30,000
1 in. = 2500 ft.
0   0.25   0.5
miles

SEE 8199 MAP

Inver Grove Heights

Eagan

Rosemount

MCDONOUGH LK

Schultz Lake Beach Rd

SCHULTZ LK

FRITZ LAKE

LEBANON HILLS REGIONAL PARK

BROADMOOR PARK

HIDDEN CORNER PARK

KEGAN LAKE

BROCKWAY GOLF CLUB

SCHWARZ POND PARK

CARROLL'S WOODS PARK

Rosemount HS

ERICKSON PARK

BISCAYNE PARK

CHIPPENDALE

A
1 Pine Cone Tr
2 Tamie Av

B
1 Cromwell Av
2 Crumfield Pth
3 Crumpet Pth
4 Cromwell Tr
5 Evermoor Pkwy
6 Crompton Av
7 Coachford Av
8 Coleshire Pth
9 Corliss Tr
10 Carrach Av
11 Corcoran Av
12 Corchman Av
13 Clare Downs Pth
14 Clare Downs Wy

C
1 Autumnwood Wy
2 Autumnwood Tr
3 Augusta Wy
4 Audobon Wy

120th St W
120th St W
MC ANDREWS RD
121st St
124th Ct W
126th St W
127th Ct W
128th St W
129th W
130th St W
131st St W
132nd St W
135th St W
136th St W
137th St W
Lower 138th St W
138th St W
139th St W
140th St W
142nd St W
143rd St W
144th St W
145TH ST W
146th St W

DODD BLVD
S ROBERT TR
BISCAYNE AV W
CONNEMARA TR
BIRCH

SEE 8284 MAP
SEE 8286 MAP
SEE C MAP

A   B   C   D   E

MAP
8286

1:30,000
1 in. = 2500 ft.
0   0.25   0.5
miles

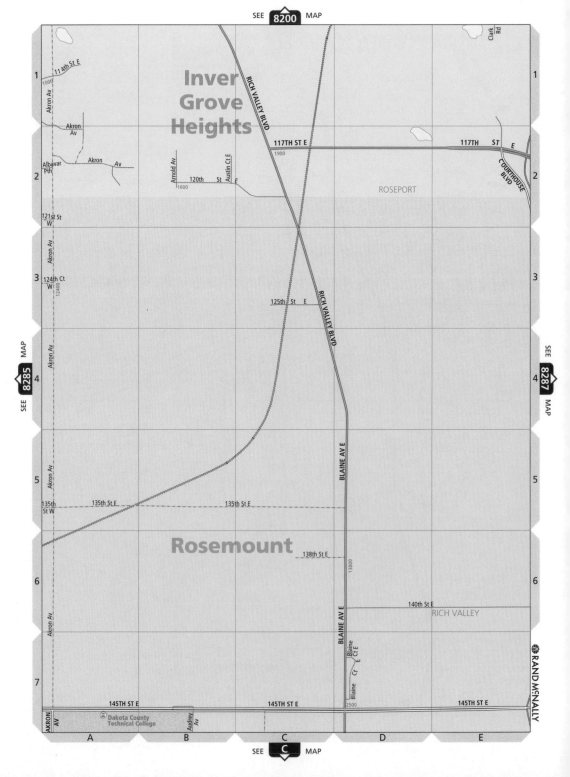

SEE ⬆ 8200 MAP

Inver Grove Heights

RICH VALLEY BLVD

Clark Rd

1

114th St E

1000

Akron Av

Akron Av

117TH ST E

117TH ST E

1900

COURTHOUSE BLVD

Albavar Pth

Akron Av

Arnold Av

120th St

Austin Ct E

ROSEPORT

2

1600

121st St W

Akron Av

3

124th Ct W

12400

125th St E

RICH VALLEY BLVD

SEE ◄ 8285 MAP

Akron Av

4

SEE ► 8287 MAP

Akron Av

BLAINE AV E

5

135th St W

135th St E

135th St E

Rosemount

138th St E

13800

6

140th St E

RICH VALLEY

Akron Av

BLAINE AV E

Blaine Ct E

7

Blaine Ct E

145TH ST E

145TH ST E

145TH ST E

AKRON AV

2500

Ⓜ Dakota County Technical College

Audrey Av

A   B   C   D   E

SEE C MAP

1:30,000
1 in. = 2500 ft.
0   0.25   0.5
miles

MAP
8287

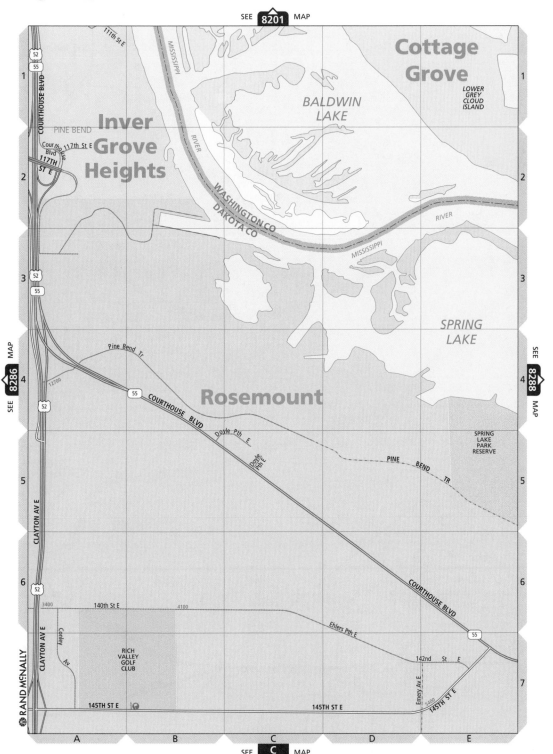

111th St E

52
55

COURTHOUSE BLVD

PINE BEND

Inver Grove Heights

Courthouse Blvd
117th St E
117TH ST E

1

52
55

2

3

SEE 8286 MAP

12700

52

Pine Bend Tr

55

COURTHOUSE BLVD

Rosemount

Doyle Pth E

Doyle Pth E

PINE BEND TR

4

SEE 8288 MAP

SPRING LAKE PARK RESERVE

5

CLAYTON AV E

52

6

3400

140th St E

4100

CLAYTON AV E

Conley Av

RICH VALLEY GOLF CLUB

Ehlers Pth E

142nd St E

Emery Av E

5400

55

COURTHOUSE BLVD

145th St E

145TH ST E

145TH ST E

MISSISSIPPI RIVER

WASHINGTON CO
DAKOTA CO

BALDWIN LAKE

Cottage Grove

LOWER GREY CLOUD ISLAND

RIVER

MISSISSIPPI

SPRING LAKE

6

7

RAND McNALLY

A   B   C   D   E

MAP
8288

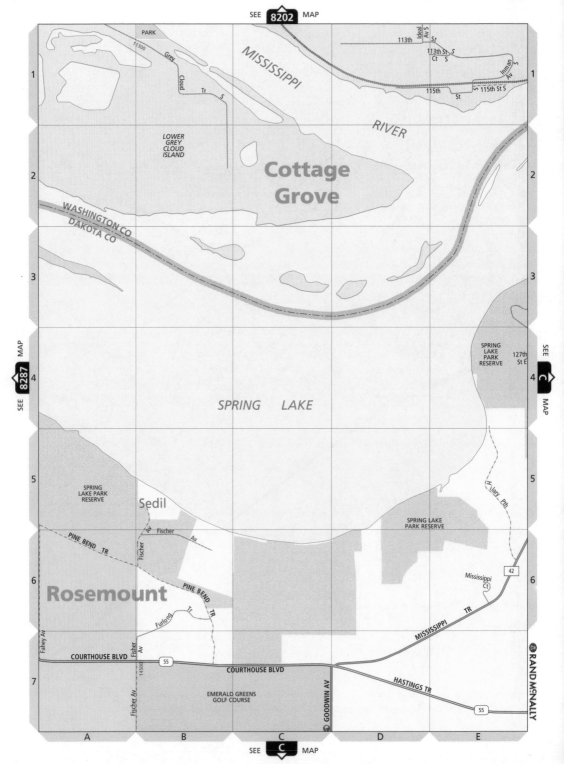

SEE 8202 MAP

PARK

11300

Grey

Cloud

Tr   S

MISSISSIPPI

113th

Ideal   Av   S   St

113th St   S
Ct   S

Inman   Av   S

1

LOWER
GREY
CLOUD
ISLAND

115th   St   S 115th St S

RIVER

Cottage
Grove

2

WASHINGTON CO
DAKOTA CO

3

SPRING   LAKE

SPRING
LAKE
PARK
RESERVE

127th
St E

SEE 8287 MAP

4

SEE C MAP

SPRING
LAKE PARK
RESERVE

Sedil

Av   Fischer   Av

Fischer

H. lary   Pth

5

SPRING LAKE
PARK RESERVE

PINE BEND   TR

Rosemount

PINE BEND   TR

Furlong   Tr

Fischer   Av

Fahey Av

COURTHOUSE BLVD

14500

55

Mississippi
Ct

42

MISSISSIPPI   TR

6

COURTHOUSE BLVD

HASTINGS TR

55

7

EMERALD GREENS
GOLF COURSE

Fischer Av

GOODWIN AV

A   B   C   D   E

SEE C MAP

List of Abbreviations

Abbr	Meaning	Abbr	Meaning	Abbr	Meaning	Abbr	Meaning
Admin	Administration	Cr	Creek	Jct	Junction	PO	Post Office
Agri	Agricultural	Cres	Crescent	Knl	Knoll	Pres	Preserve
Ag	Agriculture	Cross	Crossing	Knls	Knolls	Prov	Provincial
AFB	Air Force Base	Curv	Curve	Lk	Lake	Rwy	Railway
Arpt	Airport	Cto	Cut Off	Lndg	Landing	Rec	Recreation
Al	Alley	Dept	Department	Ln	Lane	Reg	Regional
Amer	American	Dev	Development	Lib	Library	Res	Reservoir
Anx	Annex	Diag	Diagonal	Ldg	Lodge	Rst	Rest
Arc	Arcade	Div	Division	Lp	Loop	Rdg	Ridge
Arch	Archaeological	Dr	Drive	Mnr	Manor	Rd	Road
Aud	Auditorium	Drwy	Driveway	Mkt	Market	Rds	Roads
Avd	Avenida	E	East	Mdw	Meadow	St.	Saint
Av	Avenue	El	Elevation	Mdws	Meadows	Ste.	Sainte
Bfld	Battlefield	Env	Environmental	Med	Medical	Sci	Science
Bch	Beach	Est	Estate	Mem	Memorial	Sci	Sciences
Bnd	Bend	Ests	Estates	Metro	Metropolitan	Sci	Scientific
Bio	Biological	Exh	Exhibition	Mw	Mews	Shop Ctr	Shopping Center
Blf	Bluff	Expm	Experimental	Mil	Military	Shr	Shore
Blvd	Boulevard	Expo	Exposition	Ml	Mill	Shrs	Shores
Brch	Branch	Expwy	Expressway	Mls	Mills	Skwy	Skyway
Br	Bridge	Ext	Extension	Mon	Monument	S	South
Brk	Brook	Frgds	Fairgrounds	Mtwy	Motorway	Spr	Spring
Bldg	Building	ft	Feet	Mnd	Mound	Sprs	Springs
Bur	Bureau	Fy	Ferry	Mnds	Mounds	Sq	Square
Byp	Bypass	Fld	Field	Mt	Mount	Stad	Stadium
Bywy	Byway	Flds	Fields	Mtn	Mountain	St For	State Forest
Cl	Calle	Flt	Flat	Mtns	Mountains	St Hist Site	State Historic Site
Cljn	Callejon	Flts	Flats	Mun	Municipal	St Nat Area	State Natural Area
Cmto	Caminito	For	Forest	Mus	Museum	St Pk	State Park
Cm	Camino	Fk	Fork	Nat'l	National	St Rec Area	State Recreation Area
Cap	Capitol	Ft	Fort	Nat'l For	National Forest	Sta	Station
Cath	Cathedral	Found	Foundation	Nat'l Hist Pk	National Historic Park	St	Street
Cswy	Causeway	Frwy	Freeway	Nat'l Hist Site	National Historic Site	Smt	Summit
Cem	Cemetery	Gdn	Garden	Nat'l Mon	National Monument	Sys	Systems
Ctr	Center	Gdns	Gardens	Nat'l Park	National Park	Tech	Technical
Ctr	Centre	Gen Hosp	General Hospital	Nat'l Rec Area	National Recreation Area	Tech	Technological
Cir	Circle	Gln	Glen	Nat'l Wld Ref	National Wildlife Refuge	Tech	Technology
Crlo	Circulo	GC	Golf Course	Nat	Natural	Ter	Terrace
CH	City Hall	Grn	Green	NAS	Naval Air Station	Terr	Territory
Clf	Cliff	Grds	Grounds	Nk	Nook	Theol	Theological
Clfs	Cliffs	Grv	Grove	N	North	Thwy	Throughway
Clb	Club	Hbr	Harbor/Harbour	Orch	Orchard	Toll Fy	Toll Ferry
Cltr	Cluster	Hvn	Haven	Ohwy	Outer Highway	TIC	Tourist Information Center
Col	Coliseum	HQs	Headquarters	Ovl	Oval	Trc	Trace
Coll	College	Ht	Height	Ovlk	Overlook	Trfwy	Trafficway
Com	Common	Hts	Heights	Ovps	Overpass	Tr	Trail
Coms	Commons	HS	High School	Pk	Park	Tun	Tunnel
Comm	Community	Hwy	Highway	Pkwy	Parkway	Tpk	Turnpike
Co.	Company	Hl	Hill	Pas	Paseo	Unps	Underpass
Cons	Conservation	Hls	Hills	Psg	Passage	Univ	University
Conv & Vis Bur	Convention and Visitors Bureau	Hist	Historical	Pass	Passenger	Vly	Valley
Cor	Corner	Hllw	Hollow	Pth	Path	Vet	Veterans
Cors	Corners	Hosp	Hospital	Pn	Pine	Vw	View
Corp	Corporation	Hse	House	Pns	Pines	Vil	Village
Corr	Corridor	Ind Res	Indian Reservation	Pl	Place	Wk	Walk
Cte	Corte	Info	Information	Pln	Plain	Wall	Wall
CC	Country Club	Inst	Institute	Plns	Plains	Wy	Way
Co	County	Int'l	International	Plgnd	Playground	W	West
Ct	Court	I	Island	Plz	Plaza	WMA	Wildlife Management Area
Ct Hse	Court House	Is	Islands	Pt	Point		
Cts	Courts	Isl	Isle	Pnd	Pond		

INDEX 2

Minneapolis Street Index

SR-5 Fort Rd

STREET Block City ZIP Map # Grid

HIGHWAYS

ALT - Alternate Route
BIA - Bureau of Indian Affairs
BUS - Business Route
CO - County Highway/Road
FM - Farm To Market Road
HIST - Historic Highway
I - Interstate Highway
LP - State Loop
PK - Park & Recreation Road
PROV - Provincial Highway
RTE - Other Route
SPR - State Spur
SR - State Route/Highway
TCH - Trans-Canada Highway
US - United States Highway

CO-1
- BMTN 8111 A6
- BMTN 8196 B2
- COON 7592 C1
- COON 7593 E7
- COON 7679 E1
- COON 7680 A4
- FRID 7680 B6
- FRID 7766 A5
- FRID 7852 B1

CO-1 Coon Rapids Blvd NW
- COON 7592 D2
- COON 7593 E7

CO-1 E River Rd
- FRID 7680 B6
- FRID 7766 B3
- FRID 7852 B1

CO-1 E River Rd NE
- FRID 7680 B6
- FRID 7766 A5

CO-1 E River Rd NW
- COON 7593 E7
- COON 7679 E1
- COON 7680 A4
- FRID 7680 A4

CO-1 Round Lake Blvd NW
- COON 7592 C1

CO-3
- ARDH 7681 E5
- ARDH 7682 A5
- HOPK 8021 C3
- MNDS 7681 E5
- MNTK 8021 B3
- NOAK 7683 A5
- SHVW 7681 E5
- SHVW 7682 C5
- SHVW 7683 A5

CO-3 CR-I
- MNDS 7681 E5

CO-3 CR-I W
- ARDH 7681 E5
- ARDH 7682 C5
- MNDS 7681 E5
- NOAK 7683 A5
- SHVW 7681 E5
- SHVW 7682 A5
- SHVW 7683 A5

CO-3 Excelsior Blvd
- HOPK 8021 B3
- MNTK 8021 B3

CO-3 Excelsior Blvd E
- HOPK 8021 C3
- MNTK 8021 C3

CO-3 Hamline Av N
- ARDH 7682 C5
- SHVW 7682 C5

CO-4
- EDNP 8192 B1

CO-4 Spring Rd
- EDNP 8192 B1

CO-5
- BRNV 8281 D7

CO-5 Kenwood Tr
- BRNV 8281 D7

CO-6
- PYMH 7848 E7
- PYMH 7849 A6

CO-8
- BRKP 7764 B2
- HUGO 7599 E7
- HUGO 7600 A7

CO-8 137th St N
- HUGO 7600 B7

CO-8 140th St N
- HUGO 7599 E7
- HUGO 7600 D6

CO-8 Egg Lake Rd N
- HUGO 7599 E6
- HUGO 7600 A7

CO-8 Homestead Av N
- HUGO 7600 D7

CO-9
- NWHE 7849 E2
- PYMH 7848 E2
- PYMH 7849 A2

CO-9 Rockford Rd
- NWHE 7849 E2
- PYMH 7848 E2
- PYMH 7849 A2

CO-10
- ARDH 7768 A1
- BLNE 7680 E3
- BRKC 7765 C5
- CRYS 7764 E6
- CRYS 7765 A5
- MAPG 7762 E4
- MNDS 7681 D7
- MNDS 7767 E1
- MNDS 7768 A1
- NWHE 7763 E5
- NWHE 7764 A5
- PYMH 7762 E4
- PYMH 7763 C5
- SPLP 7680 E3
- SPLP 7681 B5

CO-10 58th Av N
- BRKC 7765 C5
- CRYS 7765 A5

CO-10 89th Av NE
- BLNE 7680 C2

CO-10 Bass Lake Rd
- BRKC 7765 C5
- CRYS 7764 E6
- MAPG 7762 E4
- NWHE 7763 E5
- NWHE 7764 C6
- PYMH 7762 E4
- PYMH 7763 C5

CO-10 Orchard Av N
- BRKC 7765 A5
- CRYS 7765 A5

CO-11
- APVA 8282 E5
- BRNV 8282 E5
- COON 7593 C2
- COON 7594 B6

CO-11 Foley Blvd NW
- COON 7594 B7

CO-11 Hanson Blvd NW
- COON 7593 D2

CO-11 McAndrews Rd
- APVA 8282 E5
- BRNV 8282 E5

CO-11 McAndrews Rd E
- APVA 8282 E5
- BRNV 8282 D5

CO-11 Northdale Blvd NW
- COON 7593 E2
- COON 7594 B3

CO-12
- BLNE 7594 E4
- BLNE 7595 B4
- BLNE 7596 E4
- LINO 7596 E4

CO-12 109th Av NE
- BLNE 7594 E4
- BLNE 7595 B4
- BLNE 7596 E4
- LINO 7596 E4

CO-13B
- ELMO 7858 E2
- ODLE 7858 D3

CO-13B 50th St N
- ELMO 7858 D3
- ODLE 7858 D3

CO-13B Demontreville Tr N
- ELMO 7858 E2

CO-16
- SAVG 8279 E4
- SAVG 8280 A4
- SHKP 8278 D2
- SHKP 8279 E4

CO-16 Eagle Creek Blvd
- SAVG 8279 E4
- SHKP 8278 D2
- SHKP 8279 C4

CO-16 McColl Dr
- SAVG 8279 E4
- SAVG 8280 A4
- SHKP 8279 E4

CO-16 Quentin Av S
- SAVG 8280 E3

CO-18
- PRIO 8279 D6
- SHKP 8279 D6

CO-18 Crest Av NE
- PRIO 8279 D6
- SHKP 8279 D6

CO-20
- MINN 7937 E5
- MINN 7938 A4
- MINN 8023 E1

CO-20 Hennepin Av S
- MINN 7937 E5
- MINN 7938 A4
- MINN 8023 E1

CO-22
- CTGV 8116 A6
- SPLP 8115 E6
- SPLP 8116 A6

CO-22 70th St S
- CTGV 8116 A6
- SPLP 8115 E6
- SPLP 8116 A6

CO-22 St. Paul Park Rd
- SPLP 8115 E6

CO-23
- CIRC 7597 A6
- LINO 7597 A6

CO-23 Lake Dr
- CIRC 7597 A6
- LINO 7597 A6

CO-24
- PYMH 7848 A3

CO-25
- MINN 7937 B6
- STLP 7936 E7
- STLP 7937 A7

CO-27
- SAVG 8280 D4

CO-27 Dakota Av
- SAVG 8280 D4

CO-30
- BRKP 7677 E3
- BRKP 7678 A3
- MAPG 7676 E3
- MAPG 7677 E3
- OSSE 7677 E3
- OSSE 7678 A3

CO-30 93rd Av N
- BRKP 7677 E3
- BRKP 7678 A3
- MAPG 7676 E3
- MAPG 7677 B3
- OSSE 7677 E3
- OSSE 7678 A3

CO-30 95th Av N
- MAPG 7676 B3

CO-32
- STPL 7940 E3

CO-33
- MINN 7938 C3
- MINN 8024 C2

CO-33 Park Av S
- MINN 7938 C3
- MINN 8024 C2

CO-35
- MINN 7938 C5
- MINN 8024 C2

CO-35 Portland Av S
- MINN 7938 C5
- MINN 8024 C2

CO-38
- BRNV 8282 B5

CO-42
- BRNV 8281 E6
- BRNV 8282 A6
- NgTp 8288 E6
- PRIO 8278 E6
- PRIO 8279 C6
- PRIO 8280 C6
- SAVG 8279 E6
- SAVG 8280 C6
- SAVG 8281 C6
- SHKP 8278 A6

CO-42 140th St NE
- PRIO 8279 A6
- PRIO 8280 C6
- SAVG 8279 E6
- SAVG 8280 C6

CO-42 140th St NW
- PRIO 8278 E6
- PRIO 8279 C6
- SHKP 8278 B6

CO-42 Egan Dr
- BRNV 8281 B6
- PRIO 8280 B6
- SAVG 8280 E6
- SAVG 8281 C6

CO-42 Mississippi Tr
- NgTp 8288 E6

CO-44
- MINN 7853 C3
- MNDS 7681 B7
- NBRI 7681 B7
- NBRI 7767 B3
- STAN 7767 B2
- STAN 7853 C1

CO-44 Kenzie Ter
- MINN 7853 B4
- STAN 7853 B4

CO-44 Silver Lake Rd
- MNDS 7681 B7
- NBRI 7681 B7

CO-44 Silver Lake Rd NE
- NBRI 7767 B2
- STAN 7767 B2
- STAN 7853 C1

CO-44 Silver Lake Rd NW
- NBRI 7767 B3
- STAN 7767 C6

CO-47
- PYMH 7762 C5
- PYMH 7763 A5

CO-51
- ARDH 7682 D7
- ARDH 7768 D1
- ARDH 7854 E3
- BLNE 7682 C4
- RSVL 7854 E7
- SHVW 7682 C4
- SHVW 7768 D7
- SHVW 7854 E3
- STPL 7854 E7

CO-51 Lexington Av N
- ARDH 7682 D7
- ARDH 7768 D1
- ARDH 7854 E3
- BLNE 7682 C4
- RSVL 7854 E7
- SHVW 7682 C4
- SHVW 7768 D7
- SHVW 7854 E3
- STPL 7854 E7

CO-51 Lexington Pkwy N
- RSVL 7854 E7
- STPL 7854 E7

CO-52
- BLNE 7595 E7
- BLNE 7681 E1
- BLNE 7682 A1

CO-52 95th Av NE
- BLNE 7681 E1
- BLNE 7682 A1

CO-52 101st Av NE
- BLNE 7595 D6

CO-52 Radisson Rd NE
- BLNE 7595 E7
- BLNE 7681 E1

CO-53
- BLNE 7596 E1
- CIRC 7596 E6
- LINO 7596 E1

CO-53 Sunset Av NE
- BLNE 7596 E1
- CIRC 7596 E6
- LINO 7596 E1

CO-53 Sunset Rd
- BLNE 7596 E1
- LINO 7596 E1

CO-61
- MAPG 7677 B7
- MAPG 7763 B2
- MNTK 7934 E3
- MNTK 7935 A7
- PYMH 7762 E7
- PYMH 7763 A5
- PYMH 7848 E2
- PYMH 7849 A3
- PYMH 7934 E1

CO-61 Hemlock Ln N
- MAPG 7677 B7
- MAPG 7763 B1

CO-61 Northwest Blvd
- MAPG 7763 B4
- PYMH 7762 E7
- PYMH 7763 A5
- PYMH 7848 E2
- PYMH 7849 A3

CO-61 Plymouth Rd
- MNTK 7934 E3
- MNTK 7935 A7

CO-61 Xenium Ln N
- MNTK 7934 E2
- PYMH 7848 E4
- PYMH 7934 E1

CO-61 Xenium Ln S
- MNTK 7934 E2
- PYMH 7934 E2

CO-62
- EDNP 8020 A7
- MNTK 8020 B7

CO-62 W 62nd St
- EDNP 8020 A7
- MNTK 8020 A7

CO-62 Townline Rd
- EDNP 8020 B7
- MNTK 8020 B7

CO-65
- MPLW 7857 A7
- STPL 7857 A7
- STPL 7943 A6
- WTBL 7771 B7
- WTBL 7857 B1

CO-65 White Bear Av N
- MPLW 7857 A7
- STPL 7857 A7
- STPL 7943 A6
- WTBL 7771 B7
- WTBL 7857 B1

CO-73
- IVGH 8114 B7
- IVGH 8200 B1
- WSTP 8114 B1

CO-73 Babcock Tr E
- IVGH 8114 B7
- IVGH 8200 B1
- WSTP 8114 B1

CO-78
- COON 7593 D1

CO-78 Hanson Blvd NW
- COON 7593 D1

CO-81
- BRKP 7677 E5
- BRKP 7678 A7
- BRKP 7764 B1
- CRYS 7764 E7
- CRYS 7850 E1
- DAYT 7590 A6
- MAPG 7590 C7
- MAPG 7676 E2
- MAPG 7677 E5
- OSSE 7677 E5
- ROBB 7850 E1
- ROBB 7851 A2

CO-81 Lakeland Av N
- CRYS 7764 D7

CO-88
- MINN 7853 B4
- NBRI 7853 E1
- RSVL 7853 D3
- STAN 7853 B4

CO-88 New Brighton Blvd
- MINN 7853 B4
- RSVL 7853 D3
- STAN 7853 B4

CO-96
- ARDH 7768 A2
- NBRI 7768 A2
- NOAK 7769 B2
- NOAK 7770 A2
- SHVW 7768 E2
- SHVW 7769 A2
- VADH 7769 E2
- VADH 7770 B2
- WTBL 7770 D2
- WTBL 7771 B2
- WtBT 7770 E2
- WtBT 7771 A2

CO-96 Ramley St
- WTBL 7771 B2
- WtBT 7771 A2

CO-101
- SAVG 8279 E1
- SAVG 8280 A2
- SHKP 8192 C6
- SHKP 8193 A6
- SHKP 8279 E1

CO-103
- BRKP 7592 B7
- BRKP 7678 B1
- CHMP 7592 B7

CO-103 W Broadway Av
- BRKP 7678 B1

CO-103 Winnetka Av N
- BRKP 7592 B7
- BRKP 7678 B1
- CHMP 7592 B7

CO-104
- FRID 7766 C5

CO-104 49th Av NE
- FRID 7766 C5

CO-130
- BRKP 7677 E7
- BRKP 7678 A7
- MAPG 7676 E5
- MAPG 7677 D7

CO-130 Brooklyn Blvd
- BRKP 7677 E7
- BRKP 7678 A7

CO-130 Elm Creek Blvd N
- BRKP 7677 E7
- MAPG 7676 E5
- MAPG 7677 D7

CO-132
- COON 7680 A3

CO-132 85th Av NW
- COON 7680 A3

CO-147
- GEML 7771 A4
- WTBL 7771 A4

CO-152
- BRKP 7678 C7

CO-152 Brooklyn Blvd
- BRKP 7678 C7

CO-J
- LINO 7683 E3
- WtBT 7683 E3

CO-J Ash St
- LINO 7683 E3
- WtBT 7683 E3

I-35E
- APVA 8282 E4
- APVA 8283 A3
- BRNV 8282 E4
- BRNV 8283 B2
- EAGN 8112 E3
- EAGN 8197 E5
- EAGN 8198 A5
- EAGN 8283 D1
- LCAN 7855 E2
- LCAN 7856 A1
- LILY 8026 E6
- LILY 8027 A7
- LINO 7599 A1
- LINO 7684 D7
- MNDH 8027 A7
- MNDH 8112 E1
- MNDH 8113 A1
- MPLW 7855 E5
- STPL 7855 E7
- STPL 7941 E5
- STPL 8026 E2
- STPL 8027 B1
- VADH 7770 C5
- VADH 7856 C1
- WTBL 7770 D2
- WtBT 7684 D4
- WtBT 7770 D1

I-35E The Great River Rd
- LILY 8026 E5
- LILY 8027 A6
- MNDH 8027 A6
- STPL 8026 E4

I-35W
- ARDH 7681 E5
- ARDH 7682 A7
- ARDH 7768 A5
- BLNE 7596 A7
- BLNE 7681 E2
- BLNE 7682 A1
- BMTN 8109 E5
- BMTN 8195 E1
- BMTN 8196 A7
- BRNV 8196 A7
- BRNV 8282 A7
- LINO 7596 E4
- LINO 7597 E2
- LINO 7598 A1
- LXTN 7596 A7
- MINN 7853 E5
- MINN 7938 C4
- MINN 7939 A1
- MINN 8023 E7
- MINN 8024 B5
- MNDS 7681 E5
- MNDS 7682 A7
- MNDS 7767 E1
- MNDS 7768 A2
- NBRI 7767 E7
- NBRI 7768 A5
- NBRI 7853 E1
- RHFD 8023 E7
- RHFD 8024 A7
- RHFD 8109 E7
- RSVL 7853 E2
- RSVL 7854 A4
- SHVW 7681 E5
- STAN 7853 D5

I-35W Crosstown Hwy
- MINN 8023 E7
- MINN 8024 A7
- RHFD 8023 E7
- RHFD 8024 A7

I-94
- BRKC 7764 C3
- BRKC 7765 A3
- BRKC 7766 A6
- BRKP 7763 E2
- BRKP 7764 A3
- ELMO 7944 E6
- LNDF 7944 A6
- MAPG 7676 E7
- MAPG 7762 E1
- MAPG 7763 C1
- MINN 7766 A6
- MINN 7852 A4
- MINN 7938 A2
- MINN 7939 B4
- MPLW 7943 D6
- ODLE 7943 E6
- ODLE 7944 E6
- STPL 7939 E5
- STPL 7940 A6
- STPL 7941 C6
- STPL 7942 A6
- STPL 7943 A6
- WDBY 7943 E6
- WDBY 7944 E6

I-94 Cappelen Memorial Br
- MINN 7939 B4

I-394
- GLDV 7935 E3
- GLDV 7936 E3
- GLDV 7937 B3
- MINN 7937 E3
- MINN 7938 B2
- MNTK 7934 E3
- MNTK 7935 B3
- STLP 7935 E3
- STLP 7936 E3

I-394 Wayzata Blvd
- GLDV 7935 E3
- MINN 7937 E3
- MINN 7938 A3
- MNTK 7934 E3
- MNTK 7935 B3
- STLP 7935 D3

I-494
- BMTN 8107 E5
- BMTN 8108 E5
- BMTN 8109 C4
- BMTN 8110 C4
- BMTN 8111 B4
- EAGN 8111 E4
- EAGN 8112 A4
- EAGN 8113 C4
- EDNP 8020 E7
- EDNP 8021 A7
- EDNP 8107 A3
- HnpC 8110 E4
- HnpC 8111 B4
- IVGH 8113 E4
- IVGH 8114 D3
- MAPG 7762 E1
- MNDH 8111 E4
- MNDH 8112 E4
- MNDH 8113 A4
- MNTK 7934 D7
- MNTK 8020 D2
- MNTK 8021 A7
- MPLW 8029 D7
- NWPT 8029 E5
- NWPT 8115 D1
- ODLE 7944 C6
- PYMH 7762 E3
- PYMH 7848 E2
- PYMH 7934 D2
- RHFD 8109 E4
- RHFD 8110 C4
- SSTP 8114 D3
- SSTP 8115 C1
- SUNL 8113 E4
- SUNL 8114 B3
- WDBY 7944 C7
- WDBY 8029 E4
- WDBY 8030 A4

I-494 The Great River Rd
- NWPT 8115 D1
- SSTP 8115 B1

I-694
- ARDH 7768 C4
- BRKC 7764 C3
- BRKC 7765 A3
- BRKC 7766 E4
- BRKP 7763 E2
- BRKP 7764 A3
- FRID 7766 A4
- FRID 7767 E4
- LCAN 7769 D7
- LCAN 7855 E1
- LCAN 7856 A1
- MAHT 7858 A2
- MAPG 7676 E7
- MAPG 7762 E1
- MAPG 7763 C1
- MPLW 7856 E1
- MPLW 7857 C1
- NBRI 7767 C4
- NBRI 7768 A4
- ODLE 7857 E2
- ODLE 7858 C3
- ODLE 7944 C1
- PNSP 7858 B2
- SHVW 7768 E5
- SHVW 7769 A5
- VADH 7769 C7
- VADH 7856 C1
- WDBY 7944 C6
- WTBL 7856 E1
- WTBL 7857 C1

I-694 The Great River Rd
- BRKC 7766 A4
- FRID 7766 A4

SR-3
- EAGN 8199 C7
- EAGN 8285 C1
- IVGH 8114 A1
- IVGH 8199 E1
- IVGH 8200 A1
- RSMT 8285 B7
- STPL 7941 E7
- STPL 7942 A7
- STPL 8028 A1
- SUNL 8114 A6
- WSTP 8028 A4
- WSTP 8114 A1

SR-3 Robert St N
- STPL 7941 E7
- STPL 7942 A7

SR-3 Robert St S
- IVGH 8114 A1
- STPL 7942 A7
- STPL 8028 A1
- WSTP 8028 A4
- WSTP 8114 A1

SR-3 S Robert Tr
- EAGN 8199 C7
- EAGN 8285 C1
- IVGH 8114 A1
- IVGH 8199 E1
- IVGH 8200 A1
- RSMT 8285 A7
- SUNL 8114 A6
- WSTP 8114 A1

SR-5
- BMTN 8107 E5
- BMTN 8108 E5
- BMTN 8109 E4
- BMTN 8110 C4
- BMTN 8111 B4
- EDNP 8106 D4
- EDNP 8107 E5
- ELMO 7858 E7
- HnpC 8026 A7
- HnpC 8110 E4
- HnpC 8111 D4
- HnpC 8112 A1
- MPLW 7857 E7
- MPLW 7943 E3
- ODLE 7857 E7
- ODLE 7858 D7
- ODLE 7943 E1
- RHFD 8109 B5
- RHFD 8110 C4
- STPL 7941 E6
- STPL 7942 A5
- STPL 7943 A4
- STPL 8026 C5
- STPL 8027 A3

SR-5 W 7th St
- STPL 8026 E3
- STPL 8027 A3

SR-5 7th St E
- STPL 7941 E6
- STPL 7942 A5

SR-5 7th St W
- STPL 7941 D7
- STPL 8027 C1

SR-5 34th St N
- ELMO 7858 E7
- ODLE 7858 D7

SR-5 W 78th St
- EDNP 8106 A4

SR-5 Fort Rd
- STPL 8026 E4

INDEX 4

Aberdeen Cir NE

Minneapolis Street Index

Arcade St N

STREET Block	City	ZIP	Map #	Grid
Aberdeen Cir NE				
-	BLNE		7595	A3
Aberdeen Curv				
-	WDBY		8030	C4
Aberdeen St NE				
-	BLNE		7595	A1
Abigail Ct				
-	IVGH		8200	A4
Able St NE				
-	BLNE		7594	E2
-	BLNE		7680	E1
-	FRID		7680	E6
-	FRID		7766	E1
-	SPLP		7680	E3
Acacia Blvd				
-	MNDH		8112	C2
Acacia Dr				
-	MNDH		8112	C2
Acadia Ct				
-	BRNV		8283	A3
W Access Rd				
-	HnpC		8024	E7
-	HnpC		8025	A7
-	HnpC		8110	E1
-	MINN		8025	A7
-	RHFD		8110	E1
Acker St E				
-	STPL		7941	D4
Acker St W				
-	STPL		7941	D4
Acorn Cir				
-	BRNV		8282	E4
-	MNTK		7934	C4
Acorn Dr				
-	IVGH		8113	D4
-	SUNL		8113	D4
Acorn Ln				
-	SSTP		8028	C6
Acorn Rd				
-	RSVL		7853	E5
Acorn St				
-	EAGN		8199	C7
Ada St				
-	STPL		8028	A2
Adair Av N				
-	BRKP		7678	D5
-	BRKP		7764	D2
-	CHMP		7592	D4
-	CRYS		7764	D6
-	CRYS		7850	D3
-	GLDV		7850	D6
-	ROBB		7850	D3
Adair Cir N				
-	BRKP		7678	D5
Adair Ct N				
-	BRKP		7678	D5
Adair Ln N				
-	BRKP		7678	D5
Adam Av				
-	IVGH		8199	E5
-	IVGH		8200	A5
Adams Av				
-	EDNA		8021	E4
-	HOPK		8021	E4
Adams St				
-	ANOK		7592	B1
-	COON		7592	B1
-	MNDS		7681	E6
Adams St NE				
-	MINN		7852	D7
Adams School St				
-	COON		7679	E2
Adelbert Av				
-	IVGH		8200	A1
Adele St				
-	MPLW		7856	C7
Adeline Ct				
-	MNDH		8027	A7
-	MNTK		7934	A4
Adeline Ln				
-	MNTK		7934	A4
Adeline Ln N				
-	GLDV		7936	E1
Adell Av N				
-	GLDV		7851	A4
Admiral Ln N				
-	BRKC		7765	B5
Admiral Pl				
-	BRKC		7765	B5
Adolphus St				
-	MPLW		7855	E6
-	STPL		7855	E7
Adret Ct				
-	EDNP		8106	A1
Adrian St				
-	STPL		8026	E4
Advantage Ln				
-	EAGN		8113	B7
Aeronca Ln				
-	SSTP		8115	A4
Affirmed Dr				
-	SHKP		8192	A7
Afton Ct				
-	WDBY		8030	D3
Afton Rd				
-	WDBY		8030	E4
Agate St				
-	MPLW		7855	E7
-	STPL		7855	E7
-	STPL		7941	E4
Agatha Av				
-	IVGH		8200	A6
Aglen Av				
-	RSVL		7854	E3
Aglen St				
-	RSVL		7854	E4
Aida Pl				
-	STPL		7940	D2
Aileen Ct				
-	VADH		7770	A4
Airlift Dr				
-	HnpC		8025	D7
-	HnpC		8111	D1
Airport Dr				
-	HnpC		8111	B4
Airport Ln				
-	HnpC		8110	E4
-	HnpC		8111	A4
Airport Rd				
-	SSTP		8115	A4
-	STPL		7942	B7
-	STPL		8028	B1
Airport Rd NE				
-	BLNE		7681	B1
Akers Ln				
-	EDNA		8022	A5
Akimbo Rd				
-	WDBY		8030	C2
Akron Av				
-	IVGH		8114	A2
-	IVGH		8199	E6
-	IVGH		8200	A7
-	IVGH		8286	A2
-	RSMT		8286	A7
-	WSTP		8114	A2
Alabama Av S				
-	SAVG		8280	D4
-	STLP		7936	D7
-	STLP		8022	A2
Alabama Cir S				
-	BMTN		8194	D4
Alabama Rd S				
-	BMTN		8194	D3
Alabama St				
-	STPL		7942	A7
Aladdin St				
-	RSVL		7855	A4
Aladin Tr				
-	IVGH		8199	E4
Alameda Av				
-	IVGH		8199	E7
-	IVGH		8285	E1
-	IVGH		8286	A1
Alameda Ct				
-	IVGH		8285	E1
Alameda Pth				
-	IVGH		8199	E7
Alameda St				
-	RSVL		7855	A6
-	SHVW		7683	A4
-	STPL		7941	A1
Alamo Cir				
-	BLNE		7595	D1
Alamo Cir NE				
-	BLNE		7681	D3
Alamo Ct NE				
-	BLNE		7681	D1
Alamo St NE				
-	BLNE		7595	D5
-	BLNE		7681	D2
Alaska Av				
-	STPL		8026	E4
Alaureate Ct				
-	IVGH		8199	E5
Alaureate Trail Ct				
-	IVGH		8199	E4
Albano Tr				
-	IVGH		8199	D4
Albany Av				
-	STPL		7940	C2
Albany Cir				
-	EAGN		8199	B4
Albavar Pth				
-	IVGH		8199	D7
-	IVGH		8285	D1
-	IVGH		8286	A2
Albemarle Ct N				
-	RSVL		7855	C6
Albemarle St				
-	RSVL		7855	C6
-	STPL		7941	C1
Albert Av				
-	BLNE		7682	B2
-	FLCH		7854	C7
-	FLCH		7940	C1
-	LXTN		7682	B2
-	RSVL		7854	C7
-	STPL		7940	C1
Albert Ct				
-	LINO		7599	A7
Albert St				
-	SHVW		7682	C5
Albert St N				
-	FLCH		7940	C1
-	RSVL		7854	C2
-	STPL		7940	C1
Albert St S				
-	STPL		8026	C3
Alberta Wy				
-	IVGH		8199	D1
Alberton Ct				
-	IVGH		8199	D7
Alberton Wy				
-	IVGH		8199	D7
Albion Av				
-	STPL		8026	D4
Albright Ct				
-	IVGH		8199	D4
Alden Cir NE				
-	FRID		7680	C6
Alden Dr				
-	EDNA		8023	A3
Alden Wy NE				
-	FRID		7680	A5
-	FRID		7766	B2
Alden Pond Ln				
-	EAGN		8112	A7
Alder Ln				
-	EAGN		8197	D3
Alder St NW				
-	COON		7594	C2
Alderwood Cir				
-	WDBY		8030	B1
Alderwood Dr				
-	WDBY		8030	B1
Alderwood Plz				
-	WDBY		8030	B1
Alderwood Bay				
-	WDBY		8030	B1
Alderwood Draw				
-	WDBY		8030	B1
Aldine St				
-	ARDH		7682	B5
-	RSVL		7854	B2
-	SHVW		7682	B5
-	STPL		7940	B5
Aldrich Av N				
-	BRKC		7765	E1
-	BRKC		7766	A5
-	BRKP		7679	E7
-	BRKP		7765	E1
-	MINN		7766	A7
-	MINN		7852	A3
-	MINN		7938	A2
Aldrich Av S				
-	BMTN		8110	A7
-	BMTN		8196	A1
-	BRNV		8281	E3
-	BRNV		8282	A5
-	MINN		7938	A7
-	MINN		8023	E6
-	MINN		8024	A1
-	RHFD		8110	A1
Aldrich Cir N				
-	BRKP		7679	E7
-	BRKP		7765	E1
Aldrich Ct N				
-	BRKC		7765	E1
-	BRKP		7765	E1
-	BRKP		7766	A1
Aldrich Dr N				
-	BRKC		7766	A6
Aldrich Tr				
-	WDBY		8030	E5
Aldrin Dr				
-	EAGN		8112	E7
-	EAGN		8113	A7
Alexander Rd				
-	EAGN		8111	E7
-	EAGN		8112	A7
Alexandra Ct				
-	IVGH		8199	D7
Alexandria Ct				
-	IVGH		8285	E2
Alfa Ln				
-	IVGH		8200	A3
Alfred Rd				
-	GLDV		7850	E7
Alger Ct				
-	IVGH		8199	E3
Algonquin Av				
-	STPL		7943	B4
Alice Ct				
-	SSTP		8114	C1
-	STPL		8027	D2
Alice Ln				
-	MNDH		8113	A3
Alice St				
-	STPL		8027	D2
Alicia Cir				
-	EAGN		8199	D6
-	IVGH		8199	D6
Alimagnet Pkwy				
-	BRNV		8282	D7
Alise Pl				
-	EDNP		8193	A3
Alison Ct				
-	IVGH		8199	D7
Alison Wy				
-	IVGH		8199	D7
Alissa Ln				
-	MPLW		7943	E1
Allan Ln				
-	EAGN		8199	C7
Allen Av				
-	LCAN		7855	E2
-	LCAN		7856	B2
-	WSTP		8027	E4
Allen Blvd				
-	SAVG		8280	C7
Allen Cir				
-	NWHE		7763	E5
Allen Ct				
-	EDNP		8106	D3
-	WSTP		8027	E7
Allen Dr				
-	BRNV		8282	E2
-	BRNV		8283	A1
-	SAVG		8280	C6
Allen Pl				
-	MPLW		7856	B7
Allen Wy				
-	IVGH		8114	A7
Allendale Dr				
-	WtBT		7770	C2
Alley Rd				
-	NWPT		8115	D2
Almond Av				
-	STPL		7940	C2
Almond Av N				
-	BRKP		7679	B2
Almond Ln				
-	EDNP		8106	B7
Almquist Wy				
-	IVGH		8199	E3
Alpha Ln				
-	EDNP		8192	D2
-	SSTP		8115	A5
Alpine Av				
-	VADH		7770	C5
Alpine Dr				
-	WDBY		8030	A5
Alpine Tr				
-	EDNP		8106	A2
Alpine Wy				
-	EDNP		8106	B2
Alpine Pass				
-	GLDV		7937	A4
Alrick Dr				
-	WTBL		7771	C7
Alta Av				
-	IVGH		8114	A3
-	IVGH		8200	A2
Alta Pt				
-	EAGN		8283	E2
-	EAGN		8284	A2
Alta Vista Dr				
-	RSVL		7855	A7
Althea Ln				
-	HOPK		8021	E1
Altman Ct				
-	IVGH		8199	E3
-	WSTP		8028	A5
Alton Ct				
-	IVGH		8199	D6
Alton Rd				
-	NBRI		7767	C6
Alton St				
-	STPL		8026	C6
Altura Rd NE				
-	FRID		7766	C4
Alvarado Ct				
-	IVGH		8199	E2
Alvarado Dr				
-	MPLW		7856	C4
Alvarado Tr				
-	IVGH		8199	E3
Alvarez Av				
-	IVGH		8199	E3
Alverno Av W				
-	IVGH		8199	E3
Alvin Ct				
-	IVGH		8199	D6
Alysheba Ct				
-	SHKP		8192	A7
Alysheba Rd				
-	SHKP		8192	A7
Alyssa Rd				
-	WDBY		8030	D6
Amaryllis Ln				
-	EAGN		8198	C6
Amber Ct				
-	EAGN		8197	C6
Amber Dr				
-	EAGN		8197	C6
-	SHVW		7855	A1
Amber Ln				
-	EDNP		8106	D3
Amberjack Ln				
-	MPLW		7943	E2
Amberleaf Tr				
-	EAGN		8198	D5
Amberwood Dr				
-	WDBY		8030	E4
Amberwood Ln				
-	SAVG		8280	B6
Amble Cir				
-	ARDH		7768	D3
Amble Ct				
-	SHVW		7769	A3
Amble Dr				
-	ARDH		7768	D3
-	SHVW		7768	D3
Amble Rd				
-	ARDH		7768	D3
-	SHVW		7768	E3
-	SHVW		7769	A3
Amblewood Dr NE				
-	PRIO		8279	D7
Amelia Av				
-	WSTP		8028	A5
Amen Cir NE				
-	BLNE		7595	C4
Amen Ct NE				
-	BLNE		7595	C4
Amen Dr NE				
-	BLNE		7595	B5
American Blvd E				
-	BMTN		8110	C5
-	BMTN		8111	A5
American Blvd W				
-	BMTN		8108	D5
-	BMTN		8109	A5
-	BMTN		8110	A5
American St				
-	RSVL		7854	B4
Amery Cir				
-	IVGH		8199	D6
Amery Ct				
-	IVGH		8199	D7
Ames Av				
-	STPL		7942	E3
-	STPL		7943	A3
Ames Pl				
-	STPL		7943	A3
Amesbury Ln				
-	EDNP		8193	C1
Amethyst Ln				
-	EAGN		8197	D4
Amherst Ct				
-	IVGH		8199	E7
Amherst St				
-	STPL		8026	B1
Amherst Wy				
-	IVGH		8199	D7
Amsden Rd				
-	BMTN		8107	E7
-	BMTN		8108	A7
-	BMTN		8193	E1
Amsden Wy				
-	EDNP		8193	D1
Amsden Ridge Cir				
-	BMTN		8107	D7
Amsden Ridge Dr				
-	BMTN		8107	D7
Amundson Av				
-	EDNA		8108	C3
Amur Hill Ln				
-	EDNP		8106	C7
Amy Cir				
-	NSTP		7857	D6
Amy Ct				
-	IVGH		8200	A6
Amy Dr				
-	EDNA		8022	B6
Amy Ln				
-	BRKC		7765	D2
-	MNTK		7935	A5
Anagram Dr				
-	EDNP		8106	E4
Anapolis Ln				
-	DAYT		7590	D2
Anawanda Pth				
-	IVGH		8200	A5
Anderlie Ln				
-	WtBT		7685	A6
Anderlie Ln W				
-	WtBT		7685	A7
Anderson Ln				
-	MINN		7938	C6
-	NOAK		7684	C5
-	SHVW		7769	A2
-	WtBT		7684	C5
Anderson Lakes Pkwy				
-	BMTN		8193	E1
-	EDNP		8106	E6
-	EDNP		8107	C7
-	EDNP		8193	D1
Andes Cir				
-	IVGH		8199	D7
Andover Ct				
-	IVGH		8199	D7
Andover Rd				
-	EDNA		8108	E2
-	EDNA		8109	A2
Andrea Tr				
-	IVGH		8200	A6
Andrew Dr				
-	WDBY		8030	C7
Andrew St				
-	STPL		8028	C2
Andromeda Wy				
-	EAGN		8198	D6
Anemone Cir				
-	NOAK		7683	B6
Angela Ct				
-	MPLW		7943	E2
Angeline Av N				
-	CRYS		7764	E6
Angeline Ct N				
-	CRYS		7764	E6
Angeline Dr				
-	NWHE		7764	B7
Angell Ct				
-	SUNL		8113	E2
Angell Rd				
-	SUNL		8113	E2
Angelo Dr				
-	GLDV		7850	E7
-	GLDV		7936	E1
Angus Av				
-	IVGH		8114	A3
-	IVGH		8200	A2
Anita St				
-	STPL		8028	B2
Ann Ct				
-	EDNP		8107	A3
Ann Ln				
-	MNTK		7935	D7
Ann St				
-	STPL		8027	C1
Anna Av NE				
-	FRID		7766	B3
Annalisa Pth				
-	IVGH		8200	A2
Annapolis Cir				
-	MAPG		7762	D1
Annapolis Cir N				
-	PYMH		7848	E5
Annapolis Ln N				
-	MAPG		7676	D4
-	MAPG		7762	D2
-	PYMH		7762	D5
-	PYMH		7848	D3
Annapolis St E				
-	SSTP		8028	C3
-	STPL		8028	A3
-	WSTP		8028	A3
Annapolis St W				
-	MNDH		8027	C3
-	STPL		8027	E3
-	STPL		8028	A3
-	WSTP		8027	E3
-	WSTP		8028	A3
Annapolis St W SR-13				
-	MNDH		8027	C3
-	STPL		8027	C3
-	WSTP		8027	D3
Annapolis Wy				
-	EDNP		8107	C5
Ann Arbor St				
-	STPL		7939	E6
Annaway Dr				
-	EDNA		8022	B4
Anne Pt				
-	EAGN		8283	E3
Annette Av E				
-	IVGH		8114	B4
Ann Marie Tr				
-	IVGH		8200	A3
Anoka St NE				
-	FRID		7767	A1
Antelope Dr				
-	LINO		7597	A5
Antelope Wy				
-	MPLW		7943	D2
Anthony Ln				
-	STAN		7853	C3
Anthony Ln S				
-	STAN		7853	C4
Anthony St				
-	SSTP		8114	C1
Antler Pt				
-	EAGN		8198	A4
Antlers Rdg				
-	EDNP		8193	C3
Antoinette Av				
-	MINN		7937	B3
Antonio Dr				
-	STPL		8026	D4
Antrim Ct				
-	EDNA		8108	B3
Antrim Rd				
-	EDNA		8108	B2
Antrim Ter				
-	EDNA		8108	B3
Apache Ct				
-	MNDH		8113	C3
Apache Ln				
-	MNDH		8113	B3
Apache Rd				
-	EDNA		8107	E2
Apache Rd N				
-	NSTP		7857	D3
Apache St				
-	MNDH		8113	B3
Apex Ln NE				
-	FRID		7680	A5
Apfelridge Ct				
-	IVGH		8114	D1
-	SSTP		8114	D1
Apollo Ct				
-	LINO		7597	A3
Apollo Dr				
-	BLNE		7596	E4
-	LINO		7596	E4
-	LINO		7597	A3
Apollo Rd				
-	EAGN		8112	E7
-	EAGN		8113	A7
Appalachian Tr				
-	RSMT		8285	E3
Appaloosa Ct				
-	LINO		7597	A2
Appaloosa Ln				
-	LINO		7597	A2
Appaloosa Tr				
-	EAGN		8198	B4
Appenine Wy				
-	EAGN		8199	D7
-	IVGH		8199	D7
-	IVGH		8285	D1
Apple Ln				
-	EDNA		8022	A5
-	LINO		7683	A2
-	RHFD		8110	B1
Applegate Wy				
-	IVGH		8200	B3
Apple Orchard Ct				
-	DLWD		7686	C5
-	GRNT		7686	C5
Apple Orchard Rd				
-	DLWD		7686	C6
-	GRNT		7686	C5
Appletree Sq				
-	BMTN		8111	B5
Apple View Ln				
-	BRNV		8282	D3
Applewood Cir				
-	EDNP		8193	D3
Applewood Ct				
-	WDBY		8030	A1
Applewood Ct W				
-	RSVL		7854	C3
Applewood Rd				
-	WDBY		8030	A1
April Ct				
-	IVGH		8200	C2
April Ln				
-	MNTK		7934	E6
-	MNTK		7935	A6
Aqua Cir				
-	LINO		7597	B5
Aqua Ln				
-	LINO		7597	C5
Aquarius Ln				
-	EAGN		8198	D6
Aquila Av				
-	SAVG		8280	A6
Aquila Av N				
-	BRKP		7678	A7
-	CRYS		7850	A5
-	GLDV		7850	A7
-	NWHE		7764	A5
-	NWHE		7850	A1
Aquila Av S				
-	BMTN		8193	E4
-	HOPK		8022	A1
-	STLP		7936	A5
-	STLP		8022	A1
Aquila Cir				
-	NWHE		7850	A1
-	SAVG		8280	A5
-	STLP		8022	A1
Aquila Cir S				
-	BMTN		8193	E4
Aquila Ct				
-	SAVG		8280	A6
Aquila Dr N				
-	CHMP		7592	A6
Aquila Ln S				
-	STLP		7935	E7
-	STLP		7936	A7
Aquila Rd S				
-	BMTN		8193	E3
Arabian Cir				
-	LINO		7597	A1
Aralia Ct				
-	IVGH		8200	A3
Arbogast St				
-	SHVW		7768	E7
-	SHVW		7769	A7
Arbor Av				
-	MAHT		7772	C4
Arbor Cir				
-	MNTK		8021	B1
Arbor Ct				
-	EAGN		8199	A3
-	MNDH		8113	B4
Arbor Dr				
-	WtBT		7771	E4
Arbor Ln				
-	BRNV		8282	A4
-	EAGN		8198	B5
-	MNTK		7935	A7
-	MNTK		8021	A1
Arbor Ln S				
-	MNTK		8021	A1
Arbor St				
-	STPL		8027	A2
Arbor Glen Dr				
-	EDNP		8106	E3
Arbor Lakes Pkwy N				
-	MAPG		7676	E7
-	MAPG		7677	A7
Arbour Av				
-	EDNA		8022	C7
Arbour Ln				
-	EDNA		8022	C7
Arbre Ln N				
-	HUGO		7599	B6
Arcade St				
-	LCAN		7856	B2
-	MPLW		7856	B7
-	STPL		7856	B7
-	STPL		7942	C4
-	VADH		7856	B1
Arcade St SR-61				
-	MPLW		7856	B7
Arcade St US-61				
-	MPLW		7856	B7
-	STPL		7856	B7
-	STPL		7942	C4
Arcade St N				
-	VADH		7770	B6

STREET / Block / City / ZIP / Map # / Grid

Arcade St S — VADH 7770 B7; VADH 7856 B1
Arcadia Av — EDNA 8022 D5
Arcadia Dr — MNDH 8027 B5
Arch St E — STPL 7941 D5
Arch St W — STPL 7941 D5
Archer Av — GLDV 7850 C7
Archer Ct N — MAPG 7676 A4; PYMH 7848 A6
Archer Ln — EDNP 8193 D2
Archer Ln N — MAPG 7676 A7; MAPG 7762 A1; PYMH 7762 A7; PYMH 7848 A3; PYMH 7934 A1
Archer Pth — IVGH 8285 D1
Archers Ln — MNTK 7935 C5
Architect Av — COLH 7852 D1; MINN 7852 D2
Archwood Rd — MNTK 7935 C3
Arctic Wy — EDNA 8022 A7
Arcwood Rd — MAHT 7772 B7
Ardan Av — MNDS 7681 D4
Arden Av — EDNA 8023 A4
Arden Cir — BRNV 8282 C4; SHVW 7769 B7
Arden Pl — ARDH 7768 C7
Arden Oaks Ct — ARDH 7768 C6
Arden Oaks Dr — ARDH 7768 C6
Arden View Ct — ARDH 7768 C3
Arden View Dr — ARDH 7768 C3
Arden Vista Ct — ARDH 7768 C3
Ardmore Av — MNDS 7681 E6
Ardmore Dr — GLDV 7937 A2
Argenta Tr — EAGN 8113 D4; EAGN 8199 D2; IVGH 8113 E6; IVGH 8199 D1; MNDH 8113 D4; SUNL 8113 D4
Argonne Dr NE — COLH 7767 A5; NBRI 7767 B5
Argyle St — STPL 7940 E3
Ariel Ct N — MPLW 7857 B5; NSTP 7857 B5
Ariel St N — MPLW 7857 C2; NSTP 7857 B5
Aries Ct — EAGN 8198 D6
W Arion St — WSTP 8027 D4
Arion St E — SSTP 8028 C4; WSTP 8028 A4
Arion St W — WSTP 8027 E4
Arkansas Av — IVGH 8113 D6
Arkansas Pth — IVGH 8199 D5
Arkwright St — LCAN 7856 A4; MPLW 7856 A7; STPL 7856 A7; STPL 7942 A4
Arlene Av — IVGH 8114 B6
Arlene Ct — EAGN 8199 C4
Arlington Av E — MPLW 7943 D1; STPL 7941 D1; STPL 7942 D1; STPL 7943 B1
Arlington Av N — BRKP 7678 E7
Arlington Av W — FLCH 7940 C1; STPL 7940 C1; STPL 7941 D1
Arlington Dr — MNTK 8020 E4; MNTK 8021 A4
Arlington St — STPL 7940 E1; STPL 7941 A1
Arlington St SE — MINN 7939 A3
Arlo Ln — LINO 7597 C1
Armour Av — SSTP 8115 A1
Armour Ter — STAN 7853 C3
W Armour Ter — STAN 7853 B3
Armstrong Av — STPL 8026 E3; STPL 8027 A3
Armstrong Ct — IVGH 8285 D1
Arner Av — SHVW 7769 B2
Arnold Av — IVGH 8200 B4; IVGH 8286 B2
Arnold Palmer Ct NE — BLNE 7595 C2
Arnold Palmer Dr — BLNE 7595 B3
Arnold Palmer Tr NE — BLNE 7595 C2
Arona Av — BLNE 7682 A2; FLCH 7854 C6; FLCH 7940 C1; LXTN 7682 A2; RSVL 7854 C6; STPL 7940 C1
Arona St — FLCH 7940 C1; RSVL 7854 C2; SHVW 7682 C5; STPL 7940 C2
Arrowhead Ct — LINO 7683 C1
Arrowhead Dr — LINO 7683 B1
Arrowhead St NW — COON 7593 A4
Arrowhead Pass — EDNA 8107 E1
Arrowood Cir N — DAYT 7591 B1
Arrowood Ln N — DAYT 7591 B1; PYMH 7763 C6; PYMH 7849 C1
Arrowwood Dr — EDNP 8193 D3
Arrowwood Ln N — MAPG 7677 B2; MAPG 7763 C2
Arthur Av SE — MINN 7939 C4
Arthur Ct — CIRC 7682 D2; LINO 7599 A6
Arthur Dr — WDBY 8030 C7
Arthur Pl — MINN 7939 C4; RSVL 7854 A2
Arthur Pl NE — COLH 7767 A7
Arthur St — ARDH 7854 A2; EDNA 8022 A3; RSVL 7854 A2
Arthur St NE — COLH 7767 A7; COLH 7853 A1; FRID 7681 A6; FRID 7767 A2; MINN 7853 A3; SPLP 7681 A4
Arthur St W — MNTK 7934 E2
Arthur Ter — BRNV 8282 B6
Arundel St — STPL 7941 B1
Arvin Dr — MNDH 8027 B7; MNDH 8113 B1
Asarum Ct — SHKP 8278 B4
Asbury Av — FLCH 7854 C7; RSVL 7854 C7
Asbury St — ARDH 7682 C5; ARDH 7854 C1; FLCH 7854 C6; FLCH 7940 C1; RSVL 7854 C1; SHVW 7682 C5; STPL 7940 C1
Ascot Ct — NBRI 7767 B6
Ash Cir NE — PRIO 8279 C7
Ash Ct — FLCH 7854 A7
Ash St — CIRC 7682 E3; LINO 7682 E3; LINO 7683 A3; LINO 7684 B3; MAHT 7772 C5; NOAK 7683 E3; NOAK 7684 C3; SHVW 7682 E3; SHVW 7683 A3; WTBL 7771 D4; WtBT 7683 D3; WtBT 7684 C3
Ash St CO-J — LINO 7683 D3; WtBT 7683 E3
E Ash St — SSTP 8115 A4
W Ash St — SSTP 8114 E4
Ash St E — SHKP 8192 A6
Ashbourne Cir — SHKP 8279 A2
Ashbourne Rd — MNTK 7934 D6
Ashbury Cir — EAGN 8198 A3
Ashbury Cir N — CHMP 7591 C5
Ashbury Ct — EAGN 8198 A2
Ashbury Pl — EAGN 8198 A3
Ashbury Rd — EAGN 8197 E2; EAGN 8198 A2
Ashby Ln — EDNP 8106 A1
Ashcroft Av — EDNA 8022 E7
Ashcroft Ln — EDNA 8022 E7; EDNA 8108 E1
Ashcroft Rd — SAVG 8280 A5
Ashcroft Alcove — SAVG 8280 A5
Ashcroft Bay — SAVG 8280 A4
Asher Av — IVGH 8114 B4
Asher Ct — IVGH 8114 B4
Ashford Rd — WDBY 8030 E7
Ashland Av — SPLP 8115 E7; SPLP 8201 E1; STPL 7940 A7; STPL 7941 B7
Ashlar Dr — BMTN 8194 E6
Ashley Ct — IVGH 8285 D1
Ashley Ln — IVGH 8114 B2; MAHT 7772 B7; MAHT 7858 B1; MNDH 8027 C5; WSTP 8027 D5
Ashley Rd — EDNA 8022 A3; HOPK 8022 A3
Ashley Ter — NBRI 7767 B6
Ashley Ter N — BRKP 7679 B4
Ashton Av — IVGH 8199 D2
Ashton Av NE — FRID 7680 B4; FRID 7766 B1
Ashton Cir — SHKP 8279 B2
Ashwood Rd — WDBY 7944 B7
Asiatic Av — IVGH 8199 D2
Aspasia Cir — EDNA 8108 E3
Aspasia Ln — EDNA 8108 E3
Aspen Av NE — BLNE 7596 B7; LXTN 7596 B7; PRIO 8279 D7
Aspen Cir — EDNP 8193 D1; LCAN 7856 C1; VADH 7856 C1
Aspen Cir N — CHMP 7591 D6
Aspen Ct — EAGN 8198 B1; WDBY 8030 A1; WSTP 8027 E6; WTBL 7857 E1
Aspen Dr — BRNV 8281 B7; BRNV 8282 C3; SAVG 8280 E7; SAVG 8281 B1
Aspen Ln — LINO 7597 E7; LINO 7683 E1; NOAK 7683 E4; WtBT 7685 D5
Aspen Ln N — BRKP 7677 E5; BRKP 7764 A1; OSSE 7677 E5
Aspen Pt — LNDF 7944 A6
Aspen Rd — EDNA 8022 A7
Aspen Wy — LNDF 7944 A6; MNTK 7935 B6; ODLE 7944 A6
Aspen Cove S — CTGV 8116 B7
Aspen Grove Ln — BRNV 8281 C5
Aspen Lake Dr NE — BLNE 7595 D3
Aspen Ridge Cir — EAGN 8283 E1
Aspen Ridge Dr — MNTK 8021 A1
Aspenwood Plz — WDBY 8030 B1
Aster Dr — BRKP 7764 B3
Aston Cir — BRNV 8282 C5
Astrid Av — IVGH 8200 B5
Athena Wy — IVGH 8114 B6
Atlantic Av — IVGH 8199 D3
Atlantic St N — MPLW 7856 D5; STPL 7856 D7; STPL 7942 D1
Atlantic Hills Dr — EAGN 8199 B6
Atlas Av — IVGH 8199 D2
Atlas Cir — IVGH 8199 D3
Atrium Av — RSMT 8285 D6
Atrium Wy — MNTK 8020 C5
Atty St — STPL 7939 D6
Atwater Pth E — IVGH 8114 B2
Atwater St — HOPK 7935 D7; MNTK 7935 D7; STPL 7941 C4
Atwater Wy — RSMT 8285 D7
Atwood Av — RSMT 8285 D6
Atwood Cir — RSMT 8285 E7
Atwood Ct — RSMT 8285 D7
Atwood Dr — MNTK 7934 E7
Aubudon Rd — IVGH 8200 C3
Auburn Av — RSMT 8285 D7; WtBT 7685 C5
Auburn Ct — EAGN 8198 B6
Auburn Dr — MNTK 8021 A2
Audobon Av — IVGH 8114 B3
Audobon Wy — RSMT 8285 E7
Audrey Av — IVGH 8114 B4; RSMT 8286 B7
Audrey Av E — IVGH 8114 B1; WSTP 8114 B1
Audrey Dr — WSTP 8114 A1
Audubon Cir — IVGH 8200 B3
Audubon Ct — EDNP 8193 D4
Audubon Rd — IVGH 8200 B3
Audubon Wy — IVGH 8200 B3
Auerback Av — RSVL 7855 C5
Auger Av — WTBL 7771 B6
Auger Ln — WTBL 7771 A6
Augsburg Av — RHFD 8110 A3
August Cir — LINO 7685 A1
August Wy — IVGH 8114 B1
Augusta Ct — EAGN 8199 B5
Augusta Ln — DLWD 7686 A6; EAGN 8199 B6; EDNP 8106 A3
Augusta Wy — RSMT 8285 E7
Aurel Ln — BMTN 8110 C7
Aurora Av — RSMT 8285 D7; SPLP 8202 A1; STPL 7940 E6; STPL 7941 B6
Aurora Ln — CIRC 7596 C7
Austin Ct E — IVGH 8286 B2
Austin Ct NE — BLNE 7596 B3
Austin St NE — BLNE 7596 C6; BLNE 7682 B2; CIRC 7596 C6; LXTN 7596 B7; LXTN 7682 B2
Australian Av — LCAN 7855 D3
Austrian Pine Av N — BRKP 7679 B3
Austrian Pine Ln — MNTK 7935 A5
Auto Club Cir — BMTN 8194 A6
Auto Club Rd — BMTN 8194 B6
Auto Club Wy — STLP 8022 E2
Autumn Ct — RSMT 8285 D6
Autumn Pl — FLCH 7854 A6; RSVL 7854 A6
Autumn Pth — RSMT 8285 D6
Autumn St — FLCH 7854 A7; RSVL 7854 D7
Autumn St NE — MINN 7852 D7
Autumn Chace Cir — BMTN 8108 B6
Autumn Chace Dr — BMTN 8108 A5
Autumn Oaks Ct — EAGN 8199 C5
Autumnwood Av — RSMT 8285 D6
Autumnwood Ct — RSMT 8285 D6
Autumnwood Dr — MNTK 7935 D6
Autumnwood Ln — MNTK 7935 D6
Autumnwood Tr — RSMT 8285 E7
Autumnwood Wy — RSMT 8285 E6
Avalon Av — EAGN 8112 C5
Avalon Ct — IVGH 8199 D4
Avalon Pth — IVGH 8199 D4; RSMT 8285 D7
Avanti Av — RSMT 8285 D6
Avanti Dr — MNDH 8112 E1
Avenue B — MPLW 7943 E6
Avenue C — MPLW 7943 C6
Avenue D — MPLW 7943 D6
Avenue E — MPLW 7943 E6
Avenue F — MPLW 7943 D6
Avenue K — MPLW 7943 E6
Avenue L — MPLW 7943 D5
Avenue M — MPLW 7943 E5
Avenue O — MPLW 7943 D5
Avery Dr — IVGH 8285 D1
Aviary Pth — IVGH 8199 D3
Avignon Ct — WDBY 7944 D7
Avionics Blvd — MINN 7853 B6
Avocet Cir NW — COON 7593 D2
Avocet St NW — COON 7593 E4
Avon Ct — EAGN 8199 C4; WDBY 8030 B7
Avon Dr — WDBY 8030 B6
Avon Ln — SHKP 8278 C4
Avon St — SHVW 7769 A2
Avon St N — RSVL 7855 A2; SHVW 7855 A2; STPL 7941 A1
Avon St S — STPL 7941 A7; STPL 8027 A1
Avondale Rd — GLDV 7937 A4
Avondale St — MNTK 8020 A2
Aydee Cir — WTBL 7685 E6; WtBT 7685 E6
Ayd Mill Rd — STPL 7940 C7; STPL 8026 D1
Ayrshire Blvd — EDNA 8022 C5
Azalea Av — RSMT 8285 D6
Azalea Ct — RSMT 8285 D7
Azalea Pl — BRNV 8281 B6
Azalea Pth — RSMT 8285 D7
Azalea Tr — EDNP 8106 B7
Azalea Wy — IVGH 8199 D4
Azelia Av N — BRKC 7765 A7
Aztec Dr — EDNP 8107 A7
Aztec Ln — MNDH 8113 B2
Aztec St NW — COON 7592 C1

B

B St — HLTP 7766 E6; STPL 7943 A7; STPL 8029 A1
Babcock Tr E — IVGH 8114 B5; IVGH 8200 B1; WSTP 8114 B1
Babcock Tr E CO-73 — IVGH 8114 B5; IVGH 8200 B1; WSTP 8114 B1
Bacardi Av — IVGH 8199 D3
Bacardi Av W — EAGN 8285 D2; IVGH 8285 D2; RSMT 8285 D3
Bachelor Av — MNDH 8027 B7
Bachman Cir — IVGH 8114 B5
Bacon Av — IVGH 8114 C4; SSTP 8114 C2
Bacon Ct — IVGH 8114 C2
Bacon Dr NE — FRID 7681 A6; SPLP 7681 A6
Badger Cir NW — PRIO 8278 C7
Badger Ct — EAGN 8197 D6
Badger Ln — NOAK 7769 E1
Baffin Tr — EAGN 8199 D3; IVGH 8199 D3
Baffin Bay N — EAGN 8199 B5
Baffin Bay S — EAGN 8199 B5
Bagpipe Blvd — EDNP 8106 E3; EDNP 8107 A3
Bailey Ct — NWPT 8029 E7; NWPT 8115 E1
Bailey Rd — NWPT 8029 E7; NWPT 8030 A7; NWPT 8115 D1; STPL 8029 C7; WDBY 8030 E7
Bailey Tr — IVGH 8114 B5
Bailey Ridge Dr — WDBY 8030 E7
Baillif Pl — BMTN 8195 C4
Bainbridge Dr — EDNP 8106 A7
Baker Av — IVGH 8114 B5
Baker Av NE — FRID 7680 E6; FRID 7766 E2
Baker Ct — IVGH 8200 C4
Baker Rd — EDNP 8020 E7; EDNP 8106 E3; MNTK 8020 E2
Baker St E — STPL 8028 A2
Baker St NE — FRID 7680 E6; SPLP 7680 E6
Baker St W — STPL 8027 D2; STPL 8028 A2
Baker Tr — MNTK 8020 E2
Bakken's Wy — FRID 7680 E7; FRID 7681 A7
Bald Eagle Av — WTBL 7685 B7; WTBL 7771 B2; WtBT 7685 B7
E Bald Eagle Blvd — WtBT 7685 C6
W Bald Eagle Blvd — HUGO 7685 B2; LINO 7685 A5; WtBT 7685 B6
Bald Eagle Ct — EAGN 8198 D3
Bald Eagle Pt — HUGO 7685 C3; WtBT 7685 C3
Bald Eagle I — WtBT 7685 C4
Balder Ln — EDNA 8108 A1
Bald Lake Ct — EAGN 8199 A4
Baldwin Av — IVGH 8114 C7
Baldwin Cir — LINO 7683 A2
Baldwin Dr — CIRC 7596 E7
Baldwin Lake Rd — LINO 7682 E3; SHVW 7682 E3
Balfanz Rd — EDNA 8108 E2; EDNA 8109 A2
Balinese St — SHKP 8278 A2
Ball Rd NE — BLNE 7596 C6
Ballantine Av — IVGH 8114 C5
Ballantine Ct — IVGH 8114 C5
Ballantrae Rd — EAGN 8197 D3
Ballantyne Ln NE — SPLP 7680 C4; SPLP 7681 A4
Ballard Ct — IVGH 8114 B7
Ballard Tr — IVGH 8114 C7
Ballet Blvd NE — FRID 7680 D6
Balmoral Ln — EDNP 8193 D3
Balmoral Ln S — BMTN 8194 E5
Balsam Ln — EDNP 8193 D2
Balsam Ln N — DAYT 7591 B1; MAPG 7677 B2; MAPG 7763 B1; MNTK 7935 B2; PYMH 7763 B6; PYMH 7849 C1; PYMH 7935 B2
Balsam St — EAGN 8198 B6; STPL 7941 E6
E Balsam St — EAGN 8198 C6
Balsam Tr — SHKP 8278 B1
E Balsam Tr — EAGN 8198 C6
Balsam Fir Av N — BRKP 7679 B3
Baltic Av — EAGN 8198 A2

INDEX 6
Baltimore Ct NE

Minneapolis Street Index

Birchcrest Cir

STREET Block City ZIP Map # Grid

Baltimore Ct NE
- BLNE 7595 A1
Baltimore St NE
- BLNE 7595 A3
- BLNE 7681 A1
- SPLP 7681 A2
Bambi Ln
- WTBL 7770 D3
- WtBT 7770 D3
Bamble Cir
- EAGN 8283 E2
Banbury Ln
- MNTK 8020 A3
Bancroft Av
- STPL 8028 B2
Bancroft Wy
- IVGH 8114 C7
Bandana Blvd E
- STPL 7940 D3
Bandana Blvd N
- STPL 7940 D3
Bandana Blvd W
- STPL 7940 D3
Baneberry Cir
- SHKP 8278 B4
Baney Ct
- MNTK 8020 A7
Banfil St
- STPL 8027 B1
Banfill Cir N
- BRKP 7679 E5
SE Bank St
- MINN 7938 C1
Bankers Dr
- LCAN 7769 D7
- VADH 7769 D7
Banks Ct
- IVGH 8200 C1
Banks Pth
- IVGH 8200 C1
Banneker Av N
- MINN 7937 E1
Banning Av
- WTBL 7771 C2
Banning Wy
- IVGH 8114 C7
- IVGH 8200 C1
Bantas Point Ln
- MNTK 7934 A5
Bantas Point Rd
- MNTK 7934 A5
Banyan Ln
- EDNP 8192 B1
- RSMT 8285 C7
Banyan St
- ARDH 7768 A1
Barbara Av
- IVGH 8114 C2
- IVGH 8200 C2
Barbara Ct
- IVGH 8200 C1
- MNDH 8027 A7
Barbara Dr
- MNTK 8021 A4
Barbara Ln
- BRNV 8281 B4
- IVGH 8114 C2
- LINO 7597 C1
Barbato Ct
- IVGH 8114 C2
Barbs Cross
- RSMT 8285 A6
Barclay Av
- IVGH 8114 C5
Barclay St
- MPLW 7856 E3
- STPL 7856 E7
- STPL 7942 E2
Barge Channel Rd
- STPL 8028 C3
Barnes Av
- IVGH 8114 C6
- IVGH 8200 C3
Barnes Pl
- MINN 7937 E1
Barnes Tr
- IVGH 8200 D5
Barnes Wy E
- IVGH 8200 D6
Barn Swallow Cir
- EDNP 8193 D4
Barrett St
- STPL 7941 A3
Barrie Rd
- EDNA 8109 B1
Barrington Ct N
- BRKP 7679 B4
Barrington Pl
- MAHT 7858 A1
Barrington Ter N
- BRKP 7679 B4
Barrow Ct
- EAGN 8199 B5
Barry Dr
- NWPT 8115 D2
Barry Ln
- WtBT 7685 A6
Barrymore Ln
- WDBY 8030 D7
Bartelmy Ln
- MPLW 7857 D2
- NSTP 7857 D2
N Bartelmy Ln
- MPLW 7857 C2
Bartelmy Ln N
- MPLW 7943 D4
Bartley Ct
- IVGH 8200 C7
Barton Av SE
- MINN 7939 C4
Barton Tr
- IVGH 8200 C5
Bass Cir
- SHKP 8279 B3
Bass Ct
- SHKP 8279 B3
Bass Creek Av N
- BRKP 7763 D3
- BRKP 7764 D3
Bass Creek Cir N
- BRKP 7763 E4
- NWHE 7763 E4
Bass Creek Ct
- BRKP 7763 D3
Bassett Creek Dr
- GLDV 7850 E6
- GLDV 7851 A6
Bassett Creek Ln
- GLDV 7851 A6
Bass Lake Rd
- BRKC 7765 B5
- CRYS 7764 E6
- MAPG 7762 D3
- NWHE 7763 E5
- NWHE 7764 A5
- PYMH 7762 E4
- PYMH 7763 A4
Bass Lake Rd CO-10
- BRKC 7765 B5
- CRYS 7764 E6
- MAPG 7762 D3
- NWHE 7763 E5
- NWHE 7764 A5
- PYMH 7762 E4
- PYMH 7763 A4
Basswood Ct
- RSMT 8285 C5
Basswood Ln
- EAGN 8199 A3
- NOAK 7683 D5
Basswood Ln N
- CHMP 7591 C5
Basswood Rd
- EDNP 8107 C7
- MINN 7937 A5
- STLP 7937 B5
- WDBY 8030 A2
Bataan Ct
- BLNE 7681 D2
Bataan St NE
- BLNE 7595 D1
- BLNE 7681 D1
Batavia St
- STPL 8029 C5
Bates Av
- STPL 7942 B5
Battle Creek Ct
- STPL 7943 B5
Battle Creek Pl
- STPL 7943 B5
Battle Creek Rd
- STPL 7943 B7
- STPL 8029 B1
W Bavarian Ct
- FRID 7767 D4
E Bavarian Pass
- FRID 7767 B4
S Bavarian Pass
- FRID 7767 A4
W Bavarian Pass
- FRID 7767 A3
Baxter St N
- CHMP 7591 D2
Baxter Tr
- IVGH 8200 D5
Baxter Wy
- IVGH 8200 D3
S Bay Curv
- EDNP 8106 A5
Bay Dr
- EDNP 8106 A2
Bay Ln
- WTBL 7770 D3
- WtBT 7770 D3
W Bay Ln
- NOAK 7683 D6
Bay St
- STPL 8027 A3
Bayard Av
- STPL 8025 E3
- STPL 8026 B3
- STPL 8027 A3
Bayard Ct
- EDNP 8106 A6
Bayberry Cir
- RSMT 8285 D7
Bayberry Ct
- RSMT 8285 C7
Bayberry Dr
- WtBT 7685 D4
Bayberry Ln
- EAGN 8199 A3
Bayberry Tr
- RSMT 8285 C7
Bay Cove
- WTBL 7770 D3
Bayfield St
- STPL 7942 B7
- STPL 8028 C1
Bayhill Rd
- DLWD 7686 B4
- GRNT 7686 B4
Bayless Av
- STPL 7939 D3
Bayless Cir N
- MAPG 7677 D1
Bayless Pl
- STPL 7939 D4
Baylor Ct
- EAGN 8198 B6
Baypoint Dr
- BRNV 8283 A1
Bayridge Cir
- BMTN 8193 C2
Bayridge Ln
- BMTN 8193 E1
Bayview Cir NE
- PRIO 8279 E7
Bayview Dr
- RSVL 7855 B6
Baywood Ln
- EDNP 8106 B2
Baywood Ter
- EDNP 8106 A2
Bazaar Rd
- FLCH 7940 B2
Beach Cir
- EDNP 8107 A2
Beach Rd
- EDNP 8021 A7
- EDNP 8107 A2
- MNTK 8021 A7
- NBRI 7767 D4
Beachside Dr
- MNTK 8021 B5
Beacon Av
- STPL 7940 B6
Beacon Cir
- MNTK 8020 C5
Beacon Rd
- WDBY 8030 E7
Beacon St
- RSVL 7854 B4
Beacon St SE
- MINN 7939 B3
Beacon Hill Cir
- EAGN 8284 A1
Beacon Hill Ct
- EAGN 8198 A7
Beacon Hill Rd
- EAGN 8198 A7
- EAGN 8284 A1
- MNTK 8020 C4
Beam Av
- MPLW 7856 C2
- MPLW 7857 C2
- NSTP 7857 C2
Beam Ln
- EAGN 8112 C6
Bear Av N
- VADH 7770 A5
Bear Av S
- VADH 7769 E6
- VADH 7770 A6
Bear Ct
- WTBL 7771 D7
Beard Av N
- BRKC 7765 B3
- BRKP 7679 B7
- BRKP 7765 B1
- ROBB 7851 B1
Beard Av S
- BMTN 8109 B7
- BMTN 8195 B2
- BRNV 8281 B2
- EDNA 8023 B7
- MINN 8023 B2
Beard Ct
- EDNA 8023 B6
Beard Ct N
- BRKP 7679 B7
Beard Curv
- BMTN 8195 B3
Beard Pl
- EDNA 8023 B7
Beard Rd S
- BMTN 8109 B5
Beardsley Ct
- IVGH 8200 C3
Bear Path Tr
- EAGN 8197 D6
Bear Paw Tr
- EAGN 8199 A3
Beatrice St
- EAGN 8112 E6
Beaumont Ct
- APVA 8283 B3
Beaumont St
- MPLW 7855 D7
- STPL 7942 A5
Beaver Cir
- LINO 7683 D1
Beaver St
- WtBT 7685 C7
Beaver Tr
- LINO 7683 D1
Beaverdale Rd
- MPLW 7943 D2
Beaver Dam Ct
- EAGN 8197 D6
Beaver Dam Rd
- EAGN 8197 D6
Beaver Pond Wy
- CTRV 7598 C6
Bechtel Av
- IVGH 8200 E3
Bechtel Ct
- IVGH 8200 D2
Becker Tr
- IVGH 8113 D7
Beckman Av
- ARDH 7854 A1
- IVGH 8114 C5
Beckman Ct
- IVGH 8114 C5
Bedford Av
- EDNA 8022 D5
Bedford Ct
- MNDH 8113 C4
Bedford Dr
- EDNP 8106 D3
Bedford Ln
- SHKP 8278 A2
Bedford St
- STPL 7942 A5
Bedford St SE
- MINN 7939 D3
- STPL 7939 D5
Beebe Av
- MNDH 8027 C5
- WSTP 8027 C5
Beebe Pkwy
- MPLW 7857 C2
Beebe Rd
- MPLW 7857 C7
- NSTP 7857 C6
- STPL 7857 C7
Beech St
- STPL 7942 E4
- STPL 7943 A4
Beech St E
- STPL 7943 C4
Beech St NE
- FRID 7680 B5
Beech St W
- RSMT 8285 C7
Beechcraft Ln
- SSTP 8115 A4
Beecher Dr
- EAGN 8197 E7
Beechwood Av
- STPL 8026 B4
Beechwood Pl
- STPL 8026 D4
Beehive Ct
- EDNP 8106 E3
- EDNP 8107 A3
Behm Ln
- LINO 7597 A2
Belair Cir
- RSVL 7854 D2
Belair Ln
- EDNP 8106 A5
Belden Blvd S
- CTGV 8202 B2
Belden Dr NE
- STAN 7853 B3
Belfast Ct W
- RSMT 8285 C7
Belfast St W
- RSMT 8285 C7
Bell Ln
- IVGH 8113 D7
- STAN 7853 C3
Bellaire Av
- WTBL 7771 D6
- WTBL 7857 D1
- WtBT 7771 D6
Bellaire Av N
- MPLW 7857 D2
- NSTP 7857 D2
- WTBL 7857 D2
Bellaire Wy NE
- FRID 7680 A5
Belland Av
- VADH 7856 B1
- WTBL 7857 B1
Bellcrest Dr
- MPLW 7856 D4
Belle Ct
- RSMT 8285 C7
Belle Ln
- MNDS 7681 E6
Belle Aire Dr
- CHMP 7591 D1
Bellevue Dr
- MNTK 8020 D4
Bellflower Ct S
- CTGV 8116 A5
Bello Dr
- EDNA 8108 A2
Bell Oaks Estate Rd
- EDNP 8193 C4
Bellows St
- STPL 8027 E2
- WSTP 8027 E4
Bellvue Ln
- BRKC 7766 A6
Bellwood Av
- MPLW 7855 E7
- MPLW 7856 B7
Belmar Dr
- VADH 7856 B1
Belmont Av
- MPLW 7856 E6
Belmont Av S
- MINN 8024 B5
Belmont Ct
- APVA 8283 A4
- RSMT 8285 C6
Belmont Dr
- WDBY 8030 D2
Belmont Ln
- EDNP 8193 E3
Belmont Ln E
- MPLW 7856 D6
- MPLW 7857 C6
- NSTP 7857 E6
Belmont Ln W
- RSVL 7854 D6
- RSVL 7855 A6
Belmont Rd
- APVA 8283 A4
- MNTK 7935 D4
- STLP 7935 D4
Belmont Tr
- RSMT 8285 C6
Belmore Ln
- EDNA 8021 E3
- EDNA 8022 A4
Belt Line Blvd
- STLP 7937 A7
- STLP 8022 E1
- STLP 8023 A1
Belvidere Ct
- RSMT 8285 C6
Belvidere Ln
- EDNA 8108 E3
- EDNA 8109 A3
Belvidere St E
- STPL 8028 A3
Belvidere St W
- STPL 8027 E3
- STPL 8028 A3
- WSTP 8027 E3
Belvoir Dr
- MNTK 8020 C2
Belwood Ln
- MNTK 8020 A5
Bengal Av W
- RSMT 8285 C4
Benhill Rd
- STPL 8026 E2
Benjamin Dr
- WDBY 8030 D7
Benjamin Pl NE
- COLH 7853 A1
Benjamin St NE
- COLH 7767 B7
- COLH 7853 A2
- FRID 7767 A3
- MINN 7853 A2
- SPLP 7681 A5
Benjamin Tr
- IVGH 8200 E5
Benlana Ct
- MPLW 7943 E1
Ben More Dr NE
- FRID 7767 A2
Bennett Ct
- IVGH 8113 D7
Bennett Dr NE
- FRID 7766 D2
Bennett Pl
- EDNP 8193 C2
Benson Av
- STPL 8026 D5
Benson St
- STPL 8026 C6
Benson Wy
- IVGH 8200 E3
Bentley Wy
- RSMT 8285 C7
Benton Av
- EDNA 8022 D7
Benton Blvd
- MINN 7937 C6
Benton Cir
- IVGH 8114 C6
Benton Wy
- ARDH 7768 D7
- IVGH 8114 C6
Bent Tree Cir
- MNTK 7935 A6
Benttree Ct
- NOAK 7684 A7
Bent Tree Ln
- EAGN 8199 C6
- MNDH 8113 C2
- MNTK 7935 A5
Benttree Ln
- NOAK 7684 A7
Bent Tree Rd
- MNTK 7935 A6
Bent Tree Wy
- MNTK 7935 A6
Bent Tree Hills Dr
- NBRI 7767 B4
Bentwood Dr
- EDNP 8107 D7
Benz Rd
- NBRI 7853 D1
Berg Dr E
- SHKP 8278 A1
Berger Dr
- EDNP 8106 B6
Bergeron Ln
- WTBL 7857 C1
Berkeley Av
- STPL 8025 E1
- STPL 8026 B1
Berkeley Pl
- WILL 7772 C6
Berkshire Cir
- SHKP 8279 B2
Berkshire Ct
- EAGN 8283 D1
- MAPG 7762 D1
- SHKP 8279 C2
Berkshire Ct N
- PYMH 7848 D2
Berkshire Dr
- EAGN 8283 D1
- MNTK 8020 E3
- MNTK 8021 B3
Berkshire Ln
- EDNP 8106 E6
- SHKP 8279 B2
Berkshire Ln N
- MAPG 7676 D7
- MAPG 7762 D3
- PYMH 7762 D4
- PYMH 7848 D2
- PYMH 7934 D2
Berkshire Rd
- BMTN 8194 D3
Berkshire Wy
- EAGN 8283 D1
- MAPG 7676 D7
- MAPG 7762 D1
Berland Pl
- MPLW 8029 C1
- STPL 8029 C1
Bernard Av N
- CRYS 7764 E7
Bernard Pl
- EDNA 8022 D6
Bernard Pth
- IVGH 8200 D2
Bernard St E
- SSTP 8028 C4
- WSTP 8028 B4
Bernard St W
- WSTP 8027 E4
Berne Cir
- EDNA 8022 B6
Berne Cir E
- FRID 7767 B4
Berne Cir W
- FRID 7767 A4
Berne Rd NE
- FRID 7767 A4
Berry St
- STPL 7939 D4
Berry Ridge Rd
- EAGN 8198 C5
Bertha Ct
- MAHT 7772 B7
Berwick Cir
- SHKP 8279 B1
Berwick Knls N
- BRKP 7679 B4
Berwick Ln
- MAHT 7772 B7
- MAHT 7858 B1
Berwick Pl
- MAHT 7858 B1
E Berwood Av
- VADH 7770 C7
W Berwood Av
- VADH 7770 B7
Berwood Ct W
- VADH 7770 B7
Beryl Rd
- EAGN 8197 D4
Bester Av
- IVGH 8114 C6
Bester Av
- IVGH 8200 C1
Bester Ct
- IVGH 8114 C7
Beth Ct E
- MPLW 8029 E3
Bethel Dr
- ARDH 7768 C6
Bethia Ln N
- BRKP 7764 C2
Betty Ln
- EAGN 8199 A2
- EDNP 8107 C2
- MNDH 8027 D6
- WSTP 8027 D6
Betty Crocker Dr
- GLDV 7935 D2
- GLDV 7936 A2
- PYMH 7935 E2
- STLP 7935 D2
Betty Jane Ct
- MPLW 7857 E6
- NSTP 7857 E6
Beula Ln
- STPL 7940 D2
Beulah Ln
- STPL 7940 D3
Beverley Ln
- SAVG 8280 C7
Beverly Av
- GLDV 7937 A2
Beverly Dr
- EDNP 8192 A3
Beverly Pl
- MNTK 7934 B6
Beverly Rd
- STPL 7939 E5
Beverly Wy
- IVGH 8200 D2
Bevins Ln
- MAHT 7772 C7
- PNSP 7772 C7
Bibeau Rd
- VADH 7770 D3
- WTBL 7770 D3
- WtBT 7770 D3
Bicentennial Ct
- NBRI 7767 C6
Bichner Ln
- MAHT 7772 C7
- PNSP 7772 C7
Bidwell St
- STPL 8027 E1
- WSTP 8027 E4
- WSTP 8113 E1
Bielenberg Ct
- WDBY 8030 C3
Bielenberg Dr
- WDBY 7944 C7
- WDBY 8030 C3
Bies Dr
- GLDV 7850 A6
Big Cir Dr
- LCAN 7855 E2
Bigelow Av
- STPL 7940 D6
Big Fox Rd
- GEML 7770 D6
- VADH 7770 D6
Big Linden Curv
- WTBL 7771 C7
Biglow Ln
- STPL 7941 E1
Big Oak Dr
- BRNV 8281 D4
Big Timber Tr
- EAGN 8199 A4
Bill Bourassa Ln
- EAGN 8199 A1
Bimini Dr
- MNTK 8021 B6
Birch Blvd
- IVGH 8200 E2
Birch Ct
- IVGH 8200 E2
- LINO 7683 D1
- WTBL 7770 D3
Birch Ln
- LNDF 7944 A6
- MNTK 8020 A6
- NOAK 7769 E2
Birch Ln N
- NOAK 7683 A7
- SHVW 7683 A7
Birch Ln S
- NOAK 7683 A7
- SHVW 7683 A7
Birch Pl
- MNTK 7935 D7
Birch Pt
- EAGN 8198 C2
Birch Rd
- MNTK 8020 A5
Birch St
- ANOK 7592 B2
- BRHV 7772 A5
- COON 7592 B2
- LINO 7597 D7
- LINO 7598 A7
- LINO 7683 C1
- MAHT 7772 C5
- STPL 8029 C6
- WTBL 7771 B5
- WtBT 7771 D5
Birch St W
- RSMT 8285 C6
Birch Tr
- SHVW 7683 B5
Birch Bend Ct
- VADH 7770 C3
Birch Bend Ln
- VADH 7770 C2
- WtBT 7770 C2
Birch Briar Tr N
- PYMH 7934 A1
Birch Cove Dr
- WTBL 7770 D2
Birchcrest Cir
- EAGN 8198 E7

INDEX 7

Birchcrest Dr — Brianboru Av

Minneapolis Street Index

STREET Block	City	ZIP	Map #	Grid
Birchcrest Dr				
-	EDNA		8022	D7
-	WTBL		7770	D3
-	WtBT		7770	E3
Bircher Av				
-	SSTP		8028	C4
Birch Grove Cir N				
-	BRKP		7679	A6
Birch Island Rd				
-	EDNP		8106	C1
Birchknoll Dr				
-	WtBT		7771	E5
Birch Lake Av				
-	WTBL		7771	A2
N Birch Lake Blvd				
-	NOAK		7770	C1
-	WTBL		7770	C1
-	WtBT		7770	D1
S Birch Lake Blvd				
-	VADH		7770	C3
-	WTBL		7770	E2
-	WtBT		7770	D3
Birch Lake Blvd N				
-	WTBL		7770	E1
-	WtBT		7770	E1
Birch Lake Cir				
-	WTBL		7770	E1
Birchpond Pl				
-	EAGN		8198	A3
Birchpond Rd				
-	EAGN		8198	A2
Birch Pond Tr				
-	WtBT		7770	D3
Birch Ridge Rd				
-	VADH		7770	C3
-	WtBT		7770	B3
Birch View Ct				
-	STPL		8029	C4
Birchview Dr				
-	MPLW		7943	E2
Birchview Ln				
-	MNTK		7935	D5
Birchview Rd				
-	MAPG		7763	A2
Birchwood Av				
-	BRHV		7771	E4
-	BRHV		7772	A5
-	MAHT		7772	B6
-	RSMT		8285	C6
-	WtBT		7771	E4
Birchwood Av NE				
-	PRIO		8279	D7
Birchwood Ct				
-	BRHV		7772	A5
-	BRNV		8282	A4
Birchwood Ln				
-	BMTN		8108	A7
-	BRHV		7771	E4
-	BRNV		8282	A4
-	MNTK		8020	E4
-	WtBT		7771	E4
Birchwood Rd				
-	BRHV		7772	B6
-	MAHT		7772	B6
-	WDBY		8030	A2
Birchwood St				
-	SHVW		7682	D4
Birdsong Pth				
-	RSMT		8285	C5
Birmingham Ct				
-	RSMT		8285	C6
Birmingham St				
-	MPLW		7856	E7
-	STPL		7856	E7
-	STPL		7942	E4
Birnamwood Ct				
-	BRNV		8282	C2
Birnamwood Dr				
-	BRNV		8282	D2
Birnamwood Tr				
-	RSMT		8285	C6
Biscayne Av				
-	EAGN		8285	C2
Biscayne Av W				
-	RSMT		8285	C3
Biscayne Blvd				
-	EDNA		8021	E6
-	EDNA		8022	A6
-	EDNP		8106	A5
Biscayne Wy W				
-	RSMT		8285	C7
Bischoff Ln				
-	BMTN		8110	C7
Bishop Av				
-	IVGH		8114	C4
Bishop Ct				
-	EDNP		8193	B1
Bison Av				
-	STPL		7940	C2
Bison Dr				
-	MPLW		7943	D2
Bisset Ln				
-	IVGH		8114	D2
Bitterman Pth				
-	IVGH		8114	D2
Bittersweet Dr				
-	EDNP		8106	B4
Bittersweet Ln				
-	MPLW		7857	A4
Bittersweet St NW				
-	COON		7593	A3
Bivens Ct				
-	IVGH		8114	D2
Bixby Wy				
-	IVGH		8114	C6
Blackberry Ln				
-	MNTK		7934	B4
Blackberry Tr				
-	IVGH		8114	D4
Blackberry Wy				
-	RSMT		8285	B7
Blackberry Bridge Pth				
-	IVGH		8114	D4
Blackburn Ln				
-	IVGH		8114	C3
Black Dog Rd E				
-	BRNV		8196	B5
-	BRNV		8197	A3
-	DkaC		8197	A3
-	EAGN		8197	A3
Black Dog Rd W				
-	BRNV		8195	E6
-	BRNV		8196	A6
Black Duck Cir				
-	LINO		7597	E6
Black Duck Ct				
-	LINO		7597	E7
Black Duck Dr				
-	LINO		7597	E6
Blackduck Dr S				
-	LINO		7597	E7
Blackfoot St NW				
-	COON		7592	C3
Blackfoot Pass				
-	EDNA		8108	A1
Blackhawk Cir				
-	EAGN		8197	C1
Blackhawk Pt				
-	EAGN		8198	A3
Blackhawk Rd				
-	EAGN		8197	E6
Black Hawk Tr				
-	IVGH		8114	C6
Blackhawk Cove				
-	EAGN		8198	A3
Blackhawk Hills Rd				
-	EAGN		8198	A3
Blackhawk Lake Ct				
-	EAGN		8198	B3
Blackhawk Lake Dr				
-	EAGN		8198	A3
Blackhawk Lake Pl				
-	EAGN		8198	A3
Blackhawk Ridge Cir				
-	EAGN		8198	A4
Blackhawk Ridge Ct				
-	EAGN		8198	B3
Blackhawk Ridge Pl				
-	EAGN		8198	B3
Blackhawk Ridge Wy				
-	EAGN		8198	A3
Black Hills Dr				
-	BRNV		8281	D3
Black Lake Ct				
-	NOAK		7684	B7
Black Lake Rd				
-	NOAK		7684	B7
Black Maple Dr				
-	EDNP		8107	C7
Black Oak Dr				
-	EAGN		8113	C7
-	EAGN		8199	C1
-	MNTK		7935	B5
-	NBRI		7767	B4
Black Oak Rd				
-	NOAK		7683	C6
Black Oaks Ct N				
-	PYMH		7848	A7
Blackoaks Ct N				
-	MAPG		7676	A3
Black Oaks Ln				
-	MNTK		7934	A2
-	PYMH		7934	A2
Black Oaks Ln N				
-	PYMH		7848	A1
-	PYMH		7934	A2
Blackoaks Ln N				
-	MAPG		7676	A3
-	MAPG		7762	A1
Black Oaks Pl N				
-	PYMH		7848	A7
Blackshire Pth				
-	IVGH		8114	D4
Blackstone Av S				
-	STLP		7936	D4
Blackwell Ct				
-	IVGH		8114	C7
Blaine Av				
-	IVGH		8114	C2
-	IVGH		8200	D1
-	SSTP		8114	C1
Blaine Av E				
-	RSMT		8286	D7
Blaine Ct				
-	IVGH		8114	C7
Blaine Ct E				
-	RSMT		8286	D7
Blair Av				
-	IVGH		8200	D6
-	STPL		7940	B5
-	STPL		7941	D5
Blaisdell Av				
-	RHFD		8110	B4
Blaisdell Av S				
-	BMTN		8110	B6
-	BMTN		8196	A1
-	MINN		7938	B7
-	MINN		8024	B4
-	RHFD		8110	B1
Blaisdell Cir				
-	BMTN		8196	A1
Blake Av				
-	STPL		7939	E3
Blake Pth				
-	IVGH		8114	D7
Blake Rd N				
-	HOPK		8022	A2
-	STLP		8022	A2
Blake Rd S				
-	EDNA		8022	A4
-	HOPK		8022	A3
Blakeney Rd				
-	EDNP		8106	C7
Blake Ridge Ct				
-	EDNA		8022	B6
Blake Ridge Rd				
-	EDNA		8022	B6
Blakewood Dr				
-	SHKP		8278	C3
Blanca Av				
-	RSMT		8285	B7
Blanca Av W				
-	RSMT		8285	B3
Blanchard Av				
-	IVGH		8200	C1
Blanchard Ct				
-	IVGH		8200	D1
Blanchard Wy				
-	IVGH		8200	D1
Blaylock Cir				
-	IVGH		8114	C1
Blaylock Wy				
-	IVGH		8114	C1
Blazing Star Cir				
-	SHKP		8279	C3
Blazing Star Ct N				
-	CHMP		7591	C4
Blenheim Cir				
-	MNTK		8020	A3
Blenheim Wy				
-	MNTK		8020	A2
Bliss Ln				
-	BMTN		8195	E5
Bliss Ln Cir				
-	BMTN		8195	E5
Blomquist Av				
-	WTBL		7771	D6
Bloom Av				
-	WTBL		7771	C1
Bloom Ct				
-	LINO		7684	E2
Bloom Rd				
-	WtBT		7685	E4
Bloomberg Cir				
-	IVGH		8114	C1
Bloomberg Ln				
-	IVGH		8114	C2
-	SSTP		8114	C2
Bloomfield Ct				
-	RSMT		8285	D7
Bloomfield Pl				
-	RSMT		8285	C7
Bloomfield Pth				
-	RSMT		8285	C7
Bloomingdale's Ct				
-	BMTN		8110	D6
Bloomington Av				
-	RHFD		8110	D4
Bloomington Av S				
-	BMTN		8110	D7
-	BMTN		8196	D1
-	MINN		7938	D6
-	MINN		8024	D3
-	RHFD		8024	D7
-	RHFD		8110	D4
E Bloomington Frwy				
-	BMTN		8109	E5
-	BMTN		8195	E1
W Bloomington Frwy				
-	BMTN		8109	E7
-	BMTN		8195	E1
Bloomington Rd				
-	HnpC		8025	E7
-	HnpC		8111	D1
Bloomington Ferry Cir				
-	BMTN		8194	A6
Bloomington Ferry Rd				
-	BMTN		8193	E1
-	BMTN		8194	A3
Bloomquist Av				
-	WTBL		7771	C6
Blossom Ct				
-	EDNA		8022	C4
Blossom Ln				
-	SPLP		8202	A1
Blossom Rd				
-	EDNP		8193	C2
Bluebell Av N				
-	BRKP		7679	B3
Bluebell Ct				
-	VADH		7769	E4
Blueberry Cir				
-	EAGN		8198	D5
Blueberry Ct				
-	EAGN		8198	D5
Blueberry Knls				
-	EAGN		8198	C5
Blueberry Ln				
-	EAGN		8198	C5
Blueberry St				
-	IVGH		8200	C1
Blue Bill Cir				
-	WtBT		7685	E4
Bluebill Cir				
-	EAGN		8197	E3
Bluebill Dr				
-	EAGN		8197	E3
-	MNDH		8113	A3
Bluebird Cir				
-	MAPG		7763	B3
Bluebird Cir NW				
-	COON		7593	D1
Bluebird Dr				
-	MAPG		7763	A3
Blue Bird Ln				
-	NOAK		7683	C6
Bluebird Ln				
-	WDBY		7944	D7
Bluebird St NW				
-	COON		7593	D1
Bluebird Tr NE				
-	PRIO		8279	B6
Bluebird Alcove				
-	WDBY		7944	D7
Blue Cir Dr				
-	MNTK		8021	D7
Blue Crane Ln				
-	NOAK		7683	E6
Blue Cross Rd				
-	EAGN		8197	E2
-	EAGN		8198	A1
Blue Flag Ct				
-	NOAK		7684	A6
Blue Gentian Cir				
-	EAGN		8112	E5
Blue Gentian Rd				
-	EAGN		8112	E5
-	EAGN		8113	A4
Blue Goose Rd				
-	NOAK		7770	B1
Blue Heron Ct				
-	EAGN		8198	D2
Blue Heron Dr				
-	LINO		7597	A7
Blue Heron Ln				
-	WDBY		7944	D7
Blue Jay Ct				
-	EAGN		8198	E3
Blue Jay Ln				
-	NOAK		7769	C1
Blue Jay St				
-	SHKP		8278	A4
Blue Jay Wy				
-	EAGN		8198	E2
Blue Spruce Ct				
-	NOAK		7769	C1
Blue Stem Ln				
-	NWPT		8115	D3
Bluestem Ln				
-	EDNP		8193	C3
-	SHVW		7682	A4
Bluestem Ln S				
-	CTGV		8116	B5
Bluestem Pl N				
-	CHMP		7591	C4
Bluestem Cove S				
-	CTGV		8116	C5
Bluestone Dr				
-	EAGN		8197	C4
E Bluestone Dr				
-	EAGN		8197	E4
Bluestone Ln				
-	EAGN		8197	C4
Blue Water Rd				
-	EAGN		8112	E5
-	EAGN		8113	A5
Bluff Cir				
-	MNDH		8027	A6
Bluff Ct				
-	BRNV		8196	D6
Bluff Dr				
-	BMTN		8194	C7
Bluff Rd				
-	BMTN		8193	E4
-	EDNP		8193	D4
Bluff St				
-	MINN		7938	E3
Bluwood Av				
-	LCAN		7855	D3
Board Cir				
-	MAHT		7772	A7
Boardman St				
-	MINN		8025	B5
Boardwalk				
-	EAGN		8198	A2
Boardwalk Av				
-	MINN		7852	B3
Boardwalk Ct				
-	MNDH		8027	A6
-	SHVW		7768	E3
Boardwalk Pl				
-	MINN		7852	B3
Boatman Ln				
-	IVGH		8114	D2
Bob Pl				
-	RHFD		8110	A2
Bobcat Ln				
-	MPLW		7943	D2
Bobo Link Ln				
-	NOAK		7683	C5
Bohland Av				
-	STPL		8026	A4
Bohland Pl				
-	STPL		8026	D4
Bohn Ct				
-	SAVG		8281	A3
Bohnhof Jct				
-	FRID		7767	D3
Boiling Springs Cir				
-	SHKP		8279	D4
Boiling Springs Ln E				
-	SHKP		8279	D2
Bolivia Av W				
-	RSMT		8285	B4
Bolland Ct				
-	IVGH		8114	D5
Bolland Tr				
-	IVGH		8114	D5
Bolton Wy				
-	IVGH		8114	D7
Bona Rd				
-	MNDS		7681	D5
-	NBRI		7681	D7
Bonaire Pth W				
-	RSMT		8285	B5
Bond Wy				
-	IVGH		8114	D7
Bonner Ct				
-	IVGH		8114	D6
Bonnie Ln				
-	GLDV		7851	B6
-	STPL		8029	C5
Bonnie Brae Dr				
-	EDNA		8108	B4
Boone Av				
-	SAVG		8280	A2
Boone Av N				
-	BRKP		7678	A7
-	BRKP		7764	A4
-	GLDV		7850	A7
-	GLDV		7936	A1
-	NWHE		7764	A7
-	NWHE		7850	A4
Boone Av S				
-	PRIO		8280	A6
-	SAVG		8280	A6
-	STLP		7936	A6
-	STLP		8022	A1
Boone Cir N				
-	NWHE		7764	A7
-	NWHE		7850	A3
Boone Cir S				
-	BMTN		8193	E3
Boone Ct				
-	STLP		7936	A6
Boone Pl N				
-	NWHE		7764	A5
Booth Av				
-	IVGH		8114	D6
Borchert Ln				
-	EAGN		8113	A7
Bordeaux Ct				
-	IVGH		8114	D5
-	WDBY		7944	D7
Borden Ct				
-	IVGH		8114	D6
Borden Wy				
-	IVGH		8114	D5
Border Av N				
-	MINN		7938	A2
Bordner Dr				
-	IVGH		8114	D7
Bordner Pl				
-	STPL		8026	A5
Borealis Ln NE				
-	COLH		7766	E6
Borman Av				
-	IVGH		8114	D7
-	IVGH		8200	D6
Borman Ct				
-	IVGH		8114	D7
Borman Wy				
-	IVGH		8114	D7
Boss Cir				
-	EDNP		8193	C4
Bossard Dr				
-	RSVL		7855	B5
Bossen Ter				
-	MINN		8025	B6
Boston Cir				
-	EAGN		8198	E4
Boston Ct				
-	EAGN		8198	E4
Boston Ln				
-	LXTN		7682	B1
Boston Hill Rd				
-	EAGN		8198	E4
Boudin St NE				
-	PRIO		8280	A7
Boudreau Ct				
-	IVGH		8200	D1
Boulder Dr				
-	BRNV		8281	C6
Boulder Ln				
-	BRKC		7764	E4
-	BRNV		8281	C6
Boulder Wy				
-	MNTK		8020	C7
Boulder Bay Rd				
-	EDNP		8107	B1
Boulder Creek Dr				
-	EDNP		8020	C7
-	MNTK		8020	B7
Boulder Pointe Rd				
-	EDNP		8106	C7
Boulder Ridge Ln				
-	WDBY		8030	E4
Boulder Ridge Pt				
-	EAGN		8198	B6
Boulder Ridge Rd				
-	WDBY		8030	D4
Boulder Rise				
-	EDNP		8106	C7
Boulders Wy				
-	BRNV		8281	C6
Bouleau Rd				
-	WTBL		7770	D2
S Boulevard				
-	BMTN		8110	E5
Boundary Creek Ter				
-	MAPG		7591	C7
-	MAPG		7677	C1
Bourn Ln				
-	MNDH		8112	D4
Bourne St				
-	STPL		7939	D2
Bovey Av				
-	IVGH		8114	D7
Bowdoin St				
-	STPL		8025	E5
Bower Ct				
-	IVGH		8114	D2
-	IVGH		8200	D2
Bower Pth				
-	IVGH		8114	D2
-	IVGH		8200	D2
-	SSTP		8114	D2
Bowman Av				
-	IVGH		8114	D5
-	IVGH		8200	D1
Bowman Ct				
-	IVGH		8114	D5
-	IVGH		8200	D1
Boxman Pth				
-	IVGH		8114	D5
Boxwood Av E				
-	MPLW		8029	D5
-	STPL		8029	D5
Boxwood Pth				
-	RSMT		8285	B7
Boyce St				
-	HOPK		8022	A3
Boyd Av				
-	FLCH		7940	A2
-	IVGH		8114	D2
-	IVGH		8200	D1
Boyd Cir				
-	IVGH		8114	D7
Boyd Ct				
-	IVGH		8200	D1
Boyer Pth				
-	IVGH		8114	D5
Boys School Rd				
-	MNTK		8020	C6
Bradbury Ct				
-	IVGH		8114	D4
Braddock Tr				
-	EAGN		8199	A5
Braden Tr				
-	IVGH		8114	D7
Bradford Av N				
-	CHMP		7592	A2
Bradford Cir				
-	EAGN		8199	A4
Bradford Ct				
-	IVGH		8200	E2
Bradford Pl				
-	EAGN		8199	A4
-	EDNP		8106	C7
Bradford Rd				
-	HOPK		8021	B3
-	MNTK		8021	B3
Bradford St				
-	STPL		7939	E4
Bradley St				
-	BLNE		7596	E3
-	LINO		7596	E3
-	MPLW		7856	A7
Bradley St				
-	STPL		7942	A2
Brady Pth				
-	IVGH		8114	D7
Braeburn Cir				
-	EDNA		8108	A2
Braemar Blvd				
-	EDNA		8107	E4
-	EDNA		8108	A3
Braemar Rd				
-	WDBY		8030	C4
Braewood Cir				
-	BMTN		8194	D5
Brainard Wy				
-	NOAK		7683	B7
Brainerd Av				
-	STPL		7942	A2
Bramblewood Av				
-	VADH		7770	B3
-	WtBT		7770	B2
Branching Horn				
-	EDNP		8193	C4
Brand Av E				
-	MPLW		7943	E4
-	ODLE		7943	E4
Brandbury Wk				
-	MNTK		8020	D4
Brandlwood Ct				
-	WtBT		7684	D5
Brandlwood Rd				
-	WtBT		7684	D5
Brandywine Dr				
-	BRNV		8282	B5
Brandywine Pkwy				
-	BRKP		7679	C6
Branson Dr				
-	IVGH		8200	D3
Branson St				
-	EDNA		8023	A3
Branston St				
-	FLCH		7939	E1
-	STPL		7939	E1
Brant Cir				
-	EAGN		8197	E6
-	EAGN		8198	A6
Brant St NE				
-	BLNE		7682	C2
-	LXTN		7682	C2
Brassie Cir				
-	EDNP		8193	D2
Braun Ct				
-	EAGN		8198	C3
Bravo Ln				
-	EDNP		8192	D2
Braxton Dr				
-	EDNP		8106	A7
-	EDNP		8192	A1
Brazil Av				
-	RSMT		8285	B7
Breckenridge Rd				
-	MNTK		7935	B6
Breda Av				
-	STPL		7940	C3
Breen St				
-	STPL		7943	A2
Breezy Wy				
-	EDNP		8193	E3
Bremen Av				
-	RSMT		8285	B6
Bren Cir				
-	MNTK		8021	B7
Bren Rd				
-	MNTK		8021	B6
Bren Rd E				
-	MNTK		8021	D6
Bren Rd W				
-	EDNA		8021	D6
-	MNTK		8021	D6
Brendon Av				
-	IVGH		8114	D7
Brenlyn Ln				
-	MNTK		8021	A3
Brenner Av				
-	RSVL		7854	E2
-	RSVL		7855	A2
E Brenner Av				
-	MPLW		7857	D2
Brenner Ct				
-	RSVL		7853	D2
Brenner St				
-	RSVL		7853	D1
-	STAN		7853	D1
Brenner Pass				
-	GLDV		7937	B4
E Brenner Pass				
-	FRID		7767	D4
N Brenner Pass				
-	FRID		7767	D4
W Brenner Pass				
-	FRID		7767	D4
Brent Av				
-	IVGH		8114	D2
-	IVGH		8200	D5
Brentwood Av N				
-	CRYS		7764	C6
Brentwood Dr				
-	NBRI		7767	C6
Brentwood Ln				
-	EAGN		8199	B3
Brenwood Curv				
-	MPLW		7857	D2
Brenwood Tr				
-	MNTK		8020	E3
Brewer Dr NW				
-	PRIO		8278	D5
Brewer Ln				
-	IVGH		8114	D3
Brewster Av				
-	IVGH		8200	D2
Brewster St				
-	STPL		7939	D6
-	STPL		7940	A3
Brian Ct				
-	CTRV		7598	D5
Brian Dr				
-	CTRV		7598	D5
Brian Wy				
-	CTRV		7598	D4
Brianboru Av				
-	RSMT		8285	B6

INDEX 8

Briar Cir — Calhoun Pl

Minneapolis Street Index

STREET Block City ZIP Map # Grid

Briar Cir
- BMTN 8194 D1
Briar Ct
- BMTN 8194 D4
- BRNV 8281 E3
Briar Ln
- BMTN 8194 D1
- MNTK 7935 B4
Briar Rd
- BMTN 8194 D2
Briar Creek Rd
- EAGN 8198 E3
Briardale Ct NE
- FRID 7767 B1
Briardale Rd NE
- FRID 7767 A2
- NBRI 7767 B2
Briarknoll Cir
- ARDH 7768 C3
Briarknoll Dr
- ARDH 7768 C4
Briarwood Av
- DLWD 7772 C2
- GRNT 7772 D3
- MAHT 7772 D3
Briarwood Ct
- MNTK 8021 A3
Briarwood Dr
- MNTK 8021 A3
Briarwood Ln
- EAGN 8199 A3
- MNTK 8021 A3
Briarwood Ter
- MNTK 8021 A3
Brickstone Ct
- SHVW 7683 C5
Bridal Veil Cir
- MINN 7939 C2
Bridge Ct
- SHVW 7768 E3
Bridge Ct E
- SHVW 7769 B3
Bridge Ln
- EDNA 8023 A4
Bridge St
- ARDH 7768 E2
- EDNA 8022 E4
- EDNA 8023 A4
- MNTK 7934 E7
- SHVW 7768 E2
- SHVW 7769 C3
- VADH 7769 C3
Bridgehill Ter
- EDNP 8193 D3
Bridgepoint Curv
- SSTP 8029 A7
Bridgepoint Dr
- SSTP 8029 A6
Bridgepoint Wy
- SSTP 8029 A7
Bridgeview Ct
- MNDH 8113 B4
Bridgeview Ter
- EAGN 8112 B5
Bridgewater Cir
- VADH 7769 D4
Bridgewater Ct
- VADH 7769 D4
Bridgewater Dr
- EAGN 8199 B4
- SHVW 7769 C4
- VADH 7769 D4
Bridgewater Rd
- GLDV 7851 A7
Bridgewood Ter
- VADH 7770 C4
Bridle Ln
- HOPK 8021 D1
- STLP 8021 D1
Bridle Path Ct
- WtBT 7684 D5
Bridle Ridge Cir
- EAGN 8199 B3
Bridle Ridge Ct NE
- PRIO 8279 A7
Bridle Ridge Rd
- EAGN 8199 B4
Bridle Ridge Tr NE
- PRIO 8279 A7
Bridlewood Dr
- STPL 7943 B7
Brigadoon Cir
- SHVW 7769 A4
Brigadoon Ct
- SHVW 7769 A4
Brigadoon Dr
- SHVW 7769 A3
Brigadoon Pl NE
- FRID 7681 A6
Briggs Dr
- IVGH 8200 E7
Brighton Av NE
- MINN 7853 A4
- STAN 7853 B3
Brighton Ln
- EDNP 8193 D2
- MNDS 7681 C7
- NBRI 7681 C7
- NBRI 7767 C1
Brighton Pl
- STPL 7942 D1
Brighton Sq
- NBRI 7767 C4
Brighton Wy
- ARDH 7768 A6
Brightwood Dr
- MNTK 7934 D4
Brimhall St
- STPL 8026 C3
Brinkley Ln
- IVGH 8200 E2
Brisbin St
- ANOK 7592 B1
Bristol Av
- NBRI 7767 C6
Bristol Blvd
- EAGN 8285 C1
- EDNA 8109 A2
Bristol Cir
- EDNA 8109 A3
Bristol Hl
- EDNP 8106 C7
Bristol Ln
- MNTK 8021 A5
Bristol Pl
- WILL 7772 D6
Bristol Pth
- IVGH 8114 D4
Bristol Rd
- WDBY 8030 D5
Bristol Run
- SHVW 7768 E4
Bristol Village Curv
- BMTN 8194 A2
Bristol Village Dr
- BMTN 8194 A3
Brittany Ct
- NBRI 7767 D1
- WDBY 8030 E5
- WtBT 7684 D6
Brittany Dr N
- BRKP 7592 C6
- CHMP 7592 C6
Brittany Ln
- IVGH 8114 D7
- WDBY 8030 D5
Brittany Rd
- EDNA 8108 E2
Brittany Wy
- EDNP 8193 B4
Britton Ln
- MNTK 7934 C5
Broad Av NE
- COON 7680 A4
- FRID 7680 A4
Broadband Blvd
- SHKP 8192 D7
W Broadway
- BMTN 8110 D6
Broadway Av
- SPLP 8115 E6
W Broadway Av
- BRKP 7678 B3
- BRKP 7764 B1
- CRYS 7764 B3
- CRYS 7850 E1
- MINN 7851 C5
- MINN 7852 B6
- NWHE 7764 B5
- ROBB 7850 E2
- ROBB 7851 B4
W Broadway Av CO-103
- BRKP 7678 B3
Broadway Av NE
- MINN 7852 B6
Broadway Av W
- SPLP 8115 C6
Broadway Rd NE
- MINN 7853 B6
Broadway St
- STPL 7941 E6
- STPL 7942 A6
E Broadway St
- OSSE 7677 E4
- OSSE 7678 A4
W Broadway St
- MAPG 7677 D4
- OSSE 7677 D4
Broadway St NE
- LAUD 7853 D6
- MINN 7852 C6
- MINN 7853 C6
- RSVL 7853 D6
Brockton Cir
- EAGN 8199 A5
Brockton Curv
- EAGN 8199 C4
Broderick Blvd
- IVGH 8200 C2
Brogger Cir
- GLDV 7850 A5
- NWHE 7850 A5
Broken Oak Ct
- LINO 7598 B7
Bromley Av
- SSTP 8028 C5
Brompton Pl
- MNDH 8027 C4
Brompton St
- STPL 7939 D1
Bronson Dr
- FRID 7681 B6
- MNDS 7681 D6
Brook Av S
- EDNA 8022 E3
- STLP 8022 E3
Brook Av SE
- MINN 7939 A1
Brook Dr
- EDNA 8108 C2
Brook Ln
- SAVG 8280 D7
- STLP 8022 D3
Brookdale Cir N
- BRKP 7679 A7
Brookdale Ct N
- BRKP 7678 E7
- BRKP 7679 C7
Brookdale Ctr
- BRKC 7765 C5
Brookdale Dr N
- BRKP 7678 D7
- BRKP 7679 B7
- BRKP 7680 A7
Brookdale Ln N
- BRKP 7679 C7
- BRKP 7765 C1
Brooke Ct
- WTBL 7771 A2
Brookfield Ln
- MNDH 8113 B4
Brookline Av
- STPL 8029 C4
Brooklyn Blvd
- BRKC 7764 E1
- BRKC 7765 A2
- BRKP 7677 E7
- BRKP 7678 D7
- BRKP 7764 E1
- MINN 7765 C7
Brooklyn Blvd CO-130
- BRKP 7677 E7
- BRKP 7678 C7
Brooklyn Blvd CO-152
- BRKP 7678 C7
Brooklyn Ct
- EAGN 8285 C2
Brooklyn Dr
- BRKC 7765 C4
Brooklyn Ln
- EAGN 8285 C2
Brooklyn Pl
- BRKC 7764 D2
Brooklyn Park Dr N
- BRKP 7680 A7
- BRKP 7766 A1
Brookmere Blvd NW
- PRIO 8278 C7
Brookoak Ct N
- BRKP 7679 C7
Brookridge Av
- CRYS 7850 E6
- GLDV 7850 D6
Brooks Av E
- LCAN 7855 E4
- LCAN 7856 A4
- MPLW 7856 E4
- MPLW 7857 A4
Brooks Av W
- RSVL 7854 C4
- RSVL 7855 B4
Brooks Blvd
- IVGH 8200 D3
Brooks Cir
- RSVL 7855 C4
Brooks Ct
- MPLW 7856 C4
Brookshire Ct
- NBRI 7767 B3
Brookshire Ln
- NBRI 7767 B3
Brookside Av
- EDNA 8022 D4
- STLP 8022 D3
Brookside Av S
- BMTN 8195 C2
- STLP 8022 D3
Brookside Cir
- BMTN 8195 C3
Brookside Ct
- EDNA 8022 D3
Brookside Ln
- MNDH 8027 B5
Brookside Ter
- EDNA 8022 D4
Brookview Av
- EDNA 8023 A5
Brookview Av S
- EDNA 8023 A7
- EDNA 8109 A1
Brookview Cir
- EDNP 8193 E4
Brookview Ct N
- MPLW 7943 E7
Brookview Dr
- BRKC 7765 D6
- BRNV 8281 B4
- HOPK 8022 B2
- STLP 8022 B2
Brookview Dr E
- MPLW 7943 D7
- WDBY 7943 E7
Brookview Dr NE
- FRID 7766 E1
Brookview Pkwy
- GLDV 7936 A2
Brookwood Ter
- MINN 8023 C5
Brougham Blvd NE
- PRIO 8279 A7
Broughshane Av
- RSMT 8285 B6
Brovo Ln
- SSTP 8115 A5
Brown Av
- STPL 8028 B3
- WSTP 8028 B3
Brown Ln
- MNTK 8020 A1
Brown Bear Tr
- EAGN 8197 E3
Browndale Av
- EDNA 8022 E4
- STLP 8022 E3
Brown Farm Cir
- EDNP 8193 C4
Brownie Rd
- MINN 7937 B4
Brownlow Av
- STLP 7936 C7
- STLP 8022 C1
Brown Thrush Tr
- EDNP 8106 E1
Bruce Av
- EDNA 8023 A4
- RSVL 7854 B4
Bruce Ct
- IVGH 8200 D5
Bruce Pl
- EDNA 8023 A5
Brueberry Ln
- ARDH 7768 B4
Bruening Ct
- MAHT 7772 C7
Brunell Wy
- IVGH 8200 D3
Brunet Ct
- VADH 7770 A6
Bruns Ct
- VADH 7770 A5
Brunson St
- STPL 7942 A5
Brunsvold Rd
- MNTK 8020 C6
Brunswick Av N
- BRKP 7592 D7
- BRKP 7678 D4
- BRKP 7764 D1
- CHMP 7592 D4
- CRYS 7764 D6
- CRYS 7850 D2
- GLDV 7850 D6
- GLDV 7936 D2
Brunswick Av S
- GLDV 7936 D3
- SAVG 8280 D4
- STLP 7936 D4
- STLP 8022 A2
Brunswick Cir N
- BRKP 7678 D6
Brunswick Cir S
- BMTN 8194 D2
Brunswick Ct N
- BRKP 7592 D7
- BRKP 7678 D5
Brunswick Pth
- IVGH 8200 D3
Brunswick Rd S
- BMTN 8194 D5
Bryan Av
- IVGH 8115 B7
Bryan St
- LCAN 7855 D3
Bryant Av
- MAHT 7772 C3
- SSTP 8028 D5
Bryant Av N
- BRKC 7765 E2
- BRKP 7679 E7
- MINN 7765 E6
- MINN 7851 E3
- MINN 7937 E2
Bryant Av S
- BMTN 8109 E5
- BMTN 8195 E1
- BRNV 8281 E5
- MINN 7937 E7
- MINN 7938 A4
- MINN 8023 E4
- RHFD 8109 E1
Bryant Ct N
- BRKP 7679 E7
Bryant Ln
- BRNV 8281 C1
- BRNV 8282 A5
- IVGH 8114 D4
Bryant Pl S
- BRNV 8281 C1
Bryant Lake Dr
- EDNP 8107 C3
Bryant Lake Regional Pk Acc Rd
- EDNP 8107 B2
Bryce Av
- IVGH 8114 D2
Bryce Ct
- BRNV 8283 A3
- IVGH 8200 E2
Buchal Hts
- NOAK 7770 C1
Buchanan Ct
- EDNP 8106 C4
Buchanan Ct NE
- BLNE 7594 E1
Buchanan Pl NE
- COLH 7766 E5
Buchanan Rd NE
- BLNE 7594 E4
- BLNE 7595 A4
Buchanan St NE
- BLNE 7594 E7
- BLNE 7680 E1
- COLH 7766 E4
- COLH 7767 A5
- COLH 7852 E1
- FRID 7766 E4
- FRID 7767 A5
- MINN 7852 E1
- SPLP 7680 E5
Bucher Av
- SHVW 7682 D4
- SHVW 7683 A4
Bucher St
- SHVW 7682 D4
Buckbee Rd
- WTBL 7771 C7
Buck Hill Rd
- BRNV 8282 A7
Buckingham Ct
- VADH 7770 C3
- WDBY 8030 B5
Buckingham Dr
- EDNP 8193 D2
Buckingham Ln
- MNDS 7767 E1
Buckingham Rd
- WDBY 8030 B6
Buckingham Alcove
- WDBY 8030 B6
Buckingham Bay
- WDBY 8030 B5
Buckley Cir
- IVGH 8114 D5
Buckley Ct
- IVGH 8200 D4
Buckley Wy
- IVGH 8114 D5
Buckley Bay
- EAGN 8197 D6
Bucks Wy
- EDNP 8193 C3
Buckthorn Ln
- LINO 7598 A7
Buerkle Cir
- WTBL 7857 A1
Buerkle Rd
- VADH 7856 E1
- WTBL 7856 E1
- WTBL 7857 A1
Buffalo Ln
- SHVW 7682 D4
Buffalo Rd
- NOAK 7769 E1
Buffalo St
- STPL 7941 E4
- WtBT 7685 C6
S Buffalo St
- WtBT 7685 E6
Buffalo St NE
- FRID 7680 A5
Buffet Wy
- EAGN 8112 B5
Buffington Av
- IVGH 8115 C7
Buford Av
- FLCH 7940 A1
- STPL 7939 E1
- STPL 7940 A1
Buford Cir
- FLCH 7940 A1
Buford Pl
- FLCH 7940 A1
Buhl Av
- NSTP 7857 C3
Bulrush Blvd
- SHKP 8278 D2
Bundoran Av
- RSMT 8285 B6
Bunker Ct
- EDNP 8106 C3
Bunker Hill Dr
- MNDS 7681 E4
Bunratty Av
- RSMT 8285 B6
Burchlane Dr S
- MNTK 7935 C3
Burd Pl
- STLP 7936 A5
Burg Av
- STPL 8029 C7
Burgess St
- STPL 7940 E4
- STPL 7941 B4
Burgundy Av
- RSMT 8285 B6
Burgundy Dr
- EAGN 8197 D3
Burke Av E
- MPLW 7856 D5
- MPLW 7857 A6
- NSTP 7857 C6
Burke Av W
- RSVL 7854 C6
- RSVL 7855 C6
Burke Ct
- MPLW 7856 B5
Burke Ln
- LCAN 7855 E3
Burke Tr
- IVGH 8114 D4
Burlington Rd
- MPLW 8029 C3
- STPL 8029 C3
Burma Av W
- RSMT 8285 B7
Burma Ln
- SSTP 8028 C7
Burncrest Ct
- BRNV 8282 B4
Burnell Park Dr
- BRNV 8281 D7
Burnes Dr
- HOPK 8021 D2
Burngarten Dr
- BRNV 8281 E6
Burnham Blvd
- MINN 7937 C5
Burnham Cir
- IVGH 8114 D5
Burnham Rd
- MINN 7937 C6
Burnhaven Dr
- BRNV 8281 E6
- BRNV 8282 A7
Burnley Av W
- RSMT 8285 B7
Burnquist St N
- STPL 7942 D2
Burns Av
- MPLW 7943 C6
- STPL 7942 C6
- STPL 7943 A6
Burnside Av
- EAGN 8112 C6
Burnsville Cres
- BRNV 8282 B3
Burnsville Ctr
- BRNV 8281 E7
- BRNV 8282 A6
E Burnsville Pkwy
- BRNV 8282 B2
- BRNV 8283 A2
- EAGN 8283 B2
W Burnsville Pkwy
- BRNV 8281 D4
W Burnsville Pkwy W
- BRNV 8282 A3
W Burnsville Pkwy
- BRNV 8282 B3
Burnsville Pkwy W
- BRNV 8281 D4
- BRNV 8282 A3
Burntside Dr
- GLDV 7937 A2
Bur Oak Ct
- VADH 7770 B3
Bur Oak Dr
- VADH 7770 B3
Buron Ln
- SSTP 8115 A3
Burquest Ln
- BRKC 7765 A5
Burr St
- MPLW 7856 A5
- STPL 7942 A3
Burr Oak Av S
- CTGV 8116 B7
Burr Oak Ln
- MNTK 8021 A3
Burr Oak St
- EAGN 8283 B1
Burr Oak Cove S
- CTGV 8116 B7
Burr Ridge Ln
- EDNP 8193 C3
Burson Av
- WTBL 7771 C2
Burton Ln
- MINN 8025 D2
Burton St
- FLCH 7939 E1
- STPL 7939 E1
Burwell Dr
- MNTK 7934 E7
- MNTK 7935 A7
Bury Dr
- EDNP 8020 E7
Busch Ter
- MINN 8024 A4
Bush Av
- STPL 7942 D4
- STPL 7943 A4
Bush Av E
- MPLW 7943 D4
- STPL 7943 B4
Bush Lk
- EDNP 8106 D5
Bushaway Rd
- WAYZ 7934 A3
Bush Lake Dr
- BMTN 8194 B2
Bush Lake Rd
- BMTN 8194 B3
- EDNA 8108 D4
E Bush Lake Rd
- BMTN 8108 C5
- BMTN 8194 B2
- EDNA 8108 C5
W Bush Lake Rd
- BMTN 8108 A7
- BMTN 8194 A1
Bush Lake Rd Cir
- BMTN 8194 C1
Business Park Blvd N
- CHMP 7592 A3
Bussard Ct
- ARDH 7854 C1
Butler Av
- SSTP 8028 C4
- WSTP 8028 C4
Butler Av E
- SSTP 8028 C4
- WSTP 8028 A4
Butler Av W
- MNDH 8027 C4
- WSTP 8027 D4
- WSTP 8028 A4
Butler Pl
- MINN 7938 E4
- MINN 7939 A4
Butte Av
- APVA 8283 B3
Butterfield Ct NE
- PRIO 8279 D7
Butternut Av
- STPL 8027 A3
Butternut Av N
- BRKP 7679 B1
Butternut Cir
- MNTK 8021 A5
Butternut Cir N
- BRKP 7679 B2
Butternut Cir NW
- COON 7594 C5
Butternut Ct N
- BRKP 7679 B2
Butternut St NW
- BLNE 7594 C4
- COON 7594 C1
Butterscotch Rd
- EDNP 8106 E3
Butwin Camp Rd
- EAGN 8284 E2
- EAGN 8285 A2
- RSMT 8285 A2
Bwana Ct
- MNDH 8112 E1
Byrd Av N
- GLDV 7851 B6
- ROBB 7851 B5
Byrnes Rd S
- MNTK 7935 A5
Byron Av N
- CRYS 7850 E1
Byscane Ln
- MNTK 8020 B6
Bywood Ln
- MNTK 8020 A3
Bywood Pl
- MNTK 8020 A3
Bywood St W
- EDNA 8022 B4

C

C St
- HLTP 7766 D6
- STPL 8029 A1
Cabot Dr
- MNDS 7681 E5
Cahill Av
- IVGH 8114 E6
- IVGH 8200 E4
- SSTP 8114 E4
Cahill Ct
- IVGH 8114 E7
Cahill Ln
- EDNA 8108 C2
Cahill Rd
- EDNA 8108 C2
Cain Av
- IVGH 8114 E6
Calcite Dr
- EAGN 8197 D4
Calgary Rd
- WDBY 8030 B4
W Calhoun Blvd
- MINN 7937 C7
E Calhoun Pkwy
- MINN 7937 D6
- MINN 8023 D1
W Calhoun Pkwy
- MINN 7937 C7
- MINN 8023 C1
Calhoun Pl
- MINN 8023 D1

INDEX 10
Centerville Rd — Minneapolis Street Index — Clear Spring Dr

STREET Block | City | ZIP | Map # | Grid

Centerville Rd
- LCAN 7855 E3
- LCAN 7856 A2
- LINO 7598 C7
- LINO 7684 C4
- NOAK 7684 C7
- NOAK 7770 C1
- VADH 7770 A7
- VADH 7856 A1
- WTBL 7770 C4
- WtBT 7684 C3
- WtBT 7770 C4
Centerwood Rd
- BLNE 7596 A7
- LXTN 7596 A7
Central Av
- BRKP 7677 E3
- MAPG 7677 E3
- OSSE 7677 E4
- SSTP 8028 D6
- WTBL 7771 C1
Central Av NE
- BLNE 7595 A7
- BLNE 7681 A3
- COLH 7766 E6
- COLH 7852 E1
- FRID 7680 E5
- FRID 7681 A7
- FRID 7766 E3
- FRID 7767 A1
- HLTP 7766 E6
- MINN 7852 E2
- MINN 7938 D1
- SPLP 7680 E5
- SPLP 7681 A5
Central Av NE SR-65
- BLNE 7595 A7
- BLNE 7681 A3
- COLH 7766 E6
- COLH 7852 E1
- FRID 7680 E5
- FRID 7766 E4
- HLTP 7766 E6
- MINN 7852 E2
- MINN 7938 D1
- SPLP 7680 E5
- SPLP 7681 A3
Central Av W
- STPL 7940 E6
- STPL 7941 B6
Central Pk E
- STPL 7941 C4
Central Pkwy
- EAGN 8198 B1
Central St
- CIRC 7682 C1
- LXTN 7682 C1
Central Av Service Rd
- COLH 7766 E6
- HLTP 7766 E6
Centre St
- SHVW 7769 C7
Centre Point Dr
- RSVL 7853 E2
Centre Pointe Blvd
- MNDH 8112 D2
Centre Pointe Curv
- MNDH 8112 C1
Centre Pointe Dr
- MNDH 8112 D2
Century Av
- CTGV 8116 A5
- NWPT 8116 A5
- WDBY 8116 A5
Century Av N
- MAHT 7771 E7
- MAHT 7857 E1
- MPLW 7943 E7
- ODLE 7857 E1
- ODLE 7943 E6
- WDBY 7943 E6
- WTBL 7771 E7
- WTBL 7857 E1
Century Av N SR-120
- MAHT 7771 E7
- MAHT 7857 E1
- MPLW 7943 E6
- ODLE 7857 E1
- ODLE 7943 E6
- WDBY 7943 E6
- WTBL 7771 E7
- WTBL 7857 E1
Century Av S
- CTGV 8116 A4
- MPLW 7943 E7
- MPLW 8029 E2
- NWPT 8116 A4
- WDBY 7943 D7
- WDBY 8029 E3
- WDBY 8030 A3
- WDBY 8116 A1
Century Av S SR-120
- MPLW 7943 E7
- MPLW 8029 E2
- WDBY 7943 E7
- WDBY 8029 E2
Century Blvd
- BRKP 7764 D2
Century Cir
- WDBY 8030 A3
Century Ct
- MAHT 7857 E1
- WTBL 7857 E1
Century Pt
- EAGN 8198 A1
Century Tr
- LINO 7596 E2
- LINO 7597 A1
Cesar Chavez Av
- MINN 7938 A2
Cesar Chavez St
- STPL 8028 A2
E Cessna Dr
- NBRI 7767 D7
W Cessna Dr
- NBRI 7767 D7
Cessna Ln
- SSTP 8115 A4
Chadum Ln
- SHKP 8278 A2
Chadwell Cir
- MNTK 7934 C6
Chadwick Ct
- SAVG 8280 C7
Chadwick Dr
- SAVG 8280 C7
Chadwick Ln
- EDNP 8021 A7
Chalet Dr NE
- COLH 7767 B5
- NBRI 7767 B5
Chalet Rd
- BMTN 8108 C6
Chalice Ct
- EDNA 8021 E5
Chamber St
- MPLW 7856 D7
- STPL 7856 D7
- STPL 7942 D1
Chamberlain Cir
- WDBY 8030 A6
Chamberlain Ct
- EDNP 8107 B1
Chamberlain Rd
- WDBY 8030 A6
Chamberlain Draw
- WDBY 8030 B6
Chamber Oaks Dr NE
- SPLP 7681 A5
Chambers St
- FLCH 7940 B2
- MPLW 7856 D6
W Champion Dr
- NBRI 7767 D7
Champlin Dr
- CHMP 7591 E4
- CHMP 7592 A4
Chancellor Mnr
- BRNV 8281 D6
Chandler Av
- RSVL 7855 B7
Chandler Ct
- BRNV 8197 A5
- EDNP 8106 A1
- SHVW 7769 B2
Chandler Dr NE
- STAN 7853 C1
Chandler Ln
- IVGH 8200 E1
Chandler Rd
- SHVW 7769 B2
Channel Dr
- LINO 7684 E2
Channel Rd NE
- FRID 7766 E1
- FRID 7767 A1
Chantrey Ct
- MNTK 8020 B3
Chantrey Pl
- MNTK 8020 B4
Chantrey Rd
- EDNA 8022 C6
Chaparral Cir
- APVA 8283 A3
Chaparral Ct
- APVA 8283 B3
Chaparral Dr
- APVA 8283 A3
Chapel Ct
- EAGN 8113 C7
Chapel Dr
- EDNA 8108 B2
Chapel Ln
- EAGN 8113 B7
- EDNA 8108 B2
Chapman Ct
- IVGH 8200 E4
- IVGH 8201 A4
Chapman Pt
- EDNP 8193 C4
Chardel Ct
- WSTP 8027 D7
Charing Cross
- EDNP 8106 D2
N Charing Cross
- EDNP 8106 D1
S Charing Cross
- EDNP 8106 D2
Charing Ln
- WILL 7772 C6
Charismatic Dr
- SHKP 8192 A7
Charles Av
- EDNP 8106 E2
- STPL 7939 E4
- STPL 7940 B5
- STPL 7941 D5
E Charles St N
- NSTP 7857 E5
W Charles St N
- NSTP 7857 E5
Charles St N
- NSTP 7857 E5
Charles St NE
- FRID 7766 B3
Charles Wy
- IVGH 8200 E1
Charles Island Rd NE
- FRID 7766 B3
Charles Lake Rd
- NOAK 7683 B6
Charley Ln
- EDNP 8192 D2
Charley Lake Ct
- NOAK 7683 B6
Charlie Ln
- SSTP 8115 A5
Charlotte St
- RSVL 7854 B4
- STPL 7940 B4
Charlson Rd
- EDNP 8192 C2
Charlston Ct
- RSMT 8285 A4
Charlston Wy
- RSMT 8285 A4
Charlton Rd
- MNDH 8113 D2
- SUNL 8113 D2
Charlton Rdg
- WSTP 8113 D1
Charlton St
- STPL 8027 E2
- SUNL 8113 D1
- WSTP 8027 E2
- WSTP 8113 D1
Chartreux Av
- SHKP 8278 A2
Chase Dr
- MNTK 7934 E7
Chasewood Dr
- EDNP 8021 B7
- EDNP 8107 B1
Chasewood Pkwy
- MNTK 8021 B7
Chastek Wy
- MNTK 8020 C6
Chateau Cir
- BRNV 8282 C5
Chateau Ct
- BRNV 8282 B7
Chateau Ln
- BRNV 8282 B7
Chateau Pl
- MINN 8024 D5
Chateaulin Ln
- BRNV 8282 D4
Chatelain Ter
- GLDV 7937 A2
Chatham Av
- ARDH 7768 B6
Chatham Cir
- ARDH 7768 B6
Chatham Ct
- ARDH 7768 B6
Chatham Ct N
- BRNV 8197 A5
Chatham Ct S
- BRNV 8197 A5
Chatham Rd
- EAGN 8199 C3
- MAHT 7772 C6
- WILL 7772 C6
Chatham Rd NE
- COLH 7767 A6
Chatham Ter
- NBRI 7767 C6
Chatham Wy
- EDNP 8020 A7
- EDNP 8106 A1
- MNTK 8020 A7
Chatham Field Rd
- MNTK 7935 A3
Chatsworth Cir
- SHVW 7768 E3
Chatsworth Ct E
- SHVW 7768 E3
Chatsworth Ct W
- SHVW 7768 E3
Chatsworth Pl
- SHVW 7768 E3
Chatsworth St N
- ARDH 7768 D3
- RSVL 7854 E2
- SHVW 7682 E5
- SHVW 7768 E2
- SHVW 7854 E1
- STPL 7854 E7
- STPL 7940 E7
Chatsworth St S
- STPL 7940 E7
- STPL 8026 E1
Chatterton Ct
- EAGN 8198 C5
Chatterton Rd
- EAGN 8198 C5
Checkered Flag Blvd
- SHKP 8193 A7
Cheery Ln NE
- COLH 7766 E6
Chelmsford Rd NE
- STAN 7853 C2
Chelmsford St
- STPL 7939 E2
Chelsea Ct
- BRNV 8197 A4
- NBRI 7767 D4
Chelsea St
- MAHT 7772 D6
- STPL 7940 D1
Chelton Av
- STPL 7940 A4
Chemung St
- LILY 8027 A4
Cheney Tr
- IVGH 8200 E3
- IVGH 8201 A4
Cheri Cir NE
- FRID 7766 D4
Cheri Ct
- WTBL 7771 A6
Cheri Ln
- MNDH 8113 A3
- NWPT 8115 E1
Cheri Ln NE
- FRID 7766 D4
Cherokee Av
- STPL 8027 D5
- WSTP 8027 D3
Cherokee Dr N
- BRKP 7763 E3
- BRKP 7764 A3
Cherokee Ln N
- BRKP 7764 A3
Cherokee Pl
- GLDV 7850 E5
Cherokee Tr
- EDNA 8108 A1
- LINO 7684 A1
Cherokee Tr W
- EDNP 8107 C1
Cherokee Heights Blvd
- MNDH 8027 C3
- STPL 8027 C3
Cherry Ln
- LINO 7683 A1
- MNTK 8020 C5
Cherry St
- STPL 7942 B6
Cherry Hill Rd
- MNDH 8027 A6
- MNTK 8020 C6
Cherrywood Av N
- BRKP 7679 B3
Cherrywood Ct
- EAGN 8112 B7
Cherrywood Rd
- MNTK 7934 E5
Cherrywood Tr N
- ELMO 7858 B3
Cheryl St NE
- FRID 7680 A5
Chesapeake Ln
- EDNP 8107 C2
Chesham Ln
- WDBY 8030 C7
Cheshire Cir
- MNDS 7767 E1
Cheshire Ct
- EAGN 8199 B4
Cheshire Ln
- MNDS 7767 D1
- MNTK 7934 D3
- PYMH 7934 D3
Cheshire Ln N
- DAYT 7590 D5
- MNTK 7934 D2
- PYMH 7762 D4
- PYMH 7848 D5
- PYMH 7934 D2
Cheshire Pkwy
- MNTK 7934 D2
Chesholm Ln
- EDNP 8193 A3
Cheshunt Dr
- WDBY 8030 C7
Ches Mar Cir
- EAGN 8198 C7
Ches Mar Dr
- EAGN 8198 C7
Ches Mar Ln
- EAGN 8198 C7
Chesney Wy NE
- FRID 7680 B6
Chesshire Ct
- MAPG 7676 D7
Chesshire Ln N
- MAPG 7676 D3
- MAPG 7762 D2
Chester St
- MINN 8024 B7
- SHKP 8278 A3
- STPL 7942 B7
- STPL 8028 B1
Chestnut Av
- MINN 7938 A2
Chestnut Av N
- BRKP 7679 B2
Chestnut Av W
- GLDV 7937 C2
- MINN 7937 C2
Chestnut Cir N
- BRKP 7679 B1
- CHMP 7591 C5
Chestnut Dr
- EDNP 8106 D6
Chestnut Ln N
- BRKP 7679 B1
Chestnut Ln NE
- PRIO 8279 B7
Chestnut St
- STPL 7941 D7
Chestnut St E
- SSTP 8115 A4
Cheyenne Cir
- EDNA 8108 A2
- MNTK 7934 E5
Cheyenne Ln
- MNDH 8113 B3
Cheyenne Tr
- EDNA 8108 A2
Chianti Av W
- RSMT 8285 A7
Chicago Av
- BRNV 8282 C7
- RHFD 8110 C3
- SPLP 8202 A1
- WTBL 7685 C7
Chicago Av S
- BMTN 8110 C5
- BMTN 8196 C2
- MINN 7938 E2
- MINN 8024 C5
- RHFD 8110 C2
Chicago Cir
- BMTN 8196 C3
Chickadee Ln
- NOAK 7683 E5
Chilcombe Av
- STPL 7939 D2
Childs Rd
- STPL 7942 C7
- STPL 8028 D2
Chili Av W
- RSMT 8285 A7
Chinchilla Av
- RSMT 8285 A4
Chinchilla Ct W
- RSMT 8285 A3
Chipmunk Ct
- EAGN 8197 D5
Chipmunk Ln
- NOAK 7770 B1
Chippendale Av W
- RSMT 8285 A7
Chippenham Ln
- WILL 7772 D6
Chippewa Av
- MNDH 8027 C4
- MPLW 7857 D3
- NSTP 7857 D3
- STPL 8027 C4
Chippewa Cir
- MPLW 7857 D2
N Chippewa Ct
- MPLW 7857 D2
Chippewa Ln
- BRNV 8282 D2
Chippewa Rd
- MNTK 7935 D7
Chippewa Tr
- LINO 7683 C1
Chisholm Cir NE
- BLNE 7595 A3
Chisholm Pkwy
- MPLW 7857 C2
Chisholm St NE
- BLNE 7595 A1
Chisolm Av
- MPLW 7857 B3
- NSTP 7857 B3
Chokecherry Rd
- LINO 7598 A7
Chowen Av N
- BRKC 7765 B3
- BRKP 7593 D7
- BRKP 7679 B1
- BRKP 7765 B1
- ROBB 7851 B2
Chowen Av S
- BMTN 8109 B6
- BMTN 8195 B2
- BRNV 8281 B2
- EDNA 8023 B7
- EDNA 8109 B1
- MINN 7937 B6
- MINN 8023 B5
Chowen Bnd
- BRNV 8281 B2
Chowen Cir
- BMTN 8195 B5
Chowen Ct N
- BRKP 7593 B7
Chowen Curv
- EDNA 8023 B7
Chowen Pl
- MINN 7937 B6
Christensen Av
- IVGH 8114 B1
- STPL 8028 B4
- WSTP 8028 B4
- WSTP 8114 B1
Christensen Ct
- BRNV 8197 A6
Christenson Ct NE
- FRID 7766 C2
Christenson Ln NE
- FRID 7766 D2
Christenson Wy NE
- FRID 7766 D2
Christian Curv
- WDBY 8030 B7
Christie Pl
- STPL 7857 B6
- STPL 7943 A1
Christine Ln
- WSTP 8027 D6
Christine Pl
- WTBL 7771 C6
Christopher Ln
- RSVL 7855 A1
- SHVW 7855 A1
Christy Cir
- RSVL 7854 D4
Christy Ln
- MNTK 8020 D2
Chrome Av W
- RSMT 8284 D4
Church Ln
- MNTK 8021 B3
Church Pl
- EDNA 8108 D2
Church St SE
- MINN 7939 A3
Churchill Cir
- SHVW 7768 E1
Churchill Ct
- SHVW 7768 D1
- WDBY 8030 C6
Churchill Dr
- WDBY 8030 C6
Churchill Pl
- SHVW 7768 E3
Churchill St
- RSVL 7854 E3
- SHVW 7682 E4
- SHVW 7768 E2
- SHVW 7854 E2
- STPL 7940 E3
W Chute Rd
- SSTP 8115 A1
Cimarron Av W
- RSMT 8284 E7
Cimarron Cir
- APVA 8283 A4
- MNTK 7935 A3
Cimarron Ct
- APVA 8283 B3
Cimarron Rd
- APVA 8283 B3
Cimarron Tr
- MNTK 7935 D5
Cinnabar Ct
- EAGN 8197 D4
Cinnabar Dr
- EAGN 8197 E4
Cinnamon Ridge Cir
- EAGN 8197 B7
Cinnamon Ridge Tr
- EAGN 8197 B7
Cinnamon Teal Ct
- LINO 7597 B4
W Circle Ct
- MNDH 8112 E1
Circle Dr
- BMTN 8107 E5
- BMTN 8108 A5
- BRNV 8281 D3
- CIRC 7596 D6
- EDNA 8108 D2
- NWPT 8115 D2
- WTBL 7771 D6
Circle Dr N
- CHMP 7591 D1
Circle Ln
- BRNV 8281 E3
Circle Rd
- NWPT 8115 D2
Circle St E
- EDNA 8022 C4
Circle St W
- EDNA 8022 C4
Circle Down
- GLDV 7936 E3
- GLDV 7937 A3
Circle Terrace Blvd NE
- COLH 7766 E7
- COLH 7767 B7
- COLH 7852 E1
Citation Dr
- SHKP 8192 D7
City Centre Dr
- WDBY 8030 E3
City Heights Dr
- MPLW 7855 E7
City View Dr
- EAGN 8112 A7
- MNTK 7935 A3
- PYMH 7935 A2
City West Pkwy
- EDNP 8107 C1
Civic Center Dr
- BRNV 8282 B3
- EAGN 8198 C3
- RSVL 7854 D3
Civic Heights Cir
- CIRC 7596 A6
Civic Heights Dr
- CIRC 7596 D7
Claiborne Ln
- IVGH 8200 E1
Clare Ln
- MNTK 7934 B3
Claredon Dr
- EDNA 8108 B3
Clare Downs Pth
- RSMT 8284 E6
- RSMT 8285 E4
Clare Downs Wy
- RSMT 8284 E6
- RSMT 8285 E4
Claremont Dr
- MNDH 8113 B4
Claremore Ct
- EDNA 8108 E3
Claremore Dr
- EDNA 8109 A3
Clarence Av SE
- MINN 7939 C4
Clarence Ct
- STPL 7942 E2
Clarence St
- MPLW 7856 E3
- STPL 7856 E6
- STPL 7942 E6
- WTBL 7771 B2
Clarendon Dr
- MNTK 7934 C4
Clarion Cir
- MNTK 8021 C7
Clarion Wy
- MNTK 8021 B7
Clarion Pass
- MNTK 8021 B7
Clark Av
- WTBL 7771 C2
Clark Cir
- EDNP 8193 E1
- VADH 7770 A4
Clark Ct
- EAGN 8197 B6
Clark Rd
- IVGH 8200 E7
- IVGH 8286 E1
Clark St
- BRNV 8197 A6
- EAGN 8197 A6
- MPLW 7856 A5
- STPL 7942 A2
Clarmar Av
- RSVL 7854 C2
Clary Ct
- SHKP 8278 B4
Claude Av
- IVGH 8114 E6
Claude Wy E
- IVGH 8114 E4
Clay Av
- IVGH 8114 E6
Clay Ct
- IVGH 8114 E7
Clay Ct E
- IVGH 8114 E7
Clay St
- STPL 8027 B2
Claycross Wy
- EDNP 8020 A7
Clayland Pl
- STPL 7940 B4
Clayland St
- STPL 7940 A4
Claymore Av
- IVGH 8201 A2
Claymore Ct
- IVGH 8200 E2
Clayton Av
- IVGH 8115 A7
- IVGH 8201 A1
Clayton Av E
- RSMT 8287 A6
Clayton Av E SR-56
- RSMT 8287 A3
Clayton Av E US-52
- RSMT 8287 A6
Cleadis Av
- IVGH 8201 A2
Cleadis Wy
- IVGH 8115 A7
Clear Av
- STPL 7941 E2
- STPL 7942 C2
- STPL 7943 B2
Clear Rdg
- CTRV 7598 D4
Clearbrook Ln
- VADH 7770 B3
Clear Spring Dr
- MNTK 8020 A5

Minneapolis Street Index

STREET / Block — City — ZIP — Map # — Grid

Commerce Av NE
- SAVG 8280 B6

Commerce Blvd
- WTBL 7771 A7

Commerce Cir S
- FRID 7680 C7

Commerce Cir W
- FRID 7680 C7

Commerce Ct
- VADH 7769 E3
- VADH 7770 A3
- WTBL 7771 A7

Commerce Dr
- MNDH 8112 B3

Commerce Dr N
- CHMP 7591 A6
- CHMP 7592 A6

Commerce Ln N
- CHMP 7591 E6

Commerce Ln NE
- FRID 7680 C6

Commerce St
- RSVL 7854 C5

Commerce Wy
- EDNP 8106 C4

Commercial St
- CIRC 7682 C1
- LXTN 7682 C1
- STPL 7942 B6

Commers Dr
- EAGN 8113 A6

Commisary
- FLCH 7940 B2

Commodore Dr
- BRKC 7765 B4

Commonwealth Av
- FLCH 7940 A2
- STPL 7939 E2
- STPL 7940 A2
- WDBY 8030 D6

Commonwealth Cir
- WDBY 8030 D7

Commonwealth Ct
- WDBY 8030 D6

Commonwealth Dr
- BRNV 8282 D4
- EDNP 8107 A6

Commonwealth Rd
- WDBY 8030 D7

Commonwealth Bay
- WDBY 8030 C7

Commonwealth Draw
- WDBY 8030 D7

Community Dr
- BRNV 8282 B5

Community Center Ln
- MAPG 7676 E6

Como Av
- FLCH 7940 B2
- LAUD 7939 D1
- MINN 7939 D1
- STPL 7939 D1
- STPL 7940 D3
- STPL 7941 D5

Como Av SE
- LAUD 7939 C1
- MINN 7939 A1
- STPL 7939 C1

E Como Blvd
- STPL 7940 E1
- STPL 7941 B1

W Como Blvd
- STPL 7940 E2

Como Ln
- STPL 7941 A3

Como Pl
- STPL 7941 A3

E Como Lake Dr
- STPL 7940 E1
- STPL 7941 B1

Compass Dr
- BMTN 8194 E6

Compton Dr
- IVGH 8201 A3

Compton Ln
- IVGH 8201 A3

Computer Av
- BMTN 8108 E5
- EDNA 8108 E5

Comstock Av
- IVGH 8201 A1

Comstock Ct
- IVGH 8201 A1
- MAPG 7676 A4

Comstock Ln N
- MAPG 7676 A4
- MAPG 7762 A1
- PYMH 7762 A7
- PYMH 7848 A1
- PYMH 7934 A1

Comstock Wy E
- IVGH 8201 A2

Concerto Curv NE
- FRID 7680 D6

Concord Av
- EDNA 8022 E7

Concord Av S
- EDNA 8022 E7
- EDNA 8108 E1

Concord Blvd
- IVGH 8115 B7
- IVGH 8200 E4
- IVGH 8201 A3
- SSTP 8115 B4

Concord Ct
- IVGH 8201 A3

Concord Dr
- EDNP 8193 B4

N Concord Pl
- SSTP 8028 E6

Concord Rd
- LXTN 7682 B1

Concord St
- SSTP 8028 C3
- STPL 8028 B2

Concord St SR-156
- SSTP 8028 C3
- STPL 8028 B2

Concord St N
- SSTP 8028 D5
- SSTP 8029 A7
- STPL 8028 D5

Concord St N SR-156
- SSTP 8028 D5
- SSTP 8029 A7
- STPL 8028 D5

Concord St S
- IVGH 8115 B4
- SSTP 8029 A7
- SSTP 8115 A3

Concord St S SR-156
- SSTP 8029 A7
- SSTP 8115 A1

Concord Ter
- EDNA 8022 E6

Concord Wy
- MNDH 8113 B4

Concorde Pl
- BRNV 8282 A3

Concord Exchange N
- SSTP 8029 A6

Concord Exchange S
- SSTP 8029 A6
- SSTP 8115 A1

Concordia Av
- STPL 7940 C6
- STPL 7941 B6

Condit St
- LCAN 7855 E2

Condon Ct
- MNDH 8113 A4

Coneflower Cir N
- CHMP 7591 D6

Coneflower Ct
- EAGN 8198 E6

Coneflower Ln
- SHKP 8278 D2

Congress St
- SSTP 8028 C6

Congress St E
- STPL 8028 A2

Congress St W
- STPL 8027 E2
- STPL 8028 A2

Conley Av
- RSMT 8287 A6

Connelly Cir
- SAVG 8280 C5

Connelly Ct
- BRNV 8282 E1
- SAVG 8280 C5

Connelly Dr
- BRNV 8282 E1

Connelly Pkwy
- SAVG 8280 A6

Connelly Pl
- SAVG 8280 A6

Connelly St
- ARDH 7768 D6

Connemara Tr
- APVA 8284 D6
- RSMT 8284 E6
- RSMT 8285 A5

Conner Av E
- MPLW 7856 D4

Conner Ct
- MPLW 7856 C4

Connie Ln
- LINO 7597 A3

Conrad Av
- IVGH 8201 A5

Conroy Ct
- IVGH 8115 A7

Conroy St NE
- PRIO 8279 E6
- PRIO 8280 C5
- SAVG 8279 E6

Conroy Tr
- IVGH 8115 A7

Conroy Wy
- IVGH 8201 A1

Conservatory Ct
- STPL 7941 B2

Constance Dr E
- GLDV 7850 D7

Constance Dr W
- GLDV 7850 D7

Constellation Dr
- NOAK 7770 C1
- WtBT 7770 C1

Constitution Av
- EDNP 8106 A4
- HnpC 8025 D7

Continental Dr
- EDNA 8022 A6
- NBRI 7853 D1
- RSVL 7853 D1

Conver Av
- SSTP 8028 C4

Conver St
- WSTP 8028 A4

Conway Av E
- MPLW 7943 D5
- ODLE 7943 E5
- STPL 7943 C5

Conway St
- STPL 7942 E5
- STPL 7943 A5

Cook Av
- WTBL 7771 C1

Cook Av E
- STPL 7941 E3
- STPL 7942 A3

Cook Av W
- STPL 7941 B3

Coolidge Av
- EDNA 8022 E3
- STLP 8022 E3

Coolidge St NE
- MINN 7853 B7
- STAN 7853 B2

Cool Stream Cir
- EAGN 8197 B2

Coon Rapids Blvd NW
- ANOK 7592 B2
- BLNE 7680 C2
- COON 7592 D3
- COON 7593 A4
- COON 7594 A7
- COON 7680 B1

Coon Rapids Blvd NW CO-1
- COON 7592 D3
- COON 7593 A4

Coon Rapids Blvd Ext NW
- COON 7593 E6
- COON 7594 A6

Coon Rapids Blvd Service Dr
- COON 7593 B4

Cooper Av
- EDNA 8022 C4
- IVGH 8115 A6
- IVGH 8201 A1

Cooper Av E
- IVGH 8201 A1

Cooper Cir
- EDNA 8022 C4

Cooper Ct
- IVGH 8201 A1

Cooper Pth
- IVGH 8201 A2

Cooper St
- FLCH 7940 B1

Cooper Wy E
- IVGH 8201 A2

Cope Av E
- MPLW 7856 D5
- MPLW 7857 A5
- NSTP 7857 B5

Cope Av W
- RSVL 7855 A5

Cope Ct
- MPLW 7856 D5

Copeland Ct
- IVGH 8201 A3

Copland Wy
- IVGH 8201 A2

Copper Ct
- RSMT 8284 E6

Copper Ln
- EAGN 8197 C6

Copper Pt
- EAGN 8197 C6

Copper Cliff Tr
- WDBY 8030 B5

Copperfield Cir
- MNTK 7934 B5

Copperfield Ct
- IVGH 8201 A2

Copperfield Dr
- MNDH 8113 C3
- SUNL 8113 C3

Copperfield Pl
- MNTK 7934 C6

Copperfield Wy
- IVGH 8201 A2

Copper Oaks Cir
- WDBY 8030 D6

Copper Oaks Ct
- WDBY 8030 D6

Copper Oaks Pl
- WDBY 8030 D5

Copper Oaks Tr
- WDBY 8030 D6

Copper Oaks Alcove
- WDBY 8030 C5

Copper Oaks Draw
- WDBY 8030 D6

Coppersmith Ct
- IVGH 8201 A3

Coral Ln
- EAGN 8197 C5

Coral Sea Ct NE
- BLNE 7681 E2

Coral Sea St
- BLNE 7595 E4

Coral Sea St NE
- BLNE 7595 D1
- BLNE 7681 D1
- MNDS 7681 D4

Corchman Av
- RSMT 8285 E4

Corcoran Av
- RSMT 8285 E4

Corcoran Cir
- IVGH 8201 A2

Corcoran Pth
- IVGH 8201 A3

Cord Cir
- NBRI 7767 D7

Cord Ct NE
- BLNE 7596 C3

Cord St NE
- BLNE 7596 C7
- BLNE 7682 C3

Coren's Dr
- MNTK 7935 A3

Corey Pth
- IVGH 8201 A1

Corliss Tr
- RSMT 8285 E4

Corliss Wy
- IVGH 8115 A6

Cormack Cir
- RSMT 8284 D3
- RSMT 8285 A5

Cormorant Wy
- RSMT 8284 E7

Cornelia Cir
- EDNA 8109 A1

Cornelia Dr
- EDNA 8109 A3

Cornelia Tr
- WDBY 8030 B5

Cornell Ct
- EDNP 8193 A1

Cornell Dr
- MNDS 7681 E5

Cornwallis Ct
- EAGN 8199 A6

Coronado Ct
- BRNV 8196 D7

Coronet Dr
- MNTK 8020 D3

Corp Center Dr
- SHKP 8278 C2

Corporate Wy
- EDNP 8106 C4

Corporate Center Curv
- EAGN 8112 C5

Corporate Center Dr
- BRNV 8281 B6
- EAGN 8112 C5

Corral Ln
- EDNP 8106 B7

Cortland Pl
- STPL 7941 D4

Cortland Rd
- EDNP 8106 E6

N Cortlawn Cir
- GLDV 7936 C2

S Cortlawn Cir
- GLDV 7936 C2

W Cortlawn Cir
- GLDV 7936 C2

Corvallis Av N
- CRYS 7764 C7
- NWHE 7764 C7

Corwin Ct
- IVGH 8115 A5

Coryell Ct
- IVGH 8115 A5

Cosette Ln N
- HUGO 7599 B5

Cosette Wy N
- HUGO 7599 B6

Cosgrove St
- FLCH 7940 B2

Cosmos Ln
- EAGN 8198 C6

Costa Dr
- VADH 7856 A1

Costa Ln
- LCAN 7856 A2

Cottage Av
- WtBT 7685 A6

Cottage Av E
- STPL 7941 E2
- STPL 7942 B2
- STPL 7943 B2

Cottage Av W
- STPL 7941 C2

Cottage Cir
- NSTP 7857 C4

Cottage Ct
- WtBT 7685 A6

Cottage Dr
- NSTP 7857 C4

Cottage Ln
- MNTK 8021 B1
- WtBT 7685 A7

Cottage Pl
- SHVW 7768 E7
- SHVW 7769 A7

Cottage Downs
- HOPK 8021 D1
- STLP 8021 E1

Cottage Grove Av
- MNTK 7934 A7

Cottage Park Rd
- WTBL 7771 C3

Cottagewood Ter
- SPLP 7680 E3

Cottagewood Ter NE
- BLNE 7680 E3
- SPLP 7680 E3

Cottonwood Cir N
- DAYT 7591 B2

Cottonwood Cir NW
- COON 7594 D3

Cottonwood Ct
- CTRV 7598 E5
- SHVW 7683 A5

Cottonwood Dr
- VADH 7769 E4

Cottonwood Ln
- EDNP 8106 A7

Cottonwood Ln N
- MAPG 7677 B2
- MAPG 7763 B3
- PYMH 7763 B7
- PYMH 7849 B1
- PYMH 7935 B1

Cottonwood Pl
- VADH 7769 E4

Cottonwood St NW
- COON 7594 C1
- COON 7680 B3
- FRID 7680 B3

Couchtown Av
- RSMT 8285 A6

Couchtown Pth
- RSMT 8284 D3
- RSMT 8285 A5

Cougar Dr
- EAGN 8199 B6

Cougar Ln
- MPLW 7943 E2

Cougar Pth NW
- PRIO 8278 C7

Council Cir
- MNTK 7934 D4

Council Oaks Dr NE
- SPLP 7681 A5

Country Ct
- EAGN 8199 C5

Country Dr
- LCAN 7769 D7
- LCAN 7855 D1
- SHVW 7769 D7

Country Ln
- BRNV 8282 C5
- LINO 7597 C1
- MNTK 7935 D5

Country Pl
- BRNV 8282 C5

Country Rd
- EDNP 8020 A7
- EDNP 8106 A1

Country Club Dr
- GLDV 7936 C1

Country Club Rd
- EDNA 8022 E5
- EDNA 8023 A4

Country Creek Wy
- EAGN 8197 E3

Country Lakes Dr
- LINO 7597 D7
- LINO 7683 C1

Country Side Dr
- SHVW 7769 B1

Countryside Dr
- BMTN 8194 A4
- EAGN 8199 C5
- EDNP 8106 A1

Countryside Rd
- EDNA 8022 C7

Country View Blvd
- BRNV 8282 D3

Countryview Cir
- MPLW 7856 D2

Country View Ct
- BRNV 8282 E3

Country View Dr
- BRNV 8282 D3

Countryview Dr
- EAGN 8199 C4

Country View Ln
- BRNV 8282 D3

Country Wood Cir
- BRNV 8283 A2

Country Wood Dr
- BRNV 8283 A2

County Pkwy E
- LINO 7598 A5

County Rd
- LINO 7598 C6

E County Line Rd
- DLWD 7685 E7
- WtBT 7685 E7

E County Line Rd N
- BRHV 7771 E5
- MAHT 7771 E6
- WTBL 7771 E6
- WtBT 7771 E5

N County Line Rd
- MNDS 7681 C3

Court Pl
- BRNV 8281 B4

Court Rd
- MNTK 8020 B3

Courthouse Blvd
- EAGN 8113 D7
- IVGH 8113 D7
- IVGH 8199 D1
- IVGH 8200 E5
- IVGH 8201 A7
- IVGH 8286 E2
- IVGH 8287 A2
- NgTp 8288 B7
- RSMT 8286 E2
- RSMT 8287 B4
- RSMT 8288 A7

Courthouse Blvd SR-55
- EAGN 8113 D7
- IVGH 8113 D7
- IVGH 8199 D1
- IVGH 8200 E5
- IVGH 8201 A7
- IVGH 8287 A1
- NgTp 8288 B7
- RSMT 8287 A2
- RSMT 8288 A7

Courthouse Blvd US-52
- IVGH 8200 E5
- IVGH 8201 A7
- IVGH 8287 A1
- RSMT 8287 A2

Courthouse Ln
- EAGN 8113 B6

Courthouse Blvd Ct
- IVGH 8200 D4

Courthouse Blvd Ct E
- IVGH 8200 D4

Courtland Rd
- MNTK 8020 B3

Courtly Rd
- WDBY 8030 B4

Courtly Alcove
- WDBY 8030 A5

Cove Dr
- MNTK 7935 D6

Coventry Ct
- MNDH 8112 E1

Coventry Ln
- EDNA 8109 B3
- SHKP 8279 B2

Coventry Pkwy
- EAGN 8199 C4

Coventry Pl
- EDNA 8109 B3

Coventry Rd E
- MNTK 8020 E4

Coventry Rd W
- MNTK 8020 D4

Coventry Wy
- EDNA 8108 C4

Cove Pointe Rd
- EDNP 8106 B7

Covington Cir
- EAGN 8284 A1
- EDNP 8193 B4

Covington Ct
- EAGN 8284 A1

Covington Ln
- EAGN 8283 D1
- EAGN 8284 A1

Cowern Pl E
- NSTP 7857 D6

Coyote Cir NW
- PRIO 8278 C7

Coyote Ct
- LINO 7683 B2

Coyote Ln
- MPLW 7943 D2

Coyote Tr
- LINO 7683 B2

CR-81
- MAPG 7677 C4

CR-81 Service Rd N
- OSSE 7677 E5

CR-81 Service Rd S
- BRKP 7677 E5
- OSSE 7677 E5

CR-101
- SAVG 8279 E1
- SAVG 8280 A2
- SHKP 8279 E1

Crabapple Ln
- EDNP 8192 B3

Crackleberry Ct
- WDBY 8116 A3

Crackleberry Tr
- WDBY 8116 B3

Crackleberry Alcove
- WDBY 8116 A3

Crackleberry Bay
- WDBY 8116 A3

Craig Av
- IVGH 8115 A5

Craig Ct
- IVGH 8115 A6
- SSTP 8115 A6

Craig Dr
- EDNP 8106 A1

Craig Pl
- MPLW 7857 B5
- STPL 7857 B7
- STPL 7943 B1

Craig Wy
- IVGH 8115 A7

Craig Wy NE
- FRID 7680 B6

Craigbrook Wy NE
- FRID 7680 B5

Cranberry Wy
- RSMT 8284 E7

Cranbrook Dr
- WTBL 7771 D5

Crane St
- COON 7593 D6
- SHKP 8278 A4

Crane St NW
- COON 7593 D2

Crane Creek Ln
- EAGN 8113 C7

Crane Creek Pl
- EAGN 8113 C7

Crane Dance Tr
- EDNP 8107 D6

Cranford Cir
- RSMT 8284 D3
- RSMT 8285 A5

Crater Ct
- BRNV 8283 A3

Crawford Av
- FLCH 7854 C7

Crawford Rd
- MNTK 8021 B3

Crawford Rd W
- MNTK 8021 B3

CR-B
- LCAN 7855 D5
- MPLW 7855 D5
- RSVL 7855 B5

CR-B E
- LCAN 7855 E5
- MPLW 7855 E5
- MPLW 7856 C5
- MPLW 7857 B5
- NSTP 7857 B5

CR-B W
- RSVL 7853 E5
- RSVL 7854 A5
- RSVL 7855 A5

CR-B2 E
- LCAN 7855 D4
- LCAN 7856 B5
- MPLW 7856 B5

CR-B2 W
- LCAN 7855 D4
- RSVL 7853 E4
- RSVL 7854 B4
- RSVL 7855 B4

CR-C E
- LCAN 7855 D3
- LCAN 7856 C3
- MPLW 7856 E3
- MPLW 7857 A3
- NSTP 7857 B3

CR-C W
- LCAN 7855 D3
- RSVL 7853 D3
- RSVL 7854 E3
- RSVL 7855 D3
- STAN 7853 D3

CR-C2 W
- LCAN 7855 D2
- RSVL 7853 D2
- RSVL 7854 E2
- RSVL 7855 C2
- STAN 7853 D2

CR-D E
- LCAN 7856 A1
- MAHT 7857 E1
- MPLW 7856 E1
- MPLW 7857 A1
- VADH 7856 E1
- WTBL 7857 E1

CR-D W
- ARDH 7854 D1
- NBRI 7853 E1
- NBRI 7854 A1
- RSVL 7853 E1
- RSVL 7854 A1
- RSVL 7855 A1
- SHVW 7854 D1
- SHVW 7855 A1
- STAN 7853 D1

W CR-E
- ARDH 7768 C6
- SHVW 7768 C6
- SHVW 7769 A6

CR-E E
- GEML 7770 D6
- GEML 7771 A6
- MAHT 7771 E6
- VADH 7770 D6
- VADH 7771 A6
- WTBL 7771 E6

CR-E W
- ARDH 7768 A7
- COLH 7767 B6
- NBRI 7767 D6
- NBRI 7768 A7
- SHVW 7769 A6

INDEX 14

Dayton Av — Minneapolis Street Index — Dowlin St N

STREET Block	City	ZIP	Map #	Grid
Dayton Av				
-	STPL		7941	A7
Dayton Rd				
-	CHMP		7591	D1
Daytona Wy				
-	RSMT		8284	D6
Dealton St				
-	STPL		8026	D5
Dean Av E				
-	CHMP		7591	E2
-	CHMP		7592	A2
Dean Av W				
-	CHMP		7591	E1
Dean Ct				
-	MINN		7937	C6
Dean Pkwy				
-	MINN		7937	C6
Dean Lake Rd				
-	SHKP		8278	D2
Dean Lakes Blvd				
-	SHKP		8278	C1
Dean Lakes Tr				
-	SHKP		8278	C2
Dearborn Ct				
-	EDNA		8022	A3
Dearborn Pth				
-	RSMT		8284	D7
Dearborn St				
-	EDNA		8022	A3
Deauville Dr				
-	MPLW		7856	C4
Debra Cir				
-	SHVW		7769	A2
Debra Ct				
-	SHVW		7769	A2
Debra Ln				
-	SHVW		7769	A1
Debra St				
-	WTBL		7771	A1
Decathlon Ln				
-	SSTP		8115	A4
Decatur Av N				
-	BRKP		7763	E4
-	GLDV		7850	A5
-	GLDV		7935	E1
-	GLDV		7936	A2
-	NWHE		7763	E7
-	NWHE		7764	A5
-	NWHE		7849	E1
-	NWHE		7850	A1
Decatur Av S				
-	BMTN		8193	E1
-	STLP		7935	E5
Decatur Cir S				
-	BMTN		8193	E4
Decatur Ct N				
-	NWHE		7849	E3
Decatur Ln				
-	STLP		7935	E7
Decatur Pl N				
-	NWHE		7850	A1
Decorah Ln				
-	MNDH		8113	B3
De Courcy Cir				
-	STPL		7940	C3
Dee Pl NE				
-	SPLP		7680	E4
Deep Lake Rd N				
-	NOAK		7683	E4
-	NOAK		7684	A4
Deep Lake Rd S				
-	NOAK		7683	E5
-	NOAK		7684	A5
Deepwoods Ct				
-	RSMT		8284	D4
Deer Ct				
-	CTRV		7598	C6
Deer Ln				
-	NOAK		7770	A1
Deer Pth				
-	EDNP		8107	C7
Deer Rdg NE				
-	BLNE		7595	D3
Deer Tr				
-	WDBY		8116	C4
Deer Tr E				
-	SHVW		7683	C5
Deer Tr S				
-	SHVW		7683	C5
Deer Tr W				
-	SHVW		7683	C5
Deercliff Ct				
-	EAGN		8198	C3
Deercliff Ln				
-	EAGN		8198	C4
Deer Creek Pkwy				
-	MNTK		7934	C3
Deerfield Dr				
-	MPLW		7943	D2
Deer Hill Ct				
-	MNTK		7934	C4
Deer Hill Dr				
-	MNTK		7934	C4
Deer Hills Cir				
-	NOAK		7684	C7
Deer Hills Ct				
-	NOAK		7770	C1
Deer Hills Dr				
-	NOAK		7684	C7
-	NOAK		7770	C1
-	WtBT		7770	C1
Deer Hills Tr				
-	EAGN		8197	D5
Deer Oak Run				
-	MAHT		7772	D4
Deer Pass Dr				
-	CTRV		7598	E4
-	LINO		7598	E4
Deer Pass Tr				
-	LINO		7685	A2
Deer Pond Cir				
-	EAGN		8197	E3
Deer Pond Ct N				
-	ELMO		7858	E5
Deer Pond Tr N				
-	ELMO		7858	E5
Deerridge Ct				
-	EAGN		8198	C4
Deer Ridge Ln				
-	BMTN		8108	B7
Deer Ridge Ln				
-	MNTK		8021	B5
Deer Ridge Ln S				
-	MPLW		8029	E2
Deer Run Tr				
-	MNDH		8113	D1
-	WSTP		8113	D1
Deer Trail Cir				
-	WDBY		8116	C4
Deer Trail Ct				
-	MNDH		8027	A7
Deer Trail Pt				
-	MNDH		8027	A7
Deerwood Av N				
-	CHMP		7591	D6
Deerwood Bnd				
-	EAGN		8198	D4
Deerwood Cir				
-	LINO		7683	D1
Deerwood Cir N				
-	PYMH		7763	B4
Deerwood Ct				
-	EAGN		8198	B5
-	SSTP		8114	C1
Deerwood Dr				
-	EAGN		8197	E4
-	EAGN		8198	A4
-	MNTK		8020	E3
-	SSTP		8114	D1
Deerwood Ln				
-	EAGN		8198	D4
-	LINO		7597	B6
-	LINO		7683	D1
Deerwood Ln N				
-	DAYT		7591	B1
-	MAPG		7677	B2
-	MAPG		7763	B2
-	MNTK		7935	B2
-	PYMH		7763	B5
-	PYMH		7849	B1
-	PYMH		7935	B2
Deerwood Pl				
-	EAGN		8198	B5
Deerwood Pth				
-	EAGN		8198	B5
Deerwood Tr				
-	EAGN		8198	B4
Degrio Wy				
-	IVGH		8115	B7
Dehrer Ct				
-	IVGH		8115	B7
Dehrer Wy				
-	IVGH		8115	B7
Dejon Ct				
-	WDBY		7944	D7
DeKalb Av				
-	RSMT		8284	D7
Del Dr N				
-	NWHE		7850	B1
Delaney Av				
-	IVGH		8115	B5
Delaney Blvd				
-	EDNA		8108	C4
Delaney Cir				
-	IVGH		8201	B2
Delaney Ct				
-	IVGH		8201	B2
Delaney Dr				
-	IVGH		8201	B2
Delaney Wy				
-	IVGH		8115	B5
Delano Cir				
-	IVGH		8201	B1
Delano Ct				
-	IVGH		8201	B1
Delano Pl				
-	STPL		8026	A4
Delano St NE				
-	MINN		7853	C7
Delano Wy				
-	IVGH		8201	B1
Delany Ln				
-	SHKP		8278	A3
Delarosa Ct				
-	IVGH		8115	B6
De la Salle Dr				
-	MINN		7938	C1
Delaware Av				
-	EAGN		8113	D4
-	IVGH		8113	D4
-	MNDH		8027	D7
-	MNDH		8113	D3
-	NSTP		7857	D3
-	STPL		8027	D2
-	SUNL		8113	D3
-	WSTP		8027	D7
-	WSTP		8113	D3
Delaware St SE				
-	MINN		7939	A3
Delaware Tr				
-	EAGN		8199	D3
-	IVGH		8199	D3
Delft Av W				
-	RSMT		8284	D7
Delilah Av				
-	IVGH		8115	B5
Delina Cir				
-	LINO		7685	A1
Dell Ct N				
-	WTBL		7771	B7
Dell Ct S				
-	WTBL		7771	B7
Dell Ln				
-	MNTK		8020	A6
Dell Ln N				
-	WDBY		7944	A7
Dell Ln S				
-	WDBY		7944	A7
Dell Pl				
-	MINN		7938	A4
Dell St				
-	WTBL		7771	B7
Dellridge Av				
-	MPLW		8029	C1
-	STPL		8029	C1
Dellridge Rd				
-	BMTN		8196	D2
Dellview Av				
-	ARDH		7768	B5
Dellwood Av				
-	ARDH		7768	D7
-	DLWD		7686	A7
-	DLWD		7772	B2
-	MAHT		7772	C3
-	RSVL		7854	D3
-	SHVW		7682	D3
-	WasC		7772	B2
Dellwood Av SR-244				
-	DLWD		7686	A7
-	DLWD		7772	B2
-	MAHT		7772	C3
-	WasC		7772	B2
Dellwood Ct				
-	RSMT		8284	E5
Dellwood Dr NE				
-	FRID		7766	E2
Dellwood Ln				
-	LNDF		7944	A6
Dellwood Pl				
-	STPL		7942	B5
Dellwood Rd				
-	DLWD		7685	E7
-	WtBT		7685	E7
Dellwood Rd SR-96				
-	DLWD		7685	E7
-	WtBT		7685	E7
Dellwood Rd N				
-	DLWD		7772	E1
-	GRNT		7772	E1
Dellwood Rd N SR-96				
-	DLWD		7772	E1
-	GRNT		7772	E1
Dellwood Sq E				
-	LNDF		7944	A5
Dellwood Sq N				
-	LNDF		7944	A6
Dellwood Sq S				
-	LNDF		7944	A6
Dellwood St				
-	ARDH		7768	D3
-	RSVL		7854	D4
Dellwood Wy				
-	RSMT		8284	D5
Dellwood Cove				
-	DLWD		7686	B7
-	LNDF		7944	A4
Dellwood Rd Ct N				
-	GRNT		7772	E1
Delos St E				
-	STPL		8028	A1
Delos St W				
-	STPL		8027	E1
-	STPL		8028	A1
Delta Av				
-	MNTK		7935	D7
-	RSMT		8284	D6
Delta Ct				
-	RSMT		8284	D6
Delta Ln				
-	SSTP		8115	A5
Delta Pl				
-	RSMT		8284	D6
Delta Dental Dr				
-	EAGN		8197	E2
Demar Av				
-	SHVW		7769	C4
-	VADH		7769	C4
Demont Av E				
-	LCAN		7855	D4
-	LCAN		7856	A4
-	MPLW		7856	C4
-	MPLW		7857	A4
Demont Av W				
-	LCAN		7855	D4
-	RSVL		7855	D4
Demontreville Tr N				
-	ELMO		7858	D3
Demontreville Tr N CO-13B				
-	ELMO		7858	D3
Demontreville Cir Ct N				
-	ELMO		7858	D2
Demontreville Trail Cir N				
-	ELMO		7858	D2
Dempsey Wy				
-	IVGH		8201	B1
Den Rd				
-	EDNP		8107	B5
Denese St NE				
-	PRIO		8280	A7
Denmark Av				
-	APVA		8284	C4
-	EAGN		8112	D7
-	EAGN		8198	C1
Denmark Ct				
-	APVA		8284	D7
Denmark Ct E				
-	EAGN		8198	C3
Denmark Ct W				
-	EAGN		8198	C3
Denmark Tr E				
-	EAGN		8198	C3
Denmark Tr W				
-	EAGN		8198	C3
Dennis Av				
-	MPLW		8029	E4
Dennis Ln				
-	WTBL		7771	C6
Dennis Ln N				
-	MPLW		7943	E7
Dennis St N				
-	MPLW		7943	E2
Dennison Av				
-	SHVW		7769	C4
-	VADH		7769	C4
Denslow St				
-	STPL		7941	B4
Denton Wy				
-	IVGH		8201	B1
Denver Ct				
-	RSMT		8284	D7
Depot St				
-	MINN		7937	B6
Deppe St				
-	WSTP		8027	E3
Derby Av				
-	MINN		8024	E6
Derby Ln				
-	MAHT		7772	C6
-	SHKP		8279	B1
Derby Ln				
-	WILL		7772	C6
Derryglen Ct				
-	RSMT		8284	D5
Derrymoor Ct				
-	RSMT		8284	D5
Desnoyer Av				
-	MINN		7939	D5
-	STPL		7939	D5
Desoto St				
-	LCAN		7856	A2
-	MPLW		7856	A7
-	STPL		7856	A7
-	STPL		7942	A1
-	VADH		7770	A4
Dessa Ln				
-	SSTP		8028	C7
Deubener Pl				
-	STPL		8026	E2
Devaney St				
-	STLP		8022	E3
Deveau Pl				
-	MNTK		8020	C1
Dever Dr				
-	EDNA		8023	A6
Deville Dr				
-	EDNA		8022	A6
Devin Ln				
-	SHKP		8279	B2
Devon Dr				
-	MNTK		8020	A3
Devonshire Cir				
-	BMTN		8195	E3
-	WDBY		8030	A6
Devonshire Curv				
-	BMTN		8195	E4
Devonshire Dr				
-	WDBY		8030	B5
Devonshire Ln				
-	BMTN		8195	E4
Devonshire Pl				
-	EDNP		8193	B4
-	WDBY		8030	A6
Devonshire Rd				
-	BMTN		8195	E4
Dewerff St				
-	WSTP		8027	D4
Dewey Ct				
-	EDNP		8106	A7
Dewey St				
-	STPL		7940	A5
Dewey Hill Rd				
-	EDNA		8108	B3
Diagonal Blvd				
-	HnpC		8110	E2
-	RHFD		8110	D3
Diamond Ct				
-	APVA		8284	A4
Diamond Ct S				
-	SHKP		8278	A1
Diamond Dr				
-	BRNV		8283	A3
-	EAGN		8197	C5
Diamond Pt				
-	EAGN		8197	C4
Diamond Pth				
-	APVA		8284	C4
Diamond Pth W				
-	APVA		8284	C5
-	RSMT		8284	C5
Diamond Eight Ter				
-	STAN		7853	C1
Diamond Lake Ln				
-	MINN		8024	C7
E Diamond Lake Rd				
-	MINN		8024	B6
W Diamond Lake Rd				
-	MINN		8024	A5
Diamond Path Ct				
-	APVA		8284	C7
-	RSMT		8284	C7
Diane Dr				
-	MNTK		8021	B4
Diane Rd				
-	LILY		8027	A6
-	MNDH		8027	A6
Dianna Ln				
-	LCAN		7856	B4
Dianne St				
-	NSTP		7857	C4
Dickens Ln				
-	MNDS		7767	E1
Dickman Tr				
-	IVGH		8115	B6
-	IVGH		8201	B1
Dickson Av				
-	IVGH		8201	B1
Dickson Cir				
-	IVGH		8201	B1
Dickson Rd				
-	MNTK		8020	D5
Diego Ln				
-	MNDH		8027	C4
Dieter St				
-	MPLW		7856	E7
-	STPL		7856	E7
-	STPL		7942	E1
Diffley Rd				
-	BRNV		8197	B5
-	EAGN		8197	B5
-	EAGN		8198	A5
-	EAGN		8199	B5
Dight Av				
-	MINN		7939	A7
-	MINN		8025	A1
Dilley Av				
-	IVGH		8115	B5
Dillon St				
-	WTBL		7771	A1
-	WtBT		7685	A7
Dionne Av				
-	RSVL		7855	C7
Dionne St				
-	RSVL		7854	E7
Direct River Dr NW				
-	COON		7592	E5
-	COON		7593	A5
Disc Dr				
-	SHKP		8278	C1
Discovery Rd				
-	EAGN		8198	E1
Disk Dr				
-	BMTN		8108	E4
-	EDNA		8108	E4
Divinity Ln				
-	EDNP		8106	E3
Division Av				
-	WTBL		7685	C7
-	WTBL		7771	C1
-	WtBT		7685	C7
Division Ct				
-	WTBL		7685	C7
Division St				
-	EDNA		8022	D4
-	HOPK		8022	A1
-	STLP		8022	A1
Dixie Av				
-	IVGH		8115	B6
Dixon Dr				
-	BMTN		8109	D5
-	CTGV		8202	A2
-	SPLP		8202	A1
Doane Av				
-	IVGH		8115	B6
-	IVGH		8201	C1
-	STPL		7939	D5
Dodd Blvd				
-	EAGN		8285	B3
-	RSMT		8284	D4
-	RSMT		8285	B4
Dodd Ct				
-	RSMT		8285	A4
Dodd Ln				
-	EAGN		8113	B7
Dodd Rd				
-	EAGN		8113	A6
-	EAGN		8199	B1
-	EAGN		8285	B2
-	IVGH		8199	C4
-	MNDH		8027	B7
-	MNDH		8113	B3
-	RSMT		8285	B2
-	STPL		8027	E2
-	WSTP		8027	E3
Dodd Rd SR-55				
-	EAGN		8113	A6
Dodd Rd SR-149				
-	EAGN		8113	B7
-	EAGN		8199	B1
-	IVGH		8199	D3
-	MNDH		8027	B7
-	MNDH		8113	B3
-	WSTP		8027	D4
Dodge Ln				
-	MNDH		8113	C1
-	SUNL		8113	C1
Doe Cir				
-	WtBT		7770	D3
Doffing Av				
-	IVGH		8115	B5
Dogwood Av N				
-	BRKP		7679	B3
Dogwood Ln				
-	NOAK		7683	E7
-	NOAK		7769	E1
Dogwood St NW				
-	COON		7594	B1
Do-Little Dr				
-	MNTK		8021	A1
Dolomite Dr				
-	EAGN		8197	D4
Dolores Ln				
-	EAGN		8284	B1
Dolphin Dr				
-	MPLW		7943	D2
Dominica Av				
-	APVA		8284	C6
Dominica Ct				
-	APVA		8284	C7
Dominica Wy				
-	APVA		8284	C5
Dominick Cir				
-	MNTK		8021	A4
Dominick Dr				
-	MNTK		8021	A4
Dominick Spur				
-	MNTK		8021	A4
Dominick Wy				
-	MNTK		8021	A4
Dona Ln				
-	GLDV		7850	E5
-	GLDV		7851	A5
Donald Av				
-	EAGN		8112	A7
-	EAGN		8198	A1
Donald Ct				
-	EAGN		8198	A1
Don Bush Rd				
-	NOAK		7769	C2
Doncaster Wy				
-	EDNA		8022	C5
Donegal Cir				
-	SHVW		7683	B5
Donegal Ct				
-	EAGN		8198	A4
-	SHVW		7683	A5
Donegal Dr				
-	BRNV		8282	A4
-	NOAK		7683	B5
-	SHVW		7683	B5
-	WDBY		8030	E2
Donegal Pl				
-	WILL		7772	C6
Donegal Wy				
-	EAGN		8198	A4
Donegal Alcove				
-	WDBY		8030	C1
Donegal Bay				
-	WDBY		8030	E2
Donlea Ln				
-	EDNP		8107	A3
Donnelly Av				
-	IVGH		8115	B5
Donohue Av				
-	STPL		7940	D6
Doover Ln				
-	MAHT		7772	C5
Dora Ct E				
-	STPL		7943	A7
Dora Ct W				
-	STPL		7942	E7
Dora Ln				
-	STPL		7942	E7
Doral Rd				
-	DLWD		7686	B6
Dorchester Cir				
-	IVGH		8201	B1
Dorchester Ct				
-	APVA		8284	C3
-	EAGN		8199	C6
Dorchester Tr				
-	APVA		8284	C4
Doriann Ct				
-	EDNP		8106	C2
Doris Av				
-	SHVW		7683	A3
Dorland Ct E				
-	MPLW		8029	E2
Dorland Ct S				
-	MPLW		8029	E1
Dorland Dr E				
-	MPLW		8029	E1
Dorland Dr S				
-	MPLW		8029	E1
Dorland Ln E				
-	MPLW		8029	E1
Dorland Ln S				
-	MPLW		8029	E1
Dorland Pl E				
-	MPLW		8029	E1
Dorland Pl S				
-	MPLW		8029	C2
Dorland Rd				
-	MPLW		7857	D2
Dorland Rd S				
-	MPLW		8029	D4
Dorman Av				
-	MINN		7939	C6
Doron Dr				
-	EDNA		8108	C1
Doron Ln				
-	EDNA		8108	C1
Dorothea Av				
-	STPL		8026	A5
Dorothy Av				
-	WTBL		7771	D6
Dorothy Dr				
-	VADH		7770	A6
Dorothy Ln				
-	MNTK		7935	C6
Dorset Ln				
-	EDNP		8193	E2
Dorset Rd				
-	MNDH		8027	C5
-	WSTP		8027	D5
Dory Av				
-	APVA		8284	C4
Dory Ct				
-	APVA		8284	C7
Doswell Av				
-	FLCH		7940	A2
-	STPL		7939	D2
-	STPL		7940	A2
Dotte Ct				
-	WTBL		7771	C5
Dotte Dr				
-	WTBL		7771	C5
Douglas Av				
-	GLDV		7936	E4
-	GLDV		7937	A4
-	MINN		7937	D4
-	MINN		7938	A4
-	STLP		7936	E4
-	STLP		7937	A4
Douglas Cir N				
-	BRKP		7678	D6
Douglas Ct				
-	MNDH		8026	C7
Douglas Ct N				
-	BRKP		7678	C4
-	CHMP		7592	D6
Douglas Dr				
-	EDNP		8106	A7
-	EDNP		8192	A1
Douglas Dr N				
-	BRKP		7592	D7
-	BRKP		7678	D1
-	BRKP		7764	D1
-	CHMP		7592	D6
-	CRYS		7764	D4
-	CRYS		7850	D1
-	GLDV		7850	D7
-	GLDV		7936	D1
Douglas Ln				
-	WTBL		7771	B4
Douglas Ln N				
-	BRKP		7678	C6
Douglas Rd				
-	MNDH		8026	E7
-	MNDH		8027	A7
Douglas St				
-	STPL		8027	C1
E Douglas St				
-	SSTP		8115	A3
W Douglas St				
-	SSTP		8114	E3
Douglynn Dr				
-	MNTK		8021	B6
Douglynn Ln				
-	MPLW		8029	C5
-	STPL		8029	C5
Dousman St				
-	STPL		8027	C1
Dove Ct NE				
-	PRIO		8279	C7
Dove Ln				
-	NOAK		7770	A2
Dover Ct				
-	APVA		8284	C3
Dover Dr				
-	APVA		8284	C4
Dover St NE				
-	FRID		7680	A5
Dovre Dr				
-	EDNA		8021	E6
Dowell Av				
-	IVGH		8201	B1
Dowlin St N				
-	CHMP		7591	E2

Minneapolis Street Index

STREET Block	City	ZIP	Map #	Grid
Dowlin St N				
-	CHMP		7592	A2
Dowling Av N				
-	MINN		7851	D3
-	MINN		7852	A3
-	ROBB		7851	C3
Dowling St				
-	MINN		8025	D2
Down Rd				
-	EDNA		8108	B3
Downers Dr NE				
-	RSVL		7853	C2
-	STAN		7853	C2
Downey Tr				
-	APVA		8284	C5
Downing Av				
-	SHKP		8278	A2
Downing St				
-	MNDH		8027	C4
Downs Av				
-	MPLW		7855	E6
Downs Rd				
-	CHMP		7591	E2
-	CHMP		7592	A2
Doyle Pth E				
-	RSMT		8287	B5
Doyles Ct				
-	APVA		8284	A5
Drake Dr				
-	EAGN		8197	E6
Drake Pth				
-	APVA		8284	C7
Drake Rd				
-	GLDV		7850	E4
-	GLDV		7851	A4
-	WDBY		8030	D1
Drake St				
-	STPL		8027	B3
Drake St NW				
-	COON		7593	D1
Drake Alcove				
-	WDBY		8030	D1
Drake Bay				
-	WDBY		8030	D1
Draper Av				
-	RSVL		7853	E6
-	RSVL		7854	E6
Draper Dr				
-	RSVL		7854	A6
Dresden Ct				
-	APVA		8284	C7
-	EAGN		8198	C3
Dresden Ln				
-	GLDV		7851	A6
Dresden Wy				
-	EAGN		8198	C3
Dressen Cir				
-	EDNP		8106	A7
Drew Av N				
-	BRKC		7765	B3
-	BRKC		7851	B1
-	BRKP		7679	B7
-	BRKP		7765	B1
-	ROBB		7851	B1
Drew Av S				
-	BMTN		8195	B3
-	EDNA		8023	B7
-	EDNA		8109	B1
-	MINN		7937	B5
-	MINN		8023	B2
-	STLP		7937	B5
Drew Cir				
-	BMTN		8195	B6
Drew Cir S				
-	BMTN		8195	B1
Drewry Ln				
-	STPL		7942	B4
Drexel Ct				
-	APVA		8284	C7
-	EAGN		8198	C3
Drexell Av				
-	EDNA		8023	A4
Driftwood Cir				
-	NBRI		7767	B6
Driftwood Ct				
-	APVA		8284	C3
-	NBRI		7767	B5
Driftwood Ln				
-	APVA		8284	C3
Driftwood Rd				
-	EDNP		8107	B1
-	NBRI		7767	B5
Drillane Cir				
-	HOPK		8021	D1
Drillane Rd				
-	HOPK		8021	D1
-	MNTK		8021	D1
N Drillane Rd				
-	HOPK		8021	D1
S Drillane Rd				
-	HOPK		8021	D1
Drommond Tr				
-	APVA		8284	C6
Druid Ln				
-	MNTK		7934	A7
-	MNTK		8020	A1
Drumcliffe Cir				
-	RSMT		8284	D4
Drumcliffe Ct				
-	RSMT		8284	E4
Drumcliffe Pth				
-	RSMT		8284	E5
Drumcliffe Wy				
-	RSMT		8284	E4
Drumlin Ct				
-	APVA		8284	C7
Dublin Cir				
-	EDNA		8108	B2
Dublin Ct				
-	APVA		8284	C6
-	SHKP		8278	A2
Dublin Dr				
-	MNTK		8020	A2
Dublin Rd				
-	APVA		8284	B6
-	EDNA		8108	B2
Dublin Tr W				
-	SHKP		8278	A2
Duchess St				
-	STPL		7942	C4
Duck Lake Tr				
-	EDNP		8106	A2
Duck Pass Rd				
-	NOAK		7770	A1
Duck Pond Dr				
-	WSTP		8027	E7
-	WSTP		8113	E1
Duckwood Dr				
-	EAGN		8198	C2
Duckwood Tr				
-	EAGN		8198	D2
Dudley Av				
-	FLCH		7940	A1
-	SHVW		7769	B4
-	STPL		7939	E1
-	STPL		7940	A1
Dudley Av N				
-	CRYS		7764	C5
Duen Wy				
-	BLNE		7596	D6
-	CIRC		7596	D6
Duggan Plz				
-	EDNA		8108	D2
Duke Dr				
-	MNTK		8020	D2
Duke Dr NE				
-	BLNE		7594	D1
Duke St				
-	STPL		8027	B1
Dulcimer Wy				
-	APVA		8284	C7
Duluth Cir				
-	APVA		8284	C5
Duluth Ct				
-	APVA		8284	C6
-	MPLW		7856	D2
Duluth Dr				
-	APVA		8284	C5
-	RSMT		8284	D6
Duluth Ln				
-	GLDV		7850	D6
Duluth Pl				
-	MPLW		7856	D5
Duluth St				
-	GLDV		7849	E6
-	GLDV		7850	A6
Duluth St N				
-	MPLW		7856	D2
-	STPL		7856	D7
-	STPL		7942	D1
Dunbar Ct				
-	APVA		8284	C6
Dunbar Ct N				
-	BRKP		7679	B4
Dunbar Knls				
-	BRKP		7679	B5
-	MAHT		7858	B1
Dunbar Knls N				
-	BRKP		7679	B3
Dunbar Wy				
-	APVA		8284	C5
-	MAHT		7772	B7
-	MAHT		7858	B1
Dunbar Knoll Ct N				
-	BRKP		7679	B4
Dunbar Knolls Cir N				
-	BRKP		7679	B3
Dunberry Cir				
-	EAGN		8198	C7
-	EDNP		8193	D3
Dunberry Ln				
-	EAGN		8198	C7
-	EDNA		8108	E2
-	EDNA		8109	A2
Duncan Ln				
-	EDNA		8021	E6
Duncraig Rd				
-	EDNA		8022	C5
Dundee Rd				
-	EDNA		8022	B5
Dunes Av				
-	CTGV		8202	B4
Dunes Ct S				
-	CTGV		8202	B5
Dunes Ln				
-	CTGV		8202	B4
Dunes Wy				
-	CTGV		8202	B4
Dunham Dr				
-	EDNA		8108	E3
-	EDNA		8109	A3
Dunhill Rd				
-	EDNP		8107	B1
Dunkirk Cir NE				
-	BLNE		7595	E2
Dunkirk Ct				
-	BLNE		7681	E3
Dunkirk Ct N				
-	PYMH		7848	A3
Dunkirk Ct NE				
-	BLNE		7595	E3
-	BLNE		7681	E2
Dunkirk Ln N				
-	MAPG		7590	A7
-	MAPG		7676	A3
-	PYMH		7762	A6
-	PYMH		7848	A3
Dunkirk St NE				
-	BLNE		7595	E1
-	BLNE		7681	E1
Dunlap Av				
-	BLNE		7596	C7
-	BLNE		7682	C1
-	LXTN		7596	C7
-	LXTN		7682	C1
Dunlap Av N				
-	SHVW		7682	D5
Dunlap St N				
-	ARDH		7768	D6
-	ARDH		7854	D1
-	RSVL		7854	D4
-	STPL		7854	D7
-	STPL		7940	D7
Dunlap St S				
-	STPL		8026	D1
Dunmore Rd				
-	WDBY		8030	D3
Dunrovin Ln				
-	EAGN		8198	C6
Dunrovin Pl				
-	EAGN		8198	D6
Dunwoody Blvd				
-	MINN		7937	E3
-	MINN		7938	A3
Dupont Av N				
-	BRKC		7765	E4
-	BRKP		7679	E5
-	BRKP		7765	E1
-	MINN		7765	E7
-	MINN		7851	E1
-	MINN		7937	E1
Dupont Av S				
-	BMTN		8109	E5
-	BMTN		8195	E1
-	BRNV		8281	E2
-	MINN		7937	E4
-	MINN		8023	E4
-	RHFD		8109	E1
Dupont Ct N				
-	BRKP		7679	E7
Dupont Ln N				
-	BRKP		7679	E5
Dupont Rd S				
-	BMTN		8195	E4
Dupre Rd				
-	CTRV		7598	D5
Dupree Rd				
-	CTRV		7598	D6
Duram Ct				
-	EDNP		8107	A7
-	EDNP		8192	E1
-	EDNP		8193	A1
Durango Pl				
-	APVA		8284	C4
Durango Pt				
-	LINO		7684	A1
Durham Ct				
-	EAGN		8197	D5
Durham Rd				
-	MNTK		8020	C4
Durham Wy				
-	APVA		8284	C4
Durning Av				
-	APVA		8284	C7
Dusharme Dr				
-	BRKC		7765	B7
-	BRKC		7851	B1
Dutch Ct				
-	APVA		8284	B4
Dutton Av N				
-	BRKP		7764	C3
Duwayne Av				
-	LXTN		7682	B2
Dvorak Rd				
-	MNTK		8021	A2
Dwane St				
-	SSTP		8028	D6
Dwight Ln				
-	MNTK		7935	A5
Dwinnell Av				
-	DLWD		7772	C2
-	MAHT		7772	C2
Dylan Ct				
-	MAHT		7772	A6
Dynasty Dr				
-	MNTK		8020	A2
E				
E St				
-	HLTP		7766	D6
-	MNDT		8112	C1
-	MNTK		7935	D7
Eagandale Blvd				
-	EAGN		8112	D5
Eagandale Pl				
-	EAGN		8112	C6
Eagan Industrial Rd				
-	EAGN		8112	C5
Eagan Oaks Ct				
-	EAGN		8199	A1
Eagan Oaks Ln				
-	EAGN		8199	A1
Eagan Woods Dr				
-	EAGN		8112	B5
Eagle Av				
-	WTBL		7685	C7
-	WtBT		7685	C6
Eagle Cir				
-	COON		7593	D5
-	IVGH		8201	C1
Eagle Cir NW				
-	COON		7593	D1
Eagle Pkwy				
-	STPL		7941	D7
Eagle St NW				
-	COON		7593	D1
Eagle Tr				
-	CTRV		7598	E5
Eagle Bluff Cir				
-	BRNV		8281	D3
Eagle Bluff Dr				
-	BRNV		8281	D3
Eagle Creek Av NE				
-	PRIO		8279	A7
Eagle Creek Blvd				
-	SAVG		8279	E4
-	SHKP		8278	A1
-	SHKP		8279	A3
Eagle Creek Blvd CO-16				
-	SAVG		8279	E4
-	SHKP		8278	D2
-	SHKP		8279	A3
Eagle Creek Cir				
-	SAVG		8280	A3
Eagle Creek Pkwy				
-	SAVG		8280	A3
Eagle Crest Dr				
-	EAGN		8197	D6
N Eagle Lake Blvd				
-	MAPG		7763	C2
Eagle Lake Dr				
-	MAPG		7763	D3
-	PYMH		7763	D4
W Eagle Lake Dr				
-	MAPG		7763	C3
Eagle Point Cir				
-	ELMO		7944	E2
Eagle Ridge Cir				
-	BRNV		8282	B3
Eagle Ridge Dr				
-	BRNV		8282	B2
-	MNTK		8020	A3
Eagle Ridge Pl				
-	MNTK		8020	A3
Eagle Ridge Rd				
-	MNDH		8027	A7
-	MNDH		8113	A1
-	NOAK		7684	A7
-	NOAK		7769	E1
-	NOAK		7770	A1
-	WDBY		7944	D7
-	WDBY		8030	D1
Eagle Ridge Alcove				
-	WDBY		8030	D1
Earl Ln				
-	SSTP		8028	C7
-	WSTP		8028	C7
Earl St				
-	GLDV		7849	E6
-	PYMH		7849	E6
Earl St N				
-	STPL		7942	C4
Earle Brown Dr				
-	BRKC		7765	D4
Earley Lk				
-	BRNV		8281	E7
Earley Lake Curv				
-	BRNV		8281	E7
-	BRNV		8282	A7
Earley Shores Ln				
-	BRNV		8281	E7
Early Lake Pl				
-	BRNV		8281	E7
-	BRNV		8282	A7
East Av				
-	MAHT		7772	D4
East Ln				
-	NBRI		7767	E7
East Rd				
-	CIRC		7596	D7
East St				
-	WtBT		7685	C7
East Av Cir				
-	MAHT		7772	D4
Easter Ln				
-	EAGN		8198	C5
Eastman Dr				
-	NBRI		7767	C1
East Park Ln				
-	BRKP		7678	A6
East River Rd Service Dr				
-	FRID		7766	B5
East River Service Rd				
-	FRID		7766	B5
Eastview Ct				
-	APVA		8284	B4
Eastview Curv				
-	APVA		8284	B4
Eastview Dr				
-	EDNA		8022	D6
Eastview Ln				
-	NOAK		7683	D6
Eastway Av				
-	SHKP		8192	A7
Eastwood Ct				
-	EAGN		8199	C6
Eastwood Ln				
-	ANOK		7592	B2
Eastwood Rd				
-	MNDS		7681	C4
-	NBRI		7681	C7
Eathan Dr				
-	EAGN		8199	B5
Eaton St				
-	STPL		8028	B1
Ebba St				
-	WTBL		7771	D7
Ebertz Ct				
-	STPL		7943	B7
Ebnet Cir				
-	MNTK		8021	A4
Ebony Ln				
-	APVA		8284	B7
Echo Av				
-	STPL		7943	A3
Echo Dr				
-	BRNV		8282	D6
Echo Ln				
-	APVA		8284	B4
-	EDNP		8192	D2
-	SSTP		8115	A5
Echo St				
-	DLWD		7772	B2
-	WasC		7772	B2
Echo Lake Av				
-	MAHT		7858	A1
Echo Lake Blvd				
-	MAHT		7772	A7
Echo Park Cir				
-	BRNV		8282	D5
Echo Park Ct				
-	BRNV		8282	D5
Echo Park Ln				
-	BRNV		8282	D6
Echo Park Ter				
-	BRNV		8282	D5
Echo Shores Ct				
-	MAHT		7772	A7
Eckberg Dr				
-	BRKC		7765	A6
Eckles Av				
-	FLCH		7940	A2
Eden Av				
-	EDNA		8022	D5
Eden Cir				
-	EAGN		8199	C4
Eden Ct				
-	APVA		8284	B3
N Eden Dr				
-	EDNP		8020	B7
S Eden Dr				
-	EDNP		8020	B7
Eden Rd				
-	EDNP		8107	B5
Edenmoor St				
-	EDNA		8022	E5
Eden Prairie Ctr				
-	EDNP		8107	B5
Eden Prairie Rd				
-	EDNA		8022	B6
-	EDNP		8020	C7
-	EDNP		8106	A5
-	EDNP		8192	B1
-	MNTK		8020	C7
Edenvale Blvd				
-	EDNP		8106	C2
Edenwood Ct				
-	APVA		8284	C6
Edenwood Dr				
-	EDNP		8106	A3
Edenwood Wy				
-	APVA		8284	B6
Edgar Av				
-	STPL		7941	A3
Edgcumbe Pl				
-	STPL		8026	D4
Edgcumbe Rd				
-	STPL		8026	D4
Edge Dr				
-	BLNE		7596	E6
-	CIRC		7596	E6
Edge Pl				
-	MINN		7852	C2
Edgebrook Av				
-	MPLW		8029	C1
-	STPL		8029	C1
Edgebrook Dr				
-	STLP		8022	B1
Edgebrook Pl				
-	EDNA		8022	E5
-	EDNP		8106	E2
-	EDNP		8107	A2
Edgecumbe Dr				
-	MAHT		7772	B7
Edgehill Ct				
-	MPLW		7856	D4
Edgehill Rd				
-	MPLW		7857	A4
Edgemere Av				
-	STAN		7853	C2
Edgemont Blvd N				
-	BRKP		7763	E4
Edgemont Cir N				
-	BRKP		7763	E3
Edgemont Curv				
-	APVA		8284	B4
Edgemont St				
-	MPLW		7856	A7
-	STPL		7856	A7
-	STPL		7942	A1
-	VADH		7770	A4
Edgemont St N				
-	MPLW		7856	A6
Edgemoor Dr				
-	HOPK		8021	E1
-	MNTK		7935	E7
-	STLP		7935	E7
-	STLP		8021	E1
Edgemoor Pl NE				
-	COLH		7852	C1
Edgerton St				
-	LCAN		7856	A5
-	MPLW		7856	A6
-	STPL		7856	A7
-	STPL		7942	A4
-	VADH		7770	A7
-	VADH		7856	A2
Edgewater Av				
-	ARDH		7854	D1
-	SHVW		7854	E1
-	SHVW		7855	C1
Edgewater Blvd				
-	MINN		8024	D6
-	STPL		7943	C3
Edgewater Ln				
-	NOAK		7770	B2
Edgewater Pth				
-	APVA		8284	B4
Edgewood Av				
-	MNTK		7934	A7
-	SAVG		8280	D6
-	WDBY		7944	A7
Edgewood Av N				
-	BRKP		7678	C5
-	BRKP		7764	C1
-	CHMP		7592	D5
-	CRYS		7764	D7
-	CRYS		7850	D1
-	GLDV		7850	D7
-	GLDV		7936	D2
Edgewood Av S				
-	GLDV		7936	D2
-	STLP		7936	C4
-	STLP		8022	C2
Edgewood Cir				
-	BLNE		7596	C7
-	LXTN		7596	C7
-	SHKP		8279	E5
Edgewood Cir N				
-	CHMP		7592	D6
Edgewood Ct				
-	EDNP		8106	B2
-	WDBY		7944	A7
Edgewood Ct N				
-	CHMP		7592	D4
Edgewood Dr				
-	MNDS		7681	D5
-	NBRI		7681	D7
Edgewood Ln				
-	APVA		8282	E7
-	WSTP		8113	E1
Edgewood Ln N				
-	CHMP		7592	A4
Edgewood Pl N				
-	CHMP		7592	C5
Edgewood Rd NE				
-	BLNE		7596	B7
-	CIRC		7596	C7
-	LXTN		7596	B7
Edgewood Rd S				
-	BMTN		8194	C2
Edina Blvd				
-	EDNA		8022	E4
-	EDNA		8023	A4
Edina Ct				
-	EDNA		8023	A4
Edina Industrial Blvd				
-	EDNA		8108	D4
Edinborough Cir				
-	APVA		8284	B4
Edinborough Wy				
-	APVA		8284	B4
-	BMTN		8109	B4
-	EDNA		8109	B4
-	RHFD		8109	C4
Edinbrook Cross N				
-	BRKP		7679	B5
Edinbrook Ct N				
-	BRKP		7679	B4
Edinbrook Ln				
-	EDNA		8022	D4
Edinbrook Pkwy N				
-	BRKP		7679	D5
Edinbrook Pth				
-	APVA		8284	B4
Edinbrook Ter N				
-	BRKP		7678	E5
-	BRKP		7679	C5
Edinburgh Cir				
-	EDNP		8193	B4
Edinburgh Center Dr N				
-	BRKP		7679	D5
Edington Cir				
-	SHKP		8279	B1
Edison St NE				
-	BLNE		7595	E2
-	BLNE		7681	E1
Edith Av				
-	MAHT		7772	C7
Edith Dr				
-	WSTP		8027	D6
Edith Ln				
-	BLNE		7596	B7
-	LXTN		7596	B7
Edith St N				
-	MPLW		7943	E3
Edlin Pl				
-	MINN		7937	C4
Edmund Av				
-	STPL		7940	E5
-	STPL		7941	A5
Edmund Blvd				
-	MINN		7939	D7
-	MINN		8025	D2
Edward St				
-	MPLW		7856	D2
-	STPL		7856	D7
Edward St NE				
-	STAN		7853	B2
Edwards St				
-	IVGH		8115	B4
-	SSTP		8115	A4
Edwood Pl				
-	BMTN		8108	C5
Effress Rd				
-	WTBL		7771	E5
-	WtBT		7771	E5
Egan Av				
-	EAGN		8112	C6
Egan Dr				
-	BRNV		8281	B6
-	PRIO		8280	B6
-	SAVG		8280	B6
-	SAVG		8281	A6
Egan Dr CO-42				
-	BRNV		8281	B6
-	PRIO		8280	B6
-	SAVG		8280	B6
-	SAVG		8281	A6
Egandale Ct				
-	EAGN		8112	C6
Egg Lake Rd N				
-	HUGO		7599	E6
-	HUGO		7600	A7
Egg Lake Rd N CO-8				
-	HUGO		7599	E6
-	HUGO		7600	A7
Egret Blvd NW				
-	BLNE		7594	B5
-	COON		7593	D7
-	COON		7594	A5
Egret Ln				
-	LINO		7597	A7
Ehlers Pth E				
-	RSMT		8287	D6
Eichenwald St				
-	STPL		7942	B5
Eide Cir				
-	ARDH		7768	C4
Eide Knls				
-	EDNP		8106	B3
Eidelweiss St NW				
-	COON		7593	A2
Elaine Av				
-	SHVW		7683	B4
Elaine Ct				
-	SAVG		8280	D4
Elan Ct				
-	WDBY		7944	D7
Eland Ct				
-	APVA		8284	B3
Elderberry Ct				
-	APVA		8284	B5
Eldorado Cir				
-	DLWD		7686	B6
Eldorado Dr				
-	DLWD		7686	A6
Eldorado St NE				
-	BLNE		7595	B1
-	BLNE		7681	A2
-	SPLP		7681	B3
Eldorado St NW				
-	COON		7592	C1
E Eldorado Tr				
-	MNTK		7934	E7
Eldridge Av				
-	SSTP		8115	A3
Eldridge Av E				
-	MPLW		7856	B6
-	NSTP		7857	E6
Eldridge Av W				
-	RSVL		7854	B6
-	RSVL		7855	A6
Eleanor Av				
-	STPL		8025	E3
-	STPL		8026	B3

INDEX 16
Eleanor Ln — Fairfield Rd N

Minneapolis Street Index

STREET Block City ZIP Map # Grid

Eleanor Ln
- BRKC 7764 E4
- BRKC 7765 A4
Elfelt St
- STPL 7941 C5
Elgin Ct
- APVA 8284 B7
Elgin Pl N
- GLDV 7849 E6
- GLDV 7850 A6
Eli Rd
- LCAN 7855 E3
- LCAN 7856 A3
Eliason Dr
- BMTN 8194 D4
Eliot View Rd
- STLP 7936 C5
Elizabeth Ln
- BRNV 8282 A5
- MINN 7852 B3
- VADH 7770 B4
Elizabeth St E
- STPL 8028 A2
Elizabeth St W
- STPL 8027 E2
Elk St
- STPL 7941 E4
- WtBT 7685 C7
Elkhart Ct
- APVA 8284 B6
Elkhart Ln
- MPLW 7943 E2
Elkhart Rd
- APVA 8284 B6
Elkwood Cir
- APVA 8284 B5
Elkwood Dr
- APVA 8284 B5
Ella Ln
- MNTK 7935 A6
Ellen Ct
- LINO 7599 A7
- NWPT 8115 D2
Ellen St
- MNDH 8027 D4
- WSTP 8027 C4
Ellerdale Ln
- EDNP 8020 A7
- MNTK 8020 A7
Ellerdale Rd
- MNTK 8020 D3
Ellice Ct
- APVA 8284 A5
Ellice Tr W
- APVA 8284 A5
Elliot Av
- RHFD 8110 C3
Elliot Av S
- BMTN 8110 C6
- BMTN 8196 C1
- MINN 7938 C4
- MINN 8024 C1
- RHFD 8110 C2
Elliott Pl
- STPL 7942 C6
Ellis Av
- MINN 7939 D4
- STPL 7939 E4
- STPL 7940 A4
Ellis Ln
- GLDV 7936 B1
Ellsworth Ct
- APVA 8284 B5
Ellsworth Dr
- EDNA 8109 A3
Ellsworth Ln
- MNTK 7934 D6
Elm Av N
- BRKP 7679 B2
Elm Cir
- BRNV 8281 C4
- MNTK 8020 A4
Elm Dr
- BRNV 8282 C4
- MNTK 8020 A4
- WTBL 7771 D7
Elm Dr NE
- BLNE 7680 D3
- SPLP 7680 D3
Elm Ln
- BRNV 8281 C4
- MNTK 7934 C7
- MNTK 8020 E1
Elm Rd
- MAPG 7762 A4
Elm Rd N
- MAPG 7762 B4
Elm St
- ANOK 7592 B2
- BLNE 7596 E4
- BRNV 8281 C7
- LINO 7596 E4
- LINO 7597 A4
- MAHT 7772 C5
- MPLW 7856 E3
- STPL 8027 D1
- WTBL 7771 C7
Elm St NE
- FRID 7680 B5
Elm St SE
- MINN 7939 B1
Elm Creek Blvd N
- BRKP 7677 E7
- MAPG 7676 E4
- MAPG 7677 A7
Elm Creek Blvd N CO-130
- BRKP 7677 E7
- MAPG 7676 E4
- MAPG 7677 A7
Elm Creek Cir N
- CHMP 7591 E2
Elm Creek Pkwy
- CHMP 7591 E5
- CHMP 7592 B4
- MAPG 7591 E6
Elm Creek Rd
- CHMP 7591 E2
- DAYT 7590 E5
- DAYT 7591 A5
Elm Creek Tr N
- CHMP 7591 D5
Elm Creek Park Rd
- MAPG 7591 B7
- MAPG 7676 E2
- MAPG 7677 B1
Elmcrest Av N
- HUGO 7599 B1
- HUGO 7685 B1
- LINO 7599 B7
- LINO 7685 B1
Elmdale Rd
- GLDV 7851 A5
Elmer St W
- MPLW 7855 D6
- RSVL 7855 C6
Elmhurst Av N
- CRYS 7764 C5
Elmira Av
- APVA 8284 B7
Elmira Ct
- APVA 8284 B7
Elmo Cir
- MNTK 8021 B1
Elmo Rd
- HOPK 8021 C1
- MNTK 8021 B1
Elmo Service Rd
- HOPK 8021 C1
Elmwood Av N
- CHMP 7591 E5
Elmwood Ct
- APVA 8284 B4
Elmwood Pl
- MNTK 7934 A7
- MNTK 8020 A1
W Elmwood Pl
- MINN 8024 A5
Elmwood Pl E
- MINN 8024 B5
Elmwood St
- STPL 8029 B3
- VADH 7770 B5
Elmwood Entry N
- CHMP 7591 E5
Elodie Ln
- MNTK 8020 B5
Elrene Ct
- EAGN 8199 B3
Elrene Rd
- EAGN 8199 B4
Elrose Ct
- SSTP 8114 E4
Elroy Rd
- MINN 7938 A6
Elsberry Curv
- SHKP 8278 A4
Elsie Ct
- SPLP 8116 A6
Elsie Ln
- STPL 8025 D5
- STPL 8026 A6
Elsie Inn
- MAHT 7772 C5
Elvie Dr
- BMTN 8110 C7
Elway St
- STPL 8026 E4
Elwood Av N
- MINN 7937 D1
Ely Cir
- FRID 7680 A5
Ely St NE
- FRID 7680 A5
Elysium Pl
- APVA 8284 B7
Embassy Av
- APVA 8284 B7
Embassy Cir NE
- PRIO 8279 B6
Embassy Wy
- APVA 8284 B7
Ember Wy
- APVA 8284 B6
Embry Ct
- APVA 8284 B7
Embry Pth
- APVA 8284 B7
Embry Wy
- APVA 8284 B5
Emerald Ct
- MPLW 8029 C4
- NBRI 7767 D5
- STPL 8029 C4
Emerald Dr
- NBRI 7767 C5
- WTBL 7771 C6
Emerald Ln
- EAGN 8197 C5
- WDBY 8030 E2
Emerald Ln E
- SHKP 8278 A1
Emerald Pth
- APVA 8284 B7
Emerald Rdg
- MNTK 7934 D4
- RSVL 7855 A7
- STPL 7855 A7
SE Emerald St
- MINN 7939 D5
- STPL 7939 D5
Emerald St SE
- MINN 7939 D5
- STPL 7939 D5
Emerald Tr
- MNTK 7935 A5
Emerald Wy
- APVA 8284 B7
S Emerson Av
- MINN 7937 E3
Emerson Av E
- WSTP 8028 A5
Emerson Av N
- BRKC 7765 E2
- BRKP 7679 E7
- BRKP 7765 E1
- MINN 7765 E7
- MINN 7851 E7
- MINN 7937 E1
Emerson Av S
- BMTN 8109 E7
- BMTN 8195 E1
- MINN 7937 E5
- MINN 8023 E4
- RHFD 8109 E3
Emerson Av W
- MNDH 8027 B5
- WSTP 8027 E6
Emerson Ct
- BRNV 8281 E5
Emerson Ln
- BRNV 8281 E4
- RHFD 8109 E2
Emerson Ln N
- BRKC 7765 E2
Emerson Rd S
- BMTN 8195 E5
Emery Av E
- RSMT 8287 D7
Emil Av
- SHVW 7682 C3
- SHVW 7683 A3
Emilie Pl
- ROBB 7851 B2
Eminence Av N
- HUGO 7599 B3
Emma St
- STPL 8027 C1
Emmer Ct
- APVA 8284 B4
Emmer Pl
- APVA 8284 B4
Emmert St
- SHVW 7769 A7
- SHVW 7855 A1
Emmit Av N
- HUGO 7599 B4
Empire Av
- APVA 8284 B7
Empire Ct
- APVA 8284 B7
Empire Ct N
- MAPG 7762 D3
Empire Dr
- STPL 7941 D5
Empire Ln N
- MAPG 7762 D2
- PYMH 7762 C7
- PYMH 7848 D1
Empress Ct
- APVA 8284 B4
Empress Wy N
- HUGO 7599 B3
Emprire Ln N
- PYMH 7762 D6
Enclave Cir
- WDBY 8030 E6
Enclave Rd
- WDBY 8030 E6
Enclave Bay
- WDBY 8030 E6
Enclave Cove
- WDBY 8030 E6
Encore Cir
- MNTK 8021 B4
Endicott St
- STPL 7939 E3
Endicott Tr
- EDNP 8106 A6
Energy Ln
- STPL 7940 D3
Energy Park Dr
- STPL 7939 D3
- STPL 7940 D3
Enfield Av N
- HUGO 7599 B3
England Wy
- SHKP 8278 A2
Englert Rd
- EAGN 8198 B3
Englewood Av
- STPL 7940 B4
- STPL 7941 A4
Englewood Dr
- EDNP 8193 B4
English Cir
- GLDV 7849 E6
English St
- GEML 7770 D7
- MPLW 7856 D3
- STPL 7856 D7
- STPL 7942 D1
- VADH 7770 D7
Ensign Av
- SAVG 8279 E2
Ensign Av N
- CHMP 7591 E3
- GLDV 7849 E6
- GLDV 7935 E2
- NWHE 7763 E5
- NWHE 7849 E5
- NWHE 7850 A1
Ensign Av S
- BMTN 8193 E1
- STLP 7935 E6
Ensign Cir N
- NWHE 7849 E5
Ensign Cir S
- BMTN 8193 E2
Ensign Ct N
- NWHE 7849 D4
Ensign Curv S
- BMTN 8107 E5
Ensign Rd S
- BMTN 8107 E5
Ensley Ct
- APVA 8284 B7
Enterprise Dr
- MNDH 8112 C3
Entrevaux Dr
- EDNP 8193 C2
Equitable Dr
- EDNP 8106 D4
Ercoupe Ln
- SSTP 8115 A4
Erickson Ct N
- BRKP 7763 E3
Erickson Dr
- NWHE 7763 E7
Erickson Dr
- NWHE 7849 E1
Erickson Ln
- MNTK 8020 B2
Erickson Rd
- MNDS 7681 E6
Ericon Dr
- BRKC 7765 D6
Erie Av
- GLDV 7936 B3
Erie Ct
- EAGN 8199 C7
Erie St
- STPL 8027 B2
Erie St SE
- MINN 7939 B4
Erik Ln
- SHVW 7683 C5
Erik's Blvd
- EAGN 8284 B1
Erin Ct
- NBRI 7767 C1
Erin Dr
- EAGN 8197 B7
Erin Ln
- EAGN 8197 B7
Erin Ter
- EDNA 8108 B2
Ernal Dr
- SHVW 7769 C7
Erskin Cir NE
- BLNE 7596 C2
Erskin St NE
- BLNE 7596 C6
Erwin Ct
- EDNP 8106 D5
Escanaba Av
- STPL 7943 C4
Esk Cir
- IVGH 8199 D4
Esk Ln
- EAGN 8199 C4
- IVGH 8199 C4
Essex Av
- APVA 8284 B7
Essex Ct
- APVA 8284 B6
- EDNP 8106 E6
Essex Ln
- APVA 8284 B6
Essex Rd
- MNTK 7934 E4
Essex St SE
- MINN 7939 A3
Essex Tr
- APVA 8284 B6
Essex Wy
- APVA 8284 B4
Estabrook Dr
- STPL 7940 D2
Estate Dr
- EDNP 8193 E4
Estate Dr N
- BRKP 7679 A7
Estates Av
- APVA 8284 B7
Estates Dr
- EAGN 8283 B2
Esther Ln
- MNDH 8027 C4
- WDBY 7944 B7
- WDBY 8030 A1
Ethan Av N
- HUGO 7599 B3
- HUGO 7685 C2
Ethelton Wy
- APVA 8284 B4
Etna St
- STPL 7942 E1
Eton Pl
- EDNA 8023 B3
Euclid Av
- APVA 8284 A5
- STPL 7942 D5
Euclid Av W
- APVA 8284 B4
Euclid Ct
- APVA 8284 B6
Euclid Pl
- MINN 7937 D5
Euclid St
- STPL 7942 B6
- STPL 7943 A5
Eugene St
- WTBL 7771 A2
Eureka Ct
- APVA 8284 A7
Europa Av
- APVA 8284 A7
Europa Av N
- HUGO 7599 C3
- HUGO 7685 C2
Europa Ct
- APVA 8284 A5
Europa Ct N
- HUGO 7599 C7
- HUGO 7685 C1
Europa Tr N
- HUGO 7685 C1
Europa Wy
- APVA 8284 A7
Europa Bay N
- HUGO 7685 C1
Europa Trail Wy N
- HUGO 7685 C1
Eustis St
- LAUD 7853 D7
- LAUD 7939 D1
- RSVL 7853 D5
- STPL 7939 D2
Eva Ln
- SSTP 8028 C7
Eva St
- STPL 7942 A7
- STPL 8028 A1
Evans Av
- SSTP 8028 C4
Evans Ct
- SHVW 7769 A4
Evanswood Ln
- EDNA 8022 A5
Evar St N
- MPLW 7943 E3
Evas Dr
- MNTK 7935 A5
Eveleth Av
- APVA 8284 A4
Eveleth Ct
- APVA 8284 A6
Eveleth Pth
- APVA 8284 A4
Eveleth Wy
- APVA 8284 A5
Evelyn Ln
- MNTK 8020 C3
Evelyn St
- ARDH 7854 A2
- RSVL 7854 A2
Everest Av
- APVA 8284 A6
Everest Ct E
- APVA 8284 B3
Everest Ct N
- PYMH 7848 A4
Everest Ct W
- APVA 8284 A4
Everest Ln N
- MAPG 7676 A6
- MAPG 7762 A1
- PYMH 7848 A2
Everest Tr
- APVA 8284 A3
Everett Ct
- STPL 7939 E3
Everett Ln
- PYMH 7762 A7
Everett Pl
- EDNA 8108 D2
Evergreen Av N
- BRKP 7679 B2
Evergreen Blvd NW
- COON 7680 A1
- FRID 7680 B3
Evergreen Cir
- BRNV 8282 C6
- DLWD 7685 E6
- SHVW 7769 A5
- WtBT 7685 E6
Evergreen Cir N
- BRKP 7679 B2
Evergreen Cir NW
- COON 7594 B2
Evergreen Ct
- APVA 8284 B6
- BRNV 8282 C6
- EDNP 8106 B1
- NOAK 7769 C1
- RSVL 7854 A6
- VADH 7770 C3
- WDBY 8030 D3
Evergreen Ct N
- BRKP 7679 B2
Evergreen Dr
- BRNV 8282 C6
- EAGN 8112 A7
- EAGN 8198 A1
- LNDF 7944 A6
- MINN 7939 A5
- MNTK 8020 B2
- VADH 7770 C2
- WDBY 8030 D3
- WtBT 7770 C2
Evergreen Knls
- MNDH 8027 B7
Evergreen Ln
- CIRC 7596 E7
- NOAK 7769 D2
- SHVW 7683 B4
Evergreen Ln N
- MAPG 7677 B2
- MAPG 7763 B3
- PYMH 7763 B5
- PYMH 7849 B1
- PYMH 7935 D1
Evergreen Pl
- SHVW 7769 A5
Evergreen Rd
- DLWD 7772 D2
- GRNT 7772 D1
- NOAK 7769 D1
Evergreen St NW
- COON 7594 B1
Evergreen Tr
- APVA 8284 A7
Evergreen Alcove
- WDBY 8030 D3
Evergreen Bay
- WDBY 8030 D3
Evergreen Draw
- WDBY 8030 D3
Evergreen Echo
- WDBY 8030 D3
Evermoor Pkwy
- APVA 8284 E5
- RSMT 8284 E5
- RSMT 8285 E4
Evert Ct NE
- FRID 7681 A6
Everton Av
- APVA 8284 A4
Everton Av N
- HUGO 7599 C2
- HUGO 7685 C2
- WtBT 7685 C3
Ewald Av N
- MAPG 7763 D4
Ewald Ter
- GLDV 7936 B2
Ewing Av N
- BRKC 7765 B2
- BRKP 7679 B6
- ROBB 7851 B1
Ewing Av S
- BMTN 8195 B4
- BRNV 8281 B7
- EDNA 8023 B7
- EDNA 8109 B1
- MINN 7937 B6
- MINN 8023 B3
Ewing Av S
- STLP 7937 B5
Ewing Cir N
- BRKP 7679 B6
Ewing Cir S
- BMTN 8195 B6
- EDNA 8023 B6
Ewing Ln N
- BRKC 7765 B4
Ewing Rd
- BMTN 8109 B6
Ewing Rd S
- BMTN 8195 B4
Excelsior Blvd
- HOPK 8021 B3
- HOPK 8022 C2
- MINN 7937 B7
- MINN 8023 A1
- MNTK 8020 E4
- MNTK 8021 A3
- STLP 7937 B7
- STLP 8022 C2
- STLP 8023 A1
Excelsior Blvd CO-3
- HOPK 8021 B3
- MNTK 8021 A3
Excelsior Blvd E
- HOPK 8021 C3
- HOPK 8022 A3
- MNTK 8021 C3
- STLP 8022 B2
Excelsior Blvd E CO-3
- HOPK 8021 C3
- MNTK 8021 C3
Excelsior Cir
- MNTK 8021 A3
Excelsior Ln
- APVA 8284 A7
Excelsior Wy
- HOPK 8022 C2
- STLP 8022 C2
Exchange St E
- STPL 7941 D3
Exchange St S
- STPL 7941 D4
Exchange St W
- STPL 7941 D3
Exculpating Rd
- BRNV 8196 E7
- BRNV 8197 A6
Executive Blvd
- BRNV 8282 A7
Executive Dr
- EDNP 8106 E4
- MNDH 8112 D4
Exegesis St
- MPLW 7943 E6
Exeter Pl
- STPL 7939 E7
Exhall Av N
- HUGO 7685 C2
Exley Av
- APVA 8284 A4
Exley Ct
- APVA 8284 A6
Exley Ln
- APVA 8284 A7
Exley Wy
- APVA 8284 A6
Explorer Ct
- BRNV 8196 E6

F

F St
- HLTP 7766 D6
- MNDT 8112 C1
- MNTK 7935 D7
Faber Av
- SSTP 8028 C5
Fable Hill Cir N
- HUGO 7599 C7
Fable Hill Pkwy N
- HUGO 7599 C7
- HUGO 7685 C1
- LINO 7599 B7
Fable Hill Rd N
- HUGO 7599 B7
Fable Hill Wy N
- HUGO 7599 B7
Fable Rd Ct N
- HUGO 7599 B7
Factory St
- NWPT 8115 C5
- SPLP 8115 D6
Fahey Av
- RSMT 8288 A7
Fair Pl
- FLCH 7940 C2
- STPL 7940 C2
Fair Wy
- BRKP 7677 D3
- MAPG 7677 D3
- OSSE 7677 D3
Fairbanks Av N
- HUGO 7685 C1
Fairchild Av
- MNDS 7681 C4
- MNTK 7934 A6
Fairchild Ln
- SSTP 8115 A4
Fairfax Av
- EDNA 8023 A6
Fairfield Av E
- STPL 8028 A1
Fairfield Cir
- MNTK 7935 B3
Fairfield Cir N
- BRKP 7680 A7
Fairfield Ct
- MNTK 7935 B3
Fairfield Dr NW
- NBRI 7767 C5
Fairfield Rd
- BRKP 7679 E5
- BRKP 7680 A6
Fairfield Rd N
- BRKP 7680 A7
- BRKP 7766 A1

Minneapolis Street Index

STREET Block | City | ZIP | Map # | Grid

Forestview Cir N
- CHMP 7591 C6
- DAYT 7591 B1

Forestview Ln N
- MAPG 7677 B2
- MAPG 7763 B1
- MNTK 7935 B2
- PYMH 7763 B5
- PYMH 7849 B1
- PYMH 7935 B1

Forsham Lake Dr
- LINO 7597 B4

Forslin Dr
- EDNA 8022 D7

Forssa Wy
- EAGN 8283 E1

Forster St
- STPL 8027 A3

Fort Rd
- STPL 8026 D4

Fort Rd SR-5
- STPL 8026 D4

Foss Rd
- NBRI 7767 D7
- STAN 7767 D7
- STAN 7853 C1

Fossil Ln
- APVA 8283 D7

Foster Pl
- NOAK 7683 B7

Founders Pkwy N
- BRKP 7678 C5

Fountain Av
- APVA 8283 D6

Fountain Av N
- HUGO 7599 E6

Fountain Ct
- APVA 8283 D6

Fountain Ct N
- MAPG 7676 B7
- MAPG 7762 A3

Fountain Ln N
- MAPG 7676 A4
- MAPG 7762 A1
- PYMH 7848 A1

N Fountain Pk
- MAPG 7676 A4

Fountain Pl
- EDNP 8107 A6

Fountain Wy
- SHKP 8278 B4

Fountain Hills Ct NE
- PRIO 8279 B7

Fountain Hills Dr NE
- PRIO 8279 A7

Fountains Dr N
- MAPG 7677 B7
- MAPG 7763 B1

Fountains Wy N
- MAPG 7763 B1

Fourmes Av NE
- FRID 7766 C2

Four Oaks Rd
- EAGN 8112 A7

Four Seasons Ct
- EAGN 8283 B2

Four Seasons Dr
- EAGN 8283 B1

Fox Cir
- LINO 7683 D2

Fox Hllw
- LINO 7683 D1

Fox Hllw NW
- PRIO 8278 D7

Fox Pl
- MNDH 8113 B2

Fox Rd
- LINO 7683 D2

Fox Rdg NE
- BLNE 7595 D3

Fox Run
- CTRV 7598 D4

Fox Run NW
- PRIO 8278 C7

Fox Tr NW
- PRIO 8278 D7

Foxberry Ct
- SAVG 8280 A5

Foxberry Dr
- SAVG 8280 A4

Foxberry Rd
- SAVG 8280 A4

Foxberry Bay
- SAVG 8280 B5

Foxboro Ct
- WDBY 8030 C3

Foxboro Ln
- WDBY 8030 C3

Fox Cove
- LINO 7683 D1

Foxgate Dr
- MNTK 7934 D6

Foxglove Av N
- BRKP 7679 A3

Foxglove Ct N
- BRKP 7679 A3

Foxhall Rd
- MNTK 7935 B6

Foxhill Av N
- HUGO 7599 E3
- HUGO 7685 E2

Foxhill Cir N
- HUGO 7685 E2

Foxhollow Cir
- CHMP 7591 D6

Fox Hollow Ln N
- CHMP 7591 D6

Fox Hunt Ct NE
- PRIO 8279 B7

Fox Meadow Ln
- EDNA 8022 A5

Foxmoore Ct
- EAGN 8199 B5

Foxpoint Cir
- BRNV 8197 A5

Foxpoint Rd
- BRNV 8197 A5

Fox Ridge Ct
- EAGN 8197 D6
- WSTP 8114 A1

Fox Ridge Dr
- WSTP 8114 A1

Fox Ridge Rd
- EAGN 8197 E6

Foxridge Rd
- STPL 7943 B7

Fox Run Cir
- EDNP 8193 D1

Foxtail Ct
- APVA 8283 D7
- LINO 7685 A3

Foxtail Ct S
- CTGV 8116 B6

Foxtail Dr
- LINO 7685 A3
- WtBT 7685 A3

Foxtail Ln
- APVA 8283 D6

Fox Trot Ln
- SSTP 8115 A5

Foxtrot Ln
- EDNP 8192 D2

Foxwood Ct
- NBRI 7767 D1

Foxwood Ln
- MNDH 8027 C7

Fraizer St NE
- BLNE 7596 C6

S France Av
- GLDV 7937 B4
- MINN 7937 B4
- MINN 8023 B1
- STLP 8023 B1

France Av N
- BRKC 7765 B2
- BRKC 7851 B1
- BRKP 7593 D7
- BRKP 7679 B1
- BRKP 7765 B1
- GLDV 7851 B5
- GLDV 7937 B2
- ROBB 7851 B2

France Av S
- BMTN 8109 B3
- BMTN 8195 B2
- EDNA 8023 B7
- EDNA 8109 B2
- MINN 7937 B7
- MINN 8023 B5
- STLP 7937 B7
- STLP 8023 B3

France Pl
- BRKC 7765 A5

France's Rd
- ARDH 7682 A7

Francesca Av N
- HUGO 7599 E4

Franchise Av
- APVA 8283 D6

Francis St
- SSTP 8114 C1

Frank Ct
- MPLW 7856 D2

Frank St
- MPLW 7856 D2

Frank St N
- MPLW 7856 D7
- STPL 7856 D7
- STPL 7942 D2

Frankland St
- MAHT 7772 D6
- WILL 7772 C6

Franklin Av
- MINN 7939 D4
- STPL 7939 D4
- WtBT 7685 E6

E Franklin Av
- MINN 7938 B4
- MINN 7939 A4

SE Franklin Av
- MINN 7939 B4

W Franklin Av
- MINN 7937 E4
- MINN 7938 A4
- STLP 7935 E4
- STLP 7936 A4

Franklin Av S
- STLP 7936 B4

Franklin Av SE
- MINN 7939 C4
- STPL 7939 D4

Franklin Av W
- MINN 7937 D4
- STLP 7936 B4

Franklin Cir E
- EDNP 8106 B3

Franklin Ln
- ANOK 7591 A2

Franklin Ter
- MINN 7939 B4

Franklin Frontage Rd
- MINN 7938 E4

Frankson Av
- STPL 7940 C2

Franlo Rd
- EDNP 8107 B6
- EDNP 8193 D3

Fratallone Ln
- LCAN 7856 A2

Frear Dr
- MNTK 7934 E7

Fred St
- STPL 7942 A5

Fredeen Rd
- NBRI 7767 C3

Frederick Av
- STLP 7935 E7

Frederick Pkwy
- MPLW 7857 C2

Frederick St
- MPLW 7857 C3
- NSTP 7857 C3

Freeland Av N
- HUGO 7599 E4

Freeland Ct N
- HUGO 7599 E7

Freeport Ct
- APVA 8283 D6

Freeport Tr
- APVA 8283 D7

Freesia Wy
- APVA 8283 D7

Freeway Blvd
- BRKC 7765 D3

Freeway Rd
- MNDH 8113 B1

N Freeway Rd
- MNDH 8113 B1

S Freeway Rd
- MNDH 8113 B1

Fremont Av
- STPL 7942 E5
- STPL 7943 A5

Fremont Av E
- MPLW 7943 E5
- ODLE 7943 E5
- STPL 7943 B5

Fremont Av N
- BRKC 7765 E6
- BRKP 7679 E5
- BRKP 7765 E1
- MINN 7765 E7
- MINN 7851 E1
- MINN 7937 E2

Fremont Av S
- BMTN 8109 E5
- BMTN 8195 E1
- BRNV 8281 E4
- MINN 7937 E7
- MINN 8023 E7
- RHFD 8109 E4

Fremont Ct N
- BRKP 7765 E1

Fremont Ln
- WDBY 8030 A6

Fremont Pl
- BRNV 8281 E5

Fremont Pl N
- BRKC 7765 E2

Fremont St
- LILY 8027 C3
- MNDH 8027 C3

Fremont Alcove
- EAGN 8197 C7

French Lake Rd
- CHMP 7591 C1
- DAYT 7591 C1

E French Lake Rd
- DAYT 7590 A4

W French Lake Rd
- DAYT 7590 A5

Frenchman Rd N
- HUGO 7599 B5
- LINO 7599 B5

Fresno Ln
- APVA 8283 D7

Friar Dr
- EDNP 8193 D2

Friar Ln
- MNTK 7935 B7
- MNTK 8021 B1

Friday Ln
- APVA 8283 D7

Fridley St NE
- FRID 7767 A1

Fridley Wy
- APVA 8283 D7

Friendship Ln
- BRNV 8281 D6

Friendship Village Rd
- BMTN 8108 C6

Frisbie Av
- MPLW 7856 D7

Fromme Ct
- EAGN 8199 C4

Front Av
- STPL 7940 E3
- STPL 7941 A3

Front St
- SPLP 8115 C7

Frontage Rd
- BMTN 8108 E4
- BRKC 7765 B6
- EDNA 8108 E4
- MNDH 8113 B1
- NBRI 7767 E6
- PYMH 7849 E7
- SAVG 8280 B5
- STPL 8026 C4
- WSTP 8113 D1

E Frontage Rd
- MINN 7852 C3

N Frontage Rd
- BRNV 8281 C2
- GLDV 7936 E1
- GLDV 7937 A1
- MINN 7937 E1
- MNTK 7934 E3
- MNTK 7935 A3
- STLP 7935 D3

S Frontage Rd
- BRNV 8281 D3
- MINN 7937 E1
- MINN 7938 A2
- MINN 8025 B6
- MNTK 7935 B3

SE Frontage Rd
- BRNV 8281 D3

W Frontage Rd
- BRNV 8281 E3
- BRNV 8282 A3
- EDNA 8022 E5

Frontenac Av
- GLDV 7850 E7

Frontenac Pl
- STPL 7939 D5

Frontier Ct
- BRNV 8282 D5

Frontier Ln
- BRNV 8282 D6

Frost Av
- MPLW 7856 C6
- MPLW 7857 A6

E Frost St
- SSTP 8115 A3

W Frost St
- SSTP 8114 E3

Frost Point Wy
- APVA 8283 D4

Fry St
- FLCH 7854 B7
- RSVL 7854 B4
- STPL 7940 B7

Fulham St
- FLCH 7853 E7
- FLCH 7939 E1
- LAUD 7853 E7
- LAUD 7939 E1
- RSVL 7853 E5
- STPL 7939 E1

Fuller Av
- STPL 7940 E6
- STPL 7941 C6

Fuller Rd
- EDNP 8106 B5

W Fuller St
- EDNA 8023 B5

Fuller Wy
- VADH 7770 D7

Fulton St
- STPL 8027 A2

Fulton St SE
- MINN 7939 B3

Furlong Av
- MNDH 8112 C3

Furlong Tr
- NgTp 8288 B6
- RSMT 8288 B6

Furness Ct
- MPLW 7857 C2

Furness Pkwy
- STPL 7943 C1

Furness St
- MPLW 7857 C2
- NSTP 7857 C6

G

G St
- MNDT 8112 C1

Gaage Ln
- LINO 7598 B7

Gabbert Cir
- EAGN 8198 E7

Gabbro Tr
- EAGN 8197 E4

Gable Dr
- EDNP 8192 B2

Gable Ln
- APVA 8283 D5

Gabriel Rd
- STPL 8029 C4

Gadwall Ln
- NOAK 7770 A1

Gadwell Ct
- EAGN 8198 A6

Galaxie Av
- APVA 8283 D2
- EAGN 8197 E7
- EAGN 8283 D2

Galaxie Av W
- APVA 8283 D7
- EAGN 8283 D2

Galaxie Ct
- APVA 8283 C7
- EAGN 8197 E7

Galaxie Pl
- APVA 8283 C4

Galaxie Pt
- EAGN 8197 E7

Galaxy Dr
- BLNE 7596 C6
- CIRC 7596 C6

Gale Cir
- ARDH 7768 C4

Galena Wy
- APVA 8283 C5

Gall Av
- MPLW 7857 D1
- WTBL 7857 D1

Gallagher Dr
- EDNA 8109 B3

Galleria Pl W
- APVA 8283 C5

Gallivan Ct N
- HUGO 7685 C2

Gallup Ct
- APVA 8283 D3

Galtier Av
- RSVL 7855 C2

Galtier Cir
- RSVL 7855 C4

Galtier Dr
- BRNV 8197 A6

Galtier Pl
- BRNV 8197 A6
- NOAK 7769 C3
- SHVW 7769 C3

Galtier St
- NOAK 7769 C3
- RSVL 7855 C4
- SHVW 7769 C3
- STPL 7855 C7
- STPL 7941 C2

Galvin Av
- WSTP 8027 D4

Galway Cir
- BRNV 8282 B4
- WDBY 8030 E2

Galway Ct
- APVA 8283 C6

Galway Dr
- EDNA 8108 C2

Galway Ln
- EAGN 8198 A3

Galway Rd
- WDBY 8030 E2

Gamble Dr
- STLP 7936 E4

Gamma Wy
- APVA 8283 C5

Gannon Dr
- SHKP 8192 B7

Gannon Rd
- STPL 8026 B6

Gannon Wy
- APVA 8283 D7

Gantry Ct
- APVA 8283 C2

Gantry Ln
- APVA 8283 C3

Gantry Wy
- EDNP 8193 C4

Garbe Av
- WDBY 7944 A7

Garceau Ln
- VADH 7770 B7

Garden Av
- EDNA 8022 C6
- FLCH 7854 B7
- RSVL 7854 C7

Garden Blvd N
- ODLE 7858 B6

Garden Cir S
- BMTN 8194 B5

Garden Ct
- WDBY 8116 D4

Garden Ct N
- ODLE 7858 B6

Garden Dr
- BRNV 8282 C5
- WDBY 8116 D3

Garden Dr NE
- BLNE 7596 E3
- LINO 7596 E3

Garden Gln
- LNDF 7944 A5

Garden Ln
- EDNP 8106 E7
- EDNP 8107 A6
- LILY 8027 C4
- MNDH 8027 C4
- WTBL 7685 B7
- WtBT 7685 A7

Garden Pk
- GLDV 7936 B2

Garden Tr
- EAGN 8198 C6

Garden Wy
- HUGO 7599 B6

Garden Wy N
- HUGO 7599 B6

Gardena Av NE
- FRID 7766 E3
- FRID 7767 A3
- NBRI 7767 B3

Gardena Cir NE
- FRID 7767 A3

Gardena Ln NE
- FRID 7767 A3

Gardenette Dr N
- WTBL 7771 C4

Gardenette Dr S
- WTBL 7771 C4

Gardenia Ct
- APVA 8283 C5

Gardenia Pth
- APVA 8283 C6

Gardenview Ct
- APVA 8283 E7

Gardenview Dr
- APVA 8283 A7

Gardenwood Pkwy NE
- BLNE 7596 C2

Gardner Ln
- DLWD 7772 A2

Garfield Av
- BRNV 8282 A4
- MINN 7938 A5
- MINN 8024 A3
- RHFD 8110 A1

Garfield Av N
- CHMP 7591 D1

Garfield Av S
- BMTN 8110 A5
- BMTN 8196 A1
- RHFD 8110 A4

Garfield Cir
- EDNP 8106 B4

Garfield St
- STPL 8027 C1

Garfield St NE
- MINN 7853 A3
- SPLP 7681 A4

Garland Av
- APVA 8283 C3

Garland Ct
- EDNP 8106 D7

Garland Ln N
- MAPG 7676 A3
- PYMH 7848 A6
- PYMH 7934 A1

Garner Ct
- APVA 8283 C3

Garner Ln
- APVA 8283 C4

Garner Wy
- APVA 8283 C4

Garnet Av
- APVA 8283 C5

Garnet Ct
- BRNV 8283 B3

Garnet Dr
- EAGN 8197 C5

Garnet Ln
- EAGN 8197 C5

Garnet Pt
- EAGN 8197 C5

Garrett Av
- APVA 8283 C7

Garrett Ln
- APVA 8283 C4

Garrison Ct
- BRNV 8282 B4

Garrison Ln
- EDNA 8023 A7

Garrison Wy
- EDNP 8193 E1

Garvin Brook Ln
- APVA 8283 C4

Garwood Rd N
- BRKP 7764 D1

Gary Blvd S
- CTGV 8202 B1

Gary Dr
- SPLP 8201 E2
- SPLP 8202 A2

Gary Pl
- MPLW 7857 B7
- STPL 7857 B7
- STPL 7943 B1

Gaston Av
- NOAK 7683 A6
- SHVW 7683 A6
- WtBT 7685 D6

E Gate Rd
- STAN 7853 C3

Gate Park Rd
- EDNA 8022 C6

Gateway Blvd
- BRNV 8282 A3

Gateway Cir
- CTRV 7598 E6

Gateway Ct
- ARDH 7768 A3

Gateway Dr
- SHKP 8278 E1
- STPL 7940 E2
- STPL 7941 A3

Gateway Ln
- EDNP 8106 A7

Gatewood Cir
- MNTK 8020 C7

Gatewood Dr
- MNTK 8020 C6

Gauntlet Ct
- APVA 8283 C6

Gavotte Av
- APVA 8283 C3

Gavotte Ct
- APVA 8283 D3

Gaynor St
- MNTK 7935 D7

Gaywood Dr
- MNTK 8020 D4

Gem St N
- MPLW 7857 A3

Gemini Rd
- EAGN 8112 E7

Gemstone Ct
- APVA 8283 C5

General Miller Dr
- HnpC 8025 D7

General Mills Blvd N
- GLDV 7936 A2

Generation Av N
- HUGO 7599 D4

Generation Cir
- HUGO 7599 D4

Genesee Av
- APVA 8283 C3

Genesee Ct
- APVA 8283 C4

Genesee St
- STPL 7941 B4

Genesee Wy
- APVA 8283 C3

Geneva Av N
- HUGO 7599 E5
- HUGO 7600 A6
- MAHT 7857 E1
- MPLW 7857 E7
- MPLW 7943 E5
- NSTP 7857 E3
- ODLE 7857 E7
- ODLE 7943 E5
- WTBL 7857 E2

Geneva Av N SR-5
- MPLW 7857 E7
- MPLW 7943 E1
- ODLE 7857 E7
- ODLE 7943 E1

Geneva Av N SR-120
- MAHT 7857 E1
- MPLW 7857 E7
- MPLW 7943 E5
- NSTP 7857 E3
- ODLE 7857 E7
- ODLE 7943 E5
- WTBL 7857 E2

Geneva Av S
- CTGV 8116 A5
- CTGV 8202 A3
- GCIT 8202 A5
- NWPT 8116 A5
- SPLP 8202 A5

Geneva Blvd
- BRNV 8282 B7

Geneva Ct
- APVA 8283 C3

Geneva Ln
- APVA 8283 C2
- EAGN 8283 C2

Geneva Wy
- APVA 8283 C5

Geneva Wy N
- HUGO 7600 A6

Genevieve Av N
- NSTP 7857 E6
- ODLE 7857 E6
- ODLE 7858 A5

Genevieve Ln
- MNTK 7935 C4

Gentilly Rd
- MAPG 7763 B3

Gentry Av N
- ODLE 7858 A4
- ODLE 7944 A2

George Ct
- APVA 8283 D3

George St E
- STPL 8028 A2

George St W
- STPL 8027 D2

Georgia Av N
- BRKP 7678 C4
- BRKP 7764 C2
- CHMP 7592 C5
- CRYS 7764 C7
- CRYS 7850 C1
- GLDV 7936 C2

Georgia Av S
- STLP 7936 C6

Georgia Blvd N
- NSTP 7857 E4
- ODLE 7857 E4
- ODLE 7858 A4

INDEX 20

Granite Ct N — Minneapolis Street Index — Harbor Place Dr

Minneapolis Street Index

STREET Block | City | ZIP | Map # | Grid

Granite Ct N
- ODLE 7944 B1
Granite Dr
- EAGN 8199 B5
- SHKP 8278 A2
Granite Ln N
- ODLE 7944 A4
Granite St
- STPL 7941 E4
Grant Dr
- EDNP 8193 C3
Grant Rd
- ARDH 7768 A7
- NBRI 7768 A7
E Grant St
- MINN 7938 C4
W Grant St
- MINN 7938 B4
Grantaire Ln
- HUGO 7599 B6
Grant Alcove
- EAGN 8197 D6
Grantham St
- FLCH 7939 E1
- STPL 7939 E1
Grass Lake Ter
- MINN 8023 E7
Gray Heron Dr
- LINO 7597 B5
Grayling Cir NE
- PRIO 8280 A6
Grays Bay Blvd
- MNTK 7934 A6
Grays Landing Rd
- MNTK 7934 A5
Great Oak Pl
- EAGN 8199 A2
Great Oak Tr
- EAGN 8199 A2
Great Oaks Cir
- EAGN 8199 B2
Great Oaks Dr
- BRNV 8282 E4
Great Oaks Ln
- EAGN 8199 A2
Great Oaks Tr N
- GRNT 7686 A4
Greatview Av
- BRKC 7765 B7
Greenbriar Ct
- WDBY 8030 E7
- WtBT 7684 D4
Greenbriar Curv
- SHKP 8279 B1
Green Briar Dr
- LINO 7596 E5
- LINO 7597 A5
- MNTK 7934 D6
Green Briar Ln
- MNTK 7934 D6
Greenbriar Ln
- WDBY 8030 E6
Green Briar Rd
- BMTN 8194 D1
Greenbriar St
- VADH 7770 B7
Greenbrier Cir
- LCAN 7856 B5
Greenbrier Rd
- MNTK 7935 D6
Greenbrier St
- LCAN 7856 B2
- MPLW 7856 B6
- STPL 7942 B2
- VADH 7770 B7
- VADH 7856 B1
Green Cir Dr
- MNTK 8021 D6
Greendale Ln
- VADH 7770 B3
Greene Av N
- HUGO 7600 A4
- ODLE 7858 B7
- ODLE 7944 B4
Greene Av S
- CTGV 8202 B3
Green Farms Cir
- EDNA 8022 A4
Green Farms Ct
- EDNA 8022 A5
Green Farms Rd
- EDNA 8022 A5
Greenfield Av
- MNDS 7681 D5
Greenfield Pl
- MNDS 7681 D5
Greenhaven Cir
- VADH 7770 B4
Greenhaven Ct
- VADH 7770 A3
Green Haven Dr
- BRKP 7677 E6
- BRKP 7678 A6
Greenhaven Dr
- VADH 7770 A3
- WTBL 7770 C3
- WtBT 7770 B3
Greenhaven Ln
- MNDS 7681 E6
Greenhaven Pl
- VADH 7770 A3
Greenhaven Ter
- VADH 7770 B3
Greenland Av
- APVA 8283 B6
Greenleaf Ct
- APVA 8283 E5
E Greenleaf Dr
- EAGN 8199 B7
N Greenleaf Dr
- EAGN 8199 C7
S Greenleaf Dr
- EAGN 8199 C7
Greenleaf Dr W
- EAGN 8199 B7
Greenleaf Tr
- APVA 8283 E5
Green Oak Dr
- MNTK 8021 D6

Greenridge Ln
- BRNV 8281 C7
Green Ridge Rd
- MNTK 7935 C7
Greensboro Ct
- EAGN 8198 E3
Greensboro Dr
- EAGN 8198 E3
- EAGN 8199 A3
Greensboro Ln
- EAGN 8198 E3
Greenspruce Av N
- BRKP 7679 A2
Greenspruce Ct N
- BRKP 7679 A2
Greentree Ct
- APVA 8283 D3
Green Valley Dr
- BMTN 8108 D5
Green Valley Rd
- GLDV 7850 C7
- MNTK 8020 A4
Green View Ct
- EDNP 8106 D3
Greenview Dr
- NBRI 7767 C2
Greenview Ln
- GLDV 7850 E6
Greenway Av N
- ODLE 7944 B6
Greenway Av NE
- PRIO 8280 C5
Greenway Av S
- CTGV 8202 B3
Greenway Gables
- MINN 7938 A3
Greenwich Ct
- APVA 8283 B5
Greenwood Av
- STPL 8028 A2
Greenwood Ct
- EAGN 8198 A2
Greenwood Ct N
- EAGN 8198 A2
Greenwood Ct S
- EAGN 8198 A2
Greenwood Dr
- BRNV 8281 D2
- MNDS 7681 C4
- MNTK 8020 E3
- NBRI 7681 C7
Greenwood Ln
- LINO 7597 B1
Greenwood Rd
- MNTK 8020 E3
Greenwood St
- MAHT 7772 C5
Greenwood Tr
- MNTK 8021 A3
Gregory Dr
- NBRI 7767 C1
Gregory Rd
- GLDV 7936 A3
Grenada Pt
- EAGN 8283 E2
Grenadier Av N
- ODLE 7944 B1
Grenadier Av S
- CTGV 8202 B1
- SPLP 8202 B1
Grenadier Pl
- ODLE 7858 B6
Grenadier Tr N
- ODLE 7858 B6
Grenelefe Av N
- DLWD 7686 A5
- GRNT 7686 A5
Grenier Rd
- MNTK 8020 C6
Grenoble Av
- IVGH 8115 C7
Grenwich Av N
- ODLE 7858 B4
Grenwich Ln N
- ODLE 7858 B3
Grenwich Pl N
- ODLE 7858 B4
Grenwich Rd N
- ODLE 7858 B4
Grenwich Ter
- EDNP 8020 A7
Grenwich Tr N
- ODLE 7858 B4
Grenwich Wy N
- ODLE 7858 B4
Gresham Av N
- ODLE 7858 B6
- ODLE 7944 B1
Gresham Cir N
- ODLE 7858 B6
Gresham Ct N
- ODLE 7858 B5
Gresham Ln S
- CTGV 8202 B1
Gresham Pl N
- ODLE 7858 B6
Gresham Wy N
- ODLE 7858 B7
Gretchen Ct N
- ODLE 7858 B5
Gretchen Ln N
- ODLE 7858 B5
Gretchen Pl N
- ODLE 7858 B5
Grey Cloud Tr
- GCIT 8201 E3
- SPLP 8201 E3
Grey Cloud Tr S
- CTGV 8202 A7
- CTGV 8288 B1
- GCIT 8202 A4
- SPLP 8202 A4
Grey Cloud Island Dr S
- CTGV 8202 A7
- GCIT 8201 D5
- GCIT 8202 A6
- SPLP 8201 D2
Grey Dove Ln
- EAGN 8197 D1

Greyfield Ct
- EDNP 8193 A3
Grey Fox Rd
- ARDH 7768 D6
- SHVW 7768 D6
Greylock Ct
- APVA 8283 B3
Grey Squirrel Rd
- LINO 7597 A4
Greystone Av N
- HUGO 7686 A2
- ODLE 7944 B6
Greystone Av S
- CTGV 8202 B3
Greystone Ct N
- HUGO 7686 B1
Greystone Dr
- IVGH 8114 B3
Greystone Rdg
- EAGN 8198 A4
Grey Widgeon Pl
- EDNP 8193 A2
Grier Ln
- EDNP 8107 B6
Grieve Glen Ln
- MNDH 8113 D4
- SUNL 8113 D4
Griffin Av
- MAHT 7772 D4
Griffin Ct
- MAHT 7772 D4
Griffit St
- EDNA 8022 A4
Griffith St
- STPL 7942 D6
Griggs Av
- BLNE 7596 B7
- BLNE 7682 B2
- FLCH 7940 A2
- LXTN 7596 B7
- LXTN 7682 B1
Griggs St N
- RSVL 7854 D3
- STPL 7940 D7
Griggs St S
- STPL 8026 D3
Grimes Av N
- BRKC 7765 A2
- BRKP 7593 A7
- BRKP 7679 A1
- BRKP 7765 A2
- ROBB 7851 B1
Grimes Av S
- EDNA 8023 A3
- STLP 8023 A2
Grimes Ln
- EDNA 8023 B7
N Grimes Pl
- BRKC 7765 A3
Gristmill Rdg
- EDNP 8193 B3
Groberg St
- MNDS 7681 D6
Grospoint Av N
- ODLE 7944 B2
Grospoint Av S
- CTGV 8202 B3
Grospoint Ln N
- ODLE 7944 B5
Grothe Cir
- APVA 8283 B6
N Grotto St
- RSVL 7855 A7
- STPL 7855 A7
- STPL 7941 A3
Grotto St N
- LINO 7683 A3
- RSVL 7855 A4
- SHVW 7683 A3
- STPL 7941 A2
Grotto St S
- STPL 7941 A7
- STPL 8027 A1
Grouse Cir NW
- COON 7593 D5
Grouse Ct
- COON 7593 D6
Grouse Hllw
- CTRV 7598 D6
Grouse St NW
- COON 7593 D1
Grove Av
- NOAK 7683 A6
- SHVW 7683 A6
Grove Cir
- EDNA 8022 B6
- SHKP 8279 D2
Grove Cir N
- MAPG 7676 B2
Grove Dr
- MAPG 7676 E6
- SHKP 8279 D3
Grove Pl
- EDNA 8022 A3
- SHKP 8279 D3
Grove St
- EDNA 8022 D6
- MAHT 7772 C4
- MINN 7938 C1
- STPL 7941 E5
- STPL 7942 A5
Groveland Av
- MINN 7938 A4
Groveland Ct
- MNDS 7681 B4
Groveland Rd
- BLNE 7681 B4
- MNDS 7681 B4
Groveland Ter
- MINN 7937 E4
- MINN 7938 A4
Grovner Av N
- ODLE 7944 B6
Grovner Rd N
- ODLE 7858 B6
Gryc Ct
- MNDH 8027 B7
Guadalcanal Ct NE
- BLNE 7681 E2

Guardian Angels Av N
- ODLE 7944 E6
Guider Dr
- WDBY 8030 C2
Guild Av
- APVA 8283 B5
Guild Ct
- APVA 8283 B5
Gulden Pl
- MPLW 7856 E7
Gulf Breeze Ct
- APVA 8283 B6
Gulfstream Ln
- SSTP 8115 A4
Gull Ct
- APVA 8283 B5
Gun Club Rd
- EAGN 8285 C2
- SSTP 8115 B4
- WTBL 7770 D2
Gunflint Ct
- APVA 8283 B5
Gunflint Pth
- APVA 8283 B5
Gunflint Tr N
- BRKP 7679 C6
Gurney Ct
- APVA 8283 B6
Gurney Pth
- APVA 8283 B6
Gurney St
- MPLW 7855 D7
- STPL 7855 D7
- STPL 7941 D1
Guthrie Av
- APVA 8283 B6
Guthrie Av N
- ODLE 7944 B1
Guthrie Ct N
- ODLE 7944 A2
Guthrie Wy
- APVA 8283 B7
Gweneth Ln
- EDNP 8107 B6

H

Haas Lake Cir NW
- PRIO 8278 D6
Habitat Ct S
- EDNA 8021 E7
Hackberry Ln
- NOAK 7683 C6
- SHKP 8278 B4
Hackberry Ln N
- CHMP 7591 C5
Hackmann Av NE
- FRID 7766 E3
Hackmann Cir NE
- FRID 7766 E3
Hackmore Ct
- EAGN 8199 C6
Hackmore Dr
- EAGN 8199 B6
Haddington Rd
- RSVL 7854 B5
Hadley Av N
- DLWD 7686 B7
- GRNT 7686 B7
- MPLW 7857 E2
- ODLE 7857 E2
- ODLE 7858 A2
- ODLE 7944 B5
Hadley Av S
- CTGV 8116 B6
- CTGV 8202 B3
- SPLP 8202 A1
- WDBY 8116 B5
Hadley Cir N
- GRNT 7686 B6
- HUGO 7686 B1
- ODLE 7858 C5
Hadley Cir S
- CTGV 8116 B5
Hadley Ct N
- GRNT 7686 B7
- ODLE 7858 B6
Hadley Ct S
- CTGV 8116 B5
Hadley Ln N
- ODLE 7944 B5
Hadley St
- STPL 8029 C3
Haeg Cir
- BMTN 8109 D6
Haeg Dr
- BMTN 8109 D6
Hafner Ct
- RSVL 7854 E1
- SHVW 7854 E1
Hagen Dr N
- MPLW 7856 E7
- STPL 7856 E7
Hague Av
- STPL 7940 C7
- STPL 7941 A7
Haines St
- NBRI 7767 C7
Halcyon Ln
- MAHT 7772 D6
Halden Cir
- EAGN 8197 E7
Hale Av N
- ODLE 7858 B4
- ODLE 7944 C1
Hale Av S
- CTGV 8202 B2
Hale Ct N
- ODLE 7944 C1
Hale Ct S
- CTGV 8202 B3
Half Moon Dr
- GLDV 7936 B2
Halglo Pl
- ROBB 7851 B4
Halifax Av N
- BRKC 7765 A2
- BRKP 7679 A6
- BRKP 7765 A2
- ROBB 7851 A1

Halifax Av S
- EDNA 8023 B7
- EDNA 8109 B1
Halifax Ct N
- BRKP 7679 A6
Halifax Dr
- BRKC 7765 A4
Halifax Ln
- EDNA 8023 B6
Halifax Pl
- BRKC 7765 A5
Halite Ln
- EAGN 8197 E5
Hall Av
- BRHV 7772 A5
- MAHT 7772 B6
- STPL 8027 E4
- WSTP 8027 E3
Hall Ct
- BRHV 7772 A5
Hall Curv
- MINN 7852 B3
Hall Ln
- MINN 7852 A7
- STPL 8027 E1
- STPL 8028 A1
Hall St
- BLNE 7682 B3
- SHVW 7682 B3
Hallam Av N
- MAHT 7772 D4
Hallam Av S
- MAHT 7772 D6
Hallam Curv
- MAHT 7772 D6
Hallam St
- MAHT 7772 D4
Haller Ct S
- MPLW 8029 E7
Haller Ln E
- MPLW 8029 E7
Hallmark Av N
- ODLE 7858 C6
- ODLE 7944 C1
Hallmark Av S
- CTGV 8202 C3
Hallmark Cir N
- ODLE 7944 C3
Hallmark Ct
- APVA 8283 B5
Hallmark Ct N
- ODLE 7944 C4
Hallmark Dr
- APVA 8283 B7
- EDNP 8106 B2
Hallmark Ln N
- ODLE 7944 B3
Hallmark Wy N
- ODLE 7944 C2
Halper Pl
- WtBT 7684 D4
Halper Wy
- WtBT 7684 D4
Halsey Ln
- BMTN 8110 A7
Hamburg Ct
- APVA 8283 B4
Hamen Ct
- IVGH 8113 E4
- SUNL 8113 E4
Hames Av S
- CTGV 8202 C4
Hames Ct S
- CTGV 8202 C5
Hames Rd S
- CTGV 8202 C2
Hamilton Ct
- NBRI 7767 C2
Hamilton Dr
- EAGN 8199 A6
Hamilton Ln
- MNTK 8020 B4
- SHKP 8278 A2
Hamilton Ln N
- BRKP 7678 E7
Hamilton Rd
- EDNP 8107 D2
- MNTK 8020 B4
Hamilton St
- BRNV 8281 B2
- SAVG 8281 B2
- STLP 7936 D7
Hamlet Av
- APVA 8283 B4
Hamlet Av N
- GRNT 7686 C4
- ODLE 7858 C6
- ODLE 7944 C1
Hamlet Av S
- CTGV 8202 C5
Hamlet Ct S
- CTGV 8202 C5
Hamlet Dr
- WDBY 8030 C6
Hamlet Ln S
- CTGV 8202 C5
N Hamline Av
- ARDH 7682 C6
- ARDH 7768 C1
- SHVW 7682 C6
Hamline Av N
- ARDH 7682 C5
- ARDH 7768 C3
- ARDH 7854 C1
- BLNE 7596 B7
- BLNE 7682 B2
- FLCH 7854 D7
- FLCH 7940 D1
- LXTN 7596 B7
- LXTN 7682 B2
- RSVL 7854 C1
- SHVW 7682 C5
- STPL 7854 D7
- STPL 7940 D2
Hamline Av N CO-3
- ARDH 7682 C5
- SHVW 7682 C5
Hamline Av N SR-51
- ARDH 7768 D4

Hamline Av NE
- BLNE 7596 B7
- BLNE 7682 B1
- LXTN 7596 B7
- LXTN 7682 B1
Hamline Av S
- STPL 8026 D3
Hammer Av
- STPL 7943 A3
Hammond Rd
- WtBT 7684 E7
- WtBT 7685 A7
Hampden Av
- STPL 7939 E4
Hampshire Av
- STPL 8025 E5
- STPL 8026 B5
Hampshire Av N
- BRKP 7678 C4
- BRKP 7764 C4
- CHMP 7592 C3
- CRYS 7764 C5
- CRYS 7850 C3
- GLDV 7850 C7
- GLDV 7936 C2
Hampshire Av S
- BMTN 8194 C5
- GLDV 7936 C4
- SAVG 8280 C7
- STLP 7936 C4
- STLP 8022 C1
Hampshire Cir
- BMTN 8194 B3
Hampshire Cir N
- BRKP 7678 C7
- CHMP 7592 A4
Hampshire Ct
- MNDH 8113 C4
- STPL 8026 B5
Hampshire Ct E
- CHMP 7592 C5
Hampshire Ct N
- BRKP 7678 C6
Hampshire Ct W
- CHMP 7592 C5
Hampshire Curv
- BMTN 8194 B3
Hampshire Dr
- MINN 8024 B5
- MNDH 8113 C3
Hampshire Ln
- EDNP 8193 E2
Hampshire Ln N
- BRKP 7678 C5
- GLDV 7850 C6
Hampshire Pl
- BRNV 8282 C7
Hampshire Pl N
- GLDV 7850 C7
Hampton Ct
- MNTK 8020 A2
Hampton Ln
- SHKP 8279 B2
Hampton Rd
- GLDV 7850 E5
- GLDV 7851 A5
Hampton St NE
- PRIO 8279 C6
Hancock St
- STPL 7942 D5
Hand Av
- RSVL 7855 C5
Hankerson Av S
- EDNA 8022 D4
Hanley Rd
- GLDV 7936 A3
Hannibal Cir
- APVA 8283 B6
Hannover Av
- APVA 8283 B5
Hannover Ct
- APVA 8283 A5
Hanover Ct
- APVA 8283 A6
- EAGN 8199 C4
Hanover Ln
- APVA 8283 A7
- EDNP 8106 A6
Hanover Wy
- APVA 8283 A6
Hansen Av
- SHKP 8279 D2
Hansen Ln
- SSTP 8028 C7
Hansen Rd
- EDNA 8022 D6
Hanson Blvd NW
- COON 7593 C4
Hanson Blvd NW CO-11
- COON 7593 C2
Hanson Blvd NW CO-78
- COON 7593 C2
Hanson Ct N
- CRYS 7764 D6
Hanson Rd
- SHVW 7768 E1
Hanson St
- MAHT 7772 C4
Happy Oaks Ct
- MNTK 8021 A2
Harbor Bch NE
- PRIO 8280 C5
Harbor Cir
- SHVW 7769 B3
Harbor Ct
- SHVW 7769 B3
Harbor Ln
- SHVW 7769 B3
Harbor Ln N
- MAPG 7676 D3
- PYMH 7762 C7
- PYMH 7848 D1
- PYMH 7934 D1
Harbor Pl NE
- PRIO 8280 C5
- SAVG 8280 A6
Harborough Ct
- EDNP 8020 C7
Harbor Place Dr
- SHVW 7769 B3

STREET Block City ZIP Map # Grid

Hidden Valley Cove S
- CTGV 8116 C7

Hidden Valley Pond S
- CTGV 8116 A5

Hidden View Rd NE
- PRIO 8279 E6

Hideaway Tr
- MNTK 8020 E2
- MNTK 8021 A1

High Dr
- BRNV 8282 D5

High Rd
- IVGH 8114 A4
- SUNL 8114 A4

High St
- MINN 7938 C1
- NWPT 8115 D2

Highbury Ln
- MNTK 8020 D4

High Cir Wy
- NOAK 7683 C6

Highclere Dr
- BRNV 8282 D3

Highcourte
- RSVL 7855 B2

Highcrest Rd
- RSVL 7853 D5
- STAN 7853 D5

Highcrest Rd NE
- NBRI 7853 D1
- RSVL 7853 D1
- STAN 7853 D1

Highcroft Ct
- EAGN 8283 B1

Highland Av
- MNTK 7934 A7
- SSTP 8028 D6
- WTBL 7771 B6

Highland Blf
- MNTK 8020 B4

Highland Cir
- SHVW 7769 A4

Highland Ct
- SHVW 7769 B4

Highland Dr
- BRNV 8281 B4
- LINO 7597 C1
- SHVW 7769 A3

Highland Ln
- MNTK 8020 C3

Highland Pkwy
- STPL 8025 E3
- STPL 8026 D3

Highland Pl
- COLH 7767 A5
- MNTK 8020 B5
- SHVW 7769 A4

Highland Rd
- BMTN 8194 B5
- EDNA 8022 C7
- MNTK 8020 C3

Highland Tr
- LINO 7597 C1
- MNTK 8020 B5

Highlander Dr
- EAGN 8198 B1

Highland Heights Dr
- MNTK 8020 B5

Highland Hills Blvd
- CTGV 8116 B5

Highland Hills Ln S
- CTGV 8116 B5

Highland Lawns Ct
- MNTK 8020 B5

Highlands Rd N
- BRKP 7679 B4

Highlands Tr N
- ELMO 7858 D2
- GRNT 7858 E1
- ODLE 7858 C3

Highlands Trail Ct N
- ELMO 7858 E2

Highland View Av S
- BRNV 8196 E7
- BRNV 8282 E1

Highland View Cir
- BRNV 8283 A1

Highland View Ln
- BRNV 8196 D7
- BRNV 8283 A1

High Park Dr
- MNTK 8020 A6

High Point Cir
- EDNP 8107 D7

High Point Ct
- MNTK 8020 C3

Highpoint Ct
- WDBY 8030 D4

Highpoint Curv
- BRNV 8282 D4
- MPLW 8029 D2

High Point Rd
- DLWD 7686 C5
- GRNT 7686 C5

Highpoint Rd
- WDBY 8030 D4

High Pointe Ct
- MNDH 8113 C2

Highpointe Dr
- BMTN 8194 D2

High Pointe Rd
- MNDH 8113 C2

Highpointe Ter
- BMTN 8194 D2

Highpointe Cove
- RSVL 7855 B2

High Ridge Cir
- MNDH 8113 C1

Highridge Ct
- MPLW 7856 D1
- VADH 7856 D1

Highridge Ter
- EAGN 8112 B5

High Site Dr
- EAGN 8112 C7

Hightower
- MNTK 8020 C3

Highview Av
- EAGN 8112 B5

N Highview Cir
- MNDH 8027 A7

S Highview Cir
- MNDH 8027 A7

Highview Ct N
- CHMP 7591 D5

Highview Dr
- BRNV 8282 C4
- NBRI 7767 C4

Highview Pl
- MINN 8024 A5
- MNTK 8020 D3
- SHVW 7682 E3

Highview Ter
- EAGN 8112 B6

Highway Av
- ARDH 7682 A7
- MNDS 7681 E7
- MNDS 7682 A7

Highway Dr
- LCAN 7856 A5
- MPLW 7856 A5

N Highway Dr
- BLNE 7682 B2
- LXTN 7682 A2

S Highway Dr
- BLNE 7682 A2
- LXTN 7682 B2

Highway 10 Service Rd NE
- BLNE 7680 D3
- MNDS 7681 B4
- SPLP 7680 E3
- SPLP 7681 A4

Highwood Av E
- MPLW 8029 C4
- STPL 8029 C4
- WDBY 8029 E4

Highwood Dr
- BMTN 8107 E5
- BMTN 8108 B5
- EDNA 8022 B6
- MNTK 8020 B3

Highwood Dr W
- EDNA 8022 B5

Highwood Rd
- STLP 7937 A4

Highwood Wy
- APVA 8282 E4
- APVA 8283 A4

Hilary Pth
- NgTp 8288 E5

Hilding St
- STPL 8029 B1

Hill Av
- WTBL 7771 B5

Hill Ct
- SHVW 7682 E5

S Hill Ln
- STLP 7936 E5
- STLP 7937 A5

Hill Pl N
- CRYS 7850 C4

Hill Pt
- WDBY 8030 D7

Hill Rd
- WAYZ 7934 B3
- WDBY 8030 D7

Hill St
- HOPK 8022 A2
- STPL 7941 D7

Hill Ter
- WDBY 8030 D7

Hill Tr N
- ELMO 7858 D3

Hillaire Av
- WtBT 7771 E4

Hill-A-Way Ct
- EDNA 8108 A3

Hillcrest Av
- STPL 8026 A4

Hillcrest Ct
- BRNV 8282 B4
- WDBY 8030 B2

N Hillcrest Ct
- EDNP 8106 A2

S Hillcrest Ct
- EDNP 8106 B3

Hillcrest Dr
- DLWD 7686 C5
- GRNT 7686 C5
- SAVG 8279 E5
- WDBY 8030 B2

Hillcrest Dr N
- CHMP 7591 C5
- DLWD 7686 C4
- GRNT 7686 C4

Hillcrest Dr NE
- FRID 7767 A3

Hillcrest Ln
- BRNV 8282 B4
- CIRC 7682 D1
- EDNA 8109 A2
- EDNP 8106 A2

Hill Crest Rd
- EDNP 8106 B1

Hilldale Av NE
- STAN 7853 B3

Hilldale Dr S
- SHKP 8279 C4

Hill Farm Cir
- NOAK 7769 C1

Hill Farm Ct
- NOAK 7683 C7
- NOAK 7769 C1

Hilloway Rd
- EDNP 8106 D7

Hilloway Rd W
- MNTK 7935 A5

Hill Ridge Dr
- MNTK 7934 D4

Hillridge Dr
- EAGN 8112 A7
- EAGN 8198 A1

Hill Ridge Ter
- MNTK 7934 D3

S Hills Cir
- EAGN 8199 B3

S Hills Ct
- EAGN 8199 B3

S Hills Dr
- EAGN 8199 B3

S Hills Ln
- EAGN 8199 B3

S Hills Wy
- EAGN 8199 B3

Hillsboro Av
- SAVG 8279 E2

Hillsboro Av N
- BRKP 7591 E6
- BRKP 7763 E3
- CHMP 7591 E3
- GLDV 7849 E5
- NWHE 7763 E5
- NWHE 7849 E5

Hillsboro Av S
- STLP 7935 E4

Hillsboro Cir N
- NWHE 7763 D5

Hillsboro Ct
- SAVG 8279 E6

Hillsboro Ct N
- CHMP 7591 E6
- NWHE 7849 E3

Hillsboro Pl
- NWHE 7849 E3
- SAVG 8279 E5

Hillsboro Wy
- SAVG 8279 E5

Hillsboro Alcove
- SAVG 8279 E5

Hillscourte N
- RSVL 7855 B2

Hillscourte S
- RSVL 7855 B3

Hillsdale Av
- MPLW 8029 C1
- STPL 8029 C1

Hillshire Ln
- BRNV 8281 C7

Hillside Av
- STPL 7939 E2

Hillside Av N
- MINN 7851 D6

Hillside Cir
- EDNA 8108 C1
- MNTK 7935 C5

Hillside Cir N
- CHMP 7591 E4

Hillside Ct
- EAGN 8113 B7
- EAGN 8199 C1
- EDNA 8108 C1
- STPL 7939 D2

Hillside Dr
- EAGN 8199 C1
- EDNP 8106 C6

Hillside Dr N
- CHMP 7591 E5

Hillside Ln
- EDNA 8108 C2

Hillside Ln W
- MNTK 7935 C5

Hillside Rd
- EDNA 8022 C7
- EDNA 8108 C1
- WTBL 7771 D7

Hillside Ter
- MNTK 8020 A1

Hillside Tr S
- CTGV 8202 D2

Hillsview E
- RSVL 7855 B2

Hillsview W
- RSVL 7855 B2

Hillsview Rd
- BRKC 7765 D5

Hillswick Pl
- MAHT 7858 B1

Hillswick Ter
- MAHT 7858 B1

Hillswick Tr N
- BRKP 7679 A4

Hilltop Av
- RSVL 7855 B7

Hilltop Av N
- ELMO 7858 C3
- ODLE 7858 D3

Hilltop Ct
- MNDH 8113 B1
- MPLW 7856 D4
- NSTP 7857 D3

Hilltop Ct N
- CHMP 7591 D5

Hilltop Ln
- EAGN 8198 C5
- EDNA 8022 E4
- STPL 8026 B5

Hilltop Pt
- EAGN 8198 C5

Hilltop Rd
- BRNV 8281 E3
- EDNP 8192 A1
- MNDH 8113 A1
- MNTK 8021 B1

Hilltop St
- WTBL 7771 D7

Hilltop Ter
- MNTK 8020 A5

Hill Trail Ct N
- ELMO 7858 D3

Hillvale Av N
- ODLE 7858 D4

Hillvale Cir N
- ODLE 7858 D4

Hillvale Ct
- ODLE 7944 D1

Hillvale Tr
- ODLE 7944 D1

Hillvale Wy N
- ODLE 7858 D4

Hillview Ln
- VADH 7769 E4

Hillview Rd
- MNDS 7681 D5
- SHVW 7682 B5

Hillview Rd NE
- MNDS 7681 B5
- SPLP 7681 B5

Hillwind Rd NE
- FRID 7766 E4
- FRID 7767 A4

Hillwood Ct
- STPL 8029 C3

Hillwood Dr E
- MPLW 8029 D3
- STPL 8029 C3

Hilo Av N
- HUGO 7686 D2
- ODLE 7858 D7
- ODLE 7944 D1

Hilo Ct N
- ODLE 7944 D3

Hilo Ln S
- CTGV 8202 D2

Hilo Tr S
- CTGV 8202 D2

Hilton Ct N
- PNSP 7858 D1

Hilton Tr N
- MAHT 7772 D7
- PNSP 7772 D7
- PNSP 7858 D1

Hingham Cir
- MNDH 8027 C5

Hinkley St
- WTBL 7771 B3

Hinton Av S
- CTGV 8116 D7
- CTGV 8202 D1
- WDBY 8116 D4

Hinton Tr N
- ODLE 7944 D3

Hinton Park Av S
- CTGV 8116 D7

Hirta Pt
- EAGN 8283 E2

Historic Fort Rd
- HnpC 8025 E7
- HnpC 8026 B7

Hittner Pt
- EAGN 8283 C1

E Hobe Ct
- WtBT 7685 B4

N Hobe Ct
- LINO 7685 B3
- WtBT 7685 B3

S Hobe Ct
- WtBT 7685 B4

W Hobe Ct
- WtBT 7685 A4

Hobe Ln
- WtBT 7685 A4

N Hobe Ln
- WtBT 7685 B4

Hodges Ln
- MNDS 7681 C6

Hodgson Rd
- CIRC 7597 A6
- LINO 7597 A7
- LINO 7683 A1
- NOAK 7683 A6
- NOAK 7769 C3
- SHVW 7683 A7
- SHVW 7769 C3
- VADH 7769 C4

Hodgson Connection
- NOAK 7769 B1
- SHVW 7769 B1

Hoffman Rd
- GEML 7770 E7
- GEML 7771 A6
- VADH 7770 E7
- VADH 7771 A6
- WTBL 7771 A5
- WtBT 7771 A4

Hoffman Rd E
- VADH 7771 A7
- WTBL 7771 A7

Hokah Av
- MNDH 8113 B2

Hokah Dr
- LINO 7597 B7
- LINO 7683 B1

Holasek Ln
- EDNP 8106 E1

Holborn Av
- EDNA 8108 B1

Holden St
- MINN 7938 A2

Holdridge Cir
- WAYZ 7934 A4

Holdridge Dr
- MNTK 7934 B4

Holdridge Ln
- WAYZ 7934 B4

Holdridge Rd E
- MNTK 7934 B4
- WAYZ 7934 B4

Holdridge Rd W
- WAYZ 7934 A3

Holdridge Ter
- WAYZ 7934 B4

Holiday Cir
- MNTK 8020 A4

Holiday Ct
- APVA 8282 E3
- APVA 8283 A7
- MNTK 8020 A6

Holiday Ln
- EAGN 8113 B6

Holiday Rd
- MNTK 8020 A6
- WSTP 8028 B7

Holiday Wy
- MNTK 8020 A7

Holland Av
- APVA 8282 E7
- SSTP 8028 D5

Holland Cir
- EDNP 8193 C4

Holland Ct
- APVA 8282 E7

Holland Ln NE
- SPLP 7680 D4

Holland Jensen Park Rd
- EAGN 8284 E2
- RSMT 8284 E2

Holley Av
- SPLP 8115 E7
- SPLP 8201 E1

Hollins Ct
- APVA 8282 E5

Hollow Ln
- LINO 7683 C2

Holloway Av E
- MPLW 7857 D6
- NSTP 7857 D6
- ODLE 7857 E6

Hollow Park Ct
- BRNV 8281 C7

Hollow Park Ln
- BRNV 8281 B7

Holly Av
- STPL 7941 B7

Holly Av N
- ODLE 7944 D1

Holly Cir NW
- COON 7594 B2

Holly Ct
- LINO 7683 E2
- LINO 7684 A2

Holly Ct E
- LINO 7683 E2

Holly Dr E
- LINO 7684 C1

Holly Dr W
- LINO 7683 E3
- LINO 7684 A1
- WtBT 7683 E3

Holly Ln
- BRNV 8281 E5

Holly Ln N
- MAPG 7676 A3
- MAPG 7762 A1
- ODLE 7944 D6

Holly Rd
- EDNA 8022 A3
- EDNP 8106 D2
- HOPK 8022 A3

Holly St NW
- COON 7594 B1
- COON 7680 B1

Hollybrook Rd
- WAYZ 7934 A3

Hollyhock Cir N
- BRKP 7679 A2

Hollyhock Ln
- HOPK 8021 E2

Hollywood Av NE
- MINN 7853 A2

Hollywood Blvd NW
- COON 7592 E4
- COON 7593 A5

Hollywood Ct
- FLCH 7940 B1

Hollywood Rd
- EDNA 8022 D4

Holman Av
- IVGH 8115 B7

Holmes Av S
- MINN 7937 E7
- MINN 8023 E1

Holm Oak Ln N
- ODLE 7858 D5

Holt St N
- CHMP 7591 B2

Holton Av
- FLCH 7854 C7
- RSVL 7854 C6

Holton St
- FLCH 7940 C1
- RSVL 7854 C4
- STPL 7940 C1

Holyoke Ct
- APVA 8282 E6

Holyoke Ln
- APVA 8282 E6

Holyoke Pth
- APVA 8282 E6

Holyoke St
- APVA 8282 E6

Homedale Rd
- HOPK 8022 B3
- STLP 8022 B3

Homer Av
- SSTP 8028 C4

Homer St
- STPL 8026 D5

Homestead Av N
- HUGO 7600 D7
- HUGO 7686 D1
- ODLE 7944 E1

Homestead Av N CO-8
- HUGO 7600 D7

Homestead Av S
- CTGV 8116 D6
- CTGV 8202 D1

Homestead Cir S
- CTGV 8116 B5

Homestead Ct
- WDBY 8030 E7

Homestead Ct N
- ODLE 7944 D1

Homestead Ct S
- CTGV 8116 D7
- CTGV 8202 D1

Homestead Dr
- WDBY 8030 D7

Homestead Dr N
- HUGO 7686 D2

Homestead Ln
- MNTK 8020 E2

Homestead Ln S
- CTGV 8116 D5

Homestead Pt
- EAGN 8283 E1

Homestead Av Ct
- CTGV 8116 D5

Homeward Hills Rd
- EDNP 8107 B7
- EDNP 8193 B2

Homewood Av
- MAHT 7772 D6
- WTBL 7771 E7
- WTBL 7857 D1
- WtBT 7771 D4

Homewood Pl
- WTBL 7771 D5

Honeye Av N
- GRNT 7686 D4

Honeysuckle Av N
- BRKP 7679 A1

Honeysuckle Ct
- VADH 7769 E4

Honeysuckle Ln
- EDNP 8106 A1

Honeywood Ln
- MNTK 7935 B7

Hoover St NE
- MINN 7853 C7

Hope St
- STPL 7942 B4
- WTBL 7685 E7
- WtBT 7685 E7

Hopewood Ln N
- NWHE 7850 A2

Hopkins Cir S
- BMTN 8196 A5

Hopkins Rd
- BMTN 8196 A4

Hopkins St
- STPL 7942 A5

Hopkins Crossroad
- HOPK 7935 C6
- HOPK 8021 C1
- MNTK 7935 C7
- MNTK 8021 C1
- PYMH 7935 C2

Horizon Cir
- BRNV 8196 E7
- EAGN 8198 D7

Horizon Cir NE
- FRID 7766 C4

Horizon Cir S
- SHKP 8279 D5

Horizon Dr
- BRNV 8196 E7
- BRNV 8197 A7

Horizon Dr NE
- FRID 7766 C4
- PRIO 8279 C4
- SHKP 8279 C4

Horizon Dr S
- PRIO 8279 C4
- SAVG 8279 E5
- SHKP 8279 D5

Horizon Ln
- BRNV 8282 E1

Horizon Pl
- BRNV 8282 E1

Horizon Rd
- BRNV 8196 E7
- BRNV 8282 E1

Horizon St
- VADH 7770 C5

Horn Dr
- MNTK 7934 D3

Hornell Av S
- CTGV 8202 D1

Horseshoe Cir
- EAGN 8198 B4

Horseshoe Ct
- WtBT 7684 D4

E Horseshoe Dr
- SHVW 7769 B7
- SHVW 7855 B1

W Horseshoe Dr
- SHVW 7769 B7
- SHVW 7855 B1

Horseshoe Ln
- SUNL 8113 E4
- WDBY 8030 E5

Horseshoe Rd
- WDBY 8030 A6

Horseshoe Tr
- EDNP 8193 B3

Horten Pt
- EAGN 8283 E2

Horton Av
- STPL 7940 D2

Hosford Hills Rd
- EAGN 8198 C4

Hotel Ln
- EDNP 8192 D2
- SSTP 8115 A5

Houle Cir
- CTRV 7598 D4

Howard Av
- WTBL 7771 C6

Howard Ct
- MPLW 7857 C2
- STPL 7943 C6

Howard Ln
- EDNP 8106 C3

Howard St N
- MPLW 7857 C2
- NSTP 7857 C6
- STPL 7857 C7
- STPL 7943 C4

Howard St NE
- MINN 7852 D4

Howard St S
- STPL 8029 C3

Howe Ln
- BRKC 7764 E3

Howell Av
- FLCH 7854 A7
- STPL 8026 A4

Howell Dr N
- MINN 7937 E1

Howell St N
- STPL 7940 A7

Howell St S
- STPL 8026 A4

Howkins St
- NWPT 8116 A3
- WDBY 8116 A3

Hoxie Av
- WtBT 7685 D6

Hoyt Av E
- MPLW 7943 C1
- STPL 7941 E1
- STPL 7942 D1
- STPL 7943 C1

Hoyt Av W
- FLCH 7939 E1

STREET Block City ZIP Map # Grid

Hoyt Av W
- FLCH 7940 A1
- LAUD 7939 E1
- STPL 7939 E1
- STPL 7940 C1
- STPL 7941 C1

Hubbard Av
- STPL 7940 D4
- STPL 7941 A4

Hubbard Av N
- ROBB 7851 A3

Huber Dr
- MNDH 8113 C2
- SUNL 8113 D2

Hudalla Av N
- ODLE 7944 D3

Hudron Tr
- LINO 7684 A2

Hudson Av
- ARDH 7768 A7
- NBRI 7768 A7

Hudson Blvd N
- LNDF 7944 B6
- ODLE 7944 E6

Hudson Pl E
- MPLW 7943 D6
- STPL 7943 C6

Hudson Rd
- LNDF 7944 A6
- MPLW 7943 D7
- ODLE 7943 E6
- ODLE 7944 A6
- STPL 7942 C6
- STPL 7943 A6
- WDBY 7943 D7
- WDBY 7944 D7

Hughes Av
- FRID 7766 C5

Hughes Ct
- APVA 8282 E3

Hugo Av
- FRID 7680 A4

Hugo Ct
- WtBT 7685 D6

Hugo Rd
- HUGO 7685 C3
- WtBT 7685 C4

Hugo St NE
- FRID 7680 B4

Hull Rd
- MNTK 8020 E2
- MNTK 8021 A2

Humboldt Av
- STPL 8028 A2
- WSTP 8028 A4
- WSTP 8114 A1

Humboldt Av N
- BRKC 7765 E3
- BRKP 7679 E7
- BRKP 7765 E1
- MINN 7765 E7
- MINN 7851 E4
- MINN 7937 E1

Humboldt Av S
- BMTN 8109 E5
- BMTN 8195 E2
- BRNV 8281 E4
- MINN 7937 E5
- MINN 8023 D1
- RHFD 8109 E3

Humboldt Cir N
- BRKP 7765 D1

Humboldt Cir S
- BMTN 8195 E3

Humboldt Ln
- MINN 7765 E7

Humboldt Pl N
- BRKC 7765 D3

Humbolt Av S
- RHFD 8109 E2

Hummingbird Ct
- COON 7593 D6

Hummingbird Ct NE
- PRIO 8279 B6

Hummingbird Dr
- APVA 8282 E3

Hummingbird Ln
- APVA 8282 E3
- EAGN 8198 E2
- EDNP 8106 D1
- NOAK 7769 E2

Hummingbird St NW
- COON 7593 B1

Hummingbird Tr NE
- PRIO 8279 B7

Humphrey Dr
- HnpC 8111 B3

Hunt Pl
- STPL 7939 D4

Hunter Ln
- EAGN 8198 E3
- MNDH 8026 D7
- MNDH 8112 D1

Hunter St
- EDNA 8022 C7

Hunters Ct
- APVA 8282 E4
- APVA 8283 A4
- ARDH 7768 D7

Hunters Ln
- SAVG 8280 B7

Hunters Ovlk
- EAGN 8199 A4

Hunters Rdg
- LINO 7598 B6

Hunters Tr
- CTRV 7598 C6

Hunters Wy
- APVA 8282 E5

Hunters Glen Rd
- MNTK 7934 A3
- WAYZ 7934 A3

Hunters Ridge Ln
- CTRV 7598 C6

Hunters Ridge Rd
- MNTK 8020 D3

Huntingdon Cir
- MNTK 8021 A1

Huntingdon Dr
- MNTK 8021 A2

Huntingdon Ln
- MNTK 8021 A2

Huntington Av
- SAVG 8281 B4

Huntington Av S
- STLP 7937 A6
- STLP 8023 A1

Huntington Cir
- APVA 8282 E3
- APVA 8283 A5

Huntington Ct S
- MPLW 8029 D3

Huntington Dr
- APVA 8282 E5
- EDNP 8193 C4

Huntington Ln
- APVA 8282 E3

Huntington Ter
- APVA 8282 E5

Hunting Valley Rd
- LAUD 7939 D1
- STPL 7939 D2

Huntley Ct
- APVA 8282 E5

Hupp St NE
- BLNE 7596 D2

Hurley Av E
- WSTP 8028 A3

Hurley Av W
- WSTP 8027 D3

Huron Av
- MAHT 7772 D6

Huron Blvd SE
- MINN 7939 B3

Huron Ct
- APVA 8282 E5
- EAGN 8199 C7

Huron Pl
- EDNP 8106 B4

Huron St
- RSVL 7854 D3
- STPL 7854 D7
- STPL 7940 D1

Huron St SE
- MINN 7939 C5

Hyacinth Av E
- STPL 7941 E2
- STPL 7942 B2
- STPL 7943 B2

Hyacinth Av W
- STPL 7941 D2

Hyde Av N
- HUGO 7600 D6
- MAHT 7772 D6

Hyde Av S
- CTGV 8116 D7
- CTGV 8202 E2

Hyde Ct S
- CTGV 8202 E2

Hyde Ln S
- CTGV 8202 E2

Hyde Park Cir
- EDNA 8108 B3

Hyde Park Dr
- EDNA 8108 B3

Hyde Park Ln
- EDNA 8108 B4

Hydram Av N
- ODLE 7944 D1

Hydram Av S
- CTGV 8116 D7

Hydram Wy N
- ODLE 7944 D1

Hydram Av Ct N
- ODLE 7944 D3

Hyland Ct
- EAGN 8199 A3

Hyland Pl
- BMTN 8194 E2

Hyland Ter
- EDNP 8107 C6

Hyland Courts Dr
- BMTN 8194 D2

Hyland Creek Cir
- BMTN 8194 C1

Hyland Creek Rd
- BMTN 8108 D7
- BMTN 8194 D1

Hyland Greens Dr
- BMTN 8194 D3

Hynes Av N
- ODLE 7944 D1

Hynes Av S
- CTGV 8202 E1

Hythe St
- FLCH 7853 E6
- RSVL 7853 E6
- STPL 7939 E2

Hytrail Av N
- ELMO 7858 D2
- PNSP 7858 D1

Hytrail Av Ct N
- PNSP 7858 D1

I

I-35E
- APVA 8282 E4
- APVA 8283 A3
- BRNV 8282 B6
- BRNV 8283 B2
- EAGN 8112 E3
- EAGN 8197 E5
- EAGN 8198 A5
- EAGN 8283 D1
- LCAN 7855 E2
- LCAN 7856 A1
- LILY 8026 E6
- LILY 8027 A7
- LINO 7599 A1
- LINO 7684 D4
- MNDH 8027 A7
- MNDH 8112 E1
- MNDH 8113 A1
- MPLW 7855 E5
- STPL 7855 E7
- STPL 7941 E5
- STPL 8026 E2
- STPL 8027 B1
- VADH 7770 C5

I-35E
- VADH 7856 C1
- WTBL 7770 D2
- WtBT 7684 D7
- WtBT 7770 D1

I-35 E Service Rd
- STPL 8027 A2

I-35E The Great River Rd
- LILY 8026 E5
- LILY 8027 A6
- MNDH 8027 A6
- STPL 8026 E4

I-35W
- ARDH 7681 E5
- ARDH 7682 A7
- ARDH 7768 A5
- BLNE 7596 E4
- BLNE 7681 E2
- BLNE 7682 A1
- BMTN 8109 E5
- BMTN 8195 E1
- BMTN 8196 A7
- BRNV 8196 A7
- BRNV 8282 A7
- LINO 7596 E4
- LINO 7597 E2
- LINO 7598 A1
- LXTN 7596 A7
- MINN 7853 E5
- MINN 7938 C4
- MINN 7939 A1
- MINN 8023 E7
- MINN 8024 B1
- MNDS 7681 E5
- MNDS 7682 A7
- MNDS 7767 E1
- MNDS 7768 A2
- NBRI 7767 E7
- NBRI 7768 A5
- NBRI 7853 A1
- RHFD 8023 E7
- RHFD 8024 B7
- RHFD 8109 E2
- RSVL 7853 E2
- RSVL 7854 A4
- SHVW 7681 E5
- STAN 7853 D5

I-35W Crosstown Hwy
- MINN 8023 E7
- MINN 8024 A7
- RHFD 8023 E7
- RHFD 8024 A7

I-35W E Frontage Rd
- MINN 7938 E1

I-35W N Frontage Rd
- BRNV 8282 A1

W I-35W Service Dr NE
- BLNE 7681 E2
- BLNE 7682 A1

W I-35W Service Rd
- BLNE 7681 E4

I-35W S Frontage Rd
- BRNV 8196 A7
- BRNV 8281 E1
- BRNV 8282 A1

I-35W W Frontage Rd
- MINN 7938 E2

I-94
- BRKC 7764 C3
- BRKC 7765 A3
- BRKC 7766 A6
- BRKP 7763 E2
- BRKP 7764 A3
- ELMO 7944 E6
- LNDF 7944 A6
- MAPG 7676 E7
- MAPG 7762 E1
- MAPG 7763 C1
- MINN 7766 A6
- MINN 7852 A6
- MINN 7938 A2
- MINN 7939 B4
- MPLW 7943 D6
- ODLE 7943 E6
- ODLE 7944 E6
- STPL 7939 E5
- STPL 7940 A6
- STPL 7941 C6
- STPL 7942 A6
- STPL 7943 A6
- WDBY 7943 E6
- WDBY 7944 E6

I-94 Cappelen Memorial Br
- MINN 7939 B4

I-394
- GLDV 7935 E3
- GLDV 7936 E3
- GLDV 7937 B3
- MINN 7937 E3
- MINN 7938 B2
- STLP 7935 E3
- STLP 7936 E3

I-394 Reversible Express Ln
- GLDV 7936 E3
- GLDV 7937 A3
- MINN 7937 E3
- STLP 7936 E3

I-394 Wayzata Blvd
- GLDV 7935 E3
- MINN 7937 E3
- MINN 7938 A3
- MNTK 7934 E3
- MNTK 7935 B3
- STLP 7935 D3

I-494
- BMTN 8107 E5
- BMTN 8108 E5
- BMTN 8109 B4
- BMTN 8110 C4
- BMTN 8111 B4
- EAGN 8111 E4
- EAGN 8112 A4
- EAGN 8113 C4
- EDNP 8020 E7
- EDNP 8021 A7
- EDNP 8107 A3
- HnpC 8110 E4
- HnpC 8111 B4
- IVGH 8113 E4

I-494
- IVGH 8114 D3
- MAPG 7762 E1
- MNDH 8111 E4
- MNDH 8112 E4
- MNDH 8113 E4
- MNTK 7934 D7
- MNTK 8020 D2
- MNTK 8021 A7
- MPLW 8029 D7
- NWPT 8029 E5
- NWPT 8115 D1
- ODLE 7944 C6
- PYMH 7762 E3
- PYMH 7848 E2
- PYMH 7934 D2
- RHFD 8109 E4
- RHFD 8110 C4
- SSTP 8114 D3
- SSTP 8115 A2
- SUNL 8113 E4
- SUNL 8114 B3
- WDBY 7944 C7
- WDBY 8029 E4
- WDBY 8030 A4

I-494 The Great River Rd
- NWPT 8115 D1
- SSTP 8115 B1

I-694
- ARDH 7768 C4
- BRKC 7764 C3
- BRKC 7765 A3
- BRKC 7766 E4
- BRKP 7763 E2
- BRKP 7764 A3
- FRID 7766 B4
- FRID 7767 E4
- LCAN 7769 D7
- LCAN 7855 E1
- LCAN 7856 A1
- MAHT 7858 A2
- MAPG 7676 E7
- MAPG 7762 E1
- MAPG 7763 C1
- MPLW 7856 E1
- MPLW 7857 C1
- NBRI 7767 E4
- NBRI 7768 A4
- ODLE 7857 E2
- ODLE 7858 C3
- ODLE 7944 C1
- PNSP 7858 B2
- SHVW 7768 E5
- SHVW 7769 C7
- VADH 7769 C7
- VADH 7856 C1
- WDBY 7944 C6
- WTBL 7856 E1
- WTBL 7857 C1

I-694 Service Dr N
- MAPG 7763 C1

I-694 Service Rd
- NBRI 7767 B4

I-694 The Great River Rd
- BRKC 7766 A4
- FRID 7766 A4

Ibis Cir NW
- COON 7593 D1

Ibis St NW
- COON 7593 C5

Ice Cir Dr
- MNTK 7934 A5

Idaho Av E
- MPLW 7943 E1
- STPL 7942 D1
- STPL 7943 A1

Idaho Av N
- BRKP 7592 C6
- BRKP 7678 C6
- BRKP 7764 C3
- CHMP 7592 C6
- CRYS 7764 C5
- CRYS 7850 C3
- GLDV 7850 C7
- GLDV 7936 C1

Idaho Av S
- BMTN 8194 C6
- GLDV 7936 C4
- SAVG 8280 C7
- STLP 7936 C6

Idaho Av W
- FLCH 7940 C1
- LAUD 7939 D1
- STPL 7940 E1
- STPL 7941 C1

Idaho Cir N
- BRKP 7678 C7
- CHMP 7592 C6
- CRYS 7850 C3

Idaho Ct N
- CHMP 7592 C6

Idaho Ln N
- BRKP 7678 C7

Ide Ct
- MPLW 7856 E5

Ide St
- MPLW 7856 E7

Ideal Av N
- DLWD 7772 D1
- ELMO 7858 D6
- GRNT 7686 D7
- GRNT 7772 D2
- MAHT 7772 D3
- ODLE 7858 D7
- ODLE 7944 D6
- PNSP 7772 D6

Ideal Av S
- CTGV 8116 D6
- CTGV 8202 E1
- CTGV 8288 D1
- WDBY 8116 D4

Iden Av S
- CTGV 8116 D7
- CTGV 8202 E3

Idsen Av S
- CTGV 8116 E6

Idylwood Dr
- EDNA 8022 B5

Idylwood Ln
- EDNA 8022 A5

Idylwood Pl
- EDNA 8022 B6

Idylwood Rd
- MNTK 8020 C2

Iglehart Av
- STPL 7939 E6
- STPL 7940 B6
- STPL 7941 B6

Ikea Wy
- BMTN 8110 E5

Ikola Wy
- EDNA 8107 E3

Ilex Cir NW
- COON 7594 B2

Ilex St NW
- COON 7594 B1

Illies Av N
- GRNT 7686 D3
- HUGO 7686 D3

Illies Av S
- CTGV 8116 E7

Illion Av
- MINN 7851 D6

Imation Pl
- ODLE 7858 C6

Immanuel Av N
- ODLE 7944 E6

Immanuel Av S
- CTGV 8116 E7
- CTGV 8202 D1

Immanuel Av Ct S
- CTGV 8116 E7

Impatiens Av N
- BRKP 7678 E2
- BRKP 7679 A2

Impatiens Ct N
- BRKP 7679 A3

Impatiens Ln N
- BRKP 7679 B2

Imperial Av N
- ELMO 7944 E1
- GRNT 7686 D3
- HUGO 7686 D3
- ODLE 7944 E6

Imperial Av S
- CTGV 8116 E7
- CTGV 8202 E3

Imperial Ct N
- GRNT 7772 D4

Imperial Dr E
- WSTP 8028 A5

Imperial Dr N
- BRKP 7764 E1

Imperial Dr W
- WSTP 8027 E5
- WSTP 8028 A5

Imperial Ln
- NBRI 7767 E7
- NBRI 7853 D1

Imperial Rdg
- WSTP 8027 E5

Imperial Av Cir S
- CTGV 8116 E6

Imperial Av Ct S
- CTGV 8116 D7

Inca Ln
- NBRI 7767 C5

Indahl Av N
- GRNT 7772 E3

Indahl Av S
- CTGV 8202 E2

Indepence Av
- SHKP 8278 A4

Independence Av
- SAVG 8279 E2

Independence Av N
- BRKP 7591 E6
- CHMP 7591 E2
- GLDV 7849 E7
- NWHE 7763 E5
- NWHE 7849 E1

Independence Av S
- STLP 7935 E4
- STLP 8021 E1

Independence Cir N
- NWHE 7849 E5

Independence Ct N
- CHMP 7591 E3

Independence Ln N
- CHMP 7591 E2

India Ln
- EDNP 8192 D2

Indian Blvd S
- CTGV 8116 E7

Indian Pl
- ARDH 7768 A7

Indian Rd W
- MNTK 7934 D5

Indian Wy
- MPLW 7857 D3
- NSTP 7857 D2

Indian Wy W
- EDNA 8107 E1

Indiana Av N
- BRKC 7765 A2
- BRKC 7851 A1
- BRKP 7593 D7
- BRKP 7679 A1
- CHMP 7593 A6
- GLDV 7851 A6
- GLDV 7937 A2
- ROBB 7851 A1

Indian Blvd Ct S
- CTGV 8116 E7

Indian Chief Rd
- EDNP 8020 D7
- EDNP 8106 D1

Indian Hills Cir
- EDNA 8107 E1

Indian Hills Dr
- CIRC 7682 D3
- SHVW 7682 D3

Indian Hills Ln
- CIRC 7682 D3
- SHVW 7682 D3

Indian Hills Rd
- EDNA 8107 E1
- EDNA 8108 A1

Indian Hills Pass
- EDNA 8108 A1

Indian Oaks Cir
- ARDH 7768 D4

Indian Oaks Ct
- ARDH 7768 C4

Indian Oaks Tr
- ARDH 7768 C4

Indianola Av
- EDNA 8023 A5

Indian Pond Cir
- EDNA 8108 A1

Indian Wells Tr
- DLWD 7686 A5

Indigo Ct S
- CTGV 8116 B6

Indigo Dr
- EDNP 8192 B3

Indigo Tr N
- GRNT 7686 D7
- GRNT 7772 E1

Industrial Blvd
- PYMH 7848 D6

Industrial Blvd NE
- FRID 7766 B5
- MINN 7853 C7

Industrial Cir S
- SHKP 8192 C7

Industrial Dr
- EDNP 8020 D7
- EDNP 8106 D1

Industrial Park Blvd
- PYMH 7848 E6
- PYMH 7849 A6

Indy Blvd
- CTGV 8202 E3

Ingberg Cir N
- GRNT 7772 E4

Ingberg Ct N
- GRNT 7772 E4

Ingberg Ct S
- CTGV 8202 E3

Ingberg Tr S
- CTGV 8202 E3

Ingersoll Av N
- HUGO 7600 E1
- HUGO 7686 E1

Ingersoll Av S
- CTGV 8202 E2

Ingerson Ct
- ARDH 7854 D1

Ingerson Rd
- ARDH 7854 D1
- SHVW 7854 D1

Ingle Ct S
- CTGV 8202 E1

Ingleside Av S
- CTGV 8202 E1

Inglewood Av
- SAVG 8281 A2

Inglewood Av N
- MINN 7937 C2

Inglewood Av S
- EDNA 8023 A2
- STLP 7937 A6
- STLP 8023 A2

Inglewood Cir
- SAVG 8281 A5

Inglewood Ct
- SAVG 8281 A4

Inland Rd
- EAGN 8112 C6

Inman Av S
- CTGV 8116 E7
- CTGV 8202 E2
- CTGV 8288 E1

Inman Ct S
- CTGV 8116 E7

Inner Dr
- CIRC 7596 D7
- STPL 8025 E4

Innsbrook Ln
- BRNV 8282 B7

Innsbruck Cir W
- COLH 7767 A5

Innsbruck Ct
- NBRI 7767 B4

N Innsbruck Ct
- FRID 7767 A4

N Innsbruck Dr
- FRID 7767 A4
- NBRI 7767 A4

Innsbruck Pkwy
- COLH 7767 A5
- NBRI 7767 B5

Innsbruck Pkwy W
- COLH 7767 A5

Innsbruck Tr
- NBRI 7767 B4

Innsdale Av N
- ELMO 7858 E6
- ELMO 7944 E1

Innsdale Av S
- CTGV 8116 E5
- CTGV 8202 E1

Innsdale Av Ct S
- CTGV 8116 E6

Inskip Av S
- CTGV 8116 E5

Inskip Ct S
- CTGV 8116 E6

Inskip Tr S
- CTGV 8116 E7
- CTGV 8202 E1

Interlachen Blf
- EDNA 8022 C4

Interlachen Blvd
- EDNA 8021 E4
- EDNA 8022 B4

Interlachen Cir
- EDNA 8022 C4

Interlachen Ct
- EDNA 8021 E4
- EDNP 8106 E3

Interlachen Dr
- EAGN 8284 C1

Interlachen Rd
- HOPK 8022 B3

International Dr
- BMTN 8111 B4
- GEML 7770 E7
- VADH 7770 E7

STREET	Block	City	ZIP	Map #	Grid
Kaitlin Dr	-	VADH		7770	A4
Kale St	-	MAHT		7772	C4
Kalen Cir	-	WDBY		8116	A4
Kalen Ct	-	WDBY		8116	A4
Kalen Dr	-	NWPT		8116	A4
	-	WDBY		8116	A4
Kaltern Ln	-	GLDV		7937	B4
Kansas Av	-	STPL		8028	C2
	-	WSTP		8028	B3
Kaposia Blvd	-	SSTP		8028	E7
Kara Dr	-	EDNP		8106	C2
Karels St	-	VADH		7856	A1
Karen Cir	-	MNTK		8021	B3
Karen Ln	-	MNTK		8021	B4
Karen Ln NE	-	COLH		7852	C1
Karen Pl	-	WTBL		7771	A1
	-	WtBT		7771	A2
Kari Ln	-	NBRI		7767	D4
Kari's Wy	-	EAGN		8283	E1
Karth Rd	-	LINO		7684	B1
	-	WTBL		7857	C1
Karth Lake Cir	-	ARDH		7768	D2
Karth Lake Dr	-	ARDH		7768	D3
Karyl Dr	-	MNTK		8020	C3
Karyl Pl	-	RSVL		7854	D6
Kasota Av	-	MINN		7939	D2
	-	STPL		7939	D2
Kasota Av SE	-	MINN		7939	C2
	-	STPL		7939	C2
Kasota Cir SE	-	MINN		7939	C2
Kassan Ct	-	SSTP		8028	C4
Kassan Dr	-	SSTP		8028	C4
Kassie Ct	-	HOPK		8022	A2
Kathleen Dr	-	WSTP		8028	A7
	-	WSTP		8114	A1
Kathrene Dr	-	BRKC		7765	A4
Kathryn Cir	-	EAGN		8197	E5
Kathryn Ct	-	EDNP		8107	B7
Kathy Ln	-	WTBL		7771	B7
Kathy Ln NE	-	COLH		7852	C1
Katie Ct	-	ARDH		7854	A1
Katie Ln	-	ARDH		7854	A1
	-	NBRI		7854	A1
	-	WtBT		7685	E5
Kaufman Dr N	-	STPL		7940	D2
Kaufmanis Wy	-	EAGN		8198	D6
Kay Av	-	MNDH		8112	E1
Kaymar Dr	-	EDNA		8022	B6
Kearny Ln	-	EDNP		8193	D3
Keating Av	-	BRNV		8197	A6
Keating Cir	-	BRNV		8197	A6
Keating Ct	-	BRNV		8197	A6
Keefe St	-	EAGN		8112	E6
Keewaydin Pl	-	MINN		8025	B4
Keith Dr	-	CIRC		7596	E7
Keith Rd	-	CIRC		7596	E7
Keithson Dr	-	ARDH		7768	C3
	-	SHVW		7682	D4
Kell Av S	-	BMTN		8109	A6
	-	BMTN		8195	A1
Kell Cir	-	BMTN		8109	A7
	-	BMTN		8195	A4
Kell Rd	-	BMTN		8195	A6
Keller Pkwy	-	LCAN		7856	C4
	-	MPLW		7856	B3
Kellogg Av	-	EDNA		8023	A5
	-	EDNA		8109	A3
Kellogg Blvd E	-	STPL		7941	E7
	-	STPL		7942	A6
Kellogg Blvd W	-	STPL		7941	D7
Kellogg Pl	-	EDNA		8023	A6
Kelly Cir	-	SHKP		8279	E4
Kelly Dr N	-	GLDV		7850	B6
	-	GLDV		7936	B2
Kelsey Ct	-	EDNA		8021	E5
Kelsey Ln	-	EDNP		8106	A7
Kelsey Ter	-	EDNA		8021	E5
	-	EDNA		8022	A5
Kemrich Cir	-	MNTK		8020	A2
Kemrick Dr	-	EDNA		8108	B3
Kendon Ln	-	MNDH		8112	C3
Kenilworth Ct	-	WDBY		8030	D2
Kenilworth Dr	-	WDBY		8030	D2
Kenilworth Pl	-	MINN		7937	C5
Keniston St N	-	CHMP		7591	D1
Kenmar Cir	-	MNTK		7934	E3
Kenmare Dr	-	BMTN		8194	B6
Kennard Av	-	MPLW		7857	A3
Kennard Ct	-	STPL		7943	A7
Kennard St	-	MPLW		7857	A4
	-	STPL		7857	A7
	-	STPL		7943	A2
Kennaston Dr NE	-	FRID		7766	D1
Kennebec Dr	-	EAGN		8197	D3
Kennedy St NE	-	MINN		7853	B7
Kennelly Cir	-	BRNV		8197	A7
Kennelly Ct	-	BRNV		8283	A1
Kennelly Pl	-	BRNV		8282	E1
	-	BRNV		8283	A1
Kennelly Rd	-	BRNV		8197	A7
	-	BRNV		8282	E2
	-	BRNV		8283	A2
Kennet Cir	-	EAGN		8199	C4
Kenneth Ct	-	MNTK		7935	C5
Kenneth St	-	EAGN		8112	E5
	-	STPL		8026	A1
Kenneth Wy	-	GLDV		7850	D6
Kenney Pl	-	EDNA		8108	D1
Kenning Rd	-	EDNP		8106	A7
Kenny Ln	-	WTBL		7771	C6
Kenny Rd	-	STPL		7942	A5
Kensington Av NE	-	PRIO		8279	E6
Kensington Ct	-	MNTK		8020	A2
Kensington Dr	-	EDNP		8193	B4
Kensington Tr	-	EAGN		8198	E6
Kent Av	-	EDNA		8022	D6
Kent Cir	-	SHVW		7769	B1
Kent Ct	-	SHVW		7769	B1
Kent Dr	-	NOAK		7769	B1
	-	SHVW		7769	B1
Kent Ln	-	SHVW		7769	B7
Kent St	-	LINO		7683	B3
	-	RSVL		7855	B2
	-	SHVW		7683	B3
	-	SHVW		7769	B2
	-	STPL		7855	B7
	-	STPL		7941	B2
Kent Wy	-	SHVW		7769	B2
Kentley Av	-	GLDV		7850	E5
Kentucky Av	-	SAVG		8280	C6
Kentucky Av N	-	BRKP		7592	C6
	-	BRKP		7678	C4
	-	BRKP		7764	C2
	-	CHMP		7592	C3
	-	CRYS		7764	C5
	-	CRYS		7850	C5
	-	GLDV		7850	C5
	-	GLDV		7936	C2
Kentucky Av S	-	BMTN		8108	B5
	-	BMTN		8194	B4
	-	GLDV		7936	C2
	-	SAVG		8280	C7
	-	STLP		7936	C7
Kentucky Cir N	-	BRKP		7678	B7
	-	CHMP		7592	C3
	-	CRYS		7850	C2
Kentucky Cir S	-	BMTN		8108	B5
Kentucky Ct N	-	BRKP		7678	C5
	-	CHMP		7592	C5
Kentucky Ln	-	STLP		7936	C5
Kentwood Ct	-	BRNV		8197	A6
Kenwood Ct	-	MPLW		7856	B5
Kenwood Dr E	-	MPLW		7856	B6
Kenwood Dr W	-	MPLW		7856	B6
Kenwood Ln	-	MPLW		7856	B6
Kenwood Pkwy	-	MINN		7937	C5
	-	STPL		8027	A1
Kenwood St	-	MAHT		7772	D3
Kenwood Tr	-	BRNV		8281	D5
Kenwood Tr CO-5	-	BRNV		8281	D7
Kenwood Isles Dr	-	MINN		7937	E6
Kenyon Ct NE	-	BLNE		7595	B1
Kenyon St NE	-	BLNE		7595	B2
Kenzie Ter	-	MINN		7853	B4
	-	STAN		7853	B4
Kenzie Ter CO-44	-	MINN		7853	B4
	-	STAN		7853	B4
Keokuk Ln	-	MNDH		8113	B3
Keri Ann Ln	-	WTBL		7771	A5
Kerry Cir NE	-	FRID		7767	A2
Kerry Ct	-	MNTK		8020	A2
Kerry Ln	-	EDNP		8106	E2
	-	WDBY		8030	E3
Kerry Ln NE	-	FRID		7767	A2
Kerry Rd	-	EDNA		8108	B2
Kerry St NW	-	COON		7592	E1
Kersten Pl	-	EDNP		8193	A3
Keston St	-	STPL		7939	D1
Kestrel Tr	-	SAVG		8280	B7
Kettle Creek Rd	-	EAGN		8198	E3
Kevin Ln	-	SHVW		7769	A2
Kewanee Wy	-	GLDV		7851	B6
	-	ROBB		7851	B6
Key Cir NW	-	COON		7593	C4
Keystone Ct	-	MNTK		7935	B6
Khyber Ln NE	-	COLH		7766	E6
Kiawah Dr	-	EDNP		8107	C6
Kiersten Pl	-	EDNP		8193	A3
Kilbirnie Ter N	-	BRKP		7679	A5
Kilbirnie Wy	-	MAHT		7858	B1
Kilburn St	-	STPL		7940	E3
Killarney Dr	-	GLDV		7937	A1
Killarney Ln S	-	EDNA		8022	A7
Killarney Rd	-	WILL		7772	C6
Killdeer Ct	-	LINO		7597	E7
Killdeer Dr	-	LINO		7597	E7
	-	LINO		7683	E1
Killdeer St NW	-	COON		7593	C1
Killebrew Dr	-	BMTN		8110	E6
	-	BMTN		8111	A6
Kilmer Av	-	STLP		7935	D3
Kilmer Ln N	-	MAPG		7677	E1
	-	MAPG		7763	D1
	-	PYMH		7849	E6
Kilmer Wy	-	MAPG		7763	D3
Kilo Ln	-	EDNP		8192	D2
Kim Pl	-	STPL		7943	B7
Kimball Dr	-	CHMP		7591	E1
Kimball St NE	-	COON		7680	A4
	-	FRID		7680	A4
Kimberly Dr	-	NBRI		7767	C6
Kimberly Ln	-	ARDH		7682	E7
	-	SHVW		7682	D7
Kimberly Rd	-	MNTK		8020	A5
	-	WILL		7772	C6
Kindross Rd	-	MAHT		7772	C6
	-	WILL		7772	C6
King Av	-	SHKP		8278	A2
E King Av	-	MPLW		8029	D2
King St E	-	STPL		8028	A2
King St W	-	STPL		8027	E2
King Creek Rd	-	GLDV		7936	D2
Kingfisher Ct	-	LINO		7683	C1
Kingfisher Ln	-	EDNP		8106	E1
	-	WDBY		8030	D1
King Hill Rd	-	GLDV		7936	D2
Kinglet Ct	-	EAGN		8198	D2
Kingman Ln	-	MNTK		7935	D5
Kings Cir	-	WDBY		8030	C4
Kings Cir N	-	BRKP		7678	E5
Kings Cross N	-	BRKP		7678	E4
Kings Ct	-	SAVG		8279	E6
Kings Dr	-	MNTK		8020	D2
	-	ODLE		7858	A5
	-	WDBY		8030	C4
Kings Hwy	-	MINN		8023	E3
Kings Ln	-	ANOK		7592	B2
Kings Rd	-	EAGN		8283	C1
Kings Ter	-	WDBY		8030	C4
Kings Ter N	-	BRKP		7678	E5
Kingsberry Dr	-	EDNA		8022	A5
Kingsberry Ln	-	MNTK		8020	C4
Kingsbury Dr	-	EAGN		8198	A7
	-	EAGN		8284	A1
Kings Crst	-	EAGN		8198	B4
Kingsdale Dr	-	BMTN		8109	A7
	-	BMTN		8194	E1
Kingsford Pl	-	STPL		7943	A3
Kingslee Rd	-	BMTN		8108	C6
Kingsley Av	-	WTBL		7771	B5
Kingsley Cir N	-	LILY		8026	D7
	-	MNDH		8026	D7
Kingsley Cir S	-	MNDH		8026	C7
Kingsley Ct S	-	MNDH		8026	D7
Kingston Av	-	MPLW		7855	D7
	-	MPLW		7856	A7
	-	STPL		7855	D7
Kingston Av E	-	MPLW		7856	A7
	-	MPLW		7857	D7
Kingston Cir N	-	GLDV		7936	C2
Kingston Ct	-	EAGN		8199	B5
Kingston Dr	-	EDNP		8106	D1
Kings Valley Rd	-	GLDV		7849	E6
	-	PYMH		7849	E6
Kings Valley Rd E	-	GLDV		7849	D6
Kings Valley Rd W	-	GLDV		7849	D6
Kingsview Ct	-	MAPG		7676	C3
Kingsview Ln N	-	DAYT		7590	C2
	-	MAPG		7676	C3
	-	MAPG		7762	C3
	-	MNTK		7934	C2
	-	PYMH		7848	B2
	-	PYMH		7934	C2
Kingsway Ln	-	MNDS		7767	E1
Kings Wood Ct	-	EAGN		8198	B3
Kings Wood Ln	-	EAGN		8198	B4
Kings Wood Rd	-	EAGN		8198	B4
Kingswood Tr	-	EAGN		8198	B4
Kingswood Pond Ovlk	-	EAGN		8198	A3
Kingswood Pond Rd	-	EAGN		8198	B3
Kingview Ln	-	MAPG		7676	C4
Kingview Ln N	-	MAPG		7676	C7
Kinlock Wy	-	SHKP		8278	C2
Kinsel Rd	-	MNTK		8020	D5
Kiowa Av	-	NBRI		7767	C6
Kipling Av S	-	EDNA		8023	A2
	-	SAVG		8281	A3
	-	STLP		7937	A6
	-	STLP		8023	A2
Kipling Ct	-	SAVG		8281	A7
Kipling St	-	STPL		8029	D1
Kirby Puckett Pl	-	MINN		7938	E2
Kirchner Av	-	MNDH		8027	C4
Kirkwood Cir	-	EAGN		8198	E7
	-	MAPG		7677	A4
Kirkwood Cir N	-	PYMH		7763	A5
Kirkwood Ct	-	MAPG		7763	A1
Kirkwood Dr	-	EAGN		8198	E7
Kirkwood Ln N	-	MAPG		7677	A6
	-	MAPG		7763	A1
	-	PYMH		7763	A5
	-	PYMH		7849	A2
	-	PYMH		7935	A1
Kirkwood Wy N	-	MAPG		7677	A3
Kirsten Ct	-	EAGN		8199	B6
Kissell St NE	-	BLNE		7596	D6
Kitkerry Ct N	-	SHVW		7683	B4
Kitkerry Ct S	-	SHVW		7683	B4
Kittson St	-	STPL		7942	A5
Kittwake Cir	-	EAGN		8198	D2
Kiwi Av N	-	BRKP		7679	A2
Klainert St	-	STPL		7941	E1
Klondike Ct	-	EDNP		8106	D5
Knapp Av	-	FLCH		7940	A2
	-	STPL		7940	A2
Knapp Pl	-	STPL		7939	E2
Knapp St	-	FLCH		7940	A2
	-	STPL		7939	E2
	-	STPL		7940	A2
Knight St	-	SHVW		7682	B3
Knights Bridge Rd	-	NBRI		7767	E3
Knightsbridge Rd	-	EDNP		8193	A3
Knob Cir	-	EAGN		8198	B5
Knob Dr	-	EAGN		8198	B5
Knob Rd	-	MNDH		8113	C1
Knob Hill Ct	-	MNTK		8020	B5
Knob Hill Curv	-	MNTK		8020	B5
Knob Hill Ln	-	BRNV		8281	E4
Knob Hill Rd	-	BRNV		8281	E4
Knoble Ct	-	EDNP		8107	B7
Knoll Cir	-	MPLW		7857	D7
	-	NSTP		7857	D7
Knoll Cir E	-	BRNV		8282	B4
Knoll Cir W	-	BRNV		8282	B4
Knoll Dr	-	ARDH		7682	C5
	-	EDNA		8022	A6
	-	LINO		7597	E1
	-	MNDS		7681	D5
	-	SHVW		7682	C5
S Knoll Dr	-	EDNA		8022	A6
Knoll Ln	-	BRNV		8282	B4
Knoll Rd	-	NOAK		7770	C1
Knoll St N	-	GLDV		7850	C7
Knoll Ridge Dr	-	EAGN		8197	E3
Knollway Dr N	-	MNTK		7934	D3
Knollway Dr S	-	MNTK		7934	D3
Knollwood Ct	-	EAGN		8199	A4
	-	MNDH		8027	B5
Knollwood Ct NE	-	BLNE		7595	E3
Knollwood Dr	-	BLNE		7681	B4
	-	EDNP		8106	D7
	-	MNDS		7681	B4
	-	NBRI		7681	B7
	-	NBRI		7767	B1
Knollwood Ln	-	MNDH		8027	B5
Knottingham Cir	-	EAGN		8284	B1
S Knox Av	-	MINN		7937	D7
Knox Av N	-	BRKC		7765	D2
	-	BRKP		7679	D3
	-	BRKP		7765	D1
	-	MINN		7765	D7
	-	MINN		7851	D2
	-	MINN		7937	D1
Knox Av S	-	BMTN		8109	D5
	-	BMTN		8195	D1
	-	MINN		7937	D4
	-	MINN		8023	D4
	-	RHFD		8109	D1
Knox Cir	-	BRNV		8281	D4
Knox Dr	-	BRNV		8281	D5
Koehler Rd	-	VADH		7770	A6
Kohlman Av	-	MPLW		7856	D3
	-	MPLW		7857	B3
Kohlman Ct	-	MPLW		7856	C3
Kohlman Ln	-	MPLW		7856	C3
Kohnens Cir	-	MNTK		7935	B7
Kolff Ct	-	NWPT		8115	E2
Kolff St	-	NWPT		8115	E2
Kolstad Ln	-	EAGN		8198	C3
Kolstad Rd	-	EAGN		8198	C3
Kopp Dr	-	WSTP		8028	B5
Kove St	-	LNDF		7944	A6
E Kraft Rd	-	WSTP		8028	A7
W Kraft Rd	-	WSTP		8027	E7
	-	WSTP		8028	A7
Kraft St	-	SSTP		8028	C7
	-	SSTP		8114	C1
Kral Rd	-	MNTK		8020	C4
Kramer Av	-	IVGH		8115	C7
Krech Av	-	WTBL		7771	B2
Kresse Cir	-	EDNA		8022	A4
Kressin Av	-	MNDH		8113	A3
Krestwood Dr	-	BRNV		8282	B5
Krestwood Ln	-	EAGN		8198	C2
Krey Av	-	VADH		7770	A6
Kristen Ct	-	VADH		7770	C7
Kristin Ct	-	FRID		7767	B3
	-	NBRI		7767	B3
Kruse St	-	WSTP		8028	A4
K-Tel Dr	-	HOPK		8021	C4
	-	MNTK		8021	B4
Kumquat St NW	-	COON		7594	B7
Kurtz Cir	-	EDNP		8106	C1
Kurtz Ln	-	EDNP		8106	C1
Kutcher Ln	-	EDNP		8106	B1
Kutoff Ct	-	EAGN		8199	C1
Kyle Av N	-	BRKC		7765	A2
	-	BRKP		7593	A7
	-	BRKP		7679	A6
	-	BRKP		7765	A2
	-	CRYS		7851	A4
	-	GLDV		7851	A5
	-	ROBB		7851	A3
Kyle Pl	-	GLDV		7851	A6
Kyle Wy	-	EAGN		8197	D6
Kyllo Ln	-	EAGN		8197	E3

L

STREET	Block	City	ZIP	Map #	Grid
La Bon Ter	-	MNTK		8020	B1
Labore Av	-	LCAN		7855	D2
Labore Rd	-	GEML		7770	D6
	-	LCAN		7855	E3
	-	LCAN		7856	C1
	-	VADH		7770	C7
	-	VADH		7856	C1
Labore Industrial Ct	-	VADH		7856	C1
Lacasse Cir	-	LINO		7599	A7
Lacasse Ct	-	LINO		7599	A7
Lacasse Dr	-	LINO		7599	A7
Lacosta Cir	-	DLWD		7686	A6
La Costa Dr	-	DLWD		7686	B6
Lacota Cir	-	BRNV		8281	E4
Lacota Ln	-	BRNV		8281	D4
Lacrosse Av	-	STPL		7943	C3
Lad Pkwy	-	BRKP		7679	B6
Laddie Rd NE	-	SPLP		7680	E4
Ladino Cir	-	EDNP		8106	E7
	-	EDNP		8107	A7
Lady Bird Ln	-	BRNV		8281	E2
Ladyslipper Av N	-	BRKP		7678	E2
	-	BRKP		7679	A2
Lady Slipper Ln	-	VADH		7769	E4
Ladyslipper Ln N	-	BRKP		7679	B2
Lafayette Br	-	STPL		7942	A6
Lafayette Br US-52	-	STPL		7942	A6
Lafayette Frwy	-	IVGH		8114	C3
	-	IVGH		8200	C1
	-	SSTP		8028	C5
	-	SSTP		8114	C1

Minneapolis Street Index

STREET Block City ZIP Map # Grid

Lafayette Frwy
- STPL 7942 A7
- STPL 8028 B1
- WSTP 8028 C5
- WSTP 8114 B1

Lafayette Frwy US-52
- IVGH 8114 C3
- IVGH 8200 C1
- SSTP 8028 C5
- SSTP 8114 C1
- STPL 7942 A6
- STPL 8028 B1
- WSTP 8028 B7
- WSTP 8114 B1

Lafayette Rd N
- STPL 7942 A5

Lafayette Rd N US-52
- STPL 7942 A6

Lafayette Rd S
- SSTP 8028 C6
- STPL 7942 A7
- STPL 8028 A1
- WSTP 8028 C6

Lafayette St NE
- COON 7680 A4
- FRID 7680 A4

Lafond Av
- STPL 7940 E5
- STPL 7941 C5

Lagoon Av
- MINN 7937 D6

Laguna Cir
- EDNP 8193 B2

Laguna Dr
- EDNA 8108 E2
- EDNA 8109 A2

Lahoma Ct
- SHKP 8278 A3

Lahti Ln
- MNTK 7935 D7

Lake Av
- ARDH 7682 E6
- BRHV 7772 B5
- SHVW 7682 E6
- WtBT 7685 C4

Lake Av N
- DLWD 7685 E7
- WTBL 7685 D7
- WTBL 7771 D1
- WtBT 7685 D7

Lake Av N SR-96
- DLWD 7685 E7
- WTBL 7685 D7
- WtBT 7685 D7

Lake Av S
- WTBL 7771 B3

Lake Blvd
- MPLW 7857 E2
- NSTP 7857 E2

S Lake Blvd
- BLNE 7595 E2
- BLNE 7596 A1

W Lake Blvd
- BLNE 7595 D1

Lake Ct
- BRNV 8197 A6
- NOAK 7683 B6
- WTBL 7771 B2

Lake Dr
- BLNE 7682 A2
- CIRC 7596 E6
- CIRC 7597 A6
- CIRC 7682 C1
- LINO 7596 E6
- LINO 7597 A6
- LXTN 7682 C1
- MNDH 8113 A4

Lake Dr CO-23
- CIRC 7597 A6
- LINO 7597 C2

W Lake Dr
- NOAK 7683 B7
- SHVW 7683 B7

Lake Dr N
- MINN 7851 C1
- ROBB 7851 A2

Lake Ln
- ARDH 7768 A7
- ARDH 7854 D1
- NBRI 7767 E7

Lake Pl
- MINN 7937 D5

Lake Rd
- MPLW 8029 E3
- ROBB 7851 A1
- WDBY 8029 E3
- WDBY 8030 A4

Lake St
- LAUD 7853 D7
- LCAN 7856 B2
- MPLW 7857 E2
- NSTP 7857 E2
- RSVL 7853 D6
- STPL 7943 C4

E Lake St
- MINN 7938 E6
- MINN 7939 D6
- STPL 7939 D6

W Lake St
- MINN 7937 E6
- MINN 7938 A6
- STLP 7937 B6
- STLP 8022 B1

Lake St E
- LCAN 7855 E4

Lake St NE
- HOPK 8021 C1
- HOPK 8022 A2
- STLP 8022 B2

Lake St W
- STLP 7936 D7
- STLP 8022 C1

Lake Ter E
- WDBY 8030 B5

Lake Ter W
- WDBY 8030 B5

Lakeaires Blvd
- WTBL 7771 C5

Lake Augusta Dr
- MNDH 8112 C2

Lake Bay
- NOAK 7683 B7

Lake Bayview Ct
- SHVW 7769 B7

E Lake Beach Ct
- SHVW 7682 E6

W Lake Beach Ct
- SHVW 7682 E6

Lake Beach Dr
- ARDH 7682 E6
- SHVW 7682 E6

Lakebreeze Av N
- BRKC 7765 A7

Lakebrook Dr
- NBRI 7767 D2

Lake Cove Ct
- SHVW 7769 B7

Lake Ct Cir
- MNDS 7681 C6

Lake Ct Dr
- MNDS 7681 C6

Lake Curve Av N
- ROBB 7851 A2

Lake Curve Ln
- BRKC 7765 A5

Lake Diane Ct
- NBRI 7767 B2

Lake Fall Dr
- EDNP 8107 D7

E Lake Harriet Pkwy
- MINN 8023 E3

W Lake Harriet Pkwy
- MINN 8023 D2

Lakehill Cir
- WTBL 7771 D4

Lake Jane Tr N
- ELMO 7858 E5
- ODLE 7858 D5

Lake Johanna Blvd
- ARDH 7768 B7
- ARDH 7854 B1
- RSVL 7854 B1

Lakeland Av N
- BRKP 7678 A6
- BRKP 7764 B1
- CRYS 7764 D6
- CRYS 7850 E1
- ROBB 7850 D1
- ROBB 7851 A1

Lakeland Av N CO-81
- CRYS 7764 D7

Lakeland Cir
- CTRV 7598 C4

Lakeland Dr
- MAPG 7677 B3
- MNTK 8020 A6

Lakeland Rd
- MNTK 8020 A6

Lake Oaks Dr
- ARDH 7682 E7
- SHVW 7682 D7

E Lake of the Isles Pkwy
- MINN 7937 D6

W Lake of the Isles Pkwy
- MINN 7937 D5

Lake Park Cir
- EAGN 8198 B7

Lake Park Ct
- EAGN 8198 B7

Lake Park Dr
- EAGN 8198 B7

Lake Pine Dr
- NOAK 7683 A6
- SHVW 7683 A6

Lakepoint Ct
- SHVW 7769 A3

Lake Rd Ter
- WDBY 8030 A4

Lake Ridge Dr
- SAVG 8280 B6

Lakeridge Dr
- WTBL 7771 C4

Lake Ridge Dr N
- MAPG 7676 A5

Lake Ridge Rd
- EDNA 8022 B5

Lake Rose Cir
- MNTK 8020 B6

Lake Rose Dr
- MNTK 8020 B6

Lake Rose Ln
- MNTK 8020 B7

Lakes Pkwy
- BLNE 7595 D2

Lakes Pkwy NE
- BLNE 7595 E1
- BLNE 7596 A1

Lake Shore Av
- LCAN 7855 E3
- MNTK 8020 B6

Lake Shore Blvd
- MNTK 7934 A6

Lake Shore Dr
- MINN 7937 B6

Lakeshore Dr
- EDNP 8106 B6

Lake Shore Dr S
- RHFD 8109 E2
- RHFD 8110 A2

Lake Shore Dr W
- RHFD 8109 E3
- RHFD 8110 A2

Lakeshore Pl
- ARDH 7768 B3

Lakeshore Ter
- EAGN 8197 D7

Lakeside Av N
- BRKC 7851 A1
- CRYS 7764 E7
- MINN 7938 A2

Lakeside Cir
- EAGN 8198 C7

Lakeside Cir N
- CHMP 7591 E5

Lakeside Ct
- LCAN 7856 B3

Lakeside Ct N
- CHMP 7591 D5

Lakeside Dr
- EAGN 8198 C7

Lakeside Ln N
- MAPG 7677 A6

Lakeside Pl
- BRKC 7765 A6

Lakeside Rd NE
- FRID 7681 A6

Lakeside Tr N
- CHMP 7591 E4

Lake St Ext
- HOPK 8021 B2
- MNTK 8020 E2
- MNTK 8021 B2

Lake Summit Ct
- SHVW 7769 B7

Lake Valentine Rd
- ARDH 7768 A4
- NBRI 7768 A4

Lakeview Av
- MNDH 8112 C3
- RHFD 8109 D2
- ROBB 7851 A2
- RSVL 7854 E3
- STPL 7940 E2
- STPL 7941 A2
- WTBL 7771 C4
- WtBT 7685 A6

Lakeview Av N
- BRKC 7765 A7

Lakeview Av S
- MINN 7937 B4

Lakeview Cir S
- BMTN 8108 B6

Lake View Ct
- ARDH 7768 B5

Lakeview Ct
- WtBT 7685 A7

Lakeview Ct N
- CHMP 7591 E4

Lakeview Curv
- EAGN 8198 B3

Lakeview Dr
- APVA 8284 B5
- BRNV 8282 C4
- CIRC 7596 E6
- EDNA 8022 E6
- EDNA 8023 A6
- LINO 7596 E5
- SHVW 7769 A1

Lakeview Dr N
- MAPG 7677 A6

Lakeview Dr S
- BMTN 8108 B7

Lakeview Dr W
- MNTK 7935 D4
- STLP 7935 D4

Lakeview Ln NE
- FRID 7681 A5
- SPLP 7681 A5

Lakeview Ln W
- MNTK 7935 B4

Lakeview Pl
- MNTK 8021 A1

Lakeview Pt
- NBRI 7853 E1

Lakeview Rd
- BMTN 8108 B7

Lakeview Tr
- EAGN 8198 B2

Lake Wabasso Ct
- SHVW 7769 B7

Lakewood Av
- WTBL 7771 E5
- WtBT 7771 E4

Lakewood Ct S
- MPLW 8029 D4

Lakewood Dr N
- MPLW 7857 D2
- MPLW 7943 D1
- NSTP 7857 D6
- STPL 7943 C2

Lakewood Dr NE
- SPLP 7680 E4

Lakewood Dr S
- MPLW 8029 D3

Lakewood Ln
- BRHV 7772 A5

Lakewood Hills Rd
- EAGN 8199 A7

Lakota Tr
- LINO 7683 B1

Lambert Av
- MNDS 7681 E6

Lambert Creek Ln
- VADH 7770 A6

Lametti Cir
- ARDH 7768 C7

Lametti Ln
- ARDH 7768 C7
- SHVW 7683 B4

Lamotte Cir
- LINO 7598 C6

Lamotte Dr
- CTRV 7598 C5
- LINO 7598 C5

Lamphere Dr
- GLDV 7850 B5
- NWHE 7850 B5

Lamplight Cir
- WDBY 8030 C3

Lamplight Ct
- WDBY 8030 B3

Lamplight Dr
- WDBY 8030 B3

Lamplighter Ln
- CRYS 7850 D5
- GLDV 7850 D5

Lancaster Av
- STLP 7935 D3

Lancaster Ct
- EDNP 8106 C6

Lancaster Ln
- CHMP 7591 D1
- EAGN 8198 A7

Lancaster Ln N
- CHMP 7591 E6
- MAPG 7591 E7
- MAPG 7677 D1
- MAPG 7763 D3
- OSSE 7677 D3
- PYMH 7849 D5

Lancaster St
- MNTK 7935 D4
- STLP 7935 D5

Landau Cir
- BMTN 8194 A5

Landau Curv
- BMTN 8194 B5

Landau Dr
- BMTN 8194 A5
- WDBY 7944 D7
- WDBY 8030 D1

Landau Alcove
- WDBY 7944 D7

Landing Rd
- EDNP 8193 B4

Landmark Cir
- MNDS 7681 D6

N Landmark Tr
- HOPK 8021 C4

S Landmark Tr
- HOPK 8021 C5

Landon Av
- WDBY 8030 E7

Lane Ct N
- BRKP 7593 A7

Lane Pl N
- STPL 7942 D3

Lane St
- SSTP 8028 C5

Lanewood Cir
- EDNP 8107 C6

Lanewood Ct
- MAPG 7676 C3

Lanewood Ln N
- MAPG 7676 C3
- MAPG 7762 C1
- PYMH 7848 C2
- PYMH 7934 C2

Langdon Pl
- EDNP 8106 C7

Langer Cir
- LINO 7685 A1
- WSTP 8027 E6

Langer Ln
- LINO 7599 A7
- LINO 7685 A1

Langford Cir
- BRNV 8197 A7

Langford Ct
- EDNA 8021 E7

Langford Dr
- EDNA 8021 E7

Langford Pk E
- STPL 7939 E3

Langford Pk W
- STPL 7939 E2

Langley Ct
- EDNP 8106 E7

Lanham Ln
- EDNA 8108 B3

Lannon Ct
- BRNV 8196 D7

Lansford Ln
- MNDH 8027 B7

Lantana Ln
- EDNA 8108 E3

Lantern Cir
- LINO 7597 E7

Lantern Ct
- EAGN 8199 C5

Lantern Ln
- EAGN 8199 C5
- LINO 7597 E7

Laport Dr
- MNDS 7681 D4

Larada Ln
- EDNA 8022 A5

Laramie Tr N
- BRKP 7679 D7

Larch Cir NW
- COON 7594 A1

Larch Ln
- NOAK 7770 C1

Larch Ln N
- MAPG 7677 B6
- MAPG 7763 A2
- PYMH 7763 A7
- PYMH 7849 A1

Larch Pl N
- PYMH 7849 A2

Larch St
- STPL 7941 C4

Larch St NW
- COON 7594 A1
- COON 7680 A4
- FRID 7680 A4

Larchmore Av
- MNTK 7934 A7

Larchwood Dr
- MNTK 7934 B6
- MNTK 8020 A1

Larc Industrial Blvd
- BRNV 8196 D7
- BRNV 8282 D1

La Rivier Ct
- EDNP 8192 C1

Lark Av
- MPLW 7856 D5
- MPLW 7857 A5

Larkin Cir
- MNTK 7934 E4

Larkin Dr
- MNTK 7934 E4

Larkspur Ln
- EDNA 8108 E2
- EDNP 8107 B7
- EDNP 8193 B1
- NOAK 7769 D2

Larpenteur Av E
- MPLW 7855 D7
- MPLW 7856 D7
- MPLW 7857 A7
- ODLE 7857 E7
- STPL 7855 D7
- STPL 7856 A7
- STPL 7857 A7

Larpenteur Av W
- FLCH 7853 E7
- FLCH 7854 A7
- LAUD 7853 D7

Larpenteur Av W
- MINN 7853 D7
- MPLW 7855 D7
- RSVL 7854 E7
- RSVL 7855 C7
- STPL 7854 E7
- STPL 7855 C7

Larry Ln
- NWPT 8115 D1

Larry Ho Dr
- MPLW 7943 C7
- STPL 7943 C7

Larson Ct
- SHVW 7769 A2

Larson Ln
- SHVW 7769 A1

Larson Rd
- SHVW 7769 A1

Lasalle Av
- MINN 7938 B4

La Salle St
- STPL 7939 E5

Lassen Ct
- BRNV 8283 A3

Lasso Ln
- EAGN 8199 B6

Latta St
- WtBT 7685 A7

Laura Av
- EDNA 8022 D3

Laura Ct
- MNDH 8027 B5

Laura Ln
- MNTK 7935 A7
- MNTK 8021 A1
- SHVW 7769 B2

Laura St
- MNDH 8027 C5

Laurel Av
- GLDV 7936 D3
- SPLP 8115 E7
- SPLP 8201 E1
- STPL 7940 A7
- STPL 7941 B7

W Laurel Av
- MINN 7938 C5

Laurel Av N
- MINN 7937 E3

Laurel Av W
- MINN 7937 D3

Laurel Ct
- EAGN 8197 D3

Laurel Dr
- EDNP 8193 D2

Laurel Ln
- BMTN 8110 B7

Laurel Rd
- MAHT 7772 C2
- MNTK 7934 D4

Laurere Av
- LINO 7683 A2

Laurie Ct
- MPLW 7856 B5

Laurie Rd E
- MPLW 7856 E5
- MPLW 7857 B5
- NSTP 7857 B5

Laurie Rd W
- RSVL 7853 E5
- RSVL 7854 D5

Lavalle Ct
- WtBT 7685 A6

Lavelle Dr
- CTRV 7598 C4

Lawn Av
- GRNT 7772 D3

Lawn Ter
- GLDV 7936 E3

Lawnview Av
- SHVW 7682 E4

Lawrence Dr
- SPLP 8115 E6
- SPLP 8116 A6

Lawrence Rd
- BRKC 7765 B4

Lawson Av E
- STPL 7941 E3
- STPL 7942 A3

Lawson Av W
- STPL 7941 B3

Lawson Ln
- EDNP 8193 C3

Lawton Ln
- NOAK 7683 B7

Lawton St
- STPL 7941 B7
- STPL 8027 C2

Layman Ln
- BMTN 8196 B3

Lea Ct N
- LINO 7596 E4

Lea Rd
- BMTN 8108 B5

Leaftop Cir
- EDNP 8193 D2

Leander Ln
- COLH 7767 A7

Leann Dr
- WDBY 8030 C3

Leaping Deer Ln
- EDNP 8107 C6

Leber Ln
- GLDV 7937 A2

Lee Av
- FLCH 7940 B1

Lee Av N
- BRKC 7765 A2
- BRKP 7679 A6
- BRKP 7765 A1
- CRYS 7851 A4
- GLDV 7851 A6
- ROBB 7851 A3

Lee Dr
- EDNP 8193 D3

Lee St
- MPLW 7856 B6

Lee Wy
- MNTK 8020 C5

Leech St
- STPL 7941 D4

Leech St
- STPL 8027 C1

Leeds Pl
- WILL 7772 C6

Leesborough Av
- EDNP 8106 D1

Lee Valley Cir
- EDNA 8108 C2

Lee Valley Rd
- EDNA 8108 B3

Leeward Cir
- EDNP 8107 C7

Leeward Wy
- LCAN 7856 B2

Legend Dr
- GLDV 7851 A6

Legend Ln
- GLDV 7851 A6

Lehman Ln NE
- BLNE 7595 C3

Leibel St
- HUGO 7685 D3
- WtBT 7685 D4

Leisure Ct
- BRNV 8281 E4

Leisure Ln
- BRNV 8281 E4

Leland Rd
- MPLW 7856 D5

Leland St
- STPL 8026 D5

Lemay Av
- MNDH 8112 B3

Lemay Lake Dr
- MNDH 8112 C2

Lemay Lake Rd
- MNDH 8112 C3

Lemieux Cir
- EAGN 8198 B2

Lemire Cir
- WTBL 7771 B1

Le Mire Ln
- WTBL 7685 B7
- WTBL 7771 B1

Lena Ln
- COON 7593 D2

Lennell Dr
- MNTK 8020 D2

Lennox St
- STPL 8029 C4

Lenore Ln
- EAGN 8197 E7
- EAGN 8283 E1

Leo Ct
- EAGN 8198 D6

Leona Dr
- NBRI 7767 B1

Leona Rd
- EDNP 8107 B5

Leonard Av
- LINO 7596 E3

Leonard Ct
- MPLW 8029 C6
- STPL 8029 C6

Leonard Ln
- EAGN 8199 C4

Leone Av
- STPL 7943 A6

Leslee Ln
- EDNA 8022 B6

Lesley Ln
- EDNP 8106 C2

Letendre St
- EAGN 8198 A1

Levee Rd
- STPL 7941 E7
- STPL 8027 C2

Levenworth Av
- HnpC 8111 E1

Lever Ct NE
- BLNE 7596 D1

Lever St NE
- BLNE 7596 D6
- CIRC 7596 D6

Lewis Ct
- BRNV 8197 B6

Lewis Rd
- GLDV 7936 A1

Lewis St
- SSTP 8028 C4
- WSTP 8028 C4

Lewis Ridge Pkwy
- EDNA 8108 C3

Lexie Ct
- EAGN 8199 B5

Lexington Av
- EDNA 8022 E6
- MNTK 8020 B2

Lexington Av N
- ARDH 7682 D7
- ARDH 7768 D2
- ARDH 7854 D2
- BLNE 7596 C6
- BLNE 7682 C3
- CIRC 7596 C6
- LXTN 7596 C7
- RSVL 7854 E7
- SHVW 7682 D7
- SHVW 7768 E7
- SHVW 7854 D2
- STPL 7854 E7

Lexington Av N CO-51
- ARDH 7682 D7
- ARDH 7768 E7
- ARDH 7854 D2
- BLNE 7682 C3
- RSVL 7854 D3
- SHVW 7682 D7
- SHVW 7768 D6
- SHVW 7854 D2
- STPL 7854 E7

Lexington Av NE
- BLNE 7596 C5
- BLNE 7682 C1
- CIRC 7596 C7
- CIRC 7682 C2
- LXTN 7596 C7
- LXTN 7682 C2
- SHVW 7682 C3

Minneapolis Street Index

STREET Block	City	ZIP	Map #	Grid
Lexington Av S				
-	EAGN		8112	E7
-	EAGN		8198	E1
-	LILY		8026	E7
-	MNDH		8026	E7
-	MNDH		8112	E1
Lexington Cir				
-	MNTK		8020	B2
Lexington Dr				
-	EDNP		8107	C6
Lexington Ln				
-	SHKP		8278	A3
Lexington Pkwy N				
-	RSVL		7854	E7
-	STPL		7854	E7
-	STPL		7940	E3
Lexington Pkwy N CO-51				
-	RSVL		7854	E7
-	STPL		7854	E7
Lexington Pkwy S				
-	STPL		7940	E7
-	STPL		8026	E3
Lexington Rdg				
-	EAGN		8198	D5
Lexington St				
-	EDNA		8023	A6
Lexington Wy				
-	EAGN		8198	E5
Lexington Pointe Pkwy				
-	EAGN		8198	E6
-	EAGN		8199	A6
Lexington Ridge Ct				
-	EAGN		8198	D5
Leyte St NE				
-	BLNE		7682	A1
Liatris Ln				
-	EDNP		8192	C3
Libby Ln				
-	VADH		7856	B1
Liberty Ln				
-	EAGN		8197	B5
-	LXTN		7682	B1
Liberty Pl				
-	SSTP		8028	C7
Liberty St NE				
-	FRID		7680	A5
Library Ln				
-	STLP		7936	C7
-	STLP		8022	C1
Liggett St				
-	FLCH		7940	B2
Lightner Pl				
-	STPL		7941	D4
Lilac Dr				
-	EDNP		8192	B2
N Lilac Dr				
-	BRKC		7765	B7
-	BRKC		7851	A1
-	GLDV		7850	E7
-	GLDV		7936	E2
-	ROBB		7851	A1
Lilac Dr N				
-	BRKC		7765	E4
-	BRKC		7766	A4
-	CRYS		7850	E4
-	GLDV		7850	E4
-	GLDV		7936	E2
Lilac Dr S				
-	GLDV		7936	E4
-	GLDV		7937	A4
-	STLP		7936	E4
Lilac Ln				
-	LILY		8026	E6
-	MNDH		8026	E7
-	SHVW		7769	C4
-	WTBL		7771	C4
Lilac St				
-	BLNE		7596	E2
-	LINO		7596	E2
-	LINO		7597	B2
Lillehei Plz				
-	LCAN		7855	D5
Lillian Ln				
-	EDNP		8106	A2
Lily St NW				
-	COON		7592	E1
Lilydale Rd				
-	LILY		8027	B4
-	MNDH		8027	A5
-	STPL		8027	B4
Lily Pond Ln				
-	VADH		7769	E4
Lily Pond Rd				
-	NOAK		7770	B2
Lilywood Ln				
-	LILY		8026	E6
-	MNDH		8026	E6
Lima Ln				
-	EDNP		8192	D2
Limerick Dr				
-	EDNA		8108	C1
Limerick Ln				
-	EDNA		8108	C1
-	MNTK		8020	A2
Limestone Dr				
-	EAGN		8197	C6
Limestone Dr S				
-	SHKP		8278	A1
Limonite Ln				
-	EAGN		8197	D4
Lincoln Av				
-	CTGV		8116	A6
-	CTGV		8202	A2
-	MINN		7937	D4
-	NWPT		8116	A6
-	SPLP		8116	A6
-	SPLP		8202	A2
-	STPL		8025	E1
-	STPL		8026	A1
-	STPL		8027	A1
-	WTBL		7771	B2
Lincoln Cir				
-	EDNA		8021	E5
Lincoln Ct				
-	SPLP		8201	E2
Lincoln Ct NE				
-	BLNE		7595	A4
Lincoln Dr				
-	EDNA		8021	E6
-	RSVL		7854	B3

STREET Block	City	ZIP	Map #	Grid
Lincoln Ln				
-	EDNP		8106	A5
Lincoln Rd				
-	DLWD		7772	D2
-	GRNT		7772	D2
-	MAHT		7772	D2
Lincoln St				
-	FRID		7680	B5
NE Lincoln St				
-	MINN		7853	A6
Lincoln St NE				
-	BLNE		7594	E1
-	BLNE		7595	A5
-	BLNE		7681	A1
-	COLH		7853	A2
-	FRID		7767	A5
-	MINN		7853	A5
Lincoln Ter				
-	COLH		7766	E5
-	COLH		7767	A5
Lincolntown Av				
-	MAHT		7772	B7
-	MAHT		7858	B1
-	PNSP		7858	B1
Linda Av				
-	LINO		7683	B2
Linda Cir				
-	LINO		7683	B2
Linda Ct				
-	LINO		7683	A2
Linda Ln				
-	LINO		7683	B2
Lindau Ln				
-	BMTN		8110	E5
-	BMTN		8111	A5
Lindbergh Dr				
-	MNTK		7935	D5
Linde Ln				
-	MNTK		8021	A1
Linden Av				
-	WTBL		7771	A6
W Linden Av				
-	MINN		7937	E3
-	MINN		7938	A3
Linden Av N				
-	BRKP		7679	A2
Linden Cir S				
-	MPLW		8029	E4
Linden Ct				
-	EAGN		8199	A3
Linden Dr				
-	APVA		8282	E7
-	BMTN		8193	E2
-	EDNP		8193	D2
-	MNTK		8020	A1
-	NBRI		7767	B4
Linden Ln				
-	EAGN		8199	A3
-	LINO		7683	B2
-	LNDF		7944	A6
-	MPLW		7856	C3
Linden Ln N				
-	BRKP		7679	A2
Linden Pl				
-	WTBL		7771	C7
Linden Rd				
-	WDBY		8030	A1
Linden St				
-	IVGH		8115	A4
-	SSTP		8115	A4
-	STPL		7941	E5
-	WTBL		7771	A5
Linden Cove				
-	WTBL		7771	A6
Linden Hills Blvd				
-	MINN		8023	C3
Linder Ct				
-	STPL		7942	E5
Lindig Av				
-	FLCH		7940	A1
Lindig St				
-	FLCH		7854	A7
Lindsay St				
-	GLDV		7936	D1
Lindsey Ln				
-	HOPK		8022	A2
Lindstrom Dr				
-	BMTN		8193	E2
-	BMTN		8194	A2
Lindy Av				
-	RSVL		7854	D6
Link Rd				
-	EDNA		8022	D5
Linnea Ln				
-	MNTK		8020	B4
Linner Ct				
-	MNTK		7934	C4
Linner Rd				
-	MNTK		7934	C4
Linner Rdg				
-	MNTK		7934	C4
Linnet Cir NW				
-	COON		7593	C5
Linnet St NW				
-	COON		7593	C4
Linwood Av				
-	STPL		8026	E1
-	STPL		8027	A1
Linwood Av E				
-	MPLW		8029	D3
-	STPL		8029	C3
-	WDBY		8029	E3
Linwood Ct E				
-	MPLW		8029	D3
Lion Ln				
-	SHVW		7769	C3
Lion's Wy				
-	BRKP		7678	E5
Lisa Ct				
-	ARDH		7768	A2
Lisa Ln				
-	ARDH		7768	A2
List Pl				
-	MINN		7937	B7
Lista Pt				
-	EAGN		8283	E2
Litchfield St				
-	STPL		7941	D3
Littel St				
-	EDNA		8023	A3

STREET Block	City	ZIP	Map #	Grid
Little Av S				
-	BMTN		8195	A5
Little Cir				
-	BMTN		8109	A6
-	BMTN		8195	A2
Little Rd				
-	BMTN		8109	A6
-	BMTN		8195	A2
Little Bay Rd				
-	RSVL		7855	B2
Little Canada Rd E				
-	LCAN		7855	D3
-	LCAN		7856	A3
Little Canada Rd W				
-	LCAN		7855	D3
-	RSVL		7855	D3
Little Cir Dr				
-	LCAN		7855	D2
Little Crow Dr				
-	SSTP		8028	C5
Little Crow Dr NW				
-	PRIO		8278	D5
Little Fox Ln				
-	GEML		7770	D6
-	VADH		7770	D6
Little John Dr				
-	CIRC		7682	D2
Little Linden Curv				
-	WTBL		7771	C7
Live Oak Dr				
-	MNTK		7935	B4
Livingston Av				
-	IVGH		8114	A1
-	STPL		8028	A2
-	WSTP		8028	A5
-	WSTP		8114	A1
Livingston Av S				
-	STPL		7941	E7
-	STPL		8028	A1
Livingston Dr				
-	EAGN		8199	A6
Livingston Ln				
-	EDNP		8106	A7
Lloyd's Dr				
-	MNTK		8020	C3
Lloyd's Ln				
-	MNTK		8020	C3
Llyod Peterson Ln				
-	RHFD		8110	A4
Lobelia Ct				
-	SHKP		8279	C3
Loch Lomond Blvd N				
-	BRKP		7679	A5
Loch Lomond Ct N				
-	BRKP		7679	A4
Loch Lomond Ln				
-	BRKP		7679	A3
Lochloy Dr				
-	EDNA		8022	C5
Lochmere Ter				
-	BMTN		8108	C4
-	EDNA		8108	C4
Loch Moor Dr				
-	EDNA		8108	A3
Lochness Pk				
-	BLNE		7596	C4
Locke Lake Rd NE				
-	FRID		7766	B1
Locke Park Rd				
-	FRID		7680	E7
Lockslie Tr				
-	SAVG		8280	C7
Lockslie Wy				
-	SAVG		8280	C7
Lockwood Dr				
-	MNDH		8113	B4
Locust St				
-	MAHT		7772	C3
-	MINN		7938	E4
Lodestone Cir				
-	EAGN		8197	E3
Lodestone Ln				
-	EAGN		8197	E4
Lodge Cir				
-	BRNV		8281	B2
Lodgepole Ct				
-	EAGN		8198	B6
Lodgepole Dr				
-	EAGN		8198	B6
Loeb St				
-	STPL		7941	B3
Loftus Dr				
-	SAVG		8280	D6
Loftus Ln W				
-	SAVG		8280	C6
E Logan Av				
-	WSTP		8028	B5
Logan Av E				
-	WSTP		8028	A5
Logan Av N				
-	BRKC		7765	D2
-	BRKP		7679	D3
-	BRKP		7765	D1
-	MINN		7765	D7
-	MINN		7851	D5
-	MINN		7937	D1
Logan Av S				
-	BMTN		8109	D5
-	BMTN		8195	D1
-	MINN		7937	D4
-	MINN		8023	D5
-	RHFD		8109	D1
Logan Av W				
-	WSTP		8027	E5
-	WSTP		8028	A5
Logan Ct N				
-	BRKP		7765	D1
Logan Ln				
-	SSTP		8028	C5
Logan Pkwy NE				
-	FRID		7680	C6
Lois Av NE				
-	PRIO		8280	A7
Lois Ct				
-	SHVW		7682	D5
Lois Dr				
-	MNDS		7681	E5
-	SHVW		7682	E5
Lois Ln				
-	EDNA		8108	C2

STREET Block	City	ZIP	Map #	Grid
Lois Ln				
-	LINO		7597	B1
-	PRIO		8278	D5
-	SHVW		7682	E5
Lombard Av				
-	STPL		8026	E1
Lombardy Ln				
-	CRYS		7764	C5
-	MNTK		7935	A3
-	NWHE		7764	C5
-	WTBL		7771	B1
Londin Cir				
-	STPL		8029	C2
Londin Ct E				
-	MPLW		8029	D2
Londin Ln E				
-	MPLW		8029	C2
-	STPL		8029	C2
Londin Pl				
-	STPL		8029	C2
London Ct				
-	BRNV		8196	E5
-	BRNV		8197	A5
London Ct NE				
-	BLNE		7595	B3
London Dr				
-	BRNV		8197	A5
London Ln				
-	EAGN		8284	B1
London Rd				
-	MNDH		8027	C4
London St NE				
-	BLNE		7595	B1
Londonary Av				
-	MNDS		7767	E1
Londonderry Dr				
-	EDNA		8021	E6
Londonderry Rd				
-	EDNA		8021	E6
-	EDNA		8022	A6
-	MNTK		8021	E6
Lone Lake Rdg				
-	MNTK		8021	B6
Lone Oak Cir				
-	EAGN		8112	E6
Lone Oak Dr				
-	EAGN		8113	B6
-	MNTK		8020	E2
-	MNTK		8021	A2
-	SAVG		8280	E7
Lone Oak Ln				
-	EAGN		8112	B6
Lone Oak Pkwy				
-	EAGN		8113	B5
Lone Oak Pt				
-	EAGN		8113	C5
Lone Oak Rd				
-	EAGN		8112	B6
-	EAGN		8113	C6
-	EDNP		8106	D5
-	IVGH		8113	D6
Lonesome Pine Tr				
-	LINO		7683	B1
Long Av				
-	STPL		7939	E4
-	WTBL		7685	C7
-	WTBL		7771	C1
Long Brake Cir S				
-	EDNA		8108	C4
Long Brake Tr				
-	EDNA		8108	B4
Longfellow Av				
-	MINN		8024	E6
-	STPL		8029	C1
Longfellow Av S				
-	BMTN		8110	E7
-	HnpC		8110	E3
-	MINN		7938	E6
-	MINN		8024	E1
-	RHFD		8110	E2
Longfellow St				
-	STPL		8029	B1
Longfellow St NE				
-	FRID		7680	B5
Long Lake Ct				
-	NBRI		7767	D1
-	SHVW		7683	C5
Long Lake Rd				
-	MAHT		7858	A1
-	MNDS		7681	C3
-	NBRI		7681	C7
-	NBRI		7767	D4
-	NBRI		7853	E2
-	RSVL		7853	E1
Long Lake Rd E				
-	MAHT		7858	C1
-	PNSP		7858	C1
S Long Lake Tr				
-	NOAK		7683	D5
Long Marsh Ln				
-	NOAK		7683	B6
Long Meadow Cir				
-	BMTN		8111	A6
Longview Dr				
-	BRNV		8282	D3
-	MNDS		7681	C7
-	NBRI		7681	C7
-	NBRI		7767	C1
-	NSTP		7857	D3
Longview Ln				
-	NOAK		7683	D5
Longview Ter				
-	MINN		8024	A5
Lonsdale Cir				
-	MNTK		7935	D5
Lookout Pl				
-	COLH		7852	C1
Lookout Rd				
-	DLWD		7686	B6
Loon Ln				
-	EAGN		8112	B7
Lorane Av				
-	WtBT		7684	E7
-	WtBT		7685	A6
Lord Ct				
-	EDNP		8193	D2
Loren Dr				
-	MINN		8024	C7
-	RHFD		8024	C7

STREET Block	City	ZIP	Map #	Grid
Loren Rd				
-	RSVL		7854	A6
Lorence Rd				
-	MNTK		8020	D5
Loretta Ln				
-	MAHT		7772	A6
-	MNTK		8020	D3
Loretto St				
-	STPL		8027	D1
Lori Ln				
-	WDBY		8030	E5
Lorien St				
-	MNTK		7935	A5
L'Orient St				
-	STPL		7941	E1
Lorinda Dr				
-	SHVW		7769	A2
Loring Ln				
-	GLDV		7936	D2
-	GLDV		7937	A2
Loring Rd				
-	HOPK		7935	C7
-	MNTK		7935	C7
Lorraine Ct				
-	SHVW		7682	C4
Lorry Ln				
-	MNTK		7935	C2
-	PYMH		7935	C2
Lorry Ln W				
-	MNTK		7935	B2
Lost Lake Ct				
-	MAHT		7772	B6
Lost Lake Rd				
-	MAHT		7772	A6
Lost Rock Ln				
-	NOAK		7683	D6
Lothenbach Av				
-	WSTP		8028	A7
Lotus Ln				
-	BRNV		8281	C4
Louis Av				
-	MNTK		8020	C6
Louis Ln				
-	EAGN		8113	C7
Louis St				
-	STPL		7941	C6
Louisa Av				
-	MNDS		7681	C7
Louise Av				
-	STPL		7943	A7
Louisiana Av				
-	SAVG		8280	C2
Louisiana Av N				
-	BRKP		7678	C4
-	BRKP		7764	B1
-	CHMP		7592	C3
-	CRYS		7764	C4
-	CRYS		7850	C1
-	GLDV		7850	C7
-	GLDV		7936	C2
-	NWHE		7764	C7
-	NWHE		7850	C3
Louisiana Av S				
-	BMTN		8194	B5
-	GLDV		7936	C3
-	SAVG		8280	C7
-	STLP		7936	C6
-	STLP		8022	C1
Louisiana Cir				
-	STLP		8022	C2
Louisiana Cir N				
-	CHMP		7592	C4
Louisiana Cir S				
-	BMTN		8194	B4
Louisiana Ct E				
-	CHMP		7592	C6
Louisiana Ct N				
-	BRKP		7764	B1
Louisiana Ct S				
-	STLP		7936	B6
Louisiana Ct W				
-	CHMP		7592	C6
Louisiana Ln				
-	WtBT		7685	A7
Louisiana Ln N				
-	CHMP		7592	C6
Lourdes Pl				
-	MINN		7938	D1
Love St				
-	MAHT		7772	C3
Loveland Cir				
-	MNTK		7934	E5
Lovell Av				
-	RSVL		7855	B5
Lovell Av W				
-	RSVL		7854	E5
-	RSVL		7855	A5
Lovell Ln				
-	RSVL		7854	D5
Lovell Ln N				
-	RSVL		7854	D5
Lovell Ln S				
-	RSVL		7854	E5
Lovell Rd				
-	BLNE		7682	B1
-	CIRC		7682	C1
-	LXTN		7682	B1
Lovell Rd NE				
-	BLNE		7682	A1
-	LXTN		7682	A1
Lowell Rd				
-	CHMP		7591	E2
Lower 12th St N				
-	ODLE		7944	A4
Lower 35th St N				
-	ODLE		7858	A6
Lower 56th St N				
-	ODLE		7858	A2
Lower 57th St N				
-	ODLE		7858	A2
Lower 67th St E				
-	IVGH		8114	E6
Lower 87th St				
-	IVGH		8199	E2
Lower 94th St S				
-	CTGV		8202	C4
Lower 127th St W				
-	APVA		8283	D3
Lower 129th Ct				
-	APVA		8283	A4

STREET Block	City	ZIP	Map #	Grid
Lower 131st St Ct				
-	APVA		8284	A4
Lower 134th St				
-	SAVG		8281	A4
Lower 134th St W				
-	APVA		8283	E5
-	APVA		8284	A6
Lower 138th Ct				
-	APVA		8283	E3
Lower 138th St W				
-	RSMT		8285	B6
Lower 139th Ct W				
-	APVA		8283	B6
Lower 147th St N				
-	HUGO		7599	E5
Lower Afton Rd E				
-	MPLW		8029	C2
-	STPL		8029	D1
-	WDBY		8029	E2
Lower Buford				
-	FLCH		7940	A1
Lower Colonial Dr				
-	MNDH		8027	B6
Lower D St				
-	MNDT		8112	C1
Lower Elkwood Ct				
-	APVA		8284	B5
Lower Guthrie Ct				
-	APVA		8283	B7
Lower Hamlet Ct				
-	APVA		8283	B4
Lower Hidden Falls Dr				
-	STPL		8026	A7
Lower St. Dennis Rd				
-	STPL		8026	B5
NE Lowry Av				
-	MINN		7852	E4
-	MINN		7853	A4
-	STAN		7853	B4
Lowry Av N				
-	MINN		7851	C5
-	MINN		7852	A4
-	ROBB		7851	A4
Lowry Av NE				
-	MINN		7852	E4
-	MINN		7853	B4
-	STAN		7853	B4
Lowry Ter				
-	GLDV		7850	E4
-	GLDV		7851	A5
Lucia Ln NE				
-	FRID		7766	E1
Ludlow Av				
-	STPL		7939	E3
Ludwig Av N				
-	CHMP		7592	A3
Luella St N				
-	MPLW		7857	B7
-	STPL		7857	B7
-	STPL		7943	B1
Luella St S				
-	STPL		8029	B1
Luigi Cir S				
-	BMTN		8108	D7
Lunar Ln				
-	EAGN		8113	A7
Lund Av NE				
-	SPLP		7680	D4
Lund Pt				
-	EAGN		8283	E2
N Lund Rd				
-	EDNP		8106	B1
S Lund Rd				
-	EDNP		8106	B1
Lunski Ln				
-	EDNP		8106	D7
Luther Pl				
-	STPL		7939	E2
Luther Wy				
-	EDNP		8106	A4
Luverne Av				
-	MINN		8024	B5
Lydia Av E				
-	MPLW		7856	C2
-	MPLW		7857	B2
-	NSTP		7857	D2
Lydia Av W				
-	RSVL		7853	D2
-	RSVL		7854	E2
-	STAN		7853	D2
Lydia Cir				
-	WDBY		8030	C7
Lydia Ct				
-	RSVL		7853	D2
Lydia Dr				
-	BMTN		8110	B7
-	WDBY		8030	B7
Lydia Dr W				
-	RSVL		7854	E2
Lydia Ln				
-	WDBY		8030	B7
Lydia Alcove				
-	WDBY		8030	B7
Lydia Bay				
-	WDBY		8030	B7
Lyle Cir				
-	EDNA		8022	C6
Lyman Ln				
-	MNTK		7934	B4
Lyn Curve Av N				
-	MINN		7852	B3
E Lyndale Av N				
-	BRKC		7766	A6
-	MINN		7766	A7
-	MINN		7938	A2
S Lyndale Av				
-	MINN		7938	A4
W Lyndale Av N				
-	BRKC		7766	A6
-	MINN		7766	A6
-	MINN		7938	A2
Lyndale Av N				
-	BRKC		7766	A5
-	MINN		7766	A6
-	MINN		7852	A7
-	MINN		7938	A1
Lyndale Av S				
-	BMTN		8110	A7
-	BMTN		8196	A2
-	MINN		7938	A4

INDEX 28

Lyndale Av S — Matterhorn Ln

Minneapolis Street Index

STREET — Block, City, ZIP, Map #, Grid

Lyndale Av S
- MINN 8024 A1
- RHFD 8024 A7
- RHFD 8110 A2

Lyndale Av S SR-121
- MINN 8024 A6

Lyndale Cir
- BMTN 8196 A3
- BRNV 8281 E4

Lyndale Cir S
- BMTN 8110 A6

Lyndale Connector
- MINN 8023 E7
- MINN 8024 A6
- RHFD 8023 E7

Lyndale Connector SR-121
- MINN 8023 E7
- MINN 8024 A6
- RHFD 8023 E7

Lynde Dr NE
- FRID 7766 E4

Lynmar Ln
- EDNA 8109 B3

Lynn Av
- SAVG 8281 A3

Lynn Av S
- EDNA 8023 A2
- STLP 7937 A6
- STLP 8023 A1

Lynn Cir
- SAVG 8281 A5

Lynn Ct
- SAVG 8281 A6

Lynn Ter
- MNTK 8020 C5

Lynn Wy
- NWPT 8116 A3
- WDBY 8116 A3

Lynnhurst Av E
- STPL 7940 A5

Lynnhurst Av W
- STPL 7940 A6

Lyn Park Av N
- MINN 7852 B3

Lyn Park Cir N
- MINN 7852 B3

Lyn Park Ln N
- MINN 7852 B3

Lynwood Blvd
- RHFD 8109 E2

Lynx Ct
- EAGN 8199 B7

Lynx Rd
- WtBT 7684 E6

Lyon St
- STPL 7943 A7

Lyra Ct
- EAGN 8198 D6

Lyric Ln NE
- FRID 7680 D6

Lyton Pl
- STPL 7941 D4

M

Macalaster Dr NE
- NBRI 7767 C7
- STAN 7767 C7
- STAN 7853 C1

Macalaster St
- STPL 8026 B1

MacAlester St
- STPL 7940 B7
- STPL 8026 B1

MacArthur Av
- WSTP 8028 A4

E MacArthur St
- SSTP 8115 A4

W MacArthur St
- SSTP 8114 E3

Macbeth Cir
- WDBY 8030 B6

Macbeth Ct
- WDBY 8030 B6

Mackey Av
- EDNA 8022 E3
- STLP 8022 E3

Mackubin Cir
- SHVW 7769 B2

Mackubin Ct
- SHVW 7769 B2

Mackubin St
- LINO 7683 B3
- RSVL 7855 B3
- SHVW 7683 B4
- SHVW 7769 B2
- STPL 7855 B7
- STPL 7941 B1

MacLaren Pl
- EAGN 8199 A6

Macy's Ct
- BMTN 8110 D6

Madalyn Pl
- ROBB 7851 A1

Maddaus Ln
- GLDV 7937 A3

Maddox Ln
- EDNA 8022 D7

Madeira Av
- MINN 7937 C4

Madison Av N
- HOPK 8021 E2

Madison Av S
- EDNA 8021 E4
- HOPK 8021 E4

Madison Av W
- GLDV 7850 C5

Madison Cir N
- HOPK 8021 C1

Madison Cir S
- HOPK 8021 C1

Madison Pl NE
- COLH 7852 D2
- MINN 7852 D2

Madison St
- STPL 8026 C6

Madison St NE
- BLNE 7594 D1
- BLNE 7680 D2
- COLH 7766 D6
- COLH 7852 D1
- FRID 7680 D6
- FRID 7766 D2
- MINN 7852 D1
- SPLP 7680 D5

Magda Dr
- MAPG 7763 D4

Mager Ct
- MNDH 8113 B1

Maggie Ln
- SAVG 8279 E4

Magnetite Pt
- EAGN 8197 E5

Magnolia Av
- CTGV 8202 A2
- SPLP 8202 A2

Magnolia Av E
- MPLW 7943 D3
- STPL 7941 D3
- STPL 7942 D3
- STPL 7943 B3

Magnolia Av W
- STPL 7941 D3

Magnolia Ct
- MAPG 7677 A5

Magnolia Ct N
- CHMP 7591 D5

Magnolia Ln
- STPL 7942 D3

Magnolia Ln N
- MAPG 7677 B6
- MAPG 7763 A4
- MNTK 7935 A2
- PYMH 7763 A6
- PYMH 7849 A4
- PYMH 7935 A2

Magnolia Pl N
- PYMH 7849 A2

Magnolia St NW
- COON 7594 A1
- COON 7680 A3

Magnolia Tr
- EDNP 8106 E6
- EDNP 8107 A6

Magnolia Wy N
- MAPG 7677 C4

Magoffin Av
- STPL 8025 E5
- STPL 8026 A5

Mahle Ln
- WDBY 8030 B7

Mahogany Wy
- EAGN 8283 B1

Mahtomedi Av
- DLWD 7772 C3
- MAHT 7772 D6
- WILL 7772 D6

Mahtomedi Av SR-244
- DLWD 7772 C3
- MAHT 7772 B6

Maida Ct E
- MPLW 8029 D5

Maiden Ln
- COLH 7767 B6
- STPL 7941 C7

Mailand Ct E
- MPLW 8029 E2

Mailand Ct S
- MPLW 8029 E2

Mailand Rd E
- MPLW 8029 D2
- STPL 8029 C2

Main St
- ARDH 7682 A7
- CTRV 7598 D5
- EDNP 8106 A4
- HOPK 8021 B3
- HUGO 7599 B5
- LINO 7598 B1
- LINO 7599 A5
- NBRI 7767 E5
- SPLP 8115 D7
- SPLP 8201 D1
- STPL 7941 D7

Main St N
- MAPG 7677 A7
- MAPG 7763 A1

Main St NE
- COLH 7766 C7
- COLH 7852 C2
- FRID 7680 C5
- FRID 7766 C1
- FRID 7852 C2
- MINN 7852 C6
- MINN 7938 C1

Main St SE
- MINN 7938 D1

Mainzer St
- SSTP 8028 C4
- WSTP 8028 A4

Mait Ln
- EDNA 8022 B3

Majestic Oaks Ct
- EAGN 8199 C7

Majestic Oaks Pl
- EAGN 8199 C7

Major Av N
- BRKC 7765 A2
- BRKP 7593 A7
- BRKP 7679 A7
- BRKP 7765 A1
- CRYS 7765 A5
- CRYS 7851 A3
- GLDV 7851 A5
- ROBB 7851 A3

Major Cir
- GLDV 7851 A6

Major Dr N
- BRKP 7679 A1
- GLDV 7851 A7

Malcolm Av SE
- MINN 7939 C3

Malden St
- SSTP 8115 A3

Malibu Dr
- EDNA 8021 E5

Mallard Cir
- EAGN 8198 A7

Mallard Ct
- EAGN 8198 A6

N Mallard Ct
- NOAK 7684 B7

Mallard Dr
- EAGN 8198 A7
- WDBY 8030 A5

Mallard Ln
- LINO 7597 E6
- NOAK 7770 B1

Mallard Pl
- EAGN 8198 A6

Mallard Rd
- NOAK 7770 B1

N Mallard Rd
- NOAK 7684 B7
- NOAK 7770 B1

N Mallard Tr
- EAGN 8198 A6

S Mallard Tr
- EAGN 8198 A7

Mallard Vw
- EAGN 8198 A7

Mallard Wy
- CTRV 7598 D6

Mallard Ponds Blvd
- WtBT 7685 D4

Mallard Ponds Dr
- WtBT 7685 E3

Mallory Ln
- EDNP 8020 B7

Malmo Cir
- EAGN 8198 D6

N Malmo Ln
- EAGN 8198 C6

Malmo Pl
- EAGN 8198 C5

Maloney Av
- EDNA 8021 E4
- EDNA 8022 A4

Maltby St
- SSTP 8115 B2

Malvern St
- LAUD 7853 D7
- RSVL 7853 D6

Mamie Av E
- MPLW 8029 D4

Manchester Cir N
- GLDV 7850 C6

Manchester Dr
- GLDV 7850 D5

Manchester Ln
- EDNP 8106 D1

Mancini St
- STPL 8027 C1

Mandan Av N
- GLDV 7850 A7

Manitoba Av
- STPL 7941 D4

Manitoba Rd
- EDNP 8106 B3
- HOPK 7935 C7
- MNTK 7935 C7

Manitou Av
- STPL 7943 B4

Manitou Dr
- WTBL 7857 D1

Manitou Ln
- WTBL 7857 E1

Manitou Island Rd
- WTBL 7771 D2

Mankato St NE
- BLNE 7595 C4

Manomin Av
- STPL 8027 D2
- WSTP 8027 D3

E Manor Blvd
- BRNV 8281 D4

W Manor Blvd
- BRNV 8281 D4

Manor Dr
- BRNV 8281 D4
- EAGN 8199 C7
- EAGN 8285 C1
- GLDV 7851 B6
- MINN 7851 C6

S Manor Dr
- BRNV 8281 D4

Manor Dr NE
- SPLP 7680 D3

Manor Rd N
- EDNP 8106 A1

Manor Rd S
- EDNP 8106 A1

Manor St
- VADH 7856 B1

Manor Ct Rd
- MNTK 8020 B3

Manson St
- RSVL 7853 D2

Manton Ln
- EDNP 8193 C4

Manton St
- MPLW 7856 E7
- STPL 7856 E7
- STPL 7942 E1

Manvel St
- STPL 7939 D3

Many Levels Rd
- DLWD 7772 D2

Maple Av S
- BMTN 8195 C3

Maple Cir
- BMTN 8195 C3

Maple Ct
- FLCH 7854 A7

Maple Ln
- LCAN 7855 D2
- MNTK 8020 D3
- RSVL 7853 D2
- RSVL 7854 B2
- RSVL 7855 C2
- SHVW 7769 B7
- SHVW 7855 B1
- STAN 7853 D2

Maple Ln E
- MPLW 7857 C2

Maple Ln N
- MAPG 7676 D6

Maple Pl
- MINN 7938 C1

Maple Rd
- EDNA 8023 A4

Maple St
- GRNT 7772 D3
- MAHT 7772 D3
- MINN 7938 A3
- SHVW 7769 A1
- STPL 7942 B5

Maple St NE
- SPLP 7680 D3

Maple Tr SE
- PRIO 8280 A7

N Maplebrook Cir
- BRKP 7678 B5

S Maplebrook Cir
- BRKP 7678 B5

Maplebrook Ct N
- BRKP 7678 B4

Maplebrook Pkwy N
- BRKP 7678 B5

Maple Grove Pkwy N
- MAPG 7676 B2

Maple Hill Rd
- HOPK 8022 B3

Maple Hills Dr E
- MPLW 7856 B7

Maple Knoll Dr
- FLCH 7854 B7

Maple Knoll Wy
- MAPG 7676 D6
- MAPG 7677 B6

Maple Leaf Cir
- EAGN 8198 E7

Maple Leaf Ct
- LCAN 7856 C1
- VADH 7856 C1

Maple Park Dr
- MNDH 8027 B5

Maple Pond Ct
- SHVW 7769 A1

Maple Ridge Ct
- MNTK 8021 A5

Maple Valley Dr
- MAPG 7677 C2

Mapleview Av
- MPLW 7857 C3
- NSTP 7857 C3

Maplewood Cir N
- CHMP 7591 C4

Maplewood Dr
- MAPG 7676 D7
- MAPG 7762 D1
- MPLW 7856 D2
- VADH 7856 D2

Maplewood Dr US-61
- MPLW 7856 C6
- VADH 7856 D2

E Maplewood Dr
- BMTN 8196 B2

Maplewood Dr E
- MPLW 7856 D5

Maplewood Dr NE
- RSVL 7853 D2
- STAN 7853 C2

Maplewood Ln
- MNTK 8020 A7

Maplewood Ln N
- CHMP 7591 D5

Maras St S
- SHKP 8279 E2

Marble Ln
- EAGN 8197 C6

Marble St
- VADH 7856 B1

March Cir
- MNTK 7935 A6

Marcia Ln
- LINO 7597 A2

Marcin Hl
- BRNV 8282 B5

Marcin Ln
- BRNV 8282 B5

Marcy Ln
- MNTK 7935 D5

Maren Ln
- GLDV 7936 A1

Margaret Av E
- MPLW 7943 E5
- ODLE 7943 E5

Margaret Pl
- MNTK 8020 C1

Margaret St
- MPLW 7943 C5
- STPL 7942 E5
- STPL 7943 B5
- WTBL 7771 A3
- WtBT 7771 A3

Margaret St N
- MPLW 7857 E6
- NSTP 7857 E6

Margaret's Ln
- EDNA 8107 E1

Mari Ln
- MNTK 8021 A1

Maria Av
- STPL 7942 B6

Marian Ct
- BLNE 7682 C3
- CIRC 7682 C3

Mariann Dr
- EDNP 8106 D2

Marice Ct
- EAGN 8112 C7

Marice Dr
- EAGN 8198 C1

Maridian Ln
- STLP 8023 A1

Marie Av
- SSTP 8028 D7

Marie Av E
- WSTP 8028 A7

Marie Av W
- MNDH 8026 E7
- MNDH 8027 A7
- WSTP 8027 D7
- WSTP 8028 A7

Marie Ln E
- GLDV 7851 A5

Marie Ln W
- GLDV 7850 E5

Marigold Av
- VADH 7770 B4

Marigold Av N
- BRKP 7678 E2
- BRKP 7679 A2

Marigold Cir
- EDNP 8106 E6
- EDNP 8107 A6

Marigold Ct N
- BRKP 7679 B2

Marigold St NW
- COON 7592 E2

Marigold Ter NE
- FRID 7766 D3

Marillac Ln
- MPLW 8029 C6
- STPL 8029 C6

Marilyn Av
- EAGN 8283 B2

Marilyn Dr
- LINO 7597 C1
- MAPG 7763 A3

Mariner Dr
- MAPG 7676 C7
- MAPG 7762 C1

Mariner Pt
- MAPG 7676 C7
- MAPG 7762 C1

Marion Dr
- BRNV 8281 C4

Marion Ln W
- MNTK 7935 A3

Marion Pl
- SSTP 8028 C4

Marion Rd
- RSVL 7853 E5

Marion St
- RSVL 7855 C2
- STPL 7855 C7
- STPL 7941 C1

Mark Ct
- NWPT 8115 D2

Markay Rdg
- GLDV 7850 E6
- GLDV 7851 A6

Market Plz
- MINN 7937 B6

Market St
- GLDV 7936 C3
- MINN 7938 A2
- STPL 7941 D3

Market Place Dr
- EDNP 8107 B3
- LCAN 7855 D2
- LINO 7597 C2
- RSVL 7855 D2

Marketplace Dr N
- CHMP 7592 A5

Market Pointe Dr
- BMTN 8109 A5

Markham Pt
- EAGN 8283 E2

Mark Terrace Cir
- EDNA 8108 A2

Mark Terrace Dr
- EDNA 8108 A3

Markwood Dr
- CRYS 7850 C3
- NWHE 7850 C3

Marlboro Ct NE
- SPLP 7680 E5

Marlborough Cir
- MNTK 8020 A2

Marlborough Ct
- MNTK 8020 A3

Marlin Av
- VADH 7856 B1

Marlin Dr
- BRKC 7765 A3

Marmon St NE
- BLNE 7596 D5

Marnie Cir S
- MPLW 8029 D4

Marnie Ct S
- MPLW 8029 D5

Marnie St S
- MPLW 8029 D2

Marquette Av
- MINN 7938 B3

Marquis Pt
- EAGN 8283 E1

Marquis Rd
- GLDV 7849 E6

Marsh Wy
- MNTK 7934 C6

Marshall Av
- MINN 7939 D6
- SPLP 8116 A7
- SPLP 8202 A1
- STPL 7939 E6
- STPL 7940 A6
- STPL 7941 B6

Marshall St NE
- FRID 7766 B7
- MINN 7852 B6

Marshan Ct
- LINO 7597 C3

Marshan Ln
- LINO 7597 C3

Marsh Creek Rd
- WDBY 8030 E6

Marsh Creek Alcove
- WDBY 8030 E6

Marsh Ridge Ct
- EDNP 8106 C2

Marsh Ridge Rd
- NOAK 7770 C1

Marshview Cir N
- CHMP 7591 D5

Marshview Ln N
- CHMP 7591 D6

Marth Ct
- BMTN 8108 B4
- EDNA 8108 B4

Marth Rd
- BMTN 8107 E5
- BMTN 8108 A5

Martha Ln
- MNTK 7934 B7
- MNTK 8020 B1
- WDBY 7944 B7
- WDBY 8030 A1

Martha Lake Ct
- SHVW 7769 A2

Marthaler Ln
- WSTP 8028 B5

Martin Dr
- EDNP 8106 C4

Martin Ln
- NOAK 7769 E2

Martin St NW
- COON 7593 C1

Martin Wy
- BRHV 7771 E5
- SHVW 7769 D5
- VADH 7769 D5
- WTBL 7771 D5
- WtBT 7771 D5

Martindale St NE
- PRIO 8279 B5
- SHKP 8279 C5

Marvy St
- BLNE 7596 E3
- LINO 7596 E3
- LINO 7597 A3

Mary Ct
- MPLW 7943 D1

N Mary Ct
- MPLW 7857 D2

Mary Ln
- MPLW 7857 D2
- NSTP 7857 D2
- STPL 7940 E1

Mary Ln S
- MPLW 8029 E2

Mary Pl S
- MPLW 8029 D5

Mary St
- MPLW 7857 D2

Mary St N
- MPLW 7943 D1

Mary St S
- MPLW 8029 D2

Mary Adele Av
- MNDH 8112 E2

Mary Ann Ln
- BRNV 8282 B4

Mary Hills Dr
- GLDV 7851 B6

Maryjoe Ln
- NSTP 7857 D7

Maryknoll Av
- MPLW 7857 A7

Maryland Av
- SAVG 8280 C4

Maryland Av E
- MPLW 7943 D2
- ODLE 7943 E2
- STPL 7941 D2
- STPL 7942 A2
- STPL 7943 A2

Maryland Av N
- BRKP 7592 C6
- BRKP 7678 B4
- BRKP 7764 B2
- CHMP 7592 C6
- CRYS 7764 C5
- CRYS 7850 C1
- GLDV 7850 B6
- NWHE 7764 C6
- NWHE 7850 C3

Maryland Av S
- BMTN 8194 B4
- GLDV 7936 C3
- STLP 7936 B4

Maryland Av W
- STPL 7941 A2

Maryland Cir
- SAVG 8280 C5

Maryland Cir N
- CHMP 7592 B3

Maryland Cir S
- BMTN 8108 B6
- BMTN 8194 B4

Maryland Ct
- SAVG 8280 C5

Maryland Ct N
- BRKP 7678 C5
- CHMP 7592 B4

Maryland Ln N
- CHMP 7592 C4

Maryland Rd S
- BMTN 8108 B5
- BMTN 8194 B4

Maryland Wy N
- CHMP 7592 B5

Mary's Cir
- VADH 7770 B2

Marywood Ln
- IVGH 8113 E1
- WSTP 8113 E1

Marzitelli St
- STPL 8027 D1

Masonic Home Dr
- BMTN 8194 E6

Mason's Pointe
- EDNP 8106 C6

Massie Curv
- EDNP 8106 D5

Mathais Rd
- SHKP 8278 A3

Matilda Av
- RSVL 7855 C5

Matilda Cir
- RSVL 7855 C4

Matilda St
- RSVL 7855 C3
- STPL 7941 C1

Matterhorn Cir NE
- FRID 7767 A4

Matterhorn Dr E
- MPLW 8029 D4

Matterhorn Dr NE
- COLH 7767 A5
- FRID 7767 A5

Matterhorn Ln
- MPLW 8029 C4

INDEX 29

Matterhorn Ln

Minneapolis Street Index

Milton Datus Hammond Mem

STREET Block	City	ZIP	Map #	Grid
Matterhorn Ln				
-	STPL		8029	C4
Matthew Ct				
-	EAGN		8198	E6
Mattson Brook Ln N				
-	BRKP		7679	E5
Maureen Dr NE				
-	COLH		7766	C7
Maureen Ln NE				
-	COLH		7766	C7
Maury St				
-	STPL		7942	B5
Mavelle Dr				
-	EDNA		8109	A2
Max Metzger Wy				
-	STPL		7940	D2
Maxwell Av				
-	NWPT		8029	C7
-	NWPT		8115	C1
-	STPL		8029	C7
May St				
-	STPL		8026	E4
Mayer Ln E				
-	MPLW		7943	E7
Mayfair Av				
-	WTBL		7771	D6
Mayfair Ct				
-	MAHT		7771	E3
-	WTBL		7771	E3
Mayfair Rd				
-	GLDV		7849	D6
-	VADH		7769	D7
Mayfield Dr				
-	EDNP		8106	A7
Mayfield Rd				
-	MNTK		7934	C6
Mayfield Heights Ln				
-	MNDH		8026	E7
Mayfield Heights Rd				
-	LILY		8026	E6
-	MNDH		8026	E7
Mayflower Av				
-	MNTK		7935	B6
Mayflower Cir				
-	MNTK		7935	A5
Mayflower Pl				
-	MNTK		7935	A6
Mayhill Rd N				
-	MPLW		7943	E2
E Maynard Dr				
-	STPL		8026	B6
W Maynard Dr				
-	STPL		8026	B6
Mayo Dr				
-	BRNV		8282	B4
Mayre St				
-	STPL		7941	D2
Mayview Ct				
-	MNTK		8020	E5
Mayview Rd				
-	MNTK		8020	E5
Mayview Ter				
-	MNTK		8020	E5
Maywood Curv				
-	MNTK		8020	E5
Maywood Dr				
-	SSTP		8114	D1
Maywood Ln				
-	MNTK		8020	E4
-	MNTK		8021	A5
Maywood Pl				
-	STPL		7941	A3
Maywood St				
-	SHVW		7769	B1
-	STPL		7941	A1
McAfee Cir				
-	MPLW		7856	E5
McAfee St				
-	MPLW		7856	E7
-	STPL		7856	E7
-	STPL		7942	E1
McAndrews Rd				
-	APVA		8282	E5
-	APVA		8283	E4
-	APVA		8284	D3
-	BRNV		8282	B5
-	RSMT		8284	E3
-	RSMT		8285	B3
McAndrews Rd CO-11				
-	APVA		8282	E5
-	BRNV		8282	E5
E McAndrews Rd				
-	BRNV		8282	B5
McAndrews Rd E				
-	APVA		8282	E5
-	BRNV		8282	D5
McAndrews Rd E CO-11				
-	APVA		8282	E5
-	BRNV		8282	D5
McAndrews Rd W				
-	BRNV		8281	D6
-	BRNV		8282	B5
McBoal St				
-	STPL		8027	C1
McCallum Dr				
-	NBRI		7853	D1
-	RSVL		7853	D1
McCammon Av				
-	SPLP		8116	A7
-	SPLP		8202	A1
McCann Ct				
-	SAVG		8280	C7
N McCarron Blvd				
-	MPLW		7855	D6
-	RSVL		7855	C6
S McCarron Blvd				
-	MPLW		7855	D7
-	RSVL		7855	B7
McCarron St				
-	MPLW		7855	D6
-	RSVL		7855	C6
McCarthy Rd				
-	EAGN		8112	A7
McCarthy Rdg				
-	EAGN		8112	A7
McCauley Cir				
-	EDNA		8107	E1
McCauley Ter				
-	EDNA		8107	E1
McCauley Tr S				
-	EDNA		8107	E1
McCauley Tr W				
-	EDNA		8021	E7
-	EDNA		8107	E1
-	EDNA		8108	A1
McClelland St N				
-	MPLW		7943	E7
McClelland St S				
-	MPLW		8029	E5
McClung Dr				
-	ARDH		7768	C3
McColl Dr				
-	BRNV		8281	B3
-	SAVG		8279	E4
-	SAVG		8280	E3
-	SAVG		8281	A3
-	SHKP		8279	E4
McColl Dr CO-16				
-	SAVG		8279	E4
-	SAVG		8280	E3
-	SHKP		8279	E4
McCool Ct				
-	BRNV		8197	B4
McCool Dr E				
-	BRNV		8197	B5
McCool Dr W				
-	BRNV		8197	A5
McCoy Ct				
-	EDNP		8106	D7
McCracken Ln				
-	ARDH		7768	B6
McCracken Pl				
-	WILL		7772	D6
McCullough Park Rd				
-	SHVW		7682	E5
McFaddens Tr				
-	EAGN		8285	B1
McGinty Rd E				
-	MNTK		7934	E7
McGinty Rd W				
-	MNTK		7934	D6
-	WAYZ		7934	A4
McGregor St				
-	MAHT		7772	C5
-	WILL		7772	C6
McGuffey Rd				
-	EDNP		8106	A7
McGuire Cir				
-	SHKP		8279	D4
McGuire Ct E				
-	SHKP		8279	D4
McGuire Rd				
-	EDNA		8108	C2
McIntyre Pt				
-	EDNA		8107	E1
McKee St				
-	EAGN		8112	E6
McKenna Rd				
-	PRIO		8278	E4
-	SHKP		8278	E4
McKenna Rd NW				
-	PRIO		8278	E5
-	SHKP		8278	E5
McKenzie Blvd				
-	MNTK		8020	B2
McKinley Pl NE				
-	MINN		7853	B7
McKinley St				
-	STPL		7940	C1
McKinley St NE				
-	COLH		7853	B1
-	FRID		7681	A6
-	FRID		7767	B1
-	MINN		7853	B4
-	SPLP		7681	B5
McKnight Ln				
-	MPLW		7857	C7
McKnight Rd N				
-	MPLW		7857	C3
-	MPLW		7943	C7
-	NSTP		7857	C6
-	STPL		7857	C7
-	STPL		7943	C4
-	WTBL		7771	C4
-	WTBL		7857	C1
McKnight Rd S				
-	MPLW		8029	D5
-	STPL		8029	D5
McLean Av				
-	STPL		7942	D6
-	STPL		7943	A6
McLeod St				
-	BRNV		8197	A7
McLeod St NE				
-	COLH		7767	A7
McMenemy Cir				
-	VADH		7769	E5
McMenemy St				
-	LCAN		7855	E7
-	LCAN		7856	A4
-	MPLW		7855	E7
-	NOAK		7769	E4
-	STPL		7855	E7
-	VADH		7769	E4
McNair Av N				
-	GLDV		7851	C6
-	MINN		7851	C6
McNair Dr N				
-	GLDV		7851	B6
-	ROBB		7851	B5
McQuiston Ct				
-	SAVG		8280	D4
Mead Ct				
-	BRNV		8283	A3
Mead Dr				
-	WtBT		7685	B7
Mead St				
-	CHMP		7591	D1
Meade Ln				
-	EDNP		8193	C3
Meadow Av				
-	SHVW		7682	C4
Meadow Av NE				
-	PRIO		8279	E6
Meadow Cir				
-	CTRV		7598	C5
-	MNTK		7935	A3
Meadow Cir N				
-	BRKP		7593	B7
Meadow Cir N				
-	BRNV		8282	A5
Meadow Cir S				
-	BRNV		8282	A5
Meadow Ct				
-	CTRV		7598	D5
-	LINO		7596	E4
-	SHVW		7682	D4
-	WDBY		7944	A7
E Meadow Dr				
-	MPLW		7857	D7
-	NSTP		7857	D7
Meadow Ln				
-	CTRV		7598	D5
-	DLWD		7686	A7
-	EDNP		8106	A4
-	MNTK		7934	B6
-	MNTK		8020	A1
-	NOAK		7769	D2
-	SAVG		8280	A4
-	SHVW		7769	B2
-	WDBY		7944	A7
-	WDBY		8030	A1
-	WSTP		8028	B6
Meadow Ln N				
-	BRKP		7593	A7
-	GLDV		7937	A2
Meadow Ln NE				
-	BLNE		7596	A3
Meadow Ln S				
-	GLDV		7937	B3
Meadow Ln W				
-	MNTK		7935	A6
Meadow Pl				
-	MNTK		7935	B6
-	SAVG		8279	E4
-	SAVG		8280	A4
Meadow Rd				
-	EDNA		8023	B3
Meadow Rdg				
-	EDNA		8108	D2
Meadow Acres Pl				
-	BRNV		8282	A5
Meadowbrook Blvd				
-	STLP		8022	C2
Meadow Brook Ct				
-	WDBY		8030	D5
Meadowbrook Ct				
-	VADH		7856	B1
Meadow Brook Dr				
-	WDBY		8030	D5
Meadowbrook Ln				
-	MNTK		7934	A6
-	STLP		8022	C2
Meadowbrook Mnr				
-	STLP		8022	C2
Meadow Brook Pl				
-	WDBY		8030	D6
Meadowbrook Rd				
-	HOPK		8022	B3
-	STLP		8022	B3
Meadow Brook Alcove				
-	WDBY		8030	C5
Meadow Brook Bay				
-	WDBY		8030	C4
Meadow Grass Av S				
-	CTGV		8116	B6
Meadow Grass Ct S				
-	CTGV		8116	B7
Meadow Grass Ln S				
-	CTGV		8116	B6
Meadow Grass Cove S				
-	CTGV		8116	B7
Meadow Lake Pl				
-	NWHE		7764	A5
Meadow Lake Rd E				
-	NWHE		7764	A5
Meadow Lake Rd N				
-	NWHE		7764	A5
Meadow Lake Rd W				
-	NWHE		7764	A5
Meadowlands Dr				
-	WTBL		7770	C2
-	WtBT		7770	C2
Meadowlark Cir				
-	MAPG		7763	C3
Meadowlark Ct				
-	EAGN		8197	B2
-	LINO		7598	B6
-	MAPG		7763	C3
Meadowlark Curv				
-	EAGN		8197	E5
Meadowlark Ln				
-	EAGN		8197	B2
-	MPLW		7856	C2
-	NOAK		7769	C2
-	SHKP		8278	B4
Meadowlark Ln N				
-	MAPG		7763	A3
Meadowlark Pt				
-	EAGN		8197	E5
Meadowlark Rd				
-	EAGN		8197	E5
S Meadowlark Rd				
-	EAGN		8197	E5
Meadowlark Wy				
-	EAGN		8197	B2
Meadowlawn Tr NE				
-	PRIO		8279	C7
Meadowmoor Dr NE				
-	FRID		7681	A6
Meadowood Cir				
-	VADH		7769	E3
Meadowood Dr				
-	WDBY		8030	A1
Meadowood Ln				
-	BRNV		8282	B2
-	VADH		7769	E3
Meadowood Pl				
-	VADH		7769	E4
Meadowvale Dr				
-	EDNP		8106	B7
Meadowview Ct				
-	LINO		7684	C1
Meadowview Dr				
-	WtBT		7684	D5
Meadow View Rd				
-	EAGN		8111	E7
-	EAGN		8112	A7
Meadowview Rd				
-	BMTN		8196	E1
Meadowview Tr				
-	LINO		7597	B1
Meadow Wood Ct				
-	SAVG		8280	D7
N Meadowwood Ct				
-	BRKP		7765	C1
S Meadowwood Ct				
-	BRKP		7765	C1
Meadow Wood Dr				
-	SAVG		8280	D7
Meadowwood Dr N				
-	BRKP		7765	D1
-	BRKP		7766	A1
Meander Rd				
-	GLDV		7936	D2
Mears Av				
-	MNDH		8027	C5
-	WSTP		8027	D5
Mechanic Av				
-	STPL		7942	E3
-	STPL		7943	B3
Medallion Dr				
-	MNDH		8112	D4
Medary Dr				
-	EAGN		8197	B6
Medcom Blvd				
-	EDNP		8107	B6
E Medicine Lake Blvd				
-	PYMH		7849	C3
W Medicine Lake Dr				
-	PYMH		7848	E1
-	PYMH		7849	A4
-	PYMH		7935	D1
Medicine Lake Rd				
-	CRYS		7850	B5
-	GLDV		7849	E5
-	GLDV		7850	C6
-	NWHE		7849	E5
-	NWHE		7850	C5
-	PYMH		7849	E5
Medicine Ridge Rd N				
-	PYMH		7849	D5
Medina Rd				
-	PYMH		7848	A4
Medley Cir				
-	GLDV		7849	E5
-	NWHE		7849	E5
Medley Ln N				
-	GLDV		7849	E5
-	GLDV		7850	A5
Medley Rd				
-	GLDV		7849	E5
Medora Ct				
-	MNDH		8027	B5
Medora Rd				
-	MNDH		8027	B5
Medtronic Pkwy				
-	FRID		7766	D4
Meehan Dr				
-	WtBT		7685	D5
Meeting Pl				
-	MNTK		7934	D5
Meeting St				
-	MNTK		7934	C4
Meg Grace Ln				
-	EDNP		8107	C2
Meghan Ln				
-	EAGN		8197	C5
NW Mehigan St				
-	NBRI		7767	E6
Meister Rd				
-	FRID		7767	A4
Melbourne Av SE				
-	MINN		7939	C4
Melissa Ln				
-	WtBT		7685	A6
Melody Ct				
-	EDNP		8106	E3
Melody Dr NE				
-	FRID		7680	D6
Melody Ln				
-	BRNV		8282	D2
-	EDNA		8022	D6
-	MNTK		8020	E1
-	MNTK		8021	A1
Melody Lake Dr				
-	EDNA		8022	D6
Melrose Av S				
-	STLP		7935	D3
Mel's Wy				
-	EDNP		8107	C2
Memorial Pkwy				
-	MINN		7851	C4
-	ROBB		7851	C4
Memory Cir NE				
-	FRID		7680	D6
Memory Ct				
-	NSTP		7857	D6
Memory Ln				
-	CRYS		7850	C2
-	NSTP		7857	D6
Memory Ln NE				
-	FRID		7680	D6
Mendakota Ct				
-	MNDH		8113	A2
Mendakota Dr				
-	MNDH		8113	A2
Mendelssohn Av N				
-	BRKP		7677	E7
-	BRKP		7763	E1
-	GLDV		7849	E7
-	GLDV		7935	E1
-	PYMH		7849	E7
-	PYMH		7935	E1
Mendelssohn Ln				
-	EDNA		8022	A4
-	GLDV		7849	E6
-	PYMH		7849	E6
Mendota Br				
-	HnpC		8026	A7
-	HnpC		8112	B1
-	MNDH		8112	B1
Mendota Br SR-55				
-	HnpC		8026	A7
-	HnpC		8112	B1
-	MNDH		8112	B1
Mendota Cir				
-	STPL		7942	C4
E Mendota Rd				
-	IVGH		8114	A1
-	SSTP		8114	C1
-	WSTP		8114	A1
W Mendota Rd				
-	IVGH		8113	E1
-	MNDH		8113	D1
-	SUNL		8113	E1
-	WSTP		8113	E1
Mendota Rd W				
-	MNDH		8112	D1
-	MNDH		8113	A1
Mendota Rd W SR-110				
-	MNDH		8112	D1
-	MNDH		8113	A1
Mendota St				
-	STPL		7942	C2
Mendota Heights Cir				
-	MNDH		8113	B4
Mendota Heights Rd				
-	MNDH		8112	E4
-	MNDH		8113	A4
-	SUNL		8113	D4
Mercer St				
-	STPL		8027	A3
Mercer Wy				
-	STPL		8026	E4
Mercury Cir				
-	SHVW		7769	B1
Mercury Dr NE				
-	FRID		7766	C2
Mercury Dr W				
-	SHVW		7768	E1
-	SHVW		7769	A1
Mere Dr				
-	EDNP		8106	A1
Merganser Ct				
-	EAGN		8198	E2
-	LINO		7598	C7
Meridian Cir N				
-	MAPG		7763	D1
Meridian Ct				
-	SHKP		8192	B7
Meridian Dr				
-	GLDV		7851	B6
-	MPLW		7856	C4
-	ROBB		7851	B5
-	SHKP		8192	A7
Meridian Crossings				
-	RHFD		8109	E4
Merilane Av				
-	EDNA		8022	C4
Merilee Dr				
-	MNTK		8021	A4
Merlen Dr				
-	MNTK		7935	A6
Merlot Cove				
-	EAGN		8197	D3
Merold Dr				
-	EDNA		8022	B6
Merriam Ln				
-	STPL		7940	A6
Merriam Rd				
-	ARDH		7682	A7
-	ARDH		7768	A1
-	MNTK		8021	A2
Merriam St				
-	MINN		7938	C1
Merribee Dr				
-	GLDV		7851	A6
Merrill Av				
-	RSVL		7854	D5
Merrill St				
-	RSVL		7854	D7
-	STPL		7940	D1
Merritt Cir				
-	EDNA		8022	C6
Merrivale Av S				
-	MNTK		7935	B3
Mersey Pt				
-	EAGN		8199	C4
Mersey Wy				
-	EAGN		8199	C4
Mesabi Av				
-	MPLW		7857	B3
-	NSTP		7857	C3
Mesa Verde Ct				
-	BRNV		8283	A3
Messer Av				
-	SSTP		8115	A2
Metcalf Dr				
-	BRNV		8197	B6
-	EAGN		8197	B6
Metro Blvd				
-	EDNA		8108	E3
Metro Dr				
-	BMTN		8111	A5
Metro Pkwy				
-	BMTN		8111	A5
N Meyer Ct				
-	MPLW		7857	D2
Meyer St N				
-	MPLW		7943	D4
Mica Tr				
-	EAGN		8197	D4
Michael Av				
-	WTBL		7771	B7
Michael Dr E				
-	MPLW		7943	E1
Michael Ln				
-	MPLW		7943	D4
Michael St				
-	STPL		7943	C7
Michael Point Dr				
-	EAGN		8197	C7
Michele Ln				
-	EDNP		8106	B2
Michelle Cir				
-	BRNV		8282	D2
Michelle Dr				
-	EAGN		8198	C4
Michigan Ct				
-	EAGN		8199	C6
Michigan St				
-	STPL		8027	B1
Mickey Ln				
-	MPLW		7943	E2
Middle Ln				
-	EAGN		8285	C1
Middle St				
-	LCAN		7855	D3
Middleset Rd				
-	EDNP		8107	B5
Middleton Av				
-	STPL		8026	E4
Middletown Rd				
-	SPLP		7680	E4
Midland Av				
-	WTBL		7771	B6
-	WTBL		7857	B1
Midland Ct				
-	WTBL		7771	B7
Midland Grove Rd				
-	RSVL		7854	A5
Midland Hills Rd				
-	FLCH		7853	E6
-	RSVL		7853	E6
Midlothian Rd				
-	RSVL		7854	B6
Mid Oaks Ln				
-	FLCH		7854	B6
-	RSVL		7854	B6
Mid Oaks Rd				
-	FLCH		7854	B6
-	RSVL		7854	B7
Midvale Pl E				
-	MPLW		7943	E3
-	ODLE		7943	E3
Midway Pkwy				
-	FLCH		7940	C2
-	STPL		7940	C2
Midway St NE				
-	BLNE		7596	A1
-	BLNE		7682	A2
Mike Ln				
-	EDNP		8192	D2
Mike Collins Dr				
-	EAGN		8113	A7
-	EAGN		8199	A1
Milbert Rd				
-	MNTK		7934	E2
-	PYMH		7934	E2
Mildred Av				
-	EDNA		8022	D7
-	EDNA		8108	D1
Mildred Dr				
-	ARDH		7854	A2
-	RHFD		8109	E1
-	RSVL		7854	A2
Mildred Pl				
-	ROBB		7851	A2
Mildred Ter				
-	MNTK		7935	D5
Milford Ln				
-	WILL		7772	D6
Milford St				
-	STPL		7941	C4
Military Hwy				
-	HnpC		8025	C7
-	MINN		8025	C7
Military Rd				
-	ANOK		7592	A1
-	NWPT		8115	E1
-	NWPT		8116	A1
-	WDBY		8116	A1
Militia Dr				
-	HnpC		8025	D7
-	HnpC		8111	D1
Mill Rd				
-	CTRV		7598	D3
-	HOPK		7935	D7
-	LINO		7598	D3
Mill Run				
-	MNTK		7935	C5
Mill St				
-	STPL		8027	D1
-	WtBT		7685	A7
Mill St NE				
-	COLH		7852	D1
Mill Creek Dr				
-	EDNP		8193	B2
Miller Av				
-	WTBL		7771	C2
Miller Pkwy E				
-	EDNP		8106	A6
Miller Pkwy W				
-	EDNP		8106	A6
Miller Rd				
-	CHMP		7591	E1
Miller Crest Ln				
-	STPL		7943	A7
Millers Ln				
-	EDNA		8109	A1
Millford Dr				
-	EDNP		8106	A6
Millpond Av				
-	BRNV		8196	E7
Millpond Pl				
-	EDNA		8022	D4
Mill Run Cir				
-	EAGN		8199	B3
Mill Run Ct				
-	EAGN		8199	B3
Mill Run Ln				
-	EAGN		8199	B4
Mill Run Pth				
-	EAGN		8199	B4
Millwood Av				
-	RSVL		7853	D2
-	RSVL		7854	C2
-	RSVL		7855	A2
-	STAN		7853	D2
Milner St				
-	WtBT		7685	B7
Milton Pl				
-	RSVL		7854	E5
N Milton St				
-	RSVL		7854	E7
-	STPL		7854	E7
Milton St N				
-	RSVL		7854	E2
-	SHVW		7768	E2
-	STPL		7940	E3
Milton St S				
-	STPL		7940	E7
-	STPL		8026	E1
Milton Datus Hammond Mem Dr				
-	MINN		7852	D4

Minneapolis Street Index

STREET Block City ZIP Map # Grid

Milwaukee Av
- MINN 7938 E5

Milwaukee St
- HOPK 8021 E3

Mimosa Ln
- NBRI 7767 B5

Mina Ct
- MAHT 7772 A6

Mina St
- WSTP 8027 D4

Minea St
- WSTP 8027 E7

Minikahda Ct
- STLP 8023 A1

Mink Ln
- NOAK 7770 A1

Minnaqua Av
- GLDV 7850 E6

Minnaqua Dr
- GLDV 7850 E6

Minneapolis Av
- MINN 7939 B5

Minnehaha Av
- HnpC 8025 E7
- HnpC 8111 E1
- MINN 7938 E5
- MINN 7939 A6
- MINN 8025 D5

Minnehaha Av SR-55
- HnpC 8025 D6

Minnehaha Av E
- MPLW 7943 E4
- ODLE 7943 E4
- STPL 7941 B4
- STPL 7942 B4
- STPL 7943 A4

Minnehaha Av E SR-5
- MPLW 7943 C4
- STPL 7942 E4
- STPL 7943 A4

Minnehaha Av W
- STPL 7940 B4
- STPL 7941 B4

Minnehaha Blvd
- EDNA 8023 A5

Minnehaha Cir N
- STLP 7935 E7

Minnehaha Cir S
- STLP 7935 E7

Minnehaha Ct
- MNTK 7934 C7
- STLP 7935 D7

Minnehaha Curv
- MNTK 7934 D6

E Minnehaha Pkwy
- MINN 8024 B5
- MINN 8025 A4

W Minnehaha Pkwy
- MINN 8023 E4
- MINN 8024 A5

Minnehaha Pl
- MNTK 7934 D7

Minneral Pt
- LINO 7683 E1

Minnesota Av
- LCAN 7855 D5
- RSVL 7855 B5

Minnesota Dr
- BMTN 8109 A4
- EDNA 8109 A4

Minnesota Ln N
- MAPG 7676 C3
- MAPG 7762 C3
- PYMH 7762 C7
- PYMH 7848 C3
- PYMH 7934 C1

Minnesota St
- STPL 7941 E7

Minnesota Bluffs Dr
- BMTN 8194 B6

Minnetoga Ter
- MNTK 8020 E5

Minnetonka Blvd
- HOPK 7935 D7
- MINN 7937 B6
- MNTK 7934 A7
- MNTK 7935 A7
- MNTK 8020 B1
- STLP 7935 E6
- STLP 7936 A6
- STLP 7937 A6

Minnetonka Cir
- MNTK 8020 D1

Minnetonka Dr
- MNTK 7934 C6
- MNTK 8020 E1

Minnetonka Industrial Rd
- MNTK 8020 C1

Minnetonka Mills Rd
- HOPK 8021 D2
- MNTK 8021 B1

Minuteman Dr
- HnpC 8025 D7
- HnpC 8111 D1

Minuteman Ln
- LXTN 7682 B1

Minuteman Alcove
- EDNP 8107 C5

Miracle Ln
- MNTK 8020 A5

Mirada Ct
- BRNV 8196 D7

Miriam St
- MNDH 8027 C4

Mirror Lakes Dr
- EDNA 8022 C5

Mission Cir
- BMTN 8196 A4

Mission Ct
- NBRI 7767 B6

Mission Ln
- BMTN 8196 B4

Mission Rd W
- BMTN 8196 A4

Mission House Ln
- NBRI 7767 B5

Mission Oaks Ln
- PYMH 7849 B2

Mississippi Blvd NW
- COON 7592 E4
- COON 7593 C6
- COON 7679 E3
- COON 7680 A4
- FRID 7680 A4

Mississippi Cir
- NBRI 7767 C1

Mississippi Cir N
- BRKP 7593 B7
- BRKP 7679 B1

Mississippi Ct
- NgTp 8288 E6

Mississippi Dr
- CHMP 7592 E6

N Mississippi Dr
- BRKC 7766 A6
- MINN 7766 A7

Mississippi Dr N
- BRKP 7593 A6
- CHMP 7592 E5
- CHMP 7593 A6

Mississippi Dr NW
- COON 7592 D3

Mississippi Ln N
- BRKP 7680 A7

Mississippi Pl NE
- FRID 7766 B1

Mississippi St
- FRID 7767 B1
- LCAN 7855 E6
- MPLW 7855 E6
- NBRI 7767 C1
- STPL 7941 E1

Mississippi St NE
- FRID 7766 C1
- FRID 7767 A2
- NBRI 7767 B1

Mississippi Tr
- NgTp 8288 D7

Mississippi Tr CO-42
- NgTp 8288 D7

Mississippi Dunes Blvd
- CTGV 8202 B5

Mississippi Dunes Blvd S
- CTGV 8202 B5

Mississippi River Blvd N
- MINN 7939 D6
- STPL 7939 D6

Mississippi River Blvd S
- STPL 7939 E7
- STPL 8025 D1
- STPL 8026 A6

Mistral Ln
- EDNP 8106 A1

Misty Morning Ln
- EDNP 8193 D4

Mitchell Av
- STPL 7943 C7

Mitchell Rd
- EDNP 8106 D4
- EDNP 8192 B1

Mitchell's Ct
- MAHT 7771 E3

Mitoka Cir NE
- PRIO 8279 B7

MN-7
- MNTK 8020 B3
- MNTK 8021 A2
- STLP 7936 E7
- STLP 8022 D1

MN-13
- SAVG 8280 B7

MN-13 S
- SAVG 8280 B2

MN-13 W
- BRNV 8281 B2
- SAVG 8280 D2
- SAVG 8281 B2

N MN-13 Frontage Rd
- BRNV 8281 D3

S MN-13 Frontage Rd
- BRNV 8281 C2

MN-36 Blvd N
- ODLE 7858 A3

MN-36 Service Rd
- RSVL 7855 A5

W MN-36 Service Rd
- RSVL 7853 D5

MN-36 Service Rd S
- RSVL 7853 E5

MN-55
- HnpC 8025 E6
- MINN 8025 E6

MN-55 E
- EAGN 8113 B7
- PYMH 7848 D5
- PYMH 7849 A6
- PYMH 7935 B1

MN-55 W
- PYMH 7849 A7
- PYMH 7935 C1

MN-65 NE
- FRID 7680 E6

MN-100
- STLP 7936 E5

MN-100 S
- STLP 7936 E4

MN-101
- SHKP 8192 B6
- SHKP 8193 D7

MN-110
- IVGH 8113 E2
- IVGH 8114 A2
- MNDH 8112 E1

Moccasin Ct
- BRNV 8281 B5

Moccasin St
- DLWD 7772 C2
- MAHT 7772 C2

Moccasin Valley Rd
- EDNA 8108 A2

Mockingbird Ln
- EDNP 8106 E1

Modern Rd
- BRKP 7764 A3

Mohawk Av
- STPL 7943 C3

Mohawk Rd E
- NSTP 7857 C3

Mohawk Tr
- EDNA 8108 A2

Mohican Ct
- MNDH 8113 B3

Molan Ter
- COLH 7766 E5
- COLH 7767 A5

Molina St
- SHKP 8278 B4

Molitor Dr
- LINO 7684 D1

Monardo Ln
- EDNA 8108 E3

Mondamin St
- MINN 8025 B5

Monet Ct
- MNDH 8113 A4

Monitor St
- STLP 8022 C1

Monn Av
- VADH 7770 B7
- VADH 7856 B1
- WTBL 7771 B7

Monn Ct
- WTBL 7857 B1

Monroe Av N
- HOPK 8021 E2

Monroe Av S
- EDNA 8021 E3
- HOPK 8021 E3

Monroe Cir NE
- BLNE 7594 D2

Monroe Ct
- STPL 8026 C4
- STPL 8027 A2

Monroe Dr NE
- BLNE 7594 D4

Monroe Pl
- HOPK 8021 E2

Monroe St NE
- BLNE 7594 D1
- BLNE 7680 D1
- COLH 7766 D7
- COLH 7852 D1
- FRID 7680 D5
- FRID 7766 D4
- HLTP 7766 D6
- MINN 7852 D6
- SPLP 7680 D5

Monroe Wy
- HLTP 7766 D6

Montana Av E
- MPLW 7943 D1
- STPL 7942 B1
- STPL 7943 A1

Montana Av W
- STPL 7940 E1
- STPL 7941 D1

Montana Cir E
- MPLW 7943 D1

Montcalm Ct
- STPL 8026 D3

Montcalm Hl
- STPL 8026 D3

Montcalm Pl
- STPL 8026 D3

Montcalm Estates Rd
- STPL 8026 C4

Montclair Av
- MNDS 7681 E6

Montclair Pl
- WILL 7772 D6

Montecito Dr
- SHKP 8278 E3

Montegue Ter N
- BRKP 7679 D4

Monterey Av
- VADH 7856 B1

Monterey Av S
- EDNA 8023 A2
- SAVG 8281 A3
- STLP 7937 A6
- STLP 8023 A2

Monterey Ct
- EDNP 8106 C6

N Monterey Ct
- SHVW 7768 E2

Monterey Ct S
- SHVW 7768 E2

Monterey Dr
- SHVW 7768 E2
- STLP 8023 A1

Monterey Ln
- EAGN 8197 E2

Monterey Pkwy
- STLP 7937 A6

Montgomery Ct
- EDNP 8106 B6

Montgomery St
- STPL 7939 E5
- STPL 7940 A5

Monticello Av
- EAGN 8197 E4

Monticello Ln N
- BRKP 7677 E1
- CHMP 7591 D1
- MAPG 7591 B7
- MAPG 7677 D2
- MAPG 7763 D4
- OSSE 7677 D4

Montmorency St
- VADH 7770 E7

Montreal Av
- STPL 8026 E4

Montreal Av SR-51
- STPL 8026 C4

Montreal Cir
- STPL 8026 E4

Montreal Wy
- STPL 8026 E4

Montrose Ln
- STPL 8025 E3

Montrose Pl
- STPL 7939 E6

Montrose Rd
- WDBY 8030 C4

Mooer Ln
- EDNP 8193 A3

E Mooney Dr
- NBRI 7767 D7

W Mooney Dr
- NBRI 7767 D7

Moon Lake Cir
- WtBT 7770 C2

Moon Lake Ct
- WtBT 7770 E3

Moonlight Ln
- EDNP 8106 C3

Moonlight Hill Rd
- MNTK 8020 C3

Moonlite Dr
- CIRC 7596 D7

Moonstone Dr
- EAGN 8197 C6

Moore Av
- EDNA 8022 D3
- FLCH 7854 A7

Moore St
- STPL 7940 A7

E Moore Lake Dr
- FRID 7766 E2
- FRID 7767 A2

W Moore Lake Dr
- FRID 7766 D2

Moorland Av
- EDNA 8022 E4

Moorland Cir
- MNTK 8020 A1

Moorland Dr
- EDNP 8106 B1

Moorland Rd
- MNTK 7934 A7
- MNTK 8020 A1

Moorland Chase
- BRKP 7679 A4

Moraine Cir
- SHKP 8279 D4

Moraine Dr
- SHKP 8279 D4

Moray Av
- VADH 7856 B1

Morehead Av
- WTBL 7685 D7
- WTBL 7771 D1

Moreland Av E
- WSTP 8028 A5

Moreland Av W
- MNDH 8027 D5
- WSTP 8027 D5
- WSTP 8028 A5

Moreland Cir
- WSTP 8028 B5

Moreland Ct E
- MPLW 8029 D5
- STPL 8029 D5

Morgan Av
- BRNV 8281 D4
- STPL 8026 B5

Morgan Av N
- BRKC 7765 D6
- BRKP 7679 D3
- BRKP 7765 D1
- MINN 7765 D6
- MINN 7851 D2
- MINN 7937 D2

Morgan Av S
- BMTN 8109 D5
- BMTN 8195 D1
- BRNV 8281 D3
- MINN 7937 D3
- MINN 8023 D5
- RHFD 8023 D7
- RHFD 8109 D4

Morgan Cir N
- BRKP 7679 D6

Morgan Cir S
- BMTN 8109 D5
- BMTN 8195 D5

Morgan Ct
- BRNV 8281 D5
- MINN 8023 D7

Morgan Ln
- EDNP 8106 D6
- LINO 7597 A1

Morgan Pl
- BRNV 8281 D3

Morgan St
- DLWD 7772 C2
- MAHT 7772 C2

Mork Cir N
- CHMP 7591 E2

Morningside Av
- VADH 7770 B3

Morningside Cir
- EDNP 8021 B7
- STPL 8029 C2

Morningside Dr
- STPL 8029 D1

Morningside Pl
- VADH 7770 A3

Morningside Rd
- EDNA 8023 A3
- MINN 8023 B3
- STLP 8022 E3
- STLP 8023 A3

Morraine Wy
- EDNP 8106 B6

Morrill Ln
- MINN 8025 D2

Morris Av S
- BMTN 8109 A6
- BMTN 8195 A4

Morris Cir
- BMTN 8109 A6
- BMTN 8194 E4
- BMTN 8195 A2

Morris Ln
- BMTN 8195 A6

Morris Rd
- BMTN 8109 A6
- BMTN 8194 E4
- BMTN 8195 A4

NW Morris St
- NBRI 7767 D6

Morrison St
- LCAN 7855 E5

Morson Cir
- MNDH 8113 C4

Morton Rd
- MNTK 7934 B5

Morton St E
- STPL 8028 A3

Morton St W
- STPL 8027 D3
- STPL 8028 A3

Mosby Rd
- WTBL 7771 D7

Motor Av
- SSTP 8028 C4

Motor Pl
- MINN 8023 B3

Motor St
- EDNA 8022 D4

Mound Av
- SHVW 7769 A2

Mound Ct
- CTRV 7598 B4

Mound St
- STPL 7942 C6

Mound Tr
- CTRV 7598 A4
- LINO 7598 A4

Mounds Av
- NBRI 7767 C2

Mounds Av NW
- NBRI 7768 A2

Mounds Blvd
- STPL 7942 B5

Mounds Blvd US-61
- STPL 7942 B5

Mound Spring Ter
- BMTN 8196 C3

Moundsview Av W
- RSVL 7855 B6

Mounds View Dr
- MNDS 7681 C6

Moundsview Rd
- ARDH 7682 A7
- ARDH 7768 A1
- SHVW 7682 A7

Mount Ter
- MNTK 8020 D3

Mt Airy St
- STPL 7941 D5

Mt Curve Av
- MINN 7937 E4
- MINN 7938 A4
- STPL 8025 E1

Mt Curve Blvd
- STPL 8025 E2

Mt Curve Blvd N
- BRKP 7677 E7
- BRKP 7678 A6

Mt Curve Rd
- BMTN 8108 B7
- EDNP 8193 C1

Mounthall Ter
- MNTK 8020 D3

Mt Hope Dr
- STPL 8028 A2

Mt Hope St
- STPL 8028 A3

Mt Ida St
- STPL 7942 A4

Mt Normandale Curv
- BMTN 8108 D7

Mt Normandale Dr
- BMTN 8108 D7

Mt Ridge Rd
- ARDH 7854 A2
- RSVL 7854 A2

Mt Vernon Av
- MPLW 7855 D6
- MPLW 7856 A6

Mt View Av
- MINN 7937 C3

Mourning Dove Ct
- EAGN 8198 D3

Mourning Dove Rd
- LINO 7597 A5

MTC Rd
- HnpC 8110 E4

Muhlenhardt Rd S
- SHKP 8279 D4

Muir Ln
- BRNV 8282 D3

Mulberry Cir S
- SHKP 8278 A7

Mulberry St
- STPL 7941 C7

Mulcare Dr
- COLH 7766 E5

Mumford Rd
- BRKC 7765 B4

Munster Av
- STPL 8026 A6

Murdock Ter
- EDNP 8106 D5

Muriel Blvd
- WSTP 8028 A7
- WSTP 8114 A1

Muriel Rd
- MNTK 7934 E6
- MNTK 7935 A6

Murphy Av
- FLCH 7940 B1
- SHKP 8278 A2

Murphy Av N
- HOPK 8022 A2

Murphy Pkwy
- EAGN 8198 A4

Murray Av
- STAN 7853 B4
- WTBL 7771 B2

Murray St
- STPL 8026 A6

Muskrat Run
- LINO 7683 D1

Mustang Av
- HnpC 8025 D7
- MINN 8025 D7

Mustang Cir
- MNDS 7767 E1

Mustang Ct
- LINO 7596 E2
- LINO 7597 A2

Mustang Dr
- MNDS 7767 E1

Mustang Ln
- LINO 7596 E2
- MNDS 7767 E1
- NBRI 7767 E2

Myers Av N
- BRKP 7764 B2

Myrle Av
- WTBL 7771 D4

Myrman Av
- WSTP 8027 E5

Myrtle Av
- STPL 7939 E5

Myrtle Cir
- MNTK 8021 A2

Myrtle Ct N
- MPLW 7943 D1

Myrtle Dr
- BRNV 8281 C4

Myrtle Ln
- LINO 7597 C1

Myrtle Pl
- SSTP 8028 C7

Myrtle St
- MPLW 7857 D7
- NSTP 7857 D6

Myrtle St N
- MPLW 7857 D7
- MPLW 7943 D1

Mystic Ln
- BRNV 8282 E2

Mystic St
- STPL 8029 B2

Mystic Lake Dr NW
- PRIO 8278 C7

N

Nadeau Rd
- LCAN 7855 E2

Nagell Cir
- MAPG 7762 E1

Nancy Cir
- EAGN 8283 C1
- SHVW 7768 E4

Nancy Ct
- LINO 7597 C1

Nancy Dr
- LINO 7597 D1

Nancy Ln
- EDNA 8109 A1

Nancy Pl
- RSVL 7854 E5
- SHVW 7768 E4

Nantwick Ln
- BRKP 7679 A3

Nantwick Rdg N
- BRKP 7679 A3

Naomi Dr
- EDNA 8108 D2

Napco Av
- MINN 7938 A1

Naper St
- GLDV 7849 E6
- PYMH 7849 E7

Naper Bay
- EAGN 8197 D6

Naples St NE
- BLNE 7596 A7
- BLNE 7681 D1
- BLNE 7682 A1
- LXTN 7682 A2
- SHVW 7682 A3

Napolean Cir
- SSTP 8028 B4
- WSTP 8028 B4

Narcissus St NW
- COON 7592 E2

Narvik Ct
- EAGN 8283 E1

Narvik Dr
- EAGN 8283 E1

Nash Rd
- BRKC 7765 C4

Nashua Ln
- MNDH 8113 B3

Nason Pl
- STPL 7940 D2

Nassau Cir NE
- BLNE 7595 C3

Nassau Ct NE
- BLNE 7595 C4

Nassau St NE
- BLNE 7595 C5

Natalie Rd NE
- PRIO 8280 A7

Natchez Av
- SAVG 8281 A2

Natchez Av N
- GLDV 7937 A2

Natchez Av S
- EDNA 8023 A2
- GLDV 7937 A3
- STLP 7937 A4
- STLP 8023 A2

Natchez Cir
- SAVG 8281 B1

Natchez Ct
- SAVG 8281 B1

Natchez Ln
- SAVG 8280 E6
- SAVG 8281 A6

Natchez Pl
- SAVG 8281 B1

Nathan Ln N
- CHMP 7591 D1
- MAPG 7591 D7
- MAPG 7677 D1
- MAPG 7763 D3
- PYMH 7763 D4
- PYMH 7849 D3
- PYMH 7935 D1
- STLP 7935 D2

Nathaniel Ct
- VADH 7856 A1

National Ct NE
- BLNE 7596 D3

National St NE
- BLNE 7596 D4

Nature Ct
- WDBY 8030 C2

INDEX 31

Nature Pth — Oakland Ter

Minneapolis Street Index

STREET Block City ZIP Map # Grid

Nature Pth
- WDBY 8030 C1
Nature's Wy
- LCAN 7855 E5
Nature View Ct
- WSTP 8113 D1
Nature View Ln
- WSTP 8113 D1
Nature View Tr
- VADH 7770 C6
Nauvoo Ln
- EAGN 8285 B1
Navaho Tr
- EDNA 8108 A1
Navajo Ln
- MNDH 8113 B3
Navajo Rd
- NSTP 7857 D3
Nawadaha Blvd
- MINN 8025 C4
Nebraska Av E
- MPLW 7943 C1
- STPL 7942 D1
- STPL 7943 B1
Nebraska Av W
- FLCH 7940 C1
- STPL 7940 C1
- STPL 7941 C1
Nechas Cir
- EDNP 8106 B5
Neddersen Cir N
- BRKP 7678 C4
Neddersen Pkwy N
- BRKP 7678 C4
Neid Ln
- STPL 7942 B4
Neil Armstrong Blvd
- EAGN 8112 E7
- EAGN 8198 E1
Neill St
- STPL 7942 D7
Neill Lake Rd
- EDNP 8107 C7
- EDNP 8193 C1
Nelson Dr
- ARDH 7682 D7
- MNTK 8021 A3
- SHVW 7682 E7
Nelson St
- FLCH 7940 B2
- STPL 7943 C7
Nemec Knoll Rd
- EDNP 8193 A1
Nemitz Av E
- MPLW 8029 E5
Neptune St
- MAHT 7772 C3
Nesbitt Av S
- BMTN 8194 D5
Nesbitt Cir
- BMTN 8194 D3
Nesbitt Rd
- BMTN 8194 D1
Nestling Cir
- EAGN 8198 A6
Nettleton Av
- STPL 8026 C4
Nevada Av
- SAVG 8280 C2
Nevada Av E
- STPL 7942 A1
- STPL 7943 A1
Nevada Av N
- BRKP 7678 B3
- CHMP 7592 B4
- CRYS 7764 B5
- CRYS 7850 B1
- GLDV 7850 B6
- NWHE 7764 B7
- NWHE 7850 B4
Nevada Av S
- BMTN 8194 B6
- GLDV 7936 B3
- STLP 7936 B4
Nevada Av W
- STPL 7940 E1
- STPL 7941 A1
Nevada Cir
- SAVG 8280 B5
Nevada Cir N
- BRKP 7678 B4
- CHMP 7592 B3
Nevada Cir S
- BMTN 8108 B6
Nevada Ct
- CRYS 7850 B4
Nevada Ct N
- BRKP 7678 B4
- CHMP 7592 B3
Nevada Ln N
- CHMP 7592 B4
Neville Av
- MAHT 7772 C4
New Brighton Blvd
- MINN 7853 A6
- RSVL 7853 D3
- STAN 7853 D3
New Brighton Blvd CO-88
- MINN 7853 A6
- RSVL 7853 D3
- STAN 7853 C4
New Brighton Rd
- ARDH 7768 A6
- ARDH 7854 A1
- NBRI 7768 A7
- RSVL 7854 B1
Newbury Ct
- WDBY 8030 C7
Newbury Knl
- WDBY 8030 B7
Newbury Rd
- WDBY 8030 B7
Newbury Alcove
- WDBY 8030 C7
Newbury Draw
- WDBY 8030 C7
Newbury Echo
- WDBY 8030 C7
New Century Blvd S
- MPLW 8029 E6
- WDBY 8029 E4
New Century Ln
- MPLW 8029 E6
- WDBY 8029 E4
New Century Pl E
- MPLW 8029 E6
New Century Ter E
- MPLW 8029 E6
New Century Ter S
- MPLW 8029 E6
Newcomb St
- STPL 7942 D4
New Market Dr
- EDNP 8106 A6
Newport Dr
- EDNA 8022 A6
- EDNP 8193 C4
Newton Av
- BRNV 8281 D6
N Newton Av
- MINN 7937 D1
S Newton Av
- MINN 7937 D5
Newton Av N
- BRKC 7765 D2
- BRKP 7679 D3
- BRKP 7765 D2
- MINN 7765 D6
- MINN 7851 D2
- MINN 7937 D2
Newton Av S
- BMTN 8109 D7
- BMTN 8195 D1
- MINN 7937 D3
- MINN 8023 D5
- RHFD 8109 D1
Newtown Ct
- EAGN 8198 E4
New York Av
- EAGN 8199 A5
New York Av N
- MINN 7852 B3
Niagara Ct N
- MAPG 7762 C4
Niagara Ln N
- MAPG 7676 C3
- MAPG 7762 C1
- MNTK 7934 C2
- PYMH 7848 C1
- PYMH 7934 C2
Niblick Ln
- EDNP 8193 D2
Nicholas Ct
- WTBL 7771 B5
Nichols Ct
- SHVW 7769 C4
Nicollet Av
- BRNV 8282 B3
Nicollet Av S
- BMTN 8110 B5
- BMTN 8196 B1
- MINN 7938 B4
- MINN 8024 B4
- RHFD 8024 B4
- RHFD 8110 B4
E Nicollet Blvd
- BRNV 8282 B6
W Nicollet Blvd
- BRNV 8282 A6
Nicollet Cir
- BMTN 8196 B4
Nicollet Ct
- BRNV 8282 A7
Nicollet Ln
- BRNV 8282 B5
Nicollet St
- MINN 7938 C1
Nicols Pt
- EAGN 8283 B1
Nicols Rd
- DkaC 8197 B3
- EAGN 8197 B3
- EAGN 8283 C1
Nightingale Cir NE
- PRIO 8279 B7
Nightingale St NW
- COON 7593 C6
Niles Av
- STPL 8025 E3
- STPL 8026 B3
Nina Ct
- MNDH 8027 A7
Nina St
- STPL 7941 C7
Nine Mile Cove
- HOPK 8021 D5
Nine Mile Cove E
- HOPK 8021 D5
Nine Mile Cove N
- HOPK 8021 E5
Nine Mile Cove S
- HOPK 8021 E5
Nine Mile Cove W
- HOPK 8021 E5
Nine Mile Creek Cir
- BMTN 8108 E6
Nine Mile Creek Pkwy
- BMTN 8108 E6
- BMTN 8109 A7
Nine Oaks Cir
- BMTN 8109 A7
Nob Hill Dr
- EDNA 8108 D2
Noble Av N
- BRKC 7765 A1
- BRKP 7593 A7
- BRKP 7679 A1
- BRKP 7765 A1
- CHMP 7593 A6
- CRYS 7765 A4
- CRYS 7851 A4
- GLDV 7851 A3
- ROBB 7851 A3
Noble Ct N
- BRKP 7679 A1
Noble Dr N
- GLDV 7851 A7
Noble Ln N
- BRKC 7765 A3
Noble Pkwy N
- BRKP 7593 A7
- BRKP 7679 A3
Noble Rd
- ARDH 7768 A7
- NBRI 7768 A7
Noel Dr
- LCAN 7856 A3
Noid Dr
- BRKP 7764 A3
Nokia Wy
- EAGN 8197 E7
- EAGN 8283 E1
Nokomis Av
- MPLW 7943 C2
- STPL 7943 C3
Nokomis Av S
- MINN 8025 B3
Nokomis Cir
- MINN 8024 E6
Nokomis Ct
- MINN 8024 D6
Nokomis Ln
- MINN 8024 D6
Nokomis Pkwy E
- MINN 8024 E6
- MINN 8025 A4
Nokomis Pkwy W
- MINN 8024 E5
Nolan Dr
- MNTK 8021 B5
Norbert Ln
- STPL 8026 A5
Norbert Pl
- STPL 8026 A5
Nord Av S
- BMTN 8194 E3
- BMTN 8195 A5
Nord Cir
- BMTN 8195 B1
Nord Dr
- BMTN 8195 A5
Nord Rd
- BMTN 8194 E3
- BMTN 8195 A3
Nord Cir Dr
- NOAK 7683 E4
Nordic Cir
- EDNA 8108 B1
Nordic Dr
- EDNA 8108 B2
Nordstrom Ct
- BMTN 8110 D6
Norfolk Av
- STPL 8026 A6
Norfolk Ln
- STPL 8026 A6
Norma Av
- ARDH 7768 C4
Norma Cir
- ARDH 7768 C4
Norma Ln
- MNDH 8027 C4
- WSTP 8027 C5
Norman Dr
- MNTK 8020 C4
Norman Center Dr
- BMTN 8108 D6
Norman Creek Tr
- BMTN 8108 D5
Normandale Blvd
- BMTN 8108 E7
- BMTN 8194 E1
- EDNA 8022 E7
- EDNA 8108 E5
Normandale Blvd SR-100
- BMTN 8108 E4
- EDNA 8108 E3
Normandale Ct
- EDNA 8022 D6
Normandale Rd
- EDNA 8022 E6
- EDNA 8108 E2
Normandale Highlands Cir
- BMTN 8195 B1
Normandale Highlands Dr
- BMTN 8194 E3
- BMTN 8195 A3
Normandale Lake Blvd
- BMTN 8108 D5
Normandale Lake Dr
- BMTN 8108 C6
Normandale Service Rd
- BMTN 8108 E6
Normandy Ct
- WtBT 7684 D6
Normandy Ln
- MNTK 8020 B7
Normandy Pl
- GLDV 7850 E5
Normandy Crest
- EDNP 8193 E4
Norman Ridge Cir
- BMTN 8194 D1
Norman Ridge Dr
- BMTN 8108 D7
- BMTN 8194 D1
Norm McGrew Pl
- MINN 7938 E2
Norpac Rd
- STPL 7941 E2
Norris Cir
- STPL 7940 D4
North Av
- EDNA 8022 D4
North Cir NE
- FRID 7680 E6
North Ct
- NBRI 7767 C4
North Gdn
- BMTN 8110 D6
North Rd
- BLNE 7596 E6
- CIRC 7596 E6
- LINO 7596 E6
North Rd NE
- BLNE 7596 C6
- CIRC 7596 C6
North St
- MNTK 8020 D5
- STLP 8022 B1
- STPL 7942 B5
Northbridge Ct
- EAGN 8199 C3
Northbrook Av N
- BRKP 7763 D3
- BRKP 7764 D3
Northbrook Cir
- BRKP 7763 E4
- BRKP 7764 D4
Northco Dr NE
- FRID 7680 C7
Northdale Blvd NW
- BLNE 7594 C4
- COON 7592 E1
- COON 7593 A2
- COON 7594 B3
Northdale Blvd NW CO-11
- COON 7593 D2
- COON 7594 B3
Northern Dr
- BRNV 8282 A4
- CRYS 7850 A4
Northern Lights Blvd
- CTRV 7598 E5
- LINO 7598 E5
Northfield Av
- EDNA 8108 B1
Northgate Pkwy
- EDNP 8107 C2
North Gate Rd
- SSTP 8115 A4
Northglen Dr
- BMTN 8196 A3
Northland Cir N
- BRKP 7764 A2
Northland Ct
- BRKP 7764 A2
Northland Dr
- BMTN 8109 B5
- MNDH 8112 D4
Northland Dr N
- BRKP 7677 E7
- BRKP 7763 E1
- BRKP 7764 A2
Northland Ter N
- BRKP 7763 E1
Northmark Dr
- EDNP 8107 C6
Northport Dr
- BRKC 7765 B5
North Ridge Dr
- EAGN 8199 A4
Northridge Rd
- MNTK 7934 E3
Northrop Dr
- MINN 8025 D2
Northrup Av
- FLCH 7939 E1
- STPL 7939 E1
Northrup Ln
- MINN 7937 E4
Northrup Tr
- EDNP 8106 E7
- EDNP 8107 A7
Northtown Dr NE
- BLNE 7680 C3
Northview Dr
- EAGN 8198 E4
North View Ln
- WDBY 8030 E6
Northview St
- RSVL 7855 C2
Northview Ter
- EAGN 8198 E4
Northview Park Rd
- EAGN 8198 E4
- EAGN 8199 A4
Northway Dr
- BRKC 7765 B5
Northwest Av
- WTBL 7685 D6
- WtBT 7685 D6
Northwest Blvd
- MAPG 7763 B4
- PYMH 7762 E6
- PYMH 7763 A5
- PYMH 7848 E2
- PYMH 7849 A3
Northwest Blvd CO-61
- MAPG 7763 B4
- PYMH 7762 E6
- PYMH 7763 A5
- PYMH 7848 E2
- PYMH 7849 A3
Northwest Dr
- HnpC 8111 D2
Northwest Pkwy
- EAGN 8113 A5
Northwood Av N
- BRKP 7679 A2
Northwood Cir
- EAGN 8198 E1
- NWHE 7849 E3
Northwood Ct N
- BRKP 7678 E1
- BRKP 7679 A1
Northwood Dr
- EAGN 8198 D1
- EDNA 8022 B5
- NSTP 7857 D6
Northwood Ln N
- BRKP 7678 E1
- BRKP 7679 A2
Northwood Pkwy
- EAGN 8198 D1
- NWHE 7849 E2
- NWHE 7850 A3
Northwood Rdg
- BMTN 8108 D7
Northwoods Dr
- ARDH 7768 D5
Norton Av NE
- FRID 7680 E7
- FRID 7681 A7
Norton Dr
- SHKP 8278 A7
Norton St
- STPL 7941 B3
Nortonia Av
- STPL 7943 B4
Norway Cir
- BRNV 8283 A2
- COON 7594 A1
Norway Ct N
- CHMP 7591 D5
Norway Pt
- BRNV 8283 A2
- EAGN 8198 E1
Norway St NW
- COON 7594 A4
- COON 7680 A2
Norway Tr
- SHKP 8278 B2
Norway Pine Cir
- MNTK 7935 A4
Norway Pine Ct
- WtBT 7685 E3
Norway Pine Dr
- WtBT 7685 E4
Norwest Ct
- EAGN 8198 C1
Norwood Cir
- EAGN 8284 A1
- EDNP 8106 A6
Norwood Ct
- EAGN 8284 A1
Norwood Ct N
- MAPG 7677 A3
Norwood Dr
- EAGN 8284 A1
- MNTK 8020 A5
Norwood Ln
- MNTK 8020 A4
Norwood Ln N
- MAPG 7677 A2
- MAPG 7763 A2
- PYMH 7763 A5
- PYMH 7849 A1
Nottingham Ct
- MNTK 7935 B5
Nottingham Ln
- CIRC 7682 D2
- LINO 7597 B1
Nottingham Pkwy N
- MAPG 7676 A7
- MAPG 7762 A1
Nottingham Pl
- SHVW 7768 E1
Nottingham Tr
- EDNP 8193 D2
November Ln
- EDNP 8192 D2
Nugent St
- STPL 8027 B2
Nursery Dr
- MNTK 8020 B5
Nursery Hill Ct
- ARDH 7768 D3
Nursery Hill Ln
- ARDH 7768 D3
Nusbaumer Dr
- STPL 7940 E2
Nuthatch Ln
- NOAK 7684 A5
Nybro Cir
- EAGN 8198 C6
N Nybro Ln
- EAGN 8198 C6

O

Oak Av
- ARDH 7768 B6
Oak Cir
- CTRV 7598 D6
Oak Cir E
- MPLW 7943 D1
Oak Ct
- LINO 7597 C1
- WTBL 7771 D7
S Oak Ct
- VADH 7770 A4
Oak Dr
- EDNA 8022 E6
- EDNA 8023 A6
- EDNP 8106 C5
- MNTK 8020 A5
- WTBL 7857 E1
N Oak Dr
- VADH 7770 B4
S Oak Dr
- VADH 7770 A4
Oak Ln
- EDNA 8022 C6
- LINO 7597 C1
- MNTK 7934 C4
- WTBL 7771 D7
Oak Rd
- CIRC 7596 D7
- MNTK 8020 B2
Oak St
- MAHT 7772 C3
- SSTP 8115 B4
- WTBL 7771 D7
Oak St N
- BRKC 7765 A7
Oak St SE
- MINN 7939 B3
Oak Ter
- WTBL 7771 D6
Oak Wy
- EAGN 8283 C1
Oakbend Ln
- EDNA 8022 A4
Oak Bluff Dr
- STPL 8029 C4
Oakborough Dr
- SAVG 8280 E7
Oakbrooke Cir
- EAGN 8198 A5
Oakbrooke Ct
- EAGN 8198 A5
Oakbrooke Curv
- EAGN 8198 A5
Oakbrooke Dr
- EAGN 8198 A5
Oakbrooke Ln
- EAGN 8198 A5
Oakbrooke Ter
- EAGN 8198 B5
Oakbrooke Tr
- EAGN 8198 A5
Oakbrooke Wy
- EAGN 8198 A5
Oakbrooke Alcove
- EAGN 8198 A5
Oak Chaise Ct
- MNTK 8021 A5
Oak Chase Cir
- EAGN 8198 D7
Oak Chase Ln
- EAGN 8198 D7
Oak Chase Rd
- EAGN 8198 D7
Oak Chase Wy
- EAGN 8198 D7
Oak Cliff Dr
- EAGN 8283 B1
Oak Creek Cir
- VADH 7770 A6
Oak Creek Ct
- VADH 7770 A6
Oak Creek Dr E
- VADH 7770 A6
Oak Creek Dr S
- VADH 7770 A6
Oak Creek Dr W
- VADH 7770 A6
Oak Creek Ter
- VADH 7770 A6
Oakcrest Av
- RSVL 7854 B4
- RSVL 7855 A4
Oakcrest Dr
- VADH 7770 A4
Oakdale Av
- IVGH 8114 B1
- STPL 8028 A2
- WSTP 8028 B5
- WSTP 8114 B1
Oakdale Av N
- MINN 7851 C4
- ROBB 7851 B4
Oakdale Av S
- EDNA 8023 A3
- STLP 8023 A3
Oakdale Ct
- WSTP 8028 B6
Oakdale Dr
- MAHT 7858 B2
- PNSP 7858 B2
Oak Dr Ln
- HOPK 8021 B2
- MNTK 8021 B3
Oak Glen Dr
- HOPK 8021 D3
Oak Glen Rd
- EDNA 8108 C3
Oak Grove Blvd
- RHFD 8109 E3
- RHFD 8110 A3
Oak Grove Cir
- BMTN 8195 E4
- GLDV 7850 D7
Oak Grove Ln
- MAHT 7772 D3
Oak Grove Pkwy
- NOAK 7770 A3
- VADH 7769 E3
- VADH 7770 A3
Oak Grove Pl
- STPL 8026 D1
Oak Grove St
- MINN 7938 A4
Oak Heights Ct E
- MPLW 8029 D6
Oak Hill Ct
- EAGN 8199 A4
- EDNP 8106 E2
Oakhill Ct
- BRHV 7772 A5
- EAGN 8283 E1
Oak Hill Ct E
- MPLW 7943 E1
Oak Hill Dr
- SHVW 7683 C5
Oak Hill Pl
- NSTP 7857 D5
Oak Hollow Ln
- LINO 7683 B2
Oakhurst Av
- VADH 7770 B3
Oak Knoll Dr
- WDBY 7944 A7
- WTBL 7771 B5
Oak Knoll Plz
- WDBY 7944 A7
Oak Knoll Ter N
- MNTK 7935 C4
Oak Knoll Ter S
- MNTK 7935 C4
Oak Lake Av
- MINN 7938 D2
Oakland Av
- RHFD 8110 C3
- STPL 7941 B7
- STPL 8027 C1
Oakland Av N
- RHFD 8110 C4
Oakland Av S
- BMTN 8110 C6
- BMTN 8196 C2
- MINN 7938 C5
- MINN 8024 C2
- RHFD 8110 C2
Oakland Cir
- BRNV 8282 C3
Oakland Dr
- BRNV 8282 C5
Oakland Ln
- BRNV 8282 B5
Oakland Pl
- MNTK 7934 D5
Oakland Rd
- BMTN 8196 C3
- MNTK 7934 D4
Oakland Ter
- RHFD 8109 D2

Minneapolis Street Index

STREET / Block City ZIP Map # Grid

Overton Dr NE
- FRID 7766 D1

N Owasso Blvd
- LCAN 7769 C7
- SHVW 7769 B7

S Owasso Blvd
- LCAN 7855 D2
- RSVL 7855 C2

S Owasso Blvd E
- LCAN 7855 D2

S Owasso Blvd W
- LCAN 7855 D2
- RSVL 7855 D2

W Owasso Blvd
- RSVL 7855 A2
- SHVW 7769 A7
- SHVW 7855 A1

E Owasso Ln
- LCAN 7855 C1
- SHVW 7855 C1

Owasso St
- SHVW 7769 A7

Owasso Heights Dr
- SHVW 7855 A1

Owasso Heights Rd
- SHVW 7769 B7
- SHVW 7855 A1

Owasso Hills Dr
- RSVL 7855 B3

Owatonna Ct NE
- BLNE 7595 C2

Owatonna St NE
- BLNE 7595 C2

Oxborough Av S
- BMTN 8109 A5
- BMTN 8195 A5

Oxborough Cir
- BMTN 8194 E3

Oxborough Ct N
- BRKP 7678 E6

Oxborough Curv
- BMTN 8194 E1
- BMTN 8195 A2

Oxborough Gdns N
- BRKP 7678 E4
- BRKP 7679 A6

Oxborough Ln
- BMTN 8194 E5
- BMTN 8195 A6

Oxborough Rd
- BMTN 8194 E2
- BMTN 8195 A2

Oxbow Ct N
- CHMP 7592 D6

Oxbow Dr
- EDNP 8193 A2

Oxbow Pl N
- CHMP 7592 E6

Oxbow Tr N
- CHMP 7592 E6

Oxbow Creek Dr N
- BRKP 7592 D7
- BRKP 7593 A7

Oxbow Lake Pl N
- BRKP 7678 D2

Oxford Av
- EDNA 8022 D4

Oxford Cir
- WDBY 8030 C6

Oxford Ct
- MNDH 8112 E1
- WDBY 8030 C7

Oxford Ct N
- SHVW 7768 E4

Oxford Dr
- WDBY 8030 C6

Oxford Ln
- BRKP 7678 E6

Oxford Pl
- MNTK 8020 A3
- SHKP 8279 A2

Oxford Rd
- EAGN 8199 B5

Oxford Rd N
- SHKP 8279 A1

Oxford Rd S
- SHKP 8278 E2
- SHKP 8279 A2

Oxford St
- HOPK 8022 A1
- STLP 8022 D1

N Oxford St
- RSVL 7854 E7
- STPL 7854 E7

Oxford St N
- RSVL 7854 E2
- SHVW 7682 E4
- SHVW 7768 E1
- STPL 7940 E3

Oxford St S
- STPL 7940 E7
- STPL 8026 E1

Oxford St W
- STLP 8022 C2

Oxford Alcove
- WDBY 8030 C6

Oxford Bay
- WDBY 8030 C6

Oxford Echo
- WDBY 8030 D6

P

Pacific Av
- EAGN 8198 A2
- WTBL 7685 D7

Pacific St
- MINN 7852 B5
- STPL 7942 C6
- STPL 7943 A6

Packard St NE
- BLNE 7596 D5

Paddington Rd
- WILL 7772 D6

Paddock Ct
- EAGN 8198 D4

Paddock Rd
- EDNA 8022 C4

Page St E
- STPL 8028 A3

Page St W
- STPL 8027 E3
- STPL 8028 A3

Pagel Rd
- MNDH 8113 B3

Pahl Av
- STAN 7853 B4

Painted Turtle Rd
- LINO 7683 C1

Painters Rdg
- EDNP 8193 B1

Paisley Ln
- GLDV 7936 D2

Paiute Cir
- EDNA 8107 E2

Paiute Dr
- EDNA 8107 E2

Paiute Pass
- EDNA 8107 E2

Palace Av
- STPL 8025 E2
- STPL 8026 B2
- STPL 8027 A2

Palisade Cir
- EAGN 8197 E3

Palisade Ct NE
- BLNE 7595 C2

Palisade Pt
- EAGN 8197 E3

Palisade St NE
- BLNE 7595 C2

Palisade Wy
- EAGN 8197 E4
- EAGN 8198 A3

Pallisades Cir
- EDNP 8193 B2

Palm Cir
- MPLW 7856 C4

Palm Ct
- LCAN 7856 B4
- MPLW 7856 B4

Palm St NW
- COON 7594 A3
- COON 7680 A4

Palmer Av
- SAVG 8280 E2

Palmer Av S
- BMTN 8108 E6
- BMTN 8194 E5

Palmer Cir
- BMTN 8194 E2

Palmer Dr
- NBRI 7767 C4

Palmer Pl
- STPL 8026 E3
- STPL 8027 A3

Palmer Rd
- BMTN 8194 E1
- BMTN 8195 A7

W Palmer Lake Cir
- BRKC 7765 B2

W Palmer Lake Dr
- BRKC 7765 B2
- BRKP 7765 B2

Palmetto Dr
- EDNP 8106 B7
- EDNP 8192 B1

Palomino Dr
- APVA 8282 E5
- APVA 8283 A5
- BRNV 8282 E5

Palomino Ln
- BLNE 7596 E2
- LINO 7596 E2
- LINO 7597 A2

Palomino Tr
- EAGN 8198 B4

Pamela Ln
- MNDH 8027 B7

Pampas Ct
- SHKP 8278 A4

Pandora Dr NE
- FRID 7766 D1

Panorama Av
- FRID 7766 C5

Paola Cir S
- BMTN 8108 D6

Papa Ln
- EDNP 8192 D1

Parc Dr
- BRNV 8283 A3

Park Av
- BRHV 7772 A5
- BRNV 8281 B7
- BRNV 8282 C7
- MAHT 7772 C3
- RHFD 8110 C3
- WtBT 7685 C6

Park Av N
- RHFD 8110 C4

Park Av S
- BMTN 8110 C6
- BMTN 8196 C2
- MINN 7938 C3
- MINN 8024 C1
- RHFD 8110 C2

Park Av S CO-33
- MINN 7938 C7
- MINN 8024 C1

Park Cir
- BMTN 8196 C3
- MNDH 8027 A6

S Park Cir
- SAVG 8280 E7

Park Ct
- LINO 7597 B3
- WTBL 7770 E3

S Park Ct
- SAVG 8281 B1

Park Dr
- CIRC 7596 D7
- MINN 8023 D4
- WTBL 7771 C7
- WTBL 7857 C1

N Park Dr
- MPLW 7943 C7
- STPL 7943 C7

S Park Dr
- PRIO 8280 B7
- SAVG 8280 B7
- SAVG 8281 A7

W Park Dr
- BRNV 8281 C7

Park Dr E
- BLNE 7596 D6
- CIRC 7596 D6

Park Dr W
- BLNE 7596 D6
- CIRC 7596 D6

Park Ln
- APVA 8282 E7
- HOPK 8021 D2
- MINN 7937 C5
- MNDH 8113 C4
- MNTK 7934 A7
- SSTP 8028 E7

Park Ln NW
- COON 7593 A1

Park Ln S
- MNTK 7935 B3
- PYMH 7935 B2

Park Pl
- BRNV 8282 C6
- EAGN 8198 A2
- EDNA 8023 A6
- MAHT 7772 C5
- NWPT 8115 C4
- SHKP 8192 D7
- SHKP 8278 D1

W Park Rd
- HOPK 8021 B2
- MNTK 8021 B2

Park Rd E
- BMTN 8110 D7

Park Row
- NSTP 7857 E3

Park St
- LCAN 7855 D4
- SHVW 7682 B3
- STPL 7941 D1
- WTBL 7770 E3
- WTBL 7771 B3
- WtBT 7770 E3
- WtBT 7771 A3

Park St E
- SSTP 8115 A2

Park St W
- IVGH 8114 E2
- SSTP 8114 E2

Park Ter
- EDNA 8021 E4
- HOPK 8021 E1
- MINN 7939 D7
- MINN 8025 D1
- SPLP 7681 A3

Park Access Rd E
- CTRV 7598 B4
- LINO 7598 B4

Park Access Rd F
- LINO 7597 D5
- LINO 7598 A6

Park Access Rd G
- LINO 7597 E2
- LINO 7598 A2

Park Access Rd H
- LINO 7598 B2

Park Av Frontage Rd
- MINN 7938 C4

Park Center Blvd
- STLP 8022 E2

Park Center Dr
- EAGN 8197 C7

Parkcliff Dr
- EAGN 8198 D7
- EAGN 8284 D1

Park Commons Dr
- STLP 8022 E1
- STLP 8023 A1

Parkdale Dr
- STLP 7936 E4

Parker Av
- RSVL 7854 E6
- RSVL 7855 A6
- WtBT 7685 A7

Parker Dr
- EDNP 8193 D4

Parker Ln
- MNTK 7935 D4
- STLP 7935 D4

Parker Rd
- MAHT 7772 A7
- STLP 7935 D4

Parker's Dr
- WDBY 8030 E6

Parker's Lake Rd
- MNTK 7934 C3
- PYMH 7934 C2

Park Glen Rd
- STLP 7936 E7
- STLP 7937 A7

Park Hills Ct
- WDBY 8030 A2

W Park Hills Dr
- BMTN 8194 A5

Park Knoll Cir S
- BMTN 8108 A6

Park Knoll Dr
- EAGN 8199 A6

Parkland Ct
- STPL 7943 B7

Parklands Ln
- STLP 7937 A4

Parklands Rd
- STLP 7937 A5

Parklawn Av
- EDNA 8109 A3

Parklawn Ct
- EDNA 8109 A4

Park Nicollet Blvd
- STLP 8022 E2

Park Overlook Dr
- RSVL 7855 A1
- SHVW 7855 A1

Park Place Blvd
- GLDV 7936 E4
- STLP 7936 E4

Park Place Dr
- MNDH 8027 A6
- SHVW 7682 E5

Park Ridge Ct
- STPL 8029 B1

Parkridge Ct
- EAGN 8284 D1

Park Ridge Dr
- SHKP 8278 A1

Parkridge Dr
- EAGN 8198 D7
- EAGN 8284 D1
- WtBT 7770 D4

Park Ridge Dr W
- MNTK 7935 B5

Parkridge Knl
- BRNV 8281 C7

Parkridge Ln
- SAVG 8280 B7

Parkridge Wy
- SAVG 8280 B7

Parkshore Dr
- ARDH 7768 B4

Parkside Blvd
- HOPK 8022 A2

Parkside Cir
- BRNV 8282 C5

Parkside Cir N
- CHMP 7591 E5

Parkside Ct N
- CHMP 7591 E5

Parkside Dr
- STPL 7943 B7
- VADH 7856 B1

Parkside Ln
- EDNA 8022 D4

Parkside Tr N
- CHMP 7591 D5

Park Terrace Dr
- EDNP 8106 B2

E Park Valley Dr
- HOPK 8021 D4

Park Valley Ln
- WtBT 7770 D4

Park Valley Rd
- MNTK 7934 C6
- MNTK 8020 D1

Parkview Av
- LINO 7597 A5
- STPL 7940 E2
- STPL 7941 A2

Parkview Blvd
- GLDV 7851 B5
- MINN 7851 C5
- ROBB 7851 B5

Park View Cir
- BMTN 8195 D3

Parkview Ct
- VADH 7770 C4
- WtBT 7685 E5

Parkview Ct S
- MPLW 8029 D2

Park View Dr
- MNDS 7681 C6
- WtBT 7685 E5

Parkview Dr
- BLNE 7682 B3
- SHVW 7682 A4

Parkview Ln
- BMTN 8108 C6
- EAGN 8198 D7

Parkview Ln N
- CHMP 7591 C1

Parkview Ln NE
- COLH 7766 E6
- COLH 7767 A6

Parkview Ln S
- MPLW 8029 D2

Park View Ter
- MNDS 7681 C6

Parkview Ter
- GLDV 7937 B3

Parkway Cir
- BRKC 7765 D3

Parkway Ct
- MINN 8024 B5
- WTBL 7770 D2

Parkway Dr
- MPLW 7856 C7
- MPLW 7857 E6
- NSTP 7857 E6
- STPL 7856 B7
- STPL 7942 B1

Parkway Pl
- BRNV 8282 E2

Parkway Ponds Ln
- WtBT 7770 E4

Parkwood Cir
- VADH 7770 B6

Parkwood Ct
- BRNV 8282 D2

Parkwood Dr
- BRNV 8282 D4
- SHVW 7682 D4
- SSTP 8028 C5
- WDBY 8030 A3

Parkwood Ln
- BRNV 8282 D5
- EDNA 8021 E6
- VADH 7770 B6

Parkwood Pl
- BRNV 8282 D2

Parkwood Rd
- EDNA 8021 E5
- EDNA 8022 A5

Parkwoods Rd
- STLP 7936 E5

Parnell Av
- EDNA 8022 E7

Parnell Av S
- EDNA 8022 E7
- EDNA 8108 E1

Parsimony Ln
- EDNP 8192 C1

Partridge Cir NW
- COON 7593 B5

Partridge Ct
- LINO 7685 B2

Partridge Ct NE
- PRIO 8279 B7

Partridge Ln
- NOAK 7683 E5

Partridge Pl
- CTRV 7598 D6
- LINO 7597 E7

Partridge Rd
- RSVL 7853 E2

Partridge St NW
- COON 7593 C1

Pascal Av
- FLCH 7854 C7
- RSVL 7854 C6

N Pascal Av
- ARDH 7768 C6

Pascal Av N
- BLNE 7682 A2
- LXTN 7682 A2

Pascal St
- ARDH 7682 C5
- RSVL 7854 C3
- SHVW 7682 C5

Pascal St N
- FLCH 7854 C7
- FLCH 7940 C1
- STPL 7940 C2

Pascal St S
- STPL 8026 C2

Passfield Turn
- MAPG 7676 C6

Pathways Dr
- STPL 7943 B7

Patricia Ct
- EDNP 8106 C2

Patricia Ln
- MNTK 8020 A5

Patricia St
- MNDH 8112 E2

Patrick Rd
- EAGN 8198 E6

Patriot Ln
- LXTN 7682 B1

Patsy Ln
- GLDV 7850 A6

Patti Dr
- LINO 7597 A3

Patton Rd
- NBRI 7767 C5
- RSVL 7853 D2

Paul Dr
- BRKC 7764 E3

Paul Pkwy NE
- BLNE 7594 D1
- BLNE 7595 A1

Paul Pl
- WtBT 7685 E5

Paul St
- WDBY 8030 C3

Paul Alcove
- WDBY 8030 C3

Paul Kirkwood Dr
- ARDH 7768 C2

Pautz Pl
- MINN 7939 A4

Pawnee Rd
- EDNA 8107 E2

Payne Av
- LCAN 7856 B1
- MPLW 7856 B5
- STPL 7856 B7
- STPL 7942 A5
- VADH 7770 B7
- VADH 7856 B1

Payton Ct
- EDNA 8108 E2

Peacedale Av S
- EDNA 8023 A7
- EDNA 8109 A1

Pearl St
- STPL 7939 D3

Pearson Ct N
- BRKP 7679 D7

Pearson Dr
- BRKC 7765 B5

Pearson Dr N
- MPLW 7943 E2

Pearson Pkwy
- BRKP 7679 C6
- BRKP 7680 A6

Pearson Pl
- NOAK 7770 C1

Pearson Wy NE
- FRID 7680 A5

Pebble Ct
- CHMP 7591 D3

Pebble Rd N
- CHMP 7591 D2

Pebble Beach Wy
- EAGN 8284 C1

Pebblebrook Cir
- BMTN 8195 B1

Pebblebrook Dr
- BMTN 8195 A2

Pecks Wood Dr
- NBRI 7767 B4

Pecks Wood Turn
- NBRI 7767 B4

Pedersen St
- STPL 7943 C2

Peep O'Day Tr
- EDNP 8106 D5

Peggy Ln
- WTBL 7771 A1

Pelham Blvd
- STPL 7939 D6

Pelican Pl
- LINO 7597 A7

Pello Cir
- EAGN 8197 E7
- EAGN 8283 E1

Peltier Cir
- CTRV 7598 D4

Peltier Lake Dr
- CTRV 7598 C4
- LINO 7598 D3

Pembina Ln
- SHKP 8278 B4

Pendleton Ct
- EDNP 8193 B4

Peninsula Rd
- DLWD 7772 B2
- MEDL 7849 C6
- WasC 7772 B2

Peninsula Point Dr
- SAVG 8280 B6

Penkwe Cir
- EAGN 8284 A1

Penkwe Wy
- EAGN 8198 A7
- EAGN 8284 A1

Penn Av N
- BRKC 7765 D1
- BRKP 7679 C2
- BRKP 7765 D1
- MINN 7765 D6
- MINN 7851 D6
- MINN 7937 D1

Penn Av S
- BMTN 8109 D7
- BMTN 8195 D3
- BRNV 8281 D4
- MINN 7937 D5
- MINN 8023 D4
- RHFD 8023 D7
- RHFD 8109 D7

Penn Cir
- BMTN 8109 D6
- BMTN 8195 D2
- BRNV 8281 D4

Penn Pl
- NSTP 7857 D5

Penn Glen Pl
- BMTN 8109 D7

Pennine Pass NE
- COLH 7767 A5

Pennington Pl
- VADH 7770 B6

Penn Lake Cir
- BMTN 8109 D7

Pennock Av
- APVA 8283 B5
- STPL 7940 A4

Pennock Ct
- APVA 8283 B6

Pennsylvania Av
- EAGN 8199 B5
- SAVG 8280 B2

Pennsylvania Av E
- STPL 7941 D5

Pennsylvania Av N
- CHMP 7592 B5
- CRYS 7764 B5
- CRYS 7850 B4
- GLDV 7850 B7
- GLDV 7936 B1
- NWHE 7764 B7

Pennsylvania Av S
- BMTN 8194 B5
- GLDV 7936 B3
- STLP 7936 B4
- STLP 8022 B1

Pennsylvania Av W
- STPL 7941 D5

Pennsylvania Cir S
- BMTN 8108 B5

Pennsylvania Rd S
- BMTN 8108 B6

Penny Ln
- WDBY 8030 D4

Penny Hill Rd
- EDNP 8106 D3

Penrod Ln
- NBRI 7767 C7
- STAN 7767 C7
- STAN 7853 C1

Penstenom Ln
- SHKP 8279 C3

Pentagon Dr
- STAN 7853 D3

Penway Rd
- WILL 7772 D6

Pepperdine Ct
- EDNP 8193 A1

Pepperwood Cir
- MNTK 8020 E2

Pepperwood Ln
- MNTK 8020 E2

Pepperwood Tr
- MNTK 8020 E2

Peregrine Cir
- LINO 7684 A1

Performance Dr
- EAGN 8113 C6

Peridot Pth
- EAGN 8197 E4

W Perimeter Rd
- RSVL 7854 A5

Perron Rd
- MNDH 8112 B3

Perrot Ln
- BRNV 8197 A6
- EAGN 8197 A7

Perry Av N
- BRKC 7764 E2
- BRKP 7678 E7
- CHMP 7592 E6
- CRYS 7764 E6
- CRYS 7765 A6
- CRYS 7850 E1
- CRYS 7851 A4
- GLDV 7850 E6
- GLDV 7851 A5
- ROBB 7850 E1
- ROBB 7851 A4

Perry Cir
- CRYS 7764 E6
- CRYS 7765 A6

Perry Ct E
- BRKC 7764 E1

Perry Ct W
- BRKC 7764 E1

Perry Dr N
- BRKP 7592 E7

Perry Pl E
- BRKC 7764 D2

Perserve Cir N
- CHMP 7591 E3

Perserve Pl
- WtBT 7770 E4

Peteler Ln
- MNTK 8020 C5

Peters Pl
- COLH 7852 E1

Minneapolis Street Index

STREET Block City ZIP Map # Grid

Petersburg St NE
- BLNE 7682 A1

Peterson Pl
- NOAK 7683 B6
- SHVW 7683 B5

Peterson Rd
- WtBT 7684 D6

Peterson Tr
- CTRV 7598 D4

Pettit St
- STPL 7942 A5

Phaeton Dr
- EDNP 8193 C3

Phalen Blvd
- STPL 7941 E5
- STPL 7942 A4

Phalen Dr E
- MPLW 7856 C7
- STPL 7856 C7
- STPL 7942 C1

Phalen Pl
- MPLW 7856 D7

Pheasant Ct
- EDNA 8108 B1

Pheasant Dr
- LINO 7683 A3
- SHVW 7683 A4

Pheasant Ln
- CTRV 7598 D6
- MNTK 8021 B1
- NOAK 7770 A1

Pheasant Ln N
- MAPG 7763 C1

Pheasant Run
- BRNV 8282 C3
- LINO 7597 E7

Pheasant Run NE
- BLNE 7596 A2

Pheasant Run S
- LINO 7597 E7
- LINO 7683 E1

Pheasant Hills Cir
- LINO 7598 B7

Pheasant Hills Dr
- LINO 7598 B7
- LINO 7684 C1
- VADH 7770 C5

Pheasant Ridge Dr NE
- BLNE 7596 B5

Pheasant Ridge Dr NW
- COON 7592 D3

Pheasant Run St
- SHKP 8278 A4

Phelps Rd
- LINO 7599 A5

Philbrook Ln
- EDNA 8023 A6

Philipp Av
- SHKP 8278 B2

Philipp Dr
- SHKP 8278 B2

Philipp Wy
- SHKP 8278 A2

Phillips Pkwy
- STLP 8021 E1

Phlox Ln
- EDNA 8108 E3

Phoenix St
- GLDV 7850 C7
- GLDV 7936 D1

Phylis Ct E
- MPLW 8029 D4
- STPL 8029 C4

Picha Ln
- MNTK 8020 A6

Picha Rd
- MNTK 8020 A5

Picket Dr
- EDNP 8192 B2

Pickfair Dr
- BMTN 8108 A7

Picnic Island Rd
- HnpC 8112 A2
- MNDH 8112 A1

Picture Dr
- BMTN 8108 D5

Pierce Av N
- HOPK 8022 A3

Pierce Pl NE
- BLNE 7594 E7
- COLH 7852 E2
- MINN 7852 E2

Pierce St N
- STPL 7940 B7

Pierce St NE
- BLNE 7594 C1
- BLNE 7680 E1
- COLH 7766 E6
- COLH 7852 E2
- FRID 7766 E1
- MINN 7852 E1
- SPLP 7680 E4

Pierce Ter NE
- COLH 7766 E5
- COLH 7767 A5
- FRID 7767 A5

Pierce Butler Route
- STPL 7940 D4
- STPL 7941 A4

Pig's Eye Lake Rd
- STPL 7942 D7
- STPL 8028 D1

Pike Lake Cir
- NBRI 7767 D4

N Pike Lake Ct
- NBRI 7767 C4

Pike Lake Dr
- NBRI 7767 C4

Pike Lake Rd
- PRIO 8279 B5
- SHKP 8279 B5

Pike Lake Rd S
- PRIO 8279 B4
- SHKP 8279 B4

Pike Lake Tr NE
- PRIO 8279 B7
- SHKP 8279 B5

Pilgrim Ct N
- CHMP 7591 A2

Pilgrim Ln N
- CHMP 7591 D1
- MAPG 7591 D7
- MAPG 7677 D1
- MAPG 7763 D4
- PYMH 7763 D4
- PYMH 7849 B4

Pilgrim Wy
- MAPG 7677 D1

Pillsbury Av
- BRNV 8282 A3

Pillsbury Av S
- BMTN 8110 A6
- BMTN 8196 A1
- MINN 7938 A4
- MINN 8024 A3
- RHFD 8110 A1

Pillsbury Dr SE
- MINN 7939 A2

Pillsbury St
- STPL 7939 E5

Pilot Av
- FRID 7766 C5

Pilot Knob Rd
- APVA 8284 B5
- EAGN 8112 C7
- EAGN 8198 C1
- EAGN 8284 C1
- MNDH 8112 C4

Pilot Knob Frontage Rd
- EAGN 8284 C1

Pincherry Ln
- EDNP 8192 C3

Pine Cir
- MNTK 7935 C5

Pine Dr
- BLNE 7596 D6
- CIRC 7596 D7

S Pine Dr
- CIRC 7596 D7

Pine Ln
- EAGN 8285 C2
- MNTK 8020 A1

Pine Rd
- NOAK 7684 C7
- NOAK 7770 C1

Pine Rd NE
- PRIO 8279 C7

Pine St
- ANOK 7592 B2
- COON 7592 B2
- MAHT 7772 C3
- MNTK 8020 A2
- STPL 7941 E6
- WTBL 7771 B5

Pine Arbor Blvd S
- CTGV 8116 D6

Pine Arbor Dr S
- CTGV 8116 C6

Pine Arbor Ln S
- CTGV 8116 C6

Pine Arbor Alcove S
- CTGV 8116 C6

Pine Bend Tr
- NgTp 8288 B6
- RSMT 8287 A4
- RSMT 8288 B6

Pine Bluff Ct
- EDNP 8106 E7

Pine Cone Cir
- EAGN 8285 C1

Pine Cone Rd
- NOAK 7770 C1

Pine Cone Tr
- EAGN 8285 B1

Pinecrest Ct
- EAGN 8198 C3

Pinecrest Rd
- PNSP 7858 C1

Pine Crest Tr S
- CTGV 8116 C6

Pinefield Ct
- WtBT 7770 E3

Pine Grove Rd
- EDNA 8022 B5

Pine Hill Rd
- BMTN 8108 B7

Pine Hollow Dr
- CIRC 7596 E7

Pinehurst Av
- STPL 8025 E3
- STPL 8026 A3

Pinehurst Ct
- PNSP 7858 C1

Pinehurst Dr
- BRNV 8283 B2
- DLWD 7686 A6
- EAGN 8283 B2

Pinehurst Rd
- PNSP 7858 C1
- WDBY 8030 D2

Pinehurst Alcove
- WDBY 8030 C1

Pine Island Rd
- MNTK 7935 A5

Pine Pointe
- WTBL 7770 E2
- WtBT 7770 E2

Pine Ridge Cir
- BRNV 8282 C4

Pineridge Ct
- MAHT 7772 B7

Pine Ridge Dr
- EAGN 8112 B7
- WSTP 8113 E1

Pine Ridge Rd
- BRNV 8282 C4

Pinetree Curv
- EAGN 8198 B7
- EAGN 8284 B2

Pine Tree Dr
- ARDH 7768 D7
- MPLW 7943 E2

Pine Tree Ln
- SHKP 8278 B1

Pinetree Ln NE
- FRID 7681 A6

Pinetree Tr
- EAGN 8284 B1

Pinetree Pass
- EAGN 8284 B1

Pine Valley Dr
- DLWD 7686 B5

Pineview Ct
- MAHT 7772 B7
- RSVL 7855 A7
- STPL 8029 C4

Pineview Dr
- VADH 7770 A6

Pineview Ln N
- DAYT 7591 A1
- MAPG 7676 E6
- MAPG 7677 A3
- MAPG 7763 A1
- MNTK 7935 A2
- PYMH 7763 A7
- PYMH 7849 A1
- PYMH 7935 A2

Pinewood Cir
- MNDS 7681 D5

Pinewood Ct
- MNDS 7681 D6
- WDBY 8030 A2

Pinewood Dr
- APVA 8282 E7
- MNDS 7681 E5
- SHKP 8192 A7
- SHVW 7682 B5
- SHVW 7683 A5
- WDBY 8030 A2

Pinewood Ln
- MNTK 8020 C7

Pinewood Ln N
- PYMH 7849 A3

Pinewood Tr
- EDNA 8022 E5

Pinkspire Ln E
- MPLW 8029 E6

Pinnacle Dr
- EDNP 8106 E1

Pin Oak Av
- BRKP 7678 E2

Pin Oak Av N
- BRKP 7678 E2

Pin Oak Ct N
- BRKP 7678 E1

Pin Oak Dr
- EAGN 8283 C1

Pintail Ct
- EAGN 8198 A6

Pintail Ln
- WtBT 7685 E4

Pinto Ln
- LINO 7596 E2

Pioneer Dr
- BRNV 8197 A5

Pioneer Ln
- CTRV 7598 D5
- WtBT 7685 A7

Pioneer Rd
- MNTK 8020 E4
- MNTK 8021 A4

Pioneer Rd S
- CTGV 8202 A6
- GCIT 8201 D6
- GCIT 8202 A6

Pioneer Tr
- BMTN 8193 D3
- EDNP 8192 E2
- EDNP 8193 D3

E Piper Dr
- NBRI 7767 D7

W Piper Dr
- NBRI 7767 D7

Pitrina Wy
- LCAN 7856 A2

Pitt St
- SSTP 8028 E7
- SSTP 8029 A7

Plant Rd
- EAGN 8197 C2

Plato Blvd E
- STPL 7942 B7
- STPL 8027 E1
- STPL 8028 A1

Plato Blvd W
- STPL 8027 E1

Platwood Rd
- MNTK 7934 E5

Plaza Blvd NE
- BLNE 7681 A3
- SPLP 7681 A4

Plaza Cir
- MPLW 7856 D4

Plaza Curv NE
- FRID 7766 C1

Plaza Dr
- EAGN 8197 D7
- EAGN 8283 D1
- EDNP 8107 A4

S Plaza Dr
- MNDH 8113 B2

Pleasant Av
- BRNV 8282 A1
- SPLP 8115 E6
- SSTP 8028 D5
- STPL 7941 C7
- STPL 8026 E2
- STPL 8027 A1

E Pleasant Av S
- RHFD 8110 A1

W Pleasant Av S
- RHFD 8110 A1

Pleasant Av N
- CHMP 7592 A3

Pleasant Av S
- BMTN 8110 A5
- BMTN 8196 A4
- MINN 7938 A4
- MINN 8024 A4

Pleasant Av SE
- MINN 7939 B2

Pleasant Cir
- ARDH 7768 D3
- SHVW 7768 D3

Pleasant Ct E
- WtBT 7685 A6

Pleasant Ct W
- WtBT 7685 A6

Pleasant Dr
- ARDH 7768 D3

Pleasant Ln
- BRNV 8282 A5
- RHFD 8110 A3

Pleasant Pl
- BRNV 8282 A4

Pleasant St
- LAUD 7853 D7
- LAUD 7939 D1
- RSVL 7853 D7
- WtBT 7685 B7

Pleasant St SE
- MINN 7939 A3

Pleasant Lake Rd
- NOAK 7769 C1

E Pleasant Lake Rd
- NOAK 7683 E5
- NOAK 7684 A6
- NOAK 7769 D1

W Pleasant Lake Rd
- NOAK 7683 B7
- NOAK 7769 B1

Pleasant View Ct
- MNDS 7681 B4

Pleasant View Dr
- MNDS 7681 B4
- NBRI 7681 B7
- NBRI 7767 B1
- SPLP 7681 B4

Pleasant View Dr NE
- MNDS 7681 B4
- SPLP 7681 B5

Pleasant View Ln
- CHMP 7592 A3
- CIRC 7596 E7

Pleasantwood Rd
- MNTK 8021 B4

Pleasure Creek Cir NE
- BLNE 7594 C6

Pleasure Creek Dr
- BLNE 7594 E5
- BLNE 7680 D1

Pleasure Creek Pkwy E
- BLNE 7594 D6

Pleasure Creek Pkwy W
- BLNE 7594 C6

Plum Ln
- LINO 7683 A2

Plum St
- STPL 7942 C6

Plymouth Av
- BRNV 8282 B7

N Plymouth Av
- GLDV 7850 C7

Plymouth Av N
- GLDV 7849 E7
- GLDV 7850 B7
- GLDV 7851 C7
- MINN 7851 D7
- MINN 7852 A7
- PYMH 7849 E7

Plymouth Blvd
- PYMH 7848 B3

Plymouth Rd
- MNTK 7934 E2
- MNTK 7935 B7
- MNTK 8021 A1
- PYMH 7934 E2

Plymouth Rd CO-61
- MNTK 7934 E3
- MNTK 7935 A4

Poe Rd
- BRKC 7765 B3

Poets Grn N
- HUGO 7599 B6

Point Dr
- EDNA 8109 A2

Point Chase Rd
- EDNP 8021 C7
- EDNP 8107 C1

Pointcross Dr
- BLNE 7596 E6
- CIRC 7596 E6
- LINO 7596 E6

Point Douglas Ct
- CTGV 8202 D2

E Point Douglas Rd S
- CTGV 8202 B1

W Point Douglas Rd S
- CTGV 8202 D3

Point Douglas Rd N
- STPL 7942 D6
- STPL 7943 A7
- STPL 8029 A1

Point Douglas Rd S
- NWPT 8029 C6
- STPL 8029 A2

Pointe Pl S
- CTGV 8116 B5

Pointe Wy
- EAGN 8199 A6

Polar Cir
- EDNA 8022 A7

Polar Bear Dr
- WtBT 7685 D4

Polaris Ct
- NSTP 7857 D6

Polaris Ln N
- MAPG 7676 C2
- MAPG 7762 C1
- PYMH 7848 C1

Polaris Pl
- MPLW 7857 D6
- NSTP 7857 D6

Polk Av N
- HOPK 8022 A3

Polk Cir
- COLH 7766 E5

Polk Pl
- COLH 7766 E5

Polk St NE
- BLNE 7594 E2
- BLNE 7680 E2
- COLH 7766 E6
- COLH 7767 A7
- COLH 7852 E1
- COLH 7853 A1
- FRID 7766 E4
- MINN 7852 E3

Polk St NE
- SPLP 7680 E4

Pomander Wk
- GLDV 7936 D2

Pompano Dr
- MNTK 8021 B5

Pond Av E
- MPLW 8029 E2
- STPL 8029 C2

Pond Cir E
- MNDH 8113 C3

Pond Cir W
- MNDH 8113 C4

Pond Ct
- SHVW 7683 C4

Pond Ct S
- MPLW 8029 E1

Pond Dr
- SHVW 7683 C5

E Pond Rd
- EAGN 8198 B3

W Pond Rd
- EAGN 8198 B3

Ponderosa Cir
- EAGN 8198 B6

Pondhaven Cir
- MNDH 8113 B4

Pondhaven Ln
- MNDH 8113 B4

Ponds Ct
- SHKP 8278 A4

Ponds Dr N
- BRKC 7764 E1

Ponds Wy
- SHKP 8278 A3

Pondview Cir
- LINO 7598 B7
- MNTK 7934 C4

Pondview Cir N
- CHMP 7591 D5

Pond View Ct
- MNDH 8113 C3
- WtBT 7770 D4

Pondview Ct
- NSTP 7857 C5
- VADH 7770 C3
- WTBL 7770 C3

Pondview Ct N
- CHMP 7591 D4

Pond View Dr
- MNDH 8113 C3
- WtBT 7770 D4

Pondview Dr
- EAGN 8283 D1

Pond View Ln
- VADH 7770 D4
- WtBT 7770 D4

Pond View Pt
- EAGN 8198 B3

Pond View Ter
- MNDH 8113 D3

Pondview Ter
- MNTK 7934 C4

Pondwood Rd
- EDNA 8108 C4

Pond Wynde N
- EAGN 8198 B5

Pond Wynde S
- EAGN 8198 B5

Pontiac Pl
- MNDH 8113 B3

Pony Ct
- LINO 7596 E2

Pony Ln E
- APVA 8283 A4

Pony Ln W
- APVA 8283 A4

Poplar Av
- NSTP 7857 D3

Poplar Dr
- GLDV 7937 A2
- SHVW 7683 B5
- WDBY 8030 A1

Poplar Ln
- NOAK 7770 A2

E Poplar St
- SSTP 8115 A4

W Poplar St
- IVGH 8114 E4
- SSTP 8114 E4

Poplar Bridge Cir
- BMTN 8109 A6

Poplar Bridge Curv
- BMTN 8109 A6

Poplar Bridge Rd
- BMTN 8108 E7
- BMTN 8109 A6
- BMTN 8194 E1

Poppler Ln
- EAGN 8112 C7

Poppy Ln
- EDNA 8108 E4

Poppy St NW
- COON 7592 D1

Poppyseed Ct
- NBRI 7767 D1

Poppyseed Dr
- NBRI 7767 D1

Porchlight Ln
- EDNP 8192 B2

Porcupine Ct
- EDNP 8107 A6

Portage Ln E
- SHKP 8279 D3

Portage Ln W
- SHKP 8279 D4

Portage Wy
- CTRV 7598 D5

Portal Dr
- EDNP 8193 B2

Porter Cir N
- CHMP 7592 D4

Porter Dr
- CHMP 7592 D4

Porter Ln
- EDNA 8022 D7

Portland Av
- BRNV 8196 C7
- BRNV 8282 C3
- HUGO 7685 E5

Portland Av
- SPLP 8115 E7
- SPLP 8201 E1
- STPL 7940 A7
- STPL 7941 A7
- WtBT 7685 E7
- WtBT 7771 E5

Portland Av S
- BMTN 8110 C7
- BMTN 8196 C3
- BRNV 8282 C5
- MINN 7938 D2
- MINN 8024 C5
- RHFD 8024 C7
- RHFD 8110 C3

Portland Av S CO-35
- MINN 7938 C4
- MINN 8024 C2

Portland Cir
- BRNV 8282 B3

Portland Ct
- BRNV 8282 C2

E Portland Dr
- BRNV 8282 C2

Portland Mw
- BRNV 8282 C7

Portland Pl
- BMTN 8196 B3
- BRNV 8282 C6

Portland Woods
- WtBT 7685 E6

Port of Minneapolis Dr
- MINN 7852 A3

Post Ln
- EDNA 8107 E1

Post Rd
- HnpC 8111 D3
- LINO 7597 B4
- MNTK 7934 B4

Post Oak Rd
- ODLE 7858 B3

Potomac Tr N
- BRKP 7679 C7

Pouliot Pkwy
- WDBY 8030 A3

Powderhorn Ter
- MINN 7938 D7

Powell Rd
- HOPK 8022 B2
- STLP 8022 B2

Power St
- MINN 7938 C1

Powers Av
- STPL 7943 C7

Prairie Cir E
- EAGN 8199 C5

Prairie Cir W
- EAGN 8199 C5

Prairie Ct S
- CTGV 8116 B6

Prairie Dr
- CTRV 7598 D4

Prairie Ln
- EDNP 8106 A2

Prairie Rd
- WTBL 7771 D6

Prairie Center Dr
- EDNP 8106 E4
- EDNP 8107 A5

Prairie Flower Rd
- LINO 7683 C1

Prairie Grass Dr NW
- PRIO 8278 B7

Prairie Lakes Dr
- EDNP 8107 C6

Prairie Oak Tr
- WDBY 8030 A6

Prairie Ridge Dr
- SHVW 7682 A4

Prairie Ridge Rd
- EAGN 8199 C5

Prairie View Dr
- EDNP 8106 D3

Prairieview Ln N
- CHMP 7591 A6

Prairie View Pl
- LINO 7597 C1

Prairieview Tr N
- CHMP 7591 E5

Pratt St
- MINN 8024 A5

Preble St
- STPL 7942 B4

Prescott Cir
- EDNA 8022 A4

Prescott Ct
- BRNV 8196 E5

Prescott Dr
- EDNP 8106 A7
- MNTK 8020 D4

Prescott St
- STPL 8028 B2

Preserve Blvd
- EDNP 8107 B6

W Preserve Blvd
- BRNV 8281 B5
- SAVG 8281 B5

Preserve Cir
- SAVG 8279 E3

Preserve Ct
- SAVG 8279 E4
- SHKP 8279 D3

Preserve Ln N
- CHMP 7591 C5

Preserve Pl
- SAVG 8280 A4

Preserve Pth
- MNDH 8113 D1
- WSTP 8113 D1

Preserve Tr
- NOAK 7683 D5
- SAVG 8279 E3
- SAVG 8280 A3
- SHKP 8279 E3
- WtBT 7683 D5

Preserve Alcove
- SAVG 8279 E3

President Dr NE
- BLNE 7594 C3

INDEX 35

Prestige Ln — Rhode Island Av S

Minneapolis Street Index

STREET Block City ZIP Map # Grid

Prestige Ln
- MNTK 8021 B1

Preston Ln
- HOPK 8022 A3
- SHKP 8279 B1

Preston Rd
- MNTK 7934 E6

Prestwick Cir N
- BRKP 7678 E4
- BRKP 7679 A6

Prestwick Ct N
- BRKP 7678 E4

Prestwick Ln N
- BRKP 7678 E6

Prestwick Pkwy N
- BRKP 7678 E4
- BRKP 7679 A6

Prestwick Ter
- MAHT 7858 B1

Prestwick Ter N
- BRKP 7679 A3

Pribble St N
- CHMP 7592 B3

Price Av
- MPLW 7856 E7
- MPLW 7857 B7

Primrose Ct
- VADH 7769 E4

Primrose Ct N
- BRKP 7679 B1

Primrose Ct S
- CTGV 8116 B6

Primrose Curv
- RSVL 7854 C3

Primrose Ln
- EDNP 8107 A6

Primrose Pth
- VADH 7769 E4

Prince Pl
- MNTK 8020 D3

Prince St
- STPL 7942 A6

Princeton Av
- EDNP 8107 A7
- EDNP 8193 A1
- SAVG 8280 E2
- STPL 8025 E1
- STPL 8026 B1

Princeton Av S
- GLDV 7936 E4
- GLDV 7937 A4
- STLP 7936 E6
- STLP 7937 A4
- STLP 8022 E1

Princeton Cir
- EAGN 8198 E3
- SAVG 8280 E5

Princeton Ct
- SAVG 8280 E5
- STLP 7936 D5

Princeton Tr
- EAGN 8198 E4

Printice Ln
- MINN 7852 B3

Prior Av N
- ARDH 7768 A2
- ARDH 7854 A1
- FLCH 7854 A6
- RSVL 7854 A7
- STPL 7940 A6

Prior Av S
- STPL 7940 A7
- STPL 8026 A2

Prior Cir
- ARDH 7854 A2
- RSVL 7854 A2

Prior Ct
- ARDH 7768 A2

Priscilla St
- STPL 7939 E3

Program Av
- MNDS 7681 E7

Progress Rd
- CTRV 7598 D5

Promenade Av
- EAGN 8198 D1

Promenade Pl
- EAGN 8198 C1

Promontory Dr
- EDNP 8106 E1
- EDNP 8107 A1

Promontory Pl
- EAGN 8199 A2

Promontory Pl E
- MPLW 8029 E6

Propect Rd
- EDNP 8192 B2

Prospect Av
- MINN 8024 A5
- WtBT 7685 A6

Prospect Blvd
- STPL 8027 E1

Prospect Pl
- MNTK 7934 B6

Prospect Ter
- MINN 7939 C4

Prosperity Av
- STPL 7942 E2

Prosperity Rd
- MPLW 7857 A7
- STPL 7857 A7

Providence Ln
- EDNP 8107 C6
- SAVG 8280 E6

Pueblo Dr
- MNDH 8113 B3

Pueblo Ln
- MNDH 8113 B3

Pullman Av S
- CTGV 8202 A1
- SPLP 8201 D1
- SPLP 8202 A1

Pullman Av W
- SPLP 8201 D1

Puma Ln
- MAHT 7772 C7
- PNSP 7772 C7

Pumice Ct
- EAGN 8197 D4

Pumice Ln
- EAGN 8197 D4

Pumice Pt
- EAGN 8197 D4

Purcell Pl
- MNTK 8020 E1

Purdey Rd
- EDNP 8193 C4

Purgatory Rd
- EDNP 8193 C2

Q

Quail Av N
- BRKC 7764 E2
- BRKP 7592 E7
- BRKP 7678 E1
- CRYS 7764 E5
- CRYS 7850 E1
- GLDV 7850 E5
- ROBB 7850 E1

Quail Cir N
- BRKP 7678 E1

Quail Cir W
- BRKC 7764 E2

Quail Ct
- SHKP 8278 A3

Quail Dr
- SHKP 8278 A3

Quail Ln
- NOAK 7769 E2

Quail Rd
- DLWD 7772 C2
- GRNT 7772 C1
- MAHT 7772 C2

Quail St
- DLWD 7772 C2
- MAHT 7772 C3

Quail Hill Rd
- MAPG 7676 B5

Quail Ridge Cir
- MNDH 8113 C2

Quail Ridge Rd
- EAGN 8199 A3

Quaker Ln
- MNDS 7681 E5

Quaker Ln N
- CHMP 7591 D2
- MAPG 7591 D7
- MAPG 7677 D1
- PYMH 7763 D7
- PYMH 7849 D1
- PYMH 7935 D2

Quantico Ct
- MAPG 7762 B2

Quantico Ln N
- MAPG 7676 B2
- MAPG 7762 B1
- PYMH 7762 B7
- PYMH 7848 B1
- PYMH 7934 B2

Quarles Rd
- BRKC 7765 B3
- MAPG 7676 B5

Quarry Ct
- EAGN 8112 C7

Quarry Ln
- EAGN 8112 C7

Quarry Center Dr
- MINN 7853 A6

Quarter Horse Ct
- LINO 7597 A2

Quartz Ln
- EAGN 8197 C6

Quay St NW
- COON 7592 D1

Quebec Av
- SAVG 8280 B4

Quebec Av N
- BRKP 7592 B7
- BRKP 7764 B3
- CHMP 7592 B6
- CRYS 7764 B5
- CRYS 7850 B5
- GLDV 7850 B7
- GLDV 7936 B1
- NWHE 7764 B5
- NWHE 7850 B2

Quebec Av S
- BMTN 8194 B3
- GLDV 7936 B2
- SAVG 8280 B7
- STLP 7936 B5
- STLP 8022 B1

Quebec Cir
- BMTN 8194 B5
- EDNP 8106 B3

Quebec Cir N
- CHMP 7592 B4

Quebec Ct N
- BRKP 7678 B6

Quebec Dr
- STLP 7936 B5

Quebec Ln
- EDNP 8192 C2

Quebec Ln N
- CHMP 7592 B6

Quebec Rd
- BMTN 8194 B4

Quebec St
- CTRV 7598 D4

Quebec Wy N
- CHMP 7592 B6

Queen Av
- SHKP 8278 A2

S Queen Av
- MINN 8023 D2

Queen Av N
- BRKC 7765 D6
- BRKP 7679 D6
- MINN 7765 D6
- MINN 7851 D1
- MINN 7937 D1

Queen Av S
- BMTN 8109 D5
- BMTN 8195 D1
- MINN 7937 D3
- MINN 8023 D5
- RHFD 8109 D1

Queen Cir
- BMTN 8195 D3

Queen Ct N
- BRKP 7679 C5

Queen Rd
- BMTN 8195 D2

Queens Dr
- WDBY 8030 C2

Queens Gdns N
- BRKP 7678 E3

Queens Ln
- ANOK 7592 B2

Queens Tr
- EDNP 8106 C7
- EDNP 8192 B2

Queens Wy
- MNTK 8020 D3

Queens Gate
- NBRI 7767 E3

Quemoy Ct NE
- BLNE 7682 A1

Quemoy St NE
- BLNE 7682 A1

Quentin Av S
- GLDV 7936 E4
- SAVG 8280 E5
- STLP 7936 A4
- STLP 8022 E2

Quentin Av S CO-16
- SAVG 8280 E2

Quentin Cir
- SAVG 8280 E7

Quentin Ct
- SAVG 8280 E5
- STLP 7936 E5

Quigley Rd
- MNTK 8020 D3

Quince St NW
- COON 7594 A5
- COON 7680 A2

Quincy Blvd NE
- BLNE 7594 D4

Quincy St
- MNDS 7681 E5

Quincy St NE
- BLNE 7594 D2
- BLNE 7680 D1
- COLH 7766 D7
- COLH 7852 D1
- FRID 7680 D5
- FRID 7766 D1
- HLTP 7766 D6
- MINN 7852 D2
- SPLP 7680 D5

Quincy Wy
- HLTP 7766 D6
- WDBY 8030 D7

Quinn Av S
- BMTN 8108 E6
- BMTN 8194 E5

Quinn Cir
- BMTN 8108 E5

Quinn Rd
- BMTN 8108 E5
- BMTN 8194 E1

Quinn St NW
- COON 7593 B1

Quinwood Ln N
- MAPG 7677 A4
- MAPG 7763 A4
- PYMH 7763 A4
- PYMH 7848 E4
- PYMH 7849 A1
- PYMH 7935 A1

Quirnia St
- STPL 8026 A5

Quito St
- BLNE 7596 E6
- CIRC 7596 E6

Quito St NE
- BLNE 7596 E5

R

R St NE
- MINN 7853 C7

Rabun Dr
- EDNA 8108 D2

Rac 3 Rd
- HnpC 8110 E4

Raccoon Rd
- NOAK 7683 E7

Race St
- STPL 8026 E4

Racine St
- LCAN 7855 D2

Radatz Av
- MPLW 7857 B3
- NSTP 7857 B3

Radio Dr
- CTGV 8116 D4
- ELMO 7944 E6
- ODLE 7944 E6
- WDBY 7944 E6
- WDBY 8030 E1
- WDBY 8116 D4

Radisson Ct
- BRNV 8196 E6

Radisson Dr
- BRNV 8196 E5

Radisson Rd
- GLDV 7936 E3

Radisson Rd NE
- BLNE 7595 B1
- BLNE 7681 A2

Radisson Rd NE CO-52
- BLNE 7595 E6
- BLNE 7681 E1

Radisson Woods Dr NE
- BLNE 7595 D4

Rae Ct
- MNDH 8027 A7

Rae Dr
- RHFD 8109 E1

Rahn Rd
- EAGN 8197 D6

Rahn Wy
- EAGN 8197 C7

Rahncliff Ct
- EAGN 8197 D7

Rahncliff Ct
- EAGN 8283 D1

Rahncliff Rd
- EAGN 8197 D7
- EAGN 8283 D1

Railroad Av N
- ROBB 7850 E2
- ROBB 7851 B3

Railway Pl
- STPL 7939 E5

Rainbow Av
- NBRI 7767 C1

Rainbow Dr
- EDNP 8106 B1

Rainbow Dr NE
- FRID 7766 C2

Rainbow Ln
- MNDS 7681 C7
- NBRI 7681 C7
- NBRI 7767 C1

Raindrop Dr
- EAGN 8112 A7

Rainier Cir
- BRNV 8283 A3

Rainier Ct
- BRNV 8283 A3

Rainier Pass
- COLH 7767 A5
- FRID 7767 A5

Raleigh Av
- SAVG 8280 E7
- STPL 7940 A2

Raleigh Av S
- STLP 7936 E6
- STLP 8022 E1

Raleigh Ct
- BRNV 8196 D6

Raleigh Dr
- BRNV 8196 D6

Raleigh Ln
- EDNP 8106 A7

Raleigh Ln NE
- SPLP 7680 E5

Raleigh St
- STPL 7940 A3

Ralph St
- WtBT 7771 E4

Rambler Ct
- RSVL 7855 B3

Rambler Rd
- RSVL 7854 C3

Ramley St
- WTBL 7771 B2
- WtBT 7771 B2

Ramley St CO-96
- WTBL 7771 B2
- WtBT 7771 B2

Ramlow Pl
- STPL 8026 A5

Ramsey Cir NE
- MINN 7852 C7

Ramsey Rd
- ARDH 7682 A7
- ARDH 7768 A1

Ramsey St
- STPL 7941 D4

NE Ramsey St
- MINN 7852 B6

Ramsey St NE
- MINN 7852 C7

Ranch Rd
- WDBY 8116 D2

Ranchers Rd NE
- FRID 7680 C5

Ranchview Ct
- MNTK 7934 B2

Ranchview Ln N
- MAPG 7590 B7
- MAPG 7676 B1
- MAPG 7762 B3
- MNTK 7934 B2
- PYMH 7762 B7
- PYMH 7848 B1
- PYMH 7934 B2

Ranchview Ln S
- MNTK 7934 B2
- PYMH 7934 B2

Randall Av
- FLCH 7940 B1
- MINN 7937 B7
- STLP 7937 B7

Randall Ln
- MNTK 8020 B6

Randolph Av
- STPL 8025 E2
- STPL 8026 E2
- STPL 8027 C2

Randolph St NE
- MINN 7852 B3

Random Rd
- EAGN 8113 B7

Randy Av
- SHVW 7769 A5
- WTBL 7771 E5
- WtBT 7771 E5

Randy St
- WTBL 7771 C5

Ranier Ln
- EAGN 8112 C6

Rankin Rd
- STAN 7853 C3

Rankin St
- STPL 8026 C5

Raptor Rd
- EAGN 8197 E5

Raspberry Ct
- EAGN 8198 D5

Raspberry Ln
- EAGN 8198 C5

Raspberry Hill Rd
- EDNP 8107 B1

Rath Dr
- WDBY 8030 A1

Raven Ct
- EDNP 8106 C2

Raven Ct NE
- PRIO 8279 C7

Raven Rd
- NOAK 7769 C2

Raven St NW
- COON 7593 B2

Ravens Ct
- LINO 7683 A2

Ravenswood Ct
- SHVW 7682 D4

Ravenswood St
- SHVW 7682 D4

Ravenwood Rd N
- PYMH 7935 A1

Ravine St
- SSTP 8028 D6

Ravine Tr
- GLDV 7937 A3

Ravoux Av
- BRNV 8197 A7

Ravoux Ct
- BRNV 8197 A7

Ravoux St
- STPL 7941 C6

Rawlins Cir N
- MINN 7937 E1

Ray Pl
- FLCH 7940 A2
- STPL 7940 A2

Raymar Ct
- BRNV 8281 D4

Raymond Av
- MNDS 7681 E6
- STPL 7939 E3

Raymond Ln
- EDNP 8106 D5
- STPL 7939 D4

Raymond Pl
- STPL 7939 D1

Reading Rd
- EAGN 8199 A5

Reaney Av
- STPL 7942 B4
- STPL 7943 A4

Reaney Av E
- MPLW 7943 C4
- STPL 7943 B4

Reardon Pl
- NSTP 7857 E3

Rebecca Dr
- MPLW 7943 E1

Rebecca Ln
- EAGN 8284 B1

Reco Ln NE
- SPLP 7680 D4

Red Barn Rd
- NOAK 7769 C1

Red Birch Ct
- LINO 7597 E7

Red Cedar Cir
- EDNP 8193 D2

Red Cedar Ln
- MINN 8023 C5

Red Cedar Rd
- EAGN 8112 A7

Red Cir Dr
- MNTK 8021 C7

Red Clover Ln
- LINO 7597 A5

Redding Ridge Dr
- MNTK 8020 C2

Red Forest Hts
- NOAK 7684 A6

Red Forest Ln
- NOAK 7684 A6

Red Forest Wy
- NOAK 7684 A6

Red Fox Ct
- EDNA 8108 B1

Red Fox Dr
- MAPG 7763 B4

Red Fox Ln
- EDNA 8022 B7

Red Fox Rd
- ARDH 7768 D5
- EAGN 8197 E2
- LINO 7683 D2
- NOAK 7683 E6
- NOAK 7684 A6
- SHVW 7768 E5

Red Hawk Tr
- LINO 7683 B2

Red Maple Ln
- LINO 7683 D2
- NOAK 7683 E4

Red Oak Cir N
- BRNV 8283 A1

Red Oak Cir S
- BRNV 8283 A1

Red Oak Ct
- EAGN 8113 C7
- MNDS 7681 C4

Red Oak Ct N
- BRNV 8283 A1
- CHMP 7591 C4

Red Oak Ct S
- BRNV 8283 A1

Red Oak Dr
- EAGN 8113 C7
- EAGN 8199 C1
- EDNP 8106 B6
- MNDS 7681 C4
- NBRI 7681 C7

Red Oak Rdg
- MNTK 8020 C2

Red Oaks Dr
- VADH 7769 E3

Red Pine Blvd
- HUGO 7685 E4
- WtBT 7685 D4

Red Pine Cir E
- MPLW 8029 E4

Red Pine Ct
- EAGN 8285 C1

Red Pine Ln
- EAGN 8285 C1
- NOAK 7769 B1

Red Pine Rd
- NOAK 7769 B1

Redpine Rd S
- CTGV 8116 C7

Redpoll Ct
- EAGN 8285 C1

Red Robin Ln
- EAGN 8197 D1

Red Rock Rd
- EDNP 8106 C6
- STPL 8029 B7

Red Splender Cir E
- MPLW 8029 E6

Redwood Ln
- NBRI 7767 B5

Redwood Pl
- EAGN 8198 E2

Redwood St NW
- COON 7593 E7
- COON 7594 A2
- COON 7680 A3

Reed Pl
- WtBT 7685 A6

Reflection Rd
- APVA 8282 E6

Regal Oak
- MNTK 8021 A1

Regency Dr
- WDBY 8030 B1

Regency Ln
- EDNP 8107 C1

Regent Av N
- BRKC 7764 E2
- BRKP 7592 E7
- BRKP 7678 E6
- BRKP 7764 E1
- CHMP 7592 E6
- CRYS 7764 E6
- CRYS 7850 E1
- GLDV 7850 E6
- ROBB 7850 D1

Regent Ct N
- BRKP 7592 E7

Regent Dr
- WTBL 7771 C5

Regent Pkwy N
- BRKP 7678 D4

Regional Center Rd
- EDNP 8107 A5

Regis Dr
- WTBL 7771 C6

Regis Dr NE
- FRID 7767 A4

Regis Ln NE
- FRID 7766 E4
- FRID 7767 A4

Regis Ter NE
- FRID 7767 A4

Regis Tr NE
- FRID 7767 A4

Rehbein St
- LINO 7598 D2

Rehnberg Pl
- WSTP 8028 B6

Reid Ln
- SSTP 8028 C7

Reidmond Av
- LCAN 7856 B4

Reiland Ln
- SHVW 7769 A4

Reiling Rd
- LINO 7685 A2

Reimer Dr N
- MAPG 7676 D7

Reindeer Ln
- EAGN 8199 B7

Renaissance Ct
- HOPK 8021 C3

Rendova St NE
- BLNE 7596 A1
- BLNE 7682 A2
- LXTN 7682 A2
- SHVW 7682 A3

Republic Av
- STLP 8022 C1

Resden Rd N
- PYMH 7935 A1

Research Center Rd E
- NWHE 7763 E6
- NWHE 7764 A6

Research Center Rd W
- NWHE 7763 E6

Reservoir Blvd
- COLH 7767 A7
- COLH 7852 E1
- MINN 7852 E1

Restwood Rd
- BLNE 7682 A2
- LXTN 7682 B2

Return Ct
- STPL 8026 A5

Rev Dr Martin L King Jr Blvd
- STPL 7941 D5

Revel Wood Pl
- MAPG 7676 B6

Revere Cir N
- PYMH 7849 D5

Revere Ct
- EDNP 8106 C6

Revere Ln N
- CHMP 7591 D1
- MAPG 7677 D1
- OSSE 7677 D3
- PYMH 7849 D2
- PYMH 7935 D1

Revoir St
- CTRV 7598 D4

Rhode Island Av
- SAVG 8280 B2

Rhode Island Av N
- BRKP 7592 B7
- BRKP 7764 B4
- CHMP 7592 B5
- CRYS 7764 B5
- GLDV 7850 B7
- GLDV 7936 B1
- NWHE 7764 B6
- NWHE 7850 B6

Rhode Island Av S
- BMTN 8108 B5
- BMTN 8194 B4
- GLDV 7936 B3
- STLP 7936 B5
- STLP 8022 B1

INDEX 36

Rhode Island Cir N — Rosehill Cir

Minneapolis Street Index

STREET Block City ZIP Map # Grid

Rhode Island Cir N
- CHMP 7592 B6
Rhode Island Cir S
- BMTN 8108 A5
- BMTN 8194 A4
Rhode Island Ct N
- CHMP 7592 B5
Rhode Island Dr N
- BRKP 7678 B6
Rhode Island Rd
- BMTN 8194 B3
Rhode Island Wy N
- CHMP 7592 B5
Rice Ct
- LINO 7683 B1
Rice St
- LCAN 7769 D7
- LCAN 7855 D5
- MPLW 7855 D7
- NOAK 7769 C2
- RSVL 7855 D7
- SHVW 7769 C6
- SHVW 7855 D1
- STPL 7855 D7
- STPL 7941 D4
- VADH 7769 C6
Rice St SR-49
- LCAN 7769 D7
- LCAN 7855 D5
- MPLW 7855 D7
- RSVL 7855 D7
- SHVW 7769 D7
- SHVW 7855 D1
- STPL 7855 D7
- STPL 7941 D4
- VADH 7769 D7
Rice Creek Blvd NE
- FRID 7680 C7
- FRID 7766 C1
Rice Creek Dr NE
- FRID 7767 B1
Rice Creek Pkwy
- ARDH 7682 A5
- BLNE 7682 A3
- SHVW 7682 A5
Rice Creek Pkwy NE
- BLNE 7681 E2
Rice Creek Rd
- FRID 7767 B2
- NBRI 7767 B2
Rice Creek Rd NE
- FRID 7767 A2
- NBRI 7767 B2
Rice Creek Ter
- FRID 7767 B1
- NBRI 7767 B1
Rice Creek Ter NE
- FRID 7680 D7
- FRID 7766 E1
Rice Creek Tr
- SHVW 7682 C4
Rice Creek Wy NE
- FRID 7766 B1
Rice Creek Trail Ct
- SHVW 7682 C4
Rice Lake Cir
- MAPG 7676 D5
Rice Lake Ct
- LINO 7597 A5
Rice Lake Dr
- LINO 7597 A5
Rice Lake Ln
- LINO 7597 A5
Rice Lake Rd
- MAPG 7676 D4
Rich Av S
- BMTN 8108 E6
- BMTN 8194 E5
Rich Cir
- BMTN 8194 E3
Rich Curv
- BMTN 8194 E2
Rich Rd
- BMTN 8108 E6
- BMTN 8109 A6
- BMTN 8194 E1
Richal Dr
- WDBY 8030 C3
Richard Av
- WTBL 7771 C6
Richard Cir
- WSTP 8027 E7
Richard Ct
- WTBL 7771 A6
Richard Dr
- WtBT 7685 E5
Richard Ln
- EAGN 8284 B1
Richard P Braun Br
- BRKP 7679 E3
- COON 7679 E3
Richard P Braun Br SR-610
- BRKP 7679 E3
- COON 7679 E3
Richards Ct
- EAGN 8198 B7
Richards Dr
- MNTK 8020 C2
Richards Dr W
- MNTK 8020 C2
Richardson Av N
- CHMP 7591 B2
Richfield Rd
- MINN 8023 C2
Richmond Av
- RSVL 7854 E1
- SHVW 7768 E7
- SHVW 7854 E1
Richmond Cir
- EDNA 8022 D5
Richmond Ct
- SHVW 7768 E7
Richmond Curv
- MINN 8023 C6
Richmond Dr
- EDNA 8022 D5
Richmond Ln
- EDNA 8022 D5
Richmond St
- STPL 8027 B1
E Richmond St
- SSTP 8115 A3
W Richmond St
- SSTP 8114 E3
Rich Valley Blvd
- IVGH 8199 D4
- IVGH 8200 A4
- IVGH 8286 C3
- RSMT 8286 C3
Richwood Dr
- EDNA 8022 D5
Rickard Rd NE
- FRID 7680 B6
Ridder Cir
- STPL 7942 B7
Ridge Ct
- WtBT 7685 E6
Ridge Dr
- STLP 7936 D5
- WDBY 7944 A7
N Ridge Dr
- SAVG 8280 D7
Ridge Ln
- MNDS 7681 C7
Ridge Pl
- EDNA 8022 E4
- MNDH 8113 A1
Ridge Rd
- BRNV 8282 A4
- CIRC 7596 E7
- CIRC 7682 E1
- EDNA 8022 A4
- EDNP 8192 C1
- NOAK 7769 E2
Ridge St
- STPL 8026 D4
Ridge Wy
- MAHT 7772 A6
Ridge Cliff Dr
- EAGN 8198 A7
- EAGN 8284 A1
Ridge Creek Rd
- SHVW 7682 C3
Ridge Creek Rd Ct
- SHVW 7682 C4
Ridgecrest Ct
- EAGN 8283 E1
Ridgedale Dr
- MNTK 7934 D3
- MNTK 7935 A4
Ridgehaven Ln
- MNTK 7934 E4
Ridgemount Av W
- MNTK 7934 E2
- MNTK 7935 B2
- PYMH 7934 E2
- PYMH 7935 B2
Ridge Park Rd
- EDNA 8022 C6
Ridge Point Ct
- SAVG 8280 C4
Ridgeview Cir
- EDNA 8108 B1
Ridgeview Dr
- APVA 8282 E7
- EAGN 8198 C7
- EDNA 8108 D1
Ridgeview Tr NE
- PRIO 8279 D7
Ridgewater Dr
- MNTK 7935 B5
Ridgeway Dr
- MNTK 8020 D5
- WSTP 8028 A5
Ridgeway Pkwy NE
- MINN 7853 B6
Ridgeway Rd
- EDNA 8022 C7
- GLDV 7936 B2
Ridgeway St
- WtBT 7685 C6
Ridgewind Rd
- EDNP 8107 C6
Ridge Wind Tr
- EAGN 8283 D1
Ridgewood Av
- IVGH 8115 C7
- MINN 7938 A4
- VADH 7856 B1
- WtBT 7685 B7
Ridgewood Ct
- ARDH 7768 C7
- BRNV 8197 A5
Ridgewood Dr
- EAGN 8199 B3
- HOPK 8021 D2
- MNDH 8027 C7
Ridgewood Ln
- RSVL 7854 C6
- SAVG 8280 A6
Ridgewood Ln N
- RSVL 7854 B6
Ridgewood Ln S
- RSVL 7854 B6
Ridgewood Rd
- ARDH 7768 C7
- ARDH 7854 C1
- RSVL 7854 C1
Ridge Wy Ct
- MAHT 7772 A6
Rigby Dr
- EDNP 8193 C4
Rimbley Rd
- WDBY 8030 D3
Rimrock Dr
- APVA 8282 E6
Rindahl Ct
- MNTK 8020 B1
Ring Rd
- EDNA 8022 E6
Ringer Rd
- MNTK 7934 A4
Rio Loma Dr
- BRNV 8196 D7
Rio Loma Ln
- BRNV 8196 D7
Ripley Av
- MPLW 7856 D7
- MPLW 7857 D7
- NSTP 7857 D7
Risewood Cir
- EDNP 8193 D2
Rishworth Ln
- WTBL 7771 B4
Rita Ct
- EAGN 8113 B7
Rivendell Ln
- MNTK 7935 A5
River Cross
- SAVG 8280 E7
- SAVG 8281 B1
River Ct
- BRNV 8196 E5
River Ln
- ANOK 7592 A2
- COON 7592 B2
E River Pkwy
- CHMP 7591 E1
- CHMP 7592 A1
- MINN 7939 C4
- STPL 7939 D6
W River Pkwy
- CHMP 7591 D1
- MINN 7852 B7
- MINN 7938 B1
- MINN 7939 A4
- MINN 8025 D1
E River Rd
- ANOK 7592 B1
- COON 7592 B2
- FRID 7680 A5
- FRID 7766 B7
- FRID 7852 B1
- MINN 7852 B1
E River Rd CO-1
- FRID 7680 B6
- FRID 7766 B7
- FRID 7852 B1
E River Rd NE
- FRID 7680 B7
- FRID 7766 A4
E River Rd NE CO-1
- FRID 7680 B7
- FRID 7766 A4
E River Rd NW
- COON 7593 E7
- COON 7679 E1
- COON 7680 A4
- FRID 7680 A3
E River Rd NW CO-1
- COON 7593 E7
- COON 7679 E1
- COON 7680 A4
- FRID 7680 A4
W River Rd
- BRKC 7766 A2
- BRKP 7593 A6
- BRKP 7679 E5
- BRKP 7680 A7
- BRKP 7766 A1
- CHMP 7592 E5
- CHMP 7593 A6
- MINN 7852 B7
River Rd E
- MINN 7939 A2
N River Run
- SAVG 8281 A7
River St
- MINN 7938 B1
River Ter
- BMTN 8195 E5
River Ter E
- MINN 7939 C4
- STPL 7939 C5
River Bend Pl
- SAVG 8281 A6
River Birch Pl
- LINO 7683 C1
River Bluff Cir
- BMTN 8194 D6
River Bluff Ct
- EAGN 8198 A1
River Bluff Curv
- BMTN 8194 D7
River Bluff Dr
- BMTN 8194 D7
- EAGN 8198 A1
River Crossing Ct
- SAVG 8281 B1
Riverdale Dr N
- BRKP 7680 A7
- BRKP 7766 A1
Riverdale Rd
- BRKC 7766 A2
- BRKP 7766 A1
River Edge Wy NE
- FRID 7766 B2
E River Entry
- CHMP 7591 B2
River Heights Wy
- IVGH 8201 B3
River Hills Cir
- BRNV 8283 A1
River Hills Dr
- BRNV 8196 E6
- BRNV 8197 A7
- BRNV 8283 A1
River Hills Dr S
- BRNV 8283 A1
River Hills Dr W
- BRNV 8196 D6
River Ln Ct N
- BRKP 7680 A6
River Mews Ct
- MINN 7939 C4
River Park Plz S
- STPL 7942 A7
River Pointe Cir
- MINN 7852 B6
River Pointe Ln
- MINN 7852 B6
W River Rd Ct N
- BRKP 7766 A1
River Ridge Blvd
- BRNV 8282 A2
River Ridge Cir
- BMTN 8111 A7
- EAGN 8112 A6
N River Ridge Cir
- BRNV 8282 A2
S River Ridge Cir
- BRNV 8282 A2
River Ridge Ct
- BRNV 8282 A2
River Ridge Rd
- BMTN 8110 E7
River Run Ct
- SAVG 8281 A7
River Shore Ln N
- CHMP 7592 B3
Riverside Av
- MINN 7938 E4
- MINN 7939 A4
Riverside Dr
- SHKP 8279 D3
Riverside Pl N
- BRKP 7593 B7
River Ter Dr
- BMTN 8195 E5
River Terrace Ct E
- MINN 7939 C5
Riverton Av
- EAGN 8197 E3
- EAGN 8198 A4
Riverton Cir
- EAGN 8197 E4
Riverton Pt
- EAGN 8198 A3
River Valley Rd
- STPL 8026 E5
- STPL 8027 B4
Riverview Av
- STPL 8028 A3
Riverview Av S
- BMTN 8196 D1
Riverview Cir N
- CHMP 7592 D5
Riverview Cir S
- BMTN 8196 D1
E Riverview Dr
- EDNP 8193 B4
W Riverview Dr
- EDNP 8193 B4
Riverview Ln N
- BRKP 7679 E5
- BRKP 7680 A5
- CHMP 7592 D4
Riverview Pl NW
- COON 7593 A5
Riverview Rd
- BMTN 8193 E5
- EDNP 8192 C3
- EDNP 8193 D4
- HnpC 8025 D5
- MINN 8025 D5
Riverview Ter NE
- FRID 7680 A4
- FRID 7766 B2
Riverview Entry N
- CHMP 7592 D5
Riverwood Cir
- BRNV 8282 C1
Riverwood Dr
- BRNV 8196 C7
- BRNV 8282 D1
Riverwood Dr NE
- FRID 7680 B7
Riverwood Ln
- SAVG 8280 E4
Riverwood Ln N
- BRKC 7766 A3
Riverwood Pl
- STPL 7939 E7
River Woods Ln
- BRNV 8283 A1
Riviera Cir
- WTBL 7772 A5
Riviera Ct
- NBRI 7853 D1
- WTBL 7771 E6
Riviera Dr
- NBRI 7853 D1
Riviera Dr N
- MAHT 7772 A5
- WTBL 7771 E5
- WTBL 7772 A5
Riviera Dr S
- WTBL 7771 E6
- WTBL 7772 A6
Rivoli St
- STPL 7942 A4
Roanoak Rd
- GLDV 7937 A2
Roanoke Cir
- GLDV 7937 B2
Roanoke Rd
- SUNL 8113 E4
Robb Farm Rd
- NOAK 7769 E2
- NOAK 7770 A2
Robbins St
- MINN 8023 C5
- STPL 7939 D3
Robert Ct
- MAHT 7772 C6
- WILL 7772 C6
S Robert Ct
- IVGH 8199 E5
Robert St
- MAHT 7772 C6
- WILL 7772 B6
S Robert St
- STPL 8028 A2
Robert St N
- STPL 7941 E7
- STPL 7942 A7
Robert St N SR-3
- STPL 7941 E7
- STPL 7942 A7
Robert St S
- IVGH 8114 A1
- STPL 7942 A7
- STPL 8028 A3
- WSTP 8028 A7
- WSTP 8114 A1
Robert St S SR-3
- IVGH 8114 A1
- STPL 7942 A7
- STPL 8028 A3
- WSTP 8028 A7
- WSTP 8114 A1
S Robert Tr
- EAGN 8199 C7
- EAGN 8285 C2
- IVGH 8114 A2
- IVGH 8199 E4
- IVGH 8200 A1
- RSMT 8285 B6
- SUNL 8114 A4
- WSTP 8114 A1
S Robert Tr SR-3
- EAGN 8199 C7
- EAGN 8285 C2
- IVGH 8114 A2
- IVGH 8199 E4
- IVGH 8200 A1
- RSMT 8285 A6
- SUNL 8114 A4
- WSTP 8114 A1
Roberts Dr
- EDNP 8106 E3
- EDNP 8107 A3
Roberts Pl
- EDNA 8022 D7
Robie St E
- STPL 8028 B2
Robie St W
- STPL 8027 E2
- STPL 8028 A2
Robin Av N
- ROBB 7851 A1
Robin Cir
- MNTK 8021 A1
Robin Cir N
- ROBB 7851 A1
Robin Ct
- NBRI 7767 C4
Robin Ln
- EAGN 8197 E3
- MNDS 7681 D7
- MNTK 8021 B1
- NBRI 7681 D7
- NBRI 7767 C1
- NOAK 7769 E2
N Robin Ln
- CTRV 7598 E4
S Robin Ln
- CTRV 7598 E4
W Robin Ln
- CTRV 7598 E4
Robin Rd
- MAPG 7763 A3
Robin Rd NE
- PRIO 8279 B7
Robin St
- SHVW 7682 E4
Robinhood Cir
- SHVW 7768 E1
Robin Hood Ln
- CIRC 7682 D3
Robinhood Pl
- ARDH 7768 D1
- SHVW 7768 E1
Robin Oak Ct
- SHVW 7682 E3
Robin Oak Rd
- MNTK 7935 D5
Robin Oak Rdg
- MNTK 7935 D5
Robinson Dr
- LINO 7596 E1
- LINO 7597 A1
Robinson Dr NW
- COON 7593 C3
Robinwood Cir
- MNTK 8021 B1
Robinwood Ct
- WDBY 8030 C5
Robinwood Dr
- MNTK 8020 B1
Robinwood Ln
- HOPK 8021 C1
- MNTK 7935 B7
- MNTK 8021 C1
Robinwood Spur
- MNTK 7935 C7
Robinwood Ter
- MNTK 7935 B7
- MNTK 8021 B1
Robinwood Tr
- WDBY 8030 C5
Robinwood Wy
- WDBY 8030 C5
Robinwood Bay
- WDBY 8030 C5
Robinwood Draw
- WDBY 8030 C5
Roblyn Av
- STPL 7939 E6
- STPL 7940 A6
Rockford Rd
- NWHE 7849 E2
- PYMH 7848 A3
- PYMH 7849 D2
Rockford Rd CO-9
- NWHE 7849 E2
- PYMH 7848 A3
- PYMH 7849 C2
Rockford Rd Service Dr
- PYMH 7849 D2
Rockney St NE
- BLNE 7596 E6
Rock Ridge Cir
- SHKP 8278 C4
Rocksborough Rd
- MNTK 8020 C4
Rockstone Ct
- NBRI 7767 D1
Rockstone Ln
- NBRI 7767 D1
Rockwood Av
- STPL 8026 C6
Rocky Ln
- EAGN 8198 B4
Rocky Rapids Wy
- EAGN 8197 B3
Rodeo Ct NE
- BLNE 7596 A3
Rodeo Dr
- BRNV 8196 D7
Rodeo Dr NE
- BLNE 7595 D3
- BLNE 7596 A3
Roeder Cir
- HnpC 8025 D7
Roeller Av
- SSTP 8028 B4
- WSTP 8028 B4
Rogers Av
- MNDH 8113 A3
Rogers Ct
- EAGN 8199 A5
- MNDH 8113 A3
Rogers Dr
- MNTK 8020 E5
Rogers Rd
- EDNP 8106 A7
Rogers St
- STPL 8026 E3
Rohavic Ln
- LINO 7683 A3
Rolf Av
- EDNA 8022 E6
- EDNA 8108 D1
Roll Ln
- EAGN 8113 B7
Rolling Green Curv
- MNDH 8026 C7
- MNDH 8112 E1
Rolling Green Pkwy
- EDNA 8022 C4
Rolling Hills Cir
- EAGN 8199 D1
- IVGH 8199 D1
Rolling Hills Ct
- EAGN 8199 C1
Rolling Hills Dr
- EAGN 8113 C7
- EAGN 8199 C1
- LINO 7685 A2
- MPLW 7943 E2
Rolling Hills Pl
- EAGN 8199 C1
Rolling Hills Rd
- ARDH 7768 A5
- EDNP 8107 C6
Rolling Oaks Cir NE
- PRIO 8279 B6
Rolling Oaks Rd
- BRNV 8197 A7
Rolling View Ct
- WTBL 7771 E7
Rollingview Dr
- WTBL 7771 E7
Rollins Av SE
- MINN 7939 B1
Rolls Rd
- NBRI 7853 D1
Roma Av
- RSVL 7854 E7
- RSVL 7855 C7
Roman Rd
- FRID 7766 C5
Rome Av
- STPL 8026 A4
Romeo Ln
- EDNP 8192 C2
Romeo Rd
- WDBY 8030 B6
Ronald Av
- WTBL 7771 C6
Ronald Pl N
- BRKP 7764 C4
E Rondeau Lake Rd
- LINO 7598 B1
Rooney Pl
- WTBL 7771 A7
Roosevelt Ct NE
- STAN 7853 B2
Roosevelt St NE
- MINN 7853 B5
- STAN 7853 B2
Rosa Ct
- EAGN 8285 B1
Rosalyn Ct
- GLDV 7850 B5
- NWHE 7850 B5
Roscoe Rd
- PNSP 7858 C2
Rose Av
- STPL 7941 A3
Rose Av E
- MPLW 7943 D2
- STPL 7941 D3
- STPL 7942 D2
- STPL 7943 A2
Rose Av W
- STPL 7941 A3
Rose Ct
- EDNA 8109 A1
Rose Ct N
- BRKP 7679 B1
Rose Ln
- MINN 8023 B1
- NBRI 7767 D4
Rose Mnr
- GLDV 7850 A6
Rose Pl
- LCAN 7855 E4
- LCAN 7856 A4
- RSVL 7853 D4
- RSVL 7854 B4
- RSVL 7855 B4
Rose Pl E
- LCAN 7855 D4
Rose St
- MAHT 7772 C3
Rose St NW
- COON 7592 D1
Rosebriar Av
- VADH 7770 B3
Rosedale Dr
- FLCH 7853 E7
- RSVL 7853 E7
Rosedale Rd NE
- SPLP 7680 C5
Rosehill Cir
- LAUD 7939 D1

INDEX 37

Roselawn Av E — Minneapolis Street Index — Searle Ct

STREET Block City ZIP Map # Grid

Roselawn Av E
- MPLW 7855 D6
- MPLW 7856 A6

Roselawn Av W
- FLCH 7853 E6
- FLCH 7854 B6
- LAUD 7853 E7
- MPLW 7855 D6
- RSVL 7853 E7
- RSVL 7854 B6
- RSVL 7855 D6

Rosemary Ct
- EAGN 8199 C5

Rosemary Ln
- EDNA 8108 B2
- MNTK 7934 B5

Rosemary Rd
- EDNP 8106 D2

Rosemary Wy
- HUGO 7599 B4
- LINO 7599 B4

Rosemill Cir N
- CHMP 7591 D5

Rosemill Ct N
- CHMP 7591 D5

Rosemill Ln N
- CHMP 7591 D5

Ros Emily Ln
- EDNP 8107 C2

Rosemount Dr
- BRNV 8281 C7

Rosetown Ct
- RSVL 7855 A3

Rose Vista Ct
- RSVL 7854 D7

Roseway Rd
- MINN 8023 E2

Rosewood Av N
- MPLW 7857 A6

Rosewood Av S
- MPLW 7857 A6

Rosewood Ct
- MAPG 7677 B6
- NBRI 7767 D3

Rosewood Dr
- LCAN 7855 D3

Rosewood Ln N
- MAPG 7676 E3
- MAPG 7677 A2
- MAPG 7762 D2
- PYMH 7762 C6
- PYMH 7763 A5
- PYMH 7848 E1
- PYMH 7849 A1
- RSVL 7853 E6

Rosewood Ln S
- RSVL 7853 E6

Rosewood Rd NE
- PRIO 8279 D7

Roslyn Pl
- MINN 8024 B7

Ross Av
- STPL 7942 E4
- STPL 7943 A4

Ross Av E
- STPL 7943 B4

Ross Ln
- WtBT 7685 A6

Roth Pl
- WTBL 7771 E5
- WtBT 7771 E5

Roth St
- WTBL 7771 C5

Roundhill Rd
- MNDH 8027 B7

Round Lake Blvd NW
- COON 7592 C3

Round Lake Blvd NW CO-1
- COON 7592 C2

Round Lake Rd
- EDNP 8106 A4

Round Lake Rd W
- ARDH 7768 A3

Round Lake Tr
- LCAN 7855 D3

Rowe Pl
- STPL 7943 A7

Rowland Rd
- EDNP 8021 B7
- EDNP 8107 B1
- MNTK 8020 E5
- MNTK 8021 B7

Rowland Park Rd
- MNTK 8020 E5
- MNTK 8021 A5

Roxanna Ln
- NBRI 7767 B2

Roy St N
- STPL 7940 B6

Roy St S
- STPL 8026 B3

Royal Av
- IVGH 8115 C7

Royal Ct
- MNTK 8020 D4
- SHVW 7682 E5

Royal Ln
- ARDH 7768 C4

Royale Ct
- EAGN 8283 C2

Royale Dr
- EAGN 8283 C2

Royale Pl
- EAGN 8283 C2

Royale Tr
- EAGN 8283 C2

Royale Wy
- EAGN 8283 C2

Royal Hills Dr
- ARDH 7768 C3

Royal Link Ct
- EDNP 8106 C2

Royal Oak Cir
- EAGN 8198 B2

Royal Oak Ct NE
- FRID 7767 A3

Royal Oaks Dr
- MNTK 8021 A4
- SHVW 7682 E5

W Royal Oaks Dr
- BLNE 7682 C3
- SHVW 7682 D3

Royal Pines Pl
- LINO 7684 A2

Royalston Av N
- MINN 7938 A2

Royalton Rd NE
- PRIO 8279 D6
- SAVG 8279 E6

Roycar Rd
- EDNA 8108 E2

Royce St NE
- COLH 7767 A7

Royzelle Ln
- MNTK 8021 B1

Rozelle Dr
- STAN 7853 C4

N Ruby Ct
- EAGN 8197 D5

S Ruby Ct
- EAGN 8197 D5

Ruby Dr
- MNDH 8027 D5
- WSTP 8027 D5

Ruby Ln
- EAGN 8197 D5

Ruffed Grouse Ct
- LINO 7598 A7

Ruffed Grouse Rd
- LINO 7598 A7

Ruggles Av
- FLCH 7854 C7
- RSVL 7854 D7

Ruggles St
- RSVL 7854 D7

Runge Ln
- WSTP 8027 D6

Runnel Cir
- EDNP 8193 B2

Running Brook Rd
- EAGN 8197 B5

Runnymeade Ct
- MNTK 7935 C5

Runnymeade Ln
- MNTK 7935 C4
- STLP 7935 D4

Rupp Dr
- BRNV 8196 D7

Rush Creek Rd
- DAYT 7590 B6
- MAPG 7590 B6

Russell Av
- WDBY 8030 E7

Russell Av N
- BRKC 7765 C6
- BRKP 7679 C6
- MINN 7765 C6
- MINN 7851 C2
- MINN 7937 D1

Russell Av S
- BMTN 8109 C5
- BMTN 8195 C1
- MINN 7937 C3
- MINN 8023 C4
- RHFD 8109 C1

Russell Cir N
- BRKP 7679 C2

Russell Cir S
- BMTN 8195 D1

Russell Ct
- MINN 8023 C5
- RSVL 7854 B2

Russell St
- STPL 7942 C4

Rustad Ln
- MNDS 7681 E5

Rusten Rd
- EAGN 8283 B2

Rustic Dr
- MAHT 7772 C7

Rustic Ldg E
- MINN 8024 B4

Rustic Ln
- LINO 7596 E6
- LINO 7597 A6

Rustic Pl
- LCAN 7855 D3
- SHVW 7769 C3
- VADH 7769 C6

Rustic Rd SE
- PRIO 8280 A7
- SAVG 8280 A7

Rustic Hills Dr
- EAGN 8112 A6

W Rustic Lodge Av
- MINN 8024 A4

Rutgers St NE
- PRIO 8280 A7
- SAVG 8280 A6

Ruth Cir NE
- FRID 7680 B4

Ruth Dr
- EDNA 8022 E7

Ruth St
- LCAN 7855 D4

Ruth St N
- MPLW 7857 B7
- STPL 7857 B7
- STPL 7943 B1

Ruth St NE
- FRID 7680 A5

Ruth St S
- STPL 8029 B1

Rutledge Av
- EDNA 8022 D4

Rutledge Cir
- MNTK 7934 E7
- MNTK 7935 B7

Ryan Av
- EDNA 8022 E7
- STPL 7941 D4
- STPL 8027 D1

Ryan Av E
- MPLW 7856 D6
- NSTP 7857 D6

Ryan Av S
- EDNA 8022 E6
- EDNA 8108 E1

Ryan Av W
- RSVL 7854 C6
- RSVL 7855 B6

Ryan Cir
- BRNV 8196 D7

Ryan Ct E
- NSTP 7857 C6

Ryan Dr
- LCAN 7855 D1
- MPLW 7943 E1
- ODLE 7943 E1

Ryan Ln
- LCAN 7855 D1

Ryan Pl
- LXTN 7682 B1

Ryan St
- LAUD 7853 D6
- RSVL 7853 D6

Ryde St
- STPL 7940 E3

Rye Ct
- SHKP 8279 C3

S

Sable Dr
- BRNV 8283 A2

Sabra Ct
- APVA 8283 B4

Saddlebrooke Cir
- MNTK 7934 E6

Saddle Horn Ct
- EDNP 8192 A1

Saddlewood Dr
- EAGN 8199 B3
- MNTK 8020 A4

Saddlewood Tr
- MNTK 8020 D7

Safari Cir
- APVA 8283 D2
- EAGN 8283 D2

Safari Ct N
- EAGN 8283 D2

Safari Ct S
- EAGN 8283 D2

Safari Tr
- EAGN 8283 D1

Safari Heights Tr
- EAGN 8283 C2

Safari Pass
- APVA 8283 D2
- EAGN 8283 D2

Sailor Ln
- BRKC 7765 B6

St. Albans Cir
- EDNA 8108 A2
- SHVW 7683 A5

St. Albans Ct
- SHVW 7683 A4

E St. Albans Rd
- HOPK 7935 D7

W St. Albans Rd
- HOPK 7935 C7

St. Albans St N
- LINO 7683 A4
- RSVL 7855 A3
- SHVW 7683 A4
- STPL 7855 A7
- STPL 7941 A1

St. Albans St S
- STPL 7941 A7
- STPL 8027 A1

St. Albans Hollow Cir
- MNTK 7935 B7

St. Albans Hollow Dr
- MNTK 7935 B6

St. Albans Mill Rd
- MNTK 7935 B7

St. Andrew Blvd
- EAGN 8198 C7
- EAGN 8284 C1

St. Andrew Dr
- EDNP 8106 D3

St. Andrews Av
- EDNA 8022 E6

St. Andrews Cir NE
- BLNE 7596 D2

St. Andrews Ct NE
- BLNE 7596 D2

St. Andrews Dr
- EDNP 8106 E3

St. Andrews Dr NE
- BLNE 7596 D3

St. Anthony Av
- MINN 7939 D5
- STPL 7939 E6
- STPL 7940 A6
- STPL 7941 B6
- WtBT 7685 B7

St. Anthony Blvd
- MINN 7853 C5
- STAN 7853 C4

St. Anthony Pkwy
- MINN 7852 A2
- MINN 7853 A3
- STAN 7853 B4

St. Anthony Rd
- STAN 7853 B3

St. Charles Pl
- EAGN 8198 A2

St. Clair Av
- STPL 8025 E1
- STPL 8026 E1
- STPL 8027 A1

St. Croix Av N
- GLDV 7850 D7
- GLDV 7851 A7

St. Croix Cir
- GLDV 7851 A7

St. Croix St
- RSVL 7853 D5

St. Davids Rd
- MNTK 7934 C7
- MNTK 7935 A7

St. Dennis Ct
- STPL 8026 B5

Ste. Marie St
- SHVW 7769 C6
- VADH 7769 C6

St. Francis Wy
- EAGN 8198 D2

St. Imier Dr
- COLH 7767 B5
- FRID 7767 B5

St. Johns Av
- EDNA 8022 E6

St. John's Av S
- EDNA 8022 E7
- EDNA 8108 E1

St. John's Blvd
- MPLW 7857 A2

St. John's Dr
- EDNP 8020 E7
- EDNP 8106 E1

St. John's Rd
- HOPK 8021 D1
- MNTK 8021 D1

St. Joseph Ln
- STPL 7941 D3

St. Louis Av
- MINN 7937 B6

St. Louis St
- HOPK 8021 E3
- HOPK 8022 B3

St. Margaret Dr
- GLDV 7851 C6
- MINN 7851 C6

St. Mark's Dr
- MNTK 8020 E2

St. Mary's Av SE
- MINN 7939 B4

St. Mary's Pl
- MNTK 8020 D5

St. Mary's St
- FLCH 7854 B7

St. Michael St
- MNDS 7681 D5

St. Moritz Dr
- COLH 7767 A5
- FRID 7767 A5

St. Patrick's Ln
- EDNA 8108 B2

St. Paul Av
- MINN 7937 B6
- STPL 8026 A4

N St. Paul Rd
- MPLW 7857 B7
- NSTP 7857 B6

St. Paul Park Rd
- SPLP 8115 E6

St. Paul Park Rd CO-22
- SPLP 8115 E6

St. Peter St
- STPL 7941 D6

St. Raphael Dr
- CRYS 7764 B6
- NWHE 7764 B6

St. Stephens St
- MNDS 7681 D5
- RSVL 7853 D5

Sakpe Cir
- SHKP 8278 A7

Sakpe Dr
- SHKP 8278 A6

Salem Av
- SAVG 8280 E7

Salem Av S
- STLP 7936 E6
- STLP 8022 E2

Salem Ct
- EDNP 8193 C4
- MAHT 7772 A7

Salem Ln
- SUNL 8113 E3

Salem Pl
- BRNV 8281 C4
- MAHT 7772 A7

Salem Pt
- EAGN 8283 E1

Salem Church Rd
- IVGH 8114 A3
- MNDH 8113 D3
- SUNL 8113 D3
- SUNL 8114 A3

Sally Cir
- EAGN 8113 B7

Sally Ln
- EDNA 8107 E2

Samuel Ct
- VADH 7856 A1

Samuel Rd
- EDNA 8107 E2

Samuel St
- RSVL 7854 B6

Sanburnol Dr NE
- BLNE 7680 C3
- SPLP 7680 C3

Sanctuary Dr NE
- BLNE 7595 D5

Sandburg Ln
- CRYS 7850 C5
- GLDV 7850 C5

Sandburg Rd
- GLDV 7850 C6

Sand Creek Dr NW
- COON 7594 A2

Sandeen Rd
- ARDH 7854 B1

Sandell Av
- EDNA 8109 B2

Sander Dr
- MINN 8025 B6

Sandhill Cir
- EDNP 8106 B6

Sandhill Dr
- CIRC 7596 E7
- LINO 7596 E7
- LINO 7597 A7
- SHKP 8278 B4

Sandhoff Ln N
- PYMH 7849 D2

Sandhurst Av
- MPLW 7856 E5
- MPLW 7857 A5

Sandhurst Dr W
- RSVL 7854 E5
- RSVL 7855 A5

Sandlewood Rd
- WDBY 8030 B1

Sandpiper Ct
- EDNA 8022 B7

Sandpiper Dr
- LINO 7597 D5

E Sandpiper Dr
- BLNE 7594 E7
- BLNE 7680 E1

W Sandpiper Dr
- BLNE 7594 E7
- BLNE 7680 E1

Sand Piper Ln
- NOAK 7683 E6
- NOAK 7684 A6

Sandra Ln
- MNTK 7935 D7
- STLP 7935 D7
- WTBL 7771 A2

E Sandralee Dr
- STPL 7943 B7

W Sandralee Dr
- STPL 7943 B7

Sand Ridge Rd
- EDNP 8106 E2

Sandro Rd S
- BMTN 8108 C7

Sandstone Dr
- EAGN 8197 C6

Sandterra Cir
- WtBT 7685 E4

Sandy Ct
- SPLP 8116 A6

Sandy Hook Dr
- RSVL 7855 B2

Sandy Point Rd
- EDNP 8193 A3

Sanel Rd
- WDBY 8030 C3

Sanibel Dr
- MNTK 8021 B5

Sapphire Ln
- EAGN 8197 C5

Sapphire Pt
- EAGN 8197 D5

Saratoga Cir N
- PYMH 7849 D2

Saratoga Ln
- EDNP 8106 E6

Saratoga Ln N
- CHMP 7591 C1
- MAPG 7677 D2
- MNTK 7935 D2
- OSSE 7677 D3
- PYMH 7763 D7
- PYMH 7849 B4
- PYMH 7935 D2

Saratoga St N
- STPL 7940 C7

Saratoga St S
- STPL 8026 C3

Saratoga Wy
- MAPG 7677 C1

Sargent Av
- STPL 8025 E1
- STPL 8026 A1

Sargent Ct N
- LINO 7685 A3
- WtBT 7685 A3

Sargent Rd
- MAHT 7772 C6
- WILL 7772 C6

Sartell Av
- EAGN 8197 E4

Satellite Ln NE
- FRID 7766 C2

Saunders Av
- STPL 8026 B4

Savage Ln
- LCAN 7855 E4

Savanna Av
- WTBL 7771 A7

Savanna Ct
- LINO 7597 A4

Savanna Dr
- SHKP 8278 D2

Savannah Rd
- EAGN 8198 E4
- EAGN 8199 A4

Savannah Chace
- EDNP 8106 C6

Savannah Oaks Ln
- WDBY 8030 E5

Savannah Oaks Alcove
- WDBY 8030 E5

Savanna Oaks Dr
- SAVG 8280 B7

Saxony Ct
- WtBT 7684 D6

Saxony Rd
- EDNA 8022 B6

Scandia Rd
- EDNA 8108 A1

Scarborough Cir
- BMTN 8194 D3

Scarborough Rd
- BMTN 8194 E4

Scarlet Globe Dr
- EDNP 8106 D5
- EDNP 8193 A1

Scarlet Oak St E
- ODLE 7858 C3

Scarlet Oak St W
- ODLE 7858 B3

Scarlet Oak Crest
- ODLE 7858 B3

Scenic Cir
- MNTK 8020 A6

Scenic Ct
- MNTK 8020 A6
- SHVW 7682 E4

Scenic Dr
- MNTK 8020 A6
- SHVW 7682 E4

Scenic Ln
- MNTK 8020 A7

Scenic Ln N
- MNTK 8020 A6

Scenic Ln S
- MNTK 8020 A6

Scenic Pl
- LINO 7682 E4
- MNTK 8020 A7
- SHVW 7682 E4
- STPL 7943 C6

Scenic Heights Dr
- EDNP 8020 A7
- MNTK 8020 A7

Scenic Heights Rd
- EDNP 8106 C5

Schadt Dr E
- MPLW 8029 D5

Schaefer Cir
- EDNA 8022 A6

Schaefer Rd
- EDNA 8022 A6

Schaller Dr E
- MPLW 8029 D4

Schaller Dr S
- MPLW 8029 D4

Scheel Dr
- WDBY 7944 A7

Scheffer Av
- STPL 8025 E3
- STPL 8026 B3
- STPL 8027 B4

Scheunemann Av
- STPL 7940 D7

Schey Dr
- EDNA 8108 B3

Schifsky Rd
- SHVW 7769 A1

Schlavin Ct
- LINO 7683 A2

Schletti St
- STPL 7941 B2

Schletty Dr
- LCAN 7856 A4

Schletty Ln
- WSTP 8028 B6

Schley Av
- WSTP 8027 E4

Schmacher Rd
- SSTP 8115 B2

Schmidt Farm Rd
- CHMP 7591 C6

Schmidt Lake Rd
- NWHE 7763 E7
- PYMH 7762 B7
- PYMH 7763 C7

School Dr
- WDBY 8030 A2

School Rd
- CIRC 7682 D2
- EDNA 8022 E7
- EDNP 8106 B5

Schoolcraft Rd
- BRNV 8196 E6

Schuller's Cir
- GLDV 7936 C1

Schultz Lake Beach Rd
- EAGN 8199 A7
- EAGN 8285 A1

Schuneman Rd
- GEML 7771 A5

Schutta Rd
- ARDH 7682 A5
- SHVW 7682 A5

Science Center Dr
- NWHE 7763 E6
- NWHE 7764 A6

Scimed Pl
- MAPG 7676 C6

Scot Ter
- EDNP 8106 E3
- EDNP 8107 A3

Scotch Pine Cir
- NOAK 7769 C2

Scotch Pine Ct
- EDNP 8107 B6
- NOAK 7769 B2

Scotch Pine Ln
- NOAK 7769 C1

Scotch Pine Rd
- NOAK 7769 C2

Scotia Dr
- EDNA 8108 B2

Scotland Ct
- MNDS 7681 C6

Scott Av N
- BRKC 7764 E2
- BRKP 7592 E7
- BRKP 7678 E2
- BRKP 7764 E1
- CRYS 7764 E6
- GLDV 7850 E4
- ROBB 7850 E1

Scott Blvd S
- CTGV 8202 B1

Scott Ct
- MNTK 8020 C5

Scott Ln
- WSTP 8028 B7
- WSTP 8114 B1

Scott St
- BRNV 8281 D6

Scott Ter
- EDNA 8023 B3

Scott Tr
- EAGN 8197 C7

Scout Cir
- BRNV 8196 E6

Scriver Rd
- EDNA 8022 A5

Scudder St
- FLCH 7940 A2
- STPL 7939 E2
- STPL 7940 A2

Seabury Av
- MINN 7939 B5

Seagull Cir NE
- PRIO 8279 B7

Seal St
- STPL 7939 E4

Sean Ct
- EAGN 8198 E6

Sean's Wy N
- NSTP 7857 C4

Searle Ct
- VADH 7770 B6

Minneapolis Street Index

INDEX 40

SR-252 The Great River Rd — Minneapolis Street Index — Sunset Ct

STREET Block City ZIP Map # Grid

SR-252 The Great River Rd
- BRKP 7680 A7
- BRKP 7766 A1

SR-280
- LAUD 7853 D7
- LAUD 7939 D1
- RSVL 7853 D6
- STPL 7939 D1

SR-312
- EDNP 8106 D4

SR-610
- BLNE 7680 C1
- BRKP 7678 B2
- BRKP 7679 E2
- COON 7679 E1
- COON 7680 A1

SR-610 Richard P Braun Br
- BRKP 7679 E3
- COON 7679 E2

Stacker Blvd
- WtBT 7771 E5

Stacker Pl
- WtBT 7771 E5

Stacy Cir
- WTBL 7772 A6

Stagecoach Rd
- SHKP 8193 C7
- SHKP 8279 D1

Stage Coach Tr
- LINO 7597 B4

Stagecoach Pass
- EDNP 8193 A3

Staghorn Dr
- SHKP 8278 B4

Stallion Ln
- LINO 7597 A1

Stanbridge Av
- RSVL 7853 D2
- RSVL 7854 B2

Stanbridge Cir
- RSVL 7855 C2

Stanbury Curv
- EDNP 8106 C7

Standish Av
- MINN 8024 E6

Standish Av S
- MINN 8024 E2

Standish St
- STPL 7939 E3

Standridge Av
- MPLW 7857 D2

Standridge Pl
- MPLW 7857 C2

Stanford Av
- STPL 8025 E2
- STPL 8026 C2

Stanford Ct
- STPL 8025 E2

Stanich Ct
- MPLW 7857 B6

Stanich Pl
- MPLW 7857 B7
- STPL 7857 B7

Stanich St
- MPLW 7857 B5

Stanlen Rd
- STLP 7935 E5

Stanley Av
- SSTP 8028 C4

Stanley Av S
- BMTN 8108 E6
- BMTN 8194 E2

Stanley Cir S
- BMTN 8194 E4

Stanley Curv S
- BMTN 8194 E5

Stanley Rd S
- BMTN 8108 E6
- BMTN 8194 E5

Stanley St
- SSTP 8028 B4
- WSTP 8028 A4

Stanley Tr
- EDNP 8106 A6

Stanton Dr
- MNTK 7934 E7
- MNTK 7935 A7

Stanwich Ln
- MNDH 8027 B7

Stanwix Rd
- EAGN 8198 E4
- EAGN 8199 A4

Staples Av
- MNDH 8027 C5
- WSTP 8027 D5

Star Cir
- VADH 7769 D7

Star Ln
- SSTP 8028 C6

N Star Ln
- BLNE 7596 C6
- CIRC 7596 C6

Star Ln NE
- FRID 7766 C2

Starbridge Ct
- EAGN 8198 B5

Stardust Blvd
- CIRC 7596 C7

E Staring Ln
- EDNP 8106 C7
- EDNP 8192 C1

W Staring Ln
- EDNP 8106 C7
- EDNP 8192 C1

Staring Lake Pkwy
- EDNP 8106 D7
- EDNP 8192 C1

Stark St
- LCAN 7855 D4

Starkey St
- STPL 7941 E7
- STPL 8027 C2
- STPL 8028 A1

Starlite Blvd NE
- FRID 7766 C2

Starlite Cir NE
- FRID 7766 C2

Starrwood Cir
- EDNP 8106 D7

Stassen Dr
- WSTP 8028 B5

Stassen Ln
- WSTP 8028 B4

State St
- STPL 7942 A7
- STPL 8028 A1

State Farm Rd
- RSVL 7854 C5

State Farm Wy
- WDBY 7944 E3

State Hwy 169 Service Dr
- PYMH 7763 E7
- PYMH 7849 D2
- PYMH 7935 D1

States Av
- EAGN 8199 A5

Stauder Cir
- EDNA 8021 E6
- EDNA 8022 A6

Stavern Pt
- EAGN 8283 E2

Steele St
- MNTK 7934 B6
- MNTK 8020 B1

Steeplechase Cir
- EAGN 8284 B2

Steeplechase Ct
- EAGN 8284 B1

Steeplechase Ln
- EAGN 8284 B1

Steeplechase Wy
- EAGN 8284 C1

Steepleview Rd
- WDBY 8030 C3

Steer Dr
- WDBY 8030 B2

Stella Cir
- LINO 7685 B1

Stella Ln
- LINO 7685 B1

Stella St
- STPL 7940 A3

Stellar Ln
- EDNP 8106 C3

Stellar Pl
- STPL 7941 D4

Stephani Cir
- LCAN 7855 D5

Stephani Ct
- LCAN 7855 D5

Stephanie Cir
- EAGN 8112 A6

Stephen Cir
- SHVW 7683 B4

Stephens Dr S
- STLP 7936 E5

Sterling Av
- MPLW 8029 D7
- NWPT 8029 D7
- NWPT 8115 E1

Sterling Av N
- MPLW 7857 D7
- NSTP 7857 D7

Sterling Ct
- MAHT 7772 A7

Sterling Pl
- MPLW 8029 D6

Sterling St
- MPLW 7857 D7
- NSTP 7857 D7

Sterling St N
- MPLW 7857 D7
- MPLW 7943 D1

Sterling St S
- MPLW 8029 D4

Steven Ln
- CTRV 7598 D4

Steven Rd
- BRNV 8281 D6

Stevens Av
- MINN 8024 B4
- RHFD 8110 B2

Stevens Av S
- BMTN 8110 B7
- BMTN 8196 B1
- MINN 7938 B7
- MINN 8024 B1
- RHFD 8110 B2

Stevens St
- FLCH 7940 B2
- STPL 7940 B2

Stevens St E
- STPL 8028 A2

Stevens St W
- STPL 8027 E2

Stewart Av
- SSTP 8028 E6
- STPL 8026 D5
- STPL 8027 A3
- WTBL 7685 C7
- WTBL 7771 C1

Stewart Dr
- EDNP 8106 E3

Stewart Ln
- MNTK 8020 C5
- SSTP 8028 E6

Stewart Rd
- WILL 7772 C6

Stickney Av
- SSTP 8028 C4
- STPL 8028 C3

Stickney St
- SSTP 8028 C3
- STPL 8028 C3

Stillwater Av
- STPL 7942 E4
- STPL 7943 A4

Stillwater Av E
- MPLW 7943 C4
- STPL 7943 C4

Stillwater Blvd N
- ELMO 7858 D7
- MPLW 7943 E3
- ODLE 7858 D7
- ODLE 7943 E3
- ODLE 7944 A2

Stillwater Ct
- WtBT 7685 C7

Stillwater Rd
- GRNT 7772 D5
- MAHT 7772 C5
- WILL 7772 D5

Stillwater Rd E
- MPLW 7943 D4
- ODLE 7943 D3

Stillwater Rd E SR-5
- MPLW 7943 D4
- ODLE 7943 D3

Stillwater Rd N
- DLWD 7686 A7
- DLWD 7772 B1
- GRNT 7772 C1

Stillwater Rd N SR-96
- DLWD 7686 A7
- DLWD 7772 B1
- GRNT 7772 C1

Stillwater St
- DLWD 7685 E7
- WTBL 7685 D7
- WtBT 7684 E7
- WtBT 7685 D7

Stillwater Wy N
- ODLE 7858 D7
- ODLE 7944 E1

Stimson Tr
- WDBY 8116 B2

Stinchfield Av
- STPL 8029 C7

Stinchfield St
- STPL 8029 C7

Stinson Blvd
- COLH 7767 B6
- COLH 7853 B1
- FRID 7681 B6
- FRID 7767 B3
- MINN 7853 B7
- MNDS 7681 B6
- NBRI 7767 B3
- STAN 7767 B6
- STAN 7853 B1

Stinson Blvd NE
- COLH 7767 A7
- COLH 7853 B1
- FRID 7681 B7
- FRID 7767 B1
- MINN 7853 B7
- MNDS 7681 B7
- NBRI 7681 B7
- NBRI 7767 B1
- STAN 7853 B3

Stinson Ct
- COLH 7767 B5
- NBRI 7767 B5

Stinson Pkwy
- MINN 7853 B5
- STAN 7853 B4

Stinson St
- STPL 7940 E4
- STPL 7941 B4

Stirrup Ln
- EDNP 8192 A1

Stirrup St
- EAGN 8199 B6

Stockbridge Cir
- EDNP 8106 E5

Stockbridge Rd
- MNDH 8113 C4

Stockdale Dr
- VADH 7770 B5

Stockdale Rd
- VADH 7770 A5

Stockyards Rd
- SSTP 8029 A6
- SSTP 8115 A2

Stoddart Cir
- WtBT 7770 C2

Stoddart Ln
- WTBL 7770 C2
- WtBT 7770 C2

Stodola Rd
- MNTK 8020 A6

Stone Cir
- MNTK 7934 D6

Stone Rd
- MNDH 8113 C3
- MNTK 7934 C5

Stonebridge Blvd
- STPL 8025 E2

Stonebridge Cir
- EAGN 8199 C4

Stonebridge Dr N
- EAGN 8199 C4

Stonebridge Dr S
- EAGN 8199 B4

Stonebridge Rd
- LILY 8026 E6

Stonebrook Dr
- LINO 7684 B1

Stonecliffe Dr
- EAGN 8198 B7
- EAGN 8284 B1

Stonecrest Pth NW
- PRIO 8278 B7

Stonegate Ln
- MNTK 8020 D3

Stoneridge Ct
- LCAN 7856 C2
- VADH 7856 C2

Stone Ridge Trc
- MNTK 7934 C5

Stone Village Dr
- BRNV 8282 A7

Stonewood Ct
- EAGN 8199 C3
- EDNA 8108 B4
- EDNP 8107 A2

Stonewood Ln
- EAGN 8198 D4

Stonewood Rd
- EAGN 8199 B3

Stoney Wy
- EDNP 8193 A4

Stoneybrook Dr
- LINO 7684 B1

Stonybrook Ct
- MNTK 8020 A7

Stonybrook Dr
- MNTK 8020 A7

Stonybrook Wy NE
- FRID 7680 B6

Stony Point Rd
- EAGN 8198 E3
- EAGN 8199 A3

Storland Ct
- EAGN 8283 B2

Storland Rd
- EAGN 8283 B2

Stowe Av
- ARDH 7768 A7
- NBRI 7768 A7

Stratford Av
- MNDS 7681 E6

Stratford Cir N
- SHKP 8279 C3

Stratford Cir S
- SHKP 8279 C3

Stratford Cross N
- BRKP 7679 C5

Stratford Ct
- BRKP 7679 D4
- BRNV 8282 C2
- WDBY 8030 B6

Stratford Dr
- SHKP 8279 C2

Stratford Ln
- BRNV 8282 C1
- EAGN 8285 C1
- IVGH 8285 C1

Stratford Ln E
- BRNV 8282 C2

Stratford Ln N
- BRKP 7679 C5

Stratford Ln W
- BRNV 8282 C2

Stratford Rd
- EDNP 8106 D1
- MNDH 8112 E1
- WDBY 8030 B6

Stratford Alcove
- WDBY 8030 B6

Stratford Bay
- WDBY 8030 A6

Stratford Draw
- WDBY 8030 B6

Stratford Echo
- WDBY 8030 C6

Stratton Cir
- MNTK 7934 E6

Strawberry Ln
- EAGN 8198 C5
- GLDV 7937 A3

Street St
- ANOK 7592 A1

Stroden Cir
- GLDV 7849 E6

Strom Dr
- SAVG 8280 A2

Stryker Av
- IVGH 8113 E1
- STPL 8027 E4
- WSTP 8027 E7
- WSTP 8113 E1

Stuart Av
- EDNA 8022 C6

Stuart St
- WtBT 7684 D5

Stuber Rd
- RSVL 7855 A7

Study Ln
- BRKP 7678 C5

Sturgis St
- STPL 8027 C1

Stutz St NE
- BLNE 7596 E4

Suburban Av
- STPL 7942 C6
- STPL 7943 B6

Suburban Sq
- HOPK 8021 B3

Sucker Lake Rd
- NOAK 7769 D3
- VADH 7769 D3

Sudberry Ln
- EAGN 8199 A7

Sue Pl
- STPL 8026 A3

Sue St
- STPL 8026 A6

Sue Ann Ct
- EDNP 8106 C2

Sugarloaf Tr N
- BRKP 7679 D7

Sullivan Dr NE
- COLH 7766 D5
- FRID 7766 D5

Sullivan Ln NE
- COLH 7766 D5

Sullivan Wy NE
- COLH 7766 D4
- FRID 7766 D4

Sumac Cir
- EDNP 8193 D2
- WDBY 8030 B4
- WTBL 7857 E1

Sumac Ct
- CTRV 7598 E6
- WTBL 7857 E1

Sumac Ln
- MNTK 7935 C5
- NOAK 7683 D5

Sumac Pt
- EAGN 8198 B6

Sumac Rdg
- WTBL 7857 E1

Sumac St
- STPL 8027 A3

Sumac Wy
- WDBY 8030 B4

Sumer Ct
- MPLW 7856 A7

Summer Av
- MPLW 7855 E7
- MPLW 7856 E7
- MPLW 7857 A7

Summer Ct
- EAGN 8199 B6

Summer Ln
- EAGN 8199 B6

Summer Ln W
- MPLW 7856 A7

Summer Pl
- EAGN 8199 B6
- EDNP 8193 B3

Summer St
- FLCH 7853 E7
- FLCH 7854 A7
- LAUD 7853 D7
- RSVL 7854 D7

Summer St NE
- MINN 7852 D7
- MINN 7853 A7

Summerhill Dr
- EDNP 8106 C2

Summer Oaks Dr
- MNTK 7934 C4

Summerset Ln
- BRNV 8283 A1

Summit Av
- EDNA 8022 D4
- MAHT 7772 C4
- MINN 7937 E4
- SPLP 8115 E7
- SPLP 8201 E1
- SSTP 8028 D5
- STPL 7939 E7
- STPL 7940 E7
- STPL 7941 C6

Summit Cross
- NOAK 7770 C1

Summit Ct
- MPLW 7856 D2
- NOAK 7770 C1
- SSTP 8028 D5
- STPL 7941 B7
- STPL 8027 B1
- WSTP 8027 E6

Summit Ct S
- CTGV 8116 B5

Summit Curv S
- CTGV 8116 B4

Summit Dr
- EDNP 8106 B7

Summit Dr N
- BRKC 7765 D4

Summit Hl
- EAGN 8198 A6

Summit Hts
- NOAK 7770 C1

Summit Ln
- BRNV 8282 B5
- MNDH 8026 E7
- MNDH 8112 E1
- MNTK 8020 E1
- NOAK 7770 C1
- STPL 7941 B7
- WtBT 7771 E4

Summit Ln S
- CTGV 8116 B5

Summit Pl
- MINN 7937 E4

Summit St
- WtBT 7685 B7

Summit St NE
- COLH 7852 C1

Summit Vw
- NOAK 7770 C1

Summit Oaks Dr
- BRNV 8282 D7

Summit Pass
- EAGN 8198 B7
- EAGN 8284 B2

Summit Ridge Dr
- NOAK 7770 B1

Summit Shores Cir
- BRNV 8281 D1

Summit Shores Ct
- BRNV 8281 D1

Summit Shores Dr
- BRNV 8281 E7

Summit Shores Wy
- BRNV 8281 D1

Summit Shores Alcove
- BRNV 8281 E7

Summit Shores East
- BRNV 8281 D1

Summit Shores Vista
- BRNV 8281 D1

Summit Shores West
- BRNV 8281 D1

Sumner St
- STPL 8026 A3

Sumter Av
- SAVG 8280 B7

Sumter Av N
- BRKP 7592 B7
- BRKP 7678 B6
- BRKP 7764 B3
- CHMP 7592 B4
- CRYS 7764 B6
- CRYS 7850 B4
- GLDV 7850 B7
- GLDV 7936 B1
- NWHE 7764 B6
- NWHE 7850 B1

Sumter Av S
- BMTN 8194 A4
- GLDV 7936 B3
- STLP 7936 B5
- STLP 8022 B1

Sumter Cir
- BMTN 8194 A5

Sumter Cir N
- BRKP 7678 B5
- CHMP 7592 B4

Sumter Ct N
- CHMP 7592 B4

Sumter Ln S
- BMTN 8194 A4

Sumter Pl N
- NWHE 7764 B5

Sun Dr
- EAGN 8197 E1

Sun Rd
- EDNA 8022 B7

Sun Ter
- WTBL 7771 E6
- WTBL 7772 A6

Sunbow Ln
- MNDS 7681 D7
- NBRI 7681 D7
- NBRI 7767 C1

Sunburst Dr
- EDNP 8106 A2

Sunbury Dr
- WDBY 8030 C7

Sunbury Alcove
- WDBY 8030 C7

Sun Cliff Rd
- EAGN 8197 D6

Suncrest Ct
- EAGN 8199 A2

Sundial Ct
- EDNP 8106 D3

Sunfish Ct
- LINO 7597 A4

Sunfish Ln
- SUNL 8113 D2
- WSTP 8113 D2

Sunflower Cir
- VADH 7769 E4

Sunflower Cir S
- CTGV 8116 B6

Sunflower Ct
- BRNV 8281 B5
- VADH 7769 E4

Sunflower Ln
- LINO 7597 A4

Sunkist Blvd N
- BRKP 7680 A7

Sunkist Cir N
- BRKP 7680 A6

Sunkist Pkwy N
- BRKP 7679 E6

Sunne Pt
- EAGN 8284 A2

Sunny Ln
- BRKP 7764 B4
- NWHE 7764 B4

Sunnybrook Rd
- EDNP 8193 A1

Sunny Hill Dr
- CTGV 8116 E4
- WDBY 8116 E4

Sunnyridge Cir
- GLDV 7937 B2

Sunnyridge Ln
- GLDV 7937 B1

Sunnyside Av
- EDNA 8023 B3
- MINN 8023 B3

Sunnyside Cir
- BRNV 8281 C7

Sunnyside Ln
- HOPK 8021 C1
- SUNL 8113 E2

Sunnyside Rd
- EDNA 8022 E4
- EDNA 8023 A3
- MINN 8023 B3
- MNDS 7681 C4
- NBRI 7681 C7

Sunnyside Ter
- NBRI 7767 C1

Sunnyslope Dr
- MAPG 7762 E2

Sunnyslope Ln
- STPL 8026 B5

E Sunnyslope Rd
- EDNA 8022 E4

Sunnyslope Rd W
- EDNA 8022 E4

Sunnyvale Ln
- MNTK 7935 A2
- PYMH 7935 A2

Sunnyview Ln
- MNTK 7935 A3

E Sunrise Cir
- EDNP 8106 C7
- EDNP 8192 C1

W Sunrise Cir
- EDNP 8106 C7
- EDNP 8192 B1

Sunrise Ct
- EAGN 8197 D6
- MPLW 7856 A7
- WTBL 7771 B7

Sunrise Dr
- LCAN 7856 A4
- LINO 7596 E5
- MINN 8023 D7
- MPLW 7856 B5

Sunrise Dr E
- MNTK 8020 D1

Sunrise Dr NE
- FRID 7766 C2

Sunrise Dr W
- MNTK 8020 D1

Sunrise Ln
- MNTK 8021 A3

Sunrise Ln N
- CHMP 7591 D1

Sunrise Rd
- EAGN 8197 D6

Sunrise Ter
- BRKP 7764 A4

Sunset Av NE
- BLNE 7596 E1
- CIRC 7596 E6
- LINO 7596 E6

Sunset Av NE CO-53
- BLNE 7596 E1
- CIRC 7596 E6
- LINO 7596 E1

Sunset Blvd
- MINN 7937 B6
- STLP 7937 B6

W Sunset Blvd
- MINN 7937 B6
- STLP 7937 A6

Sunset Cir
- EDNP 8106 B1

Sunset Ct
- LCAN 7856 A4
- NOAK 7683 A7
- SHKP 8279 D4
- SHVW 7683 A7

Minneapolis Street Index

STREET Block	City	ZIP	Map #	Grid
Tibbett Pl				
-	NWPT		8115	D4
Tickseed Ln				
-	EDNP		8192	B2
Ticonderoga Tr				
-	EAGN		8198	E4
Tierney Av E				
-	MPLW		7857	D7
-	NSTP		7857	D7
Tierneys Woods Curv				
-	BMTN		8108	C6
Tierneys Woods Rd				
-	BMTN		8108	A5
Tiffany Cir N				
-	EAGN		8198	D6
Tiffany Cir S				
-	EAGN		8198	D7
Tiffany Ct				
-	BRNV		8283	B3
-	EAGN		8198	D6
Tiffany Dr				
-	EAGN		8198	D6
Tiffany Ln				
-	EDNP		8107	B6
-	SHVW		7769	C6
Tiffany Pl				
-	EAGN		8198	E6
Tiffany Pt				
-	EAGN		8198	D7
Tiflawn Ct				
-	SHKP		8278	B3
Tifton Dr				
-	EDNA		8108	D2
Tilbury Ln N				
-	CHMP		7591	D5
Tilbury Wy				
-	EAGN		8199	A4
Tilden Av N				
-	CHMP		7591	C1
Tileda Cir				
-	MNTK		8020	E2
Tiller Ln				
-	ARDH		7768	D7
-	SHVW		7768	E7
Tilsen Av E				
-	MPLW		7943	D2
-	STPL		7943	C2
Tilsen Ct E				
-	MPLW		7943	D2
Timber Av E				
-	MPLW		8029	D4
Timber Ct				
-	SHKP		8192	A6
Timber Ct E				
-	MPLW		8029	D4
Timber Ln				
-	SHVW		7855	A1
W Timber Ln				
-	MAPG		7763	A1
Timber Ln N				
-	MAPG		7763	A1
Timber Rdg				
-	EDNA		8108	A1
N Timber Rdg				
-	FRID		7767	A1
S Timber Rdg				
-	FRID		7767	A1
Timber Tr				
-	EDNA		8108	A1
Timber Tr E				
-	MPLW		8029	D4
-	STPL		8029	C4
Timber Crest Ct				
-	MAPG		7762	D2
Timber Crest Dr				
-	MAPG		7762	D2
Timber Crest Dr S				
-	CTGV		8116	C6
Timberglade Cir				
-	BMTN		8194	D3
Timberglade Dr				
-	BMTN		8194	D4
Timberglade Rd				
-	BMTN		8194	D4
Timberhill Rd				
-	MNTK		7934	C7
Timber Lake Dr				
-	EDNP		8106	A5
Timberlake Rd				
-	STPL		7941	E1
Timberland Dr				
-	BRNV		8282	A4
Timberlea Cir				
-	WDBY		8030	A6
Timberlea Dr				
-	WDBY		8030	E4
Timberline Cir N				
-	CHMP		7591	C4
Timberline Ct				
-	VADH		7769	E3
Timberline Dr N				
-	CHMP		7591	D6
Timberline Rd				
-	MNTK		7935	B4
Timberline Spur				
-	MNTK		7935	B4
Timberline Tr				
-	MNTK		7935	B4
-	VADH		7769	E2
Timber Ridge Ct S				
-	CTGV		8116	C5
Timber Ridge Dr S				
-	CTGV		8116	C6
Timber Ridge Hllw S				
-	CTGV		8116	C6
Timber Ridge Ln S				
-	CTGV		8116	C6
Timber Ridge Tr S				
-	CTGV		8116	B7
Timber Ridge Cove S				
-	CTGV		8116	C7
Timber Ridge Ln Ct S				
-	CTGV		8116	C6
Timbershore Ln				
-	EAGN		8198	C2
Timber Trail Ln S				
-	CTGV		8116	B6
Timberwolf Cir				
-	LINO		7598	B7
Timber Wolf Ct				
-	EAGN		8197	D6
Timberwolf Tr				
-	LINO		7598	B6
N Timber Wolf Tr				
-	EAGN		8197	D5
S Timber Wolf Tr				
-	EAGN		8197	D6
Timberwood Ct				
-	EAGN		8112	B7
-	WDBY		8030	A6
Timberwood Rd				
-	WDBY		8030	E5
Timberwood Tr				
-	EAGN		8112	B7
Timmy St				
-	MNDH		8112	E2
Timothy Av NE				
-	PRIO		8280	A7
-	SAVG		8280	A6
Tingdale Av				
-	EDNA		8022	D7
-	EDNA		8108	D1
Tioga Blvd				
-	NBRI		7767	C6
Tioga Ct				
-	NBRI		7767	C6
Tippecanoe St				
-	BLNE		7682	B2
-	LXTN		7682	B2
Tip Top Ln				
-	MAHT		7772	C3
Todd Av				
-	EAGN		8285	C1
Todd Ct				
-	ARDH		7768	A2
Todd Dr				
-	ARDH		7768	A2
Tofte Ln				
-	EAGN		8199	C6
Toledo Av				
-	CHMP		7592	E5
-	SAVG		8280	E6
Toledo Av N				
-	BRKC		7764	E2
-	BRKP		7678	E5
-	CRYS		7764	E7
-	GLDV		7850	E6
-	GLDV		7936	E1
-	ROBB		7850	E1
Toledo Av S				
-	BMTN		8194	E1
-	STLP		7936	E6
-	STLP		8022	E3
Toledo Cir				
-	BMTN		8194	E3
Toledo Ct				
-	BMTN		8194	E5
-	SAVG		8280	E6
Toledo Curv				
-	BMTN		8194	E5
Toledo Dr N				
-	BRKP		7592	E7
-	BRKP		7678	E2
Toledo Rd				
-	BMTN		8108	E7
-	BMTN		8194	E2
Tomahawk Ct				
-	LINO		7683	B1
Tomahawk Tr				
-	LINO		7683	C1
Tomlyn Av				
-	ARDH		7768	E2
-	SHVW		7768	E2
-	SHVW		7769	B2
Tom Thumb Blvd				
-	MNDH		8112	E2
Tonka Ln				
-	MNTK		8020	A1
Tonka Ter				
-	MNTK		7935	C3
Tonka Tr				
-	MNTK		7934	A6
Tonkadowns Dr				
-	MNTK		8020	C2
Tonkaha Dr				
-	MNTK		7934	A6
Tonkawa Tr				
-	MNTK		7934	D5
Tonkaway Rd				
-	MNTK		7934	B6
-	MNTK		8020	A1
Tonkawood Ct				
-	MNTK		8020	B3
Tonkawood Dr				
-	MNTK		8020	B1
Tonkawood Ln				
-	MNTK		8020	B2
Tonkawood Rd				
-	MNTK		8020	A3
Tony Ct				
-	WTBL		7771	A6
Top Ln				
-	WTBL		7770	E3
-	WtBT		7770	E3
Topaz Dr				
-	EAGN		8197	C5
Topel Rd				
-	GLDV		7850	E7
Tophill Cir				
-	RSVL		7855	B5
Topic Ln				
-	STPL		7942	E2
Topper Ln NE				
-	FRID		7766	C5
Topping St				
-	STPL		7940	E4
-	STPL		7941	B4
Topview Rd				
-	EDNP		8107	A3
Torchwood Cir				
-	NBRI		7767	B5
Torchwood Ct				
-	NBRI		7767	B5
Torchwood Dr				
-	NBRI		7767	B5
Toronto St				
-	STPL		8027	B2
Totem Rd				
-	STPL		8029	B2
Totem Tr				
-	LINO		7683	B1
-	MNTK		7934	D5
Tournament Players Cir N				
-	BLNE		7595	C3
Tournament Players Cir S				
-	BLNE		7595	C3
Tournament Players Ct S				
-	BLNE		7595	C3
Tournament Players Pkwy				
-	BLNE		7595	B3
Tourville Cir				
-	CTRV		7598	C6
Tower Ct				
-	WDBY		8030	D4
Tower Dr				
-	CTGV		8116	D4
-	WDBY		8030	D6
-	WDBY		8116	D4
Tower Pl NW				
-	COON		7594	B3
Tower Rd				
-	HnpC		8025	E7
-	HnpC		8026	A7
-	HnpC		8112	A1
Tower St				
-	EDNA		8022	E6
-	EDNA		8023	A6
-	STPL		7943	C6
Towers Ln				
-	EDNP		8106	D6
Tower View Cir				
-	BMTN		8195	C5
Towerview Rd				
-	EAGN		8112	B7
Town Rd				
-	ARDH		7682	A6
-	LINO		7682	E2
-	PYMH		7849	A7
-	PYMH		7935	B1
Town Center Pkwy				
-	LINO		7597	C3
Town Centre Dr				
-	EAGN		8198	C1
Towndale Ct				
-	BMTN		8109	B5
Towndale Dr				
-	BMTN		8109	B5
Towne Ter				
-	BMTN		8195	D3
Townes Cir				
-	EDNA		8023	A4
Townes Ln				
-	MNTK		7934	B2
Townes Rd				
-	EDNA		8023	A4
-	MNTK		7934	B3
-	PYMH		7934	B3
Town Line Av				
-	BMTN		8107	E7
-	BMTN		8193	E1
-	EDNP		8107	E7
-	EDNP		8193	E1
Townline Av				
-	BMTN		8107	E5
Town Line Av US-169				
-	BMTN		8107	E7
-	BMTN		8193	E1
-	EDNP		8107	E7
-	EDNP		8193	E1
Townline Rd				
-	EDNP		8020	D7
-	MNTK		8020	D7
Townline Rd CO-62				
-	EDNP		8020	D7
-	MNTK		8020	D7
Townline Rd SR-62				
-	EDNP		8020	E7
-	MNTK		8020	E7
Township Dr				
-	WtBT		7684	D6
Township Pkwy				
-	WtBT		7684	D7
-	WtBT		7770	D1
Town Square Dr NE				
-	BLNE		7595	C4
Townview Av NE				
-	STAN		7853	B3
Townview Rd				
-	MNTK		8021	A2
Tracy Av				
-	EDNA		8022	C7
-	EDNA		8108	C1
Tracy Rd				
-	WTBL		7771	C7
Traffic St NE				
-	MINN		7853	B7
Trail Ct				
-	EAGN		8199	A2
Trail Dr				
-	SHKP		8279	D5
Trail Rd				
-	MNDH		8027	B7
Trail East Rd				
-	BMTN		8196	D2
Trails End Rd				
-	EAGN		8199	A2
Trailway Dr				
-	EAGN		8197	E6
Trail West Rd				
-	BMTN		8194	E5
Trailwood N				
-	HOPK		8021	C5
Trailwood S				
-	HOPK		8021	C5
Tralee Dr				
-	EDNA		8108	B3
Tramore Pl				
-	EAGN		8198	A4
Transfer Rd				
-	STPL		7940	A4
Transit Av				
-	LCAN		7855	D4
-	RSVL		7854	D4
-	RSVL		7855	C4
Transit Av W				
-	RSVL		7855	A4
Trapp Ct				
-	FRID		7767	A4
Trapp Pt				
-	EAGN		8112	C5
Trapp Rd				
-	EAGN		8112	C5
N Trappers Cross				
-	LINO		7684	A1
S Trappers Cross				
-	LINO		7683	E1
-	LINO		7684	A2
Trappers Ct				
-	LINO		7683	E1
-	LINO		7684	A2
Travelers Tr				
-	EAGN		8283	B1
E Travelers Tr				
-	BRNV		8282	B2
W Travelers Tr				
-	BRNV		8282	A2
Traverse Pt				
-	EAGN		8283	E2
Travois Rd				
-	EDNP		8193	A2
Traymore Rd				
-	MNTK		7935	D4
Tree St				
-	MNTK		8020	C5
Tree Farm Rd				
-	EDNP		8193	A2
Trenton Cir N				
-	PYMH		7849	C1
-	PYMH		7935	C1
Trenton Ln				
-	EAGN		8198	B7
-	EDNP		8106	A7
Trenton Ln N				
-	CHMP		7591	D7
-	MAPG		7591	D7
-	MAPG		7677	C1
-	MAPG		7763	C2
-	PYMH		7763	D5
-	PYMH		7849	C3
-	PYMH		7935	C1
Trenton Rd				
-	EAGN		8199	B5
Trenton Tr				
-	EAGN		8199	A6
Tretbaugh Dr				
-	BMTN		8109	B7
Tribal Tr				
-	MNTK		7934	D5
Trillium Cir				
-	EDNP		8106	B3
Trillium Ct				
-	EAGN		8198	E5
Trillium Ct N				
-	CHMP		7591	D5
Trillium Ln				
-	EDNA		8108	E3
Trillium Ln N				
-	CHMP		7591	E5
Trim Pl				
-	WILL		7772	C5
Trinity Dr NE				
-	FRID		7766	C2
Trinity Gdns N				
-	BRKP		7678	E3
Triton Dr				
-	GLDV		7850	E5
-	GLDV		7851	A5
Trollhagen Dr				
-	FRID		7767	A5
Troon Ct				
-	DLWD		7686	C5
Troseth Rd				
-	RSVL		7853	D2
Trost Tr				
-	SAVG		8280	E5
Trotters Ct				
-	EAGN		8199	A4
Trotters Pth				
-	EDNP		8193	D4
Trotters Rdg				
-	EAGN		8199	A4
Trotters Tr NE				
-	PRIO		8279	A7
Trout Brook Cir				
-	STPL		7941	D2
Troy Dr				
-	MNDS		7681	E5
NW True St				
-	NBRI		7767	D6
Trussel Av N				
-	CHMP		7591	E2
Tuckaway Tr				
-	SHKP		8279	D4
Tucker Ln				
-	EDNA		8021	E6
Tudor Rd				
-	MNTK		7934	E4
Tulip St NW				
-	COON		7592	D2
Tupa Cir				
-	EDNA		8108	B2
Tupa Dr				
-	EDNA		8108	B3
Turin Av				
-	SSTP		8028	E6
Turnbridge Cir				
-	SHKP		8279	B3
Turnbridge Ct				
-	SHKP		8279	B3
Turners Crossroad N				
-	GLDV		7936	E2
Turners Crossroad S				
-	GLDV		7936	E3
-	STLP		7936	E3
Turnpike Rd				
-	GLDV		7936	E2
Turnstone Ct				
-	RSVL		7855	B1
Turquoise Cir				
-	EAGN		8197	E4
Turquoise Pt				
-	EAGN		8197	E4
Turquoise Tr				
-	EAGN		8197	D4
Turtle Ln				
-	ARDH		7768	E1
-	SHVW		7768	D1
Turtle Ln E				
-	SHVW		7682	E7
-	SHVW		7768	E1
Turtle Ln W				
-	SHVW		7682	E7
-	SHVW		7768	E1
Turtle Lake Rd				
-	LINO		7683	B4
-	NOAK		7683	B5
-	SHVW		7683	B5
Tuscany Wy				
-	EDNP		8193	E4
Tuscarora Av				
-	STPL		8026	E3
-	STPL		8027	A3
Tussock Ct				
-	EDNP		8107	A7
Twelve Oaks Dr				
-	MNTK		7935	A6
Twelve Oaks Center Dr				
-	MNTK		7934	B3
Twilite Ter				
-	BLNE		7596	C6
-	CIRC		7596	C6
Twin Cir Dr				
-	MNDH		8026	E7
-	MNDH		8112	E1
Twin Haven Rd				
-	MNTK		8020	E3
Twinkle Ter				
-	CIRC		7596	C6
Twin Lake Av				
-	BRKC		7765	A7
Twin Lake Blvd				
-	LCAN		7769	D7
-	VADH		7769	D7
Twin Lake Blvd E				
-	BRKC		7765	A7
Twin Lake Ct				
-	LCAN		7769	E7
-	LCAN		7855	E1
-	VADH		7769	E7
Twin Lake Rd				
-	LCAN		7769	D7
-	LCAN		7855	D1
Twin Lake Ter N				
-	BRKC		7765	A6
-	CRYS		7765	A6
Twin Lake Tr				
-	LCAN		7855	E1
Twin Lakes Av				
-	CTRV		7598	E4
Twin Lakes Cross				
-	EDNP		8106	D7
Twin Oak Dr				
-	ROBB		7851	A2
Twin Oak Ln				
-	ROBB		7851	A1
Twin Ponds Curv				
-	SAVG		8280	B7
Twins Ct				
-	EAGN		8285	C2
Tyler Av N				
-	HOPK		8022	A2
Tyler Av S				
-	EDNA		8022	A4
Tyler Ct				
-	EDNA		8022	A4
Tyler Ct NE				
-	BLNE		7594	E4
Tyler Pl NE				
-	COLH		7766	E7
Tyler St NE				
-	BLNE		7594	E6
-	BLNE		7680	E1
-	COLH		7766	E5
-	COLH		7767	A7
-	COLH		7852	E2
-	COLH		7853	A1
-	FRID		7680	E5
-	MINN		7852	E2
-	SPLP		7680	E4
Tyne Ct				
-	IVGH		8199	D4
Tyne Ln				
-	EAGN		8199	D3
-	IVGH		8199	D3
Tyrell Dr				
-	EDNP		8107	B1
Tyrol Tr				
-	GLDV		7937	B4
-	MINN		7937	B4
N Tyrol Tr				
-	GLDV		7937	A3
Tyrol Crest				
-	GLDV		7937	A4
Tyrone Dr S				
-	SHKP		8278	B2
U				
Ulmer Dr				
-	LINO		7597	A5
Ulysses St NE				
-	BLNE		7594	E2
-	BLNE		7595	A7
-	COLH		7853	A1
-	MINN		7853	A3
Undercliff St NW				
-	COON		7592	D1
Underwood Ct N				
-	PYMH		7848	E1
Underwood Ln N				
-	MAPG		7676	E4
-	PYMH		7762	E6
-	PYMH		7848	E1
Underwood St				
-	FLCH		7854	B7
-	FLCH		7940	B2
-	STPL		7940	B2
Undestad St				
-	EDNP		8106	A1
Union St SE				
-	MINN		7939	A3
Union Terrace Ct N				
-	PYMH		7763	C6
-	PYMH		7849	D3
Union Terrace Ln N				
-	CHMP		7591	C1
-	MAPG		7591	C7
Union Terrace Ln N				
-	MAPG		7677	C1
-	MAPG		7763	D2
-	PYMH		7763	C6
-	PYMH		7849	C4
-	PYMH		7935	C2
Union Terrace Wy N				
-	PYMH		7849	C3
Unique Dr				
-	BRNV		8282	A4
Unity Av				
-	CTRV		7598	E4
Unity Av N				
-	BRKC		7764	E4
-	BRKP		7678	D7
-	BRKP		7764	E1
-	CRYS		7764	E6
-	GLDV		7850	E6
-	GLDV		7936	E1
-	ROBB		7850	E2
Unity Cir N				
-	BRKC		7764	E2
Unity Cir NW				
-	COON		7593	E1
Unity Ct				
-	CRYS		7764	E6
Unity Ln N				
-	BRKP		7592	E7
Unity St NW				
-	COON		7593	E1
-	COON		7679	E1
University Av E				
-	STPL		7941	D5
-	STPL		7942	A5
University Av NE				
-	BLNE		7594	C6
-	BLNE		7680	C3
-	COLH		7766	C7
-	COLH		7852	C2
-	COON		7594	C6
-	COON		7680	C3
-	FRID		7680	C7
-	FRID		7766	C7
-	MINN		7852	C7
-	MINN		7938	D1
-	SPLP		7680	C4
University Av NE SR-47				
-	BLNE		7680	C3
-	COLH		7766	C7
-	COLH		7852	C2
-	COON		7680	C3
-	FRID		7680	C6
-	FRID		7766	C6
-	MINN		7852	C2
-	MINN		7938	D1
-	SPLP		7680	C5
University Av NW				
-	BLNE		7594	C4
-	BLNE		7680	C2
-	COON		7594	C6
-	COON		7680	C3
University Av SE				
-	MINN		7938	E1
-	MINN		7939	C3
-	STPL		7939	D4
University Av SE SR-47				
-	MINN		7938	D1
University Av W				
-	MINN		7939	D4
-	STPL		7939	D4
-	STPL		7940	E5
-	STPL		7941	D5
University Cir NE				
-	BLNE		7594	C5
Univ of Minnesota Transit Wy				
-	FLCH		7940	A3
-	MINN		7939	B3
-	STPL		7939	D3
-	STPL		7940	A3
University Service Rd				
-	BLNE		7680	C3
-	COON		7680	C3
-	FRID		7680	C3
-	SPLP		7680	C5
University Service Rd NE				
-	FRID		7680	C7
-	FRID		7766	C1
U of MN Transit Wy				
-	MINN		7939	B2
Upland Av				
-	STPL		8029	C3
Upland Ct N				
-	PYMH		7762	B6
-	PYMH		7848	B5
Upland Ln N				
-	MAPG		7676	B3
-	MAPG		7762	B4
-	PYMH		7762	B6
-	PYMH		7848	B1
-	PYMH		7934	B1
E Upland Crest				
-	COLH		7767	B5
N Upland Crest				
-	COLH		7767	A5
-	NBRI		7767	A5
W Upland Crest				
-	COLH		7767	A5
Upland Crest NE				
-	COLH		7767	A6
Uplander St NW				
-	COON		7593	B3
Upper Ter				
-	EDNA		8108	E2
Upper 5th St N				
-	ODLE		7944	B5
Upper 14th St Ct N				
-	ODLE		7944	A3
Upper 16th St N				
-	ODLE		7944	D3
Upper 17th St N				
-	ODLE		7944	D3
Upper 19th St N				
-	ODLE		7944	D2
Upper 20th St N				
-	ODLE		7944	D2
Upper 22nd St N				
-	ODLE		7944	B2
Upper 23rd St N				
-	ODLE		7944	A2

INDEX 43
Upper 24th St N — Minneapolis Street Index — Victoria Ct

Minneapolis Street Index

STREET / Block / City / ZIP / Map # / Grid

Upper 24th St N: ODLE 7944 C1
Upper 26th St N: ODLE 7944 D1
Upper 28th St N: ODLE 7944 B1
Upper 33rd St N: ODLE 7858 B7
Upper 35th St N: MPLW 7857 E6; NSTP 7857 E6; ODLE 7857 E6; ODLE 7858 A6
Upper 35th St Cir N: ODLE 7858 B6
Upper 35th St Ct N: ODLE 7858 A5
Upper 36th St N: ODLE 7858 B6
Upper 39th St N: ODLE 7858 B6
Upper 42nd St N: ODLE 7858 C5
Upper 43rd St N: ODLE 7858 C5
Upper 44th St N: ODLE 7858 A4
Upper 44th St Ct N: ODLE 7858 A5
Upper 45th St E: IVGH 8114 C1
Upper 45th St N: ODLE 7858 D4
Upper 46th St N: NSTP 7857 E4; ODLE 7857 E4; ODLE 7858 A4
Upper 47th St N: NSTP 7857 E3; ODLE 7857 E3
Upper 48th St N: ODLE 7858 A4
Upper 51st St N: NSTP 7857 E3; ODLE 7857 E3; ODLE 7858 A3
Upper 53rd St N: ODLE 7858 A3
Upper 54th St N: ODLE 7858 A2
Upper 55th St E: IVGH 8114 D4; SSTP 8114 E4
Upper 55th St N: ODLE 7858 A2
Upper 56th St N: ODLE 7858 A2
Upper 61st Pth E: IVGH 8115 B4
Upper 62nd St E: IVGH 8114 D5
Upper 64th Ct E: IVGH 8114 D5
Upper 64th Pth E: IVGH 8115 B4
Upper 65th Dr E: IVGH 8115 B4
Upper 69th St E: IVGH 8115 B6
Upper 71st St E: IVGH 8114 E7; IVGH 8115 B7
Upper 73rd St E: IVGH 8115 A7
Upper 75th St E: IVGH 8115 A7
Upper 76th St E: IVGH 8200 E1
Upper 79th Ct E: IVGH 8200 D1
Upper 84th St W: IVGH 8199 D2
Upper 85th St W: EAGN 8199 D2; IVGH 8199 D2
Upper 86th St W: IVGH 8199 E2
Upper 129th Ct: APVA 8283 B4
Upper 135th St W: APVA 8284 D5; RSMT 8284 D5
Upper 136th St W: APVA 8283 C6
Upper 136th St Ct W: APVA 8284 A5
Upper 138th Ct: APVA 8283 E3
Upper 138th St W: RSMT 8285 B6
Upper 139th Ct: APVA 8283 B6
Upper 139th St W: APVA 8283 C6
Upper 141st St W: APVA 8284 B6
Upper 143rd Ct: APVA 8283 C7
Upper 143rd St W: RSMT 8284 E7; RSMT 8285 A7
Upper 145th Ct W: APVA 8283 B7
Upper 145th St W: APVA 8283 A7; RSMT 8284 D4
Upper 146th St N: HUGO 7599 D5
Upper Afton Cir: WDBY 7944 B7; WDBY 8030 B1
Upper Afton Rd: STPL 7942 E6; STPL 7943 A7; WDBY 7944 A7; WDBY 8030 A1
Upper Afton Rd E: MPLW 7943 D7; STPL 7943 D7; WDBY 7943 E7
Upper Afton Ter: STPL 7943 A7
Upper Afton Cove: WDBY 7944 A7; WDBY 8030 A1
Upper Buford Cir: FLCH 7940 A1
Upper Colonial Dr: MNDH 8027 B6
Upper East Side: BMTN 8110 D6
Upper Elkwood Ct: APVA 8284 C6
Upper Guthrie Ct: APVA 8283 B7
Upper Hamlet Ct: APVA 8283 B4
Upper Heather Av N: HUGO 7686 C3
Upper St. Dennis Rd: STPL 8026 C5
Upper Wood Wy: BRNV 8282 B7
Upton Av N: BRKC 7765 C6; BRKP 7679 C3; MINN 7765 C7; MINN 7851 C1; MINN 7937 C1
Upton Av S: BMTN 8109 C5; BMTN 8195 C4; BRNV 8281 C2; MINN 7937 C5; MINN 8023 C2; RHFD 8023 C7; RHFD 8109 C3
Upton Cir N: BRKP 7679 C6
Upton Cir S: BMTN 8195 C2
Upton Pl: BMTN 8195 C3
Upton Rd: BMTN 8195 C2
Urban Av N: BRKC 7765 B2
Urban Pl: STPL 7942 C6
Urbank Ct NE: BLNE 7595 D4
Urbank St NE: BLNE 7595 C1
US-10: ARDH 7681 E6; ARDH 7682 A7; ARDH 7768 A1; BLNE 7594 C7; BLNE 7680 D1; BLNE 7681 E4; COON 7593 E4; COON 7594 C7; COON 7680 C1; CTGV 8116 A7; CTGV 8202 B1; LCAN 7769 C7; LCAN 7855 E3; MNDS 7681 E6; MNDS 7682 A7; MNDS 7768 A1; MPLW 7855 E5; NWPT 8029 C7; NWPT 8115 C1; SHVW 7681 E6; SHVW 7768 E5; SHVW 7769 C7; SPLP 8115 E6; SPLP 8116 A7; STPL 7855 E7; STPL 7941 E4; STPL 7942 B6; VADH 7769 C7
US-10 Frontage Rd: ARDH 7768 A2
US-10 The Great River Rd: NWPT 8029 C7; NWPT 8115 D1; STPL 7942 E7; STPL 7943 A7; STPL 8029 A1
US-12: ELMO 7944 E6; GLDV 7935 E3; GLDV 7936 A3; GLDV 7937 B3; LNDF 7944 A6; MINN 7937 E3; MINN 7938 A4; MINN 7939 A4; MPLW 7943 D6; ODLE 7943 E6; ODLE 7944 A6; STLP 7935 E3; STLP 7936 E3; STPL 7939 E5; STPL 7940 A6; STPL 7941 C6; STPL 7942 B6; STPL 7943 A6; WAYZ 7934 A3; WDBY 7943 E6; WDBY 7944 A6
US-12 Cappelen Memorial Br: MINN 7939 B4
US-12 Wayzata Blvd: GLDV 7935 E3; MINN 7937 E3; MNTK 7934 E3; MNTK 7935 A3; STLP 7935 D3; WAYZ 7934 B3
US-52: BRKC 7764 C3; BRKC 7765 A3; BRKC 7766 A7; BRKP 7763 E2; BRKP 7764 A2; MAPG 7676 E7; MAPG 7762 E1; MAPG 7763 C1; MINN 7766 A7; MINN 7852 A4; MINN 7938 A4; MINN 7939 C5; STPL 7939 E5; STPL 7940 A6; STPL 7941 E6; STPL 7942 A6
US-52 Cappelen Memorial Br: MINN 7939 B4
US-52 Clayton Av E: RSMT 8287 A3
US-52 Courthouse Blvd: IVGH 8200 E7; IVGH 8201 A7; IVGH 8287 A1; RSMT 8287 A3
US-52 Lafayette Br: STPL 7942 A6
US-52 Lafayette Frwy: IVGH 8114 C5; IVGH 8200 C1; SSTP 8028 C3; SSTP 8114 C1; STPL 7942 A6; STPL 8028 B3; WSTP 8028 B2; WSTP 8114 B1
US-52 Lafayette Rd N: STPL 7942 A6
US-61: CTGV 8116 A7; CTGV 8202 B1; GEML 7770 E6; GEML 7771 A5; HUGO 7685 D2; MPLW 7856 D2; NWPT 8029 C7; NWPT 8115 C1; SPLP 8115 E6; SPLP 8116 A7; STPL 7942 D6; VADH 7770 E6; VADH 7856 E1; WTBL 7685 C7; WTBL 7771 A5; WtBT 7685 C7
US-61 7th St E: STPL 7942 B5
US-61 Arcade St: MPLW 7856 B7; STPL 7856 B7; STPL 7942 B4
US-61 Forest Blvd N: HUGO 7599 D7; HUGO 7685 D2; WtBT 7685 D3
US-61 Frontage Rd N: VADH 7856 E1
US-61 Maplewood Dr: MPLW 7856 C6; VADH 7856 E1
US-61 Mounds Blvd: STPL 7942 B6
US-61 The Great River Rd: NWPT 8029 C7; NWPT 8115 D1; STPL 7942 E7; STPL 7943 A7; STPL 8029 A1
US-169: ANOK 7591 E1; BMTN 8107 E4; BMTN 8193 E4; BRKP 7592 A6; BRKP 7677 E6; BRKP 7678 A1; BRKP 7763 E7; CHMP 7591 E1; CHMP 7592 A5; EDNA 8021 E4; EDNA 8107 E4; EDNP 8021 E7; EDNP 8107 E1; EDNP 8193 E6; GLDV 7849 E7; GLDV 7935 E2; HOPK 8021 E1; MAPG 7677 E6; MAPG 7763 E7; MNTK 7935 E1; MNTK 8021 E5; NWHE 7763 E6; NWHE 7849 E7; OSSE 7678 A3; PYMH 7763 E7; PYMH 7849 E7; PYMH 7935 E1; SAVG 8193 E6; SHKP 8193 E3; SHKP 8278 E1; SHKP 8279 D1; STLP 7935 E1; STLP 8021 E7
US-169 S: EDNA 8107 E3
US-169 Jefferson Hwy N: CHMP 7592 A2
US-169 The Great River Rd: CHMP 7591 E1; CHMP 7592 A7
US-169 Town Line Av: BMTN 8107 E6; BMTN 8193 E1; EDNP 8107 E7; EDNP 8193 E1
US-212: EDNA 8021 E7; EDNP 8021 D7; EDNP 8107 D1
US-212 Crosstown Hwy: EDNA 8021 E7; EDNA 8022 A7; EDNP 8021 E7
US-212 Flying Cloud Dr: EDNP 8107 A7; EDNP 8192 E2; EDNP 8193 A1
Usufruct Av: MAPG 7676 E4
Utah Av: SAVG 8280 B6
Utah Av N: BRKP 7764 B4; CHMP 7592 B5; CRYS 7850 B4; NWHE 7764 B4; NWHE 7850 B1
Utah Av S: BMTN 8108 A5; BMTN 8194 A3; GLDV 7936 A3; STLP 7936 B4; STLP 8022 B1
Utah Cir S: BMTN 8194 A3
Utah Ct N: BRKP 7678 B6
Utah Dr S: STLP 7936 A4
Utah Rd S: BMTN 8194 A4
Utica Av: SAVG 8280 E4; STPL 7943 B3
Utica Av S: BMTN 8108 E7; BMTN 8194 E6; STLP 7936 E5; STLP 8022 E3
Utica Cir S: BMTN 8194 E2
Utica Rd S: BMTN 8194 E2

V

Vadnais Blvd: LCAN 7769 D7; VADH 7769 D7; VADH 7770 A7
W Vadnais Blvd: SHVW 7769 D7; VADH 7769 D7
Vadnais Dr: VADH 7770 C7
Vadnais Ln: VADH 7770 B7
Vadnais Rd: VADH 7856 A1
Vadnais Center Dr: VADH 7770 C7
Vadnais Lake Dr: VADH 7770 A7; VADH 7856 A1
Vail Dr: MNDH 8112 E1
Valders Av N: GLDV 7850 B7; GLDV 7936 A1
Vale Ct: EDNP 8106 D3
Vale St NW: COON 7593 B7
Vale Crest Rd: CRYS 7850 E6; GLDV 7850 E6
Valencour Cir: MNDH 8112 C2
Valentine Av: ARDH 7768 B5; STPL 7939 D2
Valentine Ct: ARDH 7768 B5
Valentine Ter: BMTN 8109 D6
Valentine Crest Rd: ARDH 7768 B4
Valento Cir: VADH 7770 B7
Valento Ln: LCAN 7856 B2
Valerie Ct: SPLP 8116 A6
Valerie Ln: FRID 7767 B3; NBRI 7767 B3
Valery Rd: GLDV 7851 B7
Valewood Dr: MNTK 8020 B7
Valhalla Dr: WDBY 8116 A2
Valjean Blvd N: HUGO 7599 B6
Vallacher Av: STLP 8022 E2; STLP 8023 A2
Valle Vista St: NWHE 7850 B5
Valley Ct: BRNV 8197 A6
Valley Dr: BRNV 8281 E3
Valley Ln: EDNA 8108 C1; MNDH 8027 C4
Valley Pl: CRYS 7850 B4
Valley Rd: EDNP 8192 A1; MNTK 8021 A4
Valley St: STPL 7941 D5
Valley St NE: MINN 7852 D2
Valley Wy: HOPK 8021 D1
Valley Creek Plz: WDBY 8030 B2
Valley Creek Rd: WDBY 8030 C3
Valley Creek Rd SR-120: WDBY 8030 A2
Valley Curve Rd: MNDH 8027 A7; MNDH 8113 B1
Valley Fair Dr S: SHKP 8192 E6
Valley Forge Ln N: CHMP 7591 C1; MAPG 7591 C7; MAPG 7677 C1; PYMH 7763 C7; PYMH 7849 C1
Valley Forge Pl: EAGN 8199 A6
Valley Forge Rd: EDNP 8107 C6
Valley High Dr: BMTN 8195 E5
Valley High Rd: BRNV 8282 A4
Valley Industrial Blvd N: SHKP 8192 C6
Valley Industrial Blvd S: SHKP 8192 C7
Valley Oaks Rd: VADH 7770 C3
W Valley Park Dr: HOPK 8021 D4
Valley Park Dr S: SHKP 8192 E7; SHKP 8278 E1
Valley Ridge Dr: EAGN 8112 A7; EAGN 8198 A1
Valleyside Dr: STPL 7943 B7
Valleyview Av: MPLW 8029 E4
Valley View Av E: MPLW 8029 D4; STPL 8029 C4
Valley View Ct: SHVW 7769 A5
Valleyview Ct: WSTP 8028 A6
Valley View Ct E: MPLW 8029 D4
Valley View Dr: WTBL 7771 E5
Valley View Dr N: EAGN 8197 C4
Valley View Dr S: EAGN 8197 C4
Valley View Ln: NBRI 7767 B1
Valley View Pl: MPLW 8029 C4; STPL 8029 C4
Valleyview Pl: MINN 8024 A5
Valley View Rd: EDNA 8022 D7; EDNA 8023 A7; EDNA 8107 E3; EDNA 8108 C1; EDNA 8109 A1; EDNP 8106 A3; EDNP 8107 A4
Valley View Rd E: SHKP 8278 A4
Valleywood Cir: GLDV 7936 D2
Van Buren Av: STPL 7940 E5; STPL 7941 C4
Van Buren Av N: HOPK 8021 E2
Van Buren Av S: EDNA 8021 E3; HOPK 8021 E3
Van Buren Cir NE: BLNE 7594 D5
Van Buren Ct NE: BLNE 7594 D3
N Van Buren Pl: HOPK 8021 C1
Van Buren St NE: BLNE 7594 D2; BLNE 7680 E1; COLH 7766 E7; COLH 7852 E2; FRID 7680 D5; FRID 7766 E2; HLTP 7766 E7; MINN 7852 E6; SPLP 7680 D5
N Van Buren Ter: HOPK 8021 C1
N Van Buren Tr: HOPK 8021 C1
Van Buren Wy: HLTP 7766 B5
N Van Buren Wy: HOPK 8021 C1
Vance St: STPL 8027 A2
Vancouver Rd: EDNP 8106 B3
Vandalia St: STPL 7939 E5
Vandall St: MNDH 8027 B6
Van Demark Rd: ROBB 7851 B4
Vanderbie St: LCAN 7856 A2
Vanderbilt Av: EDNP 8193 B1
Vandervork Av: EDNA 8022 D4
Van Dyke Av: MPLW 7857 B7
Van Dyke St: MPLW 7857 B3; STPL 7857 B7; STPL 7943 B6; WTBL 7771 B5
Van Nest Av: MINN 8024 B2
Van Slyke Av: STPL 7940 E2
Varner Cir N: GLDV 7936 C2
Velvetleaf Ln: LINO 7598 A7
Veness Rd: BMTN 8193 E1; BMTN 8194 A1
Ventnor Av: EAGN 8199 A5
Ventura Av NE: FRID 7766 C4
Ventura Dr: WDBY 8030 A4
Ventura Pl: SAVG 8280 B5
Venture Ln: EDNP 8106 B4
Venus Av: ARDH 7768 B5
Vera St N: CHMP 7591 D2
Vera Cruz Av N: BRKC 7764 E3; BRKP 7764 E3; CHMP 7592 E5; CRYS 7764 E7; CRYS 7850 D1; GLDV 7850 E4; ROBB 7850 E3
Vera Cruz Dr N: BRKP 7592 D7
Vera Cruz Ln N: BRKC 7764 E4; BRKP 7764 E4
Verderosa Av: SSTP 8115 B2
Verdi Rd: BMTN 8195 E4
Verdin Cir NW: COON 7593 B6
Verdin St NW: COON 7593 B3
Vermar Ter: EDNP 8106 C2
N Vermillion Ct: EAGN 8197 D3
S Vermillion Ct: EAGN 8197 D3
Vermillion Ct NE: BLNE 7595 D4
Vermillion St NE: BLNE 7595 C1
Vermont Av: EAGN 8199 A4
Vermont Av S: GLDV 7936 A3
Vermont St: STLP 8022 D3
Vernon Av: SAVG 8280 E2
Vernon Av S: EDNA 8021 E7; EDNA 8022 A7; STLP 7936 E6; STLP 8022 E3
Vernon Cir: MNTK 7935 C5; SAVG 8280 E5
Vernon Ct: SAVG 8280 E4
Vernon Ct S: EDNA 8021 E6
Vernon Dr S: MNTK 7935 C5
Vernon Ln: EDNA 8022 B6
Vernon St: STPL 8026 B1
Vernon Hills Rd S: EDNA 8021 E7
Veronica Ln: MNDH 8112 D1
Versailles Ct: EAGN 8198 C4
Vervain Dr: EDNP 8192 C3
Vervoort Ln: EDNP 8106 E3
Vessey Av S: BMTN 8194 D6
Vessey Cir S: BMTN 8194 D5
Vessey Ct S: BMTN 8194 D6
Vessey Rd: BMTN 8194 D4
Veterans Dr: HnpC 8025 D6
Viburnum Tr: EAGN 8283 C1
Viceroy Dr NE: SPLP 7680 E5
Vicki Ln: MNDH 8026 E7; MNTK 7934 E7; SHVW 7683 B4
Vickors Cross N: BRKP 7679 C4
Vickors Ln N: BRKP 7679 C5
Vicksburg Ln N: MAPG 7762 B3; PYMH 7762 B3; PYMH 7848 B1; PYMH 7934 B2
Victor Ln: MNTK 8020 C7
Victor Pth: HUGO 7599 B5
Victor Sq: HUGO 7599 B5
Victor Hugo Blvd: HUGO 7599 B5
Victor Hugo Blvd N: HUGO 7599 B5
Victoria Cir: STLP 7936 A5
Victoria Ct: MNDH 8112 E1; SHVW 7769 A4

Minneapolis Street Index

INDEX 45

Welters Wy — Minneapolis Street Index — Windemere Dr

STREET Block City ZIP Map # Grid

Welters Wy
- EDNP 8193 B1
Wendhurst Av NE
- STAN 7853 C2
Wendover Ct
- MNTK 8020 B2
Wendy Ct
- SHVW 7769 C4
- VADH 7769 C4
Wentworth Av
- BRNV 8282 A4
- MINN 8024 A7
- RHFD 8110 A3
- SSTP 8028 C6
- WSTP 8028 C6
E Wentworth Av
- SSTP 8028 C6
- WSTP 8028 A6
W Wentworth Av
- MNDH 8027 D6
- WSTP 8027 C6
Wentworth Av S
- BMTN 8110 A6
- BMTN 8196 A3
- MINN 8024 A3
- RHFD 8110 A4
Wentworth Av W
- WSTP 8027 E6
Wentworth Cir
- BMTN 8196 A3
Wentworth Ct E
- MINN 8024 B6
Wentworth Ct W
- MINN 8024 B6
Wentworth Pl
- BRNV 8282 B5
Wentworth Tr
- MNTK 7934 D7
Wenzel Av
- EAGN 8198 B5
Wescott Rd
- EAGN 8198 D3
- EAGN 8199 A3
Wescott Sq
- EAGN 8199 A1
Wescott Tr
- EAGN 8199 A2
Wescott Hills Dr
- EAGN 8198 E2
- EAGN 8199 A3
S Wescott Hills Dr
- EAGN 8199 A6
Wescott Woodlands
- EAGN 8199 A2
Wesley Ct
- MNDH 8113 B1
Wesley Dr
- GLDV 7850 A7
Wesley Ln
- MNDH 8113 B1
West Av
- WtBT 7685 B7
West Cir NE
- FRID 7680 E6
West Ct
- CIRC 7596 C7
- CIRC 7682 C1
- LXTN 7596 C7
West Ln
- NBRI 7767 E7
West Rd
- BLNE 7596 C7
- CIRC 7596 C7
- LXTN 7596 C7
West Tr
- EDNA 8107 E2
Westbend Rd
- GLDV 7850 A6
- GLDV 7851 B7
Westbrook Ln
- EDNA 8022 E4
Westbrook Rd
- GLDV 7850 D6
Westbrooke Wy
- HOPK 8021 D5
- MNTK 8021 D5
Westbury Cir
- EAGN 8198 D4
Westbury Dr
- EAGN 8198 D4
Westbury Knls
- EAGN 8198 D4
Westbury Ln
- EAGN 8198 D3
Westbury Pth
- EAGN 8198 D3
Westbury Tr
- EAGN 8198 D4
Westbury Wy
- EAGN 8198 D4
Westby Dr NE
- SPLP 7680 D5
Westchester Cir
- EAGN 8199 C6
- GLDV 7936 C2
Westchester Dr
- WSTP 8028 A5
Westchester Ln
- BRNV 8282 D1
Westchester Pl
- WSTP 8028 A5
Westchester Sq
- BRNV 8282 D1
Westcliff Ct
- SHVW 7768 E4
Westcliff Curv
- SHVW 7768 E4
Westcliffe Ct
- BRNV 8281 C7
Westcliffe Dr
- BRNV 8281 C7
Westcliffe Pl
- BRNV 8281 C7
Westcote Cir
- MNTK 7934 C6
Westergren Ct
- WtBT 7685 E5
Western Av
- GLDV 7936 B2
Western Av N
- RSVL 7855 C5
- STPL 7941 C1
Western Av S
- STPL 8027 C1
Western St N
- RSVL 7855 C6
Western Ter
- GLDV 7936 A2
Westernesse
- MNTK 7934 B3
Westfield Ln
- VADH 7770 A3
West Gate Dr
- STPL 7939 D4
Westgate Dr
- EDNP 8106 B4
Westgate Ln
- EDNP 8106 B3
Westgate Rd
- MNTK 8020 D4
Westgate Tr
- EDNP 8106 B4
Westhill Pointe
- EDNP 8106 C7
Westin Av
- WDBY 8030 E7
Westmark Cir
- MNTK 8020 C1
Westmark Dr
- MNTK 8020 C1
West Market
- BMTN 8110 D6
Westminster Cir
- EAGN 8284 B1
Westminster Rd
- MNTK 8020 D4
Westminster St
- STPL 7941 E1
- STPL 7942 A4
Westmore Wy
- GLDV 7850 D6
Westmoreland Ln
- STLP 7935 E4
- STLP 7936 A4
Weston Cir
- EDNA 8108 C2
Weston Ct N
- PYMH 7762 B7
Weston Ln N
- MAPG 7676 B4
- MAPG 7762 B2
- PYMH 7762 A7
- PYMH 7848 B1
- PYMH 7934 B1
Weston Wy
- SHVW 7768 E4
Weston Bay Rd
- EDNP 8106 A5
Weston Hills Ct
- EAGN 8199 C7
Weston Hills Dr
- EAGN 8199 C7
- EAGN 8285 C1
Weston Hills Pl
- EAGN 8285 C1
Weston Woods Wy
- WtBT 7770 B2
Westridge Blvd
- EDNA 8022 C7
- EDNA 8108 B1
Westridge Cir
- MNTK 7935 A6
Westridge Dr
- EDNP 8106 D6
Westridge Ln
- MNTK 7935 A6
- STLP 7937 A5
Westridge Rd
- MNTK 7935 A6
West River Pkwy
- HnpC 8025 E5
- MINN 7939 C6
- MINN 8025 D5
Westview Cir
- MNDH 8113 B3
Westview Ct
- SHVW 7769 B4
Westview Dr
- SHVW 7769 A4
- WSTP 8028 B7
- WSTP 8114 B1
Westview St
- CTRV 7598 C5
Westview Ter
- MNDH 8113 A4
- MNTK 7935 E5
West Virginia Av
- SAVG 8280 A6
West Virginia Ct
- SAVG 8280 A6
Westwind Cir
- EDNP 8107 C6
Westwind Dr
- EDNP 8107 B6
- LCAN 7856 C2
Westwood Cir
- FLCH 7853 E7
- MNTK 7935 C2
- PYMH 7935 D2
- RSVL 7853 E7
- SPLP 7681 A5
Westwood Ct
- EDNA 8022 A5
Westwood Dr N
- GLDV 7937 A2
Westwood Dr S
- GLDV 7937 A3
Westwood Ln
- ANOK 7592 B2
- EAGN 8197 B7
- GLDV 7937 A3
Westwood Rd
- MNTK 7935 D3
- PYMH 7935 D3
Westwood Rd N
- BRKP 7679 E6
Westwood Rd NE
- BLNE 7681 A4
- SPLP 7681 A4
Westwood Hills Curv
- STLP 7936 A4
Westwood Hills Dr
- STLP 7936 A4
Westwood Hills Rd
- STLP 7936 A4
Westwoodland Tr NW
- PRIO 8278 D6
Wewers Rd
- LCAN 7855 C3
- RSVL 7855 C3
Wexford Cir
- EAGN 8198 A6
Wexford Ct
- EAGN 8198 A6
- NBRI 7767 B6
- WDBY 8030 E3
Wexford Ln
- SHKP 8278 A3
Wexford Rd
- EDNA 8108 B3
Wexford Wy
- EAGN 8198 A6
- WDBY 8030 C2
Wexford Heights Dr
- NBRI 7767 B6
- STAN 7767 B6
Wexford Heights Ln
- NBRI 7767 B6
Whalen Av S
- BMTN 8194 D5
Wheaton Av
- RSVL 7855 A3
Wheeler Blvd
- GLDV 7849 E6
S Wheeler St
- STPL 8026 B6
Wheeler St N
- ARDH 7854 B2
- RSVL 7854 A4
- STPL 7940 B7
Wheeler St S
- STPL 7940 B7
- STPL 8026 B1
Wheelock Av
- STPL 7942 C1
Wheelock Ln
- STPL 7941 D1
Wheelock Pkwy E
- STPL 7941 D1
- STPL 7942 A1
Wheelock Pkwy W
- STPL 7941 D1
Wheelock Ridge Rd
- STPL 7942 A1
Whippoorwill Ln
- LINO 7597 B5
Whispering Ct
- EAGN 8283 B2
Whispering Tr
- EAGN 8283 B1
Whispering Wy
- EAGN 8283 B2
Whispering Oaks Tr
- SHKP 8279 D5
Whispering Oaks Alcove
- SHKP 8279 D5
Whisperwood Tr
- WtBT 7684 E5
Whitaker Ct
- WTBL 7771 A3
Whitaker St
- WTBL 7771 A3
- WtBT 7771 A3
Whitall St
- STPL 7942 A4
White Bear Av N
- MPLW 7857 B4
- STPL 7857 A7
- STPL 7943 A7
- WTBL 7771 B7
- WTBL 7857 B1
White Bear Av N CO-65
- MPLW 7857 B4
- STPL 7857 A7
- STPL 7943 A7
- WTBL 7771 B5
- WTBL 7857 B1
White Bear Av S
- STPL 8029 A1
White Bear Ct
- WTBL 7857 B1
White Bear Pkwy
- VADH 7770 D4
- WTBL 7770 D3
- WtBT 7770 D2
- WtBT 7771 A4
White Birch Ct
- LINO 7597 E7
White Birch Dr
- NOAK 7683 A6
- SHVW 7683 A6
White Birch Rd
- MNTK 7934 D4
Whited Av
- MNTK 8020 C7
White Diamond Rd NW
- PRIO 8278 E6
Whitegate Ln
- MNTK 7934 B2
Whitehall Pl
- SHKP 8279 B2
Whitehall Rd
- SHKP 8279 B2
White Oak Ct
- EAGN 8283 B1
White Oak Dr
- BRNV 8282 D7
Whiteoak Dr
- MNDH 8027 D6
- WSTP 8027 D6
White Oak Rd
- LINO 7598 A7
- LINO 7684 A1
- MNTK 8020 D3
White Oaks Ct N
- CHMP 7591 A6
White Oaks Ln
- NOAK 7683 D6
- VADH 7769 D4
White Oaks Ln
- WDBY 8030 C6
White Oaks Rd
- EDNA 8023 A4
White Oaks Tr N
- CHMP 7591 E5
White Owl Dr
- LINO 7683 C1
White Pine Cir
- LINO 7682 E2
White Pine Dr
- MNTK 7934 B4
White Pine Ln
- BRHV 7772 A5
White Pine Rd
- LINO 7682 E2
- LINO 7683 A2
- NOAK 7770 C1
White Pine Wy
- EAGN 8285 C2
White Rock Rd
- BRNV 8282 D6
White Tail Cross
- EDNP 8193 D4
Whitetail Dr
- SHKP 8278 C4
White Tail Rdg
- LINO 7685 A2
White Tail Rdg NW
- PRIO 8278 E7
Whitetail Tr
- LINO 7598 A7
- LINO 7684 A1
Whitetail Wy
- EAGN 8199 B7
Whitewater Dr
- MNTK 8021 A6
Whitewater Tr N
- BRKP 7679 D7
White Water Wy
- EAGN 8197 B3
Whitewood Dr
- BRNV 8282 C3
Whitfield Dr
- MNDH 8113 C4
Whiting Av
- EDNA 8108 D1
Whiton Av
- VADH 7769 D4
Whittington Wk
- EDNP 8020 A7
- EDNP 8106 A1
Widgeon Ct
- CTRV 7598 C6
Widgeon Wy
- EAGN 8198 D3
E Widgeon Wy
- EAGN 8198 D2
Widman Ct
- SHKP 8278 A3
Wiggins Rd
- STPL 8029 C3
Wight Bay N
- BRKP 7679 C4
Wild Canyon Cir
- WDBY 8116 A2
Wild Canyon Ct
- WDBY 8116 A2
Wild Canyon Dr
- NWPT 8116 A1
- WDBY 8116 A2
Wild Canyon Tr
- WDBY 8116 A2
Wildcrest Rd
- MNTK 8020 C3
Wild Duck Pass
- EDNP 8193 D4
Wilde Av
- SSTP 8028 C5
Wilder Dr
- EDNP 8107 B6
Wilder St
- MINN 7938 C1
Wilder St N
- ARDH 7854 A2
- RSVL 7854 A2
- STPL 7940 A7
Wilder St S
- STPL 8026 A3
Wilderness Curv
- EAGN 8198 C7
Wilderness Ln
- EAGN 8198 D5
Wilderness Cove
- EDNP 8193 A1
Wilderness Park Cir
- EAGN 8198 D6
Wilderness Park Ct
- EAGN 8198 D6
Wilderness Run Cir
- EAGN 8198 D5
Wilderness Run Ct
- EAGN 8198 D6
Wilderness Run Dr
- EAGN 8198 C6
Wilderness Run Rd
- EAGN 8198 E6
- EAGN 8199 A6
Wildflower Ct
- EAGN 8198 E6
- SHVW 7682 A4
- VADH 7769 E4
Wild Flower Dr
- LINO 7597 A5
Wildflower Dr
- EDNP 8192 C3
Wildflower Dr S
- CTGV 8116 B5
Wildflower Ln
- EAGN 8198 E5
Wildflower Pl
- NOAK 7683 B6
Wildflower Wy
- EAGN 8199 B5
- SHKP 8279 D5
N Wildflower Wy
- NOAK 7683 B6
- SHVW 7683 B6
Wild Goose Ln
- WtBT 7770 D4
Wild Heron Pt
- EDNP 8193 B3
Wild Oaks Ter NE
- PRIO 8280 C5
Wildridge Ct
- MAHT 7772 B7
Wild Ridge Ct N
- NWPT 8115 E2
Wild Ridge Ct S
- NWPT 8115 E2
Wildridge Rd
- MAHT 7772 B7
Wild Ridge Tr
- NWPT 8115 E2
- NWPT 8116 A1
- WDBY 8116 A1
Wild Rose Ct
- EAGN 8199 A2
Wildrye Cir S
- CTGV 8116 B6
Wilds Dr NW
- PRIO 8278 C7
Wilds Pkwy NW
- PRIO 8278 D7
Wilds Pth NW
- PRIO 8278 C6
Wilds Rdg
- PRIO 8278 D7
Wilds Vw NW
- PRIO 8278 D7
Wilds Ridge Ct NW
- PRIO 8278 D7
Wild Turkey Tr
- LINO 7598 A7
Wildview Av
- STPL 8029 C4
Wild Wings
- MNTK 8020 B5
Wildwood Av
- BRHV 7771 E4
- BRHV 7772 A5
- WtBT 7771 E4
Wildwood Cir
- BMTN 8194 D4
- MNTK 7935 D5
- SHKP 8279 D5
Wildwood Ct NE
- BLNE 7595 E3
Wildwood Dr
- SHKP 8279 E5
Wild Wood Rd
- WILL 7772 D6
Wildwood Rd
- BMTN 8194 D4
- MAHT 7771 E6
- MAHT 7772 A6
- WILL 7772 C6
- WTBL 7771 E6
- WTBL 7772 A6
Wildwood Rd SR-244
- MAHT 7771 E6
- MAHT 7772 A6
- WTBL 7771 E6
- WTBL 7772 A6
Wildwood St
- EAGN 8283 B1
Wildwood Tr
- MNTK 7935 D5
Wildwood Bay Dr
- MAHT 7772 C3
Wildwood Beach Rd
- MAHT 7772 B6
Wilford Wy
- EDNA 8108 E2
Wilkin St
- STPL 8027 D1
Willbrook Ct
- EAGN 8198 E3
William Av
- EDNA 8022 D5
William Ct
- MNDH 8112 E2
William St
- RSVL 7855 C6
William Berry Pkwy
- MINN 8023 D2
Williams Av
- WtBT 7685 C6
Williams Av SE
- MINN 7939 C4
Williams Dr
- BRNV 8281 B3
- SAVG 8281 B3
Williams Ln
- MNTK 8020 C7
Williams St
- SHKP 8278 A4
- VADH 7770 A5
Williamsberg Dr
- SAVG 8280 B4
Williamsburg Ct
- EDNP 8106 C6
Williams Wood Rd
- MAHT 7772 D3
William Tell Rd
- MPLW 8029 C4
- STPL 8029 C4
Willie Dr
- BRNV 8197 A5
Willins St
- STPL 7942 A6
Willis Av
- SSTP 8028 C3
- STPL 8028 C3
Williston Ln
- MNTK 8020 C4
Williston Rd
- MNTK 7934 C7
- MNTK 8020 C5
Willmatt Hl
- MNTK 8021 B2
Willoughby Wy E
- MNTK 7935 C2
- PYMH 7935 C2
Willoughby Wy W
- MNTK 7935 C3
Willow Av
- WTBL 7771 A7
Willow Av N
- MINN 7851 D6
Willow Bnd
- CRYS 7764 C6
Willow Cir
- CTRV 7598 E4
- RSVL 7854 D4
Willow Ct
- WTBL 7771 B7
Willow Ct E
- WTBL 7771 A7
Willow Ln
- BRNV 8282 C4
- MNDH 8113 B1
- RSVL 7854 D4
- WDBY 7944 B7
- WDBY 8030 A1
- WTBL 7771 C7
N Willow Ln
- STLP 7937 A5
S Willow Ln
- STLP 7937 A5
Willow Ln N
- BRKC 7766 A1
- BRKP 7766 A1
- SHVW 7682 D4
Willow Rd
- MAPG 7763 A2
- NOAK 7769 D2
Willow Rd N
- BRKP 7593 A7
Willow St S
- MINN 7938 A3
Willow Tr
- SHVW 7683 B4
Willow Wy
- EAGN 8197 D3
Willow Creek Ln
- SHVW 7682 C5
Willow Creek Rd
- BRNV 8281 C3
- EDNP 8107 C2
Willow Grove Ln
- VADH 7770 B3
Willow Lake Blvd
- VADH 7770 D7
Willow Lake Dr
- VADH 7770 C7
Willow Ln Cir
- BRNV 8282 C4
Willow Oak Ln
- MNTK 8021 A3
Willowood Dr
- EDNP 8107 C3
- MNTK 8020 B7
Willow Pond Tr
- LINO 7596 E4
Willow Wood Dr
- VADH 7769 D4
Willow Wood Rd
- EDNA 8022 A5
Wills Pl
- GLDV 7850 E7
- GLDV 7936 E1
Willson Rd
- EDNA 8022 E5
Wilryan Av
- EDNA 8022 D7
- EDNA 8108 D1
Wilshire Blvd
- CRYS 7764 D6
Wilshire Cir
- MNTK 7935 C4
- SHVW 7769 A4
Wilshire Ct
- MNDH 8113 B4
Wilshire Dr S
- MNTK 7935 C2
- PYMH 7935 C2
Wilshire Pl
- STPL 7942 C7
Wilshire Pl NE
- MINN 7853 A2
Wilshire Wk
- HOPK 8021 D1
Wilson Av
- MPLW 7943 C6
- STPL 7942 E5
- STPL 7943 C6
Wilson Dr
- EDNP 8106 D5
Wilson Rd
- ARDH 7682 A7
Wilson St
- MNTK 8020 B3
Wilson St NE
- MINN 7853 B7
- STAN 7853 B3
Wimbledon Ct
- EDNP 8193 B4
Winchell St
- STPL 7942 E1
Winchester Ln
- BRKC 7764 E3
- BRKC 7765 A3
- BRKP 7764 E3
Winchester Pl
- EDNP 8106 E6
Wind Rd
- EDNA 8022 E6
W Wind Tr
- EAGN 8283 D1
Windbreak Tr N
- ELMO 7858 E4
Wind Cave Ct
- BRNV 8283 A2
Windcrest Av
- EAGN 8198 C4
Windcrest Ct
- EAGN 8198 C4
E Windemere Cir NE
- FRID 7767 E2
W Windemere Cir NE
- FRID 7767 E2
Windemere Cir NE
- FRID 7767 E2
Windemere Curv N
- PYMH 7935 A1
Windemere Dr
- PYMH 7934 A2
- PYMH 7935 A1

INDEX 46

Windemere Dr NE

Minneapolis Street Index

Xylon Ct N

STREET Block City ZIP Map # Grid

Windemere Dr NE
- FRID 7767 A4
Windermere Pl
- MNTK 8020 A3
Windflower Pl N
- CHMP 7591 C4
Windgate Rd
- WDBY 8030 C3
Windmill Ct
- EAGN 8199 B4
Windmill Dr
- WtBT 7684 E5
Windridge Cir
- MNTK 8021 A2
Windrow Dr
- EDNP 8107 C6
- LCAN 7856 C2
Windsong Cir
- MNTK 7934 C5
Windsong Dr
- EDNP 8106 E6
Windsor Av
- EDNA 8022 D6
- SAVG 8279 E5
- SAVG 8280 A3
Windsor Cir
- SAVG 8280 A3
- SHKP 8279 B2
Windsor Ct
- BRNV 8282 C2
- EAGN 8284 B2
- NBRI 7767 C7
- SAVG 8279 E4
Windsor Dr
- SHKP 8279 B2
Windsor Dr N
- SHKP 8279 B2
Windsor Dr S
- SHKP 8279 B2
Windsor Ln
- MAHT 7858 B1
- NBRI 7767 C7
- SHKP 8279 A2
- STAN 7767 C7
- WDBY 8030 D4
Windsor Ln N
- BRKP 7679 C4
Windsor Rd
- MNTK 8020 D3
Windsor Ter
- EDNP 8193 C2
Windsor Ter N
- BRKP 7679 B3
Windsor Wy
- GLDV 7850 E6
- MNDS 7767 E1
- NBRI 7767 C7
Windsor Bay
- WDBY 8030 D5
Windsor Lake Dr
- MNTK 7935 D5
Windsor Lake Ln
- MNTK 7935 D5
Windtree Cir
- EAGN 8199 B3
Windtree Ct
- EAGN 8199 B3
Windtree Dr
- EAGN 8199 B3
Windtree Knls
- EAGN 8199 B3
Windward Cir
- EDNP 8107 B6
Windward Wy
- LCAN 7856 B2
Windwood Ct
- MNDH 8026 C7
Windy Draw
- GLDV 7936 D2
Windy Hill Ct
- SUNL 8113 E3
Windy Hill Rd
- SUNL 8113 E3
- SUNL 8114 A3
Windyhill Rd
- MNTK 7934 E3
Winfield Av
- GLDV 7850 E6
Wingard Ln
- BRKC 7764 D2
- BRKC 7765 A1
Wingard Pl
- BRKC 7764 E2
Wing Lake Dr
- MNTK 8020 B5
Wingwood Ct
- MNTK 8020 B6
Winifred St E
- STPL 8028 B2
Winifred St W
- STPL 8027 E2
- STPL 8028 A2
Winnetka Av N
- BRKP 7592 B7
- BRKP 7678 B1
- BRKP 7764 B2
- CHMP 7592 B4
- CRYS 7764 B5
- CRYS 7850 B5
- GLDV 7850 B7
- GLDV 7936 B2
- NWHE 7764 B4
- NWHE 7850 B2
Winnetka Av N CO-103
- BRKP 7592 B7
- BRKP 7678 B1
- CHMP 7592 B4
Winnetka Av S
- GLDV 7936 B3
Winnetka Cir
- BRKP 7764 A2
Winnetka Heights Dr
- GLDV 7850 A6
Winnipeg Av
- STPL 7941 D4
Winona St E
- STPL 8028 A3
Winona St W
- STPL 8027 D3
- STPL 8028 A3

Winona St W
- WSTP 8027 E3
Winpark Dr
- CRYS 7850 B4
- NWHE 7850 B4
Winsdale St N
- GLDV 7849 E7
- GLDV 7850 B7
- GLDV 7851 A7
- PYMH 7849 E7
Winslow Av
- STPL 8027 E4
- WSTP 8027 E5
Winslow Ct
- WSTP 8113 E1
Winston Cir
- MNDH 8027 C4
Winston Ct
- MNDH 8027 C4
Winston St
- FLCH 7940 B2
- STPL 7940 B3
Winter Cir
- MNTK 7934 C5
Winter Pl
- EDNP 8193 A3
Winter St
- STPL 7941 D5
Winter St NE
- MINN 7852 E7
- MINN 7853 C7
Winterberry Ln
- SHKP 8278 B3
Wintergreen St NW
- COON 7593 E2
Winterset Dr
- MNTK 8021 A4
Winterset Spur
- MNTK 8021 A3
Winthrop Ct
- MNDH 8113 C4
- STPL 8029 C3
Winthrop Dr
- MPLW 7857 C2
Winthrop Ln
- STPL 8029 C3
Winthrop St N
- MPLW 7857 C7
- STPL 7857 C7
- STPL 7943 C1
Winthrop St S
- STPL 8029 C2
Wisconsin Av N
- CHMP 7592 A3
- CRYS 7850 A4
- GLDV 7850 A6
- GLDV 7936 A1
- NWHE 7764 A6
- NWHE 7850 A3
Wisconsin Av S
- GLDV 7936 A3
Wisconsin Cir N
- NWHE 7764 A5
Wishbone Ln
- NOAK 7684 A5
Witby Dr
- EAGN 8112 B6
Witham Ln
- EAGN 8199 C5
Witt Ct
- VADH 7856 A1
Wolf Cir
- LINO 7598 B6
Wolfberry Ct
- EAGN 8199 A2
Wolfberry Ln
- GLDV 7850 D7
Wolf Ridge Av
- SHKP 8278 A6
Wolf School Tr
- EDNP 8193 B2
Wolters Blvd
- VADH 7770 E7
Wood Av
- WTBL 7685 B7
- WTBL 7771 B1
Wood Ln
- MNTK 7934 D4
- STLP 8022 D3
Wood St
- MAHT 7772 C5
- STPL 8028 A1
Wood Wy
- BRNV 8282 B7
Woodale Dr
- FRID 7681 B7
- MNDS 7681 D7
Woodbine Av
- WDBY 7943 E7
- WDBY 7944 A7
Woodbine Ct
- WDBY 7944 A7
Woodbine Ln
- BRKC 7765 E1
Woodbine Ln N
- BRKC 7765 A1
Woodbine Rd
- MNTK 8021 A2
Woodbine St NW
- COON 7592 D1
Woodbridge Cir
- RSVL 7855 C5
Woodbridge Ct
- RSVL 7855 C7
- STPL 7855 C7
Woodbridge Dr
- BMTN 8193 E2
- SAVG 8280 D7
Woodbridge Ln
- SAVG 8280 E7
Woodbridge Rd
- BMTN 8193 E1
Woodbridge St
- LCAN 7855 C5
- RSVL 7855 C2
- SHVW 7855 C1
- STPL 7941 C1
Woodbridge Tr
- MNTK 7934 E6
- MNTK 7935 A3

Woodbury Cross
- WDBY 8030 A6
Woodbury Rd
- NWPT 8115 E3
Woodbury St
- STPL 8028 B3
- WSTP 8028 B3
Woodchuck Cir
- LINO 7685 A3
Woodchuck Ct
- LINO 7685 A3
Woodchuck Tr NW
- PRIO 8278 C7
Wood Cliff Cir S
- BMTN 8108 B7
Woodcliff Ct
- EAGN 8199 A3
Wood Cliff Rd
- BMTN 8108 B7
Woodcourt Ln
- MNTK 8021 B3
Woodcrest Av
- SHVW 7682 C4
Woodcrest Dr
- BRNV 8282 A4
- CIRC 7596 E7
- CIRC 7682 D1
- EDNA 8023 A6
- MNDS 7681 B7
- STPL 7943 B7
Woodcrest Dr NW
- COON 7594 A5
Woodcrest Ln
- MNTK 7934 B3
Woodcrest Rd
- WTBL 7685 A7
- WTBL 7771 A1
Woodcroft Dr
- MNTK 8020 A1
Wooddale Av S
- EDNA 8023 A3
- EDNA 8108 E3
- EDNA 8109 A2
- STLP 7936 D7
- STLP 8022 D1
- STLP 8023 A3
Wooddale Dr
- WDBY 8030 B3
Wooddale Gln
- EDNA 8023 A5
Wooddale Ln
- EDNA 8023 A4
Wood Duck Cir
- EAGN 8197 E6
Woodduck Cir
- WDBY 7944 D7
Wood Duck Ct
- SHVW 7682 D5
Wood Duck Dr
- VADH 7770 E3
Woodduck Dr
- WDBY 7944 D7
- WDBY 8030 D1
Wood Duck Tr
- LINO 7597 B1
Wood Duck Tr E
- SHKP 8278 A5
Wood Duck Pass
- SUNL 8113 D4
Wood End Dr
- EDNA 8023 B6
Woodgate Ct
- EAGN 8197 E6
- MNTK 8020 B5
Woodgate Dr
- VADH 7856 B1
Woodgate Ln
- EAGN 8197 E6
- EAGN 8198 A6
N Woodgate Ln
- EAGN 8197 E6
- EAGN 8198 A6
Woodgate Pt
- EAGN 8197 E6
Woodgate Rd N
- MNTK 8020 B4
Woodgate Rd S
- MNTK 8020 B5
Woodhall Cir N
- BRKP 7678 D4
Woodhall Cross N
- BRKP 7678 D4
Woodhall Bay N
- BRKP 7678 D3
Woodhaven Ct N
- CHMP 7591 C4
Woodhaven Rd
- MNTK 8020 C2
Woodhill Av
- RSVL 7854 E3
Woodhill Cir
- MNTK 8020 C4
- SAVG 8280 C4
- WDBY 8030 A2
Woodhill Ct
- EAGN 8197 B7
- SAVG 8279 D6
- WDBY 8030 A2
Woodhill Dr
- RSVL 7855 B3
- SAVG 8279 E5
- SAVG 8280 C4
- WDBY 8030 A2
Woodhill Ln
- NOAK 7684 A7
Woodhill Ln NE
- BLNE 7595 D4
Woodhill Rd
- BRNV 8281 E3
- MNTK 8020 D2
Woodhill Ter
- MNTK 8020 C3
Woodhill Tr
- EDNP 8106 C2
Woodhill Wy
- EDNA 8022 E4
Woodhurst Ln
- MNTK 8020 B4
Wood Knoll Ln
- MNTK 8020 B1

Wood Lake Dr
- BRNV 8282 B1
Woodlake Dr
- RHFD 8110 A1
Woodland Av
- SHKP 8278 D2
Woodland Cir
- EDNA 8023 A6
- MNTK 8020 B7
Woodland Ct
- EAGN 8199 A2
- MAHT 7772 A7
Woodland Curv
- MNTK 8020 A4
Woodland Dr
- BRNV 8282 A4
- EDNP 8106 C2
- LINO 7598 B1
- MAHT 7771 E7
- MAHT 7772 A7
- SHVW 7769 A1
- STLP 8022 B2
- WTBL 7771 E7
Woodland Dr N
- CHMP 7591 C6
Woodland Ln
- EDNA 8023 A6
- MNTK 8020 A6
Woodland Rd
- BLNE 7682 C1
- BMTN 8108 D7
- CIRC 7682 C1
- EDNA 8023 A6
- EDNP 8020 B7
- LXTN 7682 C1
- MNTK 8020 B5
W Woodland Rd
- EDNA 8022 E6
- EDNA 8023 A6
Woodland Tr
- EAGN 8199 A2
Woodland Wy
- EAGN 8199 B7
Woodlane Ct
- WDBY 8116 B4
Woodlane Dr
- CTGV 8116 B4
- WDBY 8030 B2
- WDBY 8116 B3
Woodlane Bay
- WDBY 8116 C4
Woodlark Ln
- EAGN 8112 B7
Woodlawn Av
- STPL 8025 E1
Woodlawn Blvd
- MINN 8024 E6
- MINN 8025 A4
Woodlawn Ct
- BRNV 8282 C3
Woodlawn Ct N
- CHMP 7591 C4
Woodlawn Dr
- MNDS 7681 D5
Woodlawn Pl N
- CHMP 7591 C4
Woodlyn Av
- MPLW 7857 D2
- RSVL 7854 C1
Woodlynn Av
- LCAN 7855 D1
- RSVL 7854 E1
- RSVL 7855 C2
Woodmere Cir
- EDNP 8106 E2
Woodmere Rd
- WDBY 8030 B2
Woodpark Blvd
- WDBY 8030 D3
Woodridge Cir
- EDNP 8193 A2
- SAVG 8279 E6
- VADH 7769 E5
Woodridge Ct
- LINO 7683 A3
- MAHT 7772 B7
- MNTK 8020 D4
- SAVG 8279 E6
- VADH 7769 E5
Woodridge Dr
- EDNP 8193 A1
- MNDH 8027 B5
- VADH 7769 E5
Woodridge Ln
- IVGH 8114 A4
- LINO 7682 E3
- LINO 7683 A3
- SHVW 7683 A3
- SUNL 8114 A4
Woodridge Pth
- SAVG 8279 E6
Woodridge Rd
- MNTK 8020 D4
Woodridge Wy
- SAVG 8279 D5
Woodruff Av
- RSVL 7855 B7
Woodruff Cir
- MNTK 7934 D5
Woodruff Rd
- MNTK 7934 C5
Woodruff Spur
- MNTK 7934 C5
Woods Ct
- EAGN 8283 B2
Woods Ln
- BRNV 8196 E6
Woods Tr N
- CHMP 7591 D6
Woods Wy
- MNTK 8020 C3
Woods Edge
- MNTK 8020 C3
Woods Edge Blvd
- LINO 7597 C2
Woodside Ct
- SHKP 8192 A6
Woodside Ct NE
- FRID 7767 A2

Woodside Ln
- MNTK 8020 B3
Woodstock Av
- GLDV 7936 E2
- GLDV 7937 A2
Woodstock Curv
- BMTN 8194 C1
Woodstock Dr
- BMTN 8194 B4
Woodstone Cir
- EAGN 8198 D4
Woodthrush Ct
- EAGN 8198 E2
Wooduck Ln
- NOAK 7684 A7
Woodview Ct
- BRNV 8282 C3
- EDNA 8108 B4
- VADH 7769 E5
Woodview Dr
- BRNV 8282 C3
- VADH 7769 E5
Woodview Ln
- BRNV 8282 C3
Woodview St
- EAGN 8198 A2
Woodview St E
- EAGN 8198 A2
Woodview St W
- EAGN 8198 A2
Woodward Av
- STPL 7942 E4
Woodwatch Cir
- EDNP 8107 C7
Woodwinds Dr
- WDBY 8030 A4
Woody Ln
- MNTK 8021 B1
Woody Ln NE
- FRID 7766 E3
- FRID 7767 A3
Woody Ln NW
- COON 7593 E4
- COON 7594 A3
Worcester Av
- STPL 8026 A6
Worchester Cir
- EAGN 8199 C3
Worchester Dr
- EAGN 8199 C3
Wordsworth Av
- STPL 8026 A6
Wren Ln
- EAGN 8113 B7
- NOAK 7770 B2
Wren St NW
- COON 7593 B2
Wright Av
- FLCH 7940 B2
Wuthering Heights Rd
- EAGN 8197 C3
Wychewood Rd
- MNTK 8020 C4
Wycliff St
- STPL 7939 E3
Wycliffe Rd
- EDNA 8022 B6
Wyldwood Ln NE
- SPLP 7680 C5
- SPLP 7681 A4
Wyman Av
- EDNA 8022 D7
- EDNA 8108 D1
Wyncrest Ct
- ARDH 7768 D3
Wyncrest Ln
- ARDH 7768 D3
Wyndam Dr
- SHKP 8278 B3
Wyndemere Ln
- EAGN 8283 B1
Wyndham Cir E
- NBRI 7767 B6
Wyndham Cir W
- NBRI 7767 B6
Wyndham Wy
- WDBY 8030 C4
Wyndham Alcove
- WDBY 8030 C5
Wyndham Bay
- WDBY 8030 C6
Wyndham Hill Dr
- HOPK 8021 B2
- MNTK 8021 B2
Wyngate Ln
- MNTK 8020 B7
Wynne Av
- STPL 7940 C3
Wynnwood Rd
- GLDV 7850 A6
Wynridge Dr
- ARDH 7768 D3
Wyola Rd
- MNTK 8020 E1
Wyoming Av
- SAVG 8280 A2
Wyoming Av N
- BRKP 7678 A5
- BRKP 7764 A3
Wyoming Av S
- BMTN 8108 A5
- BMTN 8194 A1
- STLP 7936 A6
- STLP 8022 A1
Wyoming Cir S
- BMTN 8194 A2
Wyoming Ct
- BMTN 8108 A5
Wyoming Curv
- BMTN 8194 A6
Wyoming Rd S
- BMTN 8194 A4
Wyoming St E
- STPL 8028 A3
Wyoming St W
- STPL 8027 D3
- STPL 8028 A3
- WSTP 8027 E3
Wyoming Ter S
- BMTN 8194 A2

X

Xavier Av S
- BMTN 8194 D4
Xavier Cir S
- BMTN 8194 D6
Xavier Ct S
- BMTN 8194 D6
Xavier Rd S
- BMTN 8194 D6
Xavis Cir NW
- COON 7593 B3
Xavis St NW
- COON 7593 B2
Xebec St NE
- BLNE 7596 B7
- BLNE 7682 B3
- LXTN 7596 B7
- SHVW 7682 B3
Xena Ln N
- MAPG 7762 B1
Xene Ln N
- MAPG 7676 B6
- MAPG 7762 A2
- PYMH 7848 A1
- PYMH 7934 A1
Xenia Av N
- BRKP 7678 D2
- CHMP 7592 D6
- CRYS 7764 D7
- CRYS 7850 D2
- GLDV 7850 D7
- ROBB 7850 D4
Xenia Av S
- GLDV 7936 D3
- STLP 7936 D3
Xenium Ct N
- PYMH 7848 E3
Xenium Ln N
- MAPG 7676 E3
- MAPG 7762 E2
- MNTK 7934 E2
- PYMH 7762 E6
- PYMH 7848 E2
- PYMH 7934 E1
Xenium Ln N CO-61
- MNTK 7934 E2
- PYMH 7848 E7
- PYMH 7934 E1
Xenium Ln S
- MNTK 7934 E2
- PYMH 7934 E2
Xenium Ln S CO-61
- MNTK 7934 E2
- PYMH 7934 E2
Xenwood Av
- SAVG 8280 D3
Xenwood Av S
- STLP 7936 D6
- STLP 8022 D1
Xeon Blvd NW
- COON 7593 D2
Xeon St NW
- COON 7593 E3
Xerxes Av N
- BRKC 7765 C3
- BRKC 7851 C1
- BRKP 7679 B6
- BRKP 7765 C1
- GLDV 7851 C5
- GLDV 7937 C1
- MINN 7765 C7
- MINN 7851 C6
- MINN 7937 C2
- ROBB 7851 C4
Xerxes Av S
- BMTN 8109 C5
- BMTN 8195 C4
- BRNV 8281 C5
- EDNA 8023 C7
- EDNA 8109 C5
- MINN 7937 C6
- MINN 8023 C7
- RHFD 8023 C7
- RHFD 8109 C2
Xerxes Cir S
- BMTN 8109 C7
- BMTN 8195 C2
Xerxes Ct N
- BRKP 7679 B7
Xerxes Curv S
- BMTN 8195 C3
Xerxes Ln N
- BRKP 7679 C5
Xerxes Pl N
- BRKC 7765 C3
Xerxes Rd S
- BMTN 8195 C2
Ximines Ln N
- MAPG 7677 C2
- MAPG 7763 C1
- PYMH 7763 C6
- PYMH 7849 C1
Xylite Ct NE
- BLNE 7595 D4
Xylite St NE
- BLNE 7595 E1
- BLNE 7681 D3
- MNDS 7681 D3
Xylon Av N
- BRKP 7592 A6
- BRKP 7678 A5
- BRKP 7764 A3
- CHMP 7592 A5
- CRYS 7850 A4
- GLDV 7850 A6
- NWHE 7764 A5
- NWHE 7850 A5
Xylon Av S
- BMTN 8194 A6
- STLP 7936 A5
- STLP 8022 A1
Xylon Cir S
- BMTN 8108 A6
- BMTN 8194 A1
Xylon Ct N
- BRKP 7678 A5
- CHMP 7592 A6

INDEX 47

Xylon Ct S — S 5th Av SR-65

Minneapolis Street Index

STREET / Block / City / ZIP / Map # / Grid

Xylon Ct S
- BMTN 8194 A2

Xylon Ln N
- BRKP 7592 A6
- CHMP 7592 A6

Xylon Rd S
- BMTN 8193 E4
- BMTN 8194 A4

Y

Yacht Club Rd W
- STPL 8027 D1

Yale Av SE
- MINN 7939 B4

Yale Pl
- MINN 7938 B3

Yalta Ln NE
- BLNE 7682 B3

Yalta St NE
- BLNE 7596 B7
- BLNE 7682 B3
- SHVW 7682 B3

Yancey Ct
- APVA 8283 B3

Yancey Ln N
- BRKP 7679 C4

Yancy Ct NE
- BLNE 7595 D3

Yancy St NE
- BLNE 7595 D1
- BLNE 7681 D1

Yankee Dr
- EAGN 8197 E1

Yankee Pl
- EAGN 8198 D1

Yankee Doodle Ln
- EAGN 8198 A1

Yankee Doodle Rd
- EAGN 8197 E1
- EAGN 8198 A1
- EAGN 8199 A1
- IVGH 8199 C1

Yankton College Ln
- NBRI 7767 B5

Yates Av N
- BRKP 7678 D1
- CHMP 7592 D5
- CRYS 7764 D7
- CRYS 7850 D1
- ROBB 7850 D3

Yates Cir N
- CHMP 7592 D5

Yates Ct N
- BRKP 7678 D1

Yates Dr N
- BRKP 7678 D1

Yates Ter N
- BRKP 7678 D4

Yates Bay N
- BRKP 7678 D4

Yates Bay Ct N
- BRKP 7678 D4

Yellow Birch Rd
- DLWD 7772 B1

Yellow Cir Dr
- MNTK 8021 C7

Yellow Pine St NW
- COON 7593 E1

Yellowpine St NW
- COON 7593 E7

Yellowstone Tr N
- BRKP 7679 D7

Yew Pt
- EAGN 8198 B6

YMCA Ln
- MNTK 7935 B4

York Av
- GLDV 7937 C2
- STPL 7941 E4
- STPL 7942 E4
- STPL 7943 A4

York Av N
- BRKC 7765 C5
- BRKP 7679 B6
- BRKP 7765 C1
- GLDV 7851 C6
- MINN 7851 C3
- ROBB 7851 C5

York Av S
- BMTN 8109 B6
- BMTN 8195 C4
- BRNV 8281 C5
- EDNA 8023 C7
- EDNA 8109 C2
- MINN 8023 C2
- RHFD 8109 C1

York Cir
- WDBY 8030 B7

York Cir S
- BMTN 8109 C7

York Curv S
- BMTN 8195 C2

York Dr
- WDBY 8030 B6

York Ln
- BMTN 8195 B4

York Ln N
- BRKP 7679 B7

York Pl N
- BRKC 7765 C2

York Rd
- BMTN 8109 B6

York Rd S
- BMTN 8109 B7

York Ter
- EDNA 8109 C4

York Alcove
- WDBY 8030 B6

York Bay
- WDBY 8030 B6

Yorkshire Av
- STPL 8026 A4

Yorkshire Av S
- MNTK 7935 D3

Yorkshire Ct
- STPL 8026 A4

Yorkshire Ln
- EDNP 8193 A2
- SHKP 8279 C2

Yorkshire Ln N
- BRKP 7679 B3

Yorkton Blvd
- LCAN 7855 D2

Yorkton Ct
- LCAN 7855 D2

Yorkton Rdg
- LCAN 7855 E2

Yorktown Dr
- EAGN 8199 B5

Yorktown Ln N
- CHMP 7591 C1
- MAPG 7591 C7
- MAPG 7677 B1
- MAPG 7763 C2
- PYMH 7763 C6
- PYMH 7849 C1

Yorktown Pl
- EAGN 8199 B5

Yorktown Pl N
- PYMH 7763 C7

Yosemite Av N
- GLDV 7850 D7
- GLDV 7936 D2

Yosemite Av S
- EDNA 8022 D2
- SAVG 8280 D2
- STLP 7936 D6
- STLP 8022 D2

Yosemite Cir N
- GLDV 7936 D2

Yosemite Cir S
- BMTN 8194 D2
- SAVG 8280 D5

Yosemite Ct
- SAVG 8280 D6

Yosemite Rd S
- BMTN 8194 D2

Young St
- STPL 7940 B4

Youngman Av
- STPL 8026 C6

Yucca Cir
- MAPG 7762 E2

Yucca Ln N
- MAPG 7676 E3
- MAPG 7762 E1
- PYMH 7762 E5
- PYMH 7848 E5

Yucca St NW
- COON 7592 C3

Yukon Av N
- BRKP 7764 A3
- CHMP 7592 A3
- CRYS 7850 A4
- NWHE 7764 A5
- NWHE 7850 A4

Yukon Av S
- BMTN 8194 A1
- STLP 7936 A5
- STLP 8022 A1

Yukon Cir N
- CHMP 7592 A3

Yukon Cir S
- BMTN 8194 A2

Yukon Ct N
- GLDV 7850 A7

Yukon Ct S
- BMTN 8194 A2

Yukon Rd S
- BMTN 8194 A4

Yukon St NW
- COON 7593 B2

Yuma Ct N
- MAPG 7676 A6
- MAPG 7762 A1
- PYMH 7762 A7

Yuma Ln N
- MAPG 7762 B2
- PYMH 7762 B7
- PYMH 7848 A1
- PYMH 7934 A1

Yuma Wy N
- MAPG 7676 A6

Yvonne Ter
- EDNA 8022 D6

Z

Zachary Cir N
- DAYT 7591 C1

Zachary Ln N
- CHMP 7591 C6
- DAYT 7591 C6
- MAPG 7591 C6
- MAPG 7677 C7
- MAPG 7763 C1
- MNTK 7935 C2
- PYMH 7763 C6
- PYMH 7849 C2
- PYMH 7935 C2

Zachman Cir
- EDNP 8107 B7

Zane Av N
- BRKP 7678 D7
- BRKP 7764 D4
- CHMP 7592 D5
- CRYS 7764 D7
- CRYS 7850 D4
- GLDV 7850 D6
- GLDV 7936 D1
- ROBB 7850 D3

Zane Cir N
- CHMP 7592 D5

Zane Ct N
- BRKP 7678 D6
- BRKP 7764 D1

Zane Pl N
- CRYS 7764 D6

Zanzibar Ct N
- MAPG 7676 A6

Zanzibar Ln N
- DAYT 7590 A2
- MAPG 7676 A4
- MAPG 7762 A1
- PYMH 7848 A3
- PYMH 7934 A1

Zarthan Av S
- SAVG 8280 D4
- STLP 7936 D4
- STLP 8022 D1

Zarthan Cir
- SAVG 8280 D4

Zarthan Ct
- SAVG 8280 D5

Zea Cir NW
- COON 7592 C1

Zea St NW
- COON 7592 C1

Zealand Av N
- BRKP 7592 A6
- BRKP 7678 A5
- BRKP 7764 A3
- CHMP 7592 A3
- GLDV 7850 A7
- NWHE 7764 A4
- NWHE 7850 A5

Zealand Cir N
- CHMP 7592 A3

Zealand Ct N
- BRKP 7764 A3

Zealand Ln N
- BRKP 7764 A3

Zebulon Pike Av
- BRNV 8196 E6

Zehnder Rd
- IVGH 8113 E4
- SUNL 8113 E4

Zenith Av
- BRNV 8281 C2

Zenith Av N
- BRKC 7765 B2
- BRKP 7765 B1
- GLDV 7851 C6
- MINN 7851 C1
- ROBB 7851 B5

Zenith Av S
- BMTN 8109 B5
- BMTN 8195 B4
- EDNA 8023 B7
- MINN 7937 B7
- MINN 8023 B5

Zenith Cir S
- BMTN 8109 B6

Zenith Ct N
- BRKP 7679 B6

Zenith Ln
- BMTN 8195 B3
- EDNP 8106 E4

Zenith Rd
- BMTN 8109 B6
- BMTN 8195 B3

Zephyr Pl
- GLDV 7851 B6

Zieglers Dr N
- BRKP 7593 B7

Zilla St NW
- COON 7593 E2

Zinna Wy
- MAPG 7676 D7
- MAPG 7762 D1

Zinnia Ln N
- MAPG 7676 D2
- MAPG 7762 E3
- PYMH 7762 E4
- PYMH 7848 E3
- PYMH 7934 E2

N Zinnia Wy
- MAPG 7676 D5

Zinran Av
- SAVG 8280 A2

Zinran Av S
- BMTN 8194 A4
- STLP 7936 A5
- STLP 8022 A1

Zinran Cir S
- BMTN 8194 A4

Zinran Rd S
- BMTN 8194 A3

Zion Av S
- BMTN 8194 D4

Zion Cir S
- BMTN 8194 D6

Zion Rd
- BMTN 8194 D7

Zion St NW
- COON 7593 A1

Zircon Ln
- EAGN 8197 C5

Zoo Blvd
- APVA 8283 E4

Zopi Wy E
- MAPG 7591 D6

Zopi Wy W
- MAPG 7591 D6

Zumbrota Cir NE
- BLNE 7595 D1
- BLNE 7681 D2

Zumbrota Ct NE
- BLNE 7595 D4

Zumbrota St NE
- BLNE 7595 D2
- BLNE 7681 D1

#

NE
- MINN 7852 C6

1st Av
- LNDF 7944 A6
- MNDH 8027 B6
- NWPT 8115 C2
- WTBL 7771 B2
- WtBT 7685 C4

S 1st Av
- MINN 7938 B4
- MINN 8024 B5

1st Av E
- NSTP 7857 D5
- ODLE 7857 D5

1st Av N
- MINN 7938 B2
- PYMH 7934 D2

1st Av NE
- BRKP 7677 E3
- MINN 7938 D1
- OSSE 7677 E4

1st Av NW
- MAPG 7677 D3
- NBRI 7767 E3
- NBRI 7768 A5
- OSSE 7677 D3

1st Av S
- BMTN 8110 B6
- BMTN 8196 B1
- BRNV 8282 B5
- MINN 7938 B6
- MINN 8024 B4
- RHFD 8110 B1
- SSTP 8114 E2
- SSTP 8115 A2

1st Av SE
- ARDH 7768 A7
- NBRI 7768 A7
- OSSE 7677 E4

1st St
- DLWD 7685 E6
- EAGN 8112 E6
- MPLW 7943 D5
- NWPT 8115 D5
- SPLP 8115 D5
- SPLP 8201 D1
- WTBL 7685 E6
- WTBL 7771 B2
- WtBT 7685 E6

N 1st St
- MINN 7938 C1

S 1st St
- MINN 7938 C2
- MINN 8024 B7

1st St N
- HOPK 8021 C2
- MINN 7852 A3
- MNTK 8021 C2
- MPLW 7857 D6
- NSTP 7857 D3
- ODLE 7944 B6

1st St NE
- MINN 7852 C5
- OSSE 7677 E4
- OSSE 7678 A4

1st St NW
- NBRI 7767 E6
- OSSE 7677 D4
- STLP 7936 C7
- STLP 8022 A2

1st St S
- HOPK 8021 B3
- MINN 7938 C2

1st St SE
- ARDH 7768 A7
- NBRI 7768 A7
- OSSE 7677 E4

1st St SW
- NBRI 7767 E7

1 1/2 Av N
- MINN 7937 D2

1 1/2 St NE
- OSSE 7677 E4

2nd Av
- LINO 7597 A6
- LNDF 7944 B6
- MNDH 8027 B6
- NWPT 8115 C2
- ODLE 7944 A6
- SPLP 8115 C5
- WTBL 7771 B2

S 2nd Av
- ANOK 7592 A1
- MINN 8024 B6

2nd Av E
- NSTP 7857 E5
- ODLE 7857 D5

2nd Av N
- GLDV 7937 C2
- MINN 7937 E2
- MINN 7938 B2
- PYMH 7934 B2

2nd Av NE
- BRKP 7677 E4
- OSSE 7677 E4

2nd Av NW
- MAPG 7677 D3
- NBRI 7767 E3
- OSSE 7677 D4

2nd Av S
- BMTN 8110 B5
- BMTN 8196 B1
- BRNV 8282 B3
- HOPK 8021 E4
- MINN 7938 B3
- MINN 8024 B1
- RHFD 8110 B2
- SSTP 8028 E7
- SSTP 8114 E1

2nd Av SE
- ARDH 7768 A7
- MINN 7938 D1
- NBRI 7768 A7
- OSSE 7677 E4

2nd St
- MNDT 8112 C1
- NWPT 8115 D5
- SPLP 8115 D7
- SPLP 8201 D1
- WTBL 7685 E6
- WTBL 7771 A2
- WtBT 7685 E6

E 2nd St N
- NSTP 7857 D4

N 2nd St
- MINN 7852 B7
- MINN 7938 C2

S 2nd St
- MINN 7938 E3
- MINN 8024 B7

W 2nd St N
- NSTP 7857 D4

2nd St E
- STPL 7941 E7

2nd St N
- HOPK 8021 B2
- MINN 7852 A7
- MNTK 8021 B2
- MPLW 7857 D3
- NSTP 7857 D3
- ODLE 7944 A6
- SSTP 8028 D7

2nd St NE
- COLH 7766 C7
- COLH 7852 C2
- FRID 7766 C1
- HOPK 8021 E2
- HOPK 8022 A2
- MINN 7852 C7
- MINN 7938 C1
- OSSE 7677 E4

2nd St NW
- NBRI 7767 E6
- OSSE 7677 D4
- STLP 7936 C7

2nd St S
- EDNA 8021 E3
- HOPK 8021 D3
- MINN 7938 C2
- SSTP 8114 C1

2nd St SE
- ARDH 7768 A7
- EDNA 8021 C4
- HOPK 8021 C4
- MINN 7938 D1
- NBRI 7768 A7
- OSSE 7677 E5
- OSSE 7678 A5

2nd St SW
- NBRI 7767 D7

2nd Ter SW
- NBRI 7767 D7

2 1/2 St NE
- COLH 7766 C7
- COLH 7852 C2
- FRID 7766 C3
- MINN 7852 C2

3M Rd
- MPLW 7943 E6
- ODLE 7943 E6
- STPL 7943 D6

3M Center Rd
- MPLW 7943 D5
- STPL 7943 C5

3rd Av
- LNDF 7944 A6
- MNDH 8027 B6
- NWPT 8115 C2
- ODLE 7944 A6
- SPLP 8115 C5
- WTBL 7771 B2

N 3rd Av
- MINN 7938 A2

S 3rd Av
- ANOK 7592 A1
- MINN 7938 B3

3rd Av E
- NSTP 7857 E5
- ODLE 7857 E5
- SPLP 8115 D5

3rd Av N
- MINN 7937 D2
- MINN 7938 A2
- PYMH 7934 B2
- PYMH 7935 A2
- SSTP 8028 E7

3rd Av NE
- BRKP 7677 E4
- MINN 7852 D7
- MINN 7938 C1
- OSSE 7677 E4

3rd Av NW
- MAPG 7677 D4
- NBRI 7767 E4
- OSSE 7677 D4

3rd Av S
- BMTN 8110 B7
- BMTN 8196 B3
- MINN 7938 B6
- MINN 8024 B2
- RHFD 8110 B1
- SSTP 8028 E7
- SSTP 8114 E2

3rd Av S SR-65
- MINN 7938 C2

3rd Av SE
- ARDH 7768 A7
- MINN 7938 D2
- NBRI 7768 A7
- OSSE 7677 E5

3rd Av W
- SPLP 8115 C6

3rd St
- MNDT 8112 C1
- NWPT 8115 D5
- SPLP 8115 D7
- SPLP 8201 D1
- WTBL 7771 A2
- WtBT 7685 E6

N 3rd St
- MINN 7852 A4
- MINN 7938 B2

S 3rd St
- MINN 7938 E3
- MINN 8024 B7

3rd St E
- STPL 7942 B5
- STPL 7943 A5

3rd St N
- HOPK 8021 B2
- MINN 7852 A4
- MINN 7938 A1
- NSTP 7857 D4
- ODLE 7944 B6
- SSTP 8028 D7

3rd St NE
- BLNE 7594 C1
- BLNE 7680 C2
- COLH 7766 C7
- COLH 7852 C1
- FRID 7766 C2
- MINN 7852 C1
- OSSE 7677 E4
- OSSE 7678 A4

3rd St NW
- NBRI 7767 C6
- OSSE 7677 D4

3rd St S
- EDNA 8021 D3
- HOPK 8021 E3
- MINN 7938 C2
- SSTP 8114 D1

3rd St SE
- OSSE 7677 E5
- OSSE 7678 A5

3rd St SW
- NBRI 7767 D7

3rd Ter NW
- NBRI 7767 E6

3rd Av Br
- MINN 7938 C2

3rd Av Br SR-65
- MINN 7938 C2

3rd St Ct N
- ODLE 7944 B6

N 4th
- MINN 7766 A7

4th Av
- LINO 7597 B2
- MNDH 8027 B6
- NWPT 8115 D4
- SPLP 8115 D5
- WTBL 7771 B2

S 4th Av
- ANOK 7592 A1
- MINN 7938 B4

4th Av E
- NSTP 7857 E5
- ODLE 7857 E5
- SHKP 8192 A6

4th Av N
- LNDF 7944 A5
- MINN 7937 D2
- MINN 7938 B1
- PYMH 7934 A1
- SSTP 8028 E7

4th Av NE
- BRKP 7677 E3
- MINN 7852 C7
- OSSE 7677 E4

4th Av NW
- NBRI 7767 E5

4th Av S
- BMTN 8110 B6
- BMTN 8196 B2
- BRNV 8282 B4
- MINN 7938 B5
- MINN 8024 B2
- RHFD 8110 B1
- SSTP 8028 E7
- SSTP 8114 E1

4th Av S SR-65
- MINN 7938 C3

4th Av SE
- MINN 7938 D1
- OSSE 7677 E5

4th Ct NE
- BLNE 7594 C1

4th St
- MNDT 8112 C1
- MPLW 7943 D6
- NWPT 8115 D5
- SPLP 8115 D7
- SPLP 8201 D1
- WTBL 7770 E1
- WTBL 7771 A1
- WtBT 7685 E6

N 4th St
- BRKC 7766 A6
- MINN 7766 A6
- MINN 7938 B1

S 4th St
- MINN 7938 E3
- MINN 7939 A4
- MINN 8024 B7

4th St E
- MPLW 7943 B5
- STPL 7941 E7
- STPL 7942 A6
- STPL 7943 A5

4th St N
- BRKC 7766 A6
- ELMO 7944 E6
- HOPK 8021 C2
- MINN 7852 A3
- MNTK 8021 B2
- MPLW 7943 E6
- ODLE 7943 E6
- ODLE 7944 C6
- SSTP 8028 D7

4th St NE
- BLNE 7594 C2
- COLH 7766 C5
- COLH 7852 C1
- FRID 7680 C6
- FRID 7766 C1
- MINN 7852 C6
- MINN 7938 D1
- OSSE 7677 E4

4th St NW
- NBRI 7767 E6
- OSSE 7677 D4

4th St S
- SSTP 8114 D1

4th St SE
- BRKP 7677 E5
- BRKP 7678 A5
- MINN 7938 D1
- MINN 7939 B3
- OSSE 7677 E5
- OSSE 7678 A5
- STPL 7939 D3

4th St W
- STPL 7941 D7

4th St Cir N
- ODLE 7944 B6

4th St Ct N
- ODLE 7944 B6

4th St Pl N
- ODLE 7944 B6

5th Av
- LNDF 7944 A6
- NWPT 8115 D4
- SPLP 8115 D6

E 5th Av
- MPLW 7943 E5
- ODLE 7943 E5

S 5th Av
- ANOK 7592 A1
- MINN 7938 C2

S 5th Av SR-65
- MINN 7938 C2

INDEX 49

15th St Ct N — 34th Av NE

Minneapolis Street Index

STREET Block City ZIP Map # Grid

15th St Ct N
- ODLE 7944 B3

15th St Ln N
- ODLE 7944 D3

15th St Pl N
- ODLE 7944 A3

16th Av
- SPLP 8201 E2

16th Av E
- NSTP 7857 E3
- ODLE 7857 E3

16th Av N
- GLDV 7851 C7
- HOPK 8021 C2
- MINN 7851 D7
- MINN 7852 A7
- PYMH 7848 B7
- PYMH 7849 A7
- SSTP 8028 D5

16th Av NE
- MINN 7852 C6
- MINN 7853 A6

16th Av NW
- NBRI 7767 D4

16th Av S
- BMTN 8110 D6
- BMTN 8196 D1
- BRNV 8282 D1
- HOPK 8021 C4
- MINN 7938 D4
- MINN 8024 D3
- RHFD 8110 D2
- SSTP 8028 D7
- SSTP 8114 D1

16th Av SE
- MINN 7853 A7
- MINN 7939 A1

16th Av SW
- NBRI 7767 D7
- STAN 7767 C7

16th Pl N
- PYMH 7848 B7

16th St
- NWPT 8115 C3

E 16th St
- MINN 7938 B4

N 16th St
- MINN 7938 A3

W 16th St
- MNTK 7935 D4
- STLP 7935 D4
- STLP 7936 A4

16th St N
- ODLE 7944 D3

16th St NW
- FRID 7767 B3
- NBRI 7767 C3

16th St W
- STLP 7936 D4

16th Ter NW
- NBRI 7767 D3

16th Av Cir S
- BMTN 8110 D7

16th St Ct N
- ODLE 7944 C3

17th Av
- SPLP 8201 E2

N 17th Av
- MINN 7852 B7

S 17th Av
- MINN 7938 D4

17th Av E
- MPLW 7857 B3
- NSTP 7857 B3
- ODLE 7857 E3
- SHKP 8278 A2

17th Av N
- GLDV 7851 C7
- HOPK 8021 C3
- MINN 7851 C7
- MINN 7852 B7
- MNTK 8021 C1
- PYMH 7848 B7
- PYMH 7849 D6
- SSTP 8028 D7

17th Av NE
- MINN 7852 C6

17th Av NW
- MNDS 7681 D7
- NBRI 7681 D7
- NBRI 7767 C1

17th Av S
- BMTN 8110 D6
- BMTN 8196 D1
- BRNV 8282 D2
- HOPK 8021 C3
- MINN 7938 D6
- MINN 8024 D3
- RHFD 8110 D2
- SSTP 8028 D7

17th Av SE
- MINN 7939 B1

17th Av SW
- NBRI 7767 C7

17th Pl N
- PYMH 7848 B6

17th St
- MPLW 7943 E6
- NWPT 8115 D2

E 17th St
- MINN 7938 B4

17th St N
- MINN 7938 C5
- ODLE 7944 A3

17th St NW
- NBRI 7767 D2

17th Ter NW
- NBRI 7767 B3

NE 18th Av
- MINN 7852 B5

18th Av E
- NSTP 7857 E3
- ODLE 7857 E3
- SHKP 8278 B3

18th Av N
- GLDV 7851 C7
- HOPK 8021 C3
- MINN 7851 C7
- MINN 7852 A7
- PYMH 7848 B6
- PYMH 7849 A7
- SSTP 8028 C7

18th Av NE
- MINN 7852 E5
- MINN 7853 A5

18th Av NW
- NBRI 7767 C3

18th Av S
- BMTN 8110 E6
- BRNV 8282 D3
- HOPK 8021 B3
- IVGH 8114 C1
- MINN 7938 E7
- MINN 8024 E3
- RHFD 8110 E2
- SSTP 8028 C7
- SSTP 8114 C1

18th Av SE
- MINN 7939 B1

18th Pl N
- PYMH 7848 B6
- PYMH 7849 A6

18th St
- NWPT 8115 D2

E 18th St
- MINN 7938 B4

W 18th St
- MNTK 7935 D4
- STLP 7935 E4
- STLP 7936 B4

18th St N
- ODLE 7944 D3

18th St NW
- FRID 7767 B2
- NBRI 7767 C2

18th St Ct N
- ODLE 7944 D2

18 1/2 Av N
- MINN 7852 A7

18 1/2 Av NE
- MINN 7852 D5

SE 19th Av
- MINN 7939 A2

19th Av E
- NSTP 7857 D3
- ODLE 7857 E3

19th Av N
- HOPK 8021 B3
- MINN 7852 B7
- PYMH 7848 A6
- SSTP 8028 C6

19th Av NE
- MINN 7852 D5
- MINN 7853 A5

19th Av NW
- NBRI 7767 C3

19th Av S
- BMTN 8110 E7
- BRNV 8196 E6
- HOPK 8021 B3
- MINN 7938 E7
- MINN 8024 E1
- SSTP 8114 C1

19th Av SE
- MINN 7939 B1

19th Av SW
- NBRI 7767 C7

19th St
- MPLW 7943 E6
- NWPT 8115 D2

E 19th St
- MINN 7938 B4

19th St N
- ODLE 7944 C3

19th St NW
- NBRI 7767 C2

19th Ter NW
- NBRI 7767 C2

20th Av E
- NSTP 7857 E3
- ODLE 7857 E3

20th Av N
- CTRV 7598 E4
- HOPK 8021 B2
- LINO 7598 E4
- PYMH 7848 C6
- SSTP 8028 C5

20th Av NE
- MINN 7852 E5

20th Av NW
- NBRI 7767 C3

20th Av S
- BMTN 8110 E7
- CTRV 7598 E5
- HOPK 8021 B3
- LINO 7598 E7
- LINO 7684 D3
- MINN 7938 E4
- MINN 8024 E2
- MNTK 8021 B3
- SHKP 8279 C4
- SSTP 8114 C1
- WtBT 7684 D3

20th Av SE
- MINN 7939 B1

20th Av SW
- NBRI 7767 C7

20th St
- NWPT 8115 D2

20th St N
- ODLE 7944 D2

21st Av N
- CTRV 7598 E5
- GLDV 7851 C6
- HOPK 8021 B2
- LINO 7598 E5
- MINN 7851 C6
- MINN 7852 B6
- MNTK 8021 B3
- PYMH 7848 A6
- PYMH 7849 E6
- SSTP 8028 C7

21st Av NW
- NBRI 7767 C3

21st Av S
- BMTN 8110 E7
- CTRV 7598 E5
- LINO 7598 E5
- MINN 7938 E3
- MINN 8024 E2
- RHFD 8110 E1
- SHKP 8279 C4
- SSTP 8028 C7
- SSTP 8114 C1

21st Av SE
- MINN 7939 B1

21st Ln NW
- NBRI 7767 B2

21st St
- NWPT 8115 D2

E 21st St
- MINN 7938 C5

W 21st St
- MINN 7937 D5

21st St N
- ELMO 7944 E2
- ODLE 7944 B2

21st St NW
- NBRI 7767 B2

21st St W
- MINN 7937 B5

22nd Av
- BMTN 8110 D6

N 22nd Av
- MINN 7851 E6

S 22nd Av
- MINN 7938 D7
- MINN 8024 E4

22nd Av N
- MINN 7851 E6
- MINN 7852 A6
- PYMH 7848 A6
- SSTP 8028 C6

22nd Av NE
- MINN 7852 D5
- MINN 7853 A5

22nd Av NW
- NBRI 7767 C5

22nd Av S
- BMTN 8110 E6
- BRNV 8196 E6
- MINN 7938 E4
- MINN 8024 E1
- SHKP 8279 C4
- SSTP 8028 C7
- SSTP 8114 C1

22nd Av SE
- MINN 7939 B1

22nd Ct N
- ELMO 7944 E2

W 22nd Ln
- STLP 7935 E5

22nd Pl N
- PYMH 7848 B6

22nd St
- MPLW 7943 E6

E 22nd St
- MINN 7938 D5
- MINN 7939 A5

W 22nd St
- MINN 7937 B5
- MINN 7938 A5
- STLP 7935 E5
- STLP 7936 C4
- STLP 7937 B5

22nd St E
- MINN 7938 E5
- MINN 7939 A5

22nd St N
- ELMO 7944 E2
- ODLE 7944 A2

22nd Ter NW
- NBRI 7767 B1

22nd St Ct N
- ODLE 7944 A2

23rd Av N
- GLDV 7849 E6
- GLDV 7850 A6
- MINN 7851 C6
- MINN 7852 A6
- PYMH 7848 C6
- PYMH 7849 B6
- SSTP 8028 C6

23rd Av NE
- MINN 7852 E5
- MINN 7853 A5

23rd Av NW
- NBRI 7767 C3

23rd Av S
- BRNV 8196 E6
- BRNV 8282 E1
- MINN 7938 E4
- MINN 7939 A7
- MINN 8025 A1
- SSTP 8028 C7
- SSTP 8114 C1

23rd Av SE
- MINN 7939 B1

E 23rd St
- MINN 7938 D5

W 23rd St
- STLP 7935 E5
- STLP 7936 B5

23rd St N
- ODLE 7944 C2

23rd St W
- STLP 7936 C5

23rd St Cir N
- ODLE 7944 D2

24th Av N
- GLDV 7850 A6
- HUGO 7599 B2
- LINO 7599 B2
- MINN 7851 D6
- MINN 7852 A6
- PYMH 7848 E5
- PYMH 7849 A5
- SSTP 8028 C6

24th Av NE
- MINN 7852 D5

24th Av S
- BMTN 8111 A5
- BRNV 8282 E2
- HnpC 8110 E4
- HnpC 8111 A5
- HUGO 7599 B5
- LINO 7599 B5
- MINN 7939 A4
- MINN 8025 A2

24th Av SE
- MINN 7939 B1

24th Ln
- STLP 7935 E5

24th St
- MPLW 7943 E6

E 24th St
- MINN 7938 E5
- MINN 7939 B5

W 24th St
- MINN 7937 C5
- MINN 7938 A5
- STLP 7935 E5
- STLP 7936 B5

24th St N
- ODLE 7944 B1

24th St W
- MINN 7937 B5
- STLP 7936 C5
- STLP 7937 B5

25th Av N
- GLDV 7850 A5
- MINN 7851 D6
- MINN 7852 A6
- PYMH 7848 A5
- PYMH 7849 A5

25th Av S
- MINN 7939 A5
- MINN 8025 A2

25th Av SE
- MINN 7939 C1

25th Cir N
- PYMH 7848 B5

25th Ct N
- PYMH 7848 B5

25th Pl N
- PYMH 7848 B5

E 25th St
- MINN 7938 D5
- MINN 7939 A5

W 25th St
- MINN 7937 E5
- MINN 7938 A5
- STLP 7936 B5
- STLP 7937 B5

25th St N
- MPLW 7943 E1
- ODLE 7943 E1
- ODLE 7944 C1

25th St NW
- NBRI 7767 D1

25th St Cir N
- ODLE 7944 C1

25 1/2 Av NE
- MINN 7853 A4

E 25 1/2 St
- MINN 7938 E5

W 25 1/2 St
- MINN 7937 E5
- STLP 7936 E5

26th Av N
- GLDV 7849 E5
- GLDV 7851 B6
- MINN 7851 D6
- MINN 7852 A5
- NWHE 7849 E5
- PYMH 7848 B5
- PYMH 7849 D5
- ROBB 7851 B6

26th Av NE
- MINN 7852 E4
- MINN 7853 A4
- STAN 7853 A4

26th Av NW
- NBRI 7767 B1

26th Av S
- BMTN 8111 A5
- BRNV 8197 A6
- MINN 7939 A5
- MINN 8025 A2

26th Av SE
- MINN 7939 C1

E 26th St
- MINN 7938 B5
- MINN 7939 B5

W 26th St
- MINN 7937 E5
- MINN 7938 A5
- STLP 7936 E5
- STLP 7937 A5

26th St N
- ELMO 7944 E1
- ODLE 7944 A1

26th St W
- STLP 7936 C5

26th St Ct N
- ODLE 7944 A2

26 1/2 Av N
- ROBB 7851 B5

26 1/2 Av NE
- MINN 7852 C4

27th Av
- PYMH 7848 B5

S 27th Av
- MINN 7939 A4

27th Av N
- CRYS 7850 D5
- GLDV 7850 D5
- GLDV 7851 A5
- MINN 7851 C5
- MINN 7852 A5
- PYMH 7848 C5
- PYMH 7849 D5
- ROBB 7851 B5

27th Av NE
- MINN 7852 D4
- MINN 7853 A4
- STAN 7853 B4

27th Av NW
- NBRI 7767 B2

27th Av S
- BRNV 8197 A5
- MINN 7939 A5
- MINN 8025 A2

27th Av SE
- MINN 7939 C1

27th Pl
- BRNV 8197 A5

27th Pl N
- NWHE 7850 A5
- PYMH 7848 B5
- PYMH 7849 A5

E 27th St
- MINN 7938 B6
- MINN 7939 C6

W 27th St
- MINN 7937 E6
- MINN 7938 A6
- STLP 7936 D6
- STLP 7937 A6

27th St N
- ELMO 7944 E1
- ODLE 7944 D1

27th St Cir N
- ODLE 7944 C1

28th Av N
- MINN 7852 A5
- NWHE 7850 A5
- PYMH 7848 B5
- PYMH 7849 D5

28th Av NE
- MINN 7852 E4
- MINN 7853 A4

28th Av NW
- NBRI 7767 B2

28th Av S
- BMTN 8111 A5
- HnpC 8025 A7
- MINN 7939 A6
- MINN 8025 A4

28th Pl N
- PYMH 7848 D5
- PYMH 7849 A5

E 28th St
- MINN 7938 E6
- MINN 7939 B6

W 28th St
- MINN 7937 B6
- MINN 7938 A6
- STLP 7935 E6
- STLP 7936 B6
- STLP 7937 B6

28th St N
- ODLE 7944 D1

29th Av N
- CRYS 7850 C5
- GLDV 7850 D5
- MINN 7851 C5
- MINN 7852 A5
- NWHE 7849 E5
- NWHE 7850 A5
- PYMH 7848 B4
- PYMH 7849 D5
- ROBB 7851 B5

29th Av NE
- MINN 7852 C3
- MINN 7853 A4
- RSVL 7853 D3
- STAN 7853 B3

29th Av NW
- NBRI 7767 B3

29th Av S
- MINN 7939 A5
- MINN 8025 A2

29th Av SE
- MINN 7939 C1

29th Pl N
- CRYS 7850 D5

E 29th St
- MINN 7938 D6
- MINN 7939 C6

W 29th St
- MINN 7937 C6
- MINN 7938 A6
- STLP 7936 B6
- STLP 7937 A6

29th St N
- ODLE 7944 B1

29th St Cir N
- ODLE 7944 B1

29th St Pl N
- ODLE 7944 B1

NE 30th Av
- MINN 7852 D3

S 30th Av
- MINN 7939 B5

30th Av N
- CRYS 7850 B5
- MINN 7851 E5
- MINN 7852 A5
- NWHE 7849 E5
- NWHE 7850 A5
- PYMH 7848 A4
- PYMH 7849 A4
- ROBB 7851 B5

30th Av NE
- MINN 7852 B3
- MINN 7853 B3
- STAN 7853 B3

30th Av NW
- NBRI 7767 B6
- STAN 7767 B6

30th Av S
- MINN 7939 B7
- MINN 8025 A3

30th Av SE
- MINN 7939 C2

30th St N
- ODLE 7858 A7

30th St Ct N
- ODLE 7858 B7

E 30 1/2 St
- MINN 7938 E7

W 30 1/2 St
- MINN 7937 B6
- STLP 7936 A6
- STLP 7937 B6

31st Av N
- CRYS 7850 C5
- MINN 7851 E5
- MINN 7852 A5
- NWHE 7849 E5
- NWHE 7850 B5
- PYMH 7848 B4
- PYMH 7849 D4
- ROBB 7851 B5

31st Av NE
- MINN 7852 E3
- MINN 7853 A3
- STAN 7853 B3

31st Av S
- BRNV 8283 A2
- MINN 7939 B5
- MINN 8025 B1

E 31st St
- MINN 7938 E7
- MINN 7939 D7

W 31st St
- MINN 7937 B7
- MINN 7938 A7
- STLP 7935 E7
- STLP 7936 D6
- STLP 7937 A7

31st St N
- ELMO 7858 D7
- ODLE 7858 C7

31st St Cir
- ODLE 7858 C7

31st St Ct N
- ODLE 7858 D7

31st St Pl
- ODLE 7858 D7

31st St Plz N
- ODLE 7858 D7

31 1/2 Av N
- ROBB 7851 A5

32nd Av N
- CRYS 7850 C4
- GLDV 7850 E4
- NWHE 7849 E4
- NWHE 7850 B4
- PYMH 7848 C4
- PYMH 7849 C4

32nd Av NE
- MINN 7852 E3
- MINN 7853 A3
- STAN 7853 B3

32nd Av NW
- NBRI 7767 B4
- STAN 7767 B6

32nd Av S
- MINN 7939 B5
- MINN 8025 B1

32nd Cir N
- NWHE 7850 A4

32nd Ct N
- NWHE 7849 E4

32nd Pl N
- CRYS 7850 A4
- NWHE 7850 A4

E 32nd St
- MINN 7938 B7
- MINN 7939 D7

W 32nd St
- MINN 7937 B7
- MINN 7938 A7
- STLP 7936 D7
- STLP 7937 B7

32nd St E
- MINN 7939 A7

32nd St N
- ELMO 7858 D7
- ODLE 7858 A7

32nd St W
- STLP 7935 E7

W 32 1/2 St
- STLP 7936 B7

33rd Av N
- CRYS 7850 A4
- GLDV 7850 E4
- GLDV 7851 A4
- MINN 7851 E4
- MINN 7852 A4
- NWHE 7849 E4
- NWHE 7850 A4
- PYMH 7848 E4
- PYMH 7849 C4
- ROBB 7851 C4

33rd Av NE
- MINN 7852 E2
- MINN 7853 A2
- RSVL 7853 D2
- STAN 7853 A2

33rd Av S
- BRNV 8283 A2
- MINN 7939 B5
- MINN 8025 B1

33rd Av SE
- LAUD 7853 D7
- LAUD 7939 D1
- MINN 7853 D7
- MINN 7939 D1
- STPL 7939 D1

33rd Pl N
- CRYS 7850 B4
- NWHE 7850 A4

E 33rd St
- MINN 7938 B7
- MINN 7939 B7

W 33rd St
- MINN 7937 D7
- MINN 7938 A7
- STLP 7936 A7

33rd St E
- MINN 7938 B7

33rd St N
- ODLE 7858 B7

33 1/2 St
- MINN 7938 A7

33 1/2 St E
- MINN 7938 C7

34th Av N
- CRYS 7850 C4
- CRYS 7851 A4
- GLDV 7850 E4
- GLDV 7851 A4
- MINN 7851 D4
- MINN 7852 A4
- NWHE 7849 E4
- NWHE 7850 A4
- PYMH 7848 C4
- PYMH 7849 C4
- ROBB 7851 A4

34th Av NE
- MINN 7852 E2
- MINN 7853 A2
- STAN 7853 B2

Minneapolis Street Index

STREET Block	City	ZIP	Map #	Grid
34th Av S				
-	BMTN		8111	B5
-	HnpC		8111	B1
-	MINN		7939	B5
-	MINN		8025	B1
W 34th Cir				
-	MNTK		7935	D7
34th Pl N				
-	CRYS		7850	A4
E 34th St				
-	MINN		7938	C7
-	MINN		7939	B7
W 34th St				
-	MINN		7937	B7
-	MINN		7938	B7
-	MNTK		7935	D7
-	STLP		7935	E7
-	STLP		7936	A7
-	STLP		7937	B7
34th St E				
-	MINN		7938	B7
34th St N				
-	ELMO		7858	E7
-	ODLE		7858	A7
34th St N SR-5				
-	ELMO		7858	E7
-	ODLE		7858	A7
34 1/2 Av N				
-	NWHE		7849	E4
34 1/2 St				
-	MINN		8024	B1
E 34 1/2 St				
-	MINN		7938	D7
W 34 1/2 St				
-	MINN		8023	B1
-	STLP		7936	B7
35th Av N				
-	CRYS		7850	C4
-	CRYS		7851	A4
-	MINN		7851	D4
-	MINN		7852	A4
-	NWHE		7849	E4
-	NWHE		7850	B4
-	PYMH		7848	D3
-	PYMH		7849	E3
-	ROBB		7851	A4
35th Av NE				
-	MINN		7852	C2
-	MINN		7853	A2
-	STAN		7853	B2
35th Av S				
-	MINN		7939	B5
-	MINN		8025	B1
35th Pl N				
-	CRYS		7850	C3
-	PYMH		7848	E3
-	PYMH		7849	C3
E 35th St				
-	MINN		8024	C1
-	MINN		8025	B1
W 35th St				
-	MINN		8023	E1
-	MINN		8024	A1
-	STLP		7936	A7
-	STLP		7937	A7
-	STLP		8022	E1
-	STLP		8023	A1
35th St N				
-	ELMO		7858	E6
-	ODLE		7858	B6
35 1/2 Av N				
-	NWHE		7850	A3
W 35 1/2 St				
-	STLP		8022	E1
N 36 Service Dr				
-	RSVL		7854	A5
36th Av N				
-	CRYS		7850	B3
-	CRYS		7851	A3
-	MINN		7851	E3
-	MINN		7852	A3
-	NWHE		7849	E3
-	NWHE		7850	B3
-	PYMH		7848	A3
-	PYMH		7849	B3
-	ROBB		7850	E3
-	ROBB		7851	B4
36th Av NE				
-	MINN		7852	D2
-	MINN		7853	A2
-	RSVL		7853	D2
-	STAN		7853	B2
36th Av S				
-	MINN		7939	B6
-	MINN		8025	B2
36th Pl N				
-	PYMH		7848	B3
-	PYMH		7849	D3
E 36th St				
-	MINN		8024	D1
-	MINN		8025	B1
W 36th St				
-	MINN		8023	D1
-	MINN		8024	A1
-	STLP		8021	E1
-	STLP		8022	A1
-	STLP		8023	A1
36th St N				
-	ELMO		7858	D6
-	ODLE		7858	D6
36 1/2 Av NE				
-	COLH		7852	E1
-	MINN		7852	E2
36 1/2 Cir N				
-	NWHE		7850	A3
E 36 1/2 St				
-	MINN		8024	E1
-	MINN		8025	A1
36 1/2 St W				
-	STLP		8023	A1
37th Av N				
-	CRYS		7850	B3
-	MINN		7851	E3
-	MINN		7852	A3
-	NWHE		7850	B3
-	PYMH		7848	B3
-	PYMH		7849	C3
-	ROBB		7850	E3
-	ROBB		7851	B3
37th Av NE				
-	COLH		7852	E1
-	COLH		7853	A1
-	FRID		7852	A2
-	MINN		7852	E1
-	MINN		7853	A1
-	NBRI		7853	D1
-	RSVL		7853	D1
-	STAN		7853	C1
37th Av S				
-	MINN		7939	B5
-	MINN		8025	B2
37th Pl N				
-	PYMH		7848	D3
-	PYMH		7849	D3
37th Pl NE				
-	COLH		7853	A1
-	MINN		7853	A1
-	STAN		7853	B1
E 37th St				
-	MINN		8024	C1
-	MINN		8025	B1
W 37th St				
-	MINN		8023	E1
-	MINN		8024	A1
-	STLP		8022	B1
-	STLP		8023	B1
37th St N				
-	ELMO		7858	E6
-	ODLE		7858	B6
37th St W				
-	STLP		8022	D1
37th St Ct N				
-	ODLE		7858	C6
38th Av N				
-	CRYS		7850	D3
-	NWHE		7850	B3
-	PYMH		7848	C3
-	PYMH		7849	C3
-	ROBB		7850	E3
-	ROBB		7851	A3
38th Av NE				
-	COLH		7852	C1
-	COLH		7853	B1
-	STAN		7853	B1
38th Av S				
-	MINN		7939	C6
-	MINN		8025	C2
38th Ct N				
-	PYMH		7849	D3
38th Pl N				
-	PYMH		7848	C3
-	PYMH		7849	C3
38th Pl NE				
-	COLH		7852	D1
E 38th St				
-	MINN		8024	D1
-	MINN		8025	C1
W 38th St				
-	MINN		8023	B1
-	MINN		8024	A1
-	STLP		8023	B1
38th St N				
-	ELMO		7858	E6
-	ODLE		7858	E6
38th St Ct N				
-	ODLE		7858	C6
38 1/2 Av N				
-	NWHE		7850	B3
39th Av N				
-	CRYS		7850	C3
-	MINN		7851	E3
-	MINN		7852	A3
-	NWHE		7850	A3
-	PYMH		7848	B2
-	PYMH		7849	C3
-	ROBB		7850	D3
-	ROBB		7851	C3
39th Av NE				
-	COLH		7852	C1
-	COLH		7853	A1
-	STAN		7853	B1
39th Av S				
-	MINN		7939	C6
-	MINN		8025	C2
39th Pl N				
-	PYMH		7848	A2
E 39th St				
-	MINN		8024	D2
-	MINN		8025	C2
W 39th St				
-	MINN		8023	C2
-	MINN		8024	A2
-	STLP		8022	E1
-	STLP		8023	B2
39th St N				
-	ELMO		7858	E5
-	ODLE		7858	E5
39 1/2 Av N				
-	NWHE		7850	B2
-	ROBB		7851	A3
39 1/2 Av NE				
-	COLH		7853	A1
40th Av				
-	ROBB		7851	A2
40th Av N				
-	CRYS		7850	C2
-	MINN		7851	C2
-	MINN		7852	A2
-	NWHE		7849	E2
-	NWHE		7850	B2
-	PYMH		7848	B2
-	PYMH		7849	C2
-	ROBB		7850	D2
-	ROBB		7851	C2
40th Av NE				
-	COLH		7852	D1
-	COLH		7853	A1
-	FRID		7852	C1
-	STAN		7853	B1
40th Av S				
-	MINN		7939	C7
-	MINN		8025	C1
W 40th Ln				
-	EDNA		8023	A2
-	STLP		8022	E2
-	STLP		8023	A2
40th Pl N				
-	PYMH		7848	A2
-	PYMH		7849	C2
E 40th St				
-	MINN		8024	C2
-	MINN		8025	C2
W 40th St				
-	EDNA		8023	A2
-	MINN		8023	C2
-	MINN		8024	A2
-	STLP		8022	E2
-	STLP		8023	A2
40th St N				
-	ELMO		7858	D5
-	ODLE		7858	D5
40 1/2 Av N				
-	NWHE		7849	E2
-	NWHE		7850	A2
-	ROBB		7850	E2
-	ROBB		7851	A3
40 1/2 Av NE				
-	COLH		7852	C1
-	FRID		7852	C1
40 1/2 St				
-	STLP		8022	D2
41st Av N				
-	CRYS		7850	C2
-	MINN		7851	E2
-	MINN		7852	A2
-	NWHE		7849	E2
-	NWHE		7850	B2
-	PYMH		7848	B2
-	PYMH		7849	D2
-	ROBB		7850	D2
-	ROBB		7851	A2
41st Av NE				
-	COLH		7766	E7
-	COLH		7767	A7
-	FRID		7766	C7
41st Av S				
-	MINN		7939	C7
-	MINN		8025	C3
41st Pl N				
-	CRYS		7850	C2
-	PYMH		7848	B2
E 41st St				
-	MINN		8024	C2
-	MINN		8025	C2
W 41st St				
-	EDNA		8023	A2
-	MINN		8023	B2
-	MINN		8024	A2
-	STLP		8022	E2
-	STLP		8023	A2
41st St N				
-	ODLE		7858	C5
41st St Ct N				
-	ODLE		7858	C5
41 1/2 Av N				
-	ROBB		7851	A2
42nd Av N				
-	CRYS		7850	D2
-	MINN		7851	B2
-	MINN		7852	A2
-	NWHE		7849	E2
-	NWHE		7850	A2
-	PYMH		7848	D2
-	PYMH		7849	A2
-	ROBB		7850	E2
-	ROBB		7851	A2
42nd Av NE				
-	COLH		7766	E7
-	COLH		7767	A7
-	FRID		7766	C7
42nd Av S				
-	MINN		7939	C7
-	MINN		8025	C3
42nd Ct N				
-	PYMH		7849	B2
42nd Pl N				
-	PYMH		7848	E2
-	PYMH		7849	B2
E 42nd St				
-	MINN		8024	D2
-	MINN		8025	C2
W 42nd St				
-	EDNA		8023	A2
-	MINN		8023	C2
-	MINN		8024	A2
-	STLP		8022	E2
-	STLP		8023	A2
42nd St N				
-	ELMO		7858	B3
-	ODLE		7858	A5
42nd St W				
-	STLP		8022	D3
42nd St Ct N				
-	ODLE		7858	B5
42 1/2 Av				
-	NWHE		7850	B2
42 1/2 Av N				
-	ROBB		7850	E2
-	ROBB		7851	A2
42 1/2 Av NE				
-	COLH		7766	E7
-	COLH		7767	A7
42 1/2 St W				
-	STLP		8023	A3
43rd Av N				
-	CRYS		7850	C2
-	MINN		7851	E2
-	NWHE		7850	B1
-	PYMH		7848	D1
-	PYMH		7849	B2
-	ROBB		7850	D2
-	ROBB		7851	A2
43rd Av NE				
-	COLH		7766	E7
-	COLH		7767	A7
-	FRID		7766	C7
43rd Av S				
-	MINN		7939	C6
-	MINN		8025	C2
43rd Pl N				
-	PYMH		7848	C2
E 43rd St				
-	MINN		8024	E3
-	MINN		8025	C3
W 43rd St				
-	MINN		8023	C3
-	MINN		8024	A3
43rd St N				
-	ODLE		7858	C5
43 1/2 Av NE				
-	COLH		7766	E7
43 1/2 St W				
-	STLP		8022	E3
-	STLP		8023	A3
44th Av N				
-	CRYS		7850	C1
-	MINN		7851	E1
-	MINN		7852	A1
-	NWHE		7850	B1
-	PYMH		7848	E1
-	PYMH		7849	B1
-	ROBB		7850	D1
-	ROBB		7851	B1
44th Av NE				
-	COLH		7766	B7
-	COLH		7767	A7
-	FRID		7766	B7
44th Av S				
-	MINN		7939	C7
-	MINN		8025	C2
44th Cir N				
-	NWHE		7849	E1
44th Pl N				
-	PYMH		7848	D1
-	PYMH		7849	B1
E 44th St				
-	MINN		8024	C3
-	MINN		8025	C3
W 44th St				
-	EDNA		8022	E3
-	EDNA		8023	A3
-	MINN		8023	B3
-	MINN		8024	A3
-	STLP		8022	E3
-	STLP		8023	A3
44th St N				
-	ELMO		7858	D5
-	ODLE		7858	A5
44th St Ct N				
-	ODLE		7858	D5
44 1/2 Av N				
-	ROBB		7850	E1
44 1/2 Av NE				
-	COLH		7766	E7
E 45th Av				
-	MINN		8025	C5
45th Av N				
-	CRYS		7850	D1
-	MINN		7851	E1
-	MINN		7852	A1
-	NWHE		7849	E1
-	NWHE		7850	A1
-	PYMH		7848	D1
-	PYMH		7849	A1
-	ROBB		7850	E1
-	ROBB		7851	A1
45th Av NE				
-	COLH		7766	D6
-	COLH		7767	A6
-	FRID		7766	C6
-	HLTP		7766	D6
-	NBRI		7767	B6
-	STAN		7767	B6
45th Av S				
-	MINN		7939	C6
-	MINN		8025	C2
45th Pl N				
-	CRYS		7850	C1
-	PYMH		7848	C1
-	PYMH		7849	A1
E 45th St				
-	MINN		8024	B3
-	MINN		8025	C3
W 45th St				
-	EDNA		8023	B3
-	MINN		8023	B3
-	MINN		8024	A3
45th St N				
-	ODLE		7858	A4
45th St W				
-	EDNA		8023	A3
45 1/2 Av N				
-	CRYS		7850	E1
-	NWHE		7850	B1
-	ROBB		7850	E1
45 1/2 Av NE				
-	COLH		7766	E6
46th Av N				
-	CRYS		7850	C1
-	MINN		7851	E1
-	MINN		7852	A1
-	NWHE		7849	E1
-	NWHE		7850	A1
-	PYMH		7848	E1
-	PYMH		7849	A1
-	ROBB		7850	E1
-	ROBB		7851	B1
46th Av NE				
-	COLH		7766	C6
-	COLH		7767	A6
-	FRID		7766	C6
-	HLTP		7766	E6
46th Av S				
-	HnpC		8025	D7
-	MINN		7939	D7
-	MINN		8025	D6
46th Cir N				
-	ODLE		7858	C4
46th Ct E				
-	IVGH		8114	D2
46th Pl N				
-	CRYS		7850	C1
-	PYMH		7848	C1
-	PYMH		7849	C1
E 46th St				
-	MINN		8024	E3
-	MINN		8025	C3
-	STPL		8025	D4
W 46th St				
-	EDNA		8023	B3
-	MINN		8023	B3
-	MINN		8024	A3
46th St E				
-	IVGH		8114	B1
-	MINN		8024	E3
46th St N				
-	ODLE		7858	A4
46th St Ct N				
-	ODLE		7858	C4
46th St Wy N				
-	ODLE		7858	C4
46 1/2 Av N				
-	NWHE		7850	A1
-	ROBB		7851	B1
46 1/2 Av NE				
-	COLH		7766	D6
-	HLTP		7766	D6
47th Av N				
-	BRKC		7851	B1
-	CRYS		7850	C1
-	MINN		7851	C1
-	MINN		7852	A1
-	NWHE		7849	E1
-	NWHE		7850	A1
-	PYMH		7848	B1
-	PYMH		7849	A1
-	ROBB		7850	E1
-	ROBB		7851	C1
47th Av NE				
-	COLH		7766	D6
-	COLH		7767	A6
-	FRID		7766	C6
-	HLTP		7766	E6
47th Av S				
-	HnpC		8025	D5
-	MINN		7939	D7
-	MINN		8025	D1
47th Cir N				
-	ODLE		7858	C4
47th Pl N				
-	ODLE		7858	C4
-	PYMH		7849	C1
E 47th St				
-	MINN		8024	D4
-	MINN		8025	B4
W 47th St				
-	EDNA		8023	B4
-	MINN		8023	C4
-	MINN		8024	A4
-	MNTK		8021	B4
47th St E				
-	IVGH		8114	B2
-	SSTP		8114	E2
47th St N				
-	NSTP		7857	E4
-	ODLE		7857	E4
-	ODLE		7858	A4
47 1/2 Av N				
-	NWHE		7849	E1
-	NWHE		7850	A1
47 1/2 Av NE				
-	COLH		7766	D6
-	HLTP		7766	D6
47 1/2 Cir N				
-	NWHE		7850	B1
47 1/2 Pl N				
-	NWHE		7850	B1
N 48th Av				
-	MINN		7765	E7
-	MINN		7766	A7
48th Av N				
-	BRKC		7765	B7
-	BRKC		7851	B1
-	CRYS		7850	B1
-	NWHE		7763	E7
-	NWHE		7764	A7
-	NWHE		7849	E1
-	NWHE		7850	B1
-	PYMH		7762	B7
-	PYMH		7763	A7
-	PYMH		7848	B1
-	PYMH		7849	C1
48th Av NE				
-	COLH		7766	C6
-	FRID		7766	C6
-	HLTP		7766	D6
48th Av S				
-	HnpC		8025	D5
-	MINN		7939	D7
-	MINN		8025	D1
48th Cir N				
-	NWHE		7764	B7
-	PYMH		7849	A1
48th Pl N				
-	PYMH		7762	C7
-	PYMH		7763	B7
E 48th St				
-	MINN		8024	B4
W 48th St				
-	EDNA		8022	D4
-	EDNA		8023	A4
-	MINN		8023	B4
-	MINN		8024	A4
48th St N				
-	NSTP		7857	E4
-	ODLE		7857	E4
-	ODLE		7858	A4
48th St Pl N				
-	ODLE		7858	B4
49th Av N				
-	BRKC		7765	C7
-	CRYS		7764	E7
-	MINN		7765	E7
-	MINN		7766	A7
-	NWHE		7763	E7
-	NWHE		7764	B7
-	PYMH		7762	B7
-	PYMH		7763	B7
49th Av NE				
-	COLH		7766	D5
-	COLH		7767	A6
-	FRID		7766	C5
-	HLTP		7766	D5
49th Av NE CO-104				
-	FRID		7766	C5
49th Pl N				
-	PYMH		7762	A7
-	PYMH		7763	B7
E 49th St				
-	MINN		8024	C4
-	MINN		8025	B4
W 49th St				
-	EDNA		8022	D4
-	EDNA		8023	B4
-	MINN		8023	B4
-	MINN		8024	A4
49th St E				
-	IVGH		8114	D2
-	SSTP		8114	E2
49th St N				
-	ODLE		7858	A3
49th Wy E				
-	IVGH		8114	C2
49th St Ct N				
-	ODLE		7858	B3
49 1/2 N				
-	MINN		7766	A7
49 1/2 Av NE				
-	COLH		7766	D5
W 49 1/2 St				
-	EDNA		8023	A4
-	MINN		8023	B4
50th Av N				
-	BRKC		7765	A7
-	CRYS		7764	C7
-	MINN		7765	D7
-	MINN		7766	A7
-	NWHE		7763	E7
-	NWHE		7764	A7
-	PYMH		7762	B7
-	PYMH		7763	B7
50th Av NE				
-	COLH		7766	D5
-	FRID		7766	C5
50th Ct N				
-	PYMH		7763	C7
50th Pl N				
-	PYMH		7762	B7
-	PYMH		7763	B7
E 50th St				
-	MINN		8024	B4
-	MINN		8025	C4
W 50th St				
-	EDNA		8022	E5
-	EDNA		8023	A4
-	MINN		8023	B4
-	MINN		8024	A4
50th St E				
-	IVGH		8114	B2
-	MINN		8024	C5
-	MINN		8025	A4
-	SSTP		8114	D2
50th St N				
-	ELMO		7858	C3
-	ODLE		7858	C3
50th St N CO-13B				
-	ELMO		7858	D3
-	ODLE		7858	D3
50 1/2 Av NE				
-	COLH		7766	D5
51st Av N				
-	BRKC		7765	B7
-	CRYS		7764	E7
-	MINN		7765	E7
-	MINN		7766	A7
-	NWHE		7763	E7
-	NWHE		7764	A7
-	PYMH		7762	D7
-	PYMH		7763	B7
51st Av NE				
-	COLH		7766	D5
-	FRID		7766	C5
51st Ct NE				
-	COLH		7766	E5
51st Pl N				
-	CRYS		7764	D7
-	PYMH		7762	B6
-	PYMH		7763	D7
E 51st St				
-	MINN		8024	B5
-	MINN		8025	B5
W 51st St				
-	EDNA		8022	D4
-	EDNA		8023	A5
-	MINN		8023	B5
-	MINN		8024	A5
51st St E				
-	IVGH		8114	D2
-	SSTP		8114	D2
51st St N				
-	ODLE		7858	A3
51st Wy NE				
-	FRID		7766	B5
52nd Av N				
-	BRKC		7765	A7
-	CRYS		7764	C7
-	MINN		7765	C7
-	MINN		7766	A6
-	NWHE		7763	E7
-	NWHE		7764	B7
-	PYMH		7762	D7
-	PYMH		7763	C7
52nd Av NE				
-	COLH		7766	C5
-	FRID		7766	E5
E 52nd St				
-	MINN		8024	C5
-	MINN		8025	C5
W 52nd St				
-	EDNA		8022	D5
-	EDNA		8023	B5
-	MINN		8023	C5
-	MINN		8024	A5
52nd St E				
-	IVGH		8114	D3
-	SSTP		8114	D3
52nd St N				
-	NSTP		7857	E3
-	ODLE		7857	E3
-	ODLE		7858	A3
52nd St W				
-	EDNA		8023	A5
52nd Wy NE				
-	FRID		7766	B5
53rd Av N				
-	BRKC		7765	B6
-	BRKC		7766	A6
-	CRYS		7764	E6
-	MINN		7765	E6
-	MINN		7766	A6
-	NWHE		7764	C6
-	PYMH		7762	D6
-	PYMH		7763	B7
53rd Av NE				
-	COLH		7766	C4
-	FRID		7766	D4
-	FRID		7767	A4
53rd Pl N				
-	BRKC		7765	B6

Minneapolis Street Index

STREET Block · City · ZIP · Map # · Grid

E 53rd St
- MINN 8024 C5
- MINN 8025 A5
W 53rd St
- EDNA 8022 D5
- EDNA 8023 B5
- MINN 8023 D5
- MINN 8024 A5
53rd St E
- IVGH 8114 C3
53rd St N
- ELMO 7858 D3
- ODLE 7858 A3
53rd St W
- EDNA 8023 A5
- MINN 8024 A5
53rd Wy NE
- FRID 7766 B4
53 1/2 Av NE
- FRID 7766 D4
54th Av N
- BRKC 7765 B6
- CRYS 7764 C6
- NWHE 7764 A6
- PYMH 7762 D6
- PYMH 7763 C6
54th Av NE
- FRID 7766 C4
54th Pl N
- PYMH 7763 D6
54th St
- IVGH 8114 A3
E 54th St
- HnpC 8025 D5
- MINN 8024 D5
- MINN 8025 A5
W 54th St
- EDNA 8023 A5
- MINN 8023 E5
- MINN 8024 A5
54th St N
- NSTP 7857 E3
- ODLE 7857 E3
- ODLE 7858 A3
55th Av N
- BRKC 7765 B6
- BRKC 7766 A6
- CRYS 7764 C6
- NWHE 7764 B6
- PYMH 7762 E6
- PYMH 7763 A6
55th Av NE
- FRID 7766 C4
55th Pl N
- PYMH 7762 E6
- PYMH 7763 A6
E 55th St
- HnpC 8025 D6
- MINN 8024 C6
- MINN 8025 A6
W 55th St
- EDNA 8023 B6
- MINN 8023 D6
- MINN 8024 A6
55th St E
- IVGH 8114 B3
55th St N
- ODLE 7858 A2
- PNSP 7858 B2
55th St W
- EDNA 8023 A6
- IVGH 8114 A4
- SUNL 8114 A4
55th St Ct E
- IVGH 8114 B3
56th Av N
- BRKC 7765 B5
- BRKC 7766 A6
- CRYS 7765 A6
- NWHE 7764 A6
- PYMH 7762 E6
- PYMH 7763 C6
56th Av NE
- FRID 7766 C4
56th Pl N
- CRYS 7764 E6
E 56th St
- HnpC 8025 D6
- MINN 8024 E6
- MINN 8025 C6
W 56th St
- EDNA 8022 D6
- EDNA 8023 C6
- MINN 8023 E6
- MINN 8024 A6
56th St E
- IVGH 8114 A3
56th St N
- MPLW 7857 E2
- ODLE 7857 E2
- ODLE 7858 A2
56th St W
- EDNA 8022 E6
- EDNA 8023 A6
57th Av N
- BRKC 7765 E5
- BRKC 7766 A5
- CRYS 7764 D5
- CRYS 7765 A6
- PYMH 7762 D5
- PYMH 7763 B5
57th Av NE
- FRID 7766 C3
57th Pl N
- PYMH 7762 D5
- PYMH 7763 C5
57th Pl NE
- FRID 7766 C3
E 57th St
- HnpC 8025 D6
- MINN 8024 D6
- MINN 8025 C6
W 57th St
- EDNA 8022 D6
- EDNA 8023 B6
- MINN 8023 C6
- MINN 8024 A6
57 1/2 Av NE
- FRID 7766 C3
58th Av N
- BRKC 7765 D5
- BRKC 7766 A5
- CRYS 7764 B5
- CRYS 7765 A5
- NWHE 7764 A5
- PYMH 7762 D5
- PYMH 7763 A5
58th Av N CO-10
- BRKC 7765 A5
- CRYS 7765 A5
58th Av NE
- FRID 7766 D3
58th Ct E
- IVGH 8114 B4
58th Pl N
- BRKC 7765 A5
- CRYS 7764 B5
- CRYS 7765 A5
E 58th St
- HnpC 8025 D6
- MINN 8024 C6
- MINN 8025 C6
W 58th St
- EDNA 8022 E6
- EDNA 8023 C6
- MINN 8023 C6
- MINN 8024 A6
58th St E
- IVGH 8114 B4
58 1/2 Av N
- BRKC 7765 B5
58 1/2 Av NE
- FRID 7766 D3
59th Av N
- BRKC 7765 E5
- BRKC 7766 A5
- CRYS 7764 B5
- CRYS 7765 A5
- NWHE 7763 E5
- NWHE 7764 B5
- PYMH 7763 A5
59th Av NE
- FRID 7766 C3
59th Ct E
- IVGH 8114 B4
59th Pl N
- CRYS 7764 B5
- PYMH 7762 E5
E 59th St
- MINN 8024 C7
- MINN 8025 A7
W 59th St
- EDNA 8022 E7
- EDNA 8023 A7
- MINN 8023 C7
- MINN 8024 A7
59th St E
- HnpC 8025 C7
- IVGH 8115 B4
- MINN 8025 C7
59th St N
- ELMO 7858 D2
59th St W
- EDNA 8023 A7
59 1/2 Av N
- BRKC 7765 A5
- CRYS 7764 B5
- NWHE 7764 B5
E 59 1/2 St
- MINN 8025 A7
W 59 1/2 St
- MINN 8024 A7
60th Av N
- BRKC 7765 B5
- BRKC 7766 A4
- CRYS 7764 C5
- NWHE 7763 E5
- NWHE 7764 A5
- PYMH 7762 D5
- PYMH 7763 B5
60th Av NE
- FRID 7766 C3
- FRID 7767 A3
60th Ct E
- IVGH 8114 D5
60th Pl N
- PYMH 7762 E5
- PYMH 7763 A5
E 60th St
- MINN 8024 C7
W 60th St
- EDNA 8022 D7
- EDNA 8023 B7
- MINN 8023 D7
- MINN 8024 A7
60th St E
- IVGH 8114 B4
- IVGH 8115 B4
- SSTP 8115 A4
60th St N
- ELMO 7858 E1
- GRNT 7858 E1
- MAHT 7858 B1
- PNSP 7858 D1
60th St N SR-36
- ELMO 7858 D1
- GRNT 7858 D1
- PNSP 7858 D1
60th St W
- IVGH 8113 E4
- SUNL 8113 E4
60 1/2 Av N
- NWHE 7763 E5
- NWHE 7764 A5
61st Av N
- BRKC 7764 E4
- BRKC 7765 A4
- BRKC 7766 A4
- CRYS 7764 C4
- NWHE 7763 E4
- NWHE 7764 A4
- PYMH 7762 D4
- PYMH 7763 B4
61st Av NE
- FRID 7766 C2
- FRID 7767 A2
- NBRI 7767 B2
E 61st St
- MINN 8024 C7
W 61st St
- EDNA 8022 B7
- EDNA 8023 B7
- MINN 8023 C7
- MINN 8024 A7
- RHFD 8023 E7
61st St E
- IVGH 8115 A5
- SSTP 8115 A5
61st St S
- CTGV 8116 D4
61st St W
- EDNA 8023 B7
61st Wy NE
- FRID 7766 B2
61st Av Cir N
- NWHE 7763 E4
61 1/2 Av N
- NWHE 7763 E4
- NWHE 7764 A4
61 1/2 Wy NE
- FRID 7766 B2
62nd Av N
- BRKC 7764 E4
- BRKC 7765 B4
- BRKC 7766 A4
- BRKP 7763 E4
- BRKP 7764 C4
- CRYS 7764 C4
- MAPG 7762 B4
- MAPG 7763 A4
- NWHE 7763 E4
- NWHE 7764 A4
- PYMH 7762 B4
- PYMH 7763 D4
62nd Ct N
- BRKP 7764 B4
62nd Pl N
- MAPG 7762 D4
- MAPG 7763 A4
62nd St
- LINO 7683 C2
E 62nd St
- HnpC 8025 A7
- MINN 8024 D7
- MINN 8025 A7
- RHFD 8024 B7
W 62nd St
- EDNA 8022 D7
- EDNA 8023 A7
- EDNP 8020 A7
- EDNP 8021 C7
- MINN 8023 E7
- MINN 8024 A7
- MNTK 8020 A7
- MNTK 8021 C7
- RHFD 8023 D7
- RHFD 8024 A7
- RHFD 8110 A1
W 62nd St CO-62
- EDNP 8020 A7
- MNTK 8020 A7
62nd St E
- IVGH 8114 C5
62nd St N
- PNSP 7858 C1
62nd St S
- CTGV 8116 D5
62nd St W
- MINN 8023 D7
62nd Wy NE
- FRID 7766 B2
62 1/2 Av N
- BRKP 7764 B4
62 1/2 Wy NE
- FRID 7766 B2
63rd Av N
- BRKC 7764 E4
- BRKC 7765 B4
- BRKP 7763 E4
- BRKP 7764 C4
- MAPG 7762 D4
- MAPG 7763 A4
63rd Av NE
- FRID 7766 D2
63rd Ct E
- IVGH 8114 E5
63rd Ln N
- BRKC 7765 E4
63rd Pl N
- MAPG 7762 D4
- MAPG 7763 A4
E 63rd St
- HnpC 8025 B7
- HnpC 8110 E1
- HnpC 8111 B1
- MINN 8025 B7
- RHFD 8110 E1
W 63rd St
- EDNA 8108 E1
- RHFD 8109 E1
- RHFD 8110 A1
63rd St E
- IVGH 8114 B5
- IVGH 8115 A5
63rd St S
- CTGV 8116 C5
63rd Wy NE
- FRID 7766 B2
63rd St Cir S
- CTGV 8116 D5
63 1/2 Wy NE
- FRID 7766 B2
64th Av N
- BRKC 7764 E3
- BRKC 7765 A4
- BRKP 7764 A4
- MAPG 7762 D3
- MAPG 7763 D4
64th Av NE
- FRID 7766 E2
- FRID 7767 A2
64th Cir N
- MAPG 7763 D3
64th Ct E
- IVGH 8114 E5
64th Pl N
- MAPG 7762 C3
64th St
- LINO 7684 E1
E 64th St
- RHFD 8110 D1
W 64th St
- EDNA 8108 E1
- EDNA 8109 B1
- RHFD 8109 C1
- RHFD 8110 A1
64th St E
- IVGH 8114 D5
- IVGH 8115 A5
64th St N
- PNSP 7772 D7
64th St S
- LINO 7684 E1
64th St W
- EDNA 8108 D1
64th Wy NE
- FRID 7766 B2
W 64 1/2 St
- RHFD 8110 A1
64 1/2 Wy NE
- FRID 7766 B2
65th Av N
- BRKC 7764 E3
- BRKC 7765 A3
- BRKC 7766 A3
- BRKP 7764 B3
- MAPG 7763 D3
65th Pl N
- MAPG 7762 C3
- MAPG 7763 B3
65th St
- HUGO 7685 B1
- LINO 7685 B1
E 65th St
- RHFD 8110 D1
W 65th St
- EDNA 8108 E1
- EDNA 8109 B1
- RHFD 8109 C1
- RHFD 8110 A1
65th St E
- IVGH 8114 E5
- IVGH 8115 A5
65th St S
- CTGV 8116 B5
- NWPT 8116 A5
65th St W
- EDNA 8108 D1
W 65 1/2 St
- RHFD 8109 C1
65 1/2 Wy NE
- FRID 7766 B1
66th Av N
- BRKC 7764 E3
- BRKC 7765 B3
- BRKC 7766 A3
- BRKP 7763 E3
- BRKP 7764 C3
- MAPG 7762 A3
- MAPG 7763 B3
66th Av NE
- FRID 7766 E1
- FRID 7767 A1
- NBRI 7767 B1
66th Cir N
- BRKP 7763 E3
66th Pl N
- BRKP 7763 E3
- MAPG 7762 C3
- MAPG 7763 A3
E 66th St
- HnpC 8110 E1
- RHFD 8110 D1
W 66th St
- EDNA 8108 E1
- EDNA 8109 A1
- RHFD 8109 D1
- RHFD 8110 A1
66th St E
- IVGH 8115 B5
66th St N
- PNSP 7772 D7
66th St S
- CTGV 8116 D5
66th Wy NE
- FRID 7766 B1
66th St Ct S
- CTGV 8116 E5
66 1/2 Av NE
- FRID 7767 A1
- NBRI 7767 B1
66 1/2 Wy NE
- FRID 7766 B1
67th Av N
- BRKC 7764 E3
- BRKC 7765 E3
- BRKC 7766 A3
- BRKP 7763 E3
- BRKP 7764 E3
- MAPG 7762 D3
- MAPG 7763 D3
67th Av NE
- FRID 7766 E1
67th Ct E
- IVGH 8114 D6
67th Ln N
- BRKC 7765 E2
67th Pl N
- MAPG 7762 B3
- MAPG 7763 B3
E 67th St
- RHFD 8110 B2
W 67th St
- EDNA 8109 C2
- RHFD 8109 C2
- RHFD 8110 A2
67th St E
- IVGH 8114 C6
- IVGH 8115 A6
67th St S
- CTGV 8116 E5
67th Wy N
- BRKP 7764 D3
67th Wy NE
- FRID 7766 B1
67th St Ct S
- CTGV 8116 D6
67 1/2 Av N
- BRKP 7764 D3
68th Av N
- BRKC 7764 E2
- BRKC 7765 B2
- BRKP 7764 B2
- MAPG 7762 E2
68th Av NE
- FRID 7766 E1
- FRID 7767 A1
- NBRI 7767 A1
68th Ct E
- IVGH 8114 E6
68th Ln N
- BRKC 7765 E2
68th Pl N
- MAPG 7762 C2
68th Pl NE
- FRID 7766 E1
E 68th St
- RHFD 8110 D2
W 68th St
- EDNA 8108 C2
- EDNA 8109 A2
- RHFD 8109 D2
- RHFD 8110 A2
68th St E
- IVGH 8114 C6
- IVGH 8115 B6
68th St S
- CTGV 8116 E6
68th St W
- IVGH 8113 D6
68th Wy N
- BRKP 7764 D2
68th St Ct S
- CTGV 8116 D6
69th Av N
- BRKC 7764 D2
- BRKC 7765 D2
- BRKC 7766 A2
- BRKP 7764 B2
- MAPG 7762 D2
- MAPG 7763 A2
69th Av NE
- FRID 7680 C7
- FRID 7681 A7
- MNDS 7681 A7
- NBRI 7681 A7
69th Ln N
- BRKC 7765 C3
69th Pl N
- MAPG 7762 A2
- MAPG 7763 C2
69th Pl NE
- FRID 7680 C7
- FRID 7766 C1
E 69th St
- HnpC 8110 E2
- RHFD 8110 B2
W 69th St
- EDNA 8108 E2
- EDNA 8109 B2
- EDNP 8107 D2
- RHFD 8109 D2
- RHFD 8110 A2
69th St E
- IVGH 8114 E6
- IVGH 8115 A6
- SSTP 8115 A6
69th St N
- GRNT 7772 D7
- MAHT 7772 D7
69th St S
- CTGV 8116 E6
69th St W
- IVGH 8113 D6
69th Wy NE
- FRID 7680 C7
69th St Ct S
- CTGV 8116 D6
70th Av N
- BRKC 7764 E2
- BRKC 7765 D2
- BRKC 7766 A2
- BRKP 7763 E2
- BRKP 7764 D2
- MAPG 7762 A2
- MAPG 7763 A2
70th Cir N
- BRKC 7764 E2
70th Ct E
- IVGH 8114 E6
70th Ct N
- MAHT 7772 D7
70th Pl N
- MAPG 7762 A2
- MAPG 7763 B2
E 70th St
- HnpC 8111 B2
- RHFD 8110 D2
W 70th St
- EDNA 8108 C2
- EDNA 8109 A2
- EDNP 8107 D2
- RHFD 8109 C2
- RHFD 8110 A2
70th St E
- IVGH 8114 A6
- IVGH 8115 A6
- LINO 7599 A5
70th St N
- MAHT 7772 D7
70th St S
- CTGV 8116 A6
- SPLP 8115 E6
- SPLP 8116 A6
70th St S CO-22
- CTGV 8116 A6
- SPLP 8115 E6
- SPLP 8116 A6
70th St W
- EAGN 8113 D6
- IVGH 8113 E6
- SHKP 8193 B7
- SHKP 8279 B1
70th Wy NE
- FRID 7680 B7
W 70 1/2 St
- EDNA 8109 C2
- RHFD 8109 C2
71st Av N
- BRKC 7764 E2
- BRKC 7765 A2
- BRKP 7764 B2
- MAPG 7762 B2
- MAPG 7763 C2
71st Av NE
- FRID 7680 C7
71st Cir N
- BRKC 7764 E2
71st Ct E
- IVGH 8115 A6
71st Ct S
- CTGV 8116 E6
71st Pl N
- MAPG 7762 B2
- MAPG 7763 B2
E 71st St
- RHFD 8110 D3
W 71st St
- EDNA 8109 C3
- RHFD 8109 C3
- RHFD 8110 A3
71st St E
- IVGH 8114 E6
- IVGH 8115 A6
71st St N
- MAHT 7772 D6
71st St S
- CTGV 8116 C6
71st Wy NE
- FRID 7680 B7
W 71 1/2 St
- EDNA 8109 C3
- RHFD 8109 C3
71 1/2 Wy NE
- FRID 7680 B7
72nd Av N
- BRKC 7765 A2
- BRKC 7766 A2
- BRKP 7764 D1
- MAPG 7762 B1
- MAPG 7763 C1
72nd Av NE
- FRID 7680 E7
- FRID 7681 A7
72nd Cir N
- BRKC 7764 E2
72nd Cir W
- IVGH 8114 A7
72nd Ct
- MAHT 7772 D6
72nd Ct E
- IVGH 8114 C7
72nd Ln N
- BRKP 7764 D1
72nd Pl N
- MAPG 7762 A1
72nd St
- CTRV 7598 D4
E 72nd St
- HnpC 8110 E3
- HnpC 8111 B3
- RHFD 8110 D3
W 72nd St
- EDNA 8108 D3
- EDNA 8109 B3
- RHFD 8109 C3
- RHFD 8110 A3
72nd St E
- IVGH 8114 D7
- IVGH 8115 A7
72nd St N
- MAHT 7772 C6
- WILL 7772 C6
72nd St S
- CTGV 8116 E7
72nd St Ct S
- CTGV 8116 D7
72 1/2 St
- CTRV 7598 E4
W 72 1/2 St
- RHFD 8109 D3
73rd Av N
- BRKC 7765 D1
- BRKC 7766 A1
- BRKP 7763 E1
- BRKP 7764 E1
- BRKP 7765 A1
- BRKP 7766 A1
- MAPG 7762 B1
- MAPG 7763 A1
73rd Av NE
- FRID 7680 D6
- FRID 7681 A7
- MNDS 7681 B6
73rd Cir N
- MAPG 7762 B1
73rd Ct E
- IVGH 8114 C7
- IVGH 8115 A7
73rd Ct N
- BRKP 7765 D1
73rd Ln N
- BRKP 7765 B1
73rd Pl N
- MAPG 7762 A1
- MAPG 7763 A1
73rd St
- CTRV 7598 D4
- LINO 7598 E4
E 73rd St
- HnpC 8110 E3
- HnpC 8111 B3
- RHFD 8110 C3
W 73rd St
- EDNA 8108 D3
- RHFD 8109 D3
- RHFD 8110 A3
73rd St E
- IVGH 8114 D7
- IVGH 8115 A7
73rd St S
- CTGV 8116 C6
73rd Wy NE
- BRKP 7765 E1
- BRKP 7766 A1
73 1/2 Av NE
- FRID 7680 E6
- FRID 7681 A6

INDEX 52

W 73 1/2 St

Minneapolis Street Index

92nd Cir N

STREET Block	City	ZIP	Map #	Grid
W 73 1/2 St				
-	RHFD		8110	A3
74th Av N				
-	BRKP		7763	E1
-	BRKP		7764	D1
-	BRKP		7765	B1
-	BRKP		7766	A1
-	MAPG		7762	C1
-	MAPG		7763	A1
74th Av NE				
-	FRID		7680	C6
74th Cir N				
-	BRKP		7765	B1
74th Ct E				
-	IVGH		8114	D7
74th Ct N				
-	BRKP		7765	D1
74th Pl N				
-	MAPG		7762	D1
74th St				
-	LINO		7596	E3
-	LINO		7597	A3
E 74th St				
-	HnpC		8110	E3
-	RHFD		8110	C3
W 74th St				
-	EDNA		8108	D3
-	EDNA		8109	C3
-	RHFD		8109	C3
-	RHFD		8110	A3
74th St E				
-	IVGH		8114	D7
-	IVGH		8115	B7
74th St S				
-	CTGV		8116	B7
74th St W				
-	EDNA		8107	D3
-	EDNP		8107	D3
74th Wy N				
-	BRKP		7764	B1
-	BRKP		7766	A1
74th St Ct S				
-	CTGV		8116	C7
74th St Bay S				
-	CTGV		8116	B6
74 1/2 Av N				
-	BRKP		7764	C1
-	BRKP		7765	E1
75th Av N				
-	BRKP		7679	B7
-	BRKP		7763	E1
-	BRKP		7764	B1
-	BRKP		7765	C1
-	BRKP		7766	A1
-	MAPG		7762	D1
75th Av NE				
-	FRID		7680	C6
-	FRID		7681	A6
-	MNDS		7681	B6
75th Cir N				
-	BRKP		7764	B1
75th Ct E				
-	IVGH		8114	E7
75th Ct N				
-	BRKP		7679	B7
-	BRKP		7765	B1
75th Pl N				
-	MAPG		7762	D1
E 75th St				
-	HnpC		8110	E4
-	RHFD		8110	C4
W 75th St				
-	EDNA		8109	C4
-	RHFD		8109	E4
-	RHFD		8110	A4
75th St E				
-	IVGH		8114	C7
-	IVGH		8115	A7
75th St N				
-	GRNT		7772	E5
-	MAHT		7772	E5
75th St S				
-	CTGV		8116	E7
75th Wy NE				
-	FRID		7680	B6
75 1/2 Av N				
-	BRKP		7764	C1
76th Av N				
-	BRKP		7678	E7
-	BRKP		7679	A7
-	BRKP		7680	A7
-	BRKP		7764	C1
-	BRKP		7765	D1
-	BRKP		7766	A1
-	MAPG		7676	D7
76th Av NE				
-	FRID		7680	C6
-	FRID		7681	A6
76th Ct N				
-	BRKP		7679	D7
-	BRKP		7765	D1
76th Pl N				
-	BRKP		7678	E7
-	MAPG		7676	A7
E 76th St				
-	HnpC		8110	E4
-	RHFD		8110	C4
W 76th St				
-	EDNA		8108	D4
-	EDNA		8109	B4
-	RHFD		8109	D4
-	RHFD		8110	A4
76th St E				
-	IVGH		8114	D7
76th St S				
-	CTGV		8116	D7
76th St W				
-	EDNA		8107	D4
-	EDNP		8107	D4
76th Wy E				
-	IVGH		8115	B7
76th Wy NE				
-	FRID		7680	B6
77th Av N				
-	BRKP		7678	E7
-	BRKP		7679	B7
-	MAPG		7676	D7
77th Av W				
-	LINO		7597	C2
77th Blvd N				
-	BRKP		7679	C7
77th Cir N				
-	MAPG		7676	A7
77th Ct				
-	CTGV		8116	E7
-	CTGV		8202	E1
77th Pl N				
-	MAPG		7676	B7
77th St				
-	LINO		7597	D2
E 77th St				
-	HnpC		8110	E4
-	HnpC		8111	A4
-	RHFD		8110	C4
W 77th St				
-	BMTN		8109	A4
-	EDNA		8108	E4
-	EDNA		8109	A4
-	RHFD		8109	E4
-	RHFD		8110	A4
77th St E				
-	IVGH		8114	C7
-	IVGH		8201	A1
-	LINO		7598	D2
77th St S				
-	CTGV		8116	E7
-	CTGV		8202	D1
-	SPLP		8202	A1
77th St W				
-	EAGN		8199	C1
-	IVGH		8199	C1
-	LINO		7597	C2
77th Wy N				
-	BRKP		7679	E7
77th Wy NE				
-	FRID		7680	B5
77th St Ct S				
-	CTGV		8202	D1
77th St Bay S				
-	CTGV		8202	D1
78th Av N				
-	BRKP		7678	D7
-	BRKP		7679	C7
-	BRKP		7680	A7
-	MAPG		7676	A7
78th Av NE				
-	FRID		7680	B5
-	SPLP		7680	D5
78th Cir NE				
-	SPLP		7681	A5
78th Ct E				
-	IVGH		8200	C1
78th Ct N				
-	BRKP		7678	B7
-	BRKP		7679	C7
78th Ln N				
-	BRKP		7678	E7
-	BRKP		7679	A7
78th Pl N				
-	MAPG		7676	A7
E 78th St				
-	BMTN		8110	B4
-	BMTN		8111	A4
-	HnpC		8110	D4
-	RHFD		8110	C4
W 78th St				
-	BMTN		8107	E5
-	BMTN		8108	C4
-	BMTN		8109	A5
-	BMTN		8110	A4
-	EDNA		8107	E4
-	EDNA		8108	A5
-	EDNA		8109	C4
-	EDNP		8106	A4
-	EDNP		8107	A4
-	RHFD		8109	D4
-	RHFD		8110	A4
W 78th St SR-5				
-	EDNP		8106	E5
-	EDNP		8107	A4
78th St E				
-	IVGH		8200	C1
-	IVGH		8201	A1
78th St S				
-	CTGV		8202	D1
W 78th St Cir				
-	BMTN		8109	A5
78th St Ct S				
-	CTGV		8202	E1
79th Av N				
-	BRKP		7678	B7
-	BRKP		7679	C7
-	BRKP		7680	A7
-	MAPG		7676	D7
79th Av NE				
-	FRID		7680	D5
-	MNDS		7681	B5
-	SPLP		7680	D5
-	SPLP		7681	B5
79th Ct E				
-	IVGH		8200	D1
79th Ct N				
-	BRKP		7679	C7
79th Ln N				
-	BRKP		7679	A6
79th Pl N				
-	MAPG		7676	A7
79th St				
-	LINO		7597	C1
E 79th St				
-	BMTN		8111	A5
W 79th St				
-	BMTN		8109	C5
79th St E				
-	IVGH		8200	D1
-	IVGH		8201	A1
79th St S				
-	CTGV		8202	C1
79th Wy NE				
-	FRID		7680	B5
E 79 1/2 St				
-	BMTN		8110	B5
80th Av N				
-	BRKP		7678	E7
-	BRKP		7679	A6
-	MAPG		7676	B6
80th Av NE				
-	SPLP		7680	D5
-	SPLP		7681	A5
80th Cir N				
-	BRKP		7679	C6
-	MAPG		7676	E6
80th Ct E				
-	IVGH		8201	A1
80th Ct N				
-	BRKP		7679	E7
80th Pl N				
-	MAPG		7676	C6
E 80th St				
-	BMTN		8110	C5
W 80th St				
-	BMTN		8108	E5
-	BMTN		8109	E5
-	BMTN		8110	A5
80th St E				
-	BMTN		8110	D5
-	IVGH		8200	D1
-	IVGH		8201	B1
80th St N				
-	GRNT		7772	E4
-	MAHT		7772	E4
80th St S				
-	CTGV		8202	D1
W 80th St Cir				
-	BMTN		8109	A5
80 1/2 St W				
-	BMTN		8109	E5
81st Av N				
-	BRKP		7677	D6
-	BRKP		7678	A6
-	BRKP		7679	B6
-	BRKP		7680	A6
-	MAPG		7676	A6
-	MAPG		7677	D6
81st Av NE				
-	FRID		7680	B4
-	SPLP		7680	D4
-	SPLP		7681	A5
81st Cir N				
-	BRKP		7679	C6
81st Ln N				
-	BRKP		7678	E6
-	BRKP		7679	A6
81st Pl N				
-	BRKP		7678	C6
-	MAPG		7676	A6
-	MAPG		7677	A6
E 81st St				
-	BMTN		8110	C5
-	BMTN		8111	A5
W 81st St				
-	BMTN		8108	E5
-	BMTN		8109	D5
-	BMTN		8110	A5
81st St E				
-	IVGH		8200	E2
-	IVGH		8201	A1
81st St S				
-	CTGV		8202	A1
81st St W				
-	EAGN		8198	B1
81st St Ln S				
-	CTGV		8202	E2
82nd Av N				
-	BRKP		7678	E6
-	BRKP		7679	D6
-	BRKP		7680	A6
-	MAPG		7676	E6
-	MAPG		7677	A6
82nd Av NE				
-	SPLP		7680	D4
-	SPLP		7681	A4
82nd Cir N				
-	BRKP		7679	C6
82nd Ln NE				
-	BLNE		7681	E4
-	MNDS		7681	E4
82nd Pl N				
-	BRKP		7678	C5
-	MAPG		7676	A6
-	MAPG		7677	A6
E 82nd St				
-	BMTN		8110	D5
-	BMTN		8111	A5
W 82nd St				
-	BMTN		8108	B5
-	BMTN		8109	E5
-	BMTN		8110	A5
82nd St E				
-	IVGH		8200	A2
82nd St S				
-	CTGV		8202	A2
82nd St W				
-	IVGH		8199	D2
83rd Av N				
-	BRKP		7677	D6
-	BRKP		7678	A6
-	BRKP		7679	C6
-	BRKP		7680	A6
-	MAPG		7676	E6
-	MAPG		7677	D6
83rd Av NE				
-	FRID		7680	C4
-	SPLP		7680	C4
-	SPLP		7681	A4
83rd Av NW				
-	COON		7680	A4
83rd Cir N				
-	BRKP		7679	A6
83rd Ct N				
-	BRKP		7678	C6
-	BRKP		7679	C6
83rd Ln N				
-	BRKP		7679	C6
83rd Ln NW				
-	COON		7680	A4
83rd Pkwy N				
-	BRKP		7678	D6
83rd Pl N				
-	BRKP		7678	C6
-	MAPG		7676	C6
E 83rd St				
-	BMTN		8110	D6
W 83rd St				
-	BMTN		8108	D5
-	BMTN		8109	D5
-	BMTN		8110	A5
83rd St E				
-	IVGH		8201	A2
83rd St S				
-	CTGV		8202	A2
-	SPLP		8202	A2
83rd St W				
-	IVGH		8199	D2
83rd Wy N				
-	MAPG		7676	D6
83rd High Rd				
-	MAPG		7676	B6
W 83rd St Ter				
-	BMTN		8108	C6
84th Av N				
-	BRKP		7678	C5
-	BRKP		7679	D5
-	MAPG		7676	E5
-	MAPG		7677	B6
84th Av NE				
-	MNDS		7681	B3
-	SPLP		7680	D4
84th Av NW				
-	COON		7680	A4
84th Cir N				
-	BRKP		7679	B6
84th Cir NW				
-	COON		7680	A3
84th Ct N				
-	BRKP		7678	E5
-	BRKP		7679	D5
84th Ln NE				
-	BLNE		7681	E3
-	MNDS		7681	E3
84th Ln NW				
-	COON		7680	A3
84th Pl N				
-	MAPG		7676	B5
-	MAPG		7677	A5
E 84th St				
-	BMTN		8110	C6
W 84th St				
-	BMTN		8108	E6
-	BMTN		8109	C6
-	BMTN		8110	A6
84th St E				
-	IVGH		8201	A2
84th St S				
-	CTGV		8202	B2
84th St W				
-	IVGH		8199	D2
84th Wy N				
-	BRKP		7679	E5
W 84th St Cir				
-	BMTN		8108	A6
84 1/2 Av N				
-	BRKP		7678	D6
W 84 1/2 St				
-	BMTN		8109	E6
85th Av N				
-	BRKP		7677	D5
-	BRKP		7678	C5
-	BRKP		7679	A5
-	BRKP		7680	A5
-	MAPG		7676	E5
-	MAPG		7677	C5
85th Av NE				
-	BLNE		7680	B3
-	BLNE		7681	A3
-	BLNE		7682	B3
-	CIRC		7682	D3
-	FRID		7680	B3
-	LINO		7682	E3
-	MNDS		7681	C3
-	SHVW		7681	E3
-	SHVW		7682	A3
-	SPLP		7681	A3
85th Av NW				
-	BLNE		7680	C3
-	COON		7679	E3
-	COON		7680	C3
-	FRID		7680	C3
85th Av NW CO-132				
-	COON		7680	A3
85th Ct N				
-	BRKP		7678	A5
-	BRKP		7679	E6
85th Ct NE				
-	BLNE		7681	D3
85th Ln N				
-	BRKP		7679	C5
85th Ln NE				
-	BLNE		7682	C3
85th Ln NW				
-	COON		7679	E3
-	COON		7680	A3
85th Pl N				
-	MAPG		7676	E5
-	MAPG		7677	B5
E 85th St				
-	BMTN		8110	B6
W 85th St				
-	BMTN		8108	A6
-	BMTN		8109	B6
-	BMTN		8110	A6
85th St E				
-	IVGH		8200	D2
85th St S				
-	CTGV		8202	A2
-	SPLP		8202	A2
85th St W				
-	IVGH		8199	D2
W 85th St Cir				
-	BMTN		8108	A6
86th Av N				
-	BRKP		7679	E5
-	MAPG		7676	D5
-	MAPG		7677	A5
86th Av NE				
-	BLNE		7680	E3
-	BLNE		7682	B3
86th Av NW				
-	COON		7679	E3
-	COON		7680	A3
86th Ct E				
-	IVGH		8200	B2
86th Ln N				
-	BRKP		7678	D5
-	BRKP		7679	C5
86th Ln NE				
-	BLNE		7680	C2
-	BLNE		7681	B3
-	BLNE		7682	B3
-	COON		7680	C2
86th Ln NW				
-	BLNE		7680	C2
-	COON		7679	D2
-	COON		7680	A3
86th Pl N				
-	MAPG		7676	C4
-	MAPG		7677	A5
E 86th St				
-	BMTN		8110	C6
-	BMTN		8111	A6
W 86th St				
-	BMTN		8108	E6
-	BMTN		8109	E6
-	BMTN		8110	A6
86th St E				
-	IVGH		8200	D2
86th St W				
-	IVGH		8199	D2
W 86th St Cir				
-	BMTN		8108	A6
E 86 1/2 St				
-	BMTN		8110	E6
87th Av N				
-	BRKP		7679	E5
-	MAPG		7676	D5
-	MAPG		7677	A5
87th Av NE				
-	BLNE		7680	E3
-	BLNE		7681	A3
-	BLNE		7682	A3
-	CIRC		7682	C3
87th Av NW				
-	COON		7679	E3
87th Ln NE				
-	BLNE		7680	D2
-	BLNE		7682	B3
87th Ln NW				
-	COON		7679	D2
-	COON		7680	B2
87th Pl N				
-	MAPG		7676	A5
-	MAPG		7677	B5
E 87th St				
-	BMTN		8110	D6
W 87th St				
-	BMTN		8108	A6
-	BMTN		8109	D6
-	BMTN		8110	A6
87th St E				
-	IVGH		8200	D3
87th St S				
-	CTGV		8202	E3
87th St W				
-	IVGH		8199	D3
87th Tr N				
-	BRKP		7679	C5
87th Wy N				
-	MAPG		7676	E5
W 87 1/2 St				
-	BMTN		8109	C7
88th Av N				
-	BRKP		7678	B4
-	BRKP		7679	D5
-	MAPG		7676	E4
-	MAPG		7677	B5
88th Av NE				
-	BLNE		7680	D2
-	BLNE		7681	D2
-	BLNE		7682	A2
-	LXTN		7682	B2
88th Av NW				
-	COON		7679	E2
-	COON		7680	A3
88th Cres N				
-	BRKP		7678	D5
88th Ct NE				
-	BLNE		7682	B2
88th Ln NE				
-	BLNE		7681	D2
-	BLNE		7682	A2
88th Ln NW				
-	COON		7679	E2
-	COON		7680	A3
88th Pl N				
-	MAPG		7676	D4
-	MAPG		7677	A4
E 88th St				
-	BMTN		8110	E6
W 88th St				
-	BMTN		8109	A7
-	BMTN		8110	A7
88th St S				
-	CTGV		8202	E3
88th St W				
-	EAGN		8199	D3
-	IVGH		8199	D3
88th Crescent Cir N				
-	BRKP		7678	D5
88th Division Rd				
-	HnpC		8025	D7
89th Av N				
-	BRKP		7678	B4
-	BRKP		7679	D4
-	MAPG		7676	A4
-	MAPG		7677	C4
-	OSSE		7677	D4
89th Av NE				
-	BLNE		7680	E2
-	BLNE		7681	A2
-	BLNE		7682	A2
89th Av NE CO-10				
-	BLNE		7680	C2
89th Av NW				
-	COON		7679	E2
-	COON		7680	A2
89th Cir N				
-	MAPG		7676	E4
89th Cres N				
-	BRKP		7678	E4
-	BRKP		7679	A4
89th Ct E				
-	IVGH		8201	A3
89th Ct NE				
-	BLNE		7681	E2
89th Curv NE				
-	BLNE		7682	A2
-	LXTN		7682	A2
89th Dr NE				
-	BLNE		7682	A2
-	LXTN		7682	A2
89th Ln NE				
-	BLNE		7680	D2
-	BLNE		7681	D2
-	BLNE		7682	A2
-	LXTN		7682	A2
89th Ln NW				
-	COON		7679	E2
89th Pl N				
-	MAPG		7676	E4
-	MAPG		7677	A4
89th St				
-	SHKP		8279	E1
E 89th St				
-	BMTN		8110	E7
W 89th St				
-	BMTN		8109	A7
89th St E				
-	IVGH		8201	A3
89th St N				
-	GRNT		7772	D2
-	MAHT		7772	D2
89th St S				
-	CTGV		8202	C3
89th Crescent Cir N				
-	BRKP		7678	E4
90th Av N				
-	BRKP		7678	C4
-	MAPG		7676	A4
-	MAPG		7677	A4
90th Av NE				
-	BLNE		7680	C2
-	BLNE		7682	A2
-	LXTN		7682	A2
90th Av NW				
-	COON		7680	A2
90th Cres N				
-	BRKP		7679	B4
90th Ct E				
-	IVGH		8201	A3
90th Ct N				
-	MAPG		7676	A4
90th Curv NE				
-	BLNE		7682	A2
-	LXTN		7682	A2
90th Dr NE				
-	BLNE		7682	A2
-	LXTN		7682	A2
90th Ln NE				
-	BLNE		7680	C2
-	BLNE		7681	D2
-	BLNE		7682	A2
-	COON		7680	C2
-	LXTN		7682	A2
90th Pl N				
-	MAPG		7676	A4
-	MAPG		7677	A4
E 90th St				
-	BMTN		8110	D7
W 90th St				
-	BMTN		8109	C7
-	BMTN		8110	A7
90th St E				
-	IVGH		8200	A4
-	IVGH		8201	A3
90th St S				
-	CTGV		8202	B3
90th Tr N				
-	BRKP		7678	B4
91st Av N				
-	BRKP		7678	C4
-	MAPG		7676	C4
-	MAPG		7677	A4
91st Av NE				
-	BLNE		7680	C2
-	BLNE		7681	A2
-	BLNE		7682	A1
-	COON		7680	C2
-	LXTN		7682	A2
91st Cres N				
-	BRKP		7678	D4
-	BRKP		7679	C4
91st Ct NE				
-	BLNE		7682	A2
91st Curv NE				
-	BLNE		7682	A1
91st Dr NE				
-	BLNE		7682	A2
91st Ln N				
-	BRKP		7679	D4
91st Ln NE				
-	BLNE		7680	C1
-	BLNE		7681	D2
-	BLNE		7682	A1
-	COON		7680	C1
91st Pl N				
-	MAPG		7676	E4
-	MAPG		7677	A4
E 91st St				
-	BMTN		8110	D7
-	BMTN		8196	B1
W 91st St				
-	BMTN		8108	E7
-	BMTN		8109	A7
91st St E				
-	IVGH		8200	C3
91st St S				
-	CTGV		8202	C3
91st Tr N				
-	BRKP		7678	C4
W 91st St Cir				
-	BMTN		8109	C7
W 91 1/2 St				
-	BMTN		8195	D1
92nd Av N				
-	BRKP		7678	C3
-	BRKP		7679	D4
-	MAPG		7676	D3
-	MAPG		7677	A3
92nd Av NE				
-	BLNE		7680	C1
-	BLNE		7681	D1
-	BLNE		7682	A1
-	COON		7680	C1
-	LXTN		7682	A1
92nd Cir N				
-	MAPG		7676	E3

INDEX 53

92nd Cir NE

Minneapolis Street Index

111th Cir NW

STREET Block	City	ZIP	Map #	Grid
92nd Cir NE				
-	BLNE		7682	C1
-	CIRC		7682	C1
92nd Cres N				
-	BRKP		7678	E4
-	BRKP		7679	A5
92nd Ct N				
-	BRKP		7678	C4
92nd Ct NE				
-	BLNE		7682	A1
92nd Curv NE				
-	BLNE		7682	A1
92nd Dr NE				
-	BLNE		7682	A1
92nd Ln NE				
-	BLNE		7680	C1
-	BLNE		7681	A1
-	BLNE		7682	A1
-	COON		7680	C1
92nd Pl N				
-	MAPG		7676	C3
-	MAPG		7677	A3
E 92nd St				
-	BMTN		8196	D1
W 92nd St				
-	BMTN		8194	E1
-	BMTN		8195	D1
-	BMTN		8196	A1
92nd St S				
-	CTGV		8202	C4
92nd Tr N				
-	BRKP		7678	C3
W 92nd St Cir				
-	BMTN		8194	E1
E 92 1/2 St				
-	BMTN		8196	D1
93rd Av N				
-	BRKP		7677	C3
-	BRKP		7678	B3
-	BRKP		7679	A4
-	MAPG		7676	A3
-	MAPG		7677	A3
-	OSSE		7677	C3
-	OSSE		7678	B3
93rd Av N CO-30				
-	BRKP		7677	C3
-	BRKP		7678	B3
-	MAPG		7676	A3
-	MAPG		7677	A3
-	OSSE		7677	C3
-	OSSE		7678	B3
93rd Av NE				
-	BLNE		7680	C1
-	BLNE		7681	E1
-	BLNE		7682	A1
93rd Av NW				
-	COON		7679	E1
-	COON		7680	B1
93rd Cir E				
-	IVGH		8200	B4
93rd Curv NE				
-	BLNE		7682	A1
93rd Dr NE				
-	BLNE		7682	A1
93rd Ln NE				
-	BLNE		7681	A1
93rd Ln NW				
-	COON		7679	E1
-	COON		7680	A1
93rd Pl N				
-	MAPG		7676	C3
-	MAPG		7677	D3
E 93rd St				
-	BMTN		8196	C1
W 93rd St				
-	BMTN		8193	E1
-	BMTN		8194	E1
-	BMTN		8195	C1
-	BMTN		8196	A1
93rd St E				
-	IVGH		8200	A4
93rd Tr N				
-	BRKP		7679	C3
93rd Wy N				
-	BRKP		7679	C3
93rd Ln Ext NE				
-	BLNE		7681	B1
-	MNDS		7681	C3
W 93rd St Cir				
-	BMTN		8193	C2
E 93 1/2 St				
-	BMTN		8196	D1
94th Av N				
-	BRKP		7679	B3
-	MAPG		7676	C3
-	MAPG		7677	A3
94th Av NE				
-	BLNE		7680	C1
-	BLNE		7681	E1
94th Av NW				
-	COON		7679	E1
-	COON		7680	B1
94th Cir NW				
-	BLNE		7680	C1
-	COON		7680	C1
94th Ct N				
-	BRKP		7679	B3
94th Ln NE				
-	BLNE		7681	E1
94th Ln NW				
-	COON		7679	E1
94th Pl N				
-	MAPG		7676	C3
-	MAPG		7677	C3
E 94th St				
-	BMTN		8196	C1
W 94th St				
-	BMTN		8194	A1
-	BMTN		8195	E1
-	BMTN		8196	A1
94th St E				
-	IVGH		8201	A4
94th St S				
-	CTGV		8202	C4
94th Wy				
-	BRKP		7679	C3
94 1/2 St E				
-	BMTN		8196	B1
95th Av N				
-	BRKP		7679	C3
-	MAPG		7676	D3
-	MAPG		7677	B3
95th Av N CO-30				
-	MAPG		7676	A3
95th Av NE				
-	BLNE		7680	E1
-	BLNE		7681	A1
-	BLNE		7682	A1
95th Av NE CO-52				
-	BLNE		7681	E1
-	BLNE		7682	A1
95th Av NW				
-	COON		7679	E1
-	COON		7680	B1
95th Ln NE				
-	BLNE		7594	D7
-	BLNE		7595	A7
-	BLNE		7680	C1
95th Ln NW				
-	COON		7594	B7
-	COON		7680	B1
95th Pl N				
-	MAPG		7676	C3
-	MAPG		7677	C3
E 95th St				
-	BMTN		8196	C1
W 95th St				
-	BMTN		8194	A1
-	BMTN		8195	C1
-	BMTN		8196	A2
95th St S				
-	CTGV		8202	E4
E 95th St Cir				
-	BMTN		8196	B1
W 95 1/2 St				
-	BMTN		8194	E2
96th Av N				
-	BRKP		7679	D2
-	MAPG		7676	D2
-	MAPG		7677	B2
96th Av NE				
-	BLNE		7594	E7
-	BLNE		7595	A7
96th Av NW				
-	COON		7594	A7
96th Ln NE				
-	BLNE		7594	E7
-	BLNE		7595	A7
96th Ln NW				
-	COON		7593	E7
96th Pl N				
-	MAPG		7676	E2
-	MAPG		7677	D2
E 96th St				
-	BMTN		8196	B2
W 96th St				
-	BMTN		8193	E2
-	BMTN		8194	A2
-	BMTN		8195	C2
-	BMTN		8196	A2
96th St E				
-	IVGH		8200	B4
96th St S				
-	CTGV		8202	C4
96th Wy				
-	BRKP		7679	C3
W 96th St Cir				
-	BMTN		8194	E2
-	BMTN		8195	C2
97th Av N				
-	BRKP		7678	B2
-	BRKP		7679	B2
-	MAPG		7676	E2
-	MAPG		7677	A2
97th Av NE				
-	BLNE		7594	D7
-	BLNE		7595	A7
-	BLNE		7596	B7
-	COON		7594	C7
-	LXTN		7596	B7
97th Av NW				
-	BLNE		7594	C7
-	COON		7593	D7
-	COON		7594	C7
97th Ct NE				
-	BLNE		7596	B7
97th Ln NE				
-	BLNE		7594	C7
-	BLNE		7596	B7
-	CIRC		7596	C7
-	LXTN		7596	B7
97th Ln NW				
-	COON		7593	D7
-	COON		7594	B7
97th Pl N				
-	BRKP		7677	E2
-	MAPG		7676	E2
-	MAPG		7677	E2
E 97th St				
-	BMTN		8196	D2
W 97th St				
-	BMTN		8193	E2
-	BMTN		8194	C2
-	BMTN		8195	D2
-	BMTN		8196	A2
97th St E				
-	IVGH		8200	A5
97th St S				
-	CTGV		8202	C5
97th St W				
-	BMTN		8196	A2
W 97th St Cir				
-	BMTN		8193	E2
E 97 1/2 St				
-	BMTN		8196	B2
W 97 1/2 St				
-	BMTN		8193	E2
98th Av N				
-	BRKP		7679	B2
-	MAPG		7677	B2
98th Av NE				
-	BLNE		7594	E7
-	BLNE		7595	A7
-	BLNE		7596	B7
98th Av NW				
-	COON		7594	B7
98th Cir N				
-	BRKP		7679	B2
98th Ln NE				
-	BLNE		7594	E7
-	BLNE		7596	B7
98th Ln NW				
-	BLNE		7594	C7
-	COON		7593	D7
-	COON		7594	B7
98th Pl N				
-	MAPG		7677	B2
E 98th St				
-	BMTN		8196	D2
W 98th St				
-	BMTN		8193	E2
-	BMTN		8194	D2
-	BMTN		8195	A2
-	BMTN		8196	A2
98th St S				
-	CTGV		8202	C5
W 98th St Cir				
-	BMTN		8195	A2
98th St S Service Rd				
-	BMTN		8195	B1
W 98 1/2 St				
-	BMTN		8194	D2
-	BMTN		8195	C2
W 98 1/2 St Cir				
-	BMTN		8194	D2
99th Av N				
-	BRKP		7678	E2
-	BRKP		7679	A2
-	MAPG		7676	C2
-	MAPG		7677	B2
99th Av NE				
-	BLNE		7594	E7
-	BLNE		7595	A7
-	BLNE		7596	B7
-	CIRC		7596	B7
-	COON		7594	C7
99th Av NW				
-	COON		7593	C7
-	COON		7594	A7
99th Cir N				
-	BRKP		7678	E2
99th Cir NE				
-	BLNE		7594	D7
99th Cir NW				
-	COON		7593	D7
99th Cir S				
-	CTGV		8202	B5
99th Ct NE				
-	BLNE		7594	E6
-	BLNE		7595	A6
-	BLNE		7596	A7
99th Ct S				
-	CTGV		8202	B5
99th Ln NE				
-	BLNE		7594	E6
-	BLNE		7595	A6
-	BLNE		7596	B6
99th Ln NW				
-	BLNE		7594	C7
-	COON		7594	C7
99th Pl N				
-	BRKP		7677	D2
-	MAPG		7677	D2
E 99th St				
-	BMTN		8196	B2
W 99th St				
-	BMTN		8194	D2
-	BMTN		8195	B3
-	BMTN		8196	A2
99th St E				
-	IVGH		8200	C5
99th St N				
-	GRNT		7686	C7
-	GRNT		7772	C1
99th St S				
-	CTGV		8202	C5
-	GCIT		8201	D5
W 99th St Cir				
-	BMTN		8194	A3
99th St Cir N				
-	GRNT		7686	C7
-	GRNT		7772	C1
99th St Ct N				
-	GRNT		7772	C1
100th Av				
-	COON		7593	D7
100th Av N				
-	BRKP		7678	D2
-	BRKP		7679	C2
-	MAPG		7677	C1
100th Av NE				
-	BLNE		7594	E6
100th Av NW				
-	COON		7594	A6
100th Ct NE				
-	BLNE		7594	C6
-	BLNE		7595	E7
100th Dr NE				
-	BLNE		7594	E6
100th Ln N				
-	BRKP		7678	D2
100th Ln NE				
-	BLNE		7594	E6
100th Ln NW				
-	COON		7593	D6
100th Pl N				
-	MAPG		7677	B1
E 100th St				
-	BMTN		8196	D3
W 100th St				
-	BMTN		8193	E3
-	BMTN		8194	A3
-	BMTN		8195	A3
-	BMTN		8196	A3
100th St E				
-	IVGH		8200	C5
-	IVGH		8201	A5
100th St N				
-	GRNT		7686	D7
100th St S				
-	CTGV		8202	C5
W 100th St Cir				
-	BMTN		8194	B3
101st Av N				
-	BRKP		7677	C1
-	BRKP		7678	A1
-	BRKP		7679	A1
-	MAPG		7676	C1
-	MAPG		7677	C1
101st Av NE				
-	BLNE		7594	E6
-	BLNE		7595	D6
-	BLNE		7596	A6
-	COON		7594	C6
101st Av NE CO-52				
-	BLNE		7595	D6
101st Av NW				
-	BLNE		7594	C6
-	COON		7593	E6
-	COON		7594	B6
101st Ct NE				
-	BLNE		7594	C6
101st Ln N				
-	BRKP		7679	C1
101st Ln NE				
-	BLNE		7594	E6
-	BLNE		7596	C6
-	LINO		7596	E6
101st Ln NW				
-	BLNE		7594	C6
-	COON		7593	E6
-	COON		7594	C6
101st Pl N				
-	MAPG		7677	C1
E 101st St				
-	BMTN		8196	C3
W 101st St				
-	BMTN		8194	A3
-	BMTN		8195	D3
101st St N				
-	GRNT		7686	C7
W 101st St Cir				
-	BMTN		8193	E3
W 101 1/2 St				
-	BMTN		8195	B3
102nd Av N				
-	BRKP		7678	D1
-	MAPG		7677	C1
102nd Av NE				
-	BLNE		7594	E6
-	BLNE		7596	D6
102nd Av NW				
-	BLNE		7594	C6
-	COON		7593	B7
-	COON		7594	B6
102nd Cir NE				
-	BLNE		7594	E6
102nd Cir NW				
-	COON		7593	C6
102nd Ct N				
-	BRKP		7678	D1
102nd Ct W				
-	IVGH		8200	A6
102nd Ln NE				
-	BLNE		7594	E6
-	BLNE		7596	D6
-	COON		7594	C6
102nd Ln NW				
-	BLNE		7594	C6
-	COON		7594	B6
102nd Pl N				
-	MAPG		7677	D1
E 102nd St				
-	BMTN		8196	B3
W 102nd St				
-	BMTN		8194	A3
-	BMTN		8195	C3
-	BMTN		8196	A3
102nd St E				
-	IVGH		8200	A6
-	IVGH		8201	A6
102nd St W				
-	IVGH		8199	E6
-	IVGH		8200	A6
102nd Tr N				
-	BRKP		7678	E1
103rd Av N				
-	BRKP		7677	D1
-	BRKP		7678	C1
-	BRKP		7679	A1
-	MAPG		7677	D1
103rd Av NE				
-	BLNE		7594	E6
-	BLNE		7595	A6
103rd Av NW				
-	BLNE		7594	C6
-	COON		7593	A5
-	COON		7594	B6
103rd Ct NE				
-	BLNE		7595	D6
-	BLNE		7596	C6
103rd Ln NE				
-	BLNE		7595	E5
-	BLNE		7596	D6
-	LINO		7596	E6
103rd Ln NW				
-	COON		7593	E5
103rd Pl N				
-	MAPG		7591	D7
-	MAPG		7677	B1
E 103rd St				
-	BMTN		8196	C3
W 103rd St				
-	BMTN		8193	E4
-	BMTN		8194	A3
-	BMTN		8195	B3
103rd St S				
-	CTGV		8202	B6
103rd Tr N				
-	BRKP		7679	B1
103rd Wy NE				
-	BLNE		7594	E5
-	BLNE		7595	B5
W 103rd St Cir				
-	BMTN		8193	D5
104th Av N				
-	BRKP		7592	D7
-	BRKP		7593	A7
-	BRKP		7678	C1
-	BRKP		7679	A1
-	MAPG		7591	D7
-	MAPG		7677	B1
104th Av NE				
-	BLNE		7594	E5
-	BLNE		7595	A5
-	BLNE		7596	D5
-	LINO		7596	E5
104th Av NW				
-	BLNE		7594	B5
-	COON		7593	C5
-	COON		7594	B5
104th Cir N				
-	BRKP		7592	D7
-	BRKP		7678	D1
104th Ct E				
-	IVGH		8200	D6
104th Ct NE				
-	BLNE		7594	D5
-	BLNE		7595	D5
104th Ln NE				
-	BLNE		7594	D5
-	BLNE		7595	B5
-	BLNE		7596	D5
104th Ln NW				
-	BLNE		7594	C5
-	COON		7593	E5
-	COON		7594	A5
104th Pl N				
-	MAPG		7591	C7
104th Pl NE				
-	BLNE		7594	C3
-	BLNE		7595	A5
E 104th St				
-	BMTN		8196	B4
W 104th St				
-	BMTN		8193	E4
-	BMTN		8194	B4
-	BMTN		8195	E4
-	BMTN		8196	A4
104th Tr N				
-	BRKP		7593	B7
104th Wy NE				
-	BLNE		7594	C3
-	BLNE		7595	A5
W 104th St Cir				
-	BMTN		8193	E4
105th Av N				
-	BRKP		7592	B7
-	BRKP		7678	D1
-	MAPG		7590	A7
-	MAPG		7591	C7
105th Av NE				
-	BLNE		7594	C5
-	BLNE		7595	D5
-	COON		7594	C5
105th Av NW				
-	BLNE		7594	C5
-	COON		7592	D6
-	COON		7593	B6
-	COON		7594	B5
105th Ln N				
-	BRKP		7593	C7
105th Ln NE				
-	BLNE		7594	D5
-	BLNE		7596	E5
-	LINO		7596	E5
105th Ln NW				
-	BLNE		7594	C5
-	COON		7593	D5
-	COON		7594	B5
105th Pl N				
-	MAPG		7591	D7
E 105th St				
-	BMTN		8196	B4
W 105th St				
-	BMTN		8194	B4
-	BMTN		8195	E4
105th St E				
-	IVGH		8200	D6
105th St N				
-	GRNT		7686	D6
105th St S				
-	GCIT		8201	D6
105th St W				
-	IVGH		8199	E6
-	IVGH		8200	A6
105th Tr N				
-	BRKP		7593	A7
106th Av N				
-	BRKP		7591	D7
-	BRKP		7592	B7
-	BRKP		7593	A7
-	MAPG		7591	D7
106th Av NE				
-	BLNE		7594	E5
-	BLNE		7596	E5
-	COON		7594	C5
-	LINO		7596	D5
106th Av NW				
-	BLNE		7594	C5
-	COON		7593	D5
-	COON		7594	B5
106th Ln NE				
-	BLNE		7594	E5
-	BLNE		7595	C5
-	BLNE		7596	D5
106th Ln NW				
-	COON		7593	D5
-	COON		7594	B3
106th Pl N				
-	BRKP		7591	E7
-	MAPG		7590	A7
-	MAPG		7591	E7
W 106th St				
-	BMTN		8193	E4
-	BMTN		8194	E4
-	BMTN		8195	C4
-	BMTN		8196	A4
107th Av N				
-	BRKP		7592	B7
-	BRKP		7593	A7
-	MAPG		7590	A7
-	MAPG		7591	D7
107th Av NE				
-	BLNE		7594	D5
-	BLNE		7595	D5
-	BLNE		7596	D5
-	LINO		7596	E5
107th Av NW				
-	COON		7593	C5
-	COON		7594	B5
107th Cir NE				
-	BLNE		7594	D4
107th Ct NE				
-	BLNE		7594	D5
107th Ln NE				
-	BLNE		7594	E4
-	BLNE		7595	A4
107th Ln NW				
-	COON		7593	C4
-	COON		7594	B5
107th Pl N				
-	MAPG		7591	D7
W 107th St				
-	BMTN		8193	E4
-	BMTN		8194	A5
-	BMTN		8195	B4
-	BMTN		8196	A4
E 107th St Cir				
-	BMTN		8196	B4
W 107th St Cir				
-	BMTN		8194	A4
108th Av N				
-	MAPG		7591	C7
108th Av NE				
-	BLNE		7594	E4
-	BLNE		7595	A4
-	BLNE		7596	D5
-	LINO		7596	E5
108th Av NW				
-	COON		7593	B4
-	COON		7594	B4
108th Ct E				
-	IVGH		8200	C6
108th Ln NE				
-	BLNE		7595	C4
-	BLNE		7596	D4
108th Ln NW				
-	COON		7592	E4
-	COON		7593	C4
-	COON		7594	A4
108th Pl N				
-	MAPG		7591	C6
W 108th St				
-	BMTN		8194	E5
-	BMTN		8195	D5
108th St E				
-	IVGH		8200	C7
109th Av N				
-	BRKP		7591	E6
-	BRKP		7592	E6
-	BRKP		7593	A6
-	CHMP		7591	E6
-	CHMP		7592	E6
-	CHMP		7593	A6
-	DAYT		7591	C6
-	MAPG		7591	C6
109th Av NE				
-	BLNE		7594	D4
-	BLNE		7595	A4
-	BLNE		7596	D4
-	COON		7594	C4
-	LINO		7596	E4
109th Av NE CO-12				
-	BLNE		7594	D4
-	BLNE		7595	A4
-	BLNE		7596	D4
-	LINO		7596	E4
109th Av NW				
-	COON		7592	E4
-	COON		7593	E4
-	COON		7594	A4
109th Cir N				
-	CHMP		7592	B6
109th Ct NE				
-	BLNE		7595	E4
109th Ln N				
-	CHMP		7592	C6
109th Ln NE				
-	BLNE		7594	D4
-	BLNE		7595	A4
109th Ln NW				
-	COON		7592	E4
-	COON		7593	A4
-	COON		7594	A4
109th Pl N				
-	CHMP		7592	B6
W 109th St				
-	BMTN		8193	E5
-	BMTN		8194	B5
-	BMTN		8195	A5
W 109th St Cir S				
-	BMTN		8194	A5
110th Av N				
-	CHMP		7592	C6
110th Av NE				
-	BLNE		7594	D4
-	BLNE		7595	E4
110th Av NW				
-	COON		7593	B4
-	COON		7594	A4
110th Cir N				
-	CHMP		7592	B6
110th Ct NE				
-	BLNE		7595	B4
110th Ct W				
-	IVGH		8199	D7
110th Ln N				
-	CHMP		7592	C6
110th Ln NW				
-	BLNE		7594	C4
-	COON		7593	B4
-	COON		7594	C4
110th Pl N				
-	CHMP		7592	A6
W 110th St				
-	BMTN		8193	E5
-	BMTN		8194	A5
-	BMTN		8195	D5
110th St S				
-	CTGV		8202	D7
W 110th St Cir				
-	BMTN		8194	A5
111th Av N				
-	CHMP		7591	E6
-	CHMP		7592	B6
111th Av NE				
-	BLNE		7594	C4
-	BLNE		7595	B4
-	COON		7594	C4
111th Av NW				
-	COON		7592	E4
-	COON		7593	D4
-	COON		7594	B4
111th Cir NW				
-	COON		7593	B3

Street / Block	City	ZIP	Map #	Grid
W 138th St				
-	BRNV		8281	D5
-	SAVG		8279	E5
-	SAVG		8280	A5
138th St E				
-	RSMT		8286	C6
138th St N				
-	HUGO		7599	E7
138th St W				
-	APVA		8283	B6
-	APVA		8284	A6
-	RSMT		8285	B6
138th St Ct				
-	APVA		8282	E6
-	APVA		8284	A6
139th Ct				
-	APVA		8283	A6
W 139th St				
-	BRNV		8281	E5
-	SAVG		8280	E6
-	SAVG		8281	A6
139th St W				
-	APVA		8284	A6
-	RSMT		8285	B6
139th St Ct				
-	APVA		8284	A6
140th Ct				
-	APVA		8283	B6
E 140th St				
-	BRNV		8282	D6
W 140th St				
-	BRNV		8281	E6
-	BRNV		8282	A6
-	SAVG		8280	E6
-	SAVG		8281	A6
140th St E				
-	RSMT		8286	D6
-	RSMT		8287	A6
140th St N				
-	HUGO		7599	B6
-	HUGO		7600	D6
-	LINO		7599	B6
140th St N CO-8				
-	HUGO		7599	D6
-	HUGO		7600	D6
140th St NE				
-	PRIO		8279	A6
-	PRIO		8280	A6
-	SAVG		8279	E6
-	SAVG		8280	A6
140th St NE CO-42				
-	PRIO		8279	C6
-	PRIO		8280	A6
-	SAVG		8279	E6
-	SAVG		8280	A6
140th St NW				
-	PRIO		8278	A6
-	PRIO		8279	A6
-	SHKP		8278	A6
140th St NW CO-42				
-	PRIO		8278	A6
-	PRIO		8279	A6
-	SHKP		8278	A6
140th St W				
-	APVA		8282	E6
-	APVA		8283	A6
-	APVA		8284	C6
-	RSMT		8284	D6
-	RSMT		8285	C6
140th St Blvd				
-	APVA		8282	E5
140th St Ct				
-	APVA		8283	A6
141st Ct W				
-	APVA		8283	A6
E 141st St				
-	BRNV		8282	D6
W 141st St				
-	BRNV		8281	E6
-	PRIO		8279	E6
-	SAVG		8280	E6
-	SAVG		8281	A6
141st St N				
-	HUGO		7599	D6
141st St W				
-	APVA		8283	A7
-	APVA		8284	B7
141st St Cir N				
-	HUGO		7599	D6
141st St Ct				
-	RSMT		8284	D7
141st St Ct N				
-	HUGO		7599	D6
141st St Ct W				
-	APVA		8283	E7
-	RSMT		8285	D7
142nd Ct W				
-	APVA		8284	B7
142nd Pth W				
-	RSMT		8287	D7
142nd St E				
-	HUGO		7599	D6
142nd St W				
-	APVA		8283	B7
-	APVA		8284	C6
-	RSMT		8284	D7
-	RSMT		8285	A7
142nd St Ct				
-	APVA		8283	E7
142 1/2 St				
-	BRNV		8281	D6
W 142 1/2 St				
-	BRNV		8281	B6
-	SAVG		8280	E6
-	SAVG		8281	B6
143rd Cir				
-	BRNV		8281	B7
-	SAVG		8280	E7
143rd Ct				
-	SAVG		8281	B1
E 143rd Ct				
-	BRNV		8282	C7
E 143rd Ln				
-	BRNV		8282	C7
E 143rd St				
-	BRNV		8282	C6
W 143rd St				
-	BRNV		8281	D7
W 143rd St				
-	SAVG		8280	E6
-	SAVG		8281	B1
143rd St W				
-	APVA		8283	A7
-	APVA		8284	A7
-	RSMT		8284	D7
-	RSMT		8285	A7
143rd St Ct				
-	APVA		8282	E7
-	APVA		8283	C7
W 144th Ct				
-	SAVG		8280	D7
E 144th St				
-	BRNV		8282	C7
W 144th St				
-	BRNV		8281	D7
-	SAVG		8280	E7
-	SAVG		8281	A7
144th St N				
-	HUGO		7600	A5
144th St W				
-	APVA		8282	E7
-	APVA		8283	A7
-	APVA		8284	A7
-	RSMT		8284	E7
-	RSMT		8285	A7
144th St Ct				
-	APVA		8282	E7
-	APVA		8283	C7
145th Cir N				
-	HUGO		7600	B5
145th Ct				
-	BRNV		8282	C7
E 145th St				
-	BRNV		8282	B7
W 145th St				
-	BRNV		8281	B7
-	SAVG		8280	E7
-	SAVG		8281	A7
145th St E				
-	RSMT		8286	E7
-	RSMT		8287	C7
145th St N				
-	HUGO		7599	E5
-	HUGO		7600	A5
145th St W				
-	APVA		8283	D7
-	APVA		8284	B7
-	RSMT		8284	E7
-	RSMT		8285	A7
145th Alcove N				
-	HUGO		7600	A5
145th Bay N				
-	HUGO		7600	A5
E 146th St				
-	BRNV		8282	C7
W 146th St				
-	SAVG		8280	E7
146th St N				
-	HUGO		7599	B5
-	HUGO		7600	A5
146th St W				
-	APVA		8283	C7
-	RSMT		8285	A7
146th Ter				
-	SAVG		8280	B7
146th Wy W				
-	APVA		8283	C7
146th St Ct				
-	APVA		8283	D7
147th Ct				
-	SAVG		8281	B1
W 147th St				
-	SAVG		8280	E7
-	SAVG		8281	A7
147th St N				
-	HUGO		7599	E5
-	HUGO		7600	D5
147th St W				
-	APVA		8284	C7
148th St N				
-	HUGO		7599	E5
149th St N				
-	HUGO		7599	C4
150th St N				
-	HUGO		7599	E4
-	HUGO		7600	A4
150th St W				
-	RSMT		8285	C7
151st St N				
-	HUGO		7600	A4
151st St Cir N				
-	HUGO		7600	A4
152nd St N				
-	HUGO		7599	E4
-	HUGO		7600	A4
154th St N				
-	HUGO		7599	C3
155th St N				
-	HUGO		7600	E3
157th Cir N				
-	HUGO		7599	E3
157th St N				
-	HUGO		7599	C3
-	HUGO		7600	D3
157th Wy N				
-	HUGO		7599	D3
157th Wy Ct N				
-	HUGO		7599	D3
W 158th Av				
-	EDNP		8020	B7
158th St N				
-	HUGO		7599	B3
-	LINO		7599	B3
159th Cir N				
-	HUGO		7599	E3
159th Ct N				
-	HUGO		7599	E3
159th St N				
-	HUGO		7599	D2
159th Alcove N				
-	HUGO		7599	D2
165th St N				
-	HUGO		7599	D1
-	HUGO		7600	E1
-	LINO		7599	B1
168th Av W				
-	EDNP		8106	A2
180th Av N				
-	BRKP		7592	E6

Minneapolis Points of Interest Index

FEATURE NAME	CITY	MAP#	GRID
Gem Lake Hills GC	GEML	7771	A5
Glen Lake Golf & Practice Center	MNTK	8020	D7
Golden Valley Golf & CC	GLDV	7936	C1
Goodrich GC	MPLW	7857	B7
Hampton Hills GC	PYMH	7762	C6
Hayden Hills Executive GC	DAYT	7591	B1
Hiawatha GC	MINN	8024	E3
Highland National GC	STPL	8026	D4
Hillcrest GC	STPL	7943	C1
Hollydale GC	PYMH	7848	A1
Hyland Greens GC	BMTN	8194	D3
Interlachen CC	EDNA	8022	B4
Inver Wood GC	IVGH	8114	B6
Island Lake Golf Center	SHVW	7768	E5
Kate-Haven GC	BLNE	7682	C3
Keller GC	MPLW	7856	C5
Les Bolstad University GC	FLCH	7853	E7
Lost Spur GC	EAGN	8112	B5
Manitou Ridge GC	WTBL	7857	D1
Meadowbrook GC	HOPK	8022	B3
Mendakota CC	MNDH	8113	A2
Mendota Heights Par 3 GC	MNDH	8027	B7
Midland Hills CC	RSVL	7853	E6
Minikahda Club	MINN	7937	B7
Minneapolis GC	STLP	7935	E4
Minnesota Valley CC	BMTN	8194	C7
Mississippi Dunes Golf Links	CTGV	8202	B6
National Youth Golf Center	BLNE	7595	B5
New Hope Village GC	NWHE	7764	A5
North Oaks GC	NOAK	7769	E2
Oak Marsh GC	ODLE	7944	E6
Oak Ridge CC	HOPK	8021	D1
Olympic Hills GC	EDNP	8193	C2
Oneka Ridge GC	HUGO	7685	E3
Parkview GC	EAGN	8198	C7
Phalen Park GC	STPL	7942	C1
Ponds at Battle Creek GC	MPLW	8029	E3
Rich Valley GC	RSMT	8287	B7
Roseville Cedarholm GC	RSVL	7854	D5
Somerset CC	MNDH	8027	C6
Southview CC	WSTP	8114	B1
Sundance Golf & Bowl	DAYT	7590	C5
The Bridges of Mounds View	MNDS	7681	D4
Theodore Wirth GC	GLDV	7851	B7
Thompson Oaks GC	WSTP	8028	B6
Tournament Players Club Twin-Cities	BLNE	7595	C3
Town & CC	STPL	7939	D6
Valleywood GC	APVA	8284	C3
White Bear Yacht Club & GC	DLWD	7772	B1
Wilds GC	PRIO	8278	D7
Woodbury GC	WDBY	8030	C6

Historic Sites

FEATURE NAME	CITY	MAP#	GRID
Alexander Ramsey House	STPL	7941	D7
Ard Godfrey House	MINN	7938	D1
Bloomington History Clock Tower	BMTN	8196	A2
Brooklyn Park Historical Farm	BRKP	7679	A1
Historic Fort Snelling	HnpC	8026	A7
James J Hill House	STPL	7941	C7
Julian H Sleeper House	STPL	8027	A1
Sibley House Historic Site	MNDT	8112	C1
Summit Avenue Historic District	STPL	7941	C7
Warehouse Historic District-Minneapolis	MINN	7938	B1

Hospitals

FEATURE NAME	CITY	MAP#	GRID
Abbott-Northwestern Hosp	MINN	7938	C6
Fairview Ridges Hosp	BRNV	8282	B6
Fairview Riverside Hosp	MINN	7939	A4
Fairview Southdale Hosp	EDNA	8109	B1
Hennepin County Med Ctr	MINN	7938	C3
Mercy Hosp	COON	7592	C2
Methodist Hosp	STLP	8022	C2
North Memorial Health Care	ROBB	7851	B4
Regions Hosp	STPL	7941	E5
St. John's Hosp	MPLW	7857	A2
St. Joseph's Hosp	STPL	7941	D6
United Hosp	STPL	7941	C7
Unity Hosp	FRID	7680	D6
University of Minnesota Hosp &-Clinic	MINN	7939	A3
University of Minnesota Med Ctr-Riverside	MINN	7939	A4
Veterans Affairs Med Ctr	HnpC	8025	D6
Woodwinds Health Campus	WDBY	8030	A3

Law Enforcement

FEATURE NAME	CITY	MAP#	GRID
Arden Hills Police Dept	STPL	7941	E7
Blaine Police Dept	BLNE	7595	D4
Bloomington Police Dept	BMTN	8195	D3
Brooklyn Center Police Dept	BRKC	7765	D4
Brooklyn Park Police Dept	BRKP	7678	E5
Champlin Police Dept	CHMP	7592	A4
Circle Pines Police Dept	CIRC	7682	D1
Columbia Heights Police Dept	COLH	7852	D1
Coon Rapids Police Dept	COON	7593	D3
Cottage Grove Police Dept	CTGV	8202	C1
Crystal Police Dept	CRYS	7850	D2
Eagan Police Dept	EAGN	8198	C3
Eden Prairie Police Dept	EDNP	8106	D5
Edina Police Dept	EDNA	8022	E5
Fridley Police Dept	FRID	7766	C2
Golden Valley Police Dept	GLDV	7936	B1
Hennepin County Sheriff's Dept	MINN	7938	C2
Hopkins Police Dept	HOPK	8021	C3
Inver Grove Heights Police Dept	IVGH	8200	C2
Lino Lakes Police Dept	LINO	7597	C1
Maple Grove Police Dept	MAPG	7677	A7
Maplewood Police Dept	MPLW	7857	B5
Mendota Heights Police Dept	MNDH	8112	D1
Minneapolis Police Dept-3rd-Precinct	MINN	7939	A6
Minneapolis Police Dept-5th-Precinct	MINN	7938	B7
Minneapolis Police Dept-North	MINN	7937	D1
Minneapolis Police Dept-Northeast	MINN	7853	A5
Minnesota State Patrol	GLDV	7850	E6
Minnesota State Patrol	ODLE	7858	B6
Minnesota State Patrol	SSTP	8115	A2
Minnesota State Patrol	STPL	7941	E6
Minnetonka Police Dept	MNTK	8020	C1
Mounds View Police Dept	MNDS	7681	D6
New Brighton Police Dept	NBRI	7767	E5
New Hope Police Dept	NWHE	7850	A1
North St. Paul Police Dept	NSTP	7857	E5
Oakdale Police Dept	ODLE	7944	B3
Osseo Police Dept	OSSE	7677	E4
Plymouth Police Dept	PYMH	7848	C4
Ramsey County Sheriff's Dept	SHVW	7769	A6
Ramsey County Sheriff's Dept	STPL	7941	E5
Richfield Police Dept	RHFD	8110	C2
Rosemount Police Dept	RSMT	8285	B7
Roseville Police Dept	RSVL	7854	D3
St. Anthony Police Dept	STAN	7853	C2
St. Louis Park Police Dept	STLP	7936	E7
St. Paul Park Police Dept	SPLP	8115	E6
St. Paul Police Dept	STPL	7941	E6
Savage Police Dept	SAVG	8280	D4
South St. Paul Police Dept	SSTP	8028	E7
Spring Lake Park Police Dept	SPLP	7681	A4
West St. Paul Police Dept	WSTP	8028	A6
White Bear Lake Police Dept	WTBL	7771	C2
Woodbury Police Dept	WDBY	8030	E4

Libraries

FEATURE NAME	CITY	MAP#	GRID
Archbishop Ireland Memorial	STPL	7939	E7
Arden Hills	ARDH	7768	A5
Augsburg Park	RHFD	8110	B3
Bartimaeus for the Blind	BRKC	7765	B1
Brookdale	BRKC	7765	D4
Brooklyn Park	BRKP	7678	D5
Burnhaven	BRNV	8281	E6
Centennial Branch	CIRC	7596	D7
Champlin	CHMP	7591	E3
Columbia Heights Public	COLH	7852	D1
Crooked Lake Branch	COON	7593	A3
Eden Prairie	EDNP	8107	B6
Edina	EDNA	8022	D5
Franklin Community	MINN	7938	D4
Golden Valley	GLDV	7936	B1
Hopkins	HOPK	8021	C3
Inver Glen	IVGH	8200	D1
Maple Grove	MAPG	7676	E6
Maplewood	MPLW	7857	A2
Minneapolis Public-Central Branch	MINN	7938	C2
Minneapolis Public-East Lake-Branch	MINN	7939	A6
Minneapolis Public-Hosmer Branch	MINN	8024	B1
Minneapolis Public-Linden Hills-Branch	MINN	8023	C3
Minneapolis Public-Nokomis Branch	MINN	8025	B5
Minneapolis Public-Northeast-Branch	MINN	7852	E5
Minneapolis Public-North Regional-Branch	MINN	7851	E5
Minneapolis Public-Pierre Bottineau-Branch	MINN	7852	C6
Minneapolis Public-Southeast-Branch	MINN	7939	A2
Minneapolis Public-Sumner Branch	MINN	7937	E1
Minneapolis Public-Walker Branch	MINN	7937	E6
Minneapolis Public-Washburn Branch	MINN	8024	A5
Minneapolis Public-Webber Park-Branch	MINN	7851	E2
Minnesota Historical	STPL	7941	D6
Mississippi Branch	FRID	7766	C1
Mounds View	MNDS	7681	C6
North St. Paul	NSTP	7857	E4
Northtown	BLNE	7680	D3
Oakdale	ODLE	7944	D4
Osseo	OSSE	7677	D4
Oxboro	BMTN	8110	C7
Park Grove	CTGV	8202	D1
Penn Lake	BMTN	8109	D7
Plymouth	PYMH	7848	B3
Quartrefoil	STPL	7940	B7
RH Stafford	WDBY	8030	E4
Ridgedale	MNTK	7935	A4
Rockford Road	CRYS	7850	D2
Roosevelt	MINN	8025	A2
Roseville	RSVL	7854	D5
St. Anthony	STAN	7853	B4
St. Louis Park	STLP	7936	C7
St. Paul Public-Arlington Hills-Branch	STPL	7942	B3
St. Paul Public-Central Branch	STPL	7941	D7
St. Paul Public-Dayton's Bluff-Branch	STPL	7942	C4
St. Paul Public-Hamline Midway-Branch	STPL	7940	C4
St. Paul Public-Hayden Heights-Branch	STPL	7943	A1
St. Paul Public-Highland Park-Branch	STPL	8026	A4
St. Paul Public-Merriam Park-Branch	STPL	7940	B6
St. Paul Public-Rice St Branch	STPL	7941	C3
St. Paul Public-Riverview Branch	STPL	8028	A2
St. Paul Public-Rondo Community-Outreach	STPL	7941	B5
St. Paul Public-St. Anthony Park-Branch	STPL	7939	E2
St. Paul Public-Sun Ray Branch	STPL	7943	C6
St. Paul Public-W 7th St Branch	STPL	8027	B1
Savage	SAVG	8280	D4
Shoreview	SHVW	7769	A2
Southdale	EDNA	8109	C2
South St. Paul	SSTP	8028	E7
Washington County-Newport Branch	NWPT	8115	D5
Wentworth	WSTP	8028	B6
Wescott	EAGN	8198	C3
White Bear Lake	WTBL	7771	C2
Wildwood	MAHT	7772	D5

Military Installations

FEATURE NAME	CITY	MAP#	GRID
Fort Snelling Army Reserve	HnpC	8025	D7
Twin Cities Army Ammunition Plant	ARDH	7682	B6

Museums

FEATURE NAME	CITY	MAP#	GRID
American Mus of Asmat Art	SHVW	7769	A7
American Wings Air Mus	BLNE	7681	B1
Bakken Mus	MINN	8023	C1
Bear Hawk-American Indian Mus	MINN	7938	C4
Bell Mus of Natural History	MINN	7939	A2
Bloomington Art Center	BMTN	8195	D3
Czech & Slovak Culture Center	STPL	8027	B1
Dinosaur Walk Mus	BMTN	8110	E5
Eidem Homestead	BRKP	7679	A1
Fire Fighters Memorial Mus	MINN	7852	E6
Foshay Tower	MINN	7938	B3
Gibbs Mus of Pioneer And Dakotah-Life	FLCH	7853	E7
Goldstein Mus of Design	FLCH	7940	A1
Hennepin History Mus	MINN	7938	B5
John H Stevens House Mus	MINN	8025	C4
Mill City Mus	MINN	7938	D2
Minneapolis Institute of Arts	MINN	7938	B5
Minneapolis Sculpture Garden	MINN	7938	A4
Minnesota Air National Guard Mus	HnpC	8025	D6
Minnesota Center for Book Arts	MINN	7938	D3
Minnesota Center for Photography	MINN	7852	C6
Minnesota Children's Mus	STPL	7941	D7
Minnesota History Center	STPL	7941	C6
Minnesota Mus of American Art	STPL	7941	E7
Minnesota Transportation Mus	MINN	7851	C2
Minnesota Transportation Mus	STPL	7941	E4
Museum of Russian Art	MINN	8024	B6
North Star Scouting Mus	NSTP	7857	D5
Norwegian Emigrant Mus	FRID	7680	D6
Original Baseball Hall of Fame	MINN	7938	D2
Pavek Mus of Broadcasting	STLP	8022	E1
Purcell Cutts House	MINN	7937	E5
Schubert Musical Instrument Mus	STPL	7941	D7
Science Mus of Minnesota	STPL	7941	D7
The American Swedish Institute	MINN	7938	C6
The Raptor Center	FLCH	7940	A2
Walker Art Center	MINN	7938	A4
Weisman Art Mus	MINN	7939	A3

Open Space

FEATURE NAME	CITY	MAP#	GRID
Anderson Lakes Pk Preserve	EDNP	8107	D6
Bassett Nature Area	GLDV	7850	D6
Bass Lake Preserve	STLP	7937	A7
Briarwood Nature Area	GLDV	7850	E6
Bush Lake Pk Preserve	BMTN	8108	A7
Elm Creek Park Reserve	DAYT	7591	B3
Harmon Reserve	IVGH	8114	B5
Hyland Lake Pk Preserve	BMTN	8194	C2
Innsbruck Nature Center	FRID	7767	A3
Lake Elmo Regional Park Reserve	ELMO	7944	E2
Maplewood Nature Center	MPLW	7943	D4
Minnesota Valley National Wildlife-Refuge	BMTN	8193	E6
Minnesota Valley National Wildlife-Refuge	BMTN	8194	A6
Minnesota Valley National Wildlife-Refuge	BMTN	8195	C7
Minnesota Valley National Wildlife-Refuge	BMTN	8196	A5
Minnesota Valley National Wildlife-Refuge	SAVG	8280	D3
Nesbitt Preserve Pk	EDNP	8107	C6
Palmer Lake Environmental Area	BRKP	7765	C1
Paul Hugo Farms Wildlife Management-Area	HUGO	7600	C5
Spring Lake Park Reserve	NgTp	8288	E4
Tamarack Nature Preserve	WDBY	8030	D2
Westwood Hills Environmental-Education Ctr	STLP	7936	A4
Wood Lake Nature Center	RHFD	8109	E2

Other

FEATURE NAME	CITY	MAP#	GRID
Basilica of St. Mary	MINN	7938	A3
Coll of St. Catherine Astrophysical-Obsrvtry	STPL	8026	A2
Eisenhower Observatory	HOPK	8021	C1
Macalester College Observatory	STPL	8026	B1
Minneapolis Planetarium	MINN	7938	B2
Robbinsdale Schools Planetarium	NWHE	7850	B2
St. Paul Cathedral	STPL	7941	C6

Park & Ride

FEATURE NAME	CITY	MAP#	GRID
Park & Ride	APVA	8283	B4
Park & Ride	BRKP	7679	A3
Park & Ride	BRKP	7766	A1
Park & Ride	COON	7680	A1
Park & Ride	MNTK	7934	B7
Park & Ride-28th Av	BMTN	8111	A5
Park & Ride-CR-73	MNTK	7935	C3
Park & Ride-Ft Snelling Lot A	HnpC	8025	E7
Park & Ride-Ft Snelling Lot B	HnpC	8025	E7
Park & Ride-Heart of the City	BRNV	8282	B3
Park & Ride-Naples St NE	BLNE	7596	A7
Park & Ride-Northtown Transfer Hub	BLNE	7680	C3
Park & Ride-Plymouth Rd	MNTK	7934	E3
Park & Ride-Point Gouglas Rd S	STPL	8029	B3
Park & Ride-Wells Fargo History-Museum	MINN	7938	B3

Parks & Recreation

FEATURE NAME	CITY	MAP#	GRID
Abdella Memorial Pk	SPLP	8116	A7
Able Pk	SPLP	7680	D4
Acorn Pk	COON	7594	B6
Acorn Pk	RSVL	7855	C4
Adams Hill Pk	RHFD	8109	C3
Adams School Pk	COON	7680	A2
Adelmann Pk	BMTN	8109	C6
Adventure Pk	FLCH	7940	B2
Ainsworth Pk	STLP	7936	B6
Airport Pk	BLNE	7595	C5
Albert A Kordiak Pk	COLH	7767	A5
Alden Pk	EDNA	8021	E3
Alder Pk	COON	7594	B5
Al Flynn Pk	COON	7593	D6
Alimagnet Pk	BRNV	8282	D7
Ancel Glen Playfield	BMTN	8194	E4

Parks & Recreation

Minneapolis Points of Interest Index

Parks & Recreation

Parks & Recreation **Minneapolis Points of Interest Index** Parks & Recreation

Minneapolis Points of Interest Index

Schools
Minneapolis Points of Interest Index
Schools

⊛ RAND McNALLY

Thank you for purchasing this Rand McNally Street Atlas!
We value your comments and suggestions.

Please help us serve you better by completing this postage-paid reply card.
This information is for internal use ONLY and will not be distributed or sold to any external third party.

Street Atlas Title: Get Around® Twin Cities   ISBN-13# 978-0-5288-6709-5   MKT: MSP

Date: _____ Gender ☐M ☐F   Age Group ☐18-24 ☐25-31 ☐32-40 ☐41-50 ☐51-64 ☐65+

1. Where did you purchase this Street Atlas? (store name & city) _____

2. Why did you purchase this Street Atlas? _____

    Please explain: _____

3. Does this Street Atlas meet your expectations? ☐Yes ☐No

4. Do you primarily use this Street Atlas for the ☐City Maps ☐Regional Maps

5. Where do you use it? ☐Primarily in the car ☐Primarily in the office ☐Primarily at home ☐Other: _____

6. How do you use it? ☐Primarily for business ☐Both work and personal evenly ☐Primarily for personal use

7. What do you use the Street Atlas for? (mark all that apply)
    ☐Finding addresses ☐In route navigation ☐Planning routes ☐Other (please specify) _____
    ☐Finding points of interest (please specify)_____

8. Do you own a car? ☐Yes ☐No

9. How often do you use your car? ☐Daily ☐Weekly ☐Monthly ☐Other: _____

10. How often do you use public transportation? ☐Daily ☐Occasionally ☐Never

11. Do you use any of the following mapping products in addition to your Street Atlas?

    ☐Folded paper maps ☐Folded laminated maps ☐Wall maps ☐Other street atlases ☐Internet maps ☐Phone maps

12. What features or information do you find most useful in your Rand McNally Street Atlas? (please specify)

    _____

    _____

13. Please provide any additional comments or suggestions you have: _____

    _____

We strive to provide you with the most current updated information available. If you know of a map correction, please notify us here.

Where is the correction? Map Page #: _____ Grid #: _____ Index Page #: _____

Nature of the correction: ☐Street name missing ☐Street name misspelled ☐Street information incorrect
                          ☐Incorrect location for point of interest ☐Index error ☐Other: _____

Detail: _____

Yes, I would like to receive information about updated editions and special offers from Rand McNally.

☐via e-mail E-mail address: _____

☐via postal mail

Your name: _____ Company (if used for work): _____

Address: _____ City/State/ZIP: _____

Thank you for your time and help. We are working to serve you better.
This information is for internal use ONLY and will not be distributed or sold to any external third party.

SA07

CUT ALONG DOTTED LINE

get directions at
randmcnally.com

| NO POSTAGE |
| NECESSARY |
| IF MAILED |
| IN THE |
| UNITED STATES |

BUSINESS REPLY MAIL
FIRST CLASS MAIL   PERMIT NO. 388   CHICAGO, IL

POSTAGE WILL BE PAID BY ADDRESSEE

RAND McNALLY
CONSUMER AFFAIRS
PO BOX 7600
CHICAGO IL 60680-9915

⊛ RAND MℹNALLY
The most trusted name on the map.

You'll never need to ask for directions again with these Rand McNally products!

- EasyFinder® Laminated Maps
- Folded Maps
- Street Guides
- Wall Maps

- CustomView Wall Maps
- Road Atlases
- Motor Carriers' Road Atlases
- Rand McNally Traffic